אור ישראל

Ohr Yisrael

and Other Writings

by Rabbi Israel Salanter

Sefaria

מגיד
MAGGID

אור ישראל

OHR YISRAEL

and Other Writings

By Rabbi Israel Salanter

WITH A TRANSLATION AND COMMENTARY BY

Rabbi Yitz Greenberg

and

Rabbi Justin Pines

Sefaria
Maggid Books

Ohr Yisrael
and Other Writings by Rabbi Israel Salanter

First Edition, 2024

Maggid Books
An imprint of Koren Publishers Jerusalem Ltd.

POB 8531, New Milford, CT 06776-8531, USA
& POB 4044, Jerusalem 9104001, Israel
www.korenpub.com

Cover photo: Handwritten Letter by Rabbi Israel Salanter together with Rabbi Yosef Feimer, Av Beit Din of Slutsk, 1858. Photo credit to Genazym Auction House. Thank you to an anonymous owner for permission to reproduce the cover image.

The publication of this book was made possible through the generous support of *The Jewish Book Trust*.

ISBN 978-1-59264-651-7, *hardcover*

Printed and bound in the United States

Dedicated in memory of

Getzel M. Cohen, z"l

אליקים גצל בן חיים הכהן

*By his loving wife, children,
grandchildren, and great-grandchildren*

ת. נ. צ. ב. ה.

Contents

R. Salanter did not provide titles for the letters, and these brief descriptions are provided here to assist the reader.

Foreword

We deem it a privilege to present to the public the major writings of R. Israel Salanter with our new English translation and commentary. The bulk of this book (which supplies its title) consists of the writings of R. Salanter found in *Ohr Yisrael,* as edited and published by R. Salanter's disciple, R. Isaac Blazer, in 1900.[1] These include twenty-two letters written by R. Salanter to his disciples and various others;[2] "*Iggeret HaMussar,*" R. Salanter's explanation of the need and his call for a movement to practice Mussar; and four *derashot* (homilies or sermons) delivered by R. Salanter and later committed to writing by R. Blazer.[3] There are also three essays written by R. Salanter and published in a rabbinic journal, *Tevunah,* that R. Salanter edited.[4] One essay served as

1. Published by Judah Leib ben Eliezer Lipman Mats, Vilna.
2. The letters are arranged and numbered by Blazer.
3. These are referred to by Blazer as Letters 23, 26, 27, and 28.
4. As discussed in the Introduction to *Ohr Yisrael* in this volume, R. Salanter felt that rabbis must develop their thinking and communicate with the public in order to compete for the Jews' understanding and commitment, and he created *Tevunah* toward those ends. It failed after only a few issues, and reading it shows that even though R. Salanter enlisted leading rabbis to write – including such luminaries as Rabbis Isaac Elhanan Spektor, Solomon Kluger, Samuel Salant, and Tzvi Hirsch Kalischer – they submitted mostly standard responsa or talmudic commentary, which

the introduction to the publication, and two were published in various issues of *Tevunah*.

R. Blazer also included in *Ohr Yisrael* (as Letters 24 and 25) two letters written by R. Joseph Zundel of Salant. R. Salanter credits R. Zundel as the man who excited his interest in the importance of learning Mussar, thus shaping his lifetime thinking. We have included those letters, believing that they shed light on R. Zundel's thinking and, therefore, contribute to our understanding of R. Salanter's thought.

We have not included in this volume the extensive personal writings of R. Isaac Blazer on Mussar, its practices, and its values, which he included in *Ohr Yisrael*. We mean no disrespect to R. Blazer by omitting them. However, his writings about Mussar and his articulation of the Mussar movement and its practices are derivative. We want to focus readers' attention on R. Salanter's ideas. His fresh religious thinking led him to initiate the Mussar movement. We refer readers who would like to read R. Blazer's writings in *Ohr Yisrael* to the translation, annotation, and publication of R. Blazer's *Ohr Yisrael* by R. Zvi Miller, published by Targum Press/Feldheim in 2004. R. Miller's book is titled *Ohr Yisrael: The Classic Writings of Rav Yisrael Salanter and His Disciple Rav Yitzchak Blazer*. R. Miller translates all of R. Blazer's as well as R. Salanter's writing, supplying titles and headings to all units as well as occasional paraphrases and annotations to make the ideas clearer. While we hope that our readers will find that our translation of and commentary on R. Salanter's writings are illuminating and offer new insights, we stress our appreciation and continuing regard for R. Miller's volume. One of us (Yitz Greenberg) was so pleased that, after a century of neglect, a first-time English translation was finally being offered, that he helped raise the funds to enable the publication. A close friend, R. David Scheinfeld, *z"l*, gave a dedication gift. That book is dedicated to his wife Ellen Scheinfeld, *z"l*, and in part to the memory of Jonathan Joseph Greenberg, *z"l*, son of R. Yitz and Blu Greenberg. R. Scheinfeld also wrote a foreword

had little resonance with the public. All was not lost, however; R. Salanter himself wrote three essays ("*Derushim*" in his words) that make an important contribution to Jewish religious thought in the face of modernity.

on the significance of R. Israel Salanter, which will be expanded upon in the introduction to this book.

In addition to R. Salanter's *Ohr Yisrael* writings, we have translated and include his "Essay on Strengthening Those Who Learn Our Holy Torah." This essay was published in 1880 in a booklet called *Etz Peri*.[5] The book was meant to present the case and raise funds for the Kollel Perushim, an institute for advanced study of Talmud and halakha in which advanced students devoted themselves exclusively to the study of Torah and were supported by the institution of the *kollel* itself. The *kollel* was located in Kovno and was a joint project of R. Isaac Elhanan Spektor (by then the most recognized rabbinic leader of Lithuanian Jewry) and R. Salanter. R. Salanter's response to the encroachment of modernity and the spread of *Haskala* included building institutions, especially yeshivot. Instead of yeshivot growing haphazardly around a great rabbi in a particular locality, the new model was to establish yeshivot formally; a head of yeshiva would be appointed, as well as instructors for *shiurim*, and a schedule of classes would be offered as well as room and board for the students. This institutional change made the yeshiva more modern – well kept, better organized and supervised, and better able to monitor and sustain the students. The kollel was the next step in the provision of a setting in which advanced Torah scholars would develop and be taken care of financially (along with their families) so they could concentrate on furthering their learning.

The "Essay on Strengthening Those Who Learn Our Holy Torah" is one of R. Salanter's longest and most ambitious. Its tone is somewhat different from the other essays. However, in a note to the book, it is explained that R. Israel gave a sermon on the importance of Torah and the great mitzva of providing an adequate economic foundation for potential great scholars. The talk was transcribed and published under R. Israel's supervision. It has heretofore not been translated into English.

We have another motive in bringing R. Israel Salanter's ideas to the public's attention. We both feel that his emphasis on the purpose of Torah being to develop an individual of good character (a *mentsch*) and

5. By R. Salanter and R. Isaac Elhanan Spektor, published by Judah Leib ben Eliezer Lipman Mats, Vilna, 1880.

the importance of consciously working on improving one's character traits is more important than ever. R. Salanter and his disciples identified various desirable qualities of spirit to embrace and internalize. They developed practices to recognize one's flawed traits and systematically work on improving them. The authors have participated in such Mussar exercises and found them religiously inspiring and valuable for self-development. The role and practice of Mussar has diminished in the past generation, even in yeshivot where the Mussar movement once held sway. We want to invite the public to reconnect to this stream of Judaism, in order to raise personal ethical standards and develop a kinder and gentler personality and society. In R. Justin Pines's afterword to this book, the reader will find references to ongoing projects to apply Mussar in contemporary life. He also describes his experiences in developing Mussar as a course and project within a day school curriculum as well as enabling parents and laypeople in secular sectors to apply Mussar to their lives and work. In a separate personal note, R. Yitz Greenberg describes his life-changing experience of spending his college years learning in Beis Yosef Novardok, a yeshiva that simultaneously offered a classic "*lomdish*" curriculum and intensive Mussar development.

As the historical introduction will show, R. Salanter understood early on that modern culture was sweeping Europe and that traditional Jewish culture would have to transform its religious system in order to survive in the new atmosphere. His response was to create educational institutions that would guide students in internalizing the ethical and emotional dimensions of the religion, and thereby compete for loyalty and identity in the age of modernity. His educational creativity and institutional upgrading of Torah learning were ahead of their time. They are available today as models that can be applied to develop a richer religious life and higher ethical standard.

For those new to Mussar, we hope that this book will give you access to another great stream of Jewish tradition and wisdom. For those already practicing, learning, and/or teaching Mussar, we hope this book can deepen your connection with the movement and its founder. In both cases, you will meet a visionary educator, a groundbreaking thinker, and a role model for a *mentsch* inspired and shaped by Torah.

One final note on the style of this volume: The original Hebrew was written in the late nineteenth century and uses masculine pronouns as a default. We follow that convention as well, as we feel it would be anachronistic to do otherwise.

Yitz Greenberg
Justin Pines
Ellul 5784 – August 2023

Preface

My Personal Encounter with Mussar

Yitz Greenberg

I was raised in a Modern Orthodox home in Borough Park ("Boro Park"), Brooklyn. In those ancient times, Boro Park was the neighborhood to which religious immigrant families moved up socially from the Lower East Side. Despite the high level of observance, the message of making it and becoming fully American was strong. Many of my peers and counterparts in other families internalized this message and shed their traditional observances in order to become more integrated in America.

My father was a *talmid ḥakham* of awesome proportions who taught a *ḥevra Shas* (Talmud study society) every day for the last fifty years of his life, at the downstairs minyan of Temple Beth El, the fanciest Orthodox shul in Boro Park. He was a *Misnaged* (an opponent of Hasidism) by temperament, and his favorite leisure-time activity was learning Gemara with his children – so I learned a lot of Gemara with him. He was able to explain and defend Jewish observances, and my mother was a person of simple but powerfully devout faith, so they held their sons religiously better than most families could.

I attended Yeshivas Etz Chayim, the Modern Orthodox yeshiva in Boro Park. The upper grades' Talmud teacher was excellent, and he offered a voluntary summer session to study some smaller tractates in their entirety. I enjoyed this, and my learning benefited. From there I went to the newly founded Brooklyn Talmudical Academy, Yeshiva University's high school for boys. I was a successful student, but the Jewish studies and religious spirit of the school were less inspiring. In fact, we were rambunctious students, often pulling mischievous pranks and inciting students to disrupt classes – especially those of the weaker, less effective teachers. We felt that the administration was heavy-handed and did not treat the students with genuine respect. In 1949, my senior year, my plan was to attend Yeshiva College, the standard next level of education for Modern Orthodox students. I occasionally toyed with the idea of going to Brooklyn College, which offered free tuition (and would allow me to save my Regents scholarship money for graduate school). Both of my older sisters had gone to Brooklyn College and received an excellent education. They bought a lot of college-level books and created a home library which I eagerly read through. The younger of my two older sisters majored in history and raved about the department – and I was very interested in history – but I took no action in this direction.

My father walked daily from our house on 49th Street near 13th Avenue to Beth El at 48th Street and 15th Avenue. Sometimes, along the way, he would stop at Yeshivas Beis Yosef on 49th Street, between 14th and 15th Avenue, to use their library or to talk with and share in learning with its *rebbe'im*. Beis Yosef was a chief remnant of the Beis Yosef–Novardok Mussar yeshiva, which functioned in early-twentieth-century Poland and Russia. The Novardoker approach was developed by R. Yosef Yoizel Hurwitz, known as the Alter of Novardok, a primary disciple of R. Salanter.

Novardok was considered the more radical wing of the Mussar movement. At Novardok, more time was devoted to Mussar study and practice than to Talmud study. The students demonstratively wore traditional clothes and grew beards. They made no concessions to modernity in personal hygiene or social conventions. There was a strong ascetic streak in its atmosphere, and the school placed great stress on defying public opinion (even of religious Jews) as well as on breaking one's ego to become truly ethical and devout. It indoctrinated its students to "uplift the masses" by going out and creating yeshivot which offered a mix of Torah study and moral character development through Mussar exercises and study. By 1939, the movement had created more than seventy mostly elementary school-age yeshivot in Poland and the Soviet Union, in the face of Communist persecution (in Russia) and government-backed antisemitic hostility (in Poland). These schools were destroyed in the Holocaust.

After World War II, surviving remnants of the Novardok yeshiva (called Beis Yosef in honor of its founder) made their way to Eretz Yisrael, France, and England (where they founded the famed Gateshead Yeshiva). But the head of the movement, R. Avraham Jofen, the son-in-law of the Alter and the director of the Novardok network during the interwar period, came to America and settled in Boro Park, where he reestablished the yeshiva along with his son Yaakov, his son-in-law R. Yehudah Leib Nekritz, and about forty refugee students. R. Nekritz and about half of the students had survived exile to Siberia, where they were held together by R. Nekritz's leadership. The other half were survivors of various Nazi concentration camps.

Because of their radical commitment to Mussar, the Novardok yeshiva managed to keep Mussar study and activity central to its program. By contrast, many of the Mussar yeshivot in Israel and elsewhere gradually demoted Mussar to a minor part of a typical yeshiva curriculum. I knew none of this background, although I later came to see that, paradoxically, the impact of Siberia and concentration camps had somewhat "mellowed" their spirit; their exercises in ego-busting and defying conventional public opinion became less extreme.

One day, R. Jofen spoke with my father and said that they were considering taking in American boys as students – out of the belief that they must begin to sink roots in this new country. Did my father know of any boys who might be interested? Beis Yosef's leadership was deeply ambivalent about this step. They hesitated to admit outsiders who might cool off their students' fervor or dilute their passion for Mussar. They worried about bringing callow American boys into a group that was so tightly forged in the fires of Communist Siberian work camps and Nazi concentration camps.

In truth, they never quite solved their inner conflicts over this matter. They started and stopped the experiment with American boys several times. By comparison, when R. Aharon Kotler, a Holocaust survivor, came to America, he went to Lakewood, New Jersey, and threw himself into creating a New World yeshiva completely devoted to Torah study, with no secular studies. He established uncompromising standards – as high as, or higher than, the destroyed European yeshivot – and demanded unqualified commitments to these norms on the part of the American boys. He succeeded on an immense scale. Beis Yosef never made this transition. They kept vacillating on how much to expect from American-born students. In the end, they failed to establish a robust American institution.

My father came home and asked me if I would be interested in attending Beis Yosef. I said I had no idea if this was a good school. My father was a product of Lithuanian yeshivot, where he studied from childhood on. He was an orphan whose mother was so poor that she could not support him at home. My father hardly understood, and cared very little about, the Mussar angle. He said to me: "Look, I don't know. When I studied in Brisk [under R. Chaim Soloveitchik, as an older teenager – YG], they looked down on Mussar. But I have spoken with Rav Avraham [Jofen] and other *rebbe'im* in learning many times. He is a true *talmid ḥakham,* and I believe that he will give a good *shiur,* so your learning will certainly grow. Why don't you try it out?"

We decided to "look over" the yeshiva by going there for a weekday night *seder*. (There were three *sedarim,* or study sessions, each day: morning, afternoon, and night.) This was an exercise of poor judgment; there were no formal *shiurim* at night, so I could not gauge whether any of the *rebbe'im* would inspire me. Nor were there any formal Mussar *shmuessen* (discourses) in which a *mashgiaḥ* (spiritual supervisor) might teach or explore some aspect of behavioral ethics or character development. The one distinguishing feature of night *seder* – which I discovered after the fact – was that for fifteen to twenty minutes before Maariv, they learned Mussar "*behispailus*" (*behitpaalut*; with excitement and emotion). They engaged in emotional immersion in a Mussar text. For more than an hour, my father and I sat and studied Gemara together, amidst the hum of many other students learning by themselves or with a *ḥavruta* (study partner). This, of course, gave me no clue as to what learning at Beis Yosef might be like. A quarter hour before Maariv, someone gave a "*klap*" on a *shtender* (pounded on a lectern), and the room fell silent. I suddenly realized that my voice and my father's were the only sounds in the *beit midrash*. As the silence grew more intense, I fell silent.

After a few minutes, suddenly, a student sitting at a table opposite mine leaped up out of his chair and at the top of his voice began to chant: "*Hakina, hataiva, vehakavod motzi'in es haadam min haolam*" ("Jealousy, lust, and [seeking] honor drive a person from the world"; Avot 4:21). This was his text for the evening. For the next twenty minutes, he shouted, he sang, he danced, he cried, and he repeated this statement like a mantra, with all his might.

He was not alone. At a different table, another student sang out his text, rocking and weaving, never getting up but never stopping. Then another and then another student leaped up or marched back and forth, screamed and whispered, bowed his head, or cried to the heavens. There was no one text but a stunning cacophony of verses and adages that swept the *beit midrash* and swirled around my head. I felt like I was in a storm, being buffeted and overwhelmed without relief. I could barely breathe until the frenzy ended.

Never had I experienced such a flood of raw religious emotion. Never had I seen fellow yeshiva students exhibit such passion and act out with unchecked spirit and inspiration. Never had I thought of these texts as addressing one personally and demanding a response. In the silence before the *ḥazan* arose to recite "*Barkhu*" and begin Maariv, I turned to my father and said: I am going to this yeshiva.

I started Beis Yosef that fall. In doing so, I gained two immediate advantages: First, the yeshiva accepted that I would attend Brooklyn College, which offered a better and richer secular education. Due to the timing of the *shiurim*, which were generally offered in the late morning, I was able to attend Brooklyn College during the early morning hours – as long as I was fully prepared for the *shiurim*. This allowed me to take some of the best courses with the best college faculty. Secondly, the Beis Yosef students spoke Yiddish, not English. My parents spoke Yiddish to us at home, so I understood every word they spoke. But at home, I used to answer in English. To communicate with the students here, I had to learn to speak Yiddish, which I did.

Beis Yosef had recruited only a handful of Americans, so initially they set up a special *shiur* for us, though they later distributed us among the lower *shiurim*. I fell in love with the Mussar aspect of the yeshiva and with R. Yehudah Leib Nekritz, the main *mashgiaḥ*, in particular. These were the gentlest, calmest, most embracing people that I had ever met. Rav Yehudah Leib had a perpetual kind smile. He saw everything and listened to everything with total attention and unlimited patience. His second son, Daniel, was a difficult child – restless and impulsive. He was constantly coming into the *beit midrash*, often interrupting his father's *shiur*. His father listened kindly and spoke gently. I never saw a trace of anger or annoyance. Plain and simple, I wanted to be like him.

In addition to his Gemara *shiur*, Rav Nekritz gave regular *shmuessen* on Mussar and character building. The most frequent theme was honor and care for other human beings – to speak to them with respect, and even if one criticizes them, to do so without hurting feelings, and always to look out for their welfare and well-being. Love and loyalty to God are essential but are most powerfully expressed in kindness to God's creatures, our fellow human beings.

Every couple of weeks, R. Nekritz would give me an hour of "Mussar analysis." I would report to him on my Mussar activities and attempts to improve my temperament, and he would give me his assessment, and would also try to offer me analyses of problems and suggest where I should focus my efforts at self-improvement.

The whole yeshiva studied Mussar texts daily, including such classics as R. Moshe Ḥayim Luzzatto's *Mesillat Yesharim* and Rabbenu Baḥya ibn Pakuda's *Ḥovot HaLevavot* at the end of morning *seder*. The yeshiva's particular specialty was *Madregat HaAdam* (*The Stature of the Human*) by Novardok's founder, R. Yosef Yoizel Hurwitz. This book mostly focuses on character traits and critiques socialization to conventional expectations and societal standards (which were not up to religious standards). However, I most responded to its focus on "*zikui harabbim*" ("uplifting the masses") by reaching out to people to teach them Torah and Mussar. The yeshiva's stress on bringing Torah to others made a permanent mark on me. It surely played a role in my ultimate career decision to turn away from academia and instead focus on bringing Torah to American Jews and their communal leadership.

I also was introduced to R. Menachem Mendel Lefin's *Ḥeshbon HaNefesh*. In his book, Lefin lists thirteen character traits, defines them, and explains how to work on developing them. These traits include diligence, order, being just, inner tranquility, and patience. I was taught the method of working on one trait for a week. This included keeping a diary of every incident in which this trait was invoked (or was not used properly). At the end of the week, I met with an individual who reviewed my reports and critiqued what I had done or suggested where an alternate behavior would have been better. I should add that the students often told stories about especially kind or thoughtful behavior by R. Israel Salanter and by many of their teachers. The students set up an ideal model to emulate. They continually showed kindness and patience in all their interactions. There was never bickering or petty arguments or gossip or badmouthing. I wanted to be like them.

Over time, as I earned more trust, I was admitted to some inner group activities that were reserved for the original (European) students. Among these activities was working on being unaffected by the conventional opinions of others. I gather that one of the techniques used in Europe – doing public acts that seemed ridiculous, like going into a pharmacy and asking for a box of nails or a container of *yirat shamayim*, thus instilling in the students indifference to the social environment and public opinion – was no longer done. On the other hand, we practiced being unmoved by criticism or being able to go against a chorus of unanimity to offer a different response if we thought we were in the right. I believe that there were groups practicing even more private Mussar techniques to which I was never invited.

I also never encountered the exercise of the *birzhe*, for which Beis Yosef was famous in Europe. In the *birzhe* (bourse, stock exchange), students would walk around the room, like traders on the floor of the stock exchange, and talk with other individuals, exchanging views, Mussar instructions, and the latest information on personal and group religious development. I did not learn about the *birzhe* phenomenon until years after I graduated from Beis Yosef. I do not know if they no longer practiced this activity or whether I was not admitted into the group that carried on this practice.

In retrospect, the yeshiva succeeded in implanting a less extreme version of Novardoker Mussar in its students. They did less ego busting but did give over the message that it – life, one's social circle, behavior in the workplace – is not about you. They communicated that getting credit for an accomplishment was not so important; that being the center of attention was not a great achievement or proof of importance. They transmitted that the real test of rightness was not the approval of your social peers. They taught that the correct response when facing majority disapproval was to check whether you were living up to your own principles and whether you were being faithful to your values. When you faced dismissal for holding views or principles that were not the consensus, they modeled turning to God to assess whether you were in the right according to a higher authority.

There was one other spiritual service that the yeshiva provided for me. The student body's atmosphere of prayer was intense, and *tefilla* was often a deeply moving experience. The presence of the Divine was strongly felt, and the sense of connection to Hashem was intense. At Brooklyn College, in various courses, I ran into strong religious challenges. Among these "shocks" was critical historical scholarship, conflicts of science and religion, and philosophy undermining religious assumptions. The yeshiva *rebbe'im* had no familiarity with or answers for these issues. However, the religious intensity and palpable sense of connection to God sustained me and enabled me to live with the contradictions.

For years after I left the yeshiva, I felt keenly that I was walking with God in my life activities. I followed this path to a PhD and to the academic career that I had laid out for myself in my teenage years. But I wrestled internally with the urge to bring Torah to the masses and the sense that Hashem had a mission for me to bring Torah to my fellow Jews. That summons from Hashem led me to become the rabbi of Young Israel of Brookline while still in graduate school. Later, I accepted an offer to join the faculty at Yeshiva University, because it implied that I could be close to or connect to Jewish teaching as well as pure academics.

Eventually, I came to see that signals from Hashem are more complex and ambiguous than I had thought based on my Beis Yosef experiences. Sorting them out and finding their direction required more personal judgment and informed choices from me than I had naively thought. Still, I never completely lost the sense of walking with God and being sustained by Hashem's love and partnership as I pursued my life activities. I also internalized the challenge to live by a higher standard of care and respect for my fellow human beings as I made my life choices.

In summary, I found that Beis Yosef's continuous focus on improving behavior and character traits did affect me. This included learning to forgo seeking credit or being proud of an accomplishment. Most of all, I was drawn to become more like the yeshiva students who were consistently doing *ḥesed* (acts of loving-kindness) for others, while being patient, unruffled, modest, and self-effacing. Working on ethical self-improvement with a supportive but demanding group really conditioned one's personality and behavior for the better.

Although I left the yeshiva after my ordination in order to go on to graduate studies in history, the yeshiva never really left me. My experience led me to believe that Mussar could be – should be – revived as an educational technique and given a central place in religious education. That is what led me to jointly translate *Ohr Yisrael* into English and publish this volume, including personal accounts and practical advice on pursuing Mussar techniques in today's daily life.

Introduction to Ohr Yisrael

Yitz Greenberg

R. Israel Lipkin, later famous as R. Israel Salanter (of the town of Salant – today Salantai – Lithuania) was the son of R. Zev Wolf Lipkin, a noted rabbinic scholar and head of the rabbinical court (*av beit din*) in Zhagare and elsewhere in Lithuania.[1] R. Israel was a prodigious student of Torah and Talmud in the Lithuanian yeshiva style. He studied with R. Tzvi Hirsh Braude in Salant and was identified as an *ilui* (child prodigy) at an early age. The circumstances of his life were leading him to a career as a *rosh yeshiva* and a leading Torah sage – a *gadol* – in the mitnagdic tradition.

From his youth, he exhibited originality in thought and independence of mind. Two examples come to mind. The first was his early recognition of the emotional context of thinking. Lithuanian yeshiva convention takes sacred texts at face value with the reader's role seen as

1. Several academic books have been written on the life of R. Israel Salanter. See especially Immanuel Etkes, *Rabbi Israel Salanter and the Mussar Movement: Seeking the Torah of Truth* (Philadelphia: Jewish Publication Society, 1993). The present essay attempts to "read between the lines" – to interpret his life and life choices in light of what we know, and to shed light on what we might learn from his life today.

neutral – simply reading, using pure reason, and absorbing the sacred information. In his youth, mastery of dialectic (*pilpul*) was the mark of brilliance as a scholar. In *pilpul* a wide variety of themes and texts were brought together and shown to have contradictory ideas or themes that were interpreted in conflicting ways. The pilpulist could develop a new insight into the text or interpretations of themes that would reconcile and unify the clashing texts/views. Salanter was a master of this genre, able to bring a wide range of texts and themes together to generate tensions/conflicts which he would resolve with his *ḥiddushim*, his novel insights.

Yet from an early age, Israel tuned in to the emotional factor in all study, which predisposes the reader to certain understandings and may well shape (or reshape) the analysis. He also was sensitive to the character and personality traits that the Torah sought to instill in people alongside – and emerging from – the observances and behaviors of religious life. This led him to question the *pilpul* method. It seemed to him that *pilpul* glorified associative brilliance and displays of intellectual acumen over the search for truth and the plain meaning of the text. He also identified the method as designed to inspire displays of knowledge or giving honor to creators of insights. Recognition became a source of pride and honor-seeking in the pilpulist. In effect, this method of learning Torah was instilling undesirable character traits – competitiveness and one-upmanship, valorizing personal recognition, striving to impress others – rather than inspiring people to live by the ethics of the Torah or to study Torah for its own sake. Young Israel Salanter decided to give up this approach despite its prestige and to concentrate on the plain meaning of texts and on living up to the life instructions of the tradition.

Israel pursued the plain meaning method diligently. However, after further self-analysis, he concluded that he was unconsciously twisting his analysis to fit the plain meaning approach and was showing off his learning prowess while using the new method – just as he had been doing before with his *pilpulim*. He resolved to return to using the *pilpul* method of learning (which encouraged a wider range of sources and insights), but to do so more consciously, that is, being careful to check or neutralize the tendency to ostentatiously display knowledge or brilliance.[2] In

2. R. Salanter's return to *pilpul* is discussed extensively in Letter 29 of *Ohr Yisrael*.

other words, R. Salanter's approach to learning was far more conscious of psychological and other factors that affect reason or shape analysis.

A second example was R. Salanter's seeking out R. Joseph Zundel of Salant. R. Zundel was a major student of R. Chaim of Volozhin, but he was not content to simply study the standard curriculum of Talmud and halakha. He chose to study texts that spoke to the importance of fear of God and to teach such character traits as trust in God, inner tranquility, and avoiding honor and recognition. R. Zundel decided not to be an official rabbi or professional Torah teacher because this would turn his Torah into a source of income and social recognition rather than a form of service of God and studying Torah for its own sake. He became a businessman and laborer – although he restricted these activities to the minimum – while pursuing his learning and character-building efforts. R. Zundel chose to "pass" as a simple layman in daily matters and in dress while simultaneously pursuing a hidden path of advanced Torah study and character development.

At a wedding, R. Israel detected a guest who seemed to be a common layperson but whose every action and gesture bespoke that he was a great scholar and servant of God. R. Israel sought out R. Zundel, followed him, and determined to walk in his ways. When R. Israel approached him, R. Zundel told him that the key to religious life was to study Mussar texts on character building and fear of God. This initiated R. Israel into a lifelong pursuit of Mussar and character building as important elements of religious life.

R. Israel was fascinated by R. Zundel and was tempted not to go into the rabbinate or teach Torah, but to live as a layperson while secretly serving God through intense learning and higher ethical behavior. It is believed by his students that R. Salanter studied to be an accountant. To protect his disguise as an ordinary person without sacrificing devotion in prayer, he practiced praying so that he could go through the *Amida* quickly while maintaining focus on the devotional meanings that devout servants of God included in their prayer.

However, R. Salanter was increasingly aware of the coming of modernity to Eastern Europe. He grasped that dealing with the new culture would be a central challenge of Jewish life and concluded that living as a secret servant of God would be self-indulgent. If he did not go into the rabbinate or education, he could not serve or help Jewry deal with the coming crisis. This would constitute pursuing self-fulfillment in religious life while abandoning all other Jews.

R. Salanter chose to enter the rabbinate – as it were, sacrificing his soul's ideal to help Jewry. He was absolutely convinced that this was the true exercise of personal religious responsibility. Years later, when his students tried to persuade him to meet a kabbalist who served God and devoted his whole life to spiritual repair of the world, R. Salanter declined; he insisted that a true *tzaddik* would not make "Shabbat for himself" but would work publicly to strengthen the Jewish community in the face of the growing challenge of modernity.

From Salant, R. Israel went to Vilna when he was invited to serve together with R. Mordechai Meltzer as *rosh yeshiva* of R. Meile's yeshiva. When he discovered that his presence was (unintentionally) undermining R. Mordechai, he left the yeshiva and started his own *beit midrash* (study center) in the suburb of Zarzecze (today Užupis, a neighborhood in Vilna/Vilnius).

It is not clear how much R. Salanter did to advance the cause of Mussar or whether he successfully spread Mussar study during his Vilna period. What is clear retrospectively is that he recognized the advance of modern culture. R. Salanter saw that while observance and Torah values were dominant, their status was the outgrowth of a strong, entrenched traditional consensus – itself based on habit and conformity. He judged, therefore, that traditional religion would not stand up well when the new modernity brought with it choice and alternative lifestyles. Without ever saying so publicly, he took upon himself the responsibility of assuring the viability and survival of Judaism in the emerging environment.

This sense of leadership shows up in two behavior patterns in particular. The first was his focus on the broader public, and not only the scholarly elite. While teaching in his *beit midrash* in Vilna, he gave a series of *derashot* (homilies) in a wide variety of settings. These *derashot* were displays of learning to establish his credentials as a major Torah scholar, but they included much emphasis on Mussar, fear of heaven, and ethics. The *derashot* made a great impression because R. Salanter was an eloquent and brilliant speaker who spoke to the level of the public. His outreach effort to the broader community reflected his conviction that the public's religious assumptions and consensus values constituted the real basis of the dominant traditional paradigm. The scholars would lose their standing if the public (with whom they generally did not communicate much) switched its allegiance.

In 1844–1845, he also arranged for publication of a medieval Mussar classic, *Tikkun Middot HaNefesh* (*Improving the Traits of the Soul*) by R. Solomon ibn Gabirol, as well as a book called *Ḥeshbon HaNefesh* (*Accounting of the Soul*), written by Menachem Mendel Lefin, a moderate *maskil* (acolyte of the Jewish Enlightenment). The latter identified thirteen desirable character traits and a program for the individual to track them and work on their improvement. R. Salanter was always sensitive to the impact of institutional structures and settings. He created a Mussar House, where people could come and devote themselves to studying Mussar and internalizing its values through chants and actions.

R. Salanter offered a vision of strengthening Judaism by developing an internalized, committed religiosity that was as careful in observing the commandments governing human relationships and interactions as it was in ritual matters. While he did not challenge the dominant paradigm of Jewish Lithuania that placed Torah study at the center of life, he taught that religious education must include character improvement and should strongly focus on religious emotion, starting with meditation on the reward and punishment of the next world.

The other expression of his leadership was in communal affairs. He did not simply teach and speak up for his own institution and projects; he took an active part in public policy issues. The classic expression of R. Salanter's sense of leadership – and an exercise that became part of his legend in his lifetime – was his role during the cholera epidemic of 1848. Cholera was a highly contagious – and often fatal – disease, with people dying from dehydration and debilitation during its final stages. R. Salanter took seriously the Torah's overriding commitment to saving lives. He recruited yeshiva students and organized them in a kind of medical peace corps. They visited the sick, taking care of them by bringing food, water, and medication, and tended to patients by directly feeding them or offering other help. They undertook these actions at a time when many people (even family) stayed away for fear of contagion.

Every week before Shabbat, R. Salanter would give a Torah lecture reminding the corps that they must act with alacrity to carry out any and all labors ordinarily prohibited on Shabbat needed to treat the patients and prevent deterioration and death. Some rabbis and lay people were troubled by these activities, fearing that the yeshiva students' observance of Shabbat would be permanently weakened by these "deviations" from standard observance of Shabbat. R. Salanter rejected these concerns. I believe that he saw these fears as reflecting a routinized, externalized conception of observance that could be undermined by a breach of habitual action patterns. His policy was based on inculcating in the yeshiva students a Judaism solidly grounded in the deep emotion of serving God. Their commitment would only be strengthened by carrying out the Torah's profound commitment to saving lives.

As Yom Kippur approached, doctors told R. Salanter that observing the holiday posed a real danger to people's lives. Refraining from food and drink would weaken people's resistance, and they would more likely fall sick with cholera. The disease was contagious, so spending the day indoors in a crowded synagogue with many others was a health risk. It would be wise medically to cut short prayers and to spend more time outside in fresh air and not in close contact with people. Salanter watched with anxiety as the rabbis and community leaders stayed silent. When asked privately, many rabbis gave people permission not to fast. However, they were reluctant to give public exemptions that applied to everyone. Given the care with which most people observed Yom Kippur, R. Salanter felt that in the absence of public notification that it was proper not to fast, many people would choose the stringency of fasting – at the risk of getting sick. R. Salanter waited until Rosh HaShana. To his regret, no official rabbis or communal authorities made a public declaration that in light of the dangers of cholera, preserving life supersedes fasting.

R. Salanter held no official position in Vilna, but he felt a leadership responsibility. He had signs posted throughout Vilna calling on people "...not to fast on this holy and awesome day, to cut short the [recitation of] liturgical poems, and to walk outside in the city during the cool of day."[3] On Yom Kippur, following the morning service, he

3. Steinschneider, *Ir Vilna*, 130, quoted in Etkes, *Salanter*, 170.

took some baked goods, ascended the *bima*, recited the blessing over the food, and ate in the presence of the congregation so that the people would see this and do likewise. Hillel Steinschneider reports that one of the distinguished citizens of Vilna stood up and protested that the rabbis and leaders of Vilna knew the laws of saving lives yet did not permit eating in public. The entire congregation was greatly agitated.[4]

In his classic work, *Rabbi Israel Salanter and the Mussar Movement*, Professor Immanuel Etkes prefers a moderate version of this event. On the eve of Yom Kippur, R. Salanter, in coordination with halakhic authorities in Vilna, issued a ruling that people should cut short the service and stay outside in fresh air as much as possible. In addition, in the side room of synagogues, pieces of cake, cut to less than minimum size that would incur the biblical punishment for eating on Yom Kippur, should be available for people to eat when necessary. On Yom Kippur morning, R. Salanter stood up and told people that if they felt weak, they may go and eat without asking permission from a doctor.[5] Etkes's judgment as to what R. Salanter did reflects his professional commitment to treat R. Salanter with a historian's objective eye rather than incorporate the legends and hagiography that clustered around him. (Later, a Yiddish writer, David Frishman, wrote a short story, "Three Who Ate,"[6] which presented the story of that Yom Kippur even more dramatically.) I believe, given R. Salanter's sense of historic mission, deep religious emotion, and critique of the formalism and routine of most religious leadership, that the more daring version of the story should be accepted. R. Salanter's critique of the religious leadership deepened throughout his life, and I believe that the cholera incident sharpened and strengthened his critique of conventional observance.[7]

---

4. Ibid.
5. Ibid., 171.
6. A play on the first mishna in the seventh chapter of Berakhot, which discusses the obligations of a group of at least three who ate together.
7. Etkes acknowledges that Shmuel Rosenfeld, Salanter's earliest (non-disciple) biographer, accepted Steinschneider's version as did Baruch Epstein, author of the *Torah Temima*, in his memoir, *Mekor Barukh*. Dov Katz, in *Tenuat HaMussar* (the movement's "authorized" biography), also accepts the stronger version, though Katz reflects a Mussar acolyte's idealized and glorifying approach to R. Salanter.

One of R. Salanter's most important themes and discoveries was the gap between formal observance and routine conformity in religious behavior – as against deep, emotional experiences and genuine religious fervor. The Mussar movement was, in part, R. Salanter's attempt to correct this problem. This spirit is consonant with the more radical version of R. Salanter's Yom Kippur behavior.[8]

In the 1840s, the Russian government stepped up its economic and social pressure on Russian Jewry while entering into (informal) cooperation with *maskilim* to "modernize" the Jews from their traditional way of life. This policy is sometimes referred to as "Compulsory Enlightenment." Moses Montefiore, the great British philanthropist and humanitarian, came to Russia to persuade the government to soften its edicts. Yet he agreed with the government and the *maskilim* that Jews should learn to speak Russian and introduce the study of Western culture into their curriculum. The traditional leadership was inclined to temporize, outwardly agreeing to go along with Montefiore and the government while, in actuality, delaying the project. R. Salanter spoke out publicly and sharply against the proposals. The projects were eventually neutralized by delay and diversion.

By 1848, the government and *maskilim* had come up with a new idea: government-sponsored rabbinical seminaries that would include Western culture in their rabbinic training program. Graduates would be recognized as official rabbis by the government and would have official powers such as registration of population and a role setting the quota for drafting Jews. The sponsors turned to R. Salanter to give stature and legitimacy to the program. They asked him to become the teacher of Talmud in the seminary.

R. Salanter was unquestionably an Orthodox rabbi. He believed in the Talmud and its aggadic (narrative) and theological components. He taught that earning a place in the next world is the primary goal of this life, and that fear of eternal punishment was the strongest motivation of religious and ethical life. He certainly never talked of any change

8. Note that Rambam states that those who hesitate or resist performing otherwise prohibited labors to save lives on Shabbat have a theological problem in that they fail to understand God and the Torah's priority for life. See *Mishneh Torah*, Laws of Shabbat 2:2–3.

in halakha. He had spoken out against Montefiore's idea to incorporate Western culture in the traditional curriculum. Why then did the *maskilim* and government turn to him as a potential ally?

The answer lies in R. Salanter's emerging Mussar educational theory. R. Salanter offered a powerful critique that much of current observance was motivated by routine and conformity – with weak or little understanding of the values or the religious experience that underlie a compelling religion. He complained that the community neglected the mitzvot governing interpersonal relations (*bein adam leḥavero*). He also argued that schools needed better organization and supervision. As mentioned above, he arranged for a reprint of Menachem Mendel Lefin's *Ḥeshbon HaNefesh,* which offered guidelines and exercises for improving character traits and personal conduct. To *maskilim* (and the government) these ideas paralleled or echoed some of their critiques of tradition and their call for better work habits and economic productivity from the Jewish community. Hence, they saw him as a possible fellow traveler.

R. Salanter judged that the government's intentions were not honorable. The rabbis trained by these seminaries, often called "crown rabbis," would become like a "fifth column," seeking to undermine the traditional culture. He also argued that the proposed seminary students would lack sufficient knowledge of rabbinic literature to offer reliable and legitimate halakhic guidance. He resisted pressure from the government and rejected the position. When he saw that the government would not relent in its request, he left Vilna to remove himself from the line of fire. He moved to Kovno, where he lived from 1848 to 1857. It was there that he went public with his ideas for a Mussar movement – a renewal of Orthodoxy. He particularly focused on laypeople because he believed, as mentioned, that lay values and cultural consensus were the true basis of the community's religious culture, and that laypeople would be more vulnerable to modern currents of thought.

During the nine years he spent in Kovno, R. Salanter focused on developing his ideas and creating an actual movement to study and practice Mussar. He became the primary teacher and head at the Nevyozer Kloyz.[9] The *kloyz* at which Salanter taught was supported by R. Zvi

9. A *kloyz* is a small building set aside for prayer and Torah study.

Hersh Nevyozer, a wealthy layman who also was a major supporter of R. Salanter during the years he was in Kovno. Under R. Salanter's leadership, the *kloyz* attracted many high-level students. R. Salanter made Mussar study – both text and practice – a core part of the curriculum, thus putting his educational stamp on what became a leading yeshiva in Kovno. Three students who came to study with R. Salanter during this period – Isaac Blazer, Simcha Zissel Ziv, and Naphtali Amsterdam – became close disciples and actively spread the Mussar movement in their later careers. Numerous other students became rabbis and *rashei yeshiva,* and they spread R. Salanter's ideas in their work.[10] Throughout his career, R. Salanter used his prestige and standing to further his students' careers. He also reached out to nearby communities and their rabbis to incorporate Mussar study in their teaching and institutions.

R. Salanter created a Mussar House in Kovno to intensify the learning and enable experiential Mussar practice. In particular, the Mussar House provided a supportive atmosphere for learning Mussar *behitpaalut* (or "*behispailus*" in the dialect of the yeshiva).[11] This method involved fixing on a text incorporating fear of heaven or ethical guidance and studying, chanting, repeating, or even acting it out to impress its message deeply into the psyche and conduct of the student. He encouraged setting up such houses in nearby communities.

R. Israel made a special effort to reach out to laypeople, who could turn their Mussar learning into a heightened ethical practice in business and in the culture of the Jewish community. Somewhat to his frustration, he succeeded more in attracting rabbis and yeshiva teachers and fared less well with the lay public. This should not surprise us. He demanded high levels of learning and earnest efforts at character improvement, which proved to be hard standards for laypeople to live by. However, these requirements were appealing and inspiring to motivated people going into the rabbinate and teaching Torah.

The five letters that R. Israel wrote from Kovno to his followers in Vilna show that without his presence and dynamic personal influence,

---

10. See the examples cited in Etkes, *Salanter*, 181–2, 190, 193.
11. See the section titled "My Personal Encounter with Mussar" for a description of my firsthand experience with this practice.

his Mussar projects struggled and even declined. In Kovno, R. Salanter's projects became more deeply rooted, although Mussar never became a majority practice. Kovno became a Mussar stronghold – possibly because it was a newer Jewish community with less entrenched attitudes and established ways than in Vilna. The Mussar influence continued long after R. Salanter left Kovno for other cities. However, one should not exaggerate the extent of the Mussar movement. Etkes estimates that several hundred families were engaged in the movement in Kovno.[12]

In Kovno, R. Salanter also encountered opposition from leading rabbis to his proposed educational revisions (i.e., devoting substantial time to Mussar study) and the self-analysis and emotional practices of self-improvement. In the 1890s, after his death and after the Mussarists took spiritual leadership roles in various yeshivot, a serious attack on the Mussar movement was launched in Lithuania.[13] Why should a movement to increase fear of God and improve character while deepening the religious practices and emotions of individuals arouse opposition among Orthodox Jews? It would appear that R. Salanter's shift in the traditional curriculum and giving more time to Mussar (and thus less time to straight Torah study) offended some people as an unjustified "reform." This may well be a proof of R. Salanter's critique that the community was hidebound, routinized, and conformist in its religious behavior and lacking in deep religious emotion. The opponents were threatened by any proposed change or deviation from past practice – even for a positive purpose. Also, R. Salanter's attempt to generate a higher baseline of personal religious life and ethical standard – combined with rigorous modesty and self-criticism – struck some people as arrogant, as a "holier than thou" approach which they perceived as belittling them.

Finally, as Etkes suggests, the community had bitterly fought Hasidism, especially because of the Hasidim's separatism and their emotional practices and outbursts, which offended mitnagdic (non- or

12. Etkes, *Salanter*, 191. On the other hand, the proponents of Mussar took charge of or established major yeshivot in Lithuania, so the intellectual and spiritual influence of the movement was disproportionate to its size.
13. See Dov Katz, *Pulmus HaMussar* (Jerusalem, 1973). This book is written from the perspective of a full-scale partisan of Mussar, but it offers useful descriptions of the opposition and its arguments.

anti-hasidic) conceptions of decorum and, occasionally, halakhic norms such as the times for certain prayers. The Mussarists also congregated separately, in Mussar Houses, followed their mentors and guides closely, and practiced emotional excitation and outbursts (Mussar *behispailus*). All this aroused the old opposition to the new movement.

R. Salanter continued to develop his religious thinking during the Kovno years. Perhaps the most striking aspect of his approach was his focus on the Torah less as a system of learning and observance and more as an ecology designed to develop a good human being. A favorite aphorism, often quoted in his name, was: "The Torah came to make a *mensch*." Working on improving character traits became a central religious activity. Therefore, he called for setting aside time for studying Mussar and working on character improvement. Scholars who studied Torah full-time were leaving out a major part of needed religious activity. He warned that it was more difficult to correct one character trait than to go over the entire Talmud.[14] He emphasized that character improvement called for very challenging learning modes and different activities, as each person was individual and different.

From his earliest years, R. Salanter's approach differed from that of most of his scholarly peers in its basic language and metaphors. Strikingly, he did not use language (or rationales of observance) drawn from Kabbala – even though Kabbala had become the major conceptual basis for understanding the importance of Torah and mitzvot in recent centuries. He also placed little focus on the philosophic rationales and judgments that played a central role in the thought of medieval religious thinkers (such as Rambam [Maimonides]). Ultimately, his educational theory, Mussar teaching, and approach to Torah were grounded in human psychology as he understood and interpreted it.[15]

Perhaps the best snapshot of the state of his thinking in Kovno is found in his *Iggeret HaMussar* (*Letter on Mussar*), which he wrote during the period. He arranged for it to be published in 1858 – a year after leaving Kovno – as an appendix to a reprint of a sixteenth-century Mussar

14. Dov Katz, *Tenuat HaMussar*, vol. 1, 344. There is a sparkling collection of R. Salanter's pithy sayings on a variety of topics there, 342–51.
15. See Letter 6, n. 3, in this volume.

classic, *Tomer Devora.*[16] The *Iggeret HaMussar* is R. Salanter's rationale for study of Mussar literature and works that cultivate fear of God. The letter hinges on the split in every human being between the conscious mind and reason, on one hand, and the powerful desires, lusts, and drives for pleasure which are in everyone's nature, on the other. Desires are amoral and endless, and actions based on them would not stay within the bounds of morality and behaviors permitted by the Torah. Using reason, a person studies Torah and learns what is permitted and what is prohibited. God eternally rewards good behavior and eternally punishes bad behavior. The experiences in the next world, good and bad, dwarf – almost trivialize – the pleasures and pains of this world. However, the nature of desire is that it is focused on immediate gratification. It is able to distance the future so much as to render those rewards and punishments irrelevant psychologically. The typical sinner knows that the punishment and pain will far outstrip the present prohibited pleasure. But this knowledge is overwhelmed (and brushed aside) by the urgent, immediate desires and instinctual drives. Only human reason, fully informed by the Torah's guidelines and limits, and fully deployed, can check the lusts and impose the discipline of observance on the person's behaviors. The question is: Which force will win out – amoral desire or morally compelling reason? This inner conflict is the axis on which the need for Mussar study turns.

R. Salanter's famous opening line in the letter is: "The human being is free in his imagination but fettered by his reason." That is, his imagination and instinct desire without limits, but reason imposes limits and dictates that many of these desires are wicked. He continues: "His imagination leads him, undisciplined, in the path his heart desires." R. Salanter speaks of the *yetzer hara* (evil urge) and *yetzer hatov* (good urge) in every person. The inherited conventional understanding of these forces is that the *yetzer hara* is a spirit of impurity that lusts for pleasure and respects no boundaries of the Torah, and the *yetzer hatov*

16. *Tomer Devora* (*Palm Tree of Deborah*) was written by Rabbi Moses Cordovero, one of the leading kabbalists in Safed. He focuses on imitation of God through the acquisition of divine traits (especially those of the kabbalistic *sefirot*). The first edition was published in Venice in 1588.

is a spirit of purity that pushes for obedience to God and the Torah and for upholding ethical and ritual restrictions. R. Salanter proposes that one should look inward, into individual psychology, to add to this definition. The *yetzer hara* is the inner instinctual drives that desire immediate pleasure without restraint, while the *yetzer hatov* is reason, which respects limits and upholds the rules of the Torah.

However, "the imagination is a constantly flowing river, and reason will be inundated unless we guide it in a boat."[17] The "boat" is Mussar teachings – especially when internalized emotionally with "the sentiments of the soul" – the emotions that can reinforce reason and enable it to overcome the force of desires. Studying the laws and characteristics of the sin should be intensified by Mussar teachings, which also make vivid the eventual punishments. Together, these teachings will neutralize the evil drive. This will enable reason to triumph and guide toward good behavior.

The next step is to saturate the culture with these values and to make Mussar study and practice standard fare for everyone. R. Salanter calls this dissemination of Mussar action "*lezakot et harabbim*" – to bring benefit or merit to the masses. Such outreach works. He offers as proof that the laws of *kashrut* are so well entrenched in Lithuania that laypeople, the butcher and the baker who provide kosher food, avoid even marginal or doubtful cases of non-kosher rather than risk violating the rules of eating kosher. By contrast, when it comes to ethics in commerce and Torah norms in business transactions, people are lax and often willing to cut ethical corners to make money. R. Salanter insists that both ritual and ethical instructions "are equal in the Torah." Prohibitions in both areas are given equal weight.. He calls for learning all the laws and details of commerce in the Torah and backing them up with Mussar texts (including focusing on future punishment) and analyses. R. Salanter envisions a holistic religious life in which ethics in worldly matters are as rigorously and faithfully practiced as ritual matters. Here again one sees R. Salanter's focus on laypeople and his awareness that with the advent of modern economics, most people will be engaged in business or industry, and the Torah should guide them in both areas to do the right thing.

17. See *Iggeret HaMussar* in this volume.

In 1857, R. Israel Salanter left Kovno and moved west. He lived in Koenigsberg (then part of Prussia, today Kaliningrad, Russia), then in Memel (today Klaipeda, Lithuania). Both cities were geographically and culturally closer to the West. For the next two decades, he spent most of his time in similar cities in Germany in particular, working with (and living in) Jewish communities that include Berlin and Paris, where he spent two years. He regularly returned to Lithuania (especially Kovno and Vilna) for extended visits.

Why would a Torah scholar of enormous breadth and widely respected status, with mastery of Hebrew and Yiddish, the languages in which he taught his students, give up all this? In Western Europe, he did not have the local language (although he studied and learned limited German) and did not have the broad public recognition which he enjoyed in Lithuania. In effect, he chose to work with serious handicaps for the final two decades of his life rather than maximize his impact in his home location of Lithuania. Why?

R. Salanter's students and contemporary academic historians agree that his decision reflects his desire to deal with the challenge of modernity and its increasing inroads in Jewish life. However, I believe that they have not drawn the full implications of this behavior. R. Salanter's explanation is widely quoted:

> When horses begin to gallop wildly… down the hill, it is totally impossible to stop them in the middle of the mountain…. Only after the horses have gone all the way downhill, can they be stopped and calmed down. The same is true in the direction of communities. In the great cities of Russia, the communities are galloping down the mountain and are now in the middle of the descent, so it is impossible to bring about any order to them. But the communities abroad have already reached the bottom of the hill, so it is now possible to halt them and to put them in place.[18]

18. Jacob Mark, *Gedolim fun Unzerer Tsayt* (New York, 1924), Hebrew edition: *BeMeḥitzatan*, 77, quoted in Etkes, *Salanter*, 241–7.

This parable clearly reflects his sense of his mission as equipping the religious Jewish community to cope with modernity. I believe that this consciousness grew in Kovno because while he lived there, the modern economy – and, with it, the culture of modernity and the influence of the *Haskala* – grew stronger. In wrestling with this phenomenon, R. Salanter himself incorporated some new insights into his thinking. Letter 6 of *Ohr Yisrael*, while undated, is the first unit that is post-Kovno. To me, the most striking note in the letter is R. Salanter's description of the person as an "*anokhi*," that is an I, a self. He uses the term in the context of a very traditional formulation, namely, that the individual who sins in this world will suffer much greater pain in the next world. The pleasures and pains of this world are dwarfed by far by the rewards and punishments of the next. He speaks of the human as a composite of physical body and spiritual soul but states that the two together make up an *anokhi* – a self. That self does not die with the body but lives on to experience ultimate reward and punishment. Clearly, R. Salanter was affected by his exposure to modernity, where thinking of the individual as a "self" is widespread. This is in contradistinction to medieval thinkers like Rambam, who in his *Shemona Perakim* focuses on the individual as an agglomeration of separate "*middot*," or dispositions.[19]

Here we come to a fundamental divide between R. Salanter and his peers. They focused on keeping modern culture out. They sought to preserve a Jewish educational system that taught only Torah subjects and neither the language nor the culture of the country. They were relatively impervious to the emerging economy and culture of modernity, and they hoped to keep it away from their students and out of their communities. By contrast, R. Salanter saw that modernity was advancing and inescapable. As he saw it, the only adequate response was to shift Judaism from a self-evident tradition, practiced reflexively and in conformity with the religious community, into an internalized set of values and shaped character traits designed to create a good human being. Such a person would be able to uphold and practice Judaism, undeterred by the growing secularization and economic engagement of the masses in

19. The *Shemona Perakim*, or *Eight Chapters*, are Rambam's introduction to his commentary on Avot. See further in Letter 6, n. 5, of this book.

making a living. The modern world would likely pull people away from the traditional way of life by offering expanded economic activity and rewards. The new civilization wove a fabric of culture that was not supportive of traditional practice and was increasingly less focused on God and Torah. R. Salanter's envisioned transformation was the key to the tradition's capacity to live in the presence of modernity.

When R. Salanter moved from Kovno to Koenigsberg, Memel, and further west, he clearly wanted to confront the lion of modernity in its den. He sought to develop prophylactic tactics and teachings to enable people to live religiously in the midst of the new. In Koenigsberg, he worked closely with R. Yaakov Tzvi Mecklenburg, an Orthodox rabbi who fought the spread of *Haskala* and, to that end, authored a Torah commentary, *HaKetav VeHaKabbala*, to demonstrate the unity of the Written Torah and the rabbinic tradition. There, R. Salanter worked on creating informal educational activities, giving special lectures on Talmud to students in the local university – students who had a broad education but much less Jewish knowledge than his students in Lithuania – and speaking to them at their level.

When he moved to Memel in 1860, he gave weekly sermons to the public on the Torah portion of the week. He organized a *ḥevra Shas* (a daily Talmud study group) for laypeople. He organized Torah lessons for the younger generation. At the same time, he reached out to nascent Torah scholars with special classes and Mussar training. He also raised funds for these young scholars, thereby enabling them to focus on their advanced studies.

One must conclude that R. Salanter consciously chose to work on "lower level" Torah projects that could hold modernizing Jews' loyalty rather than the higher level of the renowned Lithuanian yeshivot. To be fair, some of his students enriched and reformatted these yeshivot by introducing Mussar study and practice. Moreover, three of his major disciples founded "experimental" yeshivot that introduced elements of modernity. In R. Simcha Zissel Ziv's yeshiva in Kelm (Kelmė), Russian language and mathematics were taught. R. Eliezer Gordon's yeshiva in Telz (Telšiai) introduced an entrance exam, a graded hierarchy of classes, and regular testing of students' knowledge. The culture of R. Natan Tzvi Finkel's yeshiva in Slabodka (Vilijampolė, today a neighborhood of Kovno/Kaunas) focused on instilling such "bourgeois" virtues as orderliness, personal hygiene, dignity, and restraint. Most students in these schools were clean-shaven and dressed in "modern" clothes. Yet these schools were outliers. The mainstream yeshivot – even those taken over by Mussarists – assiduously kept out all modern culture and influences as best they could.

R. Salanter clearly felt that developing new forms of Torah education – as he could not do in Eastern Europe – was essential to stem the tide of secularization and *Haskala*. The fact that he maintained this as a priority for the next twenty years of his life speaks volumes as to what he regarded as his main priority and life mission.

Let us explore another aspect of this choice: How did R. Salanter come to the German Jewish communities in the first place? R. Salanter suffered from melancholy. These bouts of depression increased as he got older. His friends advised him to see doctors and take the medicinal waters in Halberstadt, Germany, where many people went for relief from such illnesses. After spending half a year there, he decided not to return to Lithuania but to work in the modernizing German communities.

At this point, I invoke a bit of privileged information that I heard during my days studying at Yeshivas Beis Yosef. Fellow students shared with me an oral tradition: R. Salanter decided to send a disciple (who wanted to do so) to study medicine. This smacks of an experiment to see whether Western culture could be introduced into his constituency without undermining people's religious commitments. The story went that the student successfully studied medicine, but in the process broke with Jewish tradition and observance. One version of the account was that in order to advance professionally, the student converted to Christianity. Another version was that the student gave up observance to pursue his studies and be accepted by his fellow professionals.

This experience showed R. Salanter that the gap between Eastern European Orthodoxy and religious ideology, on one hand, and the emerging modernist culture and community, on the other, was too great to be successfully bridged even by elite students who had support and supervision. I conclude that since he considered solving the challenge of modernity to be an essential historical need, R. Salanter became determined to face the challenge on its home turf. Only in such an environment could he figure out the adjustments and institutional shifts that could sustain observant Jews and Torah culture in the new milieu. R. Salanter therefore sacrificed his own comfort, status, and recognition to better rescue the Torah for the emerging civilization.

I think – this is plausible, but it may be pure speculation – the failed student incident happened late in the Kovno years and led to his decision to move. The relocation enabled him to concentrate on Western Jewish communities or, more precisely, on Eastern European Jews who were moving west. This was the constituency out of which he grew, and they were experiencing the impact of modernity head on.

I am fully aware that oral traditions – especially ones passed through three generations or more – are often fanciful. Moreover, the Beis Yosef students gave no dates for this alleged incident, and there are no references in published books or volumes that offer verifiable information to corroborate the story. Nevertheless, R. Salanter's decision to live primarily in the West implies that he had an equivalent set of experiences and incidents that convinced him that such experiments could not work in Lithuania. Furthermore, there are numerous accounts that he worked with proponents of the "*Torah im Derekh Eretz*" movement in Germany, people who were trying to articulate an Orthodoxy that incorporated modern elements and whose constituents were able to participate in the new economy and culture without jettisoning traditional observance. R. Salanter met with them, encouraged them, and attended their programs to learn from them. In effect, he chose to spend the last part of his life working on their issues.

R. Salanter is quoted with some frequency as commenting that these are worthy and compelling projects, but that they could not be realized in Eastern Europe. In fact, R. Salanter continued to resist any modernization of the content of yeshiva education and communal projects in Lithuania. He also turned down a request from R. Azriel Hildesheimer, who founded an Orthodox rabbinical seminary in Berlin in the early 1870s, to solicit support for the seminary from some of R. Salanter's wealthy followers in Eastern Europe. Etkes argues that R. Salanter opposed attempts to positively modernize Orthodoxy. He permitted such activity only after the fact – as in Germany, where there was no other plausible approach – but resolutely opposed introducing these methods into Eastern Europe on principle. I argue that the last twenty years of his life are the best proof of what he really thought was essential. During these decades, he developed tactics that could bring Orthodoxy into the new culture successfully. I submit that his opposition to introducing these approaches in Eastern Europe was the outcome of his conviction that the gaps *there* were too great. Such approaches were bound to fail – and to undermine the established (if shrinking) dominance of the traditional lifestyle in Eastern Europe.

Let me cite one story that illustrates my point and then apply it again to R. Salanter's parable about runaway horses and communities. R. Yitzhak Yaakov Reines, an early Zionist and moderate modernizer, reported a conversation he had with R. Israel Salanter. R. Salanter told him of a visit to R. Hildesheimer's rabbinical seminary and then to his school for girls, praising the schools and their impact. Then he said: "... one can say with absolute certainty that this learned rabbi is doing a thing beyond value. Nevertheless, let a rabbi in our country attempt to *create a school of this type, they would insult him and chase him away,* and there is no doubt that *he would be forced to cease practicing the rabbinate,* for he would no longer be suited for it."[20]

If we look again at R. Salanter's parable of the runaway horses, we may offer the following comment: What happens when the horses bolt but *the driver has not grasped* that he no longer has control? A bystander trying to intervene at this moment would be perceived as disruptive. Indeed, the driver might be rattled by the intervention and lose any residual control that he has. The driver might well strike the bystander, believing that the would-be helper is actually endangering the driver or causing the horses to bolt!

R. Salanter's colleagues in Eastern Europe had not recognized that the horses bolted and that modernity was in the saddle. Therefore, they would likely condemn and exclude all attempts to "reform" from within as evil and motivated by bad intentions. R. Salanter's resolute opposi-

20. Reines, *Zikaron BaSefer*, n. 91, quoted in Etkes, *Salanter*, 284–5. It is worth noting that R. Reines himself tried, on two occasions, to establish a yeshiva that included some secular studies. The first attempt failed due to opposition, and even the second attempt, at Lida, achieved only a brief period of success.

tion to introducing any modernizing practices reflects his judgment that there was no chance of successfully using these tactics in Russia because of the cultural gap – and because the religious leadership's opposition would kill any marginal chance of accomplishing the goal.

There is evidence that R. Salanter felt that the quality of German neo-Orthodoxy's Torah learning (and that of its rabbis) was inferior to that of Eastern Europe and its rabbis and Torah scholars – at least at that moment. Still, he spent the next two decades with them, helping them, arranging to translate some of their material, and making it available in Hebrew and Yiddish. I believe that he hoped that someday he could use their approaches at a higher level of Torah learning, as would be appropriate for Eastern Europe. By then, presumably, people would recognize that the horses – and communities – had undeniably bolted but had reached a straightaway where a new order could be established. In the interim, R. Salanter felt that internal reward and religious deepening through Mussar (and some institutional reforms) were the only way to preserve the traditional Jewish community of Eastern Europe. Only a religious renaissance, an upgrade of religious life, would enable it to stand up to the presence of modernity, whose advent was inevitable.

What did R. Salanter do in the German communities during the last two decades of his life? As noted, his primary constituency consisted of Eastern European Jews who had migrated to Germany. These Jews were held to be culturally backward, coarse, and unenlightened by Germans – Jews, even Orthodox Jews, and gentiles alike – and they came under a great deal of pressure to become "civilized" and "useful."[21] It was here that R. Salanter felt that he could introduce a program for the educational and cultural upbuilding of Eastern European Jews in Germany that would draw on Jewish text and tradition.

He tried to strengthen communal institutions so that synagogues could provide religious services and communities could provide kosher food and social services that could meet the needs of immigrating Eastern European Jews and keep them within the Orthodox community. He facilitated the hiring of a new type of rabbi in these communities – those

21. See Steven E. Aschheim, *Brothers and Strangers: The East European Jew and German Jewish Consciousness, 1800–1923* (Madison: University of Wisconsin Press, 1982), 3–31.

who would influence laypeople and work to build a community, and not detached, scholarly rabbis – who were under his influence and who would include Mussar and character building as an important part of their rabbinate. Most of all, he tried to personally reach out – especially to the younger generation and especially to university students – to fill some of the void in their Jewish education. He offered classes of his own, and he sought out frameworks to speak personally to them.

Among other projects, R. Salanter tried to make the Talmud accessible to such audiences and considered what it would take to make Talmud attractive to them. He promoted translations of the Talmud into German, as they could facilitate the bridging of Judaism and German civilization. He even raised the idea of getting Talmud introduced into universities as part of standard humanities curricula available to any student. This would give it credibility and prestige with Jewish university students as no mere relic of a pre-modern tradition but a form of humanities and literature that modern culture respected and considered worthy of being known by an educated person. He was unable to execute these projects successfully, but these very ideas were carried out within a century, as Judaism learned to live in the presence of modernity. We should also note that were he promoting such projects in Eastern Europe, his peers might well have concluded that he was off the right path and should be disowned as endangering the tradition.

These projects show that he was convinced that the religious sources must be presented in a new light so they could resonate and be impactful within the emerging culture. Of course, he was hoping to preserve their original spirit and religious values in the process. The imagination and daring of these projects shows that he really took the matter of communicating Judaism within the culture of modernity very seriously. He also spent much time with the neo-Orthodox rabbis in Germany, with special connections to Rabbis Azriel Hildesheimer and Samson Raphael Hirsch. He attended their classes and gave them moral support. As mentioned, I envision him trying to imagine how to translate their approach into a higher level of religious efficacy which could uphold Orthodoxy in Eastern Europe.

Another example of his creativity is the journal *Tevunah*, which he founded and published during his years in Memel. He understood that one of the attractive powers of modern culture was that it generated conversations that encouraged people to develop and express opinions. This culture communicated its values through many channels and media. He felt that Orthodox rabbis needed to shift their focus and communicate more with lay people at the popular level, rather than give sermons at the rarefied level of higher learning characteristic of the Lithuanian elites and the world of the yeshivot. He came up with the idea of *Tevunah* to serve as a medium of conversation among rabbis and to stimulate them to articulate religious ideas that could reach broader swaths of their lay communities.

Unfortunately, here too, he was ahead of his time, at least in terms of Eastern Europe. Although he successfully recruited many important rabbis to submit articles for the journal, most of them produced halakhic discussions and talmudic explanations that were abstract or unrelated to the knowledge or interests of laypeople. He also overestimated his ability to enlist subscribers to the journal. As a result, he ran out of money and had to suspend publication. He never was able to reconstitute *Tevunah*, although he talked about it for years. He himself submitted an introduction and two major essays which show growth in his personal thinking. These writings might be the most important outcome of the *Tevunah* project. However, the journal's failure illustrates again how he was far ahead of his peers in understanding the power and attraction of modernity and what adjustments it would take to gain Torah a full hearing in the new culture.

The *Tevunah* essays show another way he utilized his sojourns in the West. He read nineteenth-century scientific literature, at least as it related to human psychology. In the process, the centerpiece of his thinking – the divide within human beings between instinct, lust, and desire, on one hand, and reason, common sense, and mature moral thinking, on the other, turned into a more sophisticated understanding of human psychology. He came to see that in every human being there were "dark" ("*dunkel*") forces – what we would today call unconscious forces – and "bright" ("*bahir*") forces, which are the operations of reason. The unconscious has the power to distort or reshape reason – often in ways of which the person is unaware. To R. Salanter, this awareness opened his eyes to the greater elements of subjectivity in all communication and all interpretation. Rational arguments and judgments had to be assessed to see if there were unconscious factors that were determining – even twisting – supposedly rational statements. The "self-evident" truth of Torah – just reading it and applying it – needed to be analyzed and assessed as to its being plain truth or a distortion due to emotional forces.

All mitzvot and prohibitions could not be simply assessed or judged identically. Given the psychological makeup of people, the same mitzva could be enormously hard to observe for one person and easy to uphold for another. R. Salanter speculated that God knew these undercurrents far more than individuals did and judged each person individually and distinctively based on their makeup. He also drew other challenging conclusions. A person could think they were observing Torah when in fact they were misreading the sources (or contradicting their reasoned understanding in their actual behavior patterns).

R. Salanter also came up with a more multi-factored understanding of the nature of truth – even in sacred texts. The psychological orientation of the sages of the Schools of Hillel and Shammai was a factor in their respective schools' approaches to halakha. However, this apparent undercutting of the objectivity of halakha was offset by his teaching that God understands human subjectivity and accepts that materials generated under the influence of mixed human motives and interpretations would be incorporated in divine Torah. This admixture was the inevitable outcome of giving Torah to humanity (instead of preserving its purity by keeping it in the heavens). He also came to see the value of *maḥloket* and multiple viewpoints in bringing out the full truth of Torah. Given the blind spots and emotional blockage in each individual, the best approach to understand a text was to study it in a group or by the method of *maḥloket* (dialogic argument). Each individual saw the text through his own lens. Each should argue his insights with full force. Since all are committed to observing God's Torah, they had to be willing to accept the most plausible version (or the integrated resolutions of the various viewpoints) rather than become too ego-invested and strive to make their views win out. Thus, *maḥloket* became an essential tool of bringing out the fullest (and most refined) understanding of Torah.

Each individual had to work (using Mussar) to curb and channel his emotional desires so they could be controlled, while at the same time developing the capacity to affect or neutralize the conflicting emotions and thus enable a rational judgment to be made. Of course, R. Salanter saw that many scholars never reached that point of self-abnegation (which is why Mussar training was needed). This also meant that rabbis and scholars could also be blinded or misled by ego and bias. In such cases, they would not understand Torah correctly. Sometimes, their behaviors would violate Torah norms, often behind the cover of pious words or values. This critique did not endear him or the Mussarists to their opponents or people whose piety they critiqued.

Despite living in Germany, R. Israel did not turn his back on Eastern Europe. His students continued to spread his ideas and introduce Mussar teaching there. They succeeded in reshaping certain major yeshivot into schools where Mussar was a powerful element. He continued to help his students attain rabbinical positions in communities where he had some influence, and he continued to speak out on community policies. He played a leading role (with R. Isaac Elhanan Spektor) in establishing the Kollel Perushim in Kovno, an institution that provided financial support for advanced Torah scholars to concentrate on becoming major scholars and decisors.

His essay, written in support of the kollel, notes the erosion of the community's religious value system and argues that philanthropy must take up the slack by providing economic support and assurance of livelihood to those who would become leading scholars and *poskim*. (See his final essay in this book.) He actively led the rejection of the revived idea of a new government-sponsored rabbinical seminary, advanced by the *maskilim* and Baron David Guinzberg, who was close to the Russian government. He judged that this seminary, too, was intended to be a vehicle to undermine the traditional rabbinate and community culture. While he succeeded in blocking the seminary, clearly the communal battle for tradition was being lost.

This brings us back to R. Salanter's personal life. As mentioned, he suffered from bouts of depression, which became more frequent after his wife died in 1871 (after which he traveled more and returned less often to Lithuania). Of course, one cannot fully assess rational considerations in terms of the affliction of depression. Nevertheless, I have often thought that his emotional suffering could be seen, at least in part, not as internally induced depression but as a realistic response to his life situation. He foresaw the advent of modernity and the weakening of Torah and Judaism. He even came up with strategies to preserve the tradition. But the traditional community did not see what he saw, and consequently he was unable to adequately fund his projects, leaving many of his strategies unrealized. In addition, his disciples succeeded in many areas, but they did not make significant inroads among laypeople, whom R. Salanter considered the key battleground. Add to that, that most of his avant-garde ideas to cope with modernity could not be pursued in Lithuania. In truth, his closest students could not understand or carry out his most challenging ideas. The inexorable march of modernity won out. Two of his sons were swept up by the attractions of *Haskala*. The combination of all these factors would be enough to depress a naturally happy person.

The deeper point is that the rabbinic leadership of Eastern European Jewry (which he supported even as he sought to develop alternate tactics to protect Judaism in the new culture) continued to pursue the strategy of completely maintaining the inherited traditional culture. They tried to seal it off culturally and demographically while prohibiting positive responses to modern culture. They built higher fences around their community and blocked any attempts to integrate modern elements into the tradition. They managed to hold the line with an ever-shrinking traditional community, but the majority of Jews chose paths other than strict adherence to tradition, whether by assimilating into the majority culture or by developing alternatives to traditional religious culture.

After the *Shoah*, which wiped out more than eighty percent of the traditional community, there was an important comeback, especially in the new State of Israel, where the majority treasured and supported the *ḥaredim* and underwrote their way of life economically. The net result was a demographic resurgence. However, Orthodox Judaism played little or no role in dealing with the broader challenges of modern culture and scholarship or in building economic and social infrastructure.

R. Salanter's strategy of renewing Orthodoxy, ethically and spiritually, and developing a strongly internalized religion that would adapt, even flourish, within modernity was cut short. These developments seemingly made R. Salanter's vision marginal within the Orthodox community, and the Torah, as envisioned by him, marginal in the general community of Israel. If this outcome holds, then, in my opinion, this would be tragic not only for R. Salanter personally, but for the Torah tradition as a whole, which would be left as mostly a way of life of a small tribe of Jews rather than serving as a blueprint or moving force for the repair of the world for all humanity (which the Torah seeks to be). The alternative I hope and pray for is a renaissance of Torah. One can envision a new generation rediscovering R. Salanter, taking up his Torah, deepening the religious spirit of Judaism, and renewing its ability to create deeply ethical, kind, caring human beings. This would pave the way for following through on his exploration of transmitting Torah through and in the new culture.

This is the hope that animates this English edition of the *Ohr Yisrael*!

To his credit, R. Salanter steadfastly pressed on. He lived by his vision with no consideration of his personal costs. He sacrificed communal understanding and honored status in order to serve God and save his tradition. Yet he never complained or felt deprived. His selflessness was developed to such a point that none of these setbacks deterred him. His kind and caring character, his sensitivity to people, his thoughtfulness for the poor and the marginal, and his strong commitment to ethics and faith, made him a role model and a legend in his time.

The final night of his life serves as a fitting coda to it. As R. Salanter was dying, he realized that the man assigned to be with him (and to guard his body after his death) was a simple man with a great deal of anxiety. He expressed fear of death as well as fear of demons and malign forces. Instead of turning inward, as most people do when they feel the approach of death, R. Salanter spoke with him at length. He explained that death was not to be feared, that God was with him and therefore, the demons and evil spirits would not harm him. Thus R. Salanter passed away and returned his soul to the God whom he followed, clung to, and served all his life.

אור ישראל

חֲמִשָּׁה מִכְתָּבִים הָרִאשׁוֹנִים. הֵם אֲשֶׁר כָּתַב אדמו״ר זצוק״ל בִּתְחִלַּת בּוֹאוֹ מִוִּילְנָא לְקָאוְונָא בִּשְׁנַת תר״ט. לְתַלְמִידָיו וּמְקֹרָבָיו בָּעִיר וִילְנָא.

1 This Hebrew honorific, "*admo"r*" ("***ad**oneinu, **mo**reinu, ve**r**abbenu*"), is bestowed by disciples and followers on rabbinic leaders, especially in the hasidic movement. Though neither R. Salanter nor his disciples were part of the hasidic movement, their movement, the Mussar movement, took on some of the emotional trappings of Hasidism, including emphasis on emotion and reverence for a *rebbe*. Some have referred to the Mussar movement as the "Hasidism of the *Mitnagdim*" (the opponents of Hasidism, whose primary emphasis was on Torah study as an intellectual endeavor).

2 An acronym standing for "*zekher tzaddik vekadosh livrakha*" (may the memory of the righteous and holy be for a blessing).

Ohr Yisrael

The first five letters that our master, teacher, and rabbi,[1] ztvk"l,[2] *wrote when he first came from Vilna to Kovno[3] in 5609[4] to his disciples and close associates in the city of Vilna.*

---

3 R. Salanter left Vilna for Kovno in 1848 to remove himself from the Tsarist government's pressure on him to teach Talmud in the new, state-sponsored rabbinical seminary established in Vilna in 1847. The Russian regime, under Tsar Nicholas I and his Education Minister, Sergey Uvarov, hoped to produce a more modern, educated, Russified rabbinate that would encourage greater Jewish participation in Russia's civic life. R. Salanter believed that the Tsarist government and its maskilic collaborators had an assimilationist agenda and was skeptical about the seminary's ability to train rabbis properly. He feared that graduates of such a seminary would likely weaken religious standards and beliefs. Rather than join the seminary faculty, he fled Vilna. See Etkes, *Salanter*, 145–9.

4 1848–1849 in the Gregorian calendar.

א

יְדִידַי הַנֶּאֱהָבִים אַתְחִיל לְדַבֵּר

אֶת מְגַמַּת רְצוֹנִי אֲשֶׁר הִצַּעְתִּי לִפְנֵיכֶם תָּמִיד. לָתֵת לְבַבְכֶם עֲלֵיהֶם וּלְהִתְבּוֹנֵן בָּם בִּינָה, אִם אֱמֶת יֶהְגֶּה חִכִּי? כִּמְעַט רֶגַע הָיָה נִכְנָס דְּבָרַי בְּאָזְנֵיכֶם. וְעוֹד מְעַט קָט וְאֵינֶנָּה. בְּאֹזֶן אַחַת בָּאוּ וּבְאֹזֶן אַחֶרֶת הָלְכוּ – אֵין זֹאת כִּי אִם הַחִסָּרוֹן הַמֻּרְגָּל שֶׁלֹּא לָתֵת לֵב בָּעִנְיָנִים הַנּוֹגְעִים בְּיִרְאָה וּמוּסָר, כִּי אִם לְהִתְנַהֵג בָּהֶם אַחַר הַתַּאֲוָה הַחָפְשִׁית לְפִי נְטִיַּת הָרָצוֹן כְּמַעֲשֵׂה הַבְּהֵמָה. הֲלֹא תִּרְאוּ בְּהַמִּנְהָג הַיָּדוּעַ הַמְשׁוֹטֵט עַל פְּנֵי תֵבֵל. לָתֵת עִיּוּן וְהִתְבּוֹנְנוּת בְּכָל הָעִנְיָנִים הַגַּשְׁמִיִּים. הַסּוֹחֵר בְּמַרְכֻּלְתּוֹ כַּמָּה הִתְבּוֹנְנוּת יִשְׁתַּמֵּשׁ טֶרֶם יְבַצַּע הָעֵסֶק. אִם לַעֲשׂוֹת אוֹ לַחֲדֹל. יַחְשֹׁב בְּנַפְשׁוֹ וְיִתְיָעֵץ עִם רֵעָיו הַנֶּאֱמָנִים לוֹ. יָתוּר עַל הַפְּרָטִים, יְבַקֵּשׁ מְקוֹם הַטָּעוּת, עַד יוֹצִיא הַדָּבָר לָאוֹר לְפִי

---

1. Compare Proverbs 8:7.
2. In R. Salanter's terminology, *hergel* refers to a combination of habit and routine, whereby a certain behavior has become second nature that one does without reflection. Here, *murgal* refers to behavior that has become so embedded in the culture that surrounds the individual that it is done automatically, without any dissention from that culture.

Letter 1

My beloved friends:

I will begin to speak of the goals I seek, which I have always set before you, so that you may contemplate them and analyze them to comprehend their implications. Did my mouth utter truth?[1] Barely a moment after my words entered your ears, they were gone. They went in one ear and out the other. This is none other than the problem of routinization,[2] namely, the lack of attention to matters pertaining to reverence and Mussar[3] and instead acting in these matters as unfettered instinct dictates, following the tendency[4] of one's will, as an animal does.

Consider the familiar practice that is becoming prevalent all over the world: to consider and scrutinize all material matters.[5] How much thought a merchant gives before deciding whether or not to do a transaction! He thinks to himself, consults with his most trusted friends, surveys all the details, and looks to see where he may have miscalculated, until he has illuminated the issue as best he can.

---

3. Mussar is a stream of tradition originating in medieval Judaism that focused on character building and virtue as against a primary focus on Torah learning and conventional observance.
4. A "*netiya*" is a tendency, a bias, or orientation that stems from an interest or an inner psychological attraction to acting in a certain manner.
5. In Letter 2, R. Salanter refers to this as "*ḥokhmat haolam*" ("the wisdom of the world"); in his view, one learns from and adapts standard practices from business or worldly affairs, which enables one to strengthen religious understanding and practice.

כֹּחוֹ. כֵּן בְּלִמּוּד הַתּוֹרָה הַקְּדוֹשָׁה כָּל אֶחָד לְפִי עֶרְכּוֹ. יְעַיֵּן וְיִתְבּוֹנֵן בָּהּ לְגַלּוֹת מַטְמוֹנֶיהָ, וּלְחַדֵּשׁ חִדּוּשִׁים וּלְפָרֵק הֲוָיוֹת, לֹא יְדַלֵּג בִּסְקִירָה אַחַת, לְהַחְלִיט הַדָּבָר הֶחְלֵט פְּסוּקָה.

לֹא כֵן בְּדַרְכֵי הַמּוּסָר, אֲשֶׁר הַהִתְבּוֹנְנוּת בָּהּ הַחִפּוּשׂ בְּכָל דַּרְכֵי וּמַעֲשֵׂה הָאָדָם, לְהִשָּׁמֵר מִנְּטִיַּת הָרָצוֹן, וּמֵהַיֵּצֶר הַמַּפְרִיעַ וּמוֹנֵעַ כָּל דָּבָר טוֹב וּמְעֻלֶּה, הַהֶכְרֵחִי וּמְחֻיָּב לְהַשָּׂגַת הַיִּרְאָה, וְלֹא תָּקוּם הַמּוּסָר וְהַהַנְהָגָה טוֹבָה בְּלֹא תַּחְבּוּלוֹת גְּדוֹלוֹת, לֶאֱסֹר כְּלֵי הַמֹּחַ לָזֶה עַד שֶׁיַּעֲשֶׂה רֹשֶׁם חָזָק בַּלֵּב לָתֵת עֹז וְתַעֲצוּמוֹת לָאֵבָרִים הַחִיצוֹנִים: לְהוֹצִיא לַפֹּעַל הָעִנְיָן הַמְעֻלֶּה, בַּל יַעַצְרוּהוּ תַּאֲוַת הַגּוּפָנִיּוּת הַפְּחוּתָה, הַקִּנְאָה וְהַכָּבוֹד הַבְּזוּיִים. וּבְכָל זֶה עַצְלוּת הָאָדָם רַבָּה בָּזֶה, לְמַעֲמָסָה תִּהְיֶה לוֹ אִם יַפְנֶה אֶת עַצְמוֹ זְמַן קָצָר לָזֶה. עַד אֲשֶׁר גַּם לְבִטּוּל הַזְּמַן יֵחָשֵׁב לוֹ.

עַתָּה מַה לַּעֲשׂוֹת. הַמִּלְחָמָה נְכוֹנָה, הַיֵּצֶר מְאָרֵב, הַתַּאֲוָה מְשׁוֹטֶטֶת, הַמִּדּוֹת מְרַגְּשׁוֹת, כְּלֵי הַמִּלְחָמָה אַיִן. הֲיֵעָשֶׂה כְּלִי לְמַעֲשֵׂהוּ בִּלְתִּי פּוֹעֵל נִרְצֶה לָזֶה. כֵּן אֵין תִּקְוָה לְהִנָּצֵל מִמּוֹקְשֵׁי מָוֶת בִּלְתִּי אִם נַחְזִיק בִּכְלֵי הַמִּלְחָמָה, עִנְיְנֵי הַיִּרְאָה וְהַמּוּסָר.

וְלָזֹאת אַחַת דִּבַּרְתִּי כֹּה תַּעֲשׂוּ וְטוֹב לָכֶם – הָאִישׁ הַמְטֹרָד בְּכָל אֲשֶׁר יִפְנֶה יַרְשִׁיעַ. עֲסָקָיו הוֹלְכִים קְדוֹרַנִּית, כֹּחוֹ וְשִׂכְלוֹ נְבוּכִים נְתוּנִים בְּמַאַסְרֵי הַדְּאָגָה וְהַבִּלְבּוּל. הַמְכַלֶּה אֶת כָּל כֹּחַ הָאֱנוֹשִׁי, וְהָיָה כִּי יִקְרַב אֵלָיו אִישׁ לֵאמֹר הֲלֹא חָזִיתִי לְךָ אוֹר, אִם תַּעֲשֶׂה אֶת הַדָּבָר

6. "Reverence" ("*yira*") variously refers to fear of Heaven, performing God-fearing actions, exhibiting moral awareness in behavior, and, above all, consciousness of the great reward and punishment in the afterlife for all earthly behaviors.
7. I.e., the intellect must influence the emotions.
8. Compare Job 1:7.
9. Compare Isaiah 54:16.
10. Compare Job 40:5.

So it is with respect to the study of the holy Torah – each person according to his own ability will consider and analyze it to reveal its hidden treasures, to produce novel insights, and to resolve questions. He will not skim over it at a glance and then make a definitive decision.

This is not the case with respect to the ways of Mussar. Its analysis entails searching all human paths and actions in order to guard against the tendency of the will and of the urge that disturbs and prevents all that is good and fine – an indispensable necessity to achieve reverence.[6] Mussar and good behavior will not endure without major strategies, for which one must harness the mind until it makes a strong impression on the heart[7] so that it empowers and energizes the external limbs to exercise refinement that is not impeded by lowly physical drives – contemptible envy and status-seeking. Yet, withal, humans are very lazy in this area! A person considers it a burden to devote himself [even] for a short time to this – to the point that he even considers it a waste of time.

So what shall we do? The war is upon us. The evil urge lies in ambush. Desire roams everywhere.[8] Character traits are driven by emotion. There are no weapons for this battle. Can one make an instrument fit for this work[9] without the necessary effort? Indeed, there is no hope of being saved from death traps unless we wield the weapons of war – the matters of reverence and Mussar.

To this end, there is one thing I have told you;[10] do it and it will be well with you. A preoccupied[11] person – everywhere he turns, he causes havoc.[12] His business is failing. His strength and reason are in turmoil, subject to the coils of anxiety and confusion that consume all human strength.

Now, if someone would approach this person and say, "I have seen a light for you. If you do this, then, according to an accurate assessment,

11. R. Salanter uses this term, "*mutrad*," as a concept. He often suggests that the average person in society is *mutrad* – preoccupied, overburdened, harried, and beleaguered – which enervates them, impairs their judgment, and reduces the quality of their religious activity and practice of fear of God. One of the goals of Mussar training was to develop an inner tranquility so as to make better religious, ethical, and existential decisions.
12. Compare I Samuel 14:47.

הַזֶּה לְפִי הַהַשְׁעָרָה הַנְּכוֹנָה, תּוּכַל לְהַרְוִיחַ אֶלֶף אֲלָפִים דִּינְרֵי זָהָב, לֹא יַטְרִידוּךָ הָעִנְיָן הַרְבֵּה מִתַּהֲלוּכוֹתֶיךָ וַעֲסָקֶיךָ וְלֹא תִּצְטָרֵךְ לְבַלּוֹת זְמַן הַרְבֵּה עַל זֶה – בְּוַדַּאי יִתֵּן לֵב נָבוֹן לָזֶה בְּרֹב עֹז וְתַעֲצוּמוֹת. כָּל כֹּחוֹת הַתְּבוּנָה יַצִּיק עַד אֲשֶׁר יְשָׁרֵשׁ הַדָּבָר בִּלְבָבוֹ דָּבָר נָכוֹן וּמְקֻיָּם. לְהַפְרִישׁ מְעַט זְמַן לָזֶה בְּהִתְבּוֹנְנוּת רְחָבָה, לְבַקֵּשׁ לוֹ רֵעִים כִּלְבָבוֹ אֲשֶׁר יַעַזְרוּ אוֹתוֹ לָזֶה, לֹא יָחוּשׁ עַל מְעַט בִּטּוּל הַכָּבוֹד וְהַסַּבְלָנוּת.

כֵּן אֲנַחְנוּ אֵלֶּה הַיּוֹם, מְעֻנִּים אֲנַחְנוּ בְּעִנּוּי נֶפֶשׁ, עֲוֹנוֹתֵינוּ עָבְרוּ רָאשֵׁינוּ אִישׁ אִישׁ לְפִי עֶרְכּוֹ – הַרְחֵק מְאֹד נַעֲמֹד מֵהַמֶּרְכָּז אֲשֶׁר לָזֶה נִבְרָא, וּמֵהַתַּכְלִית אֲשֶׁר בָּא לָעוֹלָם הַגַּשְׁמִי הַלָּזֶה לְהָכִין לוֹ לְאַחֲרִיתוֹ. וְעַתָּה רָאִינוּ אוֹר בָּהִיר מִתְנוֹצֵץ לְזַכּוֹת אֶת הָרַבִּים, לְחַזֵּק יָדַיִם רָפוֹת בְּלִמּוּד הַמּוּסָרִי, לָתֵת עֵצָה וְתַחְבּוּלָה לַעֲשׂוֹת מִנְהָג נָכוֹן בָּזֶה עַד אֲשֶׁר יִשְׁלֹט הַגַּאֲוָה הַמְרַחֶפֶת בָּעִנְיָן הַלֵּזוּ. לֵאמֹר וּלְהִתְפָּאֵר הַרְאִיתֶם הָאִישׁ הַלָּזֶה, כַּמָּה יָדוֹ תַּקִּיפָה בְּחָכְמַת הַיִּרְאָה וְהַמּוּסָר, אֲשֶׁר מִתּוֹךְ שֶׁלֹּא לִשְׁמָהּ יָבֹא לִשְׁמָהּ. אִם יַצְלִיחַ ד׳ אֶת דַּרְכֵּנוּ, אֵין עֲרֹךְ לְהַנּוֹלָד כַּמָּה יִגְדַּל עֶרְכּוֹ, וּבָזֹאת נִבָּנֶה גַּם אֲנַחְנוּ מָה, וְאִם מְעַט וְאִם הַרְבֵּה נֹאכַל.

לָזֹאת תִּקְבְּעוּ עֵת מוֹעֵד בְּשַׁבַּת קֹדֶשׁ לְהִתְאַסֵּף יַחַד בְּשָׁעָה מְיֻחָד, לְהִתְבּוֹנֵן בִּינָה אֵיךְ לְהַמְשִׁיךְ הָאֵיכוּת. גְּדוֹלֵי הָעִיר אֲשֶׁר אַחֲרֵיהֶם הַרְבֵּה יָרוּצוּ לְלִמּוּד הַמּוּסָרִי, תְּדַבְּרוּ דְּבָרִים בְּנַחַת וּבְיִשּׁוּב הַדַּעַת בְּלֹא שְׂחוֹק וְהִתּוּל, תַּעֲרִיכוּ מַעֲלוֹת הָאִישׁ וְחֶסְרוֹנוֹ, וּבַמֶּה יְוֻסַּר וּבַמֶּה יֵאָסֵר לָזֶה, אַל תַּחְלִיטוּ הַדָּבָר בִּסְקִירָה אַחַת. תְּחַלְּקוּ אֶת הָעֲבוֹדָה לְכֻלְּכֶם

---

13. I.e., the World to Come.
14. Compare Isaiah 35:3.
15. R. Salanter uses the Hebrew word *taḥbula* to describe a cunning strategy – one that employs human weaknesses to redirect them to good behaviors. Here, he proposes that learning Mussar be turned into a source of pride. Pride is typically not a good trait, and Mussar seeks to eliminate it. Here, however, by turning learning Mussar into a badge of honor, many more will be brought to the study of Mussar.
16. That is, teaching Mussar practice to others and working with them on improving their traits will have a positive effect on the teachers themselves.
17. In fact, leaders of the Mussar movement created a special Mussar-learning session that was held regularly on Shabbat afternoon, between sunset and the appearance

you will profit thousands upon thousands of gold pieces. It will not divert you much from your other activities and enterprises. You won't have to spend much time on it either," the preoccupied person will certainly pay real attention to this, with great energy and strength. He will mold all his powers of understanding until the matter takes root in his heart properly and enduringly. He will set aside some time for it and give it wide-ranging consideration. He will seek out like-minded friends to help him in this endeavor. He will not even notice a bit of lost status or the patience required.

Indeed, this is our present state. We are in the throes of spiritual torment. We are inundated by sin – each person to a different degree. We stand very far from the objective of our creation and from the goal for which one comes into this world: to prepare himself for his ultimate end.[13] But now we see a bright light rising to benefit the multitudes: to strengthen weak hands,[14] by Mussar study; to provide advice and strategies for establishing good practice in this respect, to the extent that the ever-present pride takes control in this area.[15] That is, people will take pride when others say: "Have you seen this man? How great he is in the wisdom of reverence and Mussar!" From this self-interested motive, he will eventually come to [reverence] for its own sake! If God grants us success, there is no limit to how valuable the result can be. And with that, we personally will also be improved somewhat, whether we achieve a little or a lot.[16]

To this end, set a meeting time on the holy Shabbat; gather together at a specific time.[17] Consider seriously how to attract the elite, the community leaders – for others will run after them to learn Mussar. Discuss these matters calmly, soberly, without frivolity or jest. Assess each person's qualities and faults, how they can be improved and how they can be harnessed to this cause. Do not make decisions after one

---

of the stars. This is a time when twilight and the subdued emotions of leaving the Shabbat behind create a mood that is receptive to introspection and self-criticism. As an educator, R. Salanter stressed the context of learning as an important influence on the individual's receptivity. In the same way, he developed the idea of a Mussar *Shtiebel* (House). The space was dedicated exclusively to Mussar study, so the environment would encourage emotional expression of self-criticism and introspection.

בִּמְעַט זְמַן וּבְלִי כֹּבֶד הָעֲבוֹדָה, וְקֹבֶץ עַל יָד יִרְבֶּה אָכֵן בְּדַעַת שְׁקֵטָה בְּיִשּׁוּב נָבוֹן וְנָכוֹן, אִישׁ אֶת רֵעֵהוּ יְחַזֵּק וְאֶת שְׁטוּת לְבָבוֹ יַרְפֶּה, אֶת עַצְלוּת הֶרְגֵּלוֹ יְבַטֵּל, בְּדֶרֶךְ אֶרֶץ וּבְנַחַת לִשְׁמֹר כָּל אֶחָד כְּבוֹד חֲבֵרוֹ בְּנַחַת וּבְסַבְלָנוּת, לֵילֵךְ אַחַר רַבִּים בְּלֹא עִקְּשׁוּת וּמַחֲלֹקֶת, וּבָזֶה יְכוֹנֵן הַמּוּסָר בְּנַפְשֵׁיכֶם עַל נָכוֹן כְּנַפְשֵׁיכֶם.

18. See Proverbs 13:11.

quick review. Divide up the work among all of you – minimizing time and effort. "He who gathers little by little, increases it [wealth]."[18] With tranquility of mind and wise and correct resolution, each person will strengthen his friend, weaken the foolishness of his heart, and break his indolent routine. With patience and serenity, follow the majority judgment without stubbornness or divisiveness. Thus, Mussar will become embedded in your souls, as is appropriate for your souls.[19]

19. In other words, the exact mix of Mussar practice will vary from person to person. This reflects R. Salanter's emphasis on the uniqueness of each person's soul and temperament.

ב

אַחַי וְרֵעַי, הֵן מִלְּפָנִים אוֹתָהּ גִּלִּיתִי, כִּי הָאִישׁ הַמְעֻנֶּה וְהַמְדֻכֶּה בְּהַבְלֵי הַתֵּבֵל הַלָּזֶה, פַּרְנָסָתוֹ דְּחוּקָה עֲמָלוֹ רַבָּה, אֵינוֹ מוֹצֵא קוֹרַת רוּחַ בְּכָל עִנְיָנָיו כַּאֲשֶׁר יִתְעוֹרֵר בְּקִרְבּוֹ אֵיזֶה דֶּרֶךְ נָכוֹן לְפָנָיו, אֲשֶׁר הַתִּקְוָה רַבָּה כִּי מְקוֹם מוֹצָא לְפָנָיו, לְהַשְׁקִיט בָּזֶה מֵהֲרַעְיוֹן רוּחַ אֲשֶׁר עָלָיו – בְּוַדַּאי לֹא יָנוּחַ וְלֹא יִשְׁקֹט, עַד אֲשֶׁר יָקִים מְזִמּוֹת לְבָבוֹ יָתֵד נֶאֱמָן בַּל יִמּוֹט, כִּי מִי הוּא פֶּתִי אֲשֶׁר בַּחֲשֵׁכִים יְהַלֵּךְ, וּלְפָנָיו יִתְנוֹצֵץ אוֹר בָּהִיר, וְלֹא יָחִישׁ מַעֲשֵׂהוּ לְהִתְקָרֵב אֵלָיו.

כֵּן אֲנַחְנוּ אֵלֶּה הַיּוֹם, בְּתַהֲלוּכוֹת עִסְקֵי נַפְשׁוֹתֵינוּ, לְהָכִין צֵידָה לְאַחֲרִיתֵנוּ, לָסוּר מִשְּׁאוֹל מַטָּה מֵרַעְיוֹן רוּחַ וּמִבֹּשֶׁת פָּנִים, בָּעוֹלָם הַנִּצְחִי לָעַד בַּל יִמּוֹט, מְעֻנִּים אֲנַחְנוּ בְּתַאֲווֹת הַמְדֻמּוֹת, הַכָּבוֹד הַמּוֹצִיא אֶת הָאָדָם מִן הָעוֹלָם מִלְּפָנֵינוּ, וְאַחֲרָיו נֵלֵךְ וּבְעִקְּבוֹתָיו נֵצֵא, מְבַלְבֵּל מֹחֵנוּ וּמְכַלֶּה כֹּחֵנוּ לְהָכִין דֵּי סִפּוּקוֹ, מְבַטֵּל אוֹתָנוּ מִן הַתּוֹרָה, אֲשֶׁר הִיא חַיֵּינוּ וְאֹרֶךְ יָמֵינוּ בָּזֶה וּבַבָּא, עוֹשֵׁק מִמֶּנּוּ הַמִּצְוֹת וְכָל מִדָּה יְקָרָה, יְנַהֲלֵנוּ לַעֲווֹנוֹת וּפְשָׁעִים אֲשֶׁר לַשָּׁמַיִם יַגִּיעוּ, אָנָה נָנוּס לְעֶזְרָה וְאֶל מִי נִפְנֶה, אִם לֹא אֶל לִמּוּד הַמּוּסָרִי, הַמְיַסֶּרֶת הָאָדָם לִזְכֹּר אַחֲרִיתוֹ, כִּי לֹא לָעַד יִחְיֶה בָּעוֹלָם הַשָּׁפָל הַלָּזֶה רַק גֵּרִים אֲנַחְנוּ בְּחַיֵּינוּ הַלָּלוּ, לַעֲסֹק בַּעֲבוֹדָתֵנוּ הַמֻּטֶּלֶת עָלֵינוּ, לְמַעַן יְשַׁלֵּם שְׂכָרֵנוּ

1. See Letter 1.
2. "*Yated ne'eman,*" lit. "a peg in a sure place" (see Is. 22:23).
3. Compare Avot 4:21.

Letter 2

My brothers, my friends:

Earlier I revealed[1] that a man who is tormented and oppressed by the vanities of this world barely earns his livelihood, works hard, [but] finds no satisfaction in his affairs. When he conceives of a right road for himself, where there is great hope that this is the way out for him, a way that will calm his troubled spirit – he will certainly not rest or be silent until he sets up these plans on a solid basis[2] that will not be moved. For who is such a fool that, walking in darkness, when suddenly a bright light shines before him, will not act quickly to get close to it?

We are such people today! – in the progression of our souls' occupation with preparing for our final end, to escape from the pit, from troubled spirit, and great shame in the eternal, everlasting world. We are tormented by illusory desires. Status-seeking, which removes a person from the world,[3] envelops us, and we pursue and track it. We are confounded and exhausted by trying to satisfy its needs. It distracts us from the Torah, which is our life and length of days[4] in this world and the next. It steals the commandments and every precious character trait from us. It leads us to sins and transgressions that reach to the heavens.

Where can we flee for help, and to whom can we turn, if not to Mussar study? It chastises a person to remember his end, that he will not live forever in this lowly world. We are only sojourners in this life, here

4. Compare *Ahavat Olam*, the second prayer in the daily evening service; compare Deuteronomy 30:20.

בִּמְקוֹמֵנוּ הָאֲמִתִּי, עַתָּה מַה כָּבוֹד נִנְחַל בָּעוֹלָם הַנָּכְרִי הַלָּזֶה, אֲשֶׁר כְּצֵל יַעֲבֹר וְלֹא יְשׁוּרֶנּוּ עוֹד.

הֵן אֵלֶּה קְצוֹת דַּרְכֵי הַמּוּסָר, אוֹר בָּהִיר הוּא וַאֲנַחְנוּ בַּחֲשֵׁכִים נְהַלֵּךְ אַחֲרֵי רְצוֹנֵנוּ הַגּוּפָנִים הַשְּׁפָלִים וְהַנִּבְזִים, אֵיךְ לֹא נָחִישׁ מַעֲשֵׂינוּ לְהִתְקָרֵב אֶל לִמּוּד הַלָּזֶה, לַעֲשׂוֹת לוֹ יְסוֹדוֹת נֶאֱמָנוֹת בַּל יִמּוֹט, לְבַל יַעֲבֹר עָלָיו מִקְרֶה רָעָה חַס וְחָלִילָה, לְהַשְׁבִּית הָרַעְיוֹן הַנִּשְׂגָּב הַלָּזֶה, לְזֹאת מְאֹד נָכוֹן הַדָּבָר לְחַזְּקוֹ בְּמַסְמְרוֹת נְטוּעִים, לִקְבֹּעַ עִתִּים סְדוּרִים לָזֶה בַּכֹּל בֵּין מִנְחָה לְמַעֲרִיב, וְאִישׁ אֶת רֵעֵהוּ יְחַזֵּק וִיזָרֵז לַעֲשׂוֹת תַּחְבּוּלוֹת לִהְיוֹת הַמּוֹעֵד נָכוֹן לָזֶה לְבַל יֶחְסַר, וְאִם יִפָּקֵד אִישׁ אוֹ אוּלַי יִהְיֶה לְשָׂטָן לָזֶה חַס וְחָלִילָה, אָז מֵהַנָּכוֹן לְפַקֵּחַ עַל זֶה הַדָּבָר, לְבַקֵּשׁ עֵצָה וְתַחְבּוּלָה לִסְבֹּל סִכְלוּתוֹ וּלְפַתּוֹת לְבָבוֹ בִּדְבָרִים רַכִּים, כָּל אֶחָד לְפִי דַּרְכּוֹ וְשִׂכְלוֹ, וּבְזֹאת יְוָסֵד הַמּוּסָרִי בְּיָתֵד נֶאֱמָן.

לְהַרְגִּיל בַּחָכְמָה הַלֵּזוּ, אֲשֶׁר דְּרָכֶיהָ יִפָּרְדוּ לִשְׁנֵי רָאשִׁים, הָאֶחָד לְהַלְהִיב הַנְּפָשׁוֹת בְּזִכּוּךְ הָרַעְיוֹן, בַּלִּמּוּדִים הַנִּשְׂגָּבִים הַלָּלוּ, לִלְמֹד בִּשְׂפָתַיִם דּוֹלְקִים, בְּרַעְיוֹן נָכוֹן, בְּצִיּוּר רָחָב לְהַרְחִיב כָּל דָּבָר, וּלְקָרְבָהּ בְּדִמְיוֹנוֹת קְרוֹבִים, עַד אֲשֶׁר יִתְלַהֵב הַלֵּב אִם מְעַט אִם הַרְבֵּה, אֲשֶׁר תּוּכַל תֵּת כֹּחָהּ לְהָכִין הָאֵבָרִים, לְהוֹצִיא כָּל מַעֲשֶׂה הַטּוֹב לְמַעֲנֵהוּ, אִם בְּרָצוֹן אוֹ בְּחָזְקָה.

וְהַשֵּׁנִי הִיא חָכְמַת הָעוֹלָם, לִהְיוֹת רוֹאֶה אֶת הַנּוֹלָדוֹת, לְפַקֵּחַ

---

5. Compare Psalms 144:4.
6. Compare Isaiah 50:10.
7. Compare the Shabbat *zemira* "Yom Shabbaton Ein Lishkoaḥ," verse 5.
8. Compare Ecclesiastes 12:11.
9. Compare Isaiah 41:6.
10. Compare Isaiah 22:23.
11. R. Salanter is referencing his educational idea that regular practice (i.e., habituation) will make it second nature and a powerful determinant of behavior.
12. I.e., impassioned singing. One of R. Salanter's creative methods to intensify the impact of Mussar learning was to chant and sing the words of the study text. He called this type of learning *hitpa'alut* (*hispailus,* in Eastern European pronunciation) – enthusiastic, active learning.

to do our assigned work so that we be paid our hire in our true place. Consider now: What honor can we really attain in this alien world, which passes like a shadow[5] and we will never see again?

Lo, these are some of the ways of Mussar. It is a bright light, while we walk in darkness,[6] following our lowly, contemptible, physical will. How can we not urgently act to draw near to this study, to place it on solid, unshakable, foundations so that no bad happenstance harm it,[7] God forbid, and stop this noble idea?

To this end, the right thing to do is to reinforce it with nails well driven.[8] Set up regular times for it between every afternoon and evening service. Each one should strengthen the other[9] and spur him on to formulate strategies; that there be a set time, which will never be missed. And if one person should be missing or should even become an opponent to this [practice], God forbid, then it is appropriate to attend to this matter, to seek counsel and strategy to defeat his foolishness and to win his heart with soft words (each one according to his own way and intelligence). Thus Mussar will be solidly established and anchored.[10]

To become habituated to this discipline[11] – there are two main paths:

The first is to fire up the spirit by refining thought through these noble studies, by studying with burning lips,[12] by [using] the right [conception], [and] by expanding on each matter with extensive illustrations and making it more persuasive with relatable analogies. [Do this] until the heart is aflame – a little or a lot – so that it can give its strength to prepare the [external] limbs to carry out all the good acts for its sake – willingly or under duress.

The second is "worldly wisdom":[13] to anticipate, to plan ahead before the bad days come,[14] to prepare counsel and strategy about how

---

13. R. Salanter concluded that people are much more strategic and analytical in their worldly/business activities, whereas religious matters were acted out unthinkingly, emotionally, and without a strategy or analysis. He coined the phrase "*ḥokhmat haolam*" ("the wisdom of the world") to capture the idea of acting in religious matters with the wisdom that people develop from their business activities and the strategic thoughtfulness that they apply in worldly matters.
14. Compare Ecclesiastes 12:1.

מֵרֹאשׁ טֶרֶם יָבוֹאוּ יְמֵי הָרָעָה, לְהָכִין עֵצָה וְתַחְבּוּלָה, אֵיךְ לְנַהֵל עַצְמוֹ וַאֲחֵרִים, וּלְהַקְטִין הַדָּבָר לְהָקֵל הַנִּסָּיוֹן, עַד אֲשֶׁר תִּגְדַּל הַיִּרְאָה מֵהַתַּאֲוָה, וְזֶה כָּל הָאָדָם לְהַגְבִּיר הַיִּרְאָה וּלְהַחְלִישׁ הַתַּאֲוָה בְּמוּסָרֵי וְחָכְמָה, לְזֹאת מַה נֶּהֱדָר הוּא, אִם יִהְיֶה לָנוּ נוֹשֵׂא עַל מַה יִּסֹּב הַלִּמּוּד וְהַהֶרְגֵּל בְּמוּסָרֵי וּבְחָכְמָה, נוֹשֵׂא הַלָּזֶה לְקָרֵב הַלְּבָבוֹת לְלִמּוּד הַמּוּסָרֵי, בְּמוּסָרֵי יוּסַד וּבְסַבְלָנוּת יֶחֱזַק, וּבְחָכְמָה יָצִיץ צִיץ וְיִגְדַּל פֶּרַח.

וּבָזֹאת אִם נִהְיֶה לְאַנְשֵׁי חַיִל, לְבַל נִקְפֹּץ לִכְעֹס עַל רֵעֵינוּ, מַדּוּעַ אָטוּם לְבָבוֹ מִלְּהָבִין מַה טִּיבוֹ שֶׁל הַלִּמּוּד הַלָּזֶה, בְּאָמְרֵנוּ הֲלֹא גַּם בָּנוּ הַסִּכְלוּת גּוֹבְרוֹת בְּעִנְיָנִים רַבִּים, בְּזֹאת נָחוֹק בְּלִבֵּנוּ נַרְגִּיל עַצְמֵנוּ בְּמִדַּת הַסַּבְלָנוּת וּבְשִׁפְלוּת הָרוּחַ, שֶׁלֹּא נַגְבִּיהַּ עַצְמֵנוּ עַל אֲחֵרִים.

עַמְקוּת הָרַעְיוֹן לְהָכִין עֵצָה וְתַחְבּוּלָה, אֵיךְ לְיַסְּרוֹ בִּדְבָרִים נְכוֹחִים, לְקָרְבוֹ אֶל אָבִינוּ שֶׁבַּשָּׁמַיִם, תּוֹסִיף תֵּת כֹּחַ לְעַצְמֵנוּ, לְהִתְעוֹרֵר לְיַסֵּר אֶת עַצְמֵנוּ בְּעִנְיָנִים רַבִּים, לְקָרֵב נַפְשׁוֹתֵינוּ אֶל עֲבוֹדָה אֲשֶׁר נִבְרֵאנוּ לָזֶה לְטוֹב לָנוּ.

וּבְיוֹתֵר כַּאֲשֶׁר נְסַפֵּר מְלַאכְתֵּנוּ לִגְבָרִים, לִהְיוֹת כָּל אֶחָד שׁוֹרֵר בְּעִנְיָנוּ הַמְסֻגָּל. זֶה יְיַסְּרֵהוּ בִּלְשׁוֹן לִמּוּדִים, וְזֶה יְקָרְבֵהוּ בְּפָנִים הַמְּאִירוֹת, זֶה יְחַזְּקֵהוּ בְּהִתְלַהֲבוּת לְבָבוֹ הַטָּהוֹר, וְזֶה יְאַסְרֵהוּ בְּתַחְבּוּלוֹתָיו הַצּוֹדְקִים וּבְחָכְמָה הַנִּדְרָשָׁה, מַה נּוֹרָא הַהֶרְגֵּל הַזֶּה לְהָקִים כָּל לִמּוּד וְכָל מִדָּה נְכוֹנָה לְסַלֵּק נִסְיוֹנוֹת רַבּוֹת הַמִּתְרַגְּשׁוֹת עַל הָאָדָם, עִנְיְנֵי פִּקּוּחַ נְפָשׁוֹת וְכַדּוֹמֶה, אֲשֶׁר בְּפֶתַע פִּתְאֹם יִרְשַׁע הָאָדָם לְמַכְבִּיר וּבְאֵין תְּקוּמָה חַס וְחָלִילָה, אָכֵן אִם נַרְגִּיל עַצְמֵנוּ

---

15. I.e., R. Salanter classifies the basic urges (which often act out lowly physical desires) as instinct. These are not rational or refined behaviors. They are driven by gut emotions and often ignore or are not constrained by Torah guidance or ethics.
16. Compare Ecclesiastes 12:13.
17. I.e., unrestrained, amoral behaviors.
18. Lit. carrier or bearer.
19. Compare Numbers 17:23.
20. Compare Deuteronomy 10:13.
21. Lit., "measure out."
22. Compare Joshua 7:14.

to lead himself and others to cut evil down to size, and so to lighten temptation to the point where reverence is more powerful than instinct.[15] This is the purpose of humankind:[16] to strengthen reverence and weaken instinct[17] with Mussar and wisdom. In this respect, how splendid would it be if we ourselves would have an axis[18] around which our learning and conditioning in Mussar and wisdom could revolve. This axis is: to bring others' hearts closer to Mussar study. It will be based on Mussar, strengthened by patience, and done with wisdom so that it will blossom and bear fruit.[19]

If we become strong in this practice, that we not leap to anger at our friend [when we wonder] why his heart is blocked from understanding the nature of this study – rather we should say that in ourselves, too, foolishness reigns in many matters – then we will inscribe on our hearts and habituate ourselves in the qualities of patience and humility, so that we do not elevate ourselves over others.

The very deepening of our thinking, in preparing counsel and strategy on how to correct the other with persuasive words to bring him closer to our Father in Heaven, will give extra strength to ourselves. It will awaken us to correct ourselves in many areas, to bring ourselves closer to the work for which we were created, to our own benefit.[20]

Moreover, assign[21] our work [among us] man by man,[22] so that each one is in charge of the area[23] he is best suited for. One can correct the other with sophisticated language. Another can bring the other closer with a smiling face. This one can strengthen him with the enthusiasm of his pure heart, and that one can capture him with correct strategies and the necessary wisdom.

How awesome is this habituation[24] for establishing all [Mussar] studies and every proper trait, and removing many temptations which come to agitate the person! These are matters of life and death and the like – for in one moment a person can sin overwhelmingly and irretrievably, God forbid. However, if we condition ourselves that our activities

---

23. Compare Esther 1:22.
24. To set up Mussar study as a regular, unbreakable routine. The goal is to make Mussar into *hergel*, a habit/routine, so that to study it becomes second nature.

לִהְיוֹת עִנְיָנֵינוּ נִפְעָלִים עַל יְדֵי רַבִּים, אִישׁ כְּפִי דַּרְכּוֹ וְעִנְיָנוֹ, מַה נָּקֵל לְהָקִים כָּל דָּבָר בִּיגִיעָה מְעֻטֶת וּבְהוֹצָאָה קְטַנָּה, לְהַחֲיוֹת נְפָשׁוֹת רַבּוֹת, וּלְקַיֵּם עוֹלָם מָלֵא, חָכְמַת הָעוֹלָם לְהָקֵל הַנִּסָּיוֹן וּלְהַקְטִין הַדָּבָר, עַד אֲשֶׁר תִּגְבַּר הַיִּרְאָה, צְרִיכָה בֵּאוּר רָחָב בְּדִמְיוֹנוֹת רַבּוֹת, לֹא נִמְצָא עִנְיָנָם בְּסִפְרֵי הַמּוּסָר, כֵּן אִישׁ אִישׁ בִּתְבוּנָתוֹ יִדְלֶנָּה, אִם תִּתְּנוּ לֵב נִסָּיוֹן לָזֶה, בְּלֹא נֶדֶר אִם יִרְצֶה הַשֵּׁם עוֹד נְדַבֵּר מִזֶּה.

25. I.e., as a group.

26. Compare the mishna in Sanhedrin 37a: "One who saves one life is considered to have sustained an entire world."

be affected by many,[25] each person in accordance with his own way and interest, how easy it will be to revive numerous souls and to sustain an entire world with slight effort and little cost.[26] [The use of] "worldly wisdom" to lighten temptation and to cut [evil] down to size so that reverence will overcome requires thorough elucidation using many analogies. We will not find [the analogies] in Mussar books. Each and every person will draw [the proper analogy] forth with his own understanding, if you will apply your experienced heart to this.

Without taking an oath,[27] God willing, we will talk about this more.

27. "*Belo neder*" – this is customary pious language. It is to say: without taking an actual oath (which would serve as a "legal guarantee" that I carry this out), I am seriously committed to following through.

ג

יְדִידַי! הִנֵּה אָנֹכִי חָשַׁבְתִּי לְמִשְׁפָּט, כִּי דִּבְרֵי הָרִאשׁוֹנִים יַסְפִּיקוּ לְמַדַּי לְעוֹרֵר לְבַבְכֶם אֶל חִזּוּק לִמּוּד הַלָּזֶה הוּא לִמּוּד הַמּוּסָרִי, אֲשֶׁר לֹא כְּכָל הַלִּמּוּדִים לִמּוּד הַמּוּסָרִי הַלָּזֶה, אֵין לְךָ לִמּוּד אֲשֶׁר יַקִּיף חִיּוּבוֹ עַל כָּל הַנְּפָשׁוֹת, הַנָּשִׁים פְּטוּרוֹת מִתַּלְמוּד תּוֹרָה, קְשֵׁי יוֹם וַחֲסְרֵי דַּעַת בִּמְצוּקוֹת רָעוֹת חַס וְחָלִילָה יֵשׁ מָקוֹם הַרְבֵּה לְפָטְרָם, אִישׁ אִישׁ לְפִי עִנְיָנוֹ יְשַׁלֵּל מֵחִיּוּבָם, לֹא רְאִי זֶה כִּרְאִי זֶה, כָּל אֲשֶׁר יַרְחִיב לָאָדָם, כֵּן יְגַדֵּל הַחִיּוּב וְכֵן יִרְבֶּה.

לֹא כֵן לִמּוּד הַלָּזֶה הוּא חִיּוּב מְקָף לְכָל הַנְּפָשׁוֹת אַחַת לֹא נֶעְדָּר, כִּי הַמִּלְחָמָה פְּרוּשָׂה עַל כָּל הַחַיִּים הַמְדַבְּרִים, הִיא מִלְחֶמֶת הַיֵּצֶר וְתַחְבּוּלוֹתָיו, תַּאֲוַת הָאָדָם וַעֲלִילוֹתָיו, אֲשֶׁר הֵמָּה יִלְכְּדוּהוּ בְּמִכְמָרֵיהֶם, לְבַל יִהְיֶה לוֹ תְּקוּמָה חַס וְחָלִילָה, אֲשֶׁר כִּמְעַט קָט יִפְשַׂע הָאָדָם לְמַרְבֶּה בְּאֵין מַעֲצוֹר לְרוּחוֹ, לְהוֹצִיא כָּל מִפְעַל רַע וְנִתְעָב לְעֵינֵי הַשֶּׁמֶשׁ, אוֹי! מַה נַּעֲשֶׂה לְיוֹם פְּקֻדָּה, כִּי יִפְקֹד ד׳ הַמִּשְׁפָּט עַל כָּל הַחַיִּים, מַעֲשֵׂה הָאָדָם וְתַחְבּוּלוֹתָיו, בַּמֶּה נֶאֱזַר עֹז וְתַעֲצוּמוֹת, לַעֲמֹד נֶגֶד הַמִּלְחָמָה הַחֲזָקָה הַלֵּזוּ, אִם לֹא בְּלִמּוּד הַלָּזֶה לִמּוּד

1. Compare *Tosefot Yom Tov* on Mishna Eiruvin 2:5, note 13.
2. Compare Bava Kamma 6a *et seriatim*.
3. Compare Isaiah 40:27.
4. Lit. "all life that speaks," a reference to the medieval definition of the superiority of human life over other animals because the human speaks.

Letter 3

My friends:

I thought[1] that my first words surely would more than suffice to awaken your heart to strengthen this learning, the study of Mussar. Mussar is not like any other study. There is no other study that is required of all people. Women are exempt from study of Torah. There is plenty of room to exempt destitute people and those who are preoccupied by desperate circumstances, God forbid. Each person, according to his own situation, may have his obligation to study Torah reduced. Each one is different.[2] The more comfortable conditions are for a person, the greater the obligation [to study Torah] grows.

Not so this [Mussar] study. This study is required of everyone; no one is excused.[3] For there is a battle hanging over all intelligent beings:[4] this is the battle with the [evil] urge and its [warped] strategies; human desire[5] and its [consequent] deeds which capture him in their traps, so that he will never recover (God forbid). For in an instant, a person will sin without limit if there is no check to his spirit. He will carry out every evil and depraved project in broad daylight. Oy! What will we do on the day of remembrance[6] [of being held accountable] when God will bring His judgment on all the living, on the work of man and his schemes?![7]

With what can we strengthen ourselves to stand up to this tremendous battle, if not with the study of Mussar to refine our thought

5. I.e., instinct.
6. Compare Isaiah 10:3.

הַמּוּסָרִי, לְזַכֵּךְ מְעַט הָרַעְיוֹן, לְהַלְהִיב מַה הַלֵּב, וְלָתֵת אַחֲרִיתֵנוּ עַל לִבֵּנוּ, לְמַעַן לִהְיוֹת לָנוּ לְאוֹר מֵאִיר, אֲשֶׁר הָאֵבָרִים הַחִיצוֹנִים לְאוֹרָם יְהַלֵּכוּ, וּבִגְבוּרָתָם יַעֲשׂוּ מִלְחַמְתָּם לְמַעַן הָאֱמֶת וְהַצֶּדֶק, כִּי זֶה כָּל פְּרִי מְגַמָּתֵנוּ, רַק עַל הָאֵבָרִים הַחִיצוֹנִים לְשָׁמְרָם מִכָּל נֶגַע רַע וּמַחֲלָה, הֵן בְּמִדּוֹת וְהֵן בְּדִינִים, אֲשֶׁר לֹא יֵאָסְרוּ כִּי אִם בְּחָזְקָה וּבְהֶרְגֵּל רַב.

אָכֵן מִי יַאַסְרֵם, מִי יִכְבְּשֵׁם, מִי יְזָרְזֵם לְכָל טוֹב וּמוֹעִיל, אִם לֹא לִמּוּד הַמּוּסָרִי, לְשַׁבֵּר הַלֵּב וּלְטַהֲרָהּ מְעַט מִזֻּהֲמָתָהּ, לְעוֹרֵר הַדַּעַת הַנָּכוֹן אֶל הַמִּלְחָמָה הַלֵּזוּ, הִיא כְּבִישַׁת הָאֵבָרִים בְּחָזְקָה, לְהִשָּׁמֵר מִכָּל נֶגַע וָחֳלִי רַע, וּבְזֹאת כָּל אֲשֶׁר יֵצֵר לְהָאָדָם עוֹד תִּרְבֶּה עָלָיו הַמִּלְחָמָה, וְיִגְדַּל הַחִיּוּב בְּלִמּוּד הַמּוּסָרִי הַלָּזֶה, וְהֵן עַתָּה הַיָּמִים לֹא טוֹבִים, הַמִּלְחָמָה מִתְגַּבֶּרֶת, כֵּן גְּדֵלָה הַחִיּוּב.

וְהִנֵּה כַּאֲשֶׁר לָקְחָה אָזְנִי, נִרְפִּים אַתֶּם נִרְפִּים בָּזֶה, לְזֹאת אָמַרְתִּי הֲלֹא חָכְמַת הַמּוּסָר, הִיא רַק הַרְחָבַת הַדְּבָרִים הַפְּשׁוּטִים וְהַנִּגְלִים, וְזֹאת אֵין טוֹב רַק לְהַרְחִיב מָה הַדִּבּוּר בְּעִנְיַן הַמִּכְתָּב הָרִאשׁוֹן.

כַּאֲשֶׁר נַשְׁקִיף עַל רְצוֹנֵנוּ וּמַאֲוַיֵּנוּ, הָעוֹלֶה עַל כָּל הִיא תַּאֲוַת הַחַיִּים הַמְדֻמִּים הַלָּזֶה, הָרָצוֹן הַלָּזֶה תָּקוּעַ בְּעֹמֶק לְבָבֵנוּ יָתֵד נֶאֱמָן, וְכָל אֲשֶׁר לָנוּ נָתֹן נִתֵּן בְּעַד נַפְשֵׁנוּ, מְסֻפָּקִים אֲנַחְנוּ לֹא נֵדַע עֵת אַחֲרִיתֵנוּ, אֵין לָנוּ לְהִשָּׁעֵן בָּזֶה אֶלָּא עַל אָבִינוּ שֶׁבַּשָּׁמַיִם, הָרוֹצֶה לְחַיּוּתֵנוּ לְמַעַן נַעֲבֹד אוֹתוֹ בֶּאֱמֶת וּבֶאֱמוּנָה, וְאִם לְקִבּוּל שְׂכָרֵנוּ בָּעוֹלָם הַהֲבָלִי הַלָּזֶה, אִם לֹא מָצָאנוּ חֵן בְּעֵינָיו. וְעַתָּה אִם נְחַפֵּשׂ מַצָּבֵנוּ רְחוֹקִים אֲנַחְנוּ מְאֹד מִמֶּרְכַּז הַחַיִּים, עֲבוֹדָתֵנוּ לֹא לַה׳ הִיא, רֹב הָעִתִּים בַּחֲשֵׁכָה נְהַלֵּךְ, לְמַלֹּאת בִּטְנֵנוּ, לִרְווֹת תַּאֲוֹתֵנוּ הַשְּׁפָלִים

---

7. Compare to the end of the liturgical poem, "*Maaseh Elokeinu,*" from the Yom Kippur *Musaf.*
8. Lit. "fruit."
9. I.e., outward behaviors.
10. I.e., routinized as to become automatic.
11. Compare Exodus 5:8.
12. See Introduction to *Mesillat Yesharim* (*Path of the Just*) by R. Moshe Ḥayim Luzzatto.
13. "*Yated ne'eman,*" lit. "a peg in a sure place" (Is. 22:23).

a bit, to arouse the heart somewhat, and to take to heart our end? [Let us study Mussar] in order that it be a shining light for us, so that the external limbs will walk by its light; and with their strength, they will battle for truth and righteousness. For this is the entire outcome[8] of our endeavor: only that the external limbs be guarded from all contagious evil and sickness – be it in character traits or be it in laws.[9] They [the limbs] can only be contained with strength and with much habituation.[10]

Indeed, who will contain them? Who will master them? Who can spur them on toward everything that is good and useful? Only the study of Mussar to break the heart and purify it a bit from its pollution; to arouse the right understanding for this battle. [It requires] strong control of the [external] limbs to hold back from all contagious evil and sickness. The more the person's evil urge intensifies its warfare, the greater the obligation grows for this Mussar study! And since these are not good days, the battle is getting harder, and the obligation [of Mussar study] has grown.

Now, as I have heard, you are idle and shirking[11] in this matter. Therefore, I said to myself: The wisdom of Mussar consists only of expounding on simple, obvious things,[12] so the best thing I can do is to expand a bit on what I dealt with in the first letter.

When we reflect on our will and urges, the strongest of all is the desire for this illusory life. This will is deeply and firmly driven in our heart.[13] Everything we have we would give for our [worldly] life.

Yet we are left in doubt. We do not know the moment of our end.

We can only rely on our Father in Heaven,[14] who wants to give us life[15] so that we serve Him truthfully and faithfully,[16] or to give us our reward in this illusory world if we do not find favor in His eyes.

Now if we examine our condition, [we find] we are far from the [true] focus of life. Our service is not to God. Most of the time we walk in darkness,[17] filling our bellies and satisfying our base desires. On top of

14. Compare Sota 49b.
15. Compare Deuteronomy 6:24.
16. Compare the opening words of the prayer immediately after the third portion of *Shema* in the evening service.
17. Compare Psalms 82:5.

וְהַנִּבְזִים, וְנוֹסָף לָזֶה בַּחֲטָאִים וּפְשָׁעִים לְמַעְלָה רֹאשׁ, הַמְּעַט אֲשֶׁר נִצְטַדַּקְנוּ שְׁבוּרִים הֵמָּה כְּשִׁבְרֵי נֵבֶל, בְּלִי רְאוּת וּבְלִי דַּעַת דֶּרֶךְ הַנָּכוֹן וְהַיָּשָׁר.

וְלָזֹאת אֵין נַחַת מוֹצֵא לַה׳ יִתְבָּרַךְ מֵחַיּוּתֵנוּ, כִּי הַכֹּל הוֹלֵךְ אַחַר הָרֹב, וְאִם לְקַבֵּל שְׂכַר מְעַט צִדְקוֹתֵינוּ, כְּדֵי בִּזָּיוֹן וָקֶצֶף, מִי יוֹדֵעַ מַעֲמָדֵנוּ בָּזֶה, אוּלַי עֲוֹנוֹתֵינוּ עָלְתָה יוֹתֵר מִידֵי צִדְקוֹתֵינוּ, כִּי חֶסְרוֹנוֹתֵינוּ בְּתַאֲווֹת הַמְדֻמּוֹת אֲשֶׁר יֶחְסַר לָנוּ, הוּא נוֹבֵעַ רַק מֵרְגָשַׁת חֶפְצַת רְצוֹנֵנוּ, וְאִם נָשׁוּבָה אָחוֹר עַל כַּמָּה מַדְרֵגוֹת פְּחוּתוֹת מֵאִתָּנוּ, מִי יוֹדֵעַ אִם לֹא עָלָה הַרְבֵּה יוֹתֵר מִדַּאי עַל כָּל צִדְקוֹתֵינוּ, וְכָל חַיּוּתֵנוּ הוּא רַחֲמֵי שָׁמַיִם, וּבְנֵס אֲנַחְנוּ עוֹמְדִים, וְאוּלַי לָאו כָּל יוֹמָא מִתְרַחֵשׁ נִסָּא, וְלָזֹאת אִם נַעֲמִיק בַּדָּבָר הַרְבֵּה בְּהִתְבּוֹנְנוּת רַב, אֲשֶׁר בְּכָל רֶגַע מָאן דְּלָא יָלִיף קְטָלָא חַיָּב, וְאֵין לְךָ שָׁעָה שֶׁאֵין הַמָּוֶת עוֹמֵד חַס וְחָלִילָה לְנֶגֶד עֵינֵינוּ – בַּמֶּה נִמְצָא תְּרוּפָה לְתַאֲוָתֵנוּ הַלָּזוֹ הִיא תַּאֲוַת הַחַיִּים, הַבּוֹעֶרֶת בְּקִרְבֵּנוּ כְּאֵשׁ בּוֹעֶרֶת לְעוֹרֵר רַחֲמֵי שָׁמַיִם, אִם לֹא שֶׁנִּמְסֹר עַצְמֵנוּ לְצִבּוּר אִם מְעַט וְאִם הַרְבֵּה, וְאֵל כַּבִּיר לֹא יִמְאַס וּבְצִלָּם נִחְיֶה, וּבִזְכוּתָם נַעֲמֹד לְאֹרֶךְ יָמִים.

---

18. Compare Isaiah 30:14.
19. See Esther 1:18.
20. Evoking Rambam's Laws of Repentance 3:2: "If a person's sins outweigh his merits, he will die immediately in his wickedness."
21. Compare to Shabbat 104a.
22. Compare, e.g., Megilla 7b, Kiddushin 29b.
23. It is noteworthy that this stinging critique of the emptiness of life and the assertion that their good deeds are outweighed by the bad to the point where God is upholding their life only out of kindness and miracle, and not on the merits, is addressed not to the public or to people of lesser standards, but to the disciples of the Mussar movement, including R. Salanter himself. Unlike the Hasidim, who felt that their opponents were living a spiritually inferior life, and unlike the *Mitnagdim* ("Opponents"), who felt that the Hasidim lacked in learning and legal discipline, the Mussarists (following R. Salanter) stressed their own flaws. R. Salanter is saying that even the "righteous" or the spiritual elite fall far short of God's minimum expectations. In part, this emphasis reflects his high standards. This passage also foreshadows the later development of his thought. There, he concludes that even people who are

that, we are steeped over our head in sins and willful acts. The little we acted righteously is smashed like fragments of a jug.[18] [We act] without seeing and without knowing the right and straight path.

That is why God does not find much satisfaction from our lives, for all [final judgment] follows the majority [of our behaviors]. And even if we receive reward for our meager [acts of] righteousness, there will be plenty of scorn and anger[19] [afterward for our bad behaviors]. Who knows where we stand on this? Perhaps our sins have outweighed our righteousness. For our shortcomings, expressed through illusory cravings, flow from the emotional [force] of our will's desire. If we look back to just a few levels from where we are now, who knows if [they] do not far outweigh all of our righteousness,[20] so that our remaining alive is entirely due to the mercies of Heaven. So we are left standing by a miracle![21] And perhaps miracles will not happen every day![22] [23]

To that end, if we delve deeply into this matter and give much thought to the notion that, at any moment, one who is not studying [Torah] is worthy of death,[24] we recognize that there is no moment when death is not staring us in the face (God forbid). How then can we find the cure for this lust, our lust for life, which burns in us as a consuming flame? [How can we] awaken the mercies of Heaven? The only way is by dedicating ourselves – some more, some less – to the community. Almighty God will not reject this,[25] and in its shadow[26] we will live;[27] in their merit we will endure for long life.

---

learned and observant, unless they improve their own character and self-awareness, may fail to live by the Torah's standards because they distort them or are blind to them. Their own character flaws lead them to distort the Torah's teachings.

This recalls the beginning of R. Salanter's aphorism: "When I first started to study Mussar, I criticized the members of the public and justified myself. As I deepened my study of Mussar, I criticized the members of the public and I criticized myself. When I completed studying Mussar, I justified the public and criticized myself."

24. See Avot 1:13.
25. Compare Job 36:5.
26. I.e., the community's merit of protection.
27. Compare Lamentations 4:20.

וּמַה נַּעֲשֶׂה כִּי דַלִּים אֲנַחְנוּ, מוֹצָא לַכֶּסֶף אֵין לְהַחְזִיק הַתּוֹרָה וְלוֹמְדֶיהָ – וְלָזֹאת נְחַפֵּשׂ דְּבָרִים לְחַזֵּק יָדַיִם רָפוֹת, לְעוֹרְרָם בְּדַעַת וּבִתְבוּנָה אֶל הַלִּמּוּד הַמּוּסָרִי, הַמְעֻתָּדָה לְכָל מַרְפֵּא לְחוֹלֵי הַנֶּפֶשׁ, לִלְמֹד וּלְלַמֵּד לִשְׁמֹר וְלַעֲשׂוֹת כְּכָל הָאָמוּר בָּהּ, לְמַעַן תִּהְיֶה תִּקְוָה טוֹבָה לְאַחֲרִיתֵנוּ, כִּי כָל אֲשֶׁר יְחֻבַּר אֶל הַחַיִּים יֵשׁ בִּטָּחוֹן, אִם בְּמוּסָרִי יְהַלֵּךְ לְהִתְהַפֵּךְ מֵרַע לְטוֹב, וּלְהוֹצִיא יָקָר מִזּוֹלֵל, וְד׳ הַטּוֹב יְחַזֵּק לְבָבֵנוּ, אִם נִהְיֶה מִמְּזַכֵּי הָרַבִּים אֲשֶׁר אֵין חֵטְא בָּא עַל יָדָם.

עַתָּה נִרְאֶה נָא בְּעַיִן חוֹדֶרֶת, הַיְהַלֵּךְ אִישׁ וְרַגְלַיִם אֵין לוֹ? הֲיַשְׁקִיף אִישׁ וְעֵינַיִם אֵין לוֹ? כֵּן לֹא יִכּוֹן הַתּוֹרָה וְהָעֲבוֹדָה, אֶל הָאָדָם הַנֶּחְלָה בְּתַחֲלוּאֵי הַיֵּצֶר, אִם לֹא בְּלִמּוּד הַמּוּסָרִי.

עַתָּה נַחְפְּשָׂה דְרָכֵינוּ וְנַחְקֹרָה, חוֹלִים אֲנַחְנוּ מִכָּל צַד וּפִנָּה, הַתַּאֲוָה וְהַכָּבוֹד יְסוֹכְכֵנוּ, הַגָּזֵל וְהָעַוְלָה יְסוֹבְבוּנוּ, הַגַּאֲוָה וְהַכַּעַס, הַקִּנְאָה וְהַקַּפְּדָנוּת, הֵם דְּרָכֵינוּ, הַלָּשׁוֹן יִשְׁלֹט בָּנוּ בְּאֵין מַעֲצוֹר, וּמַדּוּעַ לֹא נָנוּס אֶל בֵּית הָרוֹפְאִים, אוּלַי נִמְצָא אֵיזֶה מָזוֹר וּתְרוּפָה לְמַכָּתֵנוּ, כִּי מִי פֶּתִי חֲסַר לֵב אֲשֶׁר לֹא יְבַקֵּשׁ מָזוֹר לְמַחֲלָתוֹ, אֵין זֹאת כִּי אִם עֲצַת הַיֵּצֶר הַמְלֻמָּד בְּמִלְחֲמוֹתָיו, כִּי אִישׁ מִלְחָמָה מִנְּעוּרָיו הוּא, לֹא יַעַצְרוּהוּ טִרְדֵי הַבְלֵי הַזְּמַן כָּמוֹנוּ, וְכָל מְגַמּוֹתָיו הוּא רַק

---

28. Compare Isaiah 35:3.
29. Avot 5:4 (quoted in the paragraph just before the *Shema* in morning prayers).
30. Compare Jeremiah 31:17.
31. Compare Ecclesiastes 9:4. R. Salanter uses a phrase from Ecclesiastes that as long as there is life, there is hope. However, he uses the term *bitaḥon* to summon up the hope and assurance that comes through complete trust in God and God's promises. In Mussar literature of the past, *bitaḥon* is sometimes interpreted as accepting that life is completely in God's hands so there is little or no need for human action. Modern understanding of the concept minimizes the passivity aspect but stresses the sense that God is with the individual. For example, when one is under vicious attack, the cortisol is flowing and he/she feels very embattled. But if one is imbued with *bitaḥon*, one feels immersed in a pool of comfort and assurance – for God is a Presence all-around. When pushed too far, this concept can turn into the magical belief that in the battle, one cannot be killed by a bullet – especially since there is a widespread tendency in the biblical era to infer that God's Presence is a guarantee

What can we do, for we are poor? We can't find the funds to uphold the Torah and its scholars. So we must seek ways to strengthen weak hands;[28] to awaken them with wisdom and understanding, to Mussar study, which is destined to be a panacea for all sick souls; to learn and teach and observe and carry out[29] all that is stated in [the Torah] – so there will be great hope for our [final] end.[30] As long as we are reckoned among the living, there is hope[31] that we can follow the path of Mussar, transform ourselves from evil to good, and extract the precious from the vile.[32] God, most benevolent, will strengthen our hearts if we are among those who lead the public to virtue – for whom no sin can result from this work.[33]

Let us now look at this with a penetrating eye. Can a person walk if he has no feet? Can a person gaze if he has no eyes? Likewise, Torah and God's service cannot be done right by a person who is sick from the illnesses of the [evil] urge – not without Mussar study.

Let us now consider our ways and search.[34] We are sick from every side and corner. Desire and status-seeking beset us; theft and injustice surround us; pride and anger, jealousy and short-temperedness – these are our ways. Our tongue rules over us without check. So why should we not flee to the doctor's office? Maybe we will find some salve or cure for our affliction. Who is so foolish, so lacking in insight, as not to seek a cure for his sickness? This [inaction] can only be the counsel of the [evil] urge, who is schooled in warfare, for he is a warrior from his youngest days, and he is not slowed by preoccupation with worldly matters as

---

that one will be kept safe from all harm. *Bitaḥon,* then and now, also incorporates the idea of walking with God – so one never walks alone. In this more limited understanding of *bitaḥon,* it represents the trust and confidence that one is not alone and that Someone is guiding and helping you, keeping you calm, hopeful, and confident. This is comforting and strengthening.

32. Compare Jeremiah 15:19.

33. Compare Avot 5:18. Daniel 12:3 states that "those who turn many to righteousness (*matzdikei harabbim*) [shall shine] like the stars for ever and ever." Under the term *zikkui harabbim* (conferral of public benefit), the Mussarists highlighted bringing Torah and Mussar study to the broadest possible public.

34. Compare Lamentations 3:40.

לְהָסִיר מִלְּפָנֵינוּ כְּלֵי מִלְחַמְתֵּנוּ, הוּא לִמּוּד הַמּוּסָרִי, וּבָזֶה יֵאָסֵר אוֹתָנוּ לְפָנָיו וְאֵין מוֹשִׁיעַ.

לְזֹאת מִמֶּנּוּ נִלְמַד וְאֶת דְּרָכָיו נִקַּח לָנוּ לְמוֹפֵת, לְהַחְזִיק בְּמוּסָר וְלֹא נֶרֶף, לְגַדְּלוֹ וּלְהַאֲדִירוֹ לְהַלְבִּישׁוֹ בְּמַלְבּוּשֵׁי הַתַּאֲוָה הַמְדֻמָּה לְמַעַן יִשְׁלֹט בּוֹ הַשֶּׁלֹּא לִשְׁמָהּ, אֲשֶׁר מִמֶּנָּה יָבֹא הַלִּשְׁמָהּ הַצְּרוּפָה, וְכָל אֲשֶׁר יִכְבַּד עִנְיָנוֹ, אוֹת הִיא כִּי לֹא דָּבָר רֵק הוּא לְחַיּוּתֵינוּ כַּיּוֹם הַזֶּה, לְמַעַן נְלַמֵּד עַצְמֵנוּ לִכְבֹּשׁ תַּאֲווֹתֵינוּ, וּלְאַהֲבַת רֵעֵנוּ לְהַטּוֹתָם אֶל דַּרְכֵי ד׳ וְתוֹרָתוֹ, בְּצֶדֶק מִשְׁפָּט וּמֵישָׁרִים וְכָל מִדָּה יְקָרָה, וּבָזֶה נִמְצָא חֵן וְשֵׂכֶל טוֹב בְּעֵינֵי אֱלֹקִים וַאֲנָשִׁים.

אַתֶּם רֵעַי חֲנוּנִי נָא בָּזֹאת, לְהוֹדִיעֵנִי מִי וָמִי הַהוֹלְכִים לְתֻמָּם, וּמִי הֵמָּה הַנִּרְפִּים, יְדִידָם דּוֹרֵשׁ שְׁלוֹמָם וְטוֹבָתָם.

---

35. Compare Pesaḥim 50b; Sota 22b and 47a: If one starts doing good deeds with ulterior motives, it will bring him to do them for their own sake.

36. Compare Deuteronomy 32:47.

37. Lit. “good reason,” i.e., it makes common sense.

we are. His sole objective is to take away our weapons, namely, Mussar study. He thus makes us his prisoners, and no one can save us.

So let us learn from [the evil urge] and take his ways as our model. Let us hold onto Mussar and not let up, strengthening it, glorifying it, dressing it up in the accoutrements of illusory desire so that we gain control over [the evil urge] using ulterior motives, which will eventually lead to purity of motive.[35]

The more difficult it is, the more it is a sign that our work is not in vain, and it will keep us as alive as this day.[36] So we will educate ourselves to conquer our desires and to love our friends and to turn them to the ways of God and His Torah, with righteousness, judgment, equity, and every precious trait. Thus, we will find favor and approval[37] in the eyes of God and people.[38]

You, my friends, just be gracious to me in this matter.[39] Let me know who are going with us[40] wholeheartedly and who are shirking.

Your friend, who seeks your peace and well-being.

38. Compare Proverbs 3:4.
39. Compare Malachi 3:10.
40. Compare Exodus 10:8.

ד

אַתֶּם יְדִידַי!

הִנְנִי בָא לְמַלֹּאת הַבְטָחָתִי מִכְּבָר. לְהַרְחִיב הַדִּבּוּר בְּחָכְמַת הָעוֹלָם מִלֵּי דְעָלְמָא הַנִּצְרְכָה לְחָכְמַת הַמּוּסָר. וּבִלְעָדָהּ תִּכְבַּד הָעֲבוֹדָה לֹא נוֹדַע שַׁחְרָהּ. כִּי תַּחֲלוּאֵי הַנֶּפֶשׁ הַתַּאֲוָה וְהַטָּעוּת הֵמָּה בְּעוֹכְרֶיהָ. הַתַּאֲוָה בּוֹעֶרֶת וְהַנְּטִיָּה דּוֹלֶקֶת, לְטַהֵר אֶת הַשֶּׁרֶץ אֲשֶׁר טָמֵא טָמֵא יִקָּרֵא. בְּעֵת מְצוֹא לָתֵת דִּין וְחֶשְׁבּוֹן עַל פְּרִי מַעַלְלֵי אִישׁ. לְשַׁלֵּם לְאִישׁ כִּדְרָכוֹ. וּכִגְמוּל יָדָיו יֵעָשֶׂה לוֹ, כִּי הֲגַם שֶׁהַתּוֹרָה מְסוּרָה לִבְנֵי אָדָם לַחֲתֹךְ עִנְיָנָהּ כְּפִי מִשְׂרַת שֵׂכֶל אֱנוֹשִׁי, לֹא נִכְבְּשָׁה הִיא לַעֲשׂוֹת

1. Compare Isaiah 47:11.
2. I.e., these factors distort our judgment and therefore disrupt proper understanding of Torah and Mussar.
3. Recall that in R. Salanter's analysis, desire is so powerful because it is rooted in instinct. These comprise the most basic emotional forces in the human being.
4. In R. Salanter's lexicon, "tendencies" (*netiya/netiyot* in Hebrew) are those hidden biases which distort judgment. For example, if one likes sweets, one might seek out an article that says sweets are not bad for one's health, or misread an article that says sweets are bad for one's health. The tendency or bias misdirects one's reasoning or thinking. This is one of R. Salanter's main discoveries: Although humans properly use their reason to understand and to think through problems, reason itself is a flawed instrument that is constantly distorted by our unconscious, irrational drives. For example, if one's *netiya* is toward fame, then they will strive irrationally toward activities that are likely to increase their fame. They may cut corners ethically to win fame. *Netiyot* are particularly powerful because one is unaware of them even as they distort one's reason.

Letter 4

You, my friends!

I come now to fulfill my longstanding promise to speak expansively on the "wisdom of the world," the worldly wisdom that is prerequisite for the wisdom of Mussar, without which the work would be very difficult. You will not know how to shed light on it[1] because the sicknesses of the soul, desire and error, make trouble for it.[2] Desire burns[3] and tendencies[4] are inflamed – and try to declare pure[5] the crawling creature that actually must be called out as impure.[6]

[Remember:] A time will come, where an accounting will be given for the fruits of human acts – each person will be paid according to his way; and as he has done, so will be done to him. For although the Torah is given over to humans to render decisions under the direction of human intelligence,[7] it is not our captive to do with as we please,[8]

---

5. Compare Eiruvin 13b, where the Talmud states that a veteran disciple in Yavneh was capable of "proving" in 150 different ways that vermin, the *sheretz* (lit. "crawling thing"), the acme of impurity, is pure. Of R. Meir, the Talmud relates that he was able to convincingly argue that the impure was pure and the pure was impure. As a result, many of his peers became less trusting of his actual rulings. He was too sharp. The *netiya* has this same capacity to "spin" and to categorize the impure as pure.
6. The *metzora*/leper calls out that his state is "impure, impure" when he walks by (Lev. 13:45).
7. Although God knows that humans' flawed reason may distort their understanding of the Torah's message, God has given over the Torah to be applied by human judgment.
8. I.e., the Torah is not ours to shape as we please and as best fits with our desires.

בָּהּ כְּחֶפְצֵנוּ עַל פִּי תַהֲלוּכוֹת רְצוֹנֵנוּ, פִּגּוּל הוּא לֹא יֵרָצֶה לְהָשִׁיב תְּשׁוּבָה לְשׁוֹאֲלֵנוּ צֶדֶק וּלְשָׁפְטֵנוּ מֵישָׁרִים.

לָזֹאת מַה נּוֹאַלְנוּ בְּכָל דְּרָכֵינוּ. מִי יוֹרֵנוּ דֶּרֶךְ הַיְשָׁרָה, הַתַּאֲוָה וְהַכָּבוֹד הַקִּנְאָה וְהַנִּצָּחוֹן, פּוֹרְשׂוֹת כַּנְפֵיהֶם בְּכָל כְּלֵי מוֹחוֹתֵינוּ וּבְכָל מוֹסְדֵי שִׂכְלֵנוּ, אָכֵן הַיִּרְאָה עַל הַכֹּל שׁוֹלֶטֶת. עַל הַתַּאֲוָה אֲשֶׁר תְּאַסְּרֶיהָ בְּחֵיל יָדָהּ. לְבַל תַּעֲבֹר גְּבוּלֶיהָ רַק לְהִשְׁתַּמֵּשׁ הַהֶכְרֵחִי הַמֻּתֶּרֶת. וּבְהַנְּטִיָּה תִּזְרֹק חִצֶּיהָ עַל פְּנֵי הָאָדָם לְהַפְחִידוֹ בְּכָל דְּבָרָיו לְהִסְתַּכֵּל אָנֶה וָאָנָה עַד אֲשֶׁר מִמֵּילָא יִזֶּרֶה אֶת הַמּוֹץ וּבְרוּחַ יִדְּפֶנּוּ. אוּלָם אִם אֶל הַיִּרְאָה נָשִׂים פָּנֵינוּ לִהְיוֹת לִיסוֹד מוּסָד וּלְאֶבֶן בֹּחַן בְּכָל מִפְעָלֵנוּ לֹא נִטְפֹּל לָהּ דָּבָר אַחֵר. הֲלֹא מֵרָחוֹק תַּעֲמֹד עֲבוֹדָתֵנוּ, כִּי רָאִינוּ אִם לֹא שָׁמַעְנוּ וְהַנִּסָּיוֹן יוֹרֶה, כִּי מַה מְּאֹד תִּכְבַּד עַל הָאָדָם שֶׁנִּקְבַּע בִּלְבָבוֹ יָתֵד נֶאֱמָן, לִהְיוֹת יִרְאַת ה׳ פְּרוּשָׂה עַל עָקְשַׁת עָרְפּוֹ הַקָּשֶׁה. וְאִם יַעֲמֹל בָּהּ דֵּי סִפּוּקוֹ, עוֹד לֹא תְשׁוֹטֵט בְּרַעְיוֹנוֹ אַף אֶפֶס קָצֵהוּ לְעֻמַּת הַתַּאֲוָה הַגּוֹבֶרֶת וּמַה תּוּכַל תֵּת כֹּחָהּ לְעֻמַּת הַנְּטִיָּה הַמְּבַלְבֶּלֶת וְרוֹקֶדֶת בָּנוּ, וְכִשְׂחוֹק הוּא לְהָקִים כָּל מְזִמָּתָהּ.

Rather, we must try our best to understand the Torah without distortion and to come close to its expectations.

9. Heb. "*pigul*," a term that refers to a sacrifice that was disqualified because it was offered with the wrong intentions (Lev. 19:7).

10. The Torah is given into the hands of humans but we have to understand it to the best of our ability, and we should not be paralyzed by the realization that our reason is "tainted" and our judgment distorted by unconscious forces and internal biases. Nevertheless, we should remain aware of and make adjustments for the fact that we bring biases and tendencies that warp our understanding. The Torah was given by God to be judged using our best judgment. We do not have *carte blanche*. We must use Mussar to keep our *netiyot* in check. If we apply Torah thoughtlessly, our service will not be acceptable to God.

11. In this passage, R. Salanter is not dealing with the opposition of the *maskilim*, but with that of traditionally observant Jews who think they can trust their own judgment and take their readings of Torah at face value. R. Salanter offers a strong critique of this undiscerning observance. Many people who learn Torah do not recognize their

according to the dictates of our will. Such action is "offensive,[9] and will not be accepted."[10] We must give a right answer to those who ask and an equitable ruling to those who appeal to us for justice.[11]

By this standard, how wantonly we have acted[12] in all our ways! Who will show us the right way? Desire, honor-seeking, jealousy, and competitiveness spread their wings through all of our mental capacities and in all the foundations of our reason. However, fear [of God] can gain control over everything. [It can rule] over desire, which it can harness with its strong hand so that it [desire] does not overstep its bounds and is only used for what is essential and permitted.

Fear of God can fire its arrows[13] at a person's tendencies, right in front of his face, so that he act with fear [of sin] in everything and making him consider every angle, so that, in any case, he will discard the chaff and let the wind blow it away.[14]

Even so, if we look only to fear [of God] to be the bedrock foundation and the standard by which we judge all our undertakings, and we treat it with nothing else,[15] then our service will still be way off. For if we have not heard then we have seen, and experience has shown, how hard it is for a person (even when fear is anchored firmly in his heart) to have fear of God spread over [and master] his stubborn willfulness. And even if he works at it sufficiently, it will still not permeate [and channel all] his thinking, except marginally,[16] compared to overbearing desire. What can all its power give us compared to a tendency that confuses us and cavorts within us? It is child's play for [desire] to carry out its [evil] plans.

---

netiyot, which may distort their judgment about what the Torah is actually teaching. See Letter 14, which describes that the person who does not learn Mussar is governed by bad habits and by a spirit of impurity that distorts his soul and spoils his reason. Hence, they will not be capable of arriving at true repentance. This idea of overcoming bias and the need for partial purification of reason will be further developed in R. Salanter's article in *Tevunah,* Letter 30.

12. Compare Numbers 12:11 and the Rosh HaShana liturgy.
13. Compare Psalms 18:15 and 144:6.
14. I.e., he will separate the good from the bad. Compare Psalms 1:4.
15. We fail to treat it with Mussar.
16. Compare Numbers 23:13.

לָזֹאת כָּל עֲמַת שֶׁיַּעֲמֹל הָאָדָם לְהָשִׂים הָאֱמֶת לְנֶגֶד עֵינֵינוּ. וְהַתְּמִימוּת נֵר לְרַגְלֵינוּ, לְהַעֲמִיק בָּהּ לְבִלְתִּי נִהְיֶה נְבוּכִים לְחַפֵּשׂ תָּמִיד אַחַר מַעֲשֵׂינוּ וּפְרִי עֶשְׁתּוֹנוֹתֵינוּ, עַד אֲשֶׁר גָּלָה לְפָנֵינוּ מוֹרָשֵׁי לְבָבֵנוּ, עַד אֲשֶׁר נֵבוֹשׁ וְנִכָּלֵם לְהַחֲלִיף שֶׁקֶר בֶּאֱמֶת, וּלְהַלְבִּישָׁהּ מִכְסֵה הַצֶּדֶק בְּמוֹסְדֵי הַפֶּשַׁע לַהֲלֹךְ כְּעִוֵּר בָּאֲפֵלָה אֲשֶׁר לֹא יֵדַע בַּמֶּה יִכָּשֵׁל.

כֵּן נָכוֹן הַדָּבָר לְהַעֲמִיק הַתְּבוּנָה בְּתַהֲלוּכוֹת הַתֵּבֵל אֲשֶׁר בְּמִרְמָה יַהֲלֹכוּ, וּפְרִי כָּל אֱנוֹשִׁי לְצוֹדֵד נְפָשׁוֹת בְּחֶרְמוֹ. אִישׁ אִישׁ לְפִי דַּרְכּוֹ, הַכְּסִיל בְּפַעֲמוֹנֵי הַסִּכְלוּת יִתֵּן זָהָב תְּמוּרָתָהּ, הַמִּתְאַוֶּה לְמַאֲכָל וּמִשְׁתֶּה יְצוֹדֵד בְּמִכְמַרְתּוֹ. וּלְכָל אֲשֶׁר יַחְפֹּץ יִטֶּנּוּ בְּחַנְפֵי לַעֲגֵי מָעוֹג. הֶחָפֵץ בַּכָּבוֹד הַמְּדֻמֶּה, חֶפְצוֹ הִיא רִשְׁתּוֹ. וְהַחֲנִיפָה תִּלְכְּדֶנּוּ לְהַעֲנִיק לְכָל אִישׁ מְגַמַּת חֶפְצוֹ אֶת אֲשֶׁר יִהְיֶה לְאֵל יָדָיו לַעֲשׂוֹת, כֵּן כָּל אֱנוֹשׁ בְּדַרְכּוֹ יִלָּכֵד, וְאֶל תְּכוּנַת נַפְשׁוֹ יִצְפְּנוּ הָרַמָּאִים, לֵידַע וּלְהָבִין בַּמֶּה יֵאָסֵר לִפְנֵיהֶם לְמַלֹּאת דֵּי חֶפְצָם הֵן אֵלֶּה קְצוֹת דַּרְכָּם, וּמִי יְכַלְכֵּל כָּל נְתִיבוֹתֵיהֶם תִּקְצַר הַיְרִיעָה מֵהָכִיל.

גַּם זֹאת תְּכוּנַת הָאָדָם בְּעִסְקֵי הַתֵּבֵל, לְהִתְחַכֵּם לִהְיוֹת רוֹאֶה אֶת הַנּוֹלָד בְּכָל עִנְיָנָיו, לִרְאוֹת לְתַקֵּן כָּל דָּבָר טֶרֶם יָבֹא הָרָעָה כְּפִי אֲשֶׁר יִהְיֶה בְּכֹחוֹ – עִסְקֵי הַתֵּבֵל הֵמָּה יְלַמְּדוּ אֶת הָאָדָם עִנְיָנֶיהָ וְתַהֲלוּכוֹתֶיהָ. וְאִישׁ אִישׁ לְפִי טִבְעוֹ הַמְסֻגֶּלֶת כֵּן תָּקוּם בְּיָדוֹ חָכְמָתָהּ. וְהַמַּכְשֵׁלָה תַּחַת יַד הָאָדָם, וְאִם לֹא יִתֵּן מָקוֹם לְשְׁטוּתוֹ כֵּן תִּגְדַּל חָכְמָתוֹ, וְהַהֶרְגֵּל וְהַנִּסָּיוֹן בְּכָל דָּבָר מוֹשֶׁלֶת, וְלָזֹאת אִם הַתְּמִימוּת תִּהְיֶה חֲזָקָה לְבַל יִמּוֹטוּ רַגְלֵינוּ, מַה טּוֹב אִם נִשְׁתַּמֵּשׁ בְּדַרְכֵי ה׳

17. Compare Psalms 35:16.

18. In the ways of the world, people learn about other people's nature – what excites them and what their tendencies and needs are. They use this knowledge to get the other to do their will. R. Salanter proposes to do the same analysis but use it to turn the other to the service of God. Use *ḥokhmat haolam* to see analytically the inward nature of people, including ourselves. Then, channel the inward tendencies to get others and ourselves to do the right thing.

19. Compare Genesis 42:24.

20. R. Salanter makes an additional point: learning how to see through trickery and deceit, as is practiced in worldly matters, will equip us to see through the trickery and deceit of our desires and to set us on a truly righteous rational path.

So, just as it is necessary for a person to work to hold the truth up before our eyes and let wholeness illuminate our footsteps; to delve into it so that we will not be confused, always examining our actions and the fruits of our thoughts, even to the roots of our hearts, to the point where we would be embarrassed and ashamed to exchange truth for falsehood, to clothe evil actions in a righteous facade, to stumble as a blind man in darkness who knows not what he stumbles over – so is it proper to deepen [our] insight into the pathways of the world, which operate through deceit.

The effect of all human activity is to ensnare people in the net, each person in his own way: the simpleton will give gold for trinkets of foolishness; the glutton will be caught in that trap – profane, scornful mockers[17] will divert him to wherever they want him to turn. He who wants illusory honor – that desire is itself his snare; flattery will lure him into giving each person whatever they want,[18] whatever he can give them. Thus, each person, in his own way, is caught. Deceivers observe his character traits in order to know and understand how to bind him[19] so he will do as they please. These are some of the ways;[20] who can encompass all of their ways? There is not enough space to cover it all.

Another natural human trait in worldly matters is to wise up[21] so that one can anticipate what will develop in all his situations; to see and reinforce everything as best he can before troubles come.[22] Worldly occupations teach a person their ways and concerns, and each person, according to his own adaptive capacity, will retain that wisdom and identify the obstacles that he can overcome.

If he gives no quarter to his foolishness, then his wisdom will expand. Habituation (*hergel*) and experience rule everything. Thus, if we are to stand firm in our wholeness so that we do not stumble, it would be good to use these [worldly] tactics in the ways of God: to

21. Develop intellectually.
22. The wisdom of the world teaches us to systematically deal with all the difficulties and challenges that are coming in secular life. This includes anticipating problems and preparing remedies before trouble hits. This aspect of worldly wisdom is about sizing up reality more systematically and analytically. This capacity, applied to religious life, can strengthen our service of God.

בְּאֵלּוּ הַדְּבָרִים, לְהִתְחַכֵּם לֵידַע טִבְעֵי נַפְשֵׁנוּ בַּמֶּה נוּכַל לִהְיוֹת נִצָּדִים לְהַטּוֹת לְבָבֵנוּ אֶל עֲבוֹדַת הַקֹּדֶשׁ, לְהָקֵל הַנִּסָּיוֹן. וְהַיִּרְאָה תִּתֵּן עֹז וְתַעֲצוּמוֹת, וְהָאֶחָד יְחַזֵּק חֲבֵרוֹ, חָכְמַת הָעוֹלָם תָּקֵל הַמַּשָּׂא וְהַיִּרְאָה תִּסְעָדֵנוּ נִירָא וְנִפְחַד מִכָּל פֶּגַע רַע וְעָוֹן, וְלָזֹאת מֵרָחוֹק נִבְרַח מִמְּצוּדָה רָעָה.

קָצָר עִטִּי לְהָכִיל מַחְשְׁבוֹתַי, וּבָזֶה תֵּן לְחָכָם וְיֶחְכַּם עוֹד, הָעֵסֶק בְּדַרְכֵי הָעֲבוֹדָה, הֵמָּה יְלַמְּדוּ אֶת הָאָדָם תַּהֲלוּכָתָהּ. וּבְיוֹתֵר אִישׁ אֶת רֵעֵהוּ יְלַמֵּד – וְאֶל הַתְּמִימוּת יְנַהֲלֶנּוּ וּבִמְצוּדָה יִתְפְּשֶׂנּוּ, לֹא לְמַעַן קְנוֹת כָּבוֹד, רַק לְמַעַן הָאֱמֶת וְהַצֶּדֶק, וְאֶל תְּכוּנַת נַפְשׁוֹ לִצְפּוֹן לְהַטּוֹת אֶת לְבָבוֹ אֶל הַיִּרְאָה וְהַתּוֹרָה! וְהַמַּכְשֵׁלָה תִּהְיֶה נֵר מֵאִיר לַעֲמֹד עַל הָאֱמֶת. אָז יִבָּקַע כַּשַּׁחַר צִדְקֵנוּ. אִם נָשׁוּטָה נָּא עַל פְּנֵי הַתֵּבֵל לְהָבִין פְּנִיּוֹת הָאָדָם וְשִׁקְרוּתוֹ, אֲשֶׁר בָּרוּר בַּעֲלִיל יַעֲמֹד לְפָנֵינוּ. מְצֹרָף אֶל הַתְּמִימוּת הַקְּבוּעָה. זֹאת בְּכֹחָהּ לְגָרֵשׁ כָּל דָּבָר מוּזָר וּמַחְשָׁבָה בִּלְתִּי נְכוֹנָה עִם הַיִּרְאָה הָעוֹזֶרֶת. וְלָזֹאת סוֹף דָּבָר לְהַחֲזִיק בְּדַרְכֵי הַמּוּסָר, וּלְהַעֲמִיק וּלְהָבִין אֵיךְ לְהִשְׁתַּמֵּשׁ בְּחָכְמַת הָעוֹלָם, לְחַזֵּק הַמּוּסָרִי וְלֹא לַהֲרֹס חַס וְחָלִילָה, וּבְאֵין תַּחְבּוּלוֹת אֵין חָכְמָה, וּבְאֵין לִמּוּד אֵין חָכְמָה מוֹצֵאת. וְלָזֹאת הַלִּמּוּד יִהְיֶה לְקָרֵב נְפָשׁוֹת אֶל הַמּוּסָרִי וּלְיַסֵּד בְּחָכְמַת הָעוֹלָם עִם הַיִּרְאָה וְתֹקֶף הַתְּמִימוּת.

---

23. Compare Psalms 68:36.
24. Proverbs 9:9.
25. Just as involvement in worldly matters wises us up, so does systematic pursuit of service of God teach us how to do better as life and religious challenges unfold.
26. Human weakness and illicit desire are turned into a force to drive the people to Mussar and fear of God.
27. Compare Isaiah 58:8.
28. Compare the Satan in Job 1:7.
29. Worldly wisdom will give the Mussarites two legs up:

    Having learned human weaknesses and psychology, they will be able to analyze how their own desire and irrational forces may mislead them and then correct them.

    They can learn from business tactics how to systematically maximize achievement

develop intellectually so that we know our own psychology, how we can be ensnared to turn our hearts to the holy service [of God] and reduce temptation. Fear [of God] will give us strength and reinforcement,[23] and each person will strengthen his friend. Worldly wisdom will lighten the burden, and fear [of God] will strengthen us. We will be afraid and terrified of every evil act and sin. And so we will escape ensnarement by evil before it even gets close.

My pen can't contain all of my thoughts. So in this case, "give to a wise man and he adds wisdom."[24] Active involvement in the ways of service [of God] will teach a person its ways.[25] Most of all, each person should teach his friend and lead him to wholeness. He should catch him in a snare – not for the sake of attaining honor, but for the sake of truth and righteousness. He should seek to understand his psychology so that he may turn his heart to fear [of God] and Torah.

The stumbling block will instead become a shining light to arrive at the truth.[26] Then our righteousness will break forth like the dawn.[27] When we go all over the world[28] to understand each man's particular diversions and their falsity, which will clearly stand out to us when juxtaposed to enduring wholeness, it will have the power to drive away all strange things and improper thoughts, with the help of fear [of God].

Therefore, in sum: hold onto the ways of Mussar and delve into and understand how to use the wisdom of the world in order to strengthen Mussar and not to destroy it (God forbid). Without strategy, there is no wisdom, and without study, no wisdom can be found.[29] This study will serve to bring people closer to Mussar and to establish it on the basis of worldly wisdom, fear [of God], and the power of wholeness.

---

and minimize errors; strengthen weak spots before they crumble; and anticipate problems and deal with them more successfully.

These two strategies are important and they will make one's *avodat Hashem* (service of God) much stronger. One must take the insights and capabilities developed by secular activity and introduce them into one's religious and spiritual way of life.

ה

אֲנַחְנוּ בְּרוּאֵי ה׳ יִתְבָּרַךְ מְחַכֵּי חַסְדּוֹ מְיַחֲלֵי רַחֲמָיו. בַּמֶּה נִזְכֶּה בְּעֵינֵי אֲדוֹנֵנוּ, וּבַמֶּה נִמְצָא חֵן לְפָנָיו יִתְבָּרַךְ שְׁמוֹ. אִם לֹא בְּהִתְדַּמּוּת מְעַט בִּדְרָכָיו. וּבְמִדַּת טוּבוֹ הַפְּרוּשָׂה עַל כָּל הַנִּבְרָאִים, מִבְּלִי סִבָּה קְדוּמָה לָזֶה, רַק רַחֲמִים פְּשׁוּטִים בְּאֵין מְעוֹרֵר, כֵּן אֲנַחְנוּ נֵחָלֵץ חוּשִׁים לְעֶזְרַת הַחַלָּשִׁים מִבְּלִי מְבַקֵּשׁ וּמִבְּלִי מְעוֹרֵר. אָכֵן מַה כֹּחֵנוּ, עֶזְרָתֵנוּ לְהֶבֶל דָּמָה הָרַע נִפְרַץ, וְהָרִשְׁעָה גָּבְרָה, אֵין מָנוֹס וְאֵין מִפְלָט אִם לֹא בְּמַחְתֶּרֶת נְבוּאָה לְהָפֵר עֲצַת מְרֵעִים, וּבְהַשְׂכֵּל נְבַצֵּעַ מַאֲוַיֵּנוּ לִכְבֹּשׁ הָרֶשַׁע, בְּמַאֲסַר הַצֶּדֶק, בְּכַבְלֵי הַמִּדּוֹת, וּבִרְחִיקַת הַתַּאֲווֹת, זֹאת יְסוֹד הַדָּבָר לִבְנוֹת עָלָיו דַּיֵּק, אָכֵן מִי יָכִין חֹמֶר וּלְבֵנִים מִי יוֹצִיא הַדָּבָר לְמַעֲשֵׂהוּ יָשָׁר בָּאָדָם אַיִן. גַּם דַּעַת וּתְבוּנָה חָסְרוּ, וּבְזֹאת נְשׁוּבָה לְאָחוֹר הֲכִי אֵין יְרֵאִים בְּיִשְׂרָאֵל. מַדּוּעַ רָחֲקָה מָזוֹר וּתְרוּפָה, יִרְאֵי ה׳ הֵמָּה יִלְבְּשׁוּ עֹז לִכְבֹּשׁ אֶת הָרֶשַׁע בִּמְצוּדַת תַּאֲווֹתָיו. וּמַה יַּעַצְרֵם מוּכָנִים הֵמָּה לְכָל חֵפֶץ לְבָבָם לְהָקִים מְזִמָּתָם, הֲכִי הַגֶּשֶׁם יְמַנְעֵם, וְאִם הַבֹּשֶׁת וְהַכְּלִימָה יְבַלְבְּלֵם, הֲיִרְאֵי ה׳ יִקָּרְאוּ אִם כֹּה דַּרְכֵי הַתּוֹרָה,

1. Compare Psalms 33:18 and 147:11.
2. Compare Numbers 32:17.
3. Compare Tanna DeVei Eliyahu (21) and Koren Sacks Siddur (Ashkenaz), 37.
4. Compare Psalms 144:4.
5. Compare Exodus 22:1.
6. I.e., if they let themselves be intimidated.

Letter 5

We, Blessed God's creatures, anticipating His loving-kindness, hoping for His mercies[1] – how can we become worthy in the eyes of our Lord? How will we win favor before Him, blessed be His name, if not by imitating, in some small way, His ways and His quality of goodness, which is spread over all His creatures without any prior cause, just pure compassion, without any stimulus to evoke it? So we must take the initiative[2] to help the weak without being asked and without [needing] any stimulus.

Yet: What is our strength?[3] Helpfulness is like nothing.[4] Evil is rampant. Wickedness prevails. There is no safe haven and no refuge. We can only act by stealth[5] to defeat the counsels of evildoers. With intelligence, we can effectuate our longings to capture wickedness in the bonds of righteousness, in the ropes of [good] character traits, and by distancing desires. This is the base on which to build a fortification. But who will prepare mortar and bricks? Who will carry the project to its realization?

There is no upright person. Wisdom and understanding also are lacking. Then let us go back over this: Are there none in Israel who truly fear [God]? Why are remedy and medicine so far away? Let those who fear God clothe themselves in courage – to capture wickedness in the snare of its own desires.

What can stop them [who fear God]? They are ready with all their heart's desire to carry out their plans. Would the rains hold them back? Will shame and humiliation confound them? Would they be truly called "God-fearers" if these are the ways of the Torah?[6] Is not the first

הֲלֹא זֶה רֵאשִׁית דְּבַר ה' לְבַל יֵבֹשׁ מֵהַמַּלְעִיגִים, וְלִזְרוֹת הָלְאָה חֲמוּדֵי תֵּבֵל וַהֲבָלָיו וּבְזֹאת הַתְּבוּנָה וְהַחוּשׁ יִנָּגְדוּ זֶה לָזֶה.

וְלָזֹאת נְבַקֵּשׁ שָׁלוֹם וְנִרְדְּפָה. לָדַעַת מְקוֹר מוֹצָא הַיִּרְאָה, וּמֵאַיִן בָּאָה אִם מֵהֶהָרְגֵּל הַיּוֹמִי, אִם מֵהַלִּמּוּד בְּדַעַת וּבְהַשְׂכֵּל הַחוּשׁ יָעִיד כִּי דַעַת וּתְבוּנָה אַיִן מָנוֹחַ אֵין לָהּ גַּם חֵלֶק אֵין לָהּ בְּיִרְאַת ה', גַּם מֵרָחוֹק אַל תַּעֲמֹד וְלָזֹאת צָדְקוּ דִּבְרֵי הַחוּשׁ בַּל יְכַזְּבוּ וּמַה יּוֹסִיף תֵּת רַעְיוֹן הַתְּבוּנָה, אִם בִּיסוֹדֵי הַיִּרְאָה לֹא שָׁלַט כֹּחָהּ, אָכֵן מִי לֹא יָבִין כִּי הַחוּשׁ הוּא כְּלִי מוּכָן לְקַבֵּל כָּל הַצּוּרוֹת וּבְשִׁנּוּי הַצּוּרָה יִשְׁתַּנֶּה הַחוּשׁ. אִם בְּתַחְבּוּלוֹת יַעֲשֶׂה לְחַבֵּר הַתְּבוּנָה לְיִרְאָה. גַּם הַחוּשׁ יִשְׁתַּנֶּה, בְּעֵין עוֹזֵר וְסוֹמֵךְ.

וְלָזֹאת רֵאשִׁית מַעֲשֵׂינוּ לְחַזֵּק יָדַיִם רָפוֹת, לְנַהֲלֵם אֶל בֵּית הַסֵּפֶר לִמּוּד הַמּוּסָרִי, בְּהַשְׂכֵּל וָדַעַת, בְּלֵב נָכוֹן, וּבִשְׂפָתַיִם דוֹלְקִים, וְלַחֲזֹר מַאַמְרֵי חז"ל הַמַּלְהִיבִים לֵב הָאָדָם, אִישׁ אִישׁ דֵּי מַחְסוֹרוֹ אֲשֶׁר יֶחְסַר לוֹ, וְהָיָה אִם יִהְיֶה ה' עִמָּנוּ לְבַצַּע מַעֲשֵׂינוּ, וְיָכָלְנוּ עֲמֹד, וּבְזֹאת מַה נָּכוֹן הַדָּבָר לְכָל אִישׁ אֲשֶׁר קִרְבַת ה' יֶחְפָּצוּן, לִהְיוֹת שׁוֹקֵד עַל הַדָּבָר, לְהָסִיר וּלְבַטֵּל כָּל מוֹנֵעַ וּמְעַכֵּב בְּתַחְבּוּלוֹת נְכוֹנוֹת וּמוֹעִילוֹת.

אַחַת הִיא הַמְרַפֵּא כָּל נֶגַע וּמַחֲלָה רָעָה, נִגְעֵי הָאֵבָרִים וְהַנְּפָשׁוֹת, אֲשֶׁר גַּם בִּהְיוֹת הַהֶרְגֵּל עוֹזֵר לְיִרְאָה וּלְתוֹרָה, בִּלְעֲדֵי לִמּוּד הַמּוּסָרִי, רְחֵקָה מְאֹד מִמַּטָּרָה הַנִּרְצִית, הַמִּדּוֹת מְקֻלְקָלוֹת, מִלְחֶמֶת הַיֵּצֶר אֲשֶׁר לָזֶה בָּאנוּ לָעוֹלָם מֵאַיִן תִּמָּצֵא, רַק אֶל הָרָצוֹן יִפְנוּ כֹּחוֹתֵינוּ. וּמַה

7. Compare Psalms 34:15. The Hebrew word "*shalom*" in this phrase is a double-entendre. Shalom means not just peace, but also wholeness. *Shleimut* (wholeness) in Mussar is not literal. It represents purity, simplicity, wholeheartedness in seeking to do good. Note also that we must not only seek our goal but pursue it.
8. Compare Genesis 8:9.
9. Under normal circumstances, without working to achieve it, consciousness is far from reverence/fear of God.
10. Compare Exodus 2:4 and Psalms 10:1.
11. Compare Isaiah 35:3; here, "weak hands" refers to average laypersons.
12. Compare Deuteronomy 15:8 (give each poor person that which he specifically lacks).

word of God [to His prophets] to be not embarrassed by scoffers and to cast away the lures of the world and its vanities? But – in this – rational understanding and instinct are in conflict.

To this end – let us seek wholeness and pursue it,[7] to know the source out of which reverence arises and from where it comes. Is it from daily routine, or from learning with knowledge and intelligence? Instinct attests that knowledge and understanding are nothing. They have neither a foothold [in consciousness][8] nor a share in the fear of God.[9] They do not even stand at a distance.[10] In this, the words of instinct are correct; they do not mislead: What can the notion of understanding contribute if it cannot exert its power over reverence at its foundations?

Yet who does not understand that instinct is a vessel, ready to accept any shape? Change the shape, and instinct will change. If, by stratagems, you attach understanding to fear [of God], then instinct, too, will change, without any outside help or assistance.

Therefore, our first task is to strengthen weak hands,[11] to lead them to the Mussar study house, with understanding and knowledge, with ready heart, with flaming lips, and to repeatedly utter sayings of the Rabbis that enthuse the hearts of men. [Give] each person whatever he lacks.[12] If God is with us to execute our plan, then we will be able to endure.[13] Therefore, it is right that each person who seeks closeness to God[14] should hasten[15] [to work] at this to remove and nullify every obstacle and impediment, with correct and effective strategies.

There is one cure for every plague and sickness of the limbs and of the soul. Even when routine assisted fear [of God] and Torah,[16] without Mussar study, [the situation] was very far from the desired goal. Now, when character traits are corrupted, how can we find the capacity for the battle with the [evil] urge – that battle for which we come to this world? Our strength would simply follow our will [to go in the wrong

13. Compare Exodus 18:23.
14. Compare Isaiah 58:2.
15. Compare Jeremiah 1:12.
16. Until the impact of modernity, the everyday routine and surrounding culture was in harmony with Torah and fear of God.

נֹאמַר עַתָּה אֲשֶׁר הַהֶרְגֵּל מִתְנַגֵּד אֶל הַיִּרְאָה, אִם לֹא נִפְנֶה אֶל מָזוֹר הַמּוּסָרִי. אֵין מָקוֹם לַעֲבוֹדַת ה׳. וְכִמְעַט יֵאוּשׁ בַּדָּבָר.

וּבְזֹאת רְפוּאָה קַלָּה הִיא וּפִרְיָהּ רַב. מִי הָאִישׁ הֶחָפֵץ חַיִּים לִהְיוֹת מִמַּזְכֵּי הָרַבִּים, אֲשֶׁר כַּכּוֹכָבִים יַזְהִירוּ, וְצִדְקָתָם לְעוֹלָם לֹא תִמָּחֶה, לֵאוֹר בְּאוֹר הַחַיִּים, יַחְטֹף הַמִּצְוָה הַלָּזוֹ בִּזְמַנָּהּ, כִּי מִי יוֹדֵעַ מַה יּוֹלִיד יוֹם, וְאִם לֹא עַכְשָׁו אֵימָתַי, וּבָזֶה נִבְנֶה גַּם אֲנַחְנוּ לְלַטֵּשׁ הָרַעְיוֹן לִכְבֹּשׁ הַיֵּצֶר וְתַאֲווֹתָיו. וְהַבָּא לְלַמֵּד נִמְצָא לָמֵד. רֵאשִׁית דָּבָר לְהַכִּיר מַצְפּוּן אֱנוֹשׁ. מְגַמָּתוֹ חֶפְצוֹ וּרְצוֹנוֹ מַה הוּא. וְכַמָּה יִרְחַק מִן מַטְּרַת הָאֱמֶת אֲשֶׁר נִבְרָא, בַּמֶּה יֵאָסֵר תַּאֲוָתוֹ לְהַטּוֹתוֹ אֶל הָעֲבוֹדָה הַשְּׁלֵמָה הַלֵּזוּ, יְגִיעַת לִמּוּד הַמּוּסָרִי, לִהְיוֹת לִיסוֹד מוּסָד לִלְחֹם מִלְחֶמֶת חוֹבָה מִלְחֶמֶת הַיֵּצֶר, אִם בִּכְפִיַּת הָאֵבָרִים, לַעֲשׂוֹת הֵפֶךְ הָרָצוֹן וְגַם בְּלְטִישַׁת הָרַעְיוֹן, לִכְפּוֹת מְעַט הַלֵּב, אִם בַּחֲזָרַת מַאַמְרֵי חז״ל בְּמָתוּן וּבְעִיּוּן, וְאִם בְּהַעֲמָקַת הַשֵּׂכֶל בְּהַרְחָבַת הָעִנְיָנִים. לְפִי נְטִיַּת הַטֶּבַע וְהֶרְגֵּלוֹ, מַה שֶּׁגָּבוּ הָעִנְיָנִים הָאֵלֶּה. אֲשֶׁר חִיּוּבָם מְצוּדָה עַל כָּל אֲשֶׁר נִשְׁמַת רוּחַ חַיִּים בְּאַפָּיו. לִלְחֹם מִלְחַמְתּוֹ, וּבְיָדוֹ הַבְּחִירָה, לִכְבֹּשׁ הַמִּלְחָמָה לְהַטּוֹת אֵבָרָיו אֶל הַשְּׁלֵמוּת הָאֲמִתִּי.

17. With modernization, there is much more dissonance between traditional behavior and the surrounding culture in which the individual operates.
18. I.e., there is no space to operate effectively.
19. Compare Psalms 34:13.
20. Compare Daniel 12:3.
21. Compare Ben Sira 44:13. It should be noted that the Hebrew edition of Ben Sira was lost and not recovered until it was found and published after R. Salanter's lifetime. R. Salanter likely came across this phrase or paraphrase from a derivative source.
22. See Job 33:30.
23. I.e., now.
24. Compare Proverbs 27:1.
25. Avot 1:14.

direction]. Then what can we say about now, when routine opposes reverence?[17] Unless we turn to the Mussar cure, there is no room[18] for service of God. It is almost a hopeless case.

Yet with all this, there is an easy cure that bears abundant fruit. He who wants life[19] should be among those who uplift the masses, who shine like the stars,[20] and whose righteousness will never be erased.[21] So that he may bask in the light of life,[22] let him grab this mitzva in its right time.[23] For who knows what today will bring?[24] And if not now, when?[25]

With this we will also fortify ourselves to hone our thought, to conquer the [evil] urge and its desires. One who comes to teach will end up learning.

The first step is to become familiar with the psychology[26] of man – his inclination, his will, and his desire. How distanced has he become from the true purpose for which he was created? How can his desire be bound up and directed toward this wholesome service,[27] namely, the effort of Mussar study; toward becoming a solid base for fighting this "obligatory war," the war against the [evil] urge – whether by forcing the limbs to go against the will or to hone his thought so that it can compel the heart; whether by repeating sayings of the Rabbis deliberately and thoughtfully, or by deepening his thinking by broadening his study of the matter – according to his natural tendency and habit.

How lofty are these matters! The duty to fight these battles devolves upon everyone who breathes the spirit of life.[28] He can choose to conquer in the battle and direct his limbs toward true wholeness.

---

26. R. Salanter uses the term "*matzpun*" (from the root *tz-p-n*, "to hide"), which we translate as "psychology," to refer to the totality of motives that shape human behavior and decisions. These motives are "hidden" in that they are unexpressed. The subject may or may not be conscious of them; only later would R. Salanter develop his ideas about the human subconscious.
27. Note that R. Salanter has deepened his awareness that the consciousness unrefined by Mussar has distorted consciousness and can interpret and apply Torah in the wrong ways. Even the consciousness of a good person must be directed by Mussar to take a proper approach to life and a proper understanding of the Torah's instructions.
28. Compare Genesis 7:22.

ו

הָרַב בַּעַל מְסִלַּת יְשָׁרִים בְּהַקְדָּמַת סִפְרוֹ הַנִּכְבָּד, הֵחֵל לֹאמַר כִּי לֹא יִכְתֹּב רַק דְּבָרִים פְּשׁוּטִים וְנוֹדָעִים עַיֵּין שָׁם. אֵין מְסִלַּת יְשָׁרִים לְפָנַי כָּעֵת – כֵּן אָנֹכִי לֹא אֶכְתֹּב רַק אֲשֶׁר נֶאֶמְרוּ וְנִשְׁנוּ רַבּוֹת פְּעָמִים, כִּי יוֹם הַכִּפּוּרִים, לְבַד מִצְוָתוֹ הַגְּדוֹלָה, עֲשֵׂה שֶׁיֵּשׁ בָּהּ כָּרֵת וְעוֹד כוּ׳, הוּא תּוֹעֶלֶת גְּדוֹלָה לְהָאָדָם לְהַצִּילוֹ מִצָּרוֹת רַבּוֹת וְנִשְׂגָּבוֹת, אֲשֶׁר הָאָדָם

---

* Although this letter is not dated, R. Isaac Blazer, editor of *Ohr Yisrael,* published it immediately after the first five letters, which he dates to the period of R. Salanter's stay in Kovno (1848–1857). By implication, this is the next letter, chronologically. The content of the letter suggests that it was written around or during the Ten Days of Repentance, between Rosh HaShana and Yom Kippur.

1. Rabbi Moshe Ḥayim Luzzatto (1707–1746), also known as Ramḥal, a prominent Italian Jewish kabbalist, philosopher of ethics, and moralist.
2. R. Salanter highly valued this Mussar book by R. Luzzatto and arranged for its republication in Vilna in 1844–1845 in order to have the lay people and his Mussar disciples use it as a fundamental text for character building and self-improvement. It is noteworthy that he does not turn to R. Luzzatto's more kabbalistic writings as a resource for the Mussar movement. In a letter to his close friend and disciple, Eliyahu Kretinga, written in 1849 (see R. Shraga HaCohen Vilman, *Iggerot UKetavim Me'et HaGaon R. Yisrael Salanter Zt"l* [Jerusalem: Dror, 1970], 28), he writes regarding Ramḥal's kabbalistic works: "איננו שייך לי כי אינני עוסק בזה ולא ידעתי בכלל אם העת נכון לזה" – "It does not relate to me, for I do not study it and I have no idea whether the time is right for it." Educationally, one might understand

*Letter 6**

In the introduction to his important book, the rabbi,[1] author of *Mesillat Yesharim* (*Path of the Just*),[2] began by saying he will write only simple and well-known things. Take a look – I have no *Mesillat Yesharim* before me at present. I, too, will write only what has been said and repeated many times.

Yom Kippur, aside from its being a weighty mitzva – a positive commandment punishable by excision,[3] etc. – is especially useful to save a person from a great many troubles.

R. Salanter's approach as follows: R. Salanter sees the great challenge of the arrival of a new culture, i.e., modernity, in which the self-evident authority of the Torah is confronted with alternative values and authority, and the universal observance of tradition is consequently undermined. R. Salanter concluded that the inherited culture of external observance, drawing its authority from the collective consensus of the Torah's sacred status and conformity of practice and thought, could not endure in the face of choice and an alternative culture. His solution was not to reinforce traditional authority on the basis of Kabbala, but instead to develop an internalized, character-based, religious individual who chose to uphold the tradition. To do so, he drew upon classic sources and the Mussar tradition, which highlighted the values inherent in observance, as well as character building and ethics, which were found in the tradition. Benjamin Brown makes the definitive case that R. Salanter chose to focus on Mussar and not Kabbala in "'It Does Not Relate to Me': Rabbi Israel Salanter and the Kabbalah," in M. R. Niehoff, R. Meroz, and J. Garb (eds.), *VeZot LiYehuda – And This Is for Yehuda: Yehuda Liebes Jubilee Volume* (Jerusalem: Mosad Bialik, 2012), 420–39 (Hebrew).

בְּעַצְמוֹ, הוּא הָאָדָם אֲשֶׁר אֵין בְּיָדֵינוּ לְכַנּוֹתוֹ רַק – אָנֹכִי – אָנֹכִי הַלָּזֶה. הוּא הַמְדַבֵּר, הוּא הַחוֹשֵׁב, הוּא הַמִּתְאַוֶּה, הוּא הַמִּתְעַמֵּל לְהַשִּׂיג תַּאֲוָתוֹ, הוּא מִתְחַבֵּא בַּחֹמֶר הַגּוּפָנִי אֲשֶׁר בְּהִתְבַּטֵּל כֹּחוֹתָיו – הִיא הַמִּיתָה – הָאָנֹכִי הַלָּזֶה הוּא עוֹד בְּחַיּוּתוֹ וְכֹחוֹתָיו, מְפֻשָּׁט מֵעוֹלָם הַגַּשְׁמִי הוּא הִתְקַשְּׁרוּת הַנֶּפֶשׁ, הוּא הָאָנֹכִי עִם הַחֹמֶר הוּא הַגּוּף, בִּתְכוּנָה אֲשֶׁר הָאָנֹכִי הַלָּזֶה מֻכְשָׁר לְצַעַר וְעֹנֶג, לְטוֹב לוֹ אוֹ לְרַע לְצַעַר נוֹרָא וְאָיוֹם אוֹ לְעֹנֶג נִפְלָא אֲשֶׁר אֵין עֲרֹךְ לָהֶם, גְּבוֹהִים לְמַעְלָה הַרְבֵּה נֶגֶד הַצַּעַר וְהָעֹנֶג אֲשֶׁר מֻכְשָׁר הָאָנֹכִי הַלָּזֶה בָּעוֹלָם הַזֶּה, בִּהְיוֹתוֹ קָשׁוּר עִם הַגּוּף, הַצַּעַר וְהָעֹנֶג הַלָּזֶה תָּלוּי בְּהִתְנַהֲגוּת הָאָדָם הוּא הָאָנֹכִי בָּעוֹלָם הַזֶּה בִּשְׁמִירָתוֹ צִוּוּי ד׳ יִתְבָּרַךְ שְׁמוֹ, בְּהִתְקַיְּמוֹ צִוּוּיו יִתְבָּרַךְ שְׁמוֹ, יַשִּׂיג הָאָדָם הוּא הָאָנֹכִי עֹנֶג גָּדוֹל וּבְעָבְרוֹ צִוּוּיו יִתְבָּרַךְ שְׁמוֹ יַשִּׂיג צַעַר נוֹרָא.

עַל כָּל מִין עֲבֵרָה נִבְדָּל בְּתַשְׁלוּם גְּמוּל עָנְשָׁהּ בְּאֵיכוּתָהּ מֵחֲבֶרְתָּהּ לְפִי מִשְׁפָּטוֹ יִתְבָּרַךְ שְׁמוֹ, בְּכָל פְּרַט הָעֲבֵרָה נִבְדָּלִים בְּנֵי

3. The first mishna in Keritot lists only two positive commandments that are punishable by *karet* (excision) if one fails to perform them: the Paschal offering and circumcision. It is possible that the text here should be "*mitzvat lo taaseh*" ("negative commandment") instead of "*mitzvat aseh*" ("positive commandment"), and the printer made an error. Alternatively, R. Salanter may have written this letter while traveling – earlier he noted, "I have no *Mesillat Yesharim* before me at present" – so he may have simply erred or misremembered. Note that at the end of Letter 21 he mentions that he is mailing his letter immediately (by implication, not edited or proofread) and asks his students "to correct his errors."
4. R. Salanter focused on the concept of the "self" (the "*anokhi*," the ego) early in his career, though the concept was not well developed in premodern thinking. For example, Rambam's *Shemona Perakim*, the introduction to his commentary on Avot, does not describe character traits as components of an indivisible self, nor does it focus on the individual as a composite soul inside a body with specific traits, but rather as an agglomeration of separate "*middot*," or dispositions.

   Thinking of the individual as a "self" is widespread in modern culture. This reflects sociological tendencies; that is, a society that allows for more individual choice and is based on achieved status will have a more robust concept of the "self." Moreover, these developments were incorporated into psychology and the theory of the self. Modern culture thus moves toward a much stronger sense of a unitary self, and R. Salanter's use of "*anokhi*" is an example of his having internalized this emerging, more individualistic conception of human nature.

For this "person" is the subject that we can only call "the self."[4] The "self" is who speaks, thinks, and desires; the "self" is who works hard to attain the object of his desire. The self is embedded in physical matter, and when [this matter] loses its life force – that is, upon death – the self retains its vitality and life force. Removed from the material world[5] – that is, from the linkage of the soul or self with matter or the body – it still is characterized by a capacity for pain and pleasure, of the betterment or worsening of its conditions, for terrible pain or sublime, incomparable pleasure, that far surpass the pain and pleasure that the self has the capacity for in this world, when it is tethered to the body. This [ultimate] pain and pleasure depends on the behavior of the person, the self, in this world – on observing the commandments of God, blessed be His name. By fulfilling God's commandments, the person – that is, the self – will attain great pleasure; by violating God's commandments, he will suffer terribly.[6]

The recompense for each type of sin differs qualitatively from that of any other, in accordance with His judgment.[7] People differ from one

---

5. Most of R. Salanter's statements in previous letters have been tactical and common sense. His description of the "*anokhi*" is the most developed conceptual statement he has made thus far.

   Here he describes the self as enduring after the death of the body, thus identifying it with the soul. R. Salanter is thus asking his readers to think of Yom Kippur not as a set of rituals, but as a moment for self/soul-assessment. On Yom Kippur, the self is separated from the material world and views itself more as disembodied, whereas under normal circumstances, the body and its needs dominate. When one is thinking like a pure soul, one realizes that the greatest pleasure and pain will be experienced in the next world, so one wants to make sure to maintain a pure soul in this world, doing the mitzvot fully and not superficially. In this letter, in addition to focusing on the next world, as in previous letters, R. Salanter also focuses on this world and how our behavior in it affects our soul/self.

6. R. Salanter is instructing his students not to think of themselves in terms of multiple internal forces, traits, and dispositions and instead think of themselves as monistic "selves" governing everything. This "self" is the soul that survives in the next world, to be rewarded or punished in accordance with behavior as a mortal.

7. This is a another modern-oriented interpretation, in that R. Salanter focuses on the uniqueness of every individual temperament and the differing quality of every act done by different individuals. God responds and judges each person according to their individual qualities that lead to the behaviors and materially change the inner quality of each act. The individuals' actual behaviors externally may seem identical

אָדָם זֶה מִזֶּה, בְּקַבָּלַת עָנְשָׁם, לְפִי תְּכוּנָתָם וּמַצָּבָם בָּעוֹלָם הַזֶּה, עָשִׁיר וְעָנִי, חָכָם וְסָכָל, זָרִיז וְעָצֵל בְּטִבְעוֹ, וְכַיּוֹצֵא הַרְבֵּה וְהַרְבֵּה בְּחִינוֹת שׁוֹנוֹת – אוֹתוֹ הָאָדָם עַצְמוֹ – הוּא הָאָנֹכִי פְּרָטִי בְּאוֹתוֹ פְּרָט חֵלֶק מִן הָעֲבֵרָה עַצְמָהּ, נִבְדָּל בְּעָנְשָׁהּ לְפִי הִתְחַלְּפוּת תְּכוּנַת מַצָּבוֹ, מֵעֵת הַמְּנוּחָה לְעֵת הַטִּרְדָּה, מִתְּכוּנַת הַמְּנוּחָה לִתְכוּנַת הַטִּרְדָּה, מִתְּכוּנַת שְׁקִיטַת הָרַעְיוֹן לִתְכוּנַת בִּלְבּוּל הָרַעְיוֹן, וְכַיּוֹצֵא בְּחִינוֹת מִתְחַלְּפוֹת הַרְבֵּה, וְכָל אֲשֶׁר תֵּקַל לִפְנֵי הָאָדָם לְהִשָּׁמֵר מֵהָעֲבֵרָה, הֵן שֶׁלֹּא לַעֲשׂוֹת עֲבֵרָה, אוֹ שֶׁלֹּא לְבַטֵּל עֲשִׂיַּת מִצְוָה, כֵּן תִּגְדַּל עָנְשׁוֹ לְמַעְלָה, וּבְכָל בְּחִינָה וּמַדְרֵגָה אֲשֶׁר יִתְחַלֵּק מִכָּבֵד לְקַל – אֲשֶׁר יֵשׁ כָּבֵד לַקַּל מִמֶּנָּה, וְיֵשׁ קַל לַכָּבֵד מִמֶּנָּה, כֵּן תִּתְחַלֵּק הָעֳנָשִׁים, מִצַּעַר גָּדוֹל לְצַעַר קָטָן, הַגָּדוֹל נֶגֶד הַקָּטָן מִמֶּנּוּ, הַקָּטָן נֶגֶד הַגָּדוֹל מִמֶּנּוּ.

וְכַאֲשֶׁר יַשְׁקִיף הָאָדָם בְּעֵין בִּינָתוֹ, אוֹ בִּדְרִישָׁה מֵאַחֵר הַמֵּבִין יוֹתֵר מִמֶּנּוּ, עַל פְּרַט הָעֲבֵרָה הַנִּדְרֶשֶׁת לוֹ, עַד כַּמָּה תַּעֲלֶה חִיּוּב שְׁמִירָתָהּ עַל פִּי הַתּוֹרָה, אִם שֶׁלֹּא לַעֲשׂוֹת עֲבֵרָה, אוֹ שֶׁלֹּא לְבַטֵּל מִצְוָה, לְפִי מַצַּב הַכְּבֵדוּת לִשְׁמֹר כִּי יֵשׁ חִלּוּק לִדְאוֹרַיְתָא וְרַבָּנָן וְכוּ׳, וְהוּא מֻשְׂכָּל רִאשׁוֹן מוּבָן מֵעַצְמוֹ, שֶׁהָעֹנֶשׁ יִהְיֶה יוֹתֵר גָּדוֹל מִכְּבִידַת שְׁמִירַת מְנִיעַת הָעֲבֵרָה, וְאַחַר כָּךְ יֵלֵךְ הָלְאָה יִרְאֶה גַּם בְּהַשְׁקָפָה רִאשׁוֹנָה וּבִמְרוּצַת הָרַעְיוֹן, כִּי יֵשׁ הַרְבֵּה בְּחִינוֹת, יוֹתֵר גְּדוֹלִים מִמַּצָּבוֹ עַד מַצַּב הַחִיּוּב לִשְׁמִירָה, לַקַּל נֶגֶד כָּבֵד מִמֶּנָּה, וְעַל פִּי בְּחִינוֹת הַלָּלוּ

---

to someone else's. However, reflecting each person's uniqueness, the difficulty or ease of doing the action and the inner quality of the behavior vary widely. God discerns these differences and rewards/punishes accordingly.

8. I.e., it is worse for a rich person to steal.

9. *Tekhuna* (pl. *tekhunot*) is a tendency or quality in a person. *Beḥina* (pl. *beḥinot*) is a state of mind at a particular moment. A general tendency (*tekhuna*) may alter its expression to accord with the state of mind (*beḥina*) due to the exigencies of the moment.

10. There is a difference between greater and lesser anxiety, or between having greater or lesser wealth. There are different levels of physical and emotional well-being, and each level of difficulty or of ease leads to a different judgment, because they make it easier or harder to sin. Someone who loves food gets more reward for restricting

another in every detail of the sin and in receiving punishment, according to their traits and circumstances in this world: rich or poor,[8] wise or simple, energetic or lazy, and so forth with respect to innumerable different states of mind.[9] That specific person – the individual self – is different with respect to each specific detail of the sin itself, and so his punishment varies according to the changing qualities of his condition – from a time of being at peace to a time of preoccupation; from a serene tendency to one of distraction; from a temperament of tranquil contemplation to one of confused thinking, and so on, as moods are in constant flux.

[As a rule,] the easier it is for a person to have refrained from a sin – whether not to commit a transgression or not to nullify doing a mitzva – the greater his punishment. And as each circumstance and level [of difficulty] contributes to making it more difficult or easier, making that which is easy more difficult,[10] or that which is difficult easier, so will the punishment meted out be more or less painful. Greater pain corresponds to lesser [difficulty in refraining from sin] and lesser pain stems from the greater [difficulty in refraining from sin].

When a person observes, through the lens of his intelligence, or by asking someone who understands more than he does, how strong is the obligation according to the Torah to refrain from a particular sin that he wants to commit – whether not to do the sin or not to nullify a positive commandment – [the answer] hinges on the state of difficulty in observing it. There is a difference between Torah commandments and rabbinic enactments, etc., so it will be self-evident and axiomatic that the punishment will be greater than the difficulty of refraining from the sin. One can then go further and see – even at first glance and with intuitive thinking – that there are many states of mind that surpass his present state, reaching even the state of his obligation to observe and compounding its difficulty. It is in accordance with these states of mind,

---

their diet to only kosher food than would someone who does not love food. Likewise, someone who is very hungry and finds themselves in a situation with no kosher food available receives a greater reward for holding back. Thus, there are general tendencies that affect behaviors and lead to different judgments and there are situational mindsets that affect behaviors and lend to different judgments.

בְּחִינוֹת רַבּוֹת מִתְחַלְּקוֹת לַחֲלָקִים וּמַדְרֵגוֹת רַבּוֹת מְאֹד, כֵּן יִגְדַּל עָנְשׁוֹ לְמַעְלָה לְמַעְלָה, יֶחֱרַד מְאֹד לְבַב הָאָדָם הַנִּלְבָּב גַּם בְּלִי עִיּוּן וְהַעֲמָקַת הַמּוּסָרִי.

הוּא הַדָּבָר אֲשֶׁר בְּיָדֵינוּ לְהַלְבִּישׁ בְּמַאֲמַר הַכָּתוּב תְּהִלִּים צ״ד אַשְׁרֵי הַגֶּבֶר אֲשֶׁר תְּיַסְּרֶנּוּ וְגוֹ׳ וּמִתּוֹרָתְךָ תְלַמְּדֶנּוּ, הַיְנוּ כִּי עַל יְדֵי יִסּוּרֵי עוֹלָם הַזֶּה יִנָּצֵל מֵעֳנָשִׁים קָשִׁים וּמָרִים כַּנִּזְכָּר לְעֵיל, וּמֵאַיִן יֵדַע לְהָאָדָם – אִם כִּי יוֹדֵעַ הוּא כִּי עָנֹשׁ יֵעָנֵשׁ, אֲבָל לְכָל הַפָּחוֹת בְּהַשְׁקָפָה כְּלָלִית לֵידַע כִּי עָצוּם וְנוֹרָא הוּא מְאֹד לְהָאָדָם, הוּא הָאָנֹכִי הָעוֹבֵר – הוּא וּמִתּוֹרָתְךָ תְלַמְּדֶנּוּ כַּנִּזְכָּר לְעֵיל בִּדְבָרִים קְצָרִים מְעַטֵּי הַכַּמּוּת, וְרַב הָאֵיכוּת, לַמַּעֲמִיק וּמַעֲמִיק בָּהֶם.

וּבָזֹאת עֲשֶׂרֶת יְמֵי תְשׁוּבָה יְמֵי מַעֲשֶׂה הֵמָּה, לִרְאוֹת לְהֵטִיב דְּרָכֵינוּ לַשָּׁנָה הַבָּאָה לְשָׁלוֹם, כְּמַאֲמַר חֲכָמֵינוּ ז״ל בֵּינוֹנִים תְּלוּיִין וְעוֹמְדִין מֵרֹאשׁ הַשָּׁנָה עַד יוֹם הַכִּפּוּרִים זָכוּ כוּ׳ (רֹאשׁ־הַשָּׁנָה דַּף ט״ז), וְכַאֲשֶׁר הָאָדָם בָּעוֹלָם הַזֶּה שְׁתֵּי בְּחִינוֹת לְפָנָיו, הָאֶחָד אֵינוֹ בְּיָדוֹ הִיא תְּשׁוּקַת הָאָדָם לִהְיוֹת מָלֵא וְגָדוּשׁ בְּצָרְכֵי הָעוֹלָם הַזֶּה, וְהַשֵּׁנִי הִיא אֲשֶׁר בְּיָדוֹ לְפִי תְּכוּנַת מַצָּבוֹ לְמַלְּאוֹת חֶפְצוֹ וְהִצְטָרְכוּת עוֹלָם הַזֶּה, וְכָל אֲשֶׁר יִקְטַן הָאָדָם בְּמַצָּבוֹ בָּעוֹלָם הַזֶּה עוֹד יוֹתֵר יִתְעַמֵּל לְהַשִּׂיג חֶפְצוֹ, הֶעָנִי הַמַּחֲזִיר עַל הַפְּתָחִים מִתְעַמֵּל יוֹתֵר, וְאֵינֶנּוּ כָּבֵד וּמוּזָר לְפָנָיו טָרְחָתוֹ לְהַשִּׂיג מְעַט כֶּסֶף אוֹ אֹכֶל מִבַּעַל הַבַּיִת, הָאֶבְיוֹן יוֹתֵר מִבֵּינוֹנִי, הַבֵּינוֹנִי יוֹתֵר מֵעָשִׁיר, יַעַן מָה? יַעַן כִּי לְבַד הֶכְרֵחוֹ עוֹד יוֹתֵר יְקַבֵּל צַעַר מִמְּנִיעַת מְעַט הָאֹכֶל כוּ׳, הָאֶבְיוֹן בִּבְחִינַת צַעֲרוֹ מֵהַנֶּחְסָר לוֹ – הָאֶבְיוֹן יוֹתֵר מִבַּעַל הַבַּיִת כוּ׳.

כֵּן הָאָדָם בִּבְחִינַת חִיּוּב עֲבוֹדָתוֹ לַד׳ יִתְבָּרַךְ שְׁמוֹ, שְׁתֵּי בְּחִינוֹת

---

11. See Rosh HaShana 16a–b: The clearly righteous and clearly wicked receive an instant judgment. However, for the average or "in-between" person ("*beinoni*"), the judgment is delayed until Yom Kippur, to enable people to repent and/or to earn more merits.
12. "...if they are worthy they are inscribed for life; if they are not worthy they are inscribed for death."
13. The point of this paragraph is to emphasize the different states of mind of people. Everyone has a part of him that wants everything in the world, as well as a part that

the numerous mindsets that divide into many levels and parts, that his punishment grows greater and greater. Thus, the sensitive human heart will tremble even without studying or delving into Mussar.

Our conclusion can be attached to the verse in Psalm 94: "Fortunate is the man whom God chastens and teaches him from Your Torah" (94:12). That is: Through the sufferings of this world, he will be spared from hard and bitter punishment, as we mentioned above. But how will a person know this? Even if he knows that he will be punished, he should at least know in a general way how terrible it will be to the person, to this sinful self. This is what is meant by the aforementioned "and teaches him from Your Torah." Use terse statements, few in number but high in quality, to the one who will delve deeply into them.

So the Ten Days of Repentance are days of action, to see to it that we rectify our ways for the upcoming year, may it be peaceful. As the Sages, of blessed memory, say, "The average person[11] is suspended in judgment from Rosh HaShana to Yom Kippur. If they are worthy..."[12]

When a person is in this world, he has two states of mind before him. One – which he can never fulfill – is the great desire to be brimming with all the [material] goods of this world. The second is in his capacity, according to the nature of his circumstances, to fulfill his desires and make every use of this world. The worse a person's condition in this world, the harder he will have to work to attain his needs. The poor beggar who goes door-to-door works harder; his great effort to obtain a little money or food from a householder does not seem too difficult or strange in his eyes. The poor person works harder than the middle-class person; the middle-class person works harder than the wealthy. Why? Because aside from necessity, he will suffer more when even that little bit of food is withheld. The poor man's pain from lack of food is greater than that of the householder, and so on.[13]

The same is true of people with respect to their mindset toward their duty to serve God. There are two possible mindsets, and both are

---

is realistic in its wants. When the person works in a realistic frame of mind, the less they have, and the harder they work to earn at least the little that they can. They do not consider it beneath their dignity to do everything necessary. People should do the same when it comes to the service of God.

לְפָנָיו אֲשֶׁר שְׁתֵּיהֶם בְּיָדוֹ, הָאֶחָד בְּכָל הָעִתִּים כָּל אֶחָד בִּבְחִירָתוֹ לִהְיוֹת מָלֵא וְגָדוּשׁ בַּעֲבוֹדָתוֹ יִתְבָּרַךְ שְׁמוֹ, וְגַם בַּעֲשֶׂרֶת יְמֵי תְּשׁוּבָה הָאָדָם בְּיָדוֹ לְהִתְחַלֵּף לְאִישׁ אַחֵר, לִהְיוֹת צַדִּיק לַשָּׁנָה הַבָּאָה לְשָׁלוֹם. הַשֵּׁנִי הִיא הַבְּחִינָה לְפִי הַמַּצָּב בַּעֲבוֹדָתוֹ יִתְבָּרַךְ שְׁמוֹ בְּכָל הָעִתִּים, וּבִפְרָט בַּעֲשֶׂרֶת יְמֵי תְּשׁוּבָה הַיְסוֹד הָרָאשִׁי הוּא לְהַשְׁקִיף וּלְהִתְבּוֹנֵן עַל דְּרָכָיו וְלִרְאוֹת לִשְׁמֹר לְכָל הַפָּחוֹת חֵלֶק הַקַּל מִמֶּנּוּ לְפִי מַצָּבוֹ וְיִרְאָתוֹ, וּבָזֶה יִנָּצֵל מֵחֵלֶק הַיּוֹתֵר חָמוּר בְּאוֹתָהּ הָעֲבֵרָה כַּנִּזְכָּר לְעֵיל.

וְאֶפְתְּחָה בְמָשָׁל פִּי, בְּהַנּוֹגֵעַ לַלִּמּוּד הַמּוּסָרִי לֵילֵךְ לִפְעָמִים לְבֵית הַמּוּסָר, אֲשֶׁר הוּא דָּבָר נָקֵל, וְלִמּוּד הַיִּרְאָה חוֹבָה עַל הָאָדָם, וְאוּלַי תִּהְיֶה אֵיזֶה נִמְשָׁל לִדְבָרִים אֲחֵרִים הַנּוֹגֵעַ לַעֲבוֹדָתוֹ יִתְבָּרַךְ שְׁמוֹ, הַהִלּוּךְ לְבֵית הַמּוּסָרִי דָּבָר נָקֵל הוּא גַּם לַמְטֹרָד בַּעֲסָקָיו, בִּפְרָט בְּשַׁבָּת קֹדֶשׁ, אָכֵן יָדוּעַ הוּא כִּי לִמּוּד תּוֹרָה גְּמָרָא אוֹ פּוֹסֵק, הוּא יוֹתֵר גָּדוֹל וְיוֹתֵר חוֹבָה בְּשַׁבָּת קֹדֶשׁ לַטָּרוּד בַּעֲסָקָיו בְּחֹל, וְלָזֹאת טוֹב לְסַנֵּף הַבֵּית־מִדְרָשׁ דִּלְמַטָּה, אוֹ חֶדֶר הַסָּמוּךְ לְלִמּוּד הַגְּמָרָא כַּנִּזְכָּר לְעֵיל, לְמַעַן לֹא תִּהְיֶה הִתְנַגְּדוּת לְלִמּוּד הַמּוּסָרִי הָרָחוֹק מִבֵּית הַמִּדְרָשׁ הָרָגִיל לְכָל אֶחָד לְלִמּוּד הַגְּמָרָא כַּנִּזְכָּר לְעֵיל הָעִקָּרִית וְהַמּוּסָר טָפֵל אֵלָיו.

לִמּוּד הַמּוּסָרִי חוֹבָה עַל הָאָדָם, וּבְיוֹתֵר לָאָדָם הַטָּרוּד בַּעֲסָקָיו, וּמַחֲלָתוֹ גְּדוֹלָה בַּעֲבוֹדָתוֹ יִתְבָּרַךְ שְׁמוֹ, אָכֵן לֹא דָּבָר קַל הוּא לְהִשְׁתַּמֵּשׁ בִּרְפוּאַת לִמּוּד הַמּוּסָרִי, נֶגֶד מַחֲלָה הָעַזָּה הַנִּצְרֶכֶת רְפוּאוֹת גְּדוֹלוֹת.

כִּי אֲנַחְנוּ רוֹאִים בְּכֹחוֹת הָאָדָם הֵן הַנּוֹגֵעַ לַשֵּׂכֶל, כָּל לִמּוּד בְּרֵאשִׁיתוֹ הוּא בְּמַצָּב הַבָּרוּר, וּבְכָל זֶה הוֹלֵךְ בִּכְבֵדוּת, הַנַּעַר הַמַּתְחִיל

14. If he concentrates on changing what he can realistically, then at least he will avoid the worst part of the sin, because he is realistic in his self-assessment, conscious of his faults and temptations, and tries hard to reduce punishment.

15. See Psalms 78:2.

16. R. Salanter refers to "*matzav habarur*" (lit. "the level of clarity") or "*klar*" (Yiddish for the German klár) to refer to something that one does while the mind is in a state of clarity and consciousness. He refers to subconscious and unconscious levels as "*matzav hakehe*" ("the state of darkness") or "*dunkele*" (Yiddish for the German dúnkel); this refers to human reactions that are automatic or unconscious. For

attainable. One – at all times everyone has the choice to be overflowing with His service. During the Ten Days of Repentance, a person has the power to become a changed person, to be a righteous person in the upcoming year, may it be peaceful. The second is his mindset according to the actual state of his service of God at any given time. Especially during the Ten Days of Repentance, the fundamental principle is for one to observe and reflect on his own ways, and to see to it to observe at least the part that is easier for him, according to his situation and his level of reverence. With this [approach], he will at least be saved from the most severe part of that sin, as mentioned above.[14]

Let me give an example[15] pertaining to Mussar study: to go occasionally to the Mussar House, which is an easy thing to do, and the study of reverence is an obligation on everyone. Perhaps this can serve as an analogy to other matters pertaining to His service. Going to the Mussar House is easy (especially on the holy Shabbat) – even for someone preoccupied with his worldly affairs. However, it is well known that study of Torah, Talmud, or legal codes is greater, and a greater obligation, on the holy Shabbat for one who is preoccupied with his worldly affairs on weekdays. So it is good to attach the [Mussar study room] to the study hall annex, or in a room near the Talmud study hall, as suggested above. So there will be no conflict [implied] between Mussar study at a distant location from the study hall regularly used by everyone for Talmud study, as mentioned, which is primary, and to which Mussar is secondary.

Every person is obligated to study Mussar, but especially a person who is preoccupied by worldly affairs, and his service of God is significantly ailing. Indeed, it is not easy to use Mussar study to cure this fierce illness which needs strong medicine.

For we see something when it comes to human capabilities: with regard to the intellect, anything learned must begin as something at the conscious level,[16] and it proceeds with difficulty. When a child begins to

---

instance, when one is learning to ride a bicycle or play a musical instrument (or, as in R. Salanter's example, learning to read), they are very conscious of each movement. In R. Salanter's terms, they are in a "state of clarity." Once the activity has been learned and internalized, it becomes unconscious, second nature – a "state of darkness."

לִלְמֹד עִבְרִית, לֵידַע לְהַגִּיד הַמִּלּוֹת בַּתְּחִלָּה, כַּמָּה יִתְעַמֵּל עִמּוֹ מְלַמְּדוֹ לְהָאִיר לְפָנָיו הָאוֹתִיּוֹת, וְאַחַר־כָּךְ לְחַבֵּר תֵּבָה שְׁלֵמָה, בְּכָל זֹאת יִתְנַהֵג הַנַּעַר בִּכְבֵדוּת גָּדוֹל בְּקָרְאוֹ הָאוֹתִיּוֹת וְהַמִּלּוֹת, וְאַחַר־כָּךְ כְּשֶׁיִּקְנֶה הַהֶרְגֵּל הַנִּצְרָךְ לְפִי תְּכוּנָתוֹ יִקְרָא בִּמְרוּצָה בְּלִי הִתְבּוֹנְנוּת כְּלָל, הוּא אֲשֶׁר נִקְרָא אֵצֶל חוֹקְרֵי כֹּחוֹת נַפְשׁוֹת הָאָדָם, כֹּחוֹת מְאִירִים בְּרוּרִים אוֹ כֵּהִים [קְלָארֶע אוּן דוּנְקֶעלֶע], כֵּן גַּם בְּכֹחוֹת הִתְפַּעֲלוּת הַנַּפְשִׁי, יֶשְׁנָם כֹּחוֹת מְאִירִים [קְלָארֶע] וְכֵהִים [דוּנְקֶעלֶע], הַכֵּהִים הֵמָּה יוֹתֵר חֲזָקִים וּמוֹצִיאִים פְּעֻלָּתָם בְּהִתְעוֹרְרוּת מְעַט בְּחֹזֶק יָד, אַהֲבַת הָאָדָם לְצֶאֱצָאָיו כֵּהִים הֵמָּה, וְכִמְעַט בְּרֹב הָעִתִּים אֵינָם נִרְגָּשִׁים לְהָאָדָם עַצְמוֹ, וּבְהִתְעוֹרְרוּת קְטַנָּה תִּתְלַהֵב לְאֵשׁ בּוֹעֶרֶת, תַּאֲוַת הָאָדָם הֵמָּה הַכֵּהִים אֲשֶׁר בְּלִי הִתְעוֹרְרוּת מָה, כִּמְעַט אֵינָם נִרְגָּשִׁים, וְלָזֹאת גָּדוֹל כֹּחָם לִמְשֹׁל בָּאָדָם.

לִמּוּד הַמּוּסָרִי יְסוֹדוֹ וְרֵאשִׁיתוֹ בִּבְחִינַת הַבְּרֵרוֹת בְּהִתְפַּעֲלוּת הַנֶּפֶשׁ, וְלָזֹאת כִּמְעַט בְּרֹב פְּעָמִים אֵין בְּכֹחוֹ לַעֲזֹר נֶגֶד הַתַּאֲוָה בְּחִינַת הַכֵּהֶה [דוּנְקֶעלֶע] הַחֲזָקָה, אָכֵן כְּמוֹ בַּלִּמּוּד הַשִּׂכְלִי כָּל פַּעַם לִמּוּד הַבָּרוּר עוֹשֶׂה רֹשֶׁם בִּבְחִינַת הַכֵּהֶה, אֲשֶׁר בְּלֹא זֶה לֹא יִצְטָרְכוּ הַלִּמּוּדִים לְהִוָּלֵד בִּבְחִינַת הַכֵּהֶה הַגְּמוּרָה לֵידַע בִּמְרוּצָה כִּמְעַט בְּלִי הִתְבּוֹנְנוּת. וּבִתְנַאי שֶׁלֹּא יִהְיֶה הֶפְסֵק זְמַן גָּדוֹל בֵּין לִמּוּדֵי הַבָּרוּר, לְמַעַן לֹא יִתְרוֹקֵן וְיִתְבַּטֵּל רֹשֶׁם הַכֵּהֶה, כִּי אָז לִמּוּד פַּעַם הַשֵּׁנִי יִהְיֶה הָרֵאשִׁית, וְכֵן עַד אֵין סוֹף, כֵּן גַּם בְּהִתְפַּעֲלוּת נַפְשִׁי כָּל הִתְפַּעֲלוּת עוֹשָׂה רֹשֶׁם מָה בִּבְחִינַת הַכֵּהֶה, וּכְשֶׁיִּתְחַבְּרוּ הִתְפַּעֲלוּת נַפְשִׁית רַבּוֹת בְּדָבָר אֶחָד, בְּלִי הֶפְסֵק זְמַן גָּדוֹל בֵּינֵיהֶם, דְּהַיְנוּ עַל יְדֵי הִתְעוֹרְרוּת קְטַנּוֹת בֵּינֵיהֶם, כְּמוֹ בַּלִּמּוּד הַשִּׂכְלִי עַל יְדֵי תּוֹרָה מְעַט בֵּין הַלִּמּוּד בַּבָּרוּר, יִוָּלְדוּ כֹּחוֹת נְפָשׁוֹת הַכֵּהִים אֲשֶׁר חֲזָקִים הֵמָּה לְהוֹצִיא פְּעֻלָּתָם.

כֵּן בַּלִּמּוּד הַמּוּסָרִי, אִם יִתֵּן הָאָדָם אֶת נַפְשׁוֹ, לְפִי מַצַּב מַחֲלָתוֹ

---

17. *Hergel* is the habituation which makes the action second nature. It is internalized and becomes unconscious behavior.

18. We think the term in English that captures the meaning of this dark force is "unconscious." We have used "dark" and not used the term "unconscious" because we

learn Hebrew, to first know to pronounce the words, the teacher must really exert himself to illumine the letters for him, and then to combine them into a whole word. Even so, the child reads the letters and words with great difficulty. Afterward, when he has achieved the *hergel*[17] needed according to his own nature, he reads fluently without even noticing.

This is what psychologists call the illumined/conscious and dark ("clear" and "shadowy") forces.[18] It is the same with the forces of emotion: there are illumined (clear) and dark (shadowy) forces. The shadowy forces are stronger; with the slightest arousal, they respond powerfully. A person's love of his descendants is a dark force; usually, the person does not even sense it. But with the slightest provocation it blazes up into a fiery flame. Human desires are shadowy; without some stimulus, they are hardly felt, yet their power is so great that they rule over the person.

Mussar study is initially a form of conscious agitation of the psyche. Hence, in most cases, it is powerless to help against desire, instinct which is a form of the stronger, dark forces. However, as with rational study, conscious study makes some impression each time on the unconscious level as well – for were this not so, studying would not produce completely unconscious knowledge, swiftly, with barely any thought (as long as there is no long interruption between the conscious study sessions, so that the unconscious impression does not empty out and dissipate – for then the second time will really be the first and so on, *ad infinitum*). The same applies to emotional agitation (*hitpaalut*): every agitation makes some impression at the dark, unconscious level. When all of this emotional agitation is combined and focused on one thing, without large time gaps between [each exercise] – that is, by means of small arousals [of emotion] in between [major agitations], just as intellectual study [does not dissipate] with a bit of Torah between each conscious study session – it will produce unconscious psychological powers that are strong enough to manifest in action.

So it is with Mussar study. If a person devotes himself – according to the state of ailment of his service of God, blessed be His

fear that readers will identify it with the unconscious as elaborated by Freud and the Freudians. R. Salanter clearly grasps the concept of the unconscious mind present in the human self, but to make him a Freudian would be anachronistic and misguided.

בַּעֲבוֹדָתוֹ יִתְבָּרַךְ שְׁמוֹ, לִלְמוֹד מוּסָרִי בְּהִתְפַּעֲלוּת הַנֶּפֶשׁ, בְּלִי הֶפְסֵק זְמַן גָּדוֹל בֵּין הַלִּמּוּדִים, וּבְהִתְעוֹרְרוּת מְעַט בֵּין הַלִּמּוּדִים, מִזֶּה יְוָלֵד כֹּחוֹת הַכֵּהִים לַעֲזוֹר נֶגֶד הַתַּאֲוָה הַפְּרוּשָׂה – וְהִנֵּה לֹא דָבָר קַל הוּא לַטָּרוּד בַּעֲסָקָיו, וּמַחֲלָתוֹ רַבָּה, וְעִתּוֹתָיו קְצָרִים, וּמַה גַּם תּוֹרָתוֹ, קָבַעְתָּ עִתִּים לַתּוֹרָה הִיא הָרִאשׁוֹנָה לְפָנָיו.

אָכֵן לֵילֵךְ בְּשַׁבָּת קֹדֶשׁ לְבֵית הַמּוּסָר, לִלְמֹד מוּסָר בְּהִתְפַּעֲלוּת הַנֶּפֶשׁ [סְנִיף לְלִמּוּד הַגְּמָרָא הָעִקָּרִית הַנִּזְכָּר לְעֵיל] וְגַם לָרוּץ אֵיזֶה פְּעָמִים בַּשָּׁבוּעַ עַל שָׁעָה קַלָּה כִּמְעַט גַּם אֵיזֶה מִינוּטִין, לְמַעַן לֹא יִתְבַּטֵּל הָרוֹשְׁמִים הַכֵּהִים מֵאֹרֶךְ הַזְּמַן מִשַּׁבָּת קֹדֶשׁ לְשַׁבָּת קֹדֶשׁ, נָקֵל מְאֹד לַעֲשׂוֹתָהּ וּפִרְיָהּ רַב לְהוֹעִיל לִקְנוֹת בְּחִינַת כֹּחוֹת נֶגֶד הַתַּאֲוָה, לְכָל הַפָּחוֹת לְמָשָׁל לִהְיוֹת סוּר מֵרָע וַעֲשֵׂה טוֹב בַּבְּחִינוֹת הַקַּלּוֹת לִפְנֵי הָאָדָם, אֲשֶׁר הֵמָּה בְּחִינוֹת חֲמוּרוֹת יוֹתֵר וּמַזִּיקוֹת לְהָאָדָם – הוּא הָאָנֹכִי, יוֹתֵר וְיוֹתֵר בְּעוֹלָמוֹ הַחַי הָאֲמִתִּי.

הַטּוֹב לִרְאוֹת שֶׁיִּהְיֶה נָקֵל לָבֹא בְּבֵית הַמּוּסָר בְּכָל מֵעֵת לְעֵת הַיּוֹם וְהַלַּיְלָה בְּאֵין מַפְרִיעַ וְאֵין טִרְחָה, – אֲשֶׁר בְּכָל עֵת שֶׁיִּפֹּל בְּלֵב הָאָדָם לָרוּץ אֶל בֵּית הַמּוּסָר עַל אֵיזֶה מִינוּטִין, לֹא יִהְיֶה לוֹ שׁוּם מַפְרִיעַ מִצַּד בֵּית הַמּוּסָר, זֹאת כִּמְעַט סִבָּה הַטִּבְעִית, אֲשֶׁר לִמּוּד הַמּוּסָרִי אֵינוֹ פּוֹעֵל פְּעֻלָּתוֹ הַנִּדְרֶשֶׁת, מִסִּבַּת הֶפְסֵיקוֹת זְמַן אָרֹךְ בְּלִי הִתְעוֹרְרוּת קְטַנָּה בֵּינֵיהֶם. כֵּן גַּם יֵשׁ סִבּוֹת רוּחָנִיּוֹת הִיא הָעֲבֵרוֹת, הַמְטַמְטְמוֹת לִבּוֹ שֶׁל אָדָם וְהָיָה לְאֶבֶן חָלִילָה, רְפוּאָתָהּ הָעִקָּרִי לִמּוּד הַתּוֹרָה וְגַם הַתְּפִלָּה בְּהַכְנָעָה, תִּתְאַסְּפוּ נָא בַּעֲשָׂרָה תִּלְמְדוּ קֹדֶם מוּסָר אוֹ יִדְרֹשׁ אֶחָד, וְאַחַר־כָּךְ לְהִתְפַּלֵּל בְּיַחַד עַל יֵצֶר הָרוּחָנִי.

הַחוֹב הַיּוֹתֵר פְּרוּשָׂה עַל הָאָדָם הוּא לִמּוּד תּוֹרָה לִשְׁמָהּ. אוֹ

---

19. See Shabbat 31a.

20. R. Salanter is acknowledging the supreme value of Torah study. In traditional Jewish Lithuanian culture, Torah study was everything. In actual fact, R. Salanter is raising the importance of Mussar study, making it essential for achieving true Torah knowledge. Nevertheless, here he affirms Torah study above all; this is his positive response to R. Chaim of Volozhin, who makes Torah study for its own sake the highest value, almost to the exclusion of all other study. R. Salanter is struggling to

name – to learning Mussar with emotional agitation, without large intervals between study sessions, and with small arousals [of emotion] between study [sessions], it will produce unconscious powers that will help [him resist] pervasive desire.

This is not an easy thing [to do] for a person who is preoccupied with work, who is very sick, and who has limited time. And what of his Torah? Setting aside regular time for Torah[19] is his first priority.

However, to go to the Mussar House on the holy Shabbat to study Mussar with emotional agitation (attached to the aforementioned study of Talmud, which is primary), and even to run [to the Mussar House] several times a week for a short while or even a few minutes, so the impressions on the unconscious do not dissipate from one Shabbat to the next – this is an easy thing to do; and the results are very effective for acquiring unconscious dimensions [to fight] against desire. Thus he can at least control desire to the extent that he can "turn from evil and do good" (Ps. 34:15) with respect to those things that are easier for human beings, but which [if neglected] are potentially far more serious and harmful to a person – that is, to the self – in his life in the true [i.e., next] world.

The best [tactic] is to see to it that it will be easy to come to the Mussar House every day, day and night, without hindrance or preoccupation. Thus, whenever a person has an impulse to run to the Mussar House for a few minutes there will be no hindrance as far as [getting to] the Mussar House is concerned. [Otherwise,] it is only natural that Mussar study does not cause the desired effects because of long interruptions without small [emotional] arousals between sessions.

There are also spiritual factors [that make Mussar study ineffective]: i.e., sins, which desensitize the human heart, so it becomes as stone (God forbid). The main cure is Torah study[20] and humble prayer. Assemble in a *minyan*. First study some Mussar, or one of you speak about it. Then pray together about the spiritual [evil] urge.

A person's most embracing obligation is to study Torah for its own sake, or at least with the quality of practicing it for its own sake. As

---

reconcile his new educational emphasis on Mussar with the ideology of his *rebbe's rebbe*.

לְכָל הַפְּחוּת בִּתְכוּנַת עֲשִׂיָּתָהּ לִשְׁמָהּ. כְּמוֹ בְּמִצְוָה שֶׁלֹּא לִשְׁמָהּ, הַאִם מֻתָּר לַעֲשׂוֹת וּלְקַיֵּם בְּלִי תְּכוּנָתָהּ כְּמוֹ לִשְׁמָהּ, כֵּן גַּם בַּתּוֹרָה, וּמַה שֶּׁמִּנְהָגָן שֶׁל יִשְׂרָאֵל לִלְמֹד שֶׁלֹּא כְּדֶרֶךְ שֶׁלּוֹמְדִין לִשְׁמָהּ, כְּמוֹ הָעִקָּר לֵידַע דִּינֵי אֹרַח חַיִּים הַנִּצְרָכִים, אֲשֶׁר זֶהוּ הַחוֹב הָרִאשׁוֹן לַנַּעַר וְלָאַבְרֵךְ, הוּא כִּי הַיְסוֹד הָרִאשׁוֹן הוּא יְכֹלֶת הַלִּמּוּד, אֲשֶׁר לָזֶה מְסֻגָּל מְאֹד כְּפִי הַמִּנְהָג, וְאֵין לְהַאֲרִיךְ בָּזֶה כָּעֵת, רַק רָמַזְתִּי מְעַט לְמַעַן לֹא יִטְעֶה הַקּוֹרֵא בִּדְבָרַי.

הַלִּמּוּד בַּתּוֹרָה אֲשֶׁר יִקָּרֵא לִמּוּד, הוּא לִלְמֹד בַּחֲרִיפוּת הַדַּעַת [גִּיפְטִיג] כָּל אֶחָד מַחֲזִיק בְּכָל עֹז סְבָרָתוֹ. הַלִּשְׁמָהּ הִיא שְׁקִיטַת הָרוּחַ, אִם כִּדְבָרָיו וְאִם כְּדִבְרֵי חֲבֵרוֹ לִהְיוֹת שָׁוֶה בְּעֵינָיו. וְהֵמָּה כִּמְעַט דְּבָרִים מִתְנַגְּדִים זֶה לָזֶה, לָזֹאת הוֹרוּנוּ חֲכָמֵינוּ ז״ל אֵיךְ לְהִתְנַהֵג, כְּמַאֲמָרָם קִדּוּשִׁין (דַּף ל׳) אֲפִלּוּ הָאָב וּבְנוֹ הָרַב וְתַלְמִידוֹ שֶׁעוֹסְקִין בַּתּוֹרָה בְּשַׁעַר אֶחָד, נַעֲשִׂים אוֹיְבִים זֶה אֶת זֶה, וְאֵינָם זָזִים מִשָּׁם עַד שֶׁנַּעֲשִׂים אוֹהֲבִים זֶה אֶת זֶה, שֶׁנֶּאֱמַר וְאֶת וָהֵב בְּסוּפָה כו׳ עַיֵּן שָׁם, הָאֵיבָה בָּרִאשׁוֹנָה הִיא בְּחִינַת הַלִּמּוּד בַּחֲרִיפוּת הַדַּעַת [גִּיפְטִיג] כַּנִּזְכָּר לְעֵיל, וְהָאַהֲבָה בְּסוּפָהּ הִיא בְּחִינַת הַלִּשְׁמָהּ, לְבַטֵּל כָּל אֶחָד דַּעְתּוֹ לֵילֵךְ אַחַר הָרֹב אוֹ הַגָּדוֹל, אוֹ לַעֲמֹד כָּל אֶחָד בְּדַעְתּוֹ כְּמוֹ עָשׂוּ בֵּית שַׁמַּאי

21. See Pesaḥim 50b and Sanhedrin 105b.

22. R. Salanter uses the term *giftik* – toxic or poisonous – to characterize this form of study.

23. R. Salanter here is distinguishing between types of Torah learning. The type called "*limmud*," characterized by subtlety, creativity, and originality, can be an exercise in pride and self-aggrandizement and view criticism very negatively. In the opposite approach, which R. Salanter identifies with studying "*lishmah*," one views his own interpretation as one of several, equally plausible opinions and does not attempt to impose his own opinion as the correct one.

R. Salanter here presents his synthesis of these two extremes. The correct approach begins with each person seeing and analyzing the given passage from their own unique perspective. This produces the maximum insights into the Torah. The second step is to consider other viewpoints and settle differences by majority rule, by deference to a weightier argument, or by the two sides accepting their differences.

24. R. Salanter's view of Torah *lishmah* differs from the view associated with R. Chaim of Volozhin. The latter defines it as studying the theoretical Torah instead of the

in the case of doing a mitzva not for its own sake[21] – is it permitted to do and fulfill a mitzva without its essential qualities, like [doing it for] its own sake? – so it is with Torah study. And as for the custom of Jews to learn in a manner that differs from study for its own sake – rather, primarily to know the necessary laws of daily life, which is the first duty of every child or young man – this is because the ability to learn is the primary foundation [of all Torah study]. By following the custom, one is readily equipped for this purpose. (There is no need to belabor this point at this time; I have only hinted at it so that no reader will be misled by my words.)

Torah study that is called "*limmud*" refers to study with sharpness and acerbity of wit.[22] Each person holds onto his analysis with all his might. [In contrast,] "for its own sake" ["*lishmah*"] implies equanimity – it makes no difference to him whether he or his companion is correct.[23] These two views [of Torah study] are almost diametric opposites.[24] For this reason, our Sages, of blessed memory, instructed us how to behave, in accordance with their dictum in Kiddushin (30b): "Even a father and his son [or] a teacher and his student who study Torah together become enemies to each other, but they will not budge from there until they become beloved to each other, as it is said '*et Vahev beSufa*...'[25] (Num. 21:14)." The initial "enmity" is characteristic of the sharp, acerbic *limmud* mentioned above. The ultimate "love" is characteristic of *lishmah*, wherein each person abnegates his own view to follow the majority or the greater [argument]; or, alternatively, each insists their own views, as the School of Shammai practiced according

---

practical laws. Rather, R. Salanter understands "*lishmah*" to mean "disinterested," studying Torah without any personal stake in what the correct interpretation ought to be, thereby enabling the student to accept the best interpretation with equanimity, even if it is not his own interpretation. It is here that the ideal of Torah study "*lishmah*" intersects with Mussar study, for by becoming less self-centered and less driven by competitive desire for victory, one will be more likely arrive at the correct understanding of the Torah.

25. This is a play on words. The verse is literally talking about a place, "Vahev in Sufa." Homiletically it is taken to mean that these erstwhile rivals become beloved ("*ohav*") in the end ("*basof*").

כִּדְבְרֵיהֶם כוּ׳ (יְבָמוֹת דַּף י״ד), עַל פִּי הַגְּדָרִים הַמְבֹאָרִים בַּגְּמָרָא וּפוֹסְקִים בָּזֶה. אָכֵן בְּהַנְהָגַת חִבָּה וְרֵעוּת, הִיא בְּחִינַת הַלִּשְׁמָהּ, לְקַיֵּם הָאֱמֶת, הִיא בְּחִינַת הַלִּמּוּד, לְהַגִּיד וּלְחַזֵּק כָּל אֶחָד סְבָרָתוֹ הַנִּרְאֶה נָכוֹן בְּעֵינָיו, וְהַשָּׁלוֹם הִיא בְּחִינַת הַלִּשְׁמָהּ אֱהָבוּ (יְבָמוֹת שָׁם ע״ב).

כֵּן גַּם בְּכָל עִיּוּן הַשַּׁיָּךְ לַעֲבוֹדָתוֹ יִתְבָּרַךְ שְׁמוֹ, כְּמוֹ בַּמְפַקְּחִים עַל לִמּוּד לִבְנֵי עֲנִיִּים תּוֹרָה, הָעִיּוּן הִיא בְּחִינַת הַתּוֹרָה, כִּי מַה הִיא הַתּוֹרָה, הַלִּמּוּד לֵידַע אֵיךְ רְצוֹנוֹ יִתְבָּרַךְ שְׁמוֹ, כֵּן בְּכָל הָעִיּוּנִים אֲשֶׁר הֵמָּה הָעִיּוּן אֵיךְ רְצוֹנוֹ יִתְבָּרַךְ שְׁמוֹ לְהִתְנַהֵג בַּמִּצְוָה הַזֹּאת, הֵמָּה עֲנָפִים מִבְּחִינַת הַתּוֹרָה, וּצְרִיכָה לִהְיוֹת בָּרִאשׁוֹנָה בַּחֲרִיפַת הַדַּעַת, וְהַסּוֹף הַלִּשְׁמָהּ לְבַטֵּל כָּל אֶחָד דַּעְתּוֹ בְּשָׁלוֹם וְרֵעוּת לְהִתְנַהֵג אַחַר הָרֹב כַּנִּזְכָּר לְעֵיל – הָעִיּוּן אֵיךְ לְהִתְנַהֵג בְּסִדְרֵי הָעִנְיָנִים הַשַּׁיָּכִים לַעֲבוֹדָתוֹ יִתְבָּרַךְ שְׁמוֹ, נָקֵל בְּחִינַת הַלִּשְׁמָהּ לִשְׁמֹר, וְצָרִיךְ הָאָדָם לְהַרְגִּיל אֶת עַצְמוֹ לִרְאוֹת שֶׁיִּהְיֶה בִּבְחִינַת לִשְׁמָהּ – הַנִּסָּיוֹן יוֹרֵנוּ כִּי בְּלִמּוּד הַתּוֹרָה, הַחִסָּרוֹן יוֹתֵר גָּדוֹל אִם יֶחְסַר מָה בִּבְחִינַת הַלִּמּוּד מִן בְּחִינַת הַלִּשְׁמָהּ, וְצָרִיךְ הָאָדָם לִנְטוֹת יוֹתֵר אַחַר בְּחִינַת הַלִּמּוּד, וּבִשְׁאָר הָעִיּוּנִים הַחִסָּרוֹן יוֹתֵר גָּדוֹל חֶסְרוֹן בְּחִינַת לִשְׁמָהּ, וְצָרִיךְ הָאָדָם לִנְטוֹת אַחַר בְּחִינַת לִשְׁמָהּ – לָזֹאת יָשִׂים הָאָדָם לִבּוֹ וְנַפְשׁוֹ לִרְאוֹת שֶׁיִּהְיוּ הָעִיּוּנִים בַּעֲבוֹדָתוֹ יִתְבָּרַךְ שְׁמוֹ בִּבְחִינַת לִשְׁמָהּ, הַדָּבָר נָקֵל לְקַיְּמָהּ, וּבְחֶסְרוֹן בְּחִינַת לִשְׁמָהּ, הָעֲבֵרָה גְּדוֹלָה וְנִשָּׂאָה, כִּי יֻוָּלֵד חָלִילָה לְהוֹצִיא מִשְׁפָּט מְעֻקָּל בַּהַנְהָגָה נֶגֶד רְצוֹנוֹ יִתְבָּרַךְ שְׁמוֹ.

עֲבוֹדָתוֹ יִתְבָּרַךְ שְׁמוֹ הַיּוֹתֵר כְּבֵדָה עַל הָאָדָם הִיא מַשָּׂא וּמַתָּן בֶּאֱמוּנָה, אֲשֶׁר עָלָיו שׁוֹאֲלִין לְהָאָדָם – הוּא הָאָנֹכִי – בָּרִאשׁוֹנָה

26. R. Salanter does not complete the quotation, but ends it elliptically. The mishna cited in Yevamot 14a states that the School of Shammai did not refrain from marrying women from the School of Hillel, nor the School of Hillel from the School of Shammai, despite major disagreements between the two academies regarding who is deemed halakhically unfit for marriage.

27. R. Salanter emphasizes that the most basic purpose of Torah study is to know what God wants of us – what behavior or quality of character (*midda*) God prescribes through this Torah text. This corresponds to the basic education that the community is obligated to provide for its poorest members.

28. "Hergel."

to its opinions... (Yevamot 14a),[26] within the parameters explained by the Talmud and codifiers on this matter. Indeed, this loving, friendly conduct is characteristic of "*lishmah*."

In this he fulfills [the verse "Truth and peace shall you love" (Zech. 8:19)]: "Truth," the characteristic of "*limmud*," wherein each person articulates and supports his own reasoning, which seems correct to him, "and peace," the characteristic of "*lishmah*" – "shall you love" (Yevamot 14b).

So too, all intensive study connected to His service, blessed be His name, is akin to how we supervise the Torah instruction of poor children. Intensive study is Torah, for what is Torah if not learning the will of God, blessed be His name? So too, any intensive study to ascertain how He, blessed be His name, wants us to behave vis-à-vis this commandment[27] is a particular application of this aspect of Torah. Thus, it must first be undertaken with sharpness of mind, and at the end it is "*lishmah*," wherein each person abnegates his own view, peacefully and in friendship, to follow the majority as said above. In studying how to act in matters connected to His service, blessed be His name, it is easy to keep the "*lishmah*" aspects, and one should habituate[28] himself to ensure that it is done "*lishmah*."

[However,] experience shows us that when it comes to Torah study, there is a greater shortcoming if he is lacking in the "*limmud*" aspect than if he is lacking in the "*lishmah*" dimension. One must therefore incline more toward the "*limmud*" aspect. When it comes to other studies [of what God wants from us], the greater shortcoming is the lack of the "*lishmah*" dimension, so one must therefore incline more toward the "*lishmah*" dimension. Thus, a person should set his heart and mind to ensure that his studies of His service, blessed be His name, have the character of "*lishmah*." It is easy to achieve, so if the "*lishmah*" dimension is lacking, the sin is much greater, for it may happen that he produces a distorted judgment about behavior – against the will of God, blessed be His name.

For the human being, the hardest aspect of serving Him, blessed be He, is honesty in business.[29] This is the first thing the person – the

29. This is why, in Shabbat 31a, the Talmud says this is the first question asked of the soul when it arrives in the World to Come for judgment.

בְּבוֹאוֹ לָדוּן עַל הַנְהָגָתוֹ (שַׁבָּת דַּף ל"א), הַדַּעַת נוֹטָה כִּי אִם יַעֲבֹר הָאָדָם בְּמִין הָעֲבֵרָה בִּבְחִינַת הַקַּלָּה, אֲשֶׁר לְבַד עָנְשָׁהּ הֶחָמוּר יוֹתֵר מֵעֲבֵרָה בִּבְחִינַת הַכְּבֵדוּת, – גַּם כֵּן עֲשִׂיַּת הָעֲבֵרָה הָעַצְמָהּ בִּבְחִינַת הַכְּבֵדוּת, יִכָּנֵס עַל יְדֵי זֶה מָה בִּבְחִינַת הַקַּלּוּת, כִּי גַּם אִלּוּ הָיְתָה קַל לְפָנָיו הָיָה עוֹבְרָהּ. וְכֵן בַּעֲשִׂיַּת הַטּוֹב כָּל מַה שֶּׁכָּבֵד יוֹתֵר עַל הָאָדָם לְקַיְּמָהּ יִגְדַּל שְׂכָרוֹ כְּמַאֲמָרָם זַ"ל לְפוּם צַעֲרָא אַגְרָא, וּבָזֹאת בַּעֲשׂוֹתוֹ אוֹתָהּ הַמִּצְוָה בִּבְחִינַת הַקַּלּוּת, יִכָּנֵס גַּם כֵּן בִּבְחִינַת הַכְּבֵדוּת כִּי גַּם אִם הָיָה כָּבֵד לְפָנָיו הָיָה מְקַיְּמָהּ.

אוּלַי לָזֶה רָמְזוּ רַבּוֹתֵינוּ זַ"ל (סֻכָּה דַּף נ"ג) לֶעָתִיד לָבֹא מְבִיאוֹ הַקָּדוֹשׁ־בָּרוּךְ־הוּא לַיֵּצֶר הָרַע כּוּ' צַדִּיקִים נִדְמֶה לָהֶם כְּהַר גָּבוֹהַּ וּרְשָׁעִים נִדְמֶה לָהֶם כְּחוּט הַשַּׂעֲרָה כּוּ' עַיֵּן שָׁם, כִּי הַצַּדִּיק הַמְקַיֵּם גַּם בִּבְחִינַת הַכְּבֵדוּת, מַרְאִים לָהֶם שֶׁגַּם הַבְּחִינוֹת הַקַּלּוּת, בַּבְּחִינוֹת הַכְּבֵדוּת יִכָּנְסוּ. וְהָרָשָׁע הָעוֹבֵר גַּם בַּבְּחִינוֹת הַקַּלּוּת, מַרְאִים לוֹ שֶׁגַּם בְּחִינַת הַכְּבֵדוּת בִּבְחִינַת הַקַּלּוּת יִכָּנְסוּ מָה – לָזֹאת יְחַפֵּשׂ לְקַיֵּם מַשָּׂא וּמַתָּן בֶּאֱמוּנָה לְכָל הַפָּחוֹת בַּבְּחִינוֹת הַקַּלּוּת.

אָכֵן שִׁגְגַת תַּלְמוּד כּוּ' הַטּוֹב לִקְבֹּעַ שִׁעוּר לְלִמּוּד חֹשֶׁן מִשְׁפָּט, וְיָבוֹאוּ בַּעֲלֵי בָּתִּים לִפְעָמִים זֶה וְלִפְעָמִים זֶה, כִּי כָּל סָעִיף כִּמְעַט נָקֵל לְהַסְבִּירוֹ בִּפְנֵי עַצְמוֹ, וְהַבַּעֲלֵי בָּתִּים יְעַיְּנוּ אֵיךְ יִהְיֶה הַדִּין שַׁיָּךְ כָּעֵת, כִּי הָעֲסָקִים נִשְׁתַּנּוּ וְזֶה כִּמְעַט הַתְחָלַת יְדִיעַת הַלִּמּוּד בְּחֹשֶׁן מִשְׁפָּט, לֵידַע וּלְהָבִין אֵיךְ הֵם שַׁיָּכִים כָּעֵת, וּבָזֶה יִהְיֶה בְּיַד בַּעֲלֵי בָּתִּים לִדְרֹשׁ וְלַחֲקֹר אֵצֶל תּוֹפְשֵׂי הַתּוֹרָה, אֵיךְ לְקַיֵּם אֶת אֲשֶׁר יִקְרֶה לִפְנֵיהֶם לְכָל הַפָּחוֹת בַּבְּחִינוֹת הַקַּלּוּת, אִישׁ לְפִי מַצָּבוֹ וְיִרְאָתוֹ.

וּבָזֹאת כַּפָּרַת עֲוֹנוֹת בְּיוֹם הַכִּפּוּרִים הַתָּלוּי בִּתְשׁוּבָה, הִיא עֲזִיבַת הַחֵטְא תִּכְבַּד מְאֹד, אַל יֵרֶף הָאָדָם לַעֲשׂוֹת הֲכָנָה לְיוֹם הַכִּפּוּרִים לְכָל

30. Avot 5:23.

31. E.g., he receives greater punishment.

32. See Avot 4:13.

33. The section of the legal codes focused on business and commercial law.

self – is questioned about when he is judged for his behavior [in the World to Come] (Shabbat 31a).

It stands to reason that if a person violates a prohibition that is easily observed, then not only will its punishment be more severe than that of harder-to-observe prohibitions, but even a sin of the harder sort will be accounted by God as a prohibition that is easy to observe; for even if it would be easy to refrain [from that particular sin], he would violate it [anyway].

And so it is with doing good. The harder it is for a person to carry it out, the greater his reward, as they, of blessed memory, said: "According to the pain [of the effort] is the reward."[30] Thus, if he [subsequently] performs an easy mitzva, it is considered [by God] as though it is hard, for even if it would have been hard for him, he would have done it.

Perhaps our Rabbis, of blessed memory, alluded to this: "In the future, the Holy One, blessed be He, will bring the evil urge and reject it…. To the righteous, it will appear as a huge mountain; to the wicked, it will appear as a strand of hair…." (Sukka 52a). For the righteous, who observe even difficult mitzvot, are shown that even easy observances are entered as difficult ones [for purposes of reward]; and the wicked, who violate even easy observances, are shown that even the difficult commandments are weighed somewhat as easy observances.[31] Accordingly, a person should seek to be honest in business, at least as far as easy observances are concerned.

However, since errors due to lack of knowledge… [are judged as "malicious acts"[32]], the best thing is to set up a regular session to study *Ḥoshen Mishpat*.[33] Laymen will come, sometimes this one, sometimes another, since each paragraph is easily explained independently. The laymen will learn how the law applies today – for business practices have changed. This is practically the beginning level of study of *Ḥoshen Mishpat* – to know and understand how these [laws] apply today. [With this knowledge,] the layman will be able to inquire and check with the scholars of Torah how to observe at least the easy matters which come up, each according to his own condition and [level of] reverence.

Accordingly, atonement on Yom Kippur for sins that depend on repentance, that is, on abandonment of the sin, is very difficult. A person should not neglect to prepare for Yom Kippur at least with respect

הַפָּחוֹת בִּבְחִינוֹת הַקַּלּוֹת, הַיְנוּ לַעֲסֹק בַּעֲשֶׂרֶת יְמֵי תְּשׁוּבָה בְּעִנְיְנֵי הַתְּשׁוּבָה לְכָל הַפָּחוֹת בִּבְחִינוֹת הַקַּלּוֹת, לֵילֵךְ לְבֵית הַמּוּסָר בַּלַּיְלָה בְּעֵת פְּנוּי מֵעֲסָקָיו, לִלְמֹד מוּסָר בְּהִתְפַּעֲלוּת הַנֶּפֶשׁ כִּמְעַט בְּכָל לַיְלָה, אֲשֶׁר יְוָלֵד מִזֶּה אֵיזֶה בְּחִינַת כֵּהֶה [דוּנְקֶעלֶע] לְקַבָּלַת לִמּוּד הַמּוּסָר בְּלֹא נֶדֶר לְכָל הַפָּחוֹת בְּשַׁבָּת קֹדֶשׁ [סְנִיף לְלִמּוּד הַגְּמָרָא כַּנִּזְכָּר לְעֵיל] וְלָרוּץ אֵיזֶה פְּעָמִים בְּשָׁבוּעַ. לְכָל הַפָּחוֹת עַל אֵיזֶה מִינוּטִין, לְמַעַן לֹא יַשְׁבִּית רֹשֶׁם הַכֵּהֶה הֶפְסֵק הַזְּמַן כַּנִּזְכָּר לְעֵיל, וּלְהַרְגִּיל אֶת עַצְמוֹ לְהַשְׁקִיף עַל דְּרָכָיו, לְהַרְגִּישׁ לְהַבְחִין בֵּין קַל לְכָבֵד, אֲשֶׁר לְכָל הַפָּחוֹת יַעַזְרֵהוּ הַמּוּסָרִי, לִשְׁמֹר הַתּוֹרָה וְהַמִּצְוָה בִּבְחִינוֹת הַקַּלּוֹת, וְיָבֹא לִבְחִינַת בַּעַל תְּשׁוּבָה בְּיוֹם הַכִּפּוּרִים הַבָּא עָלֵינוּ לְטוֹבָה, לְכָל הַפָּחוֹת בְּקַבָּלַת עֲזִיבַת הַחֵטְא בִּבְחִינוֹת הַקַּלּוֹת, וּבָזֶה הַבָּא לִטַּהֵר יְסַיְּעֵהוּ הַקָּדוֹשׁ־בָּרוּךְ־הוּא לֵילֵךְ מִדַּרְגָּא לְדַרְגָּא לְקַיֵּם הַתּוֹרָה וְהַמִּצְוָה, גַּם בִּבְחִינוֹת הַכְּבֵדוֹת לְטוֹב לְהָאָדָם – הוּא הָאָנֹכִי – בְּעוֹלָמוֹ הַנִּצְחִי.

to easier matters – e.g., during the Ten Days of Repentance, one should study ideas of repentance, at least its simpler aspects. He should go to the Mussar House at night whenever he is free from his business, to study Mussar in a state of emotional agitation almost every night, so it produces some unconscious, "dark," effect. So should he resolve to study Mussar with all his heart and mind, at least on the holy Shabbat (in association with Talmud study, as said above), and to run there several times a week, at least for a few minutes, so that the unconscious impression is not eliminated by long interruptions, as said above. He should habituate himself to reflect upon his ways, to sense and to distinguish between easier and harder tasks. Thus, Mussar will help him observe the easier aspects of the Torah and commandments. Then he will become a [true] penitent ("*baal teshuva*") on the forthcoming Yom Kippur – at least inasmuch as he resolved to abandon the aspects of sin that are easiest [to abandon].

He who comes to purify himself will thus be helped[34] by the Holy One, blessed be He, to rise from level to level, to uphold even the harder aspects of the Torah and the commandments, for the benefit of the person – the self – in the eternal world.

34. Compare Yoma 38b; Avoda Zara 55a; Menaḥot 29b.

ז

כָּל הַדְּבָרִים שֶׁבָּעוֹלָם מֻרְכָּבִים הֵמָּה בִּיצִיאָתָם לָאוֹר מִסִּבָּה וּמְסוֹבָב, הַשָּׂגַת הַתְּבוּאָה מֵהַשָּׂדֶה הִיא מְסוֹבֶבֶת, מִסִּבּוֹת רַבּוֹת הַקּוֹדֶמֶת לָהּ זְרִיעָה חֲרִישָׁה כו׳ – קִנְיַן הַכֶּסֶף לְהָאָדָם הוּא מְסוֹבָב מִסִּבּוֹת שׁוֹנוֹת, מִסַּחַר שְׂכִירוּת וְכַיּוֹצֵא – כָּל סִבָּה הִיא מְסוֹבֶבֶת מִסִּבָּה הַקּוֹדֶמֶת לָהּ – הַזְּרִיעָה בַּשָּׂדֶה הִיא הַסִּבָּה הָרִאשׁוֹנָה לִצְמִיחַת הַתְּבוּאָה, וְהִיא מְסוֹבֶבֶת מִן הָאָדָם הַזּוֹרֵעַ, וּזְרִיעַת הָאָדָם מְסוֹבֶבֶת מִסִּבַּת חֶפְצוֹ, אִם לְהַשִּׂיג הַתְּבוּאָה, אוֹ לְהַשָּׂגַת שְׂכִירוּת בְּעַד זְרִיעָתוֹ וְכַיּוֹצֵא, סוֹף דָּבָר אֵין מְסוֹבָב בְּלִי סִבָּה לְהוֹלֵד הַמְסוֹבָב, וְאֵין סִבָּה אֲשֶׁר אֵינֶנָּה נוֹלֶדֶת מִסִּבָּה הַמְסַבַּבְתָּהּ, עַד הַסִּבָּה הָרִאשׁוֹנָה סִבָּה עַצְמִית הִיא הָאֱלֹקִית.

בְּעִנְיְנֵי תַּהֲלוּכוֹת הָאָדָם. לְצָרְכֵי גּוּפוֹ וְנַפְשׁוֹ הָאַרְצִי, הַשָּׂגַת מָמוֹן, הַשָּׂגַת כָּבוֹד וְכַיּוֹצֵא, סִבָּתָם הָרִאשׁוֹנָה (לְעֵינֵי בָשָׂר לֹא בַּשִּׂכְלִי כִּי הַכֹּל הוֹלֵךְ מִסִּבָּה הָרִאשׁוֹנָה הָאֲמִתִּית) הוּא חֵפֶץ רְצוֹנוֹ אֲשֶׁר יֵלֵךְ וְיִוָּלֵד מֵעַצְמוֹ, וּמִזֹּאת יִתְגַּלְגְּלוּ אַחַר־כָּךְ מְסוֹבָבִים אֲשֶׁר הֵמָּה סִבּוֹת לַמְסוֹבָבִים, עַד אֲשֶׁר יֵצֵא חֵפֶץ רְצוֹנוֹ לָאוֹר, אוֹ עַל יְדֵי אָדָם אַחֵר הַמְעוֹרְרוֹ אִם מִכְפִיָּה אוֹ עַל יְדֵי פִּתּוּי. לְהָעִיר חֶפְצוֹ וּרְצוֹנוֹ, וְהִיא

---

* The content of this letter suggests that it was written around or during the Ten Days of Repentance, between Rosh HaShana and Yom Kippur.

1. R. Salanter starts with analogies from *ḥokhmat haolam*.
2. This is classic medieval thinking undoubtedly drawn from Rambam's writing (which drew on Aristotelian philosophy and science).

*Letter 7**

Everything in the world initially comes into being made up of causes and effects. [For example,] obtaining a crop from a field is an effect of many prior causes: planting, plowing, etc. A person's property is the effect of various causes: commerce, wages, etc.[1] Each cause is an effect of a cause that precedes it. Sowing a field is the primary cause of the growth of the grain, yet it is the effect of the person who sows. The person's sowing is an effect of his [causal] will – whether he desires to obtain grain or to obtain wages for planting, etc. In conclusion: There is no effect without a cause that gives birth to the effect. And there is no cause that is not born of a cause that effected it – [until we get] to the "First Cause," a self-generated Cause, that is, the Divine.[2]

With respect to a person's action on behalf of his bodily and earthly needs, obtaining money, obtaining honor, etc., the first cause (as seen through mortal eyes, not through the intellect, for all really proceeds from the true First Cause)[3] is the desire of one's will, which proceeds from and is born of itself.[4] This will generate effects that are themselves causes of [further] effects, until the object of his desire comes into being. Alternatively, [the first cause is] another person who motivates him, either by coercion or by persuasion, to awaken his own

3. Objectively, using one's reason, one realizes that God is the Ultimate Cause of all. However, subjectively, one's need for earthly achievements is driven by one's desire, which is expressed in one's personal will.
4. One experiences one's will and desire as self-generated.

הַסִּבָּה הָרִאשׁוֹנָה (לְעֵינֵי בָּשָׂר) לְהָאָדָם. אֲשֶׁר תִּוָּלֵד וּתְסוֹבֵב מֵאָדָם אַחֵר, אֲשֶׁר לוֹ יֵשׁ סִבּוֹת אֲשֶׁר הֵבִיאוּ לָזֶה, לְעוֹרֵר סִבָּה רִאשׁוֹנָה לְזוּלָתוֹ.

עַתָּה נָשׁוּב וְנִרְאֶה, מַה תִּהְיֶה סִבָּה הָרִאשׁוֹנָה שֶׁיִּתְעוֹרֵר הָאָדָם לְפַקֵּחַ עַל מַעֲשָׂיו, וּלְהִתְבּוֹנֵן בַּמּוּסָר בְּחֹדֶשׁ אֱלוּל (הָעִנְיָן הַלָּזֶה שַׁיָּךְ גַּם לְכָל הַשָּׁנָה מַה שֶּׁנּוֹגֵעַ לַעֲבוֹדָתוֹ יִתְבָּרַךְ שְׁמוֹ) הֲלֹא אֵין חֵפֶץ טִבְעִי לָזֶה כְּמוֹ בְּעִנְיְנֵי הָאַרְצִי – רַבּוֹתֵינוּ הַקַּדְמוֹנִים נוּחָם עֵדֶן חָרְדוּ עַל הַדָּבָר, סָמְכוּ עַל פִּרְקֵי דְּרַבִּי אֱלִיעֶזֶר וְהִתְקִינוּ לִתְקֹעַ שׁוֹפָר בֶּאֱלוּל, וְהִיא הָיְתָה הַסִּבָּה הָרִאשׁוֹנָה לְעוֹרֵר הָאָדָם מִשְּׁנָתוֹ וּמֵהַבְלֵי טִרְדוֹתָיו לְפַקֵּחַ עַל מַעֲשָׂיו, כְּמַאֲמַר הַכָּתוּב (עָמוֹס ג׳) אִם יִתָּקַע שׁוֹפָר בְּעִיר וְהָעָם לֹא יֶחֱרָדוּ.

אָכֵן נוֹדַע כִּי מְסוֹבָב לֹא יִוָּלֵד אִם לֹא מִסִּבָּה הַדּוֹמָה לוֹ, מְסוֹבָב כָּבֵד לֹא יֵצֵא מִסִּבָּה קַלָּה.

וּבָזֹאת הַדָּבָר הַזֶּה תְּקִיעַת הַשּׁוֹפָר הָיְתָה סִבָּה הָרִאשׁוֹנָה לְהָאָדָם הַשָּׁקוּעַ מִבַּיִת וּמִחוּץ בַּעֲבוֹדָתוֹ יִתְבָּרַךְ שְׁמוֹ, וְסִבָּה קַלָּה תְּעוֹרְרֵהוּ לְפַקֵּחַ עַל עַצְמוֹ בִּבְחִינָה יוֹתֵר נַעֲלָה – אֲבָל מַה נֹּאמַר וּנְדַבֵּר, וּמַה לַּעֲשׂוֹת עַתָּה אֲשֶׁר מְשֻׁקָּעִים אֲנַחְנוּ מִבַּיִת וְחוּץ בְּהַבְלֵי טִרְדַּת הַתֵּבֵל, וְהַלֵּב מְטֻמְטָם וְקָשֶׁה כְּצוּר הַחַלָּמִישׁ, הַאִם הַהִתְעוֹרְרוּת הַקַּלָּה לְפָנֵינוּ תַּעֲשֶׂה רֹשֶׁם בָּאֶבֶן הַחֲזָקָה.

אָכֵן אִם לֹא נִמְשַׁךְ חֶבְלֵי הַיֵּצֶר עַל עַצְמֵנוּ, בְּלִי דַּעַת לַהֲפֹךְ אוֹר לְחֹשֶׁךְ, לֵאמֹר עַל הַקַּל כִּי כָבֵד הוּא – הַדָּבָר נִרְאֶה בָּעֲלִיל, כִּי לֵילֵךְ לִפְעָמִים בְּבֵית הַמּוּסָר בֶּאֱלוּל, הוּא דָּבָר קַל מְאֹד, וְעִם גֹּדֶל הַטִּרְדָּה יֵשׁ זְמַן לָזֶה בְּלִי עָמָל בַּיּוֹם אוֹ בַּלַּיְלָה, אֲשֶׁר תַּסְפִּיק לְפָנֵינוּ סִבַּת תְּקִיעַת הַשּׁוֹפָר, וְכַאֲשֶׁר יֵלֵךְ הָאָדָם אֶל בֵּית הַמּוּסָר הִיא סִבָּה גְּדוֹלָה וְנוֹרָאָה אֲשֶׁר בְּיָדָהּ לְהוֹצִיא מְסוֹבָבִים קָשִׁים וּכְבֵדִים.

הוּא מַאֲמַר חֲזַ״ל קִדּוּשִׁין (דַּף ל׳) אִם פָּגַע בְּךָ מְנֻוָּל זֶה מָשְׁכֵהוּ לְבֵית הַמִּדְרָשׁ, בָּתֵּי מִדְרָשׁ שׁוֹנוֹת יֵשׁ לִפְעָמִים, בֵּית הַמִּדְרָשׁ זֶה עִסְקוֹ

5. Chapter 46.
6. Compare Genesis 44:16.
7. Scoundrel means evil urge.

desire and will. This is the first cause (as seen through mortal eyes) for this person, which in turn [in this case] is brought into being and caused by another person – who has his own causes that brought him to this point of motivating a first cause within another.

Now let us go back and see what could be a first cause that will motivate a person to inspect his actions and to study Mussar during the month of Elul. (This matter [Mussar] applies all year round, as far as His service, blessed be His name, is concerned.) [But] there is no natural desire for this as there is in worldly matters.

Our ancient Rabbis, may they rest in [the Garden of] Eden, greatly worried about this, [so they] relied on *Pirkei DeRabbi Eliezer*[5] and instituted blowing the shofar in Elul. This was to be the primary cause that awakens a person from his slumber and from his vain occupations to inspect his actions, as the Scripture says (Amos 3:6): "Shall the shofar be blown in the city, and the people not tremble?"

However, it is known that an effect is only born of a similar cause; a weighty effect will not emerge from a light cause.

And yet, this act – shofar blowing – was a [sufficient] first cause for someone who was immersed inwardly and outwardly in His service, blessed be His name. Therefore, a minor cause stimulated him to examine himself with the most exacting standard. But what can we say and speak,[6] and what to do, now that we are sunk inwardly and outwardly in the vanities of worldly preoccupations, so the heart is stultified and hardened like flint rock? Will this mild stimulus make an impression on the hard rock?

However, let us not tie ourselves up with the ropes of the [evil] urge and unthinkingly invert light to darkness and say that the lightweight is weighty. It is patently clear that to go occasionally to the Mussar House in the month of Elul is a very easy thing. Despite our great preoccupation, there is still time for this, by day or night, without great effort. [Just as] the blowing of the shofar is sufficient cause, so when a person goes to the Mussar House, it is [equivalent to] a powerful and awesome cause, which can yield strong and weighty effects.

This is [the meaning of] the statement by the Sages, of blessed memory, in Kiddushin [30b]: "If this scoundrel[7] encounters you, draw him to the study hall." Sometimes, there are different study halls. In one

בענינים השיכים למשא ומתן באמונה, בית המדרש אחר עסקו בענינים הנוגעים באכילת כשרות וכיוצא — רפואת התורה להיצר היא כללי ופרטי, כללי תורה בעידנא דעסיק בה מגנא ומצלא, פרטי והיא הראשונה וכמעט העקרית היא למשא ומתן באמונה התורה השיך לה, לעמל פינו תורה השיך לה, ובכל פרט אשר יפגע המנוגל להאדם ילך לבית המדרש השיך לפרט הלזה — ולזאת נצרך ללמוד המוסרי הנדרשת מאד באלול. אשר פריו שתים הנה.

האחת גופני אשר האדם הוא ובני ביתו התלוים עליו בסכנה גדולה. לעת דין הגדול, היא עת תקיעת שופר בראש השנה, אשר האדם נזכר ונשפט על מעשיו. והוא בעת הלזה נדמה לכהן גדול בעת שנכנס לבית קדשי הקדשים, כמאמר חכמינו ז"ל (ראש השנה דף כ"ו) שופר בראש השנה כיון דלזכרון הוא כבפנים דמי עין שם.

ומה יחרד לב האדם האוהב את עצמו ואת בני ביתו התלוים עליו (ואם כי עיני בשר רואות אשר בני אדם יצאו לצדק בלי הכנות והתעוררות היראה והמוסר) להטיב דרכו, ולכל הפחות לשבר רוחו בשברון לבב, אשר הוא יסוד הראשי, להיות מגן על הסכנה הגדולה המרחפת, כמאמר חכמינו ז"ל ראש השנה (דף ט"ז) כל שנה שרשה בתחלתה כו', הוא שברון הלבב וכמאמרם ז"ל שם (דף כ"ו) בראש השנה כמה דכייף איניש דעתיה טפי מעלי עין שם.

הלא לכל עת (קהלת ג') והאדם לא ידע את עתו כו', לעת רעה כשפתאום תפל עליו (שם ט') בלי הכנה הדרושה להכין מגן וצנה, להשמר מהפח הוא יום הדין הנורא, כאשר גם עיני בשר רואות כי כמעט בכל ראש השנה נדונים רחמנא לצלן גם הבחורים למיתה חס

8. Sota 21a.
9. I.e., his life is at stake and any false move leads to death.
10. I.e., death.

study hall, they dealt with matters connected to honest business practices; in another one they dealt with matters regarding keeping kosher, and so on. The Torah's cure for the [evil] urge is both general and specific. Generally, "when you study Torah, it protects and saves [from sin]."[8] Specifically – and this is primary (and practically the essential) for honest business practices – [to study] the Torah which specifically applies to [business]. [Similarly,] for speech, [we must study] the Torah that applies to it. And for every specific place where one encounters the "scoundrel," one should go to the study hall [and study the Torah] that applies to this specific matter.

For this reason, we need Mussar study, which is particularly required in Elul. It will produce two outcomes.

One is physical. A person and dependent family members are in great danger at the time of the great judgment, the time of shofar blowing on Rosh HaShana, when a person is remembered and judged on his actions. At that time, he is like the High Priest when entering the Holy of Holies.[9] As the Sages, of blessed memory, say (Rosh HaShana 26a): Since the shofar on Rosh HaShana is blown so that we are remembered, it is like being in the innermost part of the Temple. See further there.

How the heart of a person who loves himself and his dependent family members should tremble (even though mortal eyes see that there are people who turn to righteousness without the preparations and awakenings of Mussar and reverence) [and how he should want] to improve his way, or at least be contrite of spirit with broken heart. For this is the first principle: to be protected against the great danger, which hovers.[10] As the Sages, of blessed memory, say in Rosh HaShana (16b): "Each year which starts in poverty [ends in wealth]…." ["Poverty"] refers to the contrition of the heart. As they, of blessed memory, say there (26b): On Rosh HaShana, "the more a person bows his spirit, the better [the year] is." See further there.

"Everything has its time" (Eccl. 3:1–2) and "a man does not know his time… [including] the bad time which will suddenly come upon him" (ibid. 9:12). [Do not be caught] without the necessary preparation, to prepare a shield and buckler, to be guarded from the snare, that is, the terrible Day of Judgment. [This is] particularly so, since even mortal eyes see that almost every Rosh HaShana, may the Merciful One save

וְשָׁלוֹם, אֲשֶׁר שְׁאָר אֲנָשִׁים כְּגִילָם נִצּוֹלוּ, וְהוּא הַדָּבָר כִּי הַקָּדוֹשׁ־בָּרוּךְ־הוּא מַאֲרִיךְ אַף עַד עֵת הַקְּצוּבָה לְפָנָיו אֲשֶׁר לְכָל אָדָם עִתּוֹ לְבַדּוֹ.

וְכַאֲשֶׁר כֹּחַ הַצִּיּוּר מוֹעִיל לַמּוּסָר, יְצַיֵּר הָאָדָם בְּעַצְמוֹ אִלּוּ הָיָה כֹּהֵן גָּדוֹל וְהָיָה צָרִיךְ לִכָּנֵס בְּיוֹם הַכִּפּוּרִים לְבֵית קָדְשֵׁי הַקֳּדָשִׁים, הָיָה חָרֵד מְאֹד לְנַפְשׁוֹ בַּל יִפְגָּעֵהוּ רָעָה חָלִילָה, כֵּן יֶחֱזַק אֱמוּנָתוֹ אֱמוּנַת חֲכָמִים רַבּוֹתֵינוּ חַכְמֵי הַתַּלְמוּד זַ"ל, אֲשֶׁר פָּסְקוּ וְחָדְלוּ שׁוֹפָר שֶׁל פָּרָה, מִשּׁוּם אֵין קָטֵיגוֹר נַעֲשֶׂה סָנֵיגוֹר, הֲגַם שֶׁבְּבֵית הַכְּנֶסֶת הַמְקֻדָּשׁ בְּבִגְדֵי זָהָב נִכְנָסִים, אָכֵן שׁוֹפָר כֵּיוָן דִּלְזִכָּרוֹן אָתֵי, וְהָאָדָם נִזְכָּר וְנִשְׁפָּט עַל כָּל מַעֲשָׂיו, כְּכֹהֵן גָּדוֹל הַנִּכְנָס לְקָדְשֵׁי הַקֳּדָשִׁים דָּמֵי, וְהַדְּבָרִים כַּהֲוָיָתָן, וּמְאֹד מְאֹד יֶחֱרַד לֵב הָאָדָם, הַמַּעֲמִיק בְּדָבָר הַנּוֹרָא הַלָּזֶה.

הַשֵּׁנִית הִיא נַפְשִׁי – יֵדַע הָאָדָם כִּי הַקָּדוֹשׁ־בָּרוּךְ־הוּא מַאֲרִיךְ אַפּוֹ וְגָבֵי דִּילֵיהּ, וְהָאָדָם בְּעַצְמוֹ הָעוֹשֶׂה דָּבָר נֶגֶד דַּעַת הַתּוֹרָה, אֲשֶׁר זֶה נֶגֶד רְצוֹנוֹ יִתְבָּרַךְ שְׁמוֹ עָנֹשׁ יֵעָנֵשׁ, כִּי גוּף הָאָדָם אֵינוֹ רַק הַלְּבוּשׁ, וְכֹחַ הָאָדָם הַמַּרְגֶּשֶׁת נֹעַם וְצַעַר, הִיא הַחַיָּה גַּם אַחַר פְּשִׁיטַת הַלְּבוּשׁ, וּמְסֻגֶּלֶת לְהַשָּׂגַת נֹעַם וָצַעַר, וּמִן קִיּוּם תּוֹרָה וּמִצְוֹת יִהְיֶה לְהָאָדָם בְּעַצְמוֹ הַמְקַיֵּם, עֹנֶג גָּדוֹל לְמַעְלָה לְמַעְלָה לְהַפְלִיא, וּמֵעֲשִׂיַּת עֲבֵרָה אוֹ בִּטּוּל תּוֹרָה וּמִצְוֹת, יִהְיֶה לְהָאָדָם בְּעַצְמוֹ הָעוֹבֵר, צַעַר גָּדוֹל וְנוֹרָא, אֲשֶׁר יִנְהַם בְּאַחֲרִיתוֹ בְּאֵין מִפְלָט, אִם לֹא יָכִין מָנוֹס לוֹ, בְּעֵת נָשְׂאוֹ הַלְּבוּשׁ הִיא הִתְקַשְּׁרוּת הַנַּפְשִׁי עִם הַחָמְרִי.

יוֹם הַכִּפּוּרִים דָּבָר טוֹב לִמְאֹד, יוֹם סְלִיחָה וְכַפָּרָה, לֹא הָיוּ יָמִים טוֹבִים לְיִשְׂרָאֵל כְּיוֹם הַכִּפּוּרִים (סוֹף תַּעֲנִית) אֵין לָנוּ דָּבָר טוֹב מִמֶּנּוּ, אִם הָיִינוּ עוֹשִׂים הַהֲכָנָה הָרְאוּיָה לְתִקּוּן דְּרָכֵינוּ, כִּי יוֹם הַכִּפּוּרִים מְכַפֵּר עִם הַתְּשׁוּבָה הִיא עֲזִיבַת הַחֵטְא – אָכֵן גַּם הַמְעַט טוֹב מְאֹד,

---

11. A reference to the Golden Calf, the ultimate act of idolatry in the desert. A cow's horn, which recalls that great sin, may not be used as a shofar to protect the Jewish people by awakening them to repentance. Instead, a ram's horn is used.
12. Rosh HaShana 26a.
13. Which also recalls the Golden Calf.
14. See Genesis Rabba 67:4.

us, even young men are condemned to death, God forbid, although the rest of the people of their age survive. This is the crux of the matter: the Holy One, blessed be His name, is patient until the allotted time before Him – and for each person there is a unique time.

Since the power of evoking imagery helps Mussar, let a person imagine to himself: if he were the High Priest and had to enter the Holy of Holies on Yom Kippur, he would be very frightened for his life, that no evil befall him, God forbid. So let him strengthen his trust in the Rabbis, our teachers, the Sages of the Talmud, of blessed memory, who decreed and stopped the use of the horn of a cow,[11] because of the principle that "a prosecutor cannot serve as defense attorney."[12] Although some enter the holy synagogue wearing articles of clothing made of gold[13] – still, since the shofar's purpose is to arouse remembrance, and the person is remembered and judged for his actions, then he is like the High Priest who enters the Holy of Holies. It is as if it were actually so. A person's heart will tremble mightily if he delves into this awesome matter.

The second [outcome produced by studying Mussar] is spiritual. A person should know that "the Holy One, blessed be He, is patient, but eventually He collects His debts."[14] And the person, himself, who does something against the Torah's view – against His will, blessed be His name – will surely be punished. For the human body is only the garment. The human faculty that feels pleasure and pain is what lives on after the garment is taken off, and it is specifically designed for feeling pleasure and pain. So, by keeping the Torah and commandments, the person who himself keeps it will receive great pleasure, so great as to astonish. By committing sin or neglecting the Torah and commandments, the person who himself violates it will receive great and awful pain. He will regret it later, but there will be no escape – unless he prepares a way out for himself while he still wears the garment, i.e., while the soul is still tied to the body.

Yom Kippur is a wonderful thing: a day of forgiveness and atonement. There were never any better days for Israel than Yom Kippur (end of Taanit [26a]). We have nothing better than it – if we would make the proper preparation to improve our way, for Yom Kippur atones [only] with repentance, i.e., abandoning the sin. However, even a little [repen-

אֵין עֲרֹךְ לָהּ בְּעִנְיְנֵי הַתֵּבֵל, לִרְאוֹת לְכָל הַפָּחוֹת שֶׁתִּהְיֶה אֵיזֶה קַבָּלָה עַל לְהַבָּא בְּיוֹם הַכִּפּוּרִים.

וְאֵין לָנוּ מִסְחָר הַנּוֹשֵׂא פְּרִי רֶוַח, כְּמוֹ לַעֲשׂוֹת הֲכָנָה בַּלִּמּוּד הַמּוּסָרִי, וּלְהִתְבּוֹנֵן לְהֵטִיב דְּרָכָיו, עַד אֲשֶׁר יָבֹא לְאֵיזֶה קַבָּלָה לְהַבָּא בְּיוֹם הַכִּפּוּרִים, וּבְכָל בְּחִינָה קְטַנָּה שֶׁבַּקְּטַנּוֹת, אֲשֶׁר יָכִין הָאָדָם אֶת עַצְמוֹ, לְהַגְדִּיל בְּחִינַת יוֹם הַכִּפּוּרִים שֶׁלּוֹ, אֵין עֲרֹךְ וְאֵין דֵּי בָּאֵר הַצְלָחַת נַפְשׁוֹ לְהִנָּצֵל מִצָּרוֹת רַבּוֹת וּנְצוּרוֹת וְאֵין לָנוּ רֶוַח גָּדוֹל מִזֶּה.

בָּזֹאת יָשִׂים הָאָדָם לִבּוֹ וְנַפְשׁוֹ, לְהַרְכִּיב שְׁנֵי הָעִנְיָנִים, וּלְחַבְּרָם בְּהִתְקַשְּׁרוּת הַגּוּף וָנֶפֶשׁ, בַּתְּחִלָּה יִשְׁבֹּר לְבָבוֹ מֵאֵימַת דִּין הַגּוּפָנִי כִּי נוֹרָא הוּא, וְחַיָּיו וְחַיֵּי בְּנֵי בֵיתוֹ וּצְרָכָיו תָּלוּי בָּזֶה, וּמִזֶּה יָבוֹא לְתַקֵּן דְּרָכָיו, וְיִהְיֶה לְהוֹעִיל לְיוֹם הַכִּפּוּרִים, אָכֵן הַמְנֻוָּל הוּא הַיֵּצֶר הַשּׂוֹנֵא וְאוֹרֵב לָאָדָם לְטַמְטֵם לְבָבוֹ, אִם פָּגַע בְּךָ מָשְׁכֵהוּ לְבֵית הַמִּדְרָשׁ הַשַּׁיָּךְ לָזֶה הוּא בֵּית הַמּוּסָר, אִם אֶבֶן הוּא עַל יְדֵי לִמּוּד הַמּוּסָר (הִיא הַתּוֹרָה לְטִמְטוּם הַלֵּב) נִמּוֹחַ כַּנִּזְכָּר לְעֵיל.

בְּכָל הַשָּׁנָה סִבָּה הָרִאשׁוֹנָה, הִיא הַיִּרְאָה הַנָּטוּעַ בְּלֵב אִישׁ הַמַּאֲמִין וְיוֹדֵעַ בִּכְלָל, כִּי רַע וָמַר תִּהְיֶה אַחֲרִיתוֹ, בְּעָזְבוֹ תּוֹרַת וּמִצְוַת ד׳ יִתְבָּרַךְ שְׁמוֹ, אָכֵן הַתַּאֲוָה בְּעָכְרָתוֹ, יַרְגִּיל הָאָדָם אֶת עַצְמוֹ בְּלִמּוּד פּוֹסְקִים [לֹא לְבַטֵּל שִׁעוּרָיו הַקְּבוּעִים לוֹ כִּי לֹא לִסְתֹּר אֱיָנָשׁ בֵּי כְּנִישְׁתָּא כו׳ בָּבָא בַּתְרָא דַּף ג׳] וּבְהַגִּיעוֹ לְדִין הַשַּׁיָּךְ לוֹ יִלְמַד מִמְּקוֹרוֹ, וְיַעֲמִיק הֵיטֵב לְפִי כֹּחוֹת תְּבוּנָתוֹ, וְדָבָר זֶה עוֹשֶׂה קִנְיָן בְּנַפְשׁוֹ לְשָׁמְרָהּ, כִּמְעַט יוֹתֵר מֵהִתְבּוֹנְנוּת הַיִּרְאָה, אָכֵן גַּם מֵהִתְבּוֹנְנוּת הַיִּרְאָה אַל יֶחְדַּל, וְאִם אֵין תּוֹרָה אֵין יִרְאָה, וְאִם אֵין יִרְאָה אֵין תּוֹרָה (אָבוֹת).

וּלְחֹלִי הַיֵּאוּשׁ בִּרְאוֹתוֹ כִּי הַתַּאֲוָה גְּדוֹלָה לְפָנָיו, וְאֵין לְךָ מַחֲלָה

---

15. A play on Isaiah 40:16.

16. The two matters are: a) the physical awareness that one is on trial for his life during the Ten Days of Repentance, and b) the spiritual awareness of the immeasurable spiritual reward and punishment in the next world for every successful repentance or failure to repent at this very moment.

17. "*Yira*" – lit. "fear or awe (of God)." These are texts which communicate the awesomeness of God and the awfulness of divine punishments in the next world.

18. Despair arises because, despite his feelings of awe and awareness of punishment, desire threatens to overwhelm his self-control.

tance] is very good. Nothing compares to it in worldly matters. See to it: on Yom Kippur, at least make some resolution for the future.

There is no enterprise as profitable as preparing with Mussar study, to be mindful and to improve one's ways, until one arrives at some resolution for the future on Yom Kippur. And in every aspect – even the smallest of the small – wherein a person prepares himself to improve his introspection on Yom Kippur, there is no comparison and no sufficient description[15] of his soul's success in being saved from many and extraordinary sorrows. And there is no greater profit than this.

Therefore, let a person put his heart and soul to fusing and combining these two matters[16] while the body and soul are together. First let him break his heart out of the fear of the physical judgment, for it is awesome, and his life and the lives of his family and their needs all depend on this. From this [awareness], he will come to correct his ways, and this will help for Yom Kippur. Therefore, this scoundrel – the [evil] urge, who hates and lies in wait for a person to stultify his heart – if he encounters you, take him to the study hall that pertains to this area, i.e., the Mussar House. Even if it is made of stone, through Mussar study (which is the Torah for a hardened heart), it will melt, as said above.

All year long, the primary cause is the fear planted in the heart of a person who believes and knows in general that his end will be bad and bitter if he abandons the Torah and commandments of God, blessed be His name. Indeed, when desire overcomes him, a person should habituate himself to study codes (but not cancel his regular studies – for "a person should not knock down an established synagogue [until he builds a new one]" [Bava Batra 3b]). When he reaches a law that applies to him, let him study it from its [primary] source. Let him delve deeply into it, in accordance with the powers of his understanding. This [action] will make his soul take possession of and observe [the law] – almost more than the study of *yira*[17] itself. However, let him not stop studying *yira* either! If there is no Torah, there will be no [true] fear [of God], and if there is no [true] fear [of God], there is no Torah (Avot [3:17]).

As for the sickness of despair, when one sees that desire looms large before him[18] – and there is no sickness so great as despair – one

כְּמוֹ הַיֵּאוּשׁ – יֵדַע הָאָדָם כִּי כָּל עֲבֵרָה תִּתְחַלֵּק לִבְחִינוֹת שׁוֹנוֹת, יֵשׁ אֲשֶׁר כָּבֵד לְפָנָיו לִשָּׁמֵר מִמֶּנָּה, וְיֵשׁ בְּאוֹתָהּ עֲבֵרָה עַצְמָהּ, אֲשֶׁר יֵקַל לְפָנָיו בְּעִתִּים שׁוֹנוֹת, אוֹ בְּמַצָּבִים שׁוֹנִים כְּמוֹ בְּבִטּוּל תּוֹרָה, הַבְּחִינָה שׁוֹנָה מִשַּׁבָּת לְחֹל, מֵעֵת הַטִּרְדָּה לְעֵת הַפְּנוּיָה, מִמַּצַּב דַּעַת הַנִּטְרֶדֶת, לְמַצַּב דַּעַת הַצְּלוּלָה וְכַיּוֹצֵא – וּבְכָל פְּרָטֵי הָעֲבֵרוֹת הָעֲבֵרָה הָאַחַת, תִּתְחַלֵּק לִבְחִינוֹת שׁוֹנוֹת לְפִי מַצַּב הָאָדָם וּתְכוּנָתוֹ. לֹא כָּל הָעִתִּים שָׁוֶה, וְלֹא כָּל הַתְּכוּנוֹת שָׁווֹת, וְכָל אֲשֶׁר יֵקַל לִפְנֵי הָאָדָם בְּאֵיזֶה בְּחִינָה לְהִשָּׁמֵר מֵהָעֲבֵרָה, תִּגְדַּל עָנְשׁוֹ לְמַעְלָה לְמַעְלָה, כְּמַאֲמַר חֲכָמֵינוּ ז״ל מְנָחוֹת (דַּף מ״ג) גָּדוֹל עָנְשׁוֹ שֶׁל לָבָן יוֹתֵר מֵעָנְשׁוֹ שֶׁל תְּכֵלֶת כו׳ עַיֵּן שָׁם.

וְלָזֹאת יַרְגִּיל הָאָדָם אֶת עַצְמוֹ לְקַיֵּם מַאֲמַר הַכָּתוּב מִשְׁלֵי אִם תְּבַקְשֶׁנָּה כַכָּסֶף וְגוֹ׳, לְהַשְׁקִיף עַל תַּהֲלוּכוֹת צָרְכֵי הַגּוּף וְלִקַּח מִמֶּנּוּ מָשָׁל וּמְלִיצָה לְנַפְשׁוֹ, הֲלֹא בְּצָרְכֵי הַגּוּף, אֵיךְ יַעֲמֹל הָאָדָם הַקְּשֵׁה יוֹם, לְהַשִּׂיג מָה לְצָרְכֵי גּוּפוֹ אִם כִּי מִצְעָר הִיא, וְאֵיךְ לֹא יִכְבַּד לִפְנֵי הָאָדָם לְהִתְעַמֵּל בְּעֵת דַּכְּאוֹ בְּיִסּוּרִים רַחֲמָנָא לִצְּלַן, לְחַפֵּשׂ וְלִרְאוֹת לְהָקֵל מַחֲלָתוֹ, וּמַדּוּעַ לֹא נַעֲשֶׂה כֹּה לְנַפְשֵׁנוּ, לִרְאוֹת לְכָל הַפָּחוֹת לְקַיֵּם הַמִּצְוֹת הַקַּלּוֹת לְפָנֵינוּ לְקַיְּמָם, וּלְהִשָּׁמֵר מֵהָעֲבֵרָה בִּבְחִינָה הַקַּלָּה, אֲשֶׁר תַּצִּילֵנוּ מִיִּסּוּרִים קָשִׁים וּמָרִים רַחֲמָנָא לִצְּלַן, וּבָזֶה אֵין מָקוֹם

19. Note this major distinctive theme in R. Salanter's teaching. Each person's nature and inner makeup is unique, and its elements are impacted (or stressed by temptation) very differently at different times, situations, and frames of mind. The net result is that similar or identical external acts of observance or violations of mitzvot will be judged very differently by Hashem and will have widely varying consequences. Thus, Mussar analysis shows the utter inadequacy of judging people simply by their external behaviors. Therefore, Mussar drives us to assess states of mind and individual character traits. We have to examine our personal motives and causes of behavior as well. In the end, this insight requires us to analyze and pass judgment even on technically proper behavior. These acts may, in fact, be "tainted" or the outcomes of conformity (meaning, spiritual laziness and lack of effort). By this standard, righteous and learned people, conforming to communal norms, may be judged as spiritually lacking or even as moral failures. This type of analysis made Mussar study a demanding discipline that took great effort to live up to. The critique of external correct behavior may also explain some of the backlash against Mussar in the yeshiva world of the 1890s. See Katz, *Pulmus HaMussar*.

should know that each sin can be divided in accordance with different aspects, some of which are difficult for him to safeguard against, and some of which, with regard to that very same sin, are easy for him [to handle] at various times, or in various situations. Like neglect of Torah study [for example]: Its aspect changes from Shabbat to weekday, from a time of preoccupation to free time, from a burdened state of mind to a clear state of mind, and so on. With all the particulars of sins, each sin divides into different aspects according to the state of a person and his disposition. Not all times are the same, and not all dispositions are the same. The easier it is for a person to refrain from some aspect of the sin, the more his punishment [for doing it] will grow and grow.[19] As our Sages, of blessed memory, say in Menaḥot 43b: "Greater is the punishment for [not wearing] the white [*tzizit*] string than the punishment for [not wearing] the sky-blue [string]."[20]

Thus, a person should habituate himself to fulfill the verse in Proverbs (2:4): "If you seek it like silver...," to reflect on the ways of attaining the bodily needs and to use it as an example and analogy for [attaining the needs of] his soul. When it comes to bodily needs, an unfortunate person will work very hard to obtain anything for his bodily needs, as painful as it may be. It is not too burdensome for him to make every effort, when he is crushed by suffering – may the Merciful One save us – to seek and make sure to alleviate his sickness. So why should we not do the same for our souls – to see to it that at least we keep the mitzvot that are easy for us to keep and refrain from sins easy [to resist]? This will save us from hard and bitter suffering, may the Merciful One save

20. The punishment for failure to attach the white *tzitzit* (fringes), which are widely available and would take little effort to obtain and attach, is greater than the punishment for failure to attach the blue fringe, since it is not available and takes much effort and expense to obtain and attach.

Note how R. Salanter has focused Torah observance on the inner dimension. The same external action carries very different rewards and punishments, commensurate with the inner quality of the observance or the difference as to difficulty or ease in observance due to difference of human nature and/or in the life situation in which the action is done. R. Salanter is also close to "modern" emphasis on the uniqueness of the individual. This leads God to judge similar behaviors by different people in very different ways.

לְיֵאוּשׁ לִפְנֵי הָאָדָם, אִם יָשִׂים לִבּוֹ וְנַפְשׁוֹ לְהַשְׁגִּיחַ בְּהַנְהָגַת צָרְכֵי הַגּוּף, לְהִשְׁתַּמֵּשׁ בָּהּ בְּצָרְכֵי הַנֶּפֶשׁ, אָכֵן מֵהַתְּשׁוּקָה וְהַחִפּוּשׂ לְקַיֵּם הַמִּצְוֹת בִּשְׁלֵמוּתָם, הֵן לִמּוּד הַתּוֹרָה וְכַיּוֹצֵא, וּלְהִשָּׁמֵר מֵהָעֲבֵרוֹת לְגַמְרֵי אַל יַנִּיחַ יָדוֹ.

כֵּן גַּם בֶּאֱלוּל אִם כִּי הָעֵת קָצָר, יִרְאֶה לִלְמֹד הַסֵּפֶר הַקָּצָר כְּמוֹ שַׁעֲרֵי תְּשׁוּבָה לְרַבֵּנוּ יוֹנָה וְכַיּוֹצֵא, הַמְדַבֵּר כִּמְעַט מִכָּל שָׁרְשֵׁי מִצְוֹת וַעֲבֵרוֹת, וּבְהַגִּיעוֹ לְדָבָר הַשַּׁיָּךְ יוֹתֵר לוֹ. יִרְאֶה לִלְמֹד בְּהַעֲמָקָה. לְפִי כֹּחוֹת תְּבוּנָתוֹ וּלְפִי מַצַּב עֵת הַקָּצָר. וְיִרְאֶה לְחַלֵּק לִבְחִינוֹת שׁוֹנוֹת כַּנִּזְכָּר לְעֵיל, וּמִזֶּה הַתִּקְוָה לָבֹא לְאֵיזֶה בְּחִינָה בְּהָעֲבֵרָה הַלָּזוֹ בְּיוֹם הַכִּפּוּרִים לְבַעַל תְּשׁוּבָה גָּמוּר, לְקַבָּלַת עֲזִיבַת הַחֵטְא, בַּבְּחִינָה הַקַּלָּה לְפָנָיו קַבָּלָה אֲמִתִּית אֲשֶׁר אֵין עֲרֹךְ לְגֹדֶל מַעֲלָתָהּ לְטוֹב לוֹ בָּזֶה וּבַבָּא.

כִּי אֲנַחְנוּ רוֹאִים בְּחוּשׁ, מַה שֶּׁהוּא כִּמְעַט טִבְעִי לְהָאָדָם לְשָׁמְרָהּ, יֵקַל לְפָנָיו לְקַיְּמָהּ גַּם אִם תִּכְבַּד לְפָנָיו, וּבָזֶה הַמְּקוֹמוֹת שׁוֹנוֹת, בִּמְדִינָתֵנוּ יֵקַל לְהָאָדָם שְׁמִירַת שַׁבָּת, וְיַעֲמֹד כִּמְעַט בְּנִסְיוֹנוֹת, וּבְאַשְׁכְּנַז לְהָפִיק שְׁמִירַת הַשַּׁבָּת יוֹתֵר כָּבֵד לִשְׁמֹר כִּמְעַט מִכָּל עֲבוֹדַת ד׳ יִתְבָּרַךְ שְׁמוֹ, וְלָזֹאת הַלִּמּוּד בְּעִיּוּן וּבְהַעֲמָקָה עוֹשֶׂה רֹשֶׁם גָּדוֹל בְּנֶפֶשׁ הָאָדָם, עַד אֲשֶׁר יִהְיֶה מְטֻבָּע בְּנַפְשׁוֹ, וְיִשְׁמֹר כִּמְעַט בְּלִי שׁוּם מוּסָר, וְיַעֲמֹד גַּם בַּנִּסָּיוֹן, לִמּוּד הַתּוֹרָה בְּעִיּוּן וּבְהַעֲמָקָה בַּדִּין הַנִּצְרָךְ לְהָאָדָם, הוּא הַיְסוֹד לִשְׁמִירָתָהּ.

---

21. Note this important theme, which becomes a staple of R. Salanter's thought. 1) One should learn from *ḥokhmat haolam,* the life wisdom one derives from dealing in business and work how to anticipate and solve difficulties and how to find ways to succeed. One should apply this wisdom and accept spiritual difficulties and solve them. 2) One should employ equivalent energy, wisdom, and strategies to prevent sins and accomplish religious goals as one does in business and other worldly matters.

22. Compare Exodus 17:11 and Ecclesiastes 7:18.

us. In this matter, there is no room for a person to despair. If he would only apply his heart and soul to observe the practices of taking care of bodily needs and use them to take care of spiritual needs.[21] Indeed, [he should never let go of] the yearning and search to keep the commandments in their totality, including study of Torah and the like; and from trying to refrain from sins entirely, he should never let up.[22]

So too in Elul, even though time is short, see to it that one studies a short book such as Rabbenu Yona's *Shaarei Teshuva*[23] and the like, which deal with almost all types of mitzvot and sins. When one reaches something that is more applicable to him, he should make sure to study it more deeply, in accordance with his powers of understanding and considering the limited time. He should make sure to divide [the sin] into different aspects, as said above. From this comes the hope to become a true penitent in some aspect of this sin on Yom Kippur, i.e., to resolve to abandon the sin – [at least] in the aspect easiest to him – with true resolve. The benefit of this to him is of immeasurable value, in this world and the next.

For we see instinctively: That which is almost natural for an individual to observe, he will find "easy" to uphold even if it is very burdensome. In this matter, locations differ. In our country, it is easy for a person to observe Shabbat, and he will withstand almost [all] temptations. In Germany, to achieve Shabbat observance is more difficult than almost anything else in the service of God, blessed be His name.

To this end, studying analytically and in depth makes a major impression on the human psyche, to the extent that it becomes imprinted on one's soul. At that point, he will observe it with barely any Mussar study and will withstand temptation. Thus, analytical, in-depth Torah study, of the laws that this person needs is the foundation of its observance.

---

23. R. Jonah ben Abraham of Girona, Catalonia (d. 1264) was an influential rabbi best known for his commentary on *Pirkei Avot* and his moralist tract *Shaarei Teshuva* (*The Gates of Repentance*), which he composed as part of his own penitence for initially opposing the philosophical works of Rambam. He also composed commentaries on several tractates of the Talmud.

ח

מִדְרָשׁ רַבָּה וַיִּקְרָא פָּרָשָׁה ב׳ חֲדָשִׁים גַּם יְשָׁנִים דּוֹדִי צָפַנְתִּי לָךְ, אַבְרָהָם יִצְחָק וְיַעֲקֹב יְשָׁנִים, עַמְרָם בֶּן קְהָת וְכָל הַכְּשֵׁרִים שֶׁהָיוּ בְּמִצְרַיִם חֲדָשִׁים, חֲבוּרָתוֹ שֶׁל מֹשֶׁה וַחֲבוּרָתוֹ שֶׁל יְהוֹשֻׁעַ, וַחֲבוּרָתוֹ שֶׁל דָּוִד וְשֶׁל חִזְקִיָּה יְשָׁנִים, חֲבוּרָתוֹ שֶׁל עֶזְרָא וְשֶׁל הִלֵּל וְשֶׁל רַבִּי יוֹחָנָן בֶּן זַכַּאי, וְשֶׁל רַבִּי מֵאִיר וַחֲבֵרָיו חֲדָשִׁים, וַעֲלֵיהֶם הוּא אוֹמֵר חֲדָשִׁים גַּם יְשָׁנִים. (פְּסָחִים דַּף קט״ז) רַבָּן גַּמְלִיאֵל הָיָה אוֹמֵר כָּל שֶׁלֹּא אָמַר שְׁלֹשָׁה דְּבָרִים אֵלּוּ בְּפֶסַח לֹא יָצָא יְדֵי חוֹבָתוֹ, וְאֵלּוּ הֵן פֶּסַח מַצָּה וּמָרוֹר, וּפֵרֵשׁ רַשְׁבַּ״ם שֶׁלֹּא פֵּרֵשׁ טַעֲמָן, וּבָזֹאת בַּמִּצְוֹת הַלָּלוּ בְּוַדַּאי הָרְשׁוּת נְתוּנָה לָתוּר וְלַחֲקֹר בְּטַעֲמֵיהֶן, וְיֵשׁ לְעַיֵּן מַדּוּעַ סִדְּרָן מָרוֹר אַחַר מַצָּה, הֲלֹא הַמַּעֲשֶׂה הָיְתָה בְּהִפּוּךְ וּלְפִי הַטַּעַם סִבַּת מָרוֹר קוֹדֶם.

1. According to this midrash, the "old ones" and "new ones" have distinctive weights – reflecting the difficulty of living up to the Torah in their circumstances, as will be explained below.
2. R. Samuel ben Meir (Troyes, 1085–1158) was a leading French Tosafist and grandson of Rabbi Shlomo Yitzḥaki (Rashi).
3. *Maror* commemorates the slavery whereas matza symbolizes the Exodus. Chronologically, slavery comes first, so it stands to reason that its commemoration should as well.

Letter 8

Leviticus Rabba, chapter 2 (section 11):

> "New ones and old ones I have held aside for you, my beloved" (Song. 7:14) – Abraham, Isaac, Jacob are "old ones"; Amram, son of Kehat, and all the righteous ones who were in Egypt are "new ones." The company of Moses and the company of Joshua, the company of David and of Hezekiah are "old ones"; the company of Ezra, of Hillel, of R. Yoḥanan ben Zakkai, of R. Meir and his colleagues are "new ones." Of all these, it is said: "New ones and old ones."[1]

Pesaḥim 116a–b:

> Rabban Gamliel used to say: Whoever does not speak of these three matters on Passover has not fulfilled his obligations: *pesaḥ* [the paschal sacrifice], matza [unleavened bread], and *maror* [bitter herbs].

Rashbam[2] explains: ["Who does not speak of" means] one who did not explain their reasons. So regarding these mitzvot, it is certainly permitted to explore and investigate their reasons. Let us look carefully: Why is *maror* placed after the matza? After all, in the actual event, [the sequence] was the opposite?[3] Likewise, the reason for eating the *maror* is first chronologically.

רַבּוֹתֵינוּ זַ"ל אָמְרוּ בְּקִדּוּשִׁין (דַּף מ') לְעוֹלָם יִרְאֶה אָדָם עַצְמוֹ, כְּאִלּוּ חֶצְיוֹ חַיָּב וְחֶצְיוֹ זַכַּאי, וְלִפְעָמִים יִרְאֶה הָאָדָם בַּעֲלִיל שֶׁאֵינוֹ כֵּן הֵן לְטוֹב וְכוּ', אָכֵן הָרַמְבַּ"ם זַ"ל כָּתַב בְּהִלְכוֹת תְּשׁוּבָה פֶּרֶק ג', כָּל אֶחָד וְאֶחָד מִבְּנֵי הָאָדָם יֵשׁ לוֹ זְכֻיּוֹת וַעֲוֹנוֹת מִי שֶׁזְּכֻיּוֹתָיו יְתֵרוֹת עַל עֲוֹנוֹתָיו צַדִּיק, וּמִי שֶׁעֲוֹנוֹתָיו יְתֵרוֹת עַל זְכֻיּוֹתָיו רָשָׁע כוּ', וְשִׁקּוּל זֶה אֵינוֹ לְפִי מִנְיַן הַזְּכֻיּוֹת וְהָעֲוֹנוֹת, אֶלָּא לְפִי גָּדְלָם, יֵשׁ זְכוּת שֶׁהוּא נֶגֶד כַּמָּה עֲוֹנוֹת כוּ', וְיֵשׁ עוֹד שֶׁהוּא נֶגֶד כַּמָּה זְכֻיּוֹת כוּ', וְאֵין שׁוֹקְלִין אֶלָּא בְּדַעְתּוֹ שֶׁל אֵל דֵּעוֹת, וְהוּא הַיּוֹדֵעַ אֵיךְ עוֹרְכִין הַזְּכֻיּוֹת נֶגֶד הָעֲוֹנוֹת עַד כָּאן לְשׁוֹנוֹ עַיֵּן שָׁם.

בְּוַדַּאי יֵשׁ בַּדָּבָר בְּחִינוֹת רַבּוֹת, מַה שֶּׁמַּגְדִּיל עֵרֶךְ הַזְּכֻיּוֹת וְהָעֲוֹנוֹת, וּנְבָאֵר מְעַט בְּחִינָה אַחַת. כִּי נוֹדַע כִּי הַמִּצְוֹת נֶעֱרָכוֹת נֶגֶד צַעַר קִיּוּמָם, כְּמַאֲמַר רַבּוֹתֵינוּ זַ"ל לְפוּם צַעֲרָא אַגְרָא, וְלָזֹאת לִפְעָמִים הָאָדָם עוֹשֶׂה מִצְוָה אַחַת בִּשְׁנֵי עִתִּים, הַשָּׁוִים בִּתְמוּנַת חָמְרָם, וּבְכָל זֶה בִּבְחִינַת צַעַר קִיּוּמָם, יֵשׁ בֵּינֵיהֶם הֶפְרֵשׁ כַּמָּה אֲלָפִים בְּחִינוֹת, כִּי כָּל דָּבָר תִּתְחַלֵּק לַחֲלָקִים דַּקִּים וְרַבִּים, כִּי בְּחִינַת הַצַּעַר תִּתְחַלֵּף לְפִי צוּרַת עֲשִׂיָּתָם, לְמָשָׁל מִי שֶׁלָּמַד בְּעֵת אַחַת שָׁעָה אַחַת. וְדַעְתּוֹ הָיְתָה אָז צְלוּלָה לַלִּמּוּד, טִבְעוֹ לֹא הָיְתָה מִתְנַגֶּדֶת לָזֶה, לֹא הִרְגִּישׁ צַעַר בְּנַפְשׁוֹ אוֹ לְכָל הַפָּחוֹת מְעַט בְּעֵת לִמּוּדוֹ, וּבְעֵת אַחֶרֶת הָיָה הַדָּבָר בְּהִפּוּךְ, כְּנֶטֶל הַחוֹל הָיְתָה עַל נַפְשׁוֹ הַלִּמּוּד, צַעֲרוֹ הָיָה לְמַכְבִּיר, הֲלֹא

---

4. Or for worse. R. Salanter deliberately elides the negative alternative.
5. Avot 5:23.
6. R. Salanter continues to shift the assessment of actions from their external performance level, in which they appear to be uniform from person to person or in the same person on different occasions and are taken at face value, to judging actions by Mussar standards, i.e., by their internal weight. Similar actions, externally, turn out to be vastly different when judged by the internal intentions and meanings brought by the individual, or in terms of the great variation between people as to their ease or propensity to observe or even within the same person on different occasions. The thrust of the Mussar approach is to turn religion into a highly individual and highly intentional set of actions and beliefs. Another far-reaching consequence of this approach is developed by R. Salanter in later letters. Actions that externally appear to be fulfillment of the

Our Rabbis, of blessed memory, said in Kiddushin (40b): "[When on trial on Rosh HaShana,] a person should always view himself as equally balanced between guilty and exonerated…" although sometimes a person sees patently that this is not so, for better etc.[4] Indeed, Rambam, of blessed memory, wrote in *Mishneh Torah*, the Laws of Repentance 3:1:

> Each individual person has merits and sins. One whose merits exceed his sins is a righteous person; one whose sins exceed his merits is a wicked man…. This weighing is not [simply] by the quantity of merits and sins, but according to their magnitude. One merit can outweigh several sins…and there are sins that outweigh several merits…. The weighing is only according to the judgment of the God of Understanding, who knows how to assess merits against sins.

See further there.

Certainly this matter has many variables that increase the value of merits and sins. Let us explain a bit about one variable. It is known that commandments are evaluated according to the pain in the effort of observing them. As the Rabbis, of blessed memory, said: "According to the pain [of the effort] is the reward."[5] Thus, sometimes a person does one mitzva at two different times. They are the same [mitzva] in outward appearance, yet with respect to the pain of observing them, the difference between them is an order of magnitude in the thousands, for everything can be broken down into many little parts, and the pain varies according to the format of the way they are done.[6] For example, one learned for one hour at one time and his mind was clear for learning; his nature did not oppose it; he felt no pain or at least only a little when he learned. At another time, [however,] the situation was quite the contrary. The learning was like a heavy burden[7] on his soul; his pain was

---

Torah's instructions may turn out to be just the opposite because of wrong intentions or because of psychological distortions, which turn the actions negative.

7. Literally, "like the weight of sand." See Proverbs 27:3.

הַחֲמוּרִי שָׁוִים לְמוֹד שָׁעָה אַחַת, אָכֵן הַצּוּרָה נִשְׁתַּנָּה הַרְבֵּה לְמַעְלָה רֹאשׁ, וְכַיּוֹצֵא בְּכָל הַדְּבָרִים, אֵין שָׁעָה דּוֹמָה לַחֲבֵרוֹ בִּבְחִינַת צוּרָתוֹ. וְלָזֹאת גַּם מַעֲשָׂיו גַּם אִם יְקַיֵּם בְּאֵין שִׁנּוּי בְּחָמְרָם, בְּכָל זֹאת בִּבְחִינַת צוּרָתָם הַהֶפְרֵשׁ בֵּינֵיהֶם מֶרְחָק רַב.

וְכֵן בְּעִנְיַן הָעֲבֵרוֹת תִּתְחַלֵּף עָנְשָׁם לְפִי גֶּדֶר עֵרֶךְ צַעַר מְנִיעַת הָעֲבֵרָה, וְכָל אֲשֶׁר תִּפְחַת בְּצַעֲרָהּ כֵּן גַּם עָנְשָׁהּ גָּדוֹל כְּמַאֲמַר רַבּוֹתֵינוּ ז"ל מְנָחוֹת (דַּף מ"ג) תַּנְיָא הָיָה רַבִּי מֵאִיר אוֹמֵר גָּדוֹל עָנְשׁוֹ שֶׁל לָבָן יוֹתֵר מֵעָנְשׁוֹ שֶׁל תְּכֵלֶת מָשָׁל כוּ' עַיֵּן שָׁם, וְלָזֹאת גַּם בְּעִנְיַן הָעֲבֵרוֹת, הֲגַם שֶׁעַל כָּל עֲבֵרָה עֹנֶשׁ יֵעָנֵשׁ הָאָדָם, אִם בָּזֶה אוֹ בַבָּא, מִכָּל מָקוֹם תִּתְחַלֵּף הָעֹנֶשׁ לְפִי צוּרָתוֹ, וְאוֹתָהּ הָעֲבֵרָה עַצְמָהּ כְּשֶׁיַּעֲשֶׂנָּה הָאָדָם, בְּעֵת אֲשֶׁר נָקֵל לְפָנָיו לְהִנָּזֵר מֵהָעֲבֵרָה כֵּן עָנְשָׁהּ תִּגְדַּל, וּלְפִי זֶה גַּם בְּעִנְיַן הָעֲבֵרוֹת, יַעֲשֶׂה הָאָדָם לִפְעָמִים עֲבֵרָה אַחַת בִּשְׁנֵי עִתִּים שָׁוִים בִּבְחִינַת חָמְרָם, וְעִם כָּל זֶה תִּתְחַלֵּף עָנְשָׁם בְּכַמָּה אֲלָפִים בְּחִינוֹת, לְפִי עֵרֶךְ הַהִתְחַלְּקוּת בְּצוּרַת הַנְּזִירָה מֵהָעֲבֵרָה אֵיךְ הָיְתָה.

וּמִזֶּה יִתְבּוֹנֵן הָאָדָם, אִם יִתֵּן לִבּוֹ לַדָּבָר לְהַעֲמִיק בָּהּ הֵיטֵב – כַּמָּה גָּדְלָה אֵיכוּת הָעֹנֶשׁ עַל עֲבֵרוֹת, אִם בַּעֲשׂוֹת מַה שֶּׁאָסְרָה תּוֹרָה, אוֹ בְּהִמָּנַע עֲשׂוֹת מַה שֶּׁצִּוְּתָה הַתּוֹרָה לַעֲשׂוֹת, כְּשֶׁיִּתְבּוֹנֵן בַּתּוֹרָה עַל פִּי הַדִּין הַמְּסוּרָה לָנוּ מֵהַגְּמָרָא וּפוֹסְקִים, עַד הֵיכָן חִיּוּבָהּ מַגַּעַת לְקַיְּמָהּ, אִם בַּעֲשׂוֹת אוֹ בִּלְי לַעֲשׂוֹת, לְהִתְנַגֵּד אֶל הַצַּעַר אֲשֶׁר יְוָּלֵד בְּקִיּוּמָהּ, וְאִם יַעֲבֹר אָז עָנֹשׁ יֵעָנֵשׁ בְּוַדַּאי בְּעֹנֶשׁ יוֹתֵר גָּדוֹל, נֶגֶד הַצַּעַר שֶׁהָיָה לוֹ אִם הָיָה מְקַיֵּם, כִּי זֶה גֶּדֶר חֲלִיפַת הָעֹנֶשׁ לְהַזְהִיר הָאָדָם לְהִשָּׁמֵר עֲבוּר זֶה מֵאֵת אֲשֶׁר נִצְטַוָּה, שֶׁיִּהְיֶה הַרְבֵּה יוֹתֵר מֵהַצַּעַר שְׁמִירַת הַצִּוּוּי, וְאַחַר כָּךְ יַשְׁקִיף לְמַטָּה כַּמָּה וְכַמָּה אֲלָפִים בְּחִינוֹת תִּמְעַט צַעֲרוֹ בִּשְׁמִירַת הַדָּבָר, וְעַל פִּי זֶה תִּכְפַּל אֶלֶף אֲלָפִים פְּעָמִים עָנְשׁוֹ.

---

8. See previous letter.

9. I.e., difficulty level.

fierce. In outward form, [the two acts] of learning one hour are equivalent. But the internal make-up has changed overwhelmingly, and so on with all matters. No hour resembles another with respect to its internal make-up. So too with his actions: even if he fulfills them with no change in their outward form, with respect to their internal make up, the difference between them is vast.

It is the same with respect to sins. Punishments vary according to the degree of pain involved in refraining from the sin. The less the pain, the greater the punishment, as the Rabbis, of blessed memory, said in Menaḥot (43b): "It was taught: R. Meir used to say: Greater is the punishment for [not wearing] the white [*tzizit*] string than the punishment for [not wearing] the sky-blue [string]…." See further there.[8] So it is with sins: although a person will be punished for every sin, whether in this [world] or the next, the punishment nevertheless varies according to context; the same sin, if committed by a person at a time when it was easy for him to refrain from the sin, will accordingly be punished more severely. Accordingly, with regard to sins, a person might commit the same sin on two different occasions that are identical with respect to severity, yet the punishment will vary on an order of magnitude in the thousands, based on different internal contexts[9] of refraining from the sin.

Based on this, one can contemplate – if he pays enough attention to delve deeply into it – the qualitative intensity of punishment for sins, be they doing what the Torah forbade, or not doing what the Torah commanded to do. When he considers the extent of his obligation to observe, whether by commission or omission, the law of the Torah, as transmitted to us from the Talmud and codes, against the pain incurred by observing it, [he will realize] that if he transgresses, his punishment will certainly be more severe than the pain he would incur by observing it, since by the very definition of variable punishment – which cautions the person to be vigilant about what he was commanded – [this pain] will be much greater than the pain of keeping the commandment. And afterward he will note how many thousands and thousands of levels his pain is lessened by keeping the commandments. And by this principle, his punishment [if he does violate] will multiply thousands upon thousands of times.

דְּבָרִים הַלָּלוּ יַכּוּ שֹׁרֶשׁ בְּלֵב הָאָדָם, אִם יָשִׂים לִבּוֹ לְהַעֲמִיק בְּלִמּוּד הַתּוֹרָה אִישׁ לְפִי עֶרְכּוֹ, לֵידַע הַחִיּוּב לְהִתְנַגֵּד אֶל הַצַּעַר, וּבִפְרָט בַּדְּבָרִים הַשַּׁיָּכִים לוֹ, כִּי כִּמְעַט לְכָל אִישׁ שַׁיָּכִים יוֹתֵר חִיּוּבִים פְּרָטִים לְפִי תְּכוּנָתוֹ וּמַצָּבוֹ, יֵשׁ אֲשֶׁר הֶכְרֵחַ לְהַעֲמִיק יוֹתֵר בְּהִלְכוֹת תַּלְמוּד תּוֹרָה, וְיֵשׁ בְּהִלְכוֹת רִבִּית, וְיֵשׁ בְּהִלְכוֹת אוֹנָאָה וְכַיּוֹצֵא.

מַה מְּאֹד עַתִּיקִין הַדְּבָרִים הַלָּלוּ בַּעֲשֶׂרֶת יְמֵי תְשׁוּבָה, לִמְצֹא דֶּרֶךְ קְצָת לַעֲזִיבַת הַחֵטְא, אֲשֶׁר הִיא הַיְסוֹד הָרִאשִׁי אֶבֶן הַפִּנָּה, וְכָבֵד לִמְצֹא דֶּרֶךְ בַּדְּבָרִים הָרְגִילִים, אָכֵן כְּשֶׁיִּתְבּוֹנֵן הָאָדָם הֵיטֵב עִנְיָנָיו בְּכָל פְּרָטֵיהֶם, בְּגֶדֶר הַקַּלּוֹת וְהַכְּבֵדוֹת נָקֵל לְפָנָיו לְקַבֵּל עַל עַצְמוֹ קַבָּלָה שֶׁל קַיָּמָא, לִשְׁמֹר אוֹתוֹ בְּגֶדֶר הַקַּלּוֹת לְפָנָיו, אֲשֶׁר לְמִין בִּפְנֵי עַצְמוֹ יֵחָשֵׁב, וּבָזֶה יִגָּזֵר כִּמְעַט מֵרֹב עֲוֹנוֹתָיו בְּנָקֵל, כִּי הָעֲבֵרוֹת בְּאֹפֶן הַקַּלּוֹת, הֵמָּה הַרְבֵּה יוֹתֵר בְּאֵיכוּתָן כַּנִּזְכָּר לְעֵיל.

נִמְצָא לְפִי זֶה בִּכְלָל נוּכַל לְחַלֵּק הַמִּצְוֹת וְהָעֲבֵרוֹת, בְּגֶדֶר הַקַּלּוֹת וְהַכְּבֵדוֹת, וּבֵינֵיהֶם פְּרָטִים רַבִּים כַּנִּזְכָּר לְעֵיל, אֲשֶׁר לִפְעָמִים יִטְעֶה הָאָדָם בָּזֶה, בְּסָבְרוֹ כִּי הַדָּבָר אֶצְלוֹ בְּגֶדֶר הַכְּבֵדוֹת, אֲשֶׁר זֹאת טוֹב לְהָאָדָם בְּאֹפֶן מִצְוָה לְהַגְדִּיל שְׂכָרוֹ, וּבְאֹפֶן עֲבֵרָה לְמַעֵט עָנְשׁוֹ, וְאֵינֶנּוּ כֵן כִּי לִפְעָמִים הַדָּבָר כָּבֵד לְהָאָדָם, לֹא מִפְּאַת מַצַּב טִבְעַת לֵידָתוֹ, רַק מִפְּאַת שֶׁהִמְשִׁיךְ עָלָיו הַיֵּצֶר, וְנַעֲשָׂה הַדָּבָר כָּבֵד לְפָנָיו, אוֹ שֶׁהִמְשִׁיךְ הַיֵּצֶר בְּדָבָר אַחֵר, אֲשֶׁר נוֹלְדָה מִמֶּנָּה הַכְּבֵדוּת גַּם בַּדָּבָר הַלָּזוּ, כִּי הַכֹּחוֹת בְּהָאָדָם מְשֻׁלָּבִים הֵמָּה וּתְלוּיִים זֶה בָּזֶה, וְאָז לֹא יֵחָשֵׁב לְהָאָדָם בְּמַצַּב הַכְּבֵדוּת רַק גֶּדֶר הַקַּלּוֹת, כֵּיוָן שֶׁבִּבְחִירָתוֹ הִמְשִׁיךְ עָלָיו הָרָעָה.

וְכֵן לְטוֹב. לִפְעָמִים יֵקַל עַל הָאָדָם עֲשׂוֹת מִצְוָה לֹא בַּעֲבוּר טוּב מִזְגּוֹ מִלֵּידָתוֹ וְכַיּוֹצֵא, רַק בַּמֶּה שֶׁקָּנָה הַיִּרְאָה וְהַמּוּסָר וְהַהֶרְגֵּל בַּדָּבָר הַלָּזֶה אוֹ בְּדָבָר מְשֻׁלָּב לָזֶה, וְאָז יֵחָשֵׁב לְהָאָדָם בְּגֶדֶר הַכְּבֵדוּת הֲגַם שֶׁנָּקֵל לְפָנָיו וּשְׂכָרוֹ מְרֻבֶּה יוֹתֵר, וְלָזֹאת אֵיכוּת הַמִּצְוָה וְהָעֲבֵרָה, אִם

These words will strike roots in a person's heart if he resolves to delve deeply into Torah study, each according to his own measure; to know to weigh obligations against pain, especially in those matters that are especially relevant to him. For almost every person, certain specific obligations apply especially to him, according to his nature and condition. For some, the obligation is to go deeper into laws of Torah study; for some it is laws of usury; for others, laws of exploitation; and the like.

These matters loom large during the Ten Days of Repentance: finding a way to abandon sin. This is the primary foundation, the cornerstone – but it is hard to find a way [to eliminate] things that are habitual. However, when a person closely scrutinizes all his activities in all their specifics, categorizing the easier and the more difficult, it will be easier for him to accept upon himself an enduring resolution to observe those that he regards as being easy, which belong in a separate category. He will thus, with relative ease, refrain from most of his sins, for the sins deemed easy are much more severe [with respect to punishment], as mentioned above.

Accordingly, we find that, in general, we can divide the commandments and the sins into categories of easier ones and more difficult ones. In each category, as noted above, there are many particulars. Sometimes a person errs, thinking this matter for him is in the difficult category, which is good for him – in a mitzva it increases his reward and in a sin it decreases punishment – but it is not so! For sometimes it is difficult for a person, not because of his inborn nature but because he attracted the [evil] urge upon himself – that is why it became difficult for him. Or, he brought the urge into another matter, which made this matter difficult, too – for human drives are connected and dependent on each other. In such a case, it is not considered a difficult condition for him but [is judged] in the "easy" category – because by his own free choice he has brought this evil upon himself.

The same is true for good. Sometimes, it is easy for a person to do a mitzva – not because of his inborn good temperament and the like, but rather by acquiring reverence, Mussar, and [proper] habituation in this matter or in something connected to this matter. Then it is considered a difficult category for him and the reward is very great – even though it is easy for him. So the quality of a mitzva or sin: whether they are

יִכָּנְסוּ בְּגֶדֶר הַכְּבֵדוֹת אוֹ הַקַּלּוֹת, וְאֵיךְ וּמַה בִּפְרָט, בַּל יְדַע לְאִישׁ אֶל נָכוֹן, וְצָדְקוּ דִּבְרֵי הָרַמְבַּ"ם שֶׁה' יִתְבָּרַךְ שְׁמוֹ הוּא יוֹדֵעַ אֵיךְ עוֹרְכִין הַמִּצְוֹת וְהָעֲבֵרוֹת.

וְנוּכַל לְהַעֲמִיס הַדָּבָר בְּדִבְרֵי רַבּוֹתֵינוּ זַ"ל בְּסֻכָּה (דַּף נ"ג) לֶעָתִיד לָבֹא מְבִיאוֹ הַקָּדוֹשׁ־בָּרוּךְ־הוּא לַיֵּצֶר הָרָע כו' צַדִּיקִים נִדְמֶה לָהֶם כְּהַר, וּרְשָׁעִים נִדְמֶה לָהֶם כְּחוּט הַשַּׂעֲרָה כו' עַיֵּן שָׁם, וְהַדָּבָר מַפְלִיא יַעַן מַה הַהִשְׁתַּנּוּת הַלָּזֶה, אָכֵן הוּא הַדָּבָר אֲשֶׁר דִּבַּרְנוּ כִּי הָרְשָׁעִים שֶׁהִמְשִׁיכוּ עֲלֵיהֶן הַיֵּצֶר, בְּוַדַּאי הָיָה קָשֶׁה לָהֶם לִמְאֹד לִכְבֹּשׁ אֶת יִצְרָם, וְסוֹבְרִים הֵמָּה הֲגַם שֶׁבְּוַדַּאי יֵעָנְשׁוּ, אָכֵן רַק בְּגֶדֶר הַכְּבֵדוֹת, וּבֶאֱמֶת הַדָּבָר אֵינוֹ כֵן, כֵּיוָן שֶׁבִּבְחִירָתָם הִמְשִׁיכוּ עֲלֵיהֶן הַיֵּצֶר, וּמִזֶּה נַעֲשָׂה הַדָּבָר כָּבֵד לִפְנֵיהֶם, וְלָזֹאת מַרְאִין לָהֶם שֶׁהַיֵּצֶר הָרָע אֶצְלָם בִּבְחִינַת חוּט הַשַּׂעֲרָה, הֶפֶךְ דִּמְיוֹנָם.

וְכֵן צַדִּיקִים אֲשֶׁר מֵהֶרְגֵּילָם נַעֲשָׂה אֶצְלָם עֲבוֹדָתוֹ יִתְבָּרַךְ שְׁמוֹ לְתַעֲנוּג, סְבוּרִים לְקַבֵּל שָׂכָר רַק בְּגֶדֶר הַקַּלּוֹת, וְהַדָּבָר אֵינוֹ כֵן כֵּיוָן שֶׁמִּבְּחִירָתָם וּמִצִּדָּם נוֹלַד, הַקַּלּוֹת לִכְבֵדוֹת יֵחָשֵׁב וּשְׂכָרָם מְרֻבֶּה, לָזֹאת מַרְאִים לָהֶם כְּהַר.

וּמַה מְּאֹד יֶחֱרַד לֵב הָאָדָם, בְּהִתְבּוֹנְנוֹ הֵיטֵב עַל מַצָּבוֹ וּתְכוּנָתוֹ, מִי יוֹדֵעַ כַּמָּה אֲלָפִים בְּחִינוֹת יֵחָשֵׁב לוֹ לְאָחוֹר לִבְחִינַת הַקַּלּוֹת, מִפְּאַת שֶׁהִמְשִׁיךְ בִּבְחִירָתוֹ עָלָיו הַכְּבֵדוֹת כַּנִּזְכָּר לְעֵיל, וְעָנְשׁוֹ יוֹתֵר וְיוֹתֵר הַרְבֵּה מְאֹת אֲשֶׁר יְדַמֶּה, עַל פִּי הַדְּבָרִים הַלָּלוּ נוּכַל לָתֵת צִיּוּר לְהַמִּשְׁנָה בְּאָבוֹת, עַל כָּרְחֲךָ אַתָּה עָתִיד לִתֵּן דִּין וְחֶשְׁבּוֹן, הַיְנוּ דִּין כְּפִי מַצַּב הָאָדָם, חֶשְׁבּוֹן מַה שֶּׁהָיָה מַצָּבוֹ אִם לֹא הִמְשִׁיךְ עָלָיו הַיֵּצֶר, וְהָיָה הַדָּבָר נָקֵל עָלָיו הַרְבֵּה.

נִמְצָא לְפִי זֶה מַה שֶּׁמַּגְדִּיל בְּחִינַת הַמִּצְוֹת הַיְנוּ בְּחִינַת הַכְּבֵדוֹת, מְמַעֵט בְּחִינַת הָעֲבֵרוֹת, וּמִצְוָה אַחַת תֵּעָרֵךְ נֶגֶד כַּמָּה עֲבֵרוֹת בַּבְּחִינָה הַלָּזוֹ, לָזֹאת בְּמִצְרַיִם שֶׁהָיָה בִּבְחִינַת הַכְּבֵדוֹת לְמַעְלָה רֹאשׁ, הָיוּ

[actually] in the difficult category or the "easy" one, and how and what is each specifically, can never be known to a person perfectly. Rambam's words are right: only God, blessed be His name, Himself knows how to assess the value of good deeds and sins.

We can hang this [idea] onto the words of the Rabbis, of blessed memory, in Sukka (52a): "In the future, the Holy One, blessed be He, will bring the evil urge [and slaughter him]…. To the righteous, [the evil urge] appears as a huge mountain; to the wicked, it appears as a strand of hair…." See further there. It is an astonishing thing – why this variance? Indeed, this is what we said: for the wicked who brought the urge on themselves, of course, it was very difficult for them to conquer their urge; so they think that although they will certainly be punished, it would only be in the category of "difficult [to resist]" sins. But in truth, it is not so, because by their choice they brought the urge on themselves, making it become difficult for them. It is shown to them that their evil urge is really only a strand of hair – the opposite of what they imagine.

Similarly, the righteous, who by conditioning made service of God, blessed be His name, a pleasure, thought they would receive reward only in the category of "easy" observance. But it is not so. Since the ease was created by their choice and efforts, their "easy" observances are weighed as difficult ones and their reward is great. So [the evil urge] is shown to them [as big] as a mountain.

How much a person's heart must tremble when he thoroughly considers his condition and nature! Who knows how many thousands of levels will afterward be considered "easy" for him [to have kept] because he brought the difficulty upon himself by his choices! His punishment will be much, much greater than he imagines. On the basis of these words, we can now illuminate the mishna in Avot (4:22): "Willing or not, in the future, you will give a reckoning and account [before the supreme King of kings]…." That is, the reckoning (*din*) is based on the state of the person, and the accounting is based on what his situation would have been had he not brought the urge upon himself, in which case it would have been much easier for him [to resist].

We find accordingly that what magnifies the aspect of a mitzva, that is, its weight, reduces the aspect of a sin. One observance will outweigh many sins in this aspect. So in Egypt, where the "difficulty" aspect

בְּמַדְרֵגָה נִשְׂגָּבָה וְזָכוּ לְנִסִּים וְנִפְלָאוֹת, הוּא מַאֲמַר הַכָּתוּב וַתַּעַל שַׁוְעָתָם גו׳ מִן הָעֲבוֹדָה, הַיְנוּ מִפְּנֵי מָה נִתְקַבְּלָה תְּפִלָּתָם אֲשֶׁר הִיא מַדְרֵגָה נִשָּׂאָה, יַעַן הָיְתָה מִן הָעֲבוֹדָה, וְעָלוּ הַמִּצְוֹת בְּאֵיכוּתָן עַל הָעֲבֵרוֹת, הֲגַם שֶׁהָיוּ מְעַטִּים בְּמִסְפָּר.

וּבָזֹאת מַצָּה הִיא הַגְּאֻלָּה הַמְסוֹבָב, מָרוֹר הַשִּׁעְבּוּד סִבָּה, וְזֹאת מוּבָן הֲגַם שֶׁבְּמַעֲשֶׂה הַסִּבָּה קוֹדֶמֶת לַמְסוֹבָב, אָכֵן בְּסִפּוּר הַדָּבָר הוּא לְהֵפֶךְ, בַּתְּחִלָּה מְסַפְּרִין הַמְסוֹבָב וְאַחַר כָּךְ סִבָּתָהּ. לָזֹאת מַצָּה וְאַחַר־כָּךְ מָרוֹר. וְהִנֵּה בְּמִצְרַיִם הָיוּ בִּבְחִינַת הַכְּבֵדוּת נֶגֶד הָאָבוֹת, וְכֵן בְּבַיִת שֵׁנִי נֶגֶד הָרִאשׁוֹן, לָזֹאת הֵמָּה בְּחִינוֹת חֲדָשׁוֹת בְּחִינָה נַעֲלָה, זֶהוּ חֲדָשִׁים גַּם יְשָׁנִים.

וּבָזֹאת גַּם אֲנַחְנוּ נֹאמַר, לִמּוּד הַמּוּסָרִי קַלָּה הִיא מִפְּאַת עַצְמָהּ לִלְמֹד לִפְעָמִים עֵת סְדוּרָה, בְּהִתְפַּעֲלוּת הַנֶּפֶשׁ, אָכֵן חֲדָשָׁה הִיא, לָזֹאת תִּכָּנֵס בִּבְחִינַת הַכְּבֵדוּת, הֶאָחֲזוּ בָהּ וְאַל תַּרְפּוּהָ וּשְׂכַרְכֶם מְרֻבֶּה, תּוֹדִיעוּנִי נָא אִם הִגִּיעֲכֶם דְּבָרִי, וְתִתְבָּרְכוּ בְּשָׁנָה טוֹבָה כְּנַפְשְׁכֶם הַטּוֹב וְנֶפֶשׁ יְדִידְכֶם דּוֹרֵשׁ שְׁלוֹמְכֶם יִשְׂרָאֵל, עֶרֶב רֹאשׁ הַשָּׁנָה תר״ך.

---

10. Numerous statements by the sages (see, for example, Rashi on Ex. 12:6) note that the Israelites in Egypt were bare of mitzvot and even indistinguishable from the Egyptians. Nevertheless, under these oppressive circumstances, every mitzva and good deed carried tremendous weight.
11. Because of the greater degree of difficulty of doing the mitzvot.
12. Because of the greater degree of difficulty of doing the mitzvot.
13. See the opening paragraph of this letter, above.
14. Notice that despite his continuing emphasis on the supremacy of Torah learning, *de facto* R. Salanter has described Mussar study as a "new one," that is to say, it is

was overwhelming, [Israel] was on so elevated a level that they were worthy of miracles and wonders. This is the [meaning of] the scriptural verse: "Their groaning went up…out of their travail" (Ex. 2:23).[10] That is, why was their prayer accepted, which evinces a high level? Because it went up "out of their travail" – so these mitzvot exceeded the sins qualitatively, even though they were few in number.

[Returning to our opening questions,] matza [represents] the redemption, which is the effect, and *maror* [represents] the oppression, which was the cause [of the redemption]. So it is understandable that although in action, the cause precedes the effect, in a story we reverse the order. First we tell the effect, then [we explain] its cause. So first comes matza, then *maror*. And in Egypt, they were considered difficult as compared to the patriarchs,[11] and so the second Temple as compared to the first.[12] So they are categorized as "new ones," a higher category, and this is the meaning of "new ones and old ones."[13]

Similarly, we can say: Mussar study in its own right is easy – to study sometimes at a set time, with enthusiasm of the soul. But it is a "new one" – so it enters into the category of difficult ones![14] Take possession of it;[15] do not let it go; and your reward will be great. Let me know if my words have reached you, and may you be blessed with a good year as good as your own good souls!

Your friend who seeks your peace.
Israel.
Erev Rosh HaShana, 1860

weightier than the "old one," Torah study. This ranking is because of the difficulties of the time, which Mussar is addressing.

15. Compare Genesis 34:10.

ט

אָמְרוּ רַבּוֹתֵינוּ זַ״ל הַכֹּל בִּידֵי שָׁמַיִם חוּץ מִיִּרְאַת שָׁמַיִם, שֶׁהִיא תְּלוּיָה בְּדַעַת וּרְשׁוּת הָאָדָם לִקְנוֹתָהּ, כְּמַאֲמַר הַכָּתוּב וְעַתָּה יִשְׂרָאֵל כּוּ׳ כִּי אִם לְיִרְאָה – הַיִּרְאָה עֹז לָהּ בְּכֹחָהּ לֶאֱסֹר עֲבוֹתוֹת הַתַּאֲוָה, בַּל יִפְרְצוּ פֶּרֶץ לְחֵטְא וְאָשָׁם, מַה נּוֹרָא חִיּוּבָהּ עַל בֶּן תְּמוּתָה, כִּי ד׳ יָבִיא בַּמִּשְׁפָּט אֶת כָּל הַמִּפְעָל, וְסוֹף דָּבָר הַכֹּל נִשְׁמָע אֶת כָּל מַעֲשֵׂה הָאָדָם, אֵין דָּבָר נִפְקָד לָתֵת דִּין וְחֶשְׁבּוֹן, וְכִגְמוּל יָדָיו יֵעָשֶׂה לוֹ בַּעֲנָשִׁים רָעִים וּמָרִים, מַה טּוֹב כִּי יִתְחַמֵּם לֵב הָאָדָם בְּעוֹדוֹ בְּאִבּוֹ בַּחַיִּים חַיּוּתוֹ לִזְכֹּר אַחֲרִיתוֹ.

עַתָּה מַה הִיא הַיִּרְאָה וּמַה קְנִיָּתָהּ – אַחַת הִיא, הַרְחָבַת הַדְּבָרִים הַנּוֹדָעִים לַכֹּל, יִרְאַת הָעֹנֶשׁ הַנּוֹגֵעַ לַגְּוִיָּה וְנֶפֶשׁ הַגְּבֹהַּ לְמַעְלָה מִכָּל יִסּוּרֵי תֵּבֵל – אָכֵן לֹא בִּידִיעָתָם יִוָּסֵר הָאָדָם, כְּמַאֲמַר רַבּוֹתֵינוּ זַ״ל בְּשַׁבָּת (דַּף ל״א) יוֹדְעִין רְשָׁעִים שֶׁדַּרְכָּם לְמִיתָה כּוּ׳ שֶׁמָּא תֹּאמַר

1. *Yira*, translated sometimes as fear and sometimes as reverence (of God), has a double meaning: awe at God's majesty, and fear of divine punishment.
2. Based on Ecclesiastes 12:13–14.
3. It is noteworthy that in Letters 6–8, R. Salanter places a rather modern emphasis on each individual's uniqueness, including the difference in weight and type of punishment for each action taken, which is dependent on individual psychology such as ease or difficulty of resisting or personal situation and frame of mind as well as different cultural circumstances. Nevertheless, R. Salanter continues to believe

Letter 9

Our Rabbis, of blessed memory, said: "Everything is in the hands of Heaven, except for the fear (*yira*) of Heaven" (Berakhot 33b, Megilla 25a), for it hinges on consciousness, and a human being is free to acquire it. As it is said in Scripture: "Now, Israel, [what does the Lord your God request of you,] except to revere (*leyira*) [the Lord your God]" (Deut. 10:12). *Yira*[1] has the power to rein in desire, that it not breach [the Torah's limits] and [consequently cause] sin and guilt.

How awesome is this obligation on every mortal! For God will bring [each person] to judgment [for] everything done. At "the end of the matter, when all is said and done... all the works of man,"[2] nothing is overlooked [on which] to give judgment and accounting, and what one has done will be returned to him in bad and bitter punishments. How good it is when the heart of man is warmed – when he is still in the spring of life – to remember his end....[3]

Now, what is *yira* and how can it be acquired? One way is to expound well-known things: the fear of punishment that affects body and soul more than any possible suffering in this world. However, knowledge of this alone will not restrain a person. As the Rabbis, of blessed memory, state in Shabbat (31b): "Wicked men know their way leads to death...,"[4]

---

that the medieval mindset and fear of punishment in the World to Come remains the most powerful motivator of good behavior among his contemporaries.

4. The wicked know that their path leads to eternal death, but they block their emotions. This prevents that realization from entering their hearts.

שְׁכוּחָה הִיא מֵהֶן תַּלְמוּד לוֹמַר וְאַחֲרֵיהֶם בְּפִיהֶם יִרְצוּ סֶלָה עַיֵּן שָׁם, וְרַק בְּהַרְחָבָה בְּהִתְפַּעֲלוּת הַנֶּפֶשׁ תּוּסַר, לְהַרְחִיב הָרַעְיוֹן בְּצִיּוּרֵי חוּשִׁי, לְעוֹרֵר הַנֶּפֶשׁ בְּרִגְשַׁת הָאֵבָרִים, לִמְשֹׁךְ בְּקִרְבָּהּ דְּבָרִים הַנּוֹדָעִים, עָנְשֵׁי הַגְּוִיָּה וְהַנֶּפֶשׁ אֲשֶׁר לֹא לַזָּר יְקוּמוּ, כִּי אִם לְהָאָדָם עַצְמוֹ הָעוֹשֶׂה הָעֲבֵרָה, הוּא בְּעַצְמוֹ יֵעָנֵשׁ בְּעֹנֶשׁ מַר בְּאֵין מְנַחֵם.

בְּזֹאת – נַחֲזִיק טוֹבָה לְרַבּוֹתֵינוּ עֵינֵי הָעֵדָה, אֲשֶׁר הִרְחִיבוּ דִּבְרֵיהֶם בְּדִבְרֵי הַמּוּסָר, לְפַתֵּחַ שַׁדְמַת לְבַב הָאֶבֶן, וַאֲנַן מַה נַּעֲנֵי אֲבַתְרֵיהֶן, לִלְמֹד וְלֶהֱגוֹת בָּהֶן, לְהוֹסִיף לֶקַח וּתְבוּנָה, בְּצִיּוּרֵי הַפְּרָטִי אֲשֶׁר לְכָל אֶחָד בְּבַיִת מְיֻחָד, בְּאֵין שָׂטָן וְאֵין פֶּגַע, לִתְנוּעַת רִגְשַׁת הָאֵבָרִים הַנִּצְרָכִים לָעִיּוּן הַגָּדוֹל הַלָּזֶה.

---

5. Lest you say that it is simply forgotten from them, the verse states: "Their end they approve with their mouth, *sela*" (Ps. 49:14). They are aware of their fate and speak of it, but it does not affect them.
6. Mussar techniques include walking back and forth, or clapping or waving hands, all while one chants the words of the text.

and if you think they have forgotten this [end], we are told: "Their end they approve with their mouth, *sela*" (Ps. 49:14).[5] See further there.

Only by expanding on this emotional Mussar learning will the soul be restrained. [One needs] to expand the conceptual understanding through concrete imagery, to arouse the psyche with the agitation of the limbs,[6] to internalize known things: the punishments of the body and the soul, which will not happen to a stranger but to the person who does the sin himself.[7] He himself will be punished with bitter punishment, without any comforter.[8]

Thus, let us be grateful to our Rabbis, the eyes of the community, who expounded words of Mussar, digging furrows even in the heart of stone. And what can we add? To learn, to meditate on them, to increase instruction and understanding, using vivid images specific to each person, in a special house,[9] without distraction or interference, to set in motion the agitation of the limbs needed for this great study.

---

7. The *anokhi*, the self, will pay the penalty for all sins committed.
8. Compare Ecclesiastes 4:1.
9. I.e., the *Beit HaMussar* (Mussar *Shtiebel* or Mussar House).

י

מִכְתַּב כְּבוֹדָם רָאִיתִי, וְשָׂמַח לְבָבִי בִּצְפִיָּתִי רוֹדְפֵי צֶדֶק קִרְבַת ה׳ יֶחְפָּצוּן, וְנַפְשִׁי תִּלְבַּשׁ גִּילָה בְּאֵין תַּאֲוָתִי חוֹצֶצֶת, וּמַה יְעַוֵּר שִׂכְלִי – מִי יִתֵּן וְהָיָה זֶה לְבָבֵנוּ לְעַצְמֵנוּ לִשְׂמֹחַ בְּיִרְאַת ה׳ בְּאֵין שִׂטְנַת הַתַּאֲוָה – אַל יֶחֶרְדוּ מִקּוֹל הֲמֻלָּה וְאַל יֵחַתּוּ – יַחֲזִיקוּ בְּעֵץ הַחַיִּים הוּא לִמּוּד הַמּוּסָרִי, הַמְחַיֶּה הַשֵּׂכֶל לְבַל יִטְבַּע בְּכֹחוֹת הַתַּאֲווֹת הָרוֹגֶלֶת.

לוֹמֵד הַמּוּסָר חַי חַי יִקָּרֵא, בְּגִדְרוֹ כָּל חַי מַרְגִּישׁ, לָשׂוּם לַלֵּב לֵידַע חֶסְרוֹנוֹתָיו לְהִשְׁתּוֹקֵק לְתִקּוּנָם – לֹא יִפֹּל בְּרֶשֶׁת הַיֵּצֶר לְהַלְעִיג עַל יִרְאַת ה׳, לִהְיוֹת לְסֵטִים לְקַפֵּחַ נְפָשׁוֹת מֵעֲבוֹדָתוֹ יִתְבָּרַךְ שְׁמוֹ,

---

1. Compare Isaiah 51:1.
2. Compare Isaiah 58:2.
3. Since my desire/instinct is not blocking, there is nothing to distort my reason. It is accurately confirming the correctness and purity of my joy over your decision to focus on learning Mussar.
4. Compare Deuteronomy 5:25.
5. I.e., one who studies Mussar is emotionally alive. R. Salanter is poetically reversing the leper's proclamation, "I am impure! I am impure!" (Lev. 13:45). See Letter 4.
6. R. Salanter here and further on sounds one of his distinctive themes, which he will return to in later letters: the person who lives the unexamined life, without reverence or Mussar study, "dies" emotionally. His reason drowns in the flood of conflicting emotions and desires. Due to his preoccupation, habituation, and worldly activity,

Letter 10

I saw your excellencies' letter, and my heart rejoiced to see pursuers of righteousness,[1] seeking closeness to God.[2] My soul clothed itself in exultation without interference from my desire. What could blind my reason?[3] Would that this would be our heart's desire for ourselves,[4] to rejoice in the fear of God without the opposition of the desire. Do not be afraid of the noise of the crowd, and do not fear. Hold fast to the tree of life, that is, Mussar study, which keeps reason alive, that it not drown in the forces of the desire which habituate us [to give in to instinct].

One who studies Mussar proclaims, "I am alive! I am alive!"[5] Within its parameters, he lives and senses everything, taking to heart knowledge of his faults [and] yearning to correct them.[6] He will not fall into the net of the [evil] urge to mock the fear of God,[7] to be an "armed bandit"[8] and divert souls from His service,[9] blessed be His name – even

---

he loses his emotional "life." His standard behaviors become routine and he is "dead" in a certain sense.

7. Some Torah scholars belittle the study of Mussar. In effect, they mock striving for fear of God as excessive.
8. An ignorant person who talks us out of studying Mussar is like a thief (who robs us of opportunity to achieve reverence of God); a Torah scholar who talks us out of studying Mussar is like an "armed bandit" – he has a loaded weapon, i.e., his Torah learning is impressive, and this convinces us to listen to him and stop our study of Mussar.
9. R. Salanter is referring to Torah scholars who state that Mussar study is a diversion from learning Torah. In so doing, they have fallen into the net of the evil urge.

גַּם בְּאֵין תַּאֲוָה מוֹצֵאת – עַיִן רוֹאָה אֶת הַחַטָּאת אֲשֶׁר לַשָּׁמַיִם יַגִּיעַ, וְהַלֵּב חוֹמֵד לְהַחֲזִיק בַּמּוּסָר לְמַעַן סוּר מִשְּׁאוֹל מָטָּה – לְעֻמָּתָם בָּרוּךְ יֹאמַר לְקָרֵב נְפָשׁוֹת לְיִרְאַת ד׳, הֶעָמָל מוּעָט וְהַשָּׂכָר הַרְבֵּה מִמַּצְדִּיקֵי הָרַבִּים אֲשֶׁר כַּכּוֹכָבִים יַזְהִירוּ.

אַל יִפֹּל לֵב הָאָדָם בְּלָמְדוֹ מוּסָר וְאֵינֶנּוּ מִתְפַּעֵל, וְאֵין רֹשֶׁם בְּנַפְשׁוֹ מוֹצֵאת לְשַׁנּוֹת דַּרְכּוֹ – יֵדַע נֶאֱמָנָה אִם כִּי לֹא נִגְלֶה לְעֵינֵי בָשָׂר הָרֹשֶׁם, עֵינֵי הַשֵּׂכֶל רוֹאוֹת, בְּרִבּוֹת הָעִתִּים, בְּרִבּוּי הַלִּמּוּד, מֵהִתְקַבְּצוּת הָרְשִׁימוֹת הַנֶּעֱלָמוֹת, לְאָדָם אַחֵר יֵהָפֵךְ, וְתַאֲוָתוֹ נֶאֶסְרָה לְבַל תִּפְרֹץ הַרְבֵּה, וְיֵשׁ אֲשֶׁר תִּבָּטֵל, וְהַנִּסָּיוֹן יָעִיד בְּהַשְׁקָפָה קַלָּה, עַל לוֹמֵד מוּסָר אִם מְעַט כו׳, בְּיֶתֶר שְׂאֵת יַעֲלֶה עַל בְּנֵי גִילוֹ בְּרַעְיוֹנוֹ וְכָל הַנְהָגָתוֹ.

הוּא הַדָּבָר נוּכַל לְהַעֲמִיס בְּדִבְרֵי חֲזַ״ל, בְּאָבוֹת דְּרַבִּי נָתָן פֶּרֶק ו׳ וְזֶה לְשׁוֹנוֹ. מֶה הָיְתָה תְּחִלָּתוֹ שֶׁל רַבִּי עֲקִיבָא, אָמְרוּ בֶּן אַרְבָּעִים שָׁנָה הָיָה וְלֹא שָׁנָה כְּלוּם, פַּעַם אַחַת הָיָה עוֹמֵד עַל פִּי הַבְּאֵר, אָמַר מִי חָקַק אֶבֶן זוֹ, אָמְרוּ לוֹ הַמַּיִם שֶׁתָּדִיר נוֹפְלִים עָלֶיהָ בְּכָל יוֹם. אָמְרוּ לוֹ עֲקִיבָא, אִי אַתָּה קוֹרֵא אֲבָנִים שָׁחֲקוּ מַיִם, מִיָּד הָיָה דָּן רַבִּי עֲקִיבָא קַל וָחֹמֶר בְּעַצְמוֹ, מָה רַךְ פָּסַל אֶת הַקָּשֶׁה, דִּבְרֵי תוֹרָה שֶׁקָּשָׁה כְּבַרְזֶל, עַל אַחַת כַּמָּה וְכַמָּה שֶׁיְּחַקְקוּ אֶת לִבִּי שֶׁהוּא בָּשָׂר וָדָם, מִיָּד חָזַר לִלְמֹד תּוֹרָה כו׳ עַיֵּן שָׁם, כִּי רַבִּי עֲקִיבָא בִּתְחִלַּת לִמּוּדוֹ, בְּאֵין רֹשֶׁם מוֹצֵאת אֶצְלוֹ, אָמַר נוֹאָשׁ לְנַפְשׁוֹ, וְהֶרְאוּ לוֹ סְתִירַת הַדָּבָר מִשְּׁפִיכַת הַמַּיִם עַל הָאֶבֶן, אֲשֶׁר לֹא יֵרָאֶה מְאוּמָה הִשְׁתַּנּוּת בְּהָאֶבֶן, וְעִם כָּל זֶה הַמְחַקְרִים בְּשִׂכְלָם גּוֹזְרִים, כִּי נַעֲשָׂה רֹשֶׁם נֶעֱלָם מֵהֶרְגֵּשׁ אֱנוֹשִׁי,

10. When instinct, desire, and evil urge are not present to block learning Mussar, those misguided Torah scholars dismiss it.

11. A reference to the chorus of angels uttering blessing, quoted from Ezekiel 3:12 in the *Kedusha* prayer.

12. Daniel 12:3.

13. Job 14:19.

when desire is not present.[10] The eye sees the sin which reaches to the heavens. And the heart desires to hold onto Mussar in order to remove itself from the pit below. [Of those pursuing the study of Mussar,] the response [I] say: "Blessed it is"[11] to bring souls close to the fear of God. The work is little but the reward is great – for "those who make the many righteous" will "shine like the stars…"[12]

A person should not be discouraged when he learns Mussar and is not stirred, and no sufficient impression is made on his psyche for him to change his way. He should know surely that even though the impression is not apparent to the human eye, the mind's eye sees. Over time, through increased study, from the accumulation of the unseen impressions he will be transformed into a different person. His desire will be reined in so it does not break out much; sometimes it even will be nullified. Experience testifies, even through cursory observation, that one who learns Mussar – a little [or a lot]… – will surpass his peers in his understanding and all his behavior.

This is something we can hang on the words of our Sages, of blessed memory, in *Avot DeRabbi Natan*, chapter 6:

> How did R. Akiva begin? They said: He was forty years old and had never learned. One time he stood at the mouth of a well. He said: "Who carved this stone?" They said to him: "The drops of water which fall on it continuously every day." They said to him: "Akiva have you not read [the verse] 'Stones rubbed out by water'?"[13] Immediately, Akiva said to himself, "*A fortiori* – if the soft [water] has carved out the hard [stone], the words of Torah, which are strong as iron, all the more so will engrave my heart which is only flesh and blood." He immediately turned to study Torah…."

See further there. For at the beginning of his learning, in the absence of visible impression on himself, R. Akiva despaired for his soul, so they showed him the refutation [of his despair] from the water pouring on the stone. For though he could not see any change in the stone, still, for all this, those who probe the matter rationally deduce that an impression not visible to human senses was being made. This was the cause of the

הִיא הַסִּבָּה לַחֲקִיקַת הָאֶבֶן, מֵרִבּוּי הַמַּיִם בִּרְבוֹת הַיָּמִים, מֵהִתְקַבְּצוּת הָרְשִׁימוֹת הַבִּלְתִּי נִרְגָּשׁוֹת.

בָּזֹאת – הָאָדָם אֲשֶׁר לֹא נִטְבַּע טְבִיעָה מִיתִית בְּרִגְשַׁת הַתַּאֲוָה, וְשִׂכְלוֹ חַי לְבַקֵּשׁ מָנוֹחַ לְנַפְשׁוֹ לְחַיֵּי עַד, וְלִבּוֹ כְּלֵב הָאֶבֶן, מַיִם הַרְבֵּה יִשְׁפֹּךְ עַל נַפְשׁוֹ, הוּא לִמּוּד הַמּוּסָרִי, וּרְשִׁימוֹת נֶעֱלָמוֹת בְּקִרְבּוֹ יָוָלְדוּ, לְנַהֲלֵהוּ לְדֶרֶךְ הַחַיִּים, הוּא לִמּוּד הַתּוֹרָה הַשְּׁקוּלָה כְּנֶגֶד כָּל הָעוֹלָם, וּמִצְוֹתֶיהָ שֶׁל תּוֹרָה (יְרוּשַׁלְמִי פֵּאָה פֶּרֶק א׳) וּמְשׁוּלָה לְמַיִם, וּמַיִם הַמְּתוּקִים הָאֵלֶּה, יַחְקְקוּ אֶת לְבָבוֹ לְשָׁמְרוֹ מִכָּל רַע וּלְשַׁנּוֹת דַּרְכּוֹ לְטוֹבָה.

hollowing out of the stone – from the multiple drops of water over many days; [the same would occur to the human] from the accumulation of the many impressions, which were not detected by the senses.

Thus, a person who has not drowned to death [emotionally] in the turbulence of desire, whose reason is still alive and is seeking a refuge for his soul in eternal life, even though his heart is still a heart of stone: let him pour a lot of water – that is, Mussar study – on his soul. Hidden impressions will be born inside him, to lead him to the way of life – that is the study of Torah, which equals the whole world and the commandments of the Torah (Y. Pe'ah 1:1). [The Torah] is compared to water. These sweet waters will engrave his heart, saving him from all evil and changing his way to the better.

יא

כְּבוֹד יְדִידַי וְרֵעַי נֵרְכֶם יָאִיר, אִישׁ לְפִי מַהֲלָלוֹ יְהֻלַּל, וִיקַבְּלוּ בִּרְכָתָם מֵאֵת ה׳ יִתְבָּרַךְ שְׁמוֹ כְּנַפְשָׁם לְטוֹב.

הִנֵּה טוֹבָה תּוֹכַחַת מְגֻלָּה, הַיּוֹצֵא מֵאַהֲבָה מְסֻתֶּרֶת, בָּאתִי לְהוֹכִיחַ אֶתְכֶם, וּלְזָרֵז אֶת כְּבוֹדְכֶם הָרָמָה, שֶׁתִּרְאוּ לְהִתְאַמֵּץ בְּכָל עֹז, אִישׁ לְפִי שִׂכְלוֹ וְעִנְיָנוֹ, לְחַזֵּק לִמּוּד הַמּוּסָרִי בְּכָל תֹּקֶף וָעֹז, וְהָעִקָּר לְהַטּוֹת לְבַב גְּדוֹלֵי הָעָם, אֲשֶׁר בֵּית יִשְׂרָאֵל יָצוּפוּ עֲלֵיהֶם וְסָרִים לְמִשְׁמַעְתָּם, שֶׁהֵמָּה יִתְּנוּ הִשְׁתַּדְּלוּתָם בָּזֶה, כְּפִי אֲשֶׁר יִהְיֶה לְאֵל יָדָם, דָּבָר קַל הוּא אִם תִּתְּנוּ לֵב לָזֶה, לַעֲשׂוֹת הַדָּבָר בְּהַשְׂכֵּל לְמַעַן הָאֱמֶת, לְהַשִּׂיג מֵהֶם מִכְתָּבִים רְאוּיִם וַהֲגוּנִים.

אַל יֵקַל נָא בְּעֵינֵיכֶם הַדָּבָר לְזַכּוֹת אֶת הָרַבִּים, לְעוֹרְרָם אֶל הַמִּלְחָמָה הַחֲזָקָה, הִיא מִלְחֶמֶת הַיֵּצֶר, אֲשֶׁר לֹא תָקוּם וְלֹא תִהְיֶה בְּלִי לִמּוּד הַמּוּסָרִי כָּרָאוּי, וְכָל הַתּוֹרָה וְהָעֲבוֹדָה זוּלַת הַיִּרְאָה, הוּא רַק מִצְוַת אֲנָשִׁים מְלֻמָּדָה, אֲשֶׁר לָזֹאת רוּחַ קַלָּה תֶּהְדְּפֶנּוּ, כְּמַאֲמַר חֲכָמֵינוּ זַ״ל כָּל שֶׁיִּרְאַת חֶטְאוֹ כוּ׳ חָכְמָתוֹ מִתְקַיֶּמֶת.

---

1. Proverbs 27:21.
2. Proverbs 27:5.
3. Or "conferring benefit on."
4. Isaiah 29:13.
5. This was one of R. Salanter's deepest criticisms of the Orthodox community of his time, the driver of his push for everyone to study and practice Mussar. The present way of life appeared to be dominant, but it was built on external observance and

Letter 11

My honored companions and friends, may your light increase! May each be praised by what makes him worthy of praise,[1] and may they receive their blessing from God, blessed be His name, for good, as they desire!

Since "open reproof that comes from hidden love is good,"[2] I have come to reprove you and to urge on your high excellencies. See to it to make an all-out effort, each according to his intellect and situation, to strengthen Mussar study with all your might and courage. The main thing is to turn the hearts of the greatest of our people, to whom the people of Israel look to and submit, that they should make efforts in this area to the extent they can. It is easily accomplished if you put your mind to it – just go about it intelligently for the sake of the truth and obtain appropriate and proper letters [of support] from them.

Do not underestimate the significance of purifying[3] the masses, of awakening them to the fierce battle, the battle with the [evil] urge, which cannot be waged or be won without proper Mussar study. Without reverence, all Torah and service is only "commandment of men learned by rote,"[4] which therefore can be blown over[5] by a slight wind. As our Sages, of blessed memory, said: "If his fear of sin [precedes his wisdom,] his wisdom will endure."[6]

---

conformity. He saw that although he and the religious leaders opposed its rising influence, modernity was coming. He warned that unless religion was deepened and internalized, the winds of modernity would blow down this house of straw.

6. Avot 3:9.

אִי לָזֹאת מִי לֹא יָבִין הַהֶכְרֵחַ הַגָּדוֹל לְלִמּוּד הַמּוּסָרִי בְּעִתּוֹתֵינוּ אֵלֶּה, אֲשֶׁר הַפַּרְנָסָה דְּחוּקָה וְהָעֲבוֹדָה מִתְמַעֶטֶת, וּמִי יִתְמֹךְ גּוֹרָלָהּ, מִי יְגַדֵּר פִּרְצוֹתֶיהָ, אִם לֹא לִמּוּד הַמּוּסָרִי, הַמְטַהֶרֶת כָּל תַּחֲלוּאֵי הַנֶּפֶשׁ לַמַּעֲמִיקִים בָּהּ כָּרָאוּי.

לָזֹאת אַשְׁרֵיכֶם, אֲשֶׁר בָּאתָה מִצְוָה רַבָּה הַלָּזוֹ לְיֶדְכֶם, מַתָּנָה גְּדוֹלָה הִיא מֵאֵת ד׳ יִתְבָּרַךְ שְׁמוֹ, תְּקַבְּלוּהָ בְּאַהֲבָה וְתַעֲשׂוּ בְּנֶפֶשׁ חֲפֵצָה, בְּכָל עֹז וְתַעֲצוּמוֹת, וּתְקַבְּלוּ שְׂכַר כֻּלָּם בָּזֶה וּבַבָּא כְּנַפְשׁוֹתֵיכֶם וּכְנֶפֶשׁ יְדִידְכֶם דּוֹרֵשׁ טוֹבַתְכֶם. יִשְׂרָאֵל.

7. R. Salanter seems to be referring to the increasing penetration of the modern economy into the Jewish community. This unsettled some traditional livelihoods and generated economic pressures within the community, which lessened study of Torah and/or lessened observance.

Accordingly, who cannot grasp the great need to study Mussar in these, our times, when livelihood is difficult and service [of God] is diminishing?[7] Who will uphold [service of God's] future? Who will repair its breaches – if not Mussar study, which cures all sicknesses of the soul for those who delve into it properly!

So you are fortunate! This great mitzva has come into your hands. It is a great gift to you from God, blessed be His name. Accept it with love and do it willingly, with all strength and might. Then you will receive the reward of all [of them][8] in this world and the next – as you desire, and as your friend, who seeks your welfare, desires for you –

Israel

8. This is in accordance with R. Salanter's teaching that one who turns another person to good deeds and commandments is rewarded by God for those good deeds and commandments as well.

יב

הִנְנִי בָּא לְמַלְּאוֹת דִּבְרֵי אֲשֶׁר נִדְבַּרְנוּ טֶרֶם נְסִיעָתִי, וּלְעוֹרֵר עַל דְּבַר חִזּוּק בֵּית הַמִּדְרָשׁ לְהַרְחִיב תּוֹרָה, אֵין עַל עָפָר מָשְׁלָה, אָכֵן גַּם הַיִּרְאָה וְלִמּוּד הַמּוּסָר רֵאשִׁיתָהּ, כַּאֲשֶׁר הֶאֱרִיכוּ רַבּוֹתֵינוּ נוּחֵי נֶפֶשׁ זי״ע הֲלֹא בְּסִפְרֵיהֶם, וּבְאֵין מָקוֹם פַּסּוּ שׁוֹחֲרֶיהָ, לָזֹאת בִּהְיוֹת יְמִינְכֶם פְּשׁוּטָה, לְהַחֲזִיק בְּעֵץ הַחַיִּים, אִכְלוּ וִחְיוּ לְעוֹלָם, לְהַרְחִיב מָקוֹם לַתּוֹרָה וְלַתְּעוּדָה, תְּנוּ נָא יָד, לִתְמֹךְ אֲחוֹתָהּ הַצְּעִירָה הַנּוֹפֶלֶת, אֲשֶׁר מֵעָפָר תְּשַׁח אֲמָרֶיהָ לֵאמֹר, סַמְּכוּנִי נָא סַמְּכוּנִי בְּמָקוֹם צַר.

וְהָיָה הָאִישׁ רַךְ הַלֵּבָב, אֲשֶׁר יָנוּעַ לְבָבוֹ וְיָסוּר שָׁמָּה לְהָבִיא מִנְחָה טְהוֹרָה, לִשְׁפֹּךְ נַפְשׁוֹ אֶל ד׳ יִתְבָּרַךְ שְׁמוֹ, בְּשִׁבִירַת הַלֵּבָב אֲשֶׁר לֹא יִבְזֶה, אָז אֶשָּׂא רֹאשׁ וְאֵדַע כִּי נִשְׁרַשׁ זֶרַע לְצֶדֶק, אוֹ אָז יִכָּנַע לְבָבוֹ לְהֵטִיב מְעַט דְּרָכָיו וּלְיַשֵּׁר מַעֲלָלָיו, הֲלֹא הִצְלִיחַ דַּרְכֵּי לְהוֹצִיא פְּרִי יָקָר לְמַעֲנֵהוּ – שִׁמְעוּ נָא לְקוֹלָהּ וְיִשְׁמַע אֲלֵיכֶם ד׳, לְהַצְלִיחֲכֶם בְּכָל אֲשֶׁר תִּפְנוּ לְטוֹבָה, וַתְּרוּ נָא וְאַל תַּעַמְדוּ עַל הַמִּקָּח.

---

1. I.e., to include Mussar study in the basic Torah study curriculum for everyone.
2. Compare Genesis 3:22.
3. Compare Isaiah 29:4.
4. Compare Song of Songs 2:5.
5. Compare Deuteronomy 20:8.
6. Compare Psalms 51:19.
7. Compare Psalms 97:11; if his students can establish the study of Mussar in the *beit*

Letter 12

I have come to fulfill my word as we agreed before I departed and to spur you to strengthen the *beit midrash* through expanded Torah study.[1] There is nothing on earth to compare to it. However, reverence and study of Mussar is the beginning, as our Rabbis, may their souls rest in peace and may their merit protect us, expounded at great length in their books. In the absence of a place [for Mussar study], those who seek it are few. So, since your right hand is extended to grasp the tree of life – eat and live forever![2] – expand the place for Torah and law, but please give a hand to uphold its falling younger sister [i.e., Mussar], who, from the dust, cries[3] and says: "Strengthen me; uphold me[4] in my dire situation."

It will come to be, that a soft-hearted person,[5] whose heart is moved, will turn [to the Mussar House] to bring a pure offering, pouring out his soul to God, blessed be His name, with a broken heart, which God will not despise.[6] Then I will lift my head and know that the seed planted for the righteous person is rooted.[7] For then his[8] heart will humble itself[9] to improve his ways a bit and to straighten his actions. Then my way will have succeeded in bringing him good results.

Hearken to [Mussar's] voice and God will listen to you – so that you may succeed in everything good that you turn to.

---

midrash, then R. Salanter will know that his work was not in vain, and that Mussar study will continue to expand, even where he is no longer present.

8. The lay student of Mussar.
9. Compare Leviticus 26:41.

הָקֵלּוּ נָא בְּהַפְּרָטִים, כִּי דוֹרְשָׁיו מוּעָטִים וַחֲלָשִׁים, פֶּן תִּדְחָקוּן וְיִנָּזוֹרוּ הָלְאָה – אַמְּצוּ בִּרְכַּיִם כּוֹשְׁלוֹת, וְחַזְּקוּ יָדַיִם רָפוֹת, לְיִרְאָה אֶת ד׳ וּלְהַלֵּךְ בִּדְרָכָיו לְטוֹב כָּל הַיָּמִים.

יְדִידְכֶם הַמְבָרְכֶם לְשָׁנָה טוֹבָה

דּוֹרֵשׁ שְׁלוֹמְכֶם בְּכָבוֹד

Compromise a bit, and don't insist on your own terms. Be flexible about the details, for those who seek [Mussar] are few and weak, lest you push them away, and they become further alienated. Encourage failing knees and strengthen weak hands to fear God and to walk in His ways for good all the time.[10]

Your friend who blesses you with a good year, who seeks your well-being.

Respectfully...

10. Compare Deuteronomy 10:12–13.

יג

מעמיל שְׁנַת תר״ך כו׳.

רָאִיתִי דְּבָרָיו, הַרְבֵּה עָשׂוּ וְלֹא עָלְתָה בְּיָדָם, וְגָרְמוּ חִלּוּל הַשֵּׁם, וְיָרֵאתִי לְהַלְבִּישׁ אֶת עַצְמִי, בְּאִצְטְלָא שֶׁאֵינָהּ רְאוּיָה לִי עַד כָּאן לְשׁוֹנוֹ – עַל סוֹף דְּבָרָיו אֶתְוַכַּח, כִּי נָפַל בְּטָעוּת הָעוֹלָם לְהַחֲזִיק לִמּוּד הַמּוּסָר בְּבַיִת מְיֻחָד לָזֶה, לְאֵיזֶה מַדְרֵגָה אוֹ לְמִדַּת חֲסִידוּת, בְּזֹאת כַּאֲשֶׁר יִרְאוּ אֶחָד הוֹלֵךְ לְבֵית הַמּוּסָר, יִרְמְזוּן עָלָיו בְּעֵינֵיהֶם, מִי הוּא זֶה אֲשֶׁר מְלָאוֹ לִבּוֹ לַעֲשׂוֹת וּלְהַחֲזִיק בַּמַּדְרֵגָה, וִידַקְדְּקוּ עַל הַנְהָגָתוֹ, הָאִישׁ כָּזֶה יַעֲשֶׂה כָּכָה.

לֹא כֵן אַחַי הַדָּבָר, אֵין זֶה מַעֲלָה וְלֹא מַדְרֵגָה רַק הֶכְרֵחִי – לָאִישׁ הַחוֹלֶה נָגוּעַ בַּעֲוֹנוֹת וּפְשָׁעִים, אֲשֶׁר מָרָה תִּהְיֶה בָּאַחֲרוֹנָה, לֵילֵךְ שָׁמָּה לִשְׁפֹּךְ נַפְשׁוֹ בְּלִמּוּד הַמּוּסָר, אוּלַי תַּצִּילֵהוּ מְעַט מִצָּרָתוֹ, תַּכְנִיעַ מַה יִּצְרוֹ, לְבַל יֵלֵךְ שׁוֹבָב בְּדֶרֶךְ לִבּוֹ, וּבֶאֱמֶת אֵין מָקוֹם לָחוּשׁ לְחִלּוּל ה׳, אֵין כָּאן מְקוֹמוֹ, כִּי גֶּדֶר שְׁמִירַת חִלּוּל ה׳, לְהַחֲזִיק יוֹתֵר בִּשְׁמִירַת הַתּוֹרָה וְהַמִּצְוָה, לֹא לְמַעְטָה, הִיא רַק תַּאֲוָה מַה שֶּׁהָאָדָם

1. Compare Berakhot 35b, where the Talmud records a dispute between R. Yishmael and R. Shimon bar Yoḥai. R. Shimon ruled that one should study Torah all the time and not spend time pursuing a livelihood. R. Yishmael asserted that one must work for a living. Abaye concludes the discussion by saying that "many tried to act according to R. Shimon's view but did not succeed, and many acted according to R. Yishmael and succeeded." The recipient of this letter has reported to R. Salanter that the people in the community were comparing the idea of serious study of Mussar to R. Shimon's utopian and unworkable idea of exclusively learning Torah. This

Letter 13

Memel, 1860...

I have seen your words: "Many tried to do it but did not succeed,[1] and they caused a desecration of [God's] name. So I feared to dress myself in a garment of which I am not worthy."[2] It is with your last statement that I take issue, for you have fallen into the same mistake the world makes: to consider Mussar study in a house set aside for it as achieving some exalted level or pious virtue. Therefore, when they see someone going to the Mussar House, they raise their eyebrows at him: "Who is this who presumes to do this[3] and hold himself on an exalted level?" So they nit-pick his every behavior: "How can a person like this do such a thing!?"

This is not the way it is, my brother. [Learning Mussar] is no [act of] superiority, no exalted state, but a necessity for a sick person, plagued with transgressions and sins that will [lead to a] bitter end, to go there to pour out his soul in study of Mussar. Perhaps it will save him a little from his troubles and subdue his [evil] urge somewhat so that he does not go, uncontrolled, in the way of his heart. In truth, there is no room for concern about the desecration of [God's] name. It is out of place here. The parameter of guarding against the desecration of God's name is that it leads one to hold more strongly to observance – not to

student was concerned that pursuing a policy of serious Mussar study will fail, and the backfire will damage the credibility of any learning of Mussar.

2. I.e., one who studies Mussar seriously appears to be posturing as a paragon of piety, which he is not. Compare Bava Metzia 113b and *Shita Mekubetzet* on Bava Metzia 114a.

אֵינוֹ רוֹצֶה שֶׁיִּלְעֲגוּ עָלָיו חֲבֵרָיו, פּוֹשֶׁטֶת טְלָפֶיהָ לְהַלְבִּישָׁהּ בִּמְעִיל הַצֶּדֶק.

מַה יִּתֵּן וּמַה יּוֹסִיף דְּבָרִים, אִם הָאָדָם יִשְׁכַּח אַחֲרִיתוֹ, לְבַל לְחַפֵּשׂ אֵיזֶה תְּעָלָה לְנַפְשׁוֹ אִם מְעַט כּוּ׳. בְּצָרְכֵי הַגּוּפָנִי וּבְחָלְיוֹ, הָאָדָם מְחַפֵּשׂ בְּכָל עֹז, אֶת אֲשֶׁר יִהְיֶה לְאֵל יָדוֹ, לְכָל הַפָּחוֹת לְהָקֵל מָה עָנְיוֹ וּמְרוּדוֹ וּמַחֲלָתוֹ, וּמַדּוּעַ לֹא יַעֲשֶׂה הָאָדָם כֹּה לְנַפְשׁוֹ – הַחוֹלֶה לֹא יִתְבַּיֵּשׁ עֲשׂוֹת דְּבָרִים, אֲשֶׁר אֵינָם לְפִי כְּבוֹדוֹ, וּמַדּוּעַ לְנַפְשׁוֹ יָצִיץ וְיַשְׁגִּיחַ עַל דִּבְרַת הָאָדָם, אֲשֶׁר אֵינָם יוֹדְעִים מְאוּמָה מַה הוּא – הוּא רַק טִפּוּל הָאָדָם, בְּטִרְדַּת רַעְיוֹנוֹ לְמַעְלָה רֹאשׁ, לְהַרְבּוֹת צָרְכֵי הַגּוּפָנִי, אֲשֶׁר תְּטַמְטֵם אֶת לֵב הָאָדָם, מִבְּלִי לְהַשְׁגִּיחַ עַל תַּכְלִיתוֹ הַנִּצְחִי.

אַחַת הִיא לְהָאָדָם, בִּפְרָט לְהֶעָמוּס בְּמַשָּׂא וּמַתָּן, לַעֲשׂוֹת חֹק חָזָק לֵילֵךְ לְבֵית הַמּוּסָר, לִשְׁפֹּךְ נַפְשׁוֹ וְרוּחוֹ, וְכָל הָרוּחוֹת שֶׁבָּעוֹלָם לֹא יְנִזְוֻנּוּ אָחוֹר מְאוּמָה מִזֶּה, אָז חַי יִקָּרֵא, לֹא מֵת חַס וְשָׁלוֹם שֶׁאֵינוֹ מַרְגִּישׁ מְאוּמָה, וְכָל אֲשֶׁר אֶל הַחַיִּים יְחֻבַּר יֵשׁ בִּטָּחוֹן.

---

3. Compare Esther 7:5.
4. Lit. "sticks out its hooves" – as a non-kosher pig "hypocritically" shows off its split hooves as if it were a kosher animal.
5. In *Halakhic Man*, R. Joseph B. Soloveitchik reports R. Chaim Soloveitchik's (of Brisk) rejection of R. Isaac Blazer's proposal to introduce the study of Mussar at the Volozhin Yeshiva. R. Blazer, one of R. Salanter's preeminent students, was attempting to spread the Mussar movement through the Lithuanian yeshivot at the end of the nineteenth century. R. Hayim replied: "If a person is sick, we prescribe castor oil for him. However, it is certain that if a healthy person ingests castor oil, he will become very sick" (Philadelphia: Jewish Publication Society, 1983, p.75). In the view of the Lithuanian yeshiva establishment, the average healthy religious person can meet all of his spiritual needs by studying Torah regularly. In fact, by implication, the study of Mussar may encourage or induce spiritual illness. Only a person who is spiritually troubled or sick needs to study Mussar. R. Salanter, for

diminish. This [argument expresses] only the desire of a person not wanting his peers to mock him – [a desire that] hypocritically[4] dresses itself in clothes of righteousness.

What can words give or add? If a person forgets his end and does not seek any help, small or great, for his soul ... ? With regard to physical needs, or when sick, a person seeks with all his might to do whatever he can to at least lighten his distress and suffering and sickness. Why wouldn't a person do the same for his soul?[5] A sick person would not be ashamed to do things that are beneath him, so why, when it comes to his soul, should he look at or pay attention to the talk of people who know nothing about this! [This hesitation] is only like diverting a man by inundating and preoccupying his mind with the proliferation of bodily needs that stultify the human heart, so he does not pay attention to his eternal purpose.

There is only one way for a person – especially one overloaded by business: to make a hard-and-fast rule to go to the Mussar House, to pour out his soul and spirit. All the winds in the world must not blow him back from this at all. Then he can be called "alive," not an unfeeling corpse (God forbid).[6] And as long as he is connected to life, he can rest assured.[7]

---

his part, is convinced that everyone is troubled spiritually and falling short of the Torah's ideal. Therefore, Mussar is a necessity, not a pious luxury and certainly not a spiritual excess. Further historical development showed that, when not fortified by Mussar study and the internalization of the religious way, both yeshiva students and the laity were more vulnerable to being religiously undermined by the modern cultural values that conflicted with tradition.

6. R. Salanter returns to one of his central images: a person who learns Mussar – is self-critical, grows emotionally, and improves his character – is alive, with genuine emotions such as guilt and yearning for improvement. One who is complacent and not self-critical, even if he is going through the motions of doing good things, is really "dead" and not sensitive to the need for kindness or the need for repentance; a kind of zombie. Compare elements of Letters 1, 2, 3, 6, and 9.
7. This inner assurance and rootedness in life enables the person to be indifferent to the opinions and dismissals of others.

יד

ב״ה. רְאֵה – בְּרָכָה.

מִלְּפָנִים כַּאֲשֶׁר יָדַעְתִּי – כָּל אִישׁ אֲחָזוֹ פַּלָּצוּת, מִקּוֹל הַקּוֹרֵא קָדוֹשׁ אֱלוּל. הַחֲרָדָה הַלָּזוֹ נָשְׂאָה פִּרְיָהּ לְהִתְקָרֵב לַעֲבוֹדָתוֹ יִתְבָּרַךְ שְׁמוֹ, אִישׁ לְפִי עֶרְכּוֹ – אָכֵן לֹא לְפִי מֻשְׂכָּל הָרִאשׁוֹן, אֲשֶׁר לְהָאִישׁ אֲשֶׁר בְּכָל הַשָּׁנָה נִתְרַחֵק מֵעֲבוֹדָתוֹ יִתְבָּרַךְ שְׁמוֹ, תִּלְבָּשֶׁנּוּ הַפַּחַד וְהַדְּאָגָה יוֹתֵר מֵאֵימַת הַדִּין. אֲשֶׁר רַק הַתּוֹרָה וְהַמַּעֲשִׂים טוֹבִים הֵמָּה הַתְּרִיס מֵהַפֻּרְעָנוּת רַחֲמָנָא לִצְלַן, וְנֶהְפַּךְ הָיְתָה, שִׁנּוּי הַמַּעֲשֶׂה לְטוֹבָה, הַתְרָאָה בְּכִפְלַיִם, בְּהָאִישׁ אֲשֶׁר כָּל הַשָּׁנָה אָחַז דַּרְכּוֹ בַּקֹּדֶשׁ – לְפִי עֶרְכּוֹ – מֵהָאִישׁ אֲשֶׁר כָּל הַשָּׁנָה הָלַךְ חֲשֵׁכִים בְּאֵין נֹגַהּ – לְפִי עֶרְכּוֹ.

סִבַּת הִתְחַלְּפוּת הַלָּזֶה, שׁוֹנוֹת הֵנָּה גַּשְׁמִיּוּת וְרוּחָנִיּוּת, קֹטֶב סִבַּת הַגַּשְׁמִיּוּת, הוּא מֵהֶהָרְגֵּל הַשּׁוֹלֵט עַל כָּל הֵן לְטוֹב כו׳ וְכַיּוֹצֵא, סִבַּת הָרוּחָנִיּוּת פְּשׁוּטָה הִיא, כִּי הָאָדָם בְּחֶטְאוֹ, מַמְשִׁיךְ עָלָיו רוּחַ הַטֻּמְאָה, הַמְעַכֵּר רוּחוֹ וּמְבַלְבֵּל שִׂכְלוֹ, כְּמַאֲמַר חֲכָמֵינוּ ז״ל אֵין אָדָם עוֹבֵר עֲבֵרָה אֶלָּא אִם כֵּן נִכְנְסָה בּוֹ רוּחַ שְׁטוּת, הַיְנוּ נֶגֶד דַּרְכֵי הַשֵּׂכֶל.

---

1. This letter was apparently written during the week when the Torah portion of *Re'eh* is read. Typically, this occurs in the month of Elul, when religious seekers turn their attention to the coming Days of Judgment and the Ten Days of Repentance, which is a theme in the letter.
2. The Torah portion *Re'eh* opens with the declaration: "Behold! I place before you today, blessing and curse" (Deut. 11:26). R. Salanter is expressing the wish that the recipient will behold blessing, and not curse.

Letter 14

With the help of God. *Re'eh* [Behold][1] – *Berakha* [Blessing].[2]

In the past, as I knew it, each person was seized with terror from [hearing] the proclamation sanctifying Elul.[3] This trembling bore fruit, bringing each person, at his own level, closer to His service, blessed be His name.

However, it was not as expected, namely, that a person who all year was far from His service, blessed be His name, would clothe himself in greater dread and worry of fear of judgment – for only Torah and good deeds can offer protection from retribution, may the Merciful One save us. On the contrary![4] The improvement of actions was twice as evident in the person who all year long held onto his holy way, according to his level, than in the person who all year long walked in darkness without light, according to his level.

The reasons for this reversal are several, both physical and spiritual. The main physical cause is habit (*hergel*) which rules over everything for better [or worse], and the like. The spiritual cause is very simple – by sinning, a person draws upon himself a spirit of impurity, which troubles his spirit and confuses his reason. As in the saying of our Sages, of blessed memory, "No person commits a sin unless a spirit of foolishness enters him,"[5] i.e., [sin] is irrational.

---

3. For this meant that the Day of Judgment was only a month away.
4. Compare Esther 9:1.
5. Compare Sota 3a.

וּמִי שֶׁעָסַק מְעַט בְּלִמּוּד הַמּוּסָרִי, רָאָה בְּחוּשׁ כִּי סִבַּת הָרוּחָנִי, עוֹמֶדֶת לְפָנָיו לְשָׂטָן לְטַמְטֵם לִבּוֹ, נֶגֶד תַּהֲלוּכוֹת הַשֵּׂכֶל לְפִי יָדְעוֹ אֱמוּנָתוֹ כַּנִּזְכָּר לְעֵיל, וּבְוַדַּאי גַּם דַּרְכֵי הַתֵּבֵל וְהַפּוּכָה שׁוֹלֶטֶת בַּדָּבָר, וְלָזֹאת עַתָּה לְבַד סִבַּת הַגַּשְׁמִיּוּת הִיא הַהִתְדַּמּוּת, אֲשֶׁר הָאָדָם הָעִקָּר הוּא רַק כְּקוֹף לַעֲשׂוֹת כְּמַעֲשֵׂה אֲחֵרִים בְּמַלְבּוּשִׁים וְכַיּוֹצֵא.

בָּזֹאת, כַּאֲשֶׁר סָפוּ תַּמּוּ גְּדוֹלֵי הַיְרֵאִים, אֲשֶׁר חֶרְדָּתָם מֵאֵימַת הַמִּשְׁפָּט הִתְרָאָה עַל פְּנֵיהֶם, וְעָשְׂתָה רֹשֶׁם בְּלֵב הַסָּרִים אַחֲרֵיהֶם, אִם אֵין שֹׁרֶשׁ מֵאַיִן יָבוֹאוּ עָלַיִן – אָכֵן סִבַּת הָרוּחָנִיּוּת הִיא סִבָּה הָעִקָּרִית, לְפִי הָרְאוּת – אֲשֶׁר חֶרְדַּת הָאֱלוּל כִּמְעַט נִכְבְּתָה רַחֲמָנָא לִצְלַן – אָכֵן כַּאֲשֶׁר נַפְשִׁיט מֵעָלֵינוּ לְפִי שָׁעָה, מַלְבּוּשִׁים הַנִּגְאָלוֹת וְנִלְבַּשׁ מַחֲלָצוֹת, נִרְאֶה בַּעֲלִיל כִּי יֵשׁ לִפְחֹד וְלִרְתֹּת עַתָּה כָּל אֶחָד לְפִי עֶרְכּוֹ, בְּכִפְלֵי כִּפְלֵי כִּפְלַיִם מֵאֵת אֲשֶׁר לְפָנִים – וּבִכְלָל – מַה לַּעֲשׂוֹת? הַפְּרָטִים רַבִּים הֵמָּה אִישׁ לְפִי מַצָּבוֹ וּתְכוּנָתוֹ.

אָכֵן בִּכְלָל נוֹדַע אִם כִּי הַנִּסָּיוֹן יוֹרֵנוּ, לִהְיוֹת עוֹבֵד ה׳ יִתְבָּרַךְ שְׁמוֹ גַּם בְּמַדְרֵגָה נִשָּׂאָה, בְּלִי לִמּוּד הַמּוּסָרִי. אָכֵן הַהִתְהַפְּכוּת מֵרַע לְטוֹב בְּלִי מוּסָרִי. (אִם מוּסָר שְׁמֵימִי כּוּ׳ הַמְשַׁבֶּרֶת לִבּוֹ שֶׁל אָדָם וְהוֹפְכָתוֹ לְטוֹב אִם הַיְסוֹד הוּא לִמּוּד הַמּוּסָרִי) הִיא כְּמוֹ בַּקָּשַׁת הָרְאִיָּה בְּלִי עַיִן וּשְׁמִיעָה בְּלִי אֹזֶן – וְלָזֹאת כָּתְבוּ הַפּוֹסְקִים אֲשֶׁר בַּיָּמִים הַנּוֹרָאִים הַלָּלוּ – עֵת הַהֲכָנָה לָבֹא אֶל הַמִּשְׁפָּט בְּרֹאשׁ הַשָּׁנָה, וּבְיוֹתֵר הַהֲכָנָה עַל יוֹם הַכִּפּוּרִים, אֲשֶׁר אֵין דַּי בָּאֵר הָעֵסֶק הַגָּדוֹל לִפְנֵי הָאָדָם, לְהָכִין אֶת עַצְמוֹ לִפְנֵי בּוֹאוֹ.

כִּי אִי אֶפְשָׁר לְתָאֵר אֶת גֹּדֶל הַהֶבְדֵּל, לְהִנָּצֵל מִפֻּרְעָנוּת גְּדוֹלוֹת רַחֲמָנָא לִצְלַן בָּעוֹלָם הָאֲמִתִּי, כַּאֲשֶׁר יַגְדִּיל אֶצְלוֹ בְּחִינַת יוֹם הַכִּפּוּרִים מְעַט גָּבוֹהַּ יוֹתֵר בְּמַדְרֵגַת הַתְּשׁוּבָה, יִקְבַּע כָּל אֶחָד עֵת לִלְמֹד בְּסִפְרֵי הַיְרֵאִים.

---

6. See Letters 7 and 13.
7. One of the major themes that emerged in Mussar education and training was for an individual to develop an internal compass, so as not to be swayed by the attitudes or conventions of others.
8. I.e., clean/pure.
9. Compare Zechariah 3:4.

Anyone who has engaged at all in Mussar study has seen palpably that this spiritual cause stands as an obstacle; it stultifies his heart against the progression of reason (to the extent that he truly understands the state of his belief, as mentioned above[6]). And certainly, the ways of the world and what it would take to reverse them also govern [behavior] in this matter. Thus, in addition to the physical cause [of *hergel*] there is also [the cause of] imitation, according to which the essential human is like an ape, doing exactly as others do, in their dress and the like.[7]

So, now that the men of great reverence are gone, whose trembling in awe of judgment was apparent on their faces – and made an impression on the hearts of their followers – in the absence of the root, where will the leaves come from?

Still, the spiritual cause is the main cause; it would appear that the trembling of Elul is almost extinguished, may the Merciful One save us. However, for a moment, when we take off the filthy clothes and put on priestly[8] robes,[9] we see clearly that one should fear and shudder now, each on his own level, many, many, many times more than before. In general – what is to be done? There are many details, each person according to his situation and nature.

In general, it is known, and experience teaches us, that to be a servant of God, blessed be His name, even at a high level, without Mussar study – and to transform evil to good without Mussar (be it heavenly chastisement … that breaks a person's heart and makes it good, or it be based on Mussar study) – is like trying to see without an eye or hear without an ear. Therefore, the decisors have written that in these Days of Awe – the time of preparing to go to judgment on Rosh HaShana, and especially the preparation for Yom Kippur (one can't explain enough[10] the importance of the task before the person: to prepare himself before he comes [to judgment], for it is impossible to describe the great difference, how much more he will be saved from terrible retributions [may the Merciful One save us] in the true world, if he increases for himself the quality of Yom Kippur, and attains even a slightly higher level of repentance) – each person should set aside time to study the books of reverence.[11]

---

10. A play on Isaiah 40:16.
11. This last clause is a direct continuation of "the decisors have written …"

אָכֵן מַה לַּעֲשׂוֹת לְכֹתֶל בַּרְזֶל הַמַּפְסִיק – הִיא רוּחַ הַטֻּמְאָה הַמְלַפֶּפֶת וּמְעַכֶּרֶת רוּחַ הָאָדָם, לִבְלִי תַּעֲשֶׂינָה יָדָיו תּוּשִׁיָּה, לָתֵת פְּרִי מִלִּמּוּד הַמּוּסָר, לְהֵטִיב דַּרְכֵי הָאָדָם לְקָרְבוֹ לַעֲבוֹדָתוֹ יִתְבָּרַךְ שְׁמוֹ.

אַחַת הִיא – אֲשֶׁר גַּם הַנִּסָּיוֹן יוֹרֵנוּ – הִיא לִשְׁפֹּךְ הַנֶּפֶשׁ אֶל ד׳ יִתְבָּרַךְ שְׁמוֹ בַּעֲשָׂרָה, אֶל מֶרְכָּז הַלָּזֶה לָקוֹב חוֹר קָטָן בְּכֹתֶל הַבַּרְזֶל הַלָּזֶה, דָּבָר קָטָן וְנִקְלֶה הוּא וּפִרְיוֹ רַב.

וְכַאֲשֶׁר אָנֹכִי כָּעֵת אִישׁ נוֹדֵד מִמְּקוֹמוֹ, אֵין בְּיָדִי לְהַשִּׂיג לָזֶה עֲשָׂרָה, בָּזֹאת הִנְנִי לְהַזְכִּיר אֶת כְּבוֹדְכֶם, וּלְזָרְזְכֶם בְּעֵת אֲשֶׁר מָצוּי לָכֶם וְעוֹדְכֶם בְּיֶדְכֶם (שַׁבָּת דַּף קנ״א) לְהִתְאַסֵּף בַּעֲשָׂרָה כַּנִּזְכָּר לְעֵיל, וְאוּלַי אִבָּנֶה גַּם אָנֹכִי בִּתְפִלָּתִי בְּיָחִיד בְּלִי נֶדֶר, אֲשֶׁר הִיא לִפְנֵי הַרְבֵּה נֶגֶד כוּ׳, וְלֹא הִסְכַּנְתִּי מֵעוֹדִי בָּזֶה בְּיְחִידוּת, אֲבָל מַה לְּפָנַי לַעֲשׂוֹת כָּעֵת – יְדִידְכֶם יִשְׂרָאֵל. מוֹצָאֵי שַׁבַּת קֹדֶשׁ.

12. Compare Berakhot 32b.

13. I.e., a *minyan*.

But what shall we do about the iron wall that separates[12] – the impure spirit that surrounds and disturbs the human spirit [by] not letting him achieve wise counsel [and not letting him] get results from his study of Mussar in order to improve a person's ways to get closer to His service, blessed be His name?

There is one way. Experience shows it too. It is to pour out one's soul to God, blessed be His name, in the presence of ten.[13] To this purpose, pierce a small hole in this iron wall. It is a small, easy thing, but it bears much fruit.

Since I am currently a man wandering from his place, I can't get ten for this purpose. With this [letter] I remind your excellencies and encourage you – while you still can and it's still in your hands (Shabbat 151b) – gather in a group of ten, as mentioned above. Perhaps I, too, will achieve something[14] in my individual prayer (without making promises) which feels like facing a lot of counterforces.... I was never used[15] to doing this alone, but this is what I must do now.

Your friend, Israel, [written] on the night after Holy Shabbat

---

14. Compare Genesis 30:3.
15. Compare Numbers 22:30.

טו

ב"ה. כְּבוֹד כו' יִתְבָּרְכוּ לִגְמַר חֲתִימָה טוֹבָה.

אִם כִּי לְמַצַּב בְּרִיאוּתִי דְּבָרַי לָעוּ, כַּאֲשֶׁר אָמַרְתִּי לִכְבוֹדָם, בְּכָל זֶה לְשִׂמְחַת לְבָבִי, כִּי הִגִּיעַנִי מִכְתָּב כִּי הֻסְכַּם לִבְנוֹת כו'. אֲשֶׁר הַדָּבָר נוֹגֵעַ גַּם לְדִידִי, לֹא נְגִיעָה גּוּפָנִית רַק נַפְשִׁית – נִתְעוֹרֵר בִּלְבָבִי לִכְתֹּב בִּקְצָרָה דָּבָר בְּעִתּוֹ.

הֵן יְסוֹד יְמֵי הַתְּשׁוּבָה, קַבָּלַת עֲזִיבַת הַחֵטְא, וְהִיא הַקָּשָׁה מִכָּל הָעֲבוֹדוֹת שֶׁבְּיוֹם הַכִּפּוּרִים הַבָּא עָלֵינוּ לְטוֹבָה, וְהַכְּבֵדָה מִכֹּל הִיא עֲוֹן גָּזֵל, אֲשֶׁר קֻפָּה מְלֵאָה עֲוֹנוֹת מִי מְקַטְרֵג בָּרֹאשׁ גָּזֵל, וְהָאָדָם צָרִיךְ לְחַפֵּשׂ לַעֲשׂוֹת תְּשׁוּבָה לְכָל הַפָּחוֹת, בַּחֵלֶק הַיּוֹתֵר חָמוּר, וְהוּא לְפִי הַנּוֹשֵׂא וְהַנָּשׂוּא, לְפִי הַנּוֹשֵׂא הוּא כָּל מַה שֶּׁנָּקֵל לְפִי שֶׁהָאָדָם לְהִשָּׁמֵר מֵעֲבֵרָה הוּא יוֹתֵר חָמוּר, וְעָנְשׁוֹ גָּדוֹל יוֹתֵר, כְּמַאֲמָרָם זַ"ל מְנָחוֹת דַּף מ"ג קָשֶׁה עָנְשׁוֹ שֶׁל לָבָן יוֹתֵר מֵעָנְשׁוֹ שֶׁל תְּכֵלֶת כו' עַיֵּן שָׁם – לְפִי הַנָּשׂוּא קָשֶׁה יוֹתֵר גָּזֵל מֵהֶעָנִי כו'.

וּמַה מְּאֹד כָּבֵד לִפְנֵי הָאָדָם לִמְצֹא דֶּרֶךְ בָּזֶה, וְאוֹי לְאוֹתָהּ בּוּשָׁה כו' אֲשֶׁר בְּעָוֹן גָּדוֹל כָּזֶה, לֹא יְקַיֵּם הָאָדָם לְכָל הַפָּחוֹת חֵלֶק

---

1. Lit. "seal." The favorable ruling for a good year, prayed for on Rosh HaShana, is sealed on Yom Kippur. This formula, "*Gemar ḥatima tova*" in Hebrew, is a standard greeting during the days between Rosh HaShana and Yom Kippur.
2. Compare Proverbs 15:23.
3. Compare Leviticus Rabba 33.
4. See Letter 7, n. 20.

Letter 15

With the help of God. Honored [recipients]….
May they be blessed [to receive] the final
confirmation[1] *of a good year.*

As for the state of my health, words fail, as I said to your honored selves. Yet my heart rejoices, nevertheless, because I received the letter that an agreement to build [a house of Mussar was reached]…. Since this affects me too – not physically but spiritually – my heart was stirred to write a brief, timely word.[2]

The basic principle of the Days of Repentance is resolving to turn away from the sin. This is the most difficult of every form of worship on the coming Yom Kippur (may it be for the good). The most grave [sin] of all is theft: "In a basket full of sins, which accuses us first? Theft."[3] One must seek to repent at least in the most severe aspects, according to the subject and the object. According to the subject – the easier it is for a person to observe, the more severe [the sin] and the greater the punishment. As [the Sages], of blessed memory, say in Menaḥot 43b, the punishment for white is greater than the punishment for indigo…. See further there.[4] As for the object – stealing from a pauper is more severe [than stealing from one who has more resources]….

How hard it is for a person to find his way in this! "And woe to that shame!…,"[5] if with respect to so great a sin, one does not undertake,

5. Bava Batra 75a.

מָה בְּקַבָּלָה גְּמוּרָה עַל הֶעָתִיד, לָזֹאת מַה טּוֹב אֲשֶׁר בָּא לְפָנֵינוּ תִּקּוּן חֲשַׁשׁ גָּזֵל, אֲשֶׁר נִקְבְּצוּ בּוֹ שְׁנֵי הָעִנְיָנִים בְּיַחַד, מִצַּד הַנּוֹשֵׂא לֹא קָשָׁה הִיא כוּ׳ בְּנִיַּן הַבַּיִת כוּ׳, וּמִצַּד הַנָּשׁוּא אוּלַי יִמָּצֵא גַּם אֶחָד אֲשֶׁר יִהְיֶה בִּרְצוֹנוֹ לִשְׁפֹּךְ נַפְשׁוֹ כוּ׳, וְלֹא יַעֲלֶה בְּיָדוֹ חָלִילָה בִּשְׁלֵמוּת אִם הָיוּ כוּ׳ – אֵין לִפְטֹר בָּזֶה רַק כָּל אֶחָד לְפִי מַצָּבוֹ וְעִנְיָנוֹ, הַהֶכְרֵחַ לְחַפֵּשׂ דְּרָכִים, אֵיךְ לְקַיֵּם קַבָּלַת עֲזִיבַת הַחֵטְא, בַּעֲוֹן גָּזֵל לְכָל הַפָּחוֹת בַּחֵלֶק הַיּוֹתֵר חָמוּר לְפִי הַנּוֹשֵׂא וְהַנָּשׁוּא כַּנִּזְכָּר לְעֵיל.

וְכֵן בִּשְׁאָרֵי עֲבֵרוֹת, כְּמוֹ בִּטּוּל תּוֹרָה הַחֲמוּרָה מִכֹּל. כַּמְבֹאָר בְּשַׁעֲרֵי תְּשׁוּבָה בְּשֵׁם הַסִּפְרֵי עַיֵּן שָׁם, אֲשֶׁר חֵלֶק הַיּוֹתֵר חָמוּר בֶּעָוֹן הַגָּדוֹל הַלָּזֶה, הוּא לְפִי הַנּוֹשֵׂא וְהַנָּשׁוּא, לְפִי הַנּוֹשֵׂא כָּל מַה שֶּׁיּוֹתֵר נָקֵל לְהָאָדָם לִלְמֹד לְפִי הָעֵת כְּמוֹ בְּשַׁבָּת כוּ׳, לְפִי הַמַּצָּב עֵת הַפְּנוּיָה כוּ׳ הָעֹנֶשׁ יוֹתֵר גָּדוֹל – לְפִי הַנָּשׁוּא עֹנֶשׁ בִּטּוּל הַלִּמּוּד הַנִּצְרָךְ לְהָאָדָם לְמַעֲשֶׂה, אִם לֵידַע בְּעַצְמוֹ מִזֶּה אֵיךְ לַעֲשׂוֹת, אוֹ לֵידַע עַל יְדֵי זֶה אֵיךְ לִשְׁאֹל מִגָּדוֹל מִמֶּנּוּ אֵיךְ לַעֲשׂוֹת כוּ׳, וְכֵן בְּכָל הַתּוֹרָה וְהַמִּצְוָה זֶה הַכְּלָל לְכָל פְּרָט בִּטּוּל הַתּוֹרָה וְהַמִּצְוָה, אִם בְּמַעֲשֶׂה אִם בְּשֵׁב וְאַל תַּעֲשֶׂה, יֵעָנֵשׁ הָאָדָם בְּעָבְרוֹ עֲלֵיהֶם, אָכֵן מַה שֶּׁיּוֹתֵר נָקֵל לִפְנֵי הָאָדָם לְקַיֵּם, יֵעָנֵשׁ יוֹתֵר וְיוֹתֵר.

וְהָאָדָם צָרִיךְ לְחַפֵּשׂ דְּרָכָיו לַעֲשׂוֹת קַבָּלָה חֲזָקָה, כִּמְעַט בְּכָל פְּרָטֵי עִנְיָנָיו, לְהִשָּׁמֵר לְכָל הַפָּחוֹת אֶת אֲשֶׁר נָקֵל לְפָנָיו בְּכָל פְּרָטֵי הַתּוֹרָה וְהַמִּצְוָה, וּבָזֶה יֵשׁ דֶּרֶךְ אֲשֶׁר יְקַיֵּם מִצְוַת הַתְּשׁוּבָה בְּרֹב חֶלְקֵי עֲוֹנוֹתָיו, כִּי הָרִבּוּי בְּהָעֲוֹנוֹת אֵינָם הוֹלְכִים אַחַר הַכַּמּוּת – לְפִי הַמִּנְיָן – רַק לְפִי הָאֵיכוּת, (עַיֵּן רַמְבַּ״ם הִלְכוֹת תְּשׁוּבָה פ״ג) הַיְנוּ מַה שֶּׁנָּקֵל לִפְנֵי הָאָדָם לְקַיֵּם, עֲבֵרָה אַחַת חָמוּר יוֹתֵר מִכַּמָּה עֲבֵרוֹת אֲשֶׁר כָּבֵד לְפָנָיו, וְכֵן בְּאוֹתָהּ עֲבֵרָה עַצְמָהּ חֵלֶק קָטָן מִמֶּנָּה הַנָּקֵל

6. *Shaarei Teshuva* is a treatise on penitence authored by R. Jonah of Girona (d. 1264) to atone, it is thought, for his earlier attacks on Rambam.

at least in some small part, a firm resolution [to change] for the future. Thus, how fortunate that we now have an opportunity to correct a case of possible theft, in which both of these matters [i.e., building a Mussar House and resolving to correct the sin of theft] come together. With respect to the subject, it is not difficult [to be honest] when building the [Mussar] House, [because it is not your money]. As for the object, perhaps even one person who wants to pour out his soul… will not be able to do so completely, God forbid, [because of lack of a building,] [so building this house is a mitzva]….

So no one is exempt in this matter. Rather, each one according to his own circumstances and situation must seek out ways to establish a resolution to turn from the sin of theft – at least in the most serious area (defined by the criteria of subject and object), as said above.

So too with other sins, such as neglecting Torah study, which is the gravest of all, as explained in *Shaarei Teshuva* (*The Gates of Repentance*)[6] quoting *Sifrei*. See further there. The gravest aspect of this great sin depends on the subject and the object. According to the subject – the easier it would have been for the person to learn, whether due to time, as on Shabbat, etc., or circumstance, as when he has free time, etc., the greater the punishment. According to object – the punishment is greater for neglecting to learn what is needed by the person in practice, whether to know from study what to do himself or to know by means of it how to ask someone greater than himself how to act, etc. So too, this is the principle with respect to all of the Torah and every commandment, with respect to acts of omission and acts of commission: a person will be punished for his violation, and the easier it would have been for him to fulfill, and greater the punishment will be.

A person must search his ways to make a firm resolution, in almost every part of his business, to observe, at least, all the details of the Torah and commandment that are easy for him. This is the way to fulfill the mitzva of repentance in most aspects of his sins, for proliferation of sin does not follow quantity – the number – but quality (see Rambam, Laws of Repentance, ch. 3). That is, regarding whatever is easy for a person to observe, one sin is graver than several sins in matters that are difficult for him to observe. Likewise, regarding that sin itself, [there may be] a small detail which is easier for him to observe – so it is graver and its

לִפְנֵי הָאָדָם לְקַיֵּם, יוֹתֵר חָמוּר וְעָנְשָׁהּ גָּדוֹל מֵהַרְבֵּה חֲלָקִים אֲשֶׁר בְּהָעֲבֵרָה אֲשֶׁר כָּבֵד לְקַיֵּם.

כְּמוֹ בְּמִצְוַת לִמּוּד הַתּוֹרָה, נָקֵל מְאֹד לְאָדָם גַּם מִי שֶׁהוּא שַׁכְחָן גָּדוֹל, לַחֲזֹר הַרְבֵּה פְּעָמִים עַל לְשׁוֹן זַארְגָּאן (מוּטְטֶער שְׁפְּרָאךְ) לְאַט לְאַט לִמּוּדוֹ בַּגְּמָרָא וְכַיּוֹצֵא, כִּמְעַט רַק יְדִיעַת הַשֵּׂכֶל לְבַד – בְּלִי יְדִיעַת הַתַּנָּא וְהָאָמוֹרָא כַּנִּזְכָּר לְעֵיל, וְלַחֲשֹׁב בָּהֶם בְּעֵת הִלּוּכוֹ בַּשּׁוּק בְּמָקוֹם נָקִי, בְּעֵת יֵשְׁבוֹ בָּעֲגָלָה כו׳, וְגַם כִּמְעַט בְּאֶמְצַע עִסְקוֹ כַּנִּזְכָּר לְעֵיל, וְדָבָר זֶה נָקֵל יוֹתֵר לְאִישׁ סוֹחֵר, מֵהָאִישׁ הַיּוֹשֵׁב עַל הַתּוֹרָה, אֲשֶׁר אֵין עִתּוֹתָיו בְּיָדוֹ לַחֲזֹר הַרְבֵּה לֵידַע בְּעַל פֶּה, לְמַעַן לֹא יְבַטְּלֶנּוּ הַרְבֵּה מִלִּמּוּדוֹ הָעִקָּרִית. לֹא כֵן אִישׁ הַסּוֹחֵר, אֲשֶׁר אִם יַחֲזֹר רַק אֵיזֶה פְּעָמִים עַל הַדַּף בְּלָמְדוֹ בַּשָּׁעָה הַפְּנוּיָה לְפָנָיו, כִּמְעַט רֹב הַיּוֹם לְפָנָיו לַחֲזֹר כַּמָּה פְּעָמִים בְּמַחֲשַׁבְתּוֹ.

וְצָרִיךְ אִישׁ הַטָּרוּד לְהִתְחַזֵּק מְאֹד בַּדָּבָר הַגָּדוֹל הַלָּזֶה, אֲשֶׁר נָקֵל הִיא מְאֹד לְפִי הַטֶעאָרִי (מַחֲשֶׁבֶת הַדַּעַת), לִרְאוֹת שֶׁיִּהְיֶה נָקֵל לְפָנָיו גַּם הַפְּרַאקְטִישׁ (הַמַּעֲשֶׂה), וְאַל יִפְתֶּה בְּשְׁטוּת יִצְרוֹ כִּי כְּבֵדָה הִיא! לְאַט לְאַט יִרְאֶה לֵידַע בְּעַל פֶּה, תּוֹרָה בִּלְשׁוֹן זַרְגָּאן שֵׂכֶל הַתּוֹרָה, אֲשֶׁר הוּא נָקֵל מְאֹד גַּם לְשַׁכְחָן גָּדוֹל, וּבְיוֹתֵר לְאִישׁ טָרוּד אֲשֶׁר עִתּוֹתָיו בְּיָדוֹ לַחֲזֹר בָּהֶם בְּמַחֲשַׁבְתּוֹ, גַּם לְפִי טִרְדָּתוֹ הָעֲצוּמָה.

---

7. This emphasis on the inner quality of a mitzva or a sin and on the uniqueness of each person doing the act based on individual levels of ease or difficulty is a kind of climax of R. Salanter's teaching that God recognizes every individual temperament and judges every individual act uniquely, even though the external act may be the same. By this same Mussar analysis, both mitzvot and sins may carry much greater weight than their external appearances suggest. Thus, working on character and personal characteristics becomes more and more important. As a result of such development, each individual act may carry much greater or much lesser weight than routine and external judgment may recognize.
8. Lit. "*zhargon*" ("jargon") or "mother tongue." The Jewish language of Yiddish was, at the time, considered a coarse corruption of German. Unlearned Jews spoke and understood Yiddish, but not necessarily Hebrew.

punishment is much greater than in many aspects of the transgression that are hard to observe.[7]

For example, with respect to the mitzva of studying Torah, it is very easy, even for someone who easily forgets, to review the Talmud or similar that he studied – many times, slowly, and in Yiddish.[8] At a minimum, he can know the cognitive flow without knowing the specific *Tanna* or *Amora*. He can meditate on it while he walks on the street through clean places,[9] or when he rides in a wagon, etc. Perhaps even in the course of his work, as mentioned; this is even easier for a merchant than for a Torah scholar who does not have many leisure opportunities to review often and to memorize – because he does not want to neglect his primary studies. Not so the merchant. If he can only go over the actual page of Talmud when he has a free hour, then he has most of the day before him to go over it in his mind several times.[10]

A busy person must strengthen himself in this great matter, which is easy in theory, to make sure that it becomes easy for him in practice, too. Let him not be seduced by the foolishness of his [evil] urge to think that it is "difficult." Little by little, let him see to it that he memorizes Torah – the logical flow of the Torah – in Yiddish, which is easy even for a very forgetful person, and especially for a busy person who has time to review the learning mentally, despite being so busy.

9. There are public places, such as privies or manure piles, where it is prohibited to study Torah.

10. R. Salanter is writing a guide for lay people who are not able to study Torah for long periods of time every day because they have to make a living. On the one hand, he is legitimating their right to go to work and earn an income in order to support their families. This is in contrast with the approach of his own *rebbe*, R. Joseph Zundel of Salant (1786–1866) and others, who argued that one should engage in as little work or business as possible, and to trust God to provide. On the other hand, R. Salanter is saying that they should use their hours in business to learn Torah by mental review, even as they are engaged externally with business matters. This letter shows that his Mussar movement (or at least the person that R. Salanter is writing to) is still engaged with lay people whom he seeks to mobilize for this movement, rather than with yeshiva students who would still be able to study Torah full time (while being supported by the community).

וְהַטּוֹב לִלְמֹד עַל זֶה סִפְרֵי מוּסָר, הַמְדַבְּרִים בְּגֹדֶל עֲוֹן בִּטּוּל תּוֹרָה, לַעֲשׂוֹת חִזּוּק בְּנַפְשׁוֹ, לְבִלִי לֵילֵךְ זְמַן גָּדוֹל בָּטֵל מֵהַתּוֹרָה, אֲשֶׁר הִיא חַיֵּי הָאָדָם – יְדִידָם יִשְׂרָאֵל – אוֹר ח׳ תִּשְׁרֵי תרל״ז.

The best thing is to study Mussar books on this, which talk about the greatness of the sin of neglecting Torah – so as to strengthen his soul not to neglect Torah for a significant period, for [Torah] is the life of a person.

Your friend, Israel; the night of 8 Tishrei, 5637 (1876)

טז

בָּאוּ יְמֵי הָרָעָה אֵלּוּ יְמֵי הַזִּקְנָה, רַעְיוֹנַי בִּלְתִּי מְסֻדָּרִים, כָּבֵד לְפָנַי לָתֵת לֵב לְהָשִׁיב בִּשְׁאֵלָה כְּבֵדָה, לְבַעֵר הַיֵּצֶר אֲשֶׁר נוֹצַרְנוּ לִלְחֹם מִלְחַמְתּוֹ, אֵין סֵדֶר בַּמִּלְחָמָה, וְאֵין בִּטָּחוֹן, הַרְבּוֹת בְּמוּסָר בְּעֵת מְצוֹא – יָמִים הַמְקֻדָּשִׁים לָהּ שׁוּמָה מִסִּפְרֵי הַפּוֹסְקִים, בִּהְיוֹת הָאָדָם מְעֻתָּד לְמִשְׁפָּט אִם לְחַיִּים כוּ׳.

וּבַמֶּה יִתְרַצֶּה הָעֶבֶד אֶל אֲדוֹנָיו, אִם לֹא בְּלֵב נִשְׁבָּר, אֲשֶׁר הָאֱלֹהִים לֹא תִבְזֶה, הַנּוֹדָע מִמְּקוֹר שְׁקִידָה הַגְּדוֹלָה בְּסִפְרֵי הַיְרֵאִים, בִּשְׁפִיכַת הַנֶּפֶשׁ לַד׳ יִתְבָּרַךְ שְׁמוֹ – אִם כֹּה יַעֲשֶׂה הָאָדָם וָחַי, גַּם לְאַחַר עֲבוֹר יְמֵי הַמִּשְׁפָּט, עוֹד רִשְׁמֵי הַמּוּסָר יְדַפְּקוּ – חִיּוּב לְמוּדָהּ תִּבְעַר בְּלֵב נִלְבָּב, לְהַחֲזִיק בָּהּ בְּאֵין רִפְיוֹן – יְדִידָם הַמְבָרְכָם לְשָׁנָה טוֹבָה.

דָּבָר הַמַּחֲזִיק בְּקִרְבָּהּ הַרְבֵּה מִיסוֹד הָאֵשׁ, הֲגַם כִּי הָאֵשׁ אֵינוֹ נִכָּר, אַךְ עַל יְדֵי נִיצוֹץ אֵשׁ תִּתְלַקַּח וְתִתְלַהֵב, כֵּן הֲגַם כִּי אֵין מַצָּבִי עַתָּה לְהַאֲרִיךְ בִּדְבָרִים, בְּכָל זֹאת הַתִּקְוָה כִּי בִּדְבָרִים קְצָרִים, יַזְכִּירוּ וְיִתְעוֹרְרוּ, אֶת אֲשֶׁר דָּרַשְׁתִּי לִפְנֵי כְּבוֹדְכֶם מִכְּבָר, אֲשֶׁר בֶּטַח נִכְנְסוּ הַדְּבָרִים בְּעֹמֶק לְבָבָם, לֵילֵךְ לְבֵית הַמּוּסָר וּבִפְרָט בַּעֲשֶׂרֶת יְמֵי תְּשׁוּבָה,

---

1. Compare Ecclesiastes 12:1.
2. See Shabbat 151b.
3. *Sifrei HaPoskim* – lit. "The Books of the Decisors."

Letter 16

"'The bad days have come...'[1] – these are the days of old age."[2] My thoughts are disorganized. It is hard for me to concentrate and answer a difficult question: [How] to destroy the [evil] urge, [i.e.,] wage the war for which we were created to fight. There is no order in this battle. There is no guarantee. Learn a lot of Mussar when you can. Days devoted to [Mussar] are needed according to the codes,[3] for a person is destined for judgment, whether for life [or death].

With what can a servant win favor in the eyes of his master, if not with a broken heart – which the Lord will not scorn[4] – stemming from a source of great application to books of reverence, through pouring out the soul to God, blessed be His name? If a person will do this, he will live. Even after the days of judgment pass, the effects of Mussar will beat on [in his mind and heart]. The sense of obligation to learn [Mussar] will burn on in a heart aflame – to hold onto it without weakening.

Your friend, who blesses you for "a good year."

Something that embodies much of the element of fire, even when the fire is not visible, will ignite and become inflamed with one spark. So although I am in no condition to write at length, I hope that these brief words will remind you and awaken in you what I preached [at length] before to your excellencies. Certainly, those words entered deeply into your hearts: to go to the House of Mussar, especially during

4. Compare Psalms 51:19.

לִלְמֹד מוּסָר בְּהִתְפַּעֲלוּת הַנֶּפֶשׁ, וְגַם הַתְּפִלָּה אֲשֶׁר יוֹתֵר טוֹב בַּעֲשָׂרָה (עַיֵּן תַּעֲנִית ח׳ כָּאן בְּצִבּוּר וְכוּ׳) וְהַהִתְעוֹרְרוּת הַפְּנִימִי יִתְגַּבְּרוּ עַל כָּל הַהִתְנַגְּדוּת.

the Ten Days of Repentance, and learn Mussar with emotional enthusiasm (*hitpaalut*), and also with prayer, which is better done with a group of ten (see Taanit 8a – "This case [refers to] prayer in a congregation [which will not be rejected by God] …"), so the inward awakening will overcome all opposition.

יז

גֶּדֶר הָאָדָם לִהְיוֹת תַּהֲלוּכָתוֹ וְעִנְיָנָיו אַחַר הַשֵּׂכֶל הַנָּכוֹן, וּבָזֹאת נִבְדָּל מִן בַּעֲלֵי חַיִּים אֲשֶׁר תַּהֲלוּכָתָם אַחַר טִבְעָם וּמִזְגָּם, וְזֶה הוּא כְּבִישַׁת הַיֵּצֶר, לִבְלִי הָלוֹךְ אַחַר נְטִיַּת הַטֶּבַע אִם רַע חַס וְשָׁלוֹם, כִּי הָאָדָם בְּכֹחוֹ בְּמֶמְשֶׁלֶת שִׂכְלוֹ לִשְׁלֹט עַל אֵבָרָיו כִּרְצוֹן חָכְמָתוֹ, וְזֶה הוּא גְּבוּרָתוֹ, כְּמַאֲמָרָם זַ"ל אֵיזֶהוּ גִּבּוֹר הַכּוֹבֵשׁ אֶת יִצְרוֹ, וְיֵשׁ בָּזֶה שְׁתֵּי בְּחִינוֹת, הָאֶחָד לַעֲצֹר טִבְעוֹ לִבְלִי עֲשׂוֹת רַע, וְהַשֵּׁנִי לַהֲפֹךְ טִבְעוֹ לַעֲשׂוֹת הַטּוֹב, וְהַבְּחִינָה הַשְּׁנִיָּה קָשָׁה מִן הָרִאשׁוֹנָה, כִּי כָּבֵד יוֹתֵר לְשַׁנּוֹת אֶת טִבְעוֹ, מִלַּעֲצֹר בְּעַד טִבְעוֹ, וְהָאָדָם צָרִיךְ לֵילֵךְ בְּהַדְרָגָה, בַּתְּחִלָּה לִהְיוֹת סָר מֵרָע, הִיא הַבְּחִינָה הָאַחַת, וְאַחַר כָּךְ עֲשֵׂה טוֹב הִיא הַבְּחִינָה הַשְּׁנִיָּה.

וּבָזֶה יֵשׁ לְבָאֵר הַמִּשְׁנָה בְּאָבוֹת פֶּרֶק ב׳ הֱוֵי מְחַשֵּׁב הֶפְסֵד מִצְוָה כְּנֶגֶד שְׂכָרָהּ, וּשְׂכַר עֲבֵרָה כְּנֶגֶד הֶפְסֵדָהּ, אֲשֶׁר לִכְאוֹרָה יִפָּלֵא הֲלֹא גַּם עַל מְנִיעַת הַמִּצְוָה עָנֹשׁ יֵעָנֵשׁ הָאָדָם, אִם בָּעוֹלָם הַזֶּה כְּמַאֲמָרָם זַ"ל בִּמְנָחוֹת דַּף מ"א בִּזְמַן דְּאִיכָּא רִתְחָא עָנְשִׁינַן אַעֲשֵׂה, אִם בָּעוֹלָם הַנִּצְחִי, כְּמַאֲמַר הַכָּתוּב גַּם מִתְרַפֶּה בִמְלַאכְתּוֹ אָח הוּא לְבַעַל מַשְׁחִית, וְגַם עַל מְנִיעַת הָרַע יֵשׁ קִבּוּל שָׂכָר, כְּמַאֲמָרָם זַ"ל בְּקִדּוּשִׁין דַּף ל"ט,

1. Avot 4:1.
2. Psalms 34:15.
3. Ibid.
4. Proverbs 18:9.

Letter 17

The definition of a human is that his behavior and concerns follow correct reason. In this way, he is different from other living creatures, whose behavior follows their nature and temperament. This [overcoming of nature and temperament through reason] is the "conquering of the urge" so as not to follow the natural tendency if it is to evil, God forbid. For a human has the power to govern his limbs by the rule of his reason, in accordance with the [free] will of his wisdom. This is his strength, as [the Sages], of blessed memory, said: "Who is [truly] strong? One who conquers his urges."[1]

There are two aspects in this. The first is to arrest his nature and not to do evil; the second is to transform his nature to do good. The second aspect is harder than the first, for it is harder to change his nature than to check it. A person must proceed gradually, first to become one who "shuns evil"[2] – which is the first aspect – and then to "do good"[3] – that is the second aspect.

With this we can explain the mishna in Avot 2:1: "Always weigh the cost of doing a mitzva against its reward, and the gain in doing a sin as against its loss." At first glance, it is a surprising statement; after all, a person is also punished for failing to do a good deed – whether in this world, as [the Sages], of blessed memory, said in Menaḥot 41a: "In a time of [God's] anger, there is punishment for not having done a positive commandment," or in the eternal world, as the Scripture says: "One who is lazy in his work is a brother to one who is destructive [in his work]."[4] Similarly, there is reward for not doing evil, as [the Sages],

יָשַׁב וְלֹא עָבַר עֲבֵרָה נוֹתְנִין לוֹ שָׂכָר כְּעוֹשֶׂה מִצְוָה, וְאִם כֵּן לָמָּה חִלְּקָה הַמִּשְׁנָה, לַחֲשֹׁב עַל מִצְוָה שְׂכָרָהּ וְעַל עֲבֵרָה עָנְשָׁהּ

אָכֵן עַל פִּי הַנִּזְכָּר לְעֵיל יֵשׁ לוֹמַר שֶׁהַמִּשְׁנָה אָחֲזָה בְּכָל אֶחָד הַבְּחִינָה הַגְּדוֹלָה, כִּי נוֹדַע כִּי לְפִי גֹּדֶל צַעַר הַמִּצְוָה יִגְדַּל שְׂכָרָהּ כְּמַאֲמָרָם זַ״ל בְּאָבוֹת, לְפוּם צַעֲרָא אַגְרָא, וְכָל אֲשֶׁר תִּקְטַן צַעַר עֲשִׂיַּת הַמִּצְוָה יִגְדַּל עֹנֶשׁ בִּטּוּלָהּ, כְּמַאֲמָרָם זַ״ל בִּמְנָחוֹת דַּף מ״ג קָשֶׁה עָנְשָׁהּ שֶׁל לָבָן יוֹתֵר מֵעָנְשָׁהּ שֶׁל תְּכֵלֶת כו׳, לִהְיוֹת צַעַר הַנָּחַת הַלָּבָן קְטַנָּה מִצַּעַר הַנָּחַת הַתְּכֵלֶת הַיְקָרָה בְּדָמִים, וְכֵן לְעִנְיַן הָעֲבֵרָה, כָּל אֲשֶׁר תִּקְטַן צַעַר מְנִיעַת עֲשִׂיַּת הָעֲבֵרָה, כֵּן יִגְדַּל עֹנֶשׁ עֲשִׂיָּתָהּ, וְכָל אֲשֶׁר יִקְשֶׁה לִפְנֵי הָאָדָם לִפְרֹשׁ מִן הָעֲבֵרָה, כֵּן תִּגְדַּל שְׂכָרָהּ אִם יִכְבֹּשׁ יִצְרוֹ לְבַל לְהִתְגָּאֵל בְּתַאֲוָתוֹ.

וְהִנֵּה בְּסוּר מֵרַע הַבְּחִינָה הָאַחַת, תִּגְדַּל הָעֹנֶשׁ בַּעֲשִׂיָּתָהּ, בְּעֵרֶךְ בְּחִינָה הַשְּׁנִיָּה עֹנֶשׁ מְנִיעַת עֲשֵׂה טוֹב, לִהְיוֹתָהּ קַלָּה מִבְּחִינָה הַשְּׁנִיָּה. וּבַשָּׂכָר הוּא לְהֵפֶךְ, שְׂכַר הַבְּחִינָה הַשְּׁנִיָּה הִיא עֲשִׂיַּת הַטּוֹב, גְּדֹלָה מִשְּׂכַר בְּחִינָה הָאַחַת מְנִיעַת הָרַע, לִהְיוֹתָהּ קָשָׁה מִבְּחִינָה הָאַחַת, וְלָזֶה אָחֲזָה הַמִּשְׁנָה בְּכָל אַחַת, הַדָּבָר הַיּוֹתֵר גָּדוֹל מֵחֲבֶרְתָּהּ, הַיְנוּ בַּעֲשִׂיַּת הַמִּצְוָה שְׂכָרָהּ לִהְיוֹתָהּ בַּמַּדְרֵגָה הַגְּבוֹהָה, וּבַעֲשִׂיַּת הָרַע הָעֹנֶשׁ הִיא הַמַּדְרֵגָה הַגְּבוֹהָה, וּלְפִי זֶה יֶשְׁנוֹ שְׁתֵּי מַדְרֵגוֹת בַּשָּׂכָר וְכֵן בָּעֹנֶשׁ.

וּבָזֹאת הֲלֹא נוֹדַע. כִּי אָדָם לְעָמָל יוּלָּד, לִלְחֹם מִלְחֶמֶת מִצְוָה, וְהַחוֹבָה עָלָיו לְהִתְיַגֵּעַ בַּעֲבוֹדַת ד׳, לֹא רַק לִשְׁמֹר מַה שֶׁטִּבְעוֹ מַנִּיחוֹ מֵעַצְמוֹ, וּמַה שֶּׁהוּא קְצָת כְּבֵדוּת לְהַזְנִיחַ, כִּי בָּזֶה הָאֹפֶן אֵין הָאָדָם עוֹבֵד ה׳ רַק הַטֶּבַע עוֹשֶׂה שֶׁלָּהּ, וְיוּכַל לְהִקָּרֵא חָלִילָה פּוֹרֵק עֹל,

5. That is, the mishna ignores the punishment for not doing a mitzva and the reward for not committing a transgression.

6. Job 5:7.

of blessed memory, say in Kiddushin 39b: "If he sat and did not commit a transgression, he is given a reward as one who did a mitzva." If so, why did the mishna make this distinction to [only focus on] calculating the reward of a good deed and the punishment of a transgression?[5]

However, according to what was mentioned above, we can say that in each [type] the mishna grasped the major aspect. It is known that the more painful doing a mitzva is, the greater its reward grows, as [the Sages], of blessed memory, say in Avot [5:23]: "According to the pain [of the effort] is the reward." The less painful the performance of a mitzva, the greater the punishment for not doing it, as they, of blessed memory, say in Menaḥot 43b: "Greater is the punishment for [not wearing] the white [*tzizit*] string than the punishment for [not wearing] the sky-blue [string]," for the difficulty of putting on the white is much less than the difficulty of putting on the blue, which is expensive.

The same applies to transgression. The less painful it is to hold back from committing a transgression, the greater the punishment grows for doing it. The more painful it is for a person to separate from the sin, the greater the reward grows if he conquers his urge by not being soiled through [acting on] his desire.

In the first aspect, "shun evil," the punishment is greater if you do the [evil] act, compared to the second aspect, the punishment for failure to "do good," because the first aspect is easier [to do] than the second aspect. With reward, the situation is reversed. Reward for the second aspect – doing good – is greater than the reward for the first aspect – not doing evil – for [the second aspect] is more difficult than the first aspect. For this reason, the mishna grasped, with regard to each aspect, that which is greater than the other. That is, in doing a mitzva, the reward is at a higher level [than refraining from doing a transgression], and in doing evil, the punishment is at a higher level [than refraining from doing good]. Accordingly, there are two levels of reward and two of punishment.

It is known that "a person is born to toil,"[6] to fight the war that is a mitzva to fight [against the evil urge]. He is obligated to exert himself in the service of God – not just to observe what his nature lets him do naturally and to neglect whatever is somewhat difficult. A person who serves in this manner is no servant of God; rather nature takes its course.

כַּאֲשֶׁר לֹא יִתֵּן שׁוּם יְגִיעָה לַעֲבוֹדַת ד׳ יִתְבָּרַךְ שְׁמוֹ, רַק לִשְׁמֹר מַה שֶּׁאֵין עָלָיו עֹל, וְזֹאת הוּא הַיְסוֹד מֵעֲבוֹדַת הָאָדָם לְבוֹרְאוֹ יִתְבָּרַךְ שְׁמוֹ, לִשְׁמֹר וְלַעֲשׂוֹת, גַּם מַה שֶּׁאֵין לִבּוֹ חָפֵץ, כִּי אִם לֹא יָשִׂים הָאָדָם לִבּוֹ וְנַפְשׁוֹ, לַעֲשׂוֹת נֶגֶד רְצוֹן לְבָבוֹ, הֲרֵי הוּא עָלוּל לְכָל עֲבֵרוֹת שֶׁבַּתּוֹרָה רַחֲמָנָא לִצְלַן, גַּם אוֹתָן שֶׁאֵינוֹ עוֹבֵר עֲלֵיהֶן מִצַּד הֶרְגֵּלוֹ וְטִבְעוֹ.

כִּי הַהֶרְגֵּל וְהַטֶּבַע מִתְחַלְּפִים מִסִּבּוֹת צְדָדִיּוֹת כַּאֲשֶׁר יְאַלְּצֵם כֹּחַ אַחֵר הַמְנַגֵּד לָזוֹ, כַּדּוֹמֶה הָאִישׁ הַמַּתְמִיד בְּלִמּוּדוֹ מִצַּד הֶרְגֵּלוֹ וְטִבְעוֹ, וְיֵשׁ לוֹ כֹּחַ נִסְתָּר הַמִּשְׁתּוֹקֵק לְכֶסֶף, וְהַכֹּחַ אֵינוֹ נִכָּר, יַעַן כִּי אֵין לוֹ דֶּרֶךְ לָזֶה, כִּי מַצָּבוֹ וְתַהֲלוּכָתוֹ אֵינוֹ דֶּרֶךְ הַמִּסְחוֹר, וְלֹא רָאָה כֶּסֶף מִיָּמָיו, מִמֵּילָא אֵין לְהַכֹּחַ נוֹשֵׂא בַּמֶּה לְהֵאָחֵז, כִּי הַכֹּחוֹת שֶׁבָּאָדָם כָּל זְמַן שֶׁאֵין לָהֶם דָּבָר חוּשִׁי בַּמֶּה לְהֵאָחֵז, נִסְתָּרִים הֵמָּה בִּפְנִימִיּוּת הַנֶּפֶשׁ, בַּל יֵרָאוּ הַחוּצָה גַּם בַּל נוֹדָעוּ.

אָכֵן כַּאֲשֶׁר יִהְיֶה אֵיזֶה סִבָּה שֶׁיִּצְטָרֵךְ לֶאֱחֹז מָה בְּמִסְחוֹר לְטֶרֶף בֵּיתוֹ וְכַיּוֹצֵא, יוּכַל לְהִתְפָּרֵץ כֹּחַ הַלָּזֶה בְּקֻשַּׁת הַכֶּסֶף, עַד אֲשֶׁר יַזְנִיחַ כִּמְעַט תַּלְמוּדוֹ לְגַמְרֵי מֵחֲמַת הַכֹּחַ הַלָּזֶה, אֲשֶׁר לֹא הָיָה מַאֲמִין עַל עַצְמוֹ בְּשׁוּם אֹפֶן אֵיךְ יוּכַל לִהְיוֹת שֶׁיַּזְנִיחַ כָּל כָּךְ לִמּוּדוֹ, וְכֵן בְּכָל הַכֹּחוֹת וְהָעִנְיָנִים הַטּוֹבִים שֶׁבָּאָדָם, יוּכְלוּ לִהְיוֹת מוּפָרִים מִכֹּחוֹת מִתְנַגְּדִים אֲשֶׁר בְּסִבָּה קְטַנָּה יִתְעוֹרְרוּ בְּחָזְקָה לְהָפֵר כָּל נֵתַח טוֹב.

לָזֹאת גַּם אִם הָעֲבֵרוֹת הָרְגִילוֹת אֲשֶׁר נַעֲשִׂים כְּהֶתֵּר רַחֲמָנָא לִצְלַן. לֹא יְעוֹרְרוּ אֶת נֶפֶשׁ הָאָדָם לַעֲסֹק בְּלִמּוּד יִרְאַת שָׁמַיִם (לִזְכֹּר אַחֲרִיתוֹ יְמֵי הַחֹשֶׁךְ כִּי הַרְבֵּה יִהְיוּ, וְעַל כָּל עֲבֵרָה בִּפְרָט, עָנֹשׁ יֵעָנֵשׁ בַּעֲנָשִׁים קָשִׁים וּמָרִים רַחֲמָנָא לִצְלַן כְּמַאֲמָרָם ז״ל, כָּל הָאוֹמֵר

7. Earlier, R. Salanter suggested that a person work on his nature and improve his personal *middot*. Otherwise, the Torah he learns may be tainted. Driven by the needs of his ego, he may distort his understanding of the Torah's instructions until they fit his desire, rather than do what God wants him to do. In this letter, R. Salanter goes a step further and suggests that if one has not changed his nature and *middot* through the self-critique that Mussar supplies, then he is in danger of really not serving God in any way. He is only doing what his nature and desire want him to do. R. Salanter's definition of being a servant of God is that one has overcome his desires and unimproved nature, enabling him to do the genuine will of God.

Perhaps he should be called "one who throws off the yoke of [God]" since he makes no effort to serve God, blessed be His name, but only keeps whatever is not a burden to him.[7] This is the basic principle of a person's service to his Creator, blessed be His name: to observe and do even that which his heart does not want to do. For if a person does not put his heart and soul into doing some things against his heart's [natural] desire, he is prone to every sin in the Torah, may the Merciful One save us – even those that, out of nature and habit, he does not violate [currently].

Habit and nature change from incidental causes, [i.e.,] when compelled by a force opposing them. For example, a man learns diligently out of habit and nature, but he has a hidden drive that yearns for money. The drive is not discernible because he has no access to it. His situation and behavior are not in the realm of commerce, and he has never seen money. Consequently, this drive has nothing to latch on to, for as long as human drives have nothing palpable to latch on to, they remain hidden in the inner recesses of the psyche, not manifesting externally and not even recognized.

However, whenever any cause arises that requires him to take on some business, to feed his family or the like, this money-seeking drive can burst forth, to the point that he abandons his learning almost entirely because of this drive. He would never have believed about himself, in any way, that he could be so neglectful of his learning! So it is with all the good drives and concerns in a person – they can be breached by opposing drives that are stirred up powerfully at the slightest trigger, to break apart every bit of goodness.

[The same happens] if the transgressions become so routine that they "become as if permitted,"[8] may the Merciful One save us. [The commission of these sins] will not arouse a person's soul to engage in the study of fear of Heaven (to remember his end, the dark days, which will be numerous; and for each particular sin, he will be punished with hard and bitter punishments, may the Merciful One save us. As they, of blessed memory, say: "Whoever says God waives [those punishments],

8. Ḥullin 4b.

הַקָּדוֹשׁ־בָּרוּךְ־הוּא וַתְּרָן הוּא יְוַתְּרוּ חַיּוֹהִי אֶלָּא מַאֲרִיךְ אַפֵּיהּ וְגָבֵי דִּילֵיהּ, וּמִי יוֹדֵעַ עַד כַּמָּה תִּגְדַּל הָעֹנֶשׁ אֲשֶׁר שׁוּם אַחֵר לֹא יִסְבֹּל רַק הָאָדָם לְבַדּוֹ הָעוֹשֶׂה הָעֲבֵרוֹת) לִהְיוֹתָם נַעֲשִׂים כְּהֶתֵּר. אֵין רוֹאֶה וְאֵין מַרְגִּישׁ הָאָדָם בָּהֶם.

אַךְ זֶה יוּכַל לְעוֹרֵר לְהָאָדָם, בְּהִתְבּוֹנְנוֹ חִלּוּפֵי הַזְּמַן וּמִקְרֵי הָעִתִּים אֲשֶׁר עִם דָּבָר קָטָן יוּכַל הַטֶּבַע לְהִשְׁתַּנּוֹת וְלִפֹּל בַּעֲבֵרוֹת רָמוֹת, אֲשֶׁר הַהֶרְגֵּשׁ עֲדַיִן בְּתָקְפּוֹ כִּי עֲבֵרוֹת הֵמָּה, וְיִרְאָתָם מְרַחֶפֶת עַל פָּנָיו, לָזֹאת יַקְדִּים הָאָדָם רְפוּאָה לְעַצְמוֹ לַעֲסֹק בְּלִמּוּד הַיִּרְאָה וְהַמּוּסָר לְהָעִיר וּלְעוֹרֵר אֶת רוּחוֹ שֶׁיּוּכַל לַעֲשׂוֹת נֶגֶד רְצוֹנוֹ.

9. Bava Kamma 50a.

10. Initially R. Salanter argued for the need for Mussar to supplement standard Torah study, in order to identify accurately and to properly practice the good life (see Letter 6). In subsequent letters, R. Salanter emphasized that without Mussar and self-analysis, a person may not accurately establish what is truly the will of God and the message of the Torah. In this letter, R. Salanter comes close to saying that without changing one's character through Mussar, one's understanding of Torah (and the proper practices of the good life) is likely tainted and distorted.

his life will be waived! Rather, God is patient, but He collects His debts!"[9] Who knows how great will be the punishment? No one else will suffer but the person himself who commits the sins.) Since they have become as if permitted, the person neither sees them nor feels them anymore.[10]

Only this can awaken the person: when he considers the changes that accrue over time and the incidents that occurred at various times, [and notes] that with something small, nature can change and cause a fall into terrible sins – which he still senses at the time to be sins, and fear of them still hovers over him. So let that person prepare a cure for himself preemptively: to engage in study of reverence and Mussar to arouse and awaken his spirit so he can defy his desires.[11]

11. R. Salanter is stressing that there are powerful unconscious drives in a person that may overwhelm his current positive behavior patterns. Therefore, it is necessary for everyone to engage in the disciplined study of Mussar and transformation of his nature to want the good that the Torah recommends. He should engage in this study now, lest some new force or life experience unleash the hitherto unconscious negative drives and take over his life. If he has not studied Mussar in advance, it may be too late to check the outbursts of these drives.

יח

מָה אוֹסִיף עַל דְּבָרַי. אֲשֶׁר נִדְבַּרְנוּ בִּהְיוֹת כְּבוֹד תּוֹרָתוֹ אֶצְלִי. וְהוּא – הַמַּעֲשֶׂה קוֹדֵם לַמַּחֲשָׁבָה. הַלִּמּוּד קוֹדֵם לַמַּעֲשֶׂה. קְנִיַּת דַּרְכֵי הַלִּמּוּד הוּא הַפֶּתַח לְהִכָּנֵס בְּדַרְכֵי עֲבוֹדָתוֹ יִתְבָּרַךְ שְׁמוֹ. מֵעֵת חֲתִימַת הַתַּלְמוּד נִנְעֲלוּ דַּרְכֵי הַתּוֹרָה לְהָבִין וּלְהוֹרוֹת מִכִּתְבֵי הַקֹּדֶשׁ עַל פִּי הַמִּדּוֹת הַמְּסוּרוֹת מִסִּינַי. וְרַק אֶל הַתַּלְמוּד עֵינֵינוּ צוֹפִיּוֹת לִשְׁאֹב מִמֶּנָּה תּוֹרַת ה׳ וּדְרָכָיו. וְגַם הָאָדָם הַגָּדוֹל בָּעֲנָקִים אֵין בְּיָדוֹ רַק לְחַפֵּשׂ וּלְגַלּוֹת תַּעֲלוּמוֹת סִתְרָהּ. וְעַל הַתַּלְמוּד אֵין לְהוֹסִיף וְאֵין לִגְרֹעַ מְאוּמָה.

לָזֹאת הַתַּלְמוּד אֶצְלֵנוּ כְּמוֹ בְּחִינַת מִקְרָא בִּימֵי חֲכָמֵינוּ זַ״ל. וְלִמּוּד הַמִּקְרָא אֶצְלֵנוּ כְּמוֹ בְּחִינַת א״ב בִּימֵי חֲכָמֵינוּ זַ״ל לָבֹא עַל יָדוֹ לְלִמּוּד הַתַּלְמוּד. וְסִפְרֵי גְּדוֹלֵי הַפּוֹסְקִים רִאשׁוֹנִים וְאַחֲרוֹנִים. הוּא כְּמוֹ בְּחִינַת מִשְׁנָה בִּימֵי חֲכָמֵינוּ זַ״ל. אֲשֶׁר בְּיַד הָאָדָם הָרָאוּי וּמֻכְשָׁר לְכָךְ. לַחֲלֹק וּלְשַׁנּוֹת עַל פִּי תְּנָאִים הָרְצוּיִם לְהַכְרִיעַ אִם יִמָּצֵא

1. *"Kevod Torato"* (lit. "the honor of his Torah") is a traditional formal mode of address. In this letter, addressed to an individual, R. Salanter refers to the recipient in the third person, out of respect. Most letters in this collection are addressed to groups of disciples and friends and use the second person plural. We have translated the honorific as "your honor," which preserves the formality of the original.
2. I.e., the Talmud's.
3. Compare Deuteronomy 4:2.

Letter 18

What can I add to my words from our discussion when [your] honor[1] visited me? Namely, that deed precedes thought; study precedes deed; mastering methods of learning is the entrance gate to methods of serving Him, blessed be His name.

Since the time of the sealing of the Talmud, the Torah ways of understanding and instructing [directly] from Scripture, according to the [hermeneutic] principles given at Sinai, have been locked away. We can only look to the Talmud to draw therefrom God's Torah and His ways. Even a giant of a person can only search and uncover her[2] hidden mysteries. One cannot add or subtract anything from the Talmud.[3]

Thus, the Talmud for us is as Scripture was for the Sages, of blessed memory. Study of Scripture for us is in the same category as learning the alphabet in the days of the Sages, of blessed memory – a prerequisite for studying the Talmud. And the books of the great codifiers, *Rishonim* and *Aḥaronim*,[4] are in the same category as the Mishna in the days of the Sages, of blessed memory – a person worthy and trained to do it can disagree and change things according to the desired conditions for rendering decisions, if he finds an authority upon whom to rely.

---

4. The great talmudic commentators and halakhic authorities of medieval times are called "*Rishonim*" (lit. "early ones"), and those since early modernity are referred to as "*Aḥaronim*" (lit. "the latter ones"). These titles signify their stature and highlight the periodization of halakhic authority, with each successive period considered less authoritative than earlier periods.

פּוֹסֵק לִסְמֹךְ עָלָיו. וְאוּלַי לְאָדָם גָּדוֹל גַּם לַחֲלֹק כְּמוֹ רַב תַּנָּא וּפָלִיג כו׳ – וְאַחַר הַבְּקִיאוּת הַנּוֹרָאָה בְּתַלְמוּד בַּבְלִי וִירוּשַׁלְמִי כו׳. וְהַיְדִיעָה הַנְּכוֹנָה בִּגְדוֹלֵי הַפּוֹסְקִים כו׳. וִידִיעַת לִמּוּד הַתּוֹסָפוֹת עַל כֻּלָּנָה. אָז יָבֹא הָאָדָם לְלִמּוּד הַתַּלְמוּד (הִיא כְּמוֹ בְּחִינַת הַתַּלְמוּד בִּימֵי חֲכָמֵינוּ זַ״ל) הוּא הָעִיּוּן הַנָּכוֹן לִשְׁאֹב יְסוֹדוֹת הַתַּלְמוּד בִּפְרָטָיו מִמְּקוֹמוֹת הַמְפֻזָּרִים וּלְהָבִין וּלְהוֹרוֹת כַּדָּת. וְזֶה הוּא בְּחִינַת תּוֹרַת אֱמֶת הַנִּקְנֶה בַּמִּקְרָא (הִיא הַבְּקִיאוּת בְּשַׁ״ס וִירוּשַׁלְמִי כו׳) וּבַמִּשְׁנָה (הִיא הַיְדִיעָה בְּחִבּוּרֵי גְּדוֹלֵי הָרִאשׁוֹנִים וְהָאַחֲרוֹנִים כו׳) וְזֹאת הִיא שִׁמּוּשׁ תַּלְמִידֵי חֲכָמִים. וְקָרָא וְשָׁנָה וְלֹא שִׁמֵּשׁ תַּלְמִידֵי חֲכָמִים הֲרֵי זֶה עַם הָאָרֶץ.

וְעַל כָּל אֵלֶּה חִדּוּד הַשֵּׂכֶל. וְהַהִתְבּוֹנְנוּת דַּרְכֵי הַמִּדּוֹת לֵידַע דַּרְכֵי הַנְּטִיָּה לְמַעַן יֵלֵךְ הַשֵּׂכֶל יָשָׁר דַּרְכּוֹ. וְיִרְאַת ד׳ הִיא אוֹצָרוֹ. לְקַבֵּל עֹל הַיְגִיעָה. לְהַעֲמִיק בְּתוֹרַת ה׳ יִתְבָּרַךְ שְׁמוֹ. גַּם בְּדִבּוּק חֲבֵרִים וּבְפִלְפּוּל הַתַּלְמִידִים בְּשׁוּבָה וָנַחַת.

עַתָּה בָּרוּךְ ד׳ עֶלֶם רַךְ כמי״ב. יֵדַע וְיָבִין דַּרְכּוֹ עַל מַה הַטִּבְעוֹ. וְעַל מַה יָּסֹבּוּ דַּלְתֵי רַעְיוֹנָיו וּמַאֲוָיו. יִתֵּן הַשֵּׁם יִתְבָּרַךְ וְיַעֲלֶה לְגֶפֶן אַדֶּרֶת כְּנַפְשׁוֹ הַטּוֹב וְנֶפֶשׁ תִּדְרְשֶׁנּוּ. יְדִידוֹ יִשְׂרָאֵל.

5. See Eiruvin 50b. Rav, an early *Amora* (sage from the talmudic era), disagrees with a *Tanna* (sage from the mishnaic era, whose authority is greater than that of an *Amora*) even without the support of another *Tanna,* because his stature granted him the authority to dispute even a *Tanna.*
6. Berakhot 47b.
7. Isaiah 33:6.
8. I.e., exchanging views.
9. See Avot 6:6.
10. At first glance, this letter is intended to guide R. Salanter's student as to how to initiate a new young student in the proper way of learning Torah and Mussar. However, one can speculate that this is also an answer to those who questioned the justification

And maybe a great man can even disagree [without an authority upon whom to rely] – as in "Rav is a *Tanna* and disagrees."[5] After achieving awesome fluency in the Babylonian and Palestinian Talmudim, etc., proper knowledge of the great codifiers, etc., and, above all, the knowledge from learning the *Tosafot*, one can reach the study of Talmud (as the Talmud was [studied] in the days of the Sages, of blessed memory). This is the proper study to draw out the basic principles of the Talmud, through its details from scattered places, and thus to understand and instruct properly.

This is the idea of "the Torah of truth," mastered by [study of] Scripture (that is, [for us] fluency in the Babylonian and Palestinian Talmudim, etc.), and Mishna (that is, [for us] knowing the works of the greatest *Rishonim* and *Aḥaronim*, etc.). And this is "apprenticeship under Torah scholars." For, "one who read [Scripture] and studied [Mishna] but did not apprentice under Torah scholars is an ignoramus."[6]

On top of all this, [he needs] keenness of reason and contemplation of the ways of character traits to know the nature of bias, so that reason can proceed straight on its path. "And the fear of God is his treasure"[7] to take on the yoke of the effort to delve deeply into the Torah of God, blessed be His name. Likewise, through close association with colleagues[8] and argumentation with students,[9] with repetition and patience.

Now, thank God, a young man – may there be many like him in Israel – will know and understand his path: what is his nature and what activates his ideas and desires. May God grant that this young man grow into a vine as glorious as [yourself] – whose well-being is sought by [your] friend, Israel.[10]

---

and the authority of R. Salanter and his students to add a major, new corpus (i.e., Mussar) to the curriculum and to judge and sometimes find inadequate the piety of those who do not learn Mussar.

יט

יְקָרָתוֹ מִן י״א דְּנָא נָכוֹן הִגִּיעַנִי הַיּוֹם. נִמְצֵאתִי נָכוֹן לִכְתֹּב לִכְבוֹד תּוֹרָתוֹ לִבְלִי לְאַחֵר מִפְּנֵי הַכָּבוֹד. כִּי לֹא הֵשַׁבְתִּי עַל מִכְתָּבָיו הַקּוֹדְמִים. רָאִיתִי אֹמֶץ תְּשׁוּקָתוֹ לְהִתְרָאוֹת אִתִּי וְהַדִּין עִמּוֹ כְּמַאֲמַר הַכָּתוּב בִּישִׁישִׁים חָכְמָה.

וַאֲפָרֵשׁ שִׂיחָתִי. הַחָכְמוֹת וְהַמַּדָּעִים הֵמָּה טֶעהָארִי (עִיּוּן). וּפְרַאקְטִיק (חִנּוּךְ הַמַּעֲשֶׂה). הַחָכְמוֹת אֲשֶׁר יְסוֹדָתָם הַמּוֹפֵת וְהָרְאָיוֹת הַיְסוֹד בָּהֶם הָעִיּוּן. אוּלָם אֶת אֲשֶׁר נוֹפְלִים רַק תַּחַת הַהַשְׁעָרָה הַנְּכוֹנָה. הַיְסוֹד בָּהֶם חִנּוּךְ הַמַּעֲשֶׂה. הַטֶעהָארִי (עִיּוּן) אֵינָהּ נוֹפֶלֶת תַּחַת הַשָּׁנִים כִּי יֵשׁ קַנְקָן חָדָשׁ כו׳. וְשֵׂכֶל צְעִיר הַיָּמִים תְּבָרֵר יוֹתֵר מִזָּקֵן חֲלוּשׁ הַדַּעַת וְהַתְּבוּנָה. אָכֵן הַפְּרַאקְטִיק (חִנּוּךְ הַמַּעֲשֶׂה) בְּיָמִים יָבוֹאוּ וּבִזְקְנָה תִּתְכּוֹנֵן. תְּבוּנָה (שֵׁם חָכְמָה) נוֹפֵל עַל הַהַשְׁעָרָה הַנְּכוֹנָה לָזֶה אָמַר הַכָּתוּב בִּישִׁישִׁים כו׳.

וְהִנֵּה לִמּוּד הַתּוֹרָה הַיְסוֹד הוּא (הַטֶעהָארִי). הַחֲרִיפוּת וְהַבְּקִיאוּת וְהָעִיּוּן הַיָּשָׁר. לְבָרֵר דָּבָר עַל אָפְנָיו בְּדַרְכֵי הַהוֹכָחוֹת

---

1. This letter, like the previous, is addressed to the recipient in the third person.
2. That is, he is right to want to talk with an elder sage.
3. Job 12:12.
4. It would appear from this letter and the next that R. Salanter had been reading some general works on the nature of scientific evidence. He seeks to apply these approaches to the understanding of the ways of Torah and Mussar.
5. See Avot 4:20.

Letter 19

[Your][1] precious letter of the eleventh of this month reached me today. I find it proper to write to [your] honor without delay, out of respect, for I did not reply to [your] earlier letters. I see [your] intense longing to meet with me. The law accords with [you],[2] as it says in Scripture: "With the venerable ones is understanding [found]."[3]

I will explain my words. [Branches of] wisdom and the sciences are "theory" (abstract learning) and "practice" (learning through action, i.e., experience).[4] [Branches of] wisdom that are based on demonstration and proof are founded upon theory. However, those [branches of wisdom and science] that emerge from good assessments are based on practical experience. Theory does not emerge with time alone, for "there is a new pitcher [full of old, i.e., rare, wine]...."[5] The reason of a young person may clarify more than an old man who is weak in mind and understanding. However, practical experience comes with time, and is established in old age. "Understanding" (the name of a branch of wisdom) refers to good assessment.[6] Therefore Scripture says: "With venerable ones is understanding [found]."

When it comes to Torah study, the foundation is theory: keenness, encyclopedic knowledge, and straightforward analysis to clarify matters in a fitting manner,[7] with evidence and proof in line with the

6. ...which reaches its conclusions based on the evidence that accumulates with experience.

7. See Proverbs 25:11.

וְהָרְאָיוֹת לְרַגְלֵי דַּרְכֵי הַתּוֹרָה וְתַהֲלוּכוֹתֶיהָ. כְּפִי אֲשֶׁר הוֹרוּנוּ גְּדוֹלֵי הָרִאשׁוֹנִים וְהָאַחֲרוֹנִים זַ"ל. אָכֵן הַמּוּסָרִי וְדַרְכֵי הַמִּדּוֹת. הַיְסוֹד בָּהֶם הַפְּרַאקְטִיק – וּבָזֹאת כְּבוֹד תּוֹרָתוֹ שׁוֹאֵל מִמֶּנִּי כַּהֹגֶן וְאָנֹכִי נִצָּב מִנֶּגֶד – מַה זֶּה וְלָמָּה?

אָכֵן הוּא הַדָּבָר אֲשֶׁר דִּבַּרְתִּי. בַּמּוּסָרִי וְדַרְכֵי הַמִּדּוֹת הַיְסוֹד בָּהֶם הַפְּרַאקְטִיק. (נִסְיוֹן אִישׁ פְּרָטִי אֲשֶׁר הֻסְכַּן בִּימֵי חֶלְדּוֹ. אֵין דֶּרֶךְ כְּבוּשָׁה לְמוּסָרִים לִפְנֵי אָדָם גָּדוֹל כמי"ב) וְכִמְעַט קָרוֹב לְהֶפְסֵד חָלִילָה. כִּי כָּל אָדָם וּבִפְרָט אָדָם גָּדוֹל הוּא עוֹלָם בִּפְנֵי עַצְמוֹ לְפִי כֹּחוֹתָיו כֹּחוֹת נֶפֶשׁ שִׂכְלוֹ כו'. תְּכוּנַת מִדּוֹתָיו וְהִתְפַּעֲלוּתוֹ כו' מַצַּב עִנְיָנוֹ כו'.

וְהִנֵּה בִּדְבַר רְפוּאַת הַגּוּף אֲשֶׁר הַפְּרַאקְטִישׁ גְּדֹלָה לִמְאֹד. הַנּוֹלְדָה מִפְּרַאקְטִישׁ חָכְמַת הַטֶּעהָארִי הַנִּפְלָאָה חָכְמַת הָרְפוּאָה הָרְחָבָה. אָכֵן בִּרְפוּאַת הַנֶּפֶשׁ אֶצְלֵנוּ. אֲשֶׁר אֵין בָּהֶם פְּרַאקְטִישׁ מֵאִישׁ לְרֵעֵהוּ לֵידַע וּלְהוֹדִיעַ. הַחָכְמָה מֵאַיִן תִּמָּצֵא לְהָשִׁיב לַשּׁוֹאֵל עַל אָפְנָיו. יְהִי נָא כְּבוֹד תּוֹרָתוֹ שָׁקוּט בִּמְעוֹנוֹ בִּמְנוּחַת נַפְשׁוֹ. אָנֹכִי בְּדַעְתִּי לִהְיוֹת אִם יִרְצֶה ה' כו'. אָז נִתְרָאֶה אִם יִרְצֶה ה' בְּלֹא נֶדֶר לָשׂוּם רַעְיוֹנֵינוּ בִּדְבַר תַּהֲלוּכוֹת כְּבוֹד תּוֹרָתוֹ וּמַאֲוָיו. עַל מַה צְּפוּנָה עִיּוּנָיו בִּדְבַר תַּהֲלוּכוֹת הַמּוּסָרִי וְהַמִּדּוֹת. לְפִי דְּרָכָיו וְדַרְכֵי הַזְּמַן לְטוֹב לְפִי הַשְׁעָרָה הַנְּכוֹחָה. וַה' יִתְבָּרַךְ שְׁמוֹ יִהְיֶה בְּעֶזְרָתֵנוּ לְטוֹב וּמֵטִיב. יְדִידוֹ דּוֹרֵשׁ שְׁלוֹמוֹ יִשְׂרָאֵל.

ways and procedures of the Torah, as we were taught by the great *Rishonim* and *Aḥaronim*, of blessed memory. However, the foundation of Mussar and the nature of character traits is practical. [Your] honor rightfully questions me [on this difference], yet I stand fast on this counter position – what is this, and why?

Indeed, it is as I have told [you].[8] In Mussar and the ways of character traits, the foundation is practice (the experience of an individual who lives out his vulnerable mortal days on earth is not a well-troden path for Mussar for a great man, may there be many like him in Israel). It is almost a lost cause – for every person, and especially a great man, is a world unto himself, according to his talents, the powers of his soul and intelligence, etc., the qualities of his character, his capacity for sentiment, etc., the state of his engagement, etc.

Regarding the cure of the body, practical experience has grown dramatically, and out of practice was born the wondrous theoretical wisdom, the broad wisdom of medicine. However, when it comes to our interest, the healing of the soul, there is no "practice" to know and communicate from one person to another. So how can we find the wisdom to answer to each questioner in accordance with his ways?

Let [your] honor be at ease in dwelling in the tranquility of his soul. I plan to be [in his vicinity] with the help of God.... Then we will meet, God willing, without taking an oath, to put our minds to his honor, [great in] Torah's ways and hopes: on what hidden [forces] his analysis should focus on, on the mysteries of Mussar and character traits – according to his ways and the vicissitudes of time, in accordance with the present assessment. And God, blessed be His name, will help us to be good and do good.

His friend who seeks his well-being, Israel

8. Compare Genesis 42:14.

כ

יְקָרַת מִכְתַּב כְּבוֹד תּוֹרָתוֹ מִן כ"ב שְׁבָט נָכוֹן הִגִּיעַנִי. אָנֹכִי נָחוּץ לְהָשִׁיב לִכְבוֹד תּוֹרָתוֹ. כְּבָר כָּתַבְתִּי כִּי בְּדַרְכֵי תַּהֲלוּכוֹת הַמּוּסָרִי הַיְסוֹד הַפְּרַאקְטִישׁ. וְאֵין לָתֵת גֶּדֶר נָכוֹן בָּזֶה כְּמוֹ בְּתַהֲלוּכוֹת הַמִּסְחָר. וּבִפְרָט לְאָדָם גָּדוֹל כמי"ב. כָּבֵד הַדָּבָר לִמְאֹד (וְאוּלַי קָרוֹב לְהֶפְסֵד חַס וְחָלִילָה) לִכְתֹּב בָּזֶה אֶת אֲשֶׁר יְנַקְּרוּ בְּמַשְׂכִּיּוֹת לְבַב אִישׁ פְּרָטִי.

וּבִכְלָל בְּכֹחוֹת נֶפֶשׁ הָאָדָם. אֵין לְדַמּוֹת מִלְּתָא לְמִלְּתָא. יֵשׁ אֲשֶׁר בְּדָבָר אֶחָד נָקֵל לְפָנָיו. וּבְדָבָר אַחֵר כָּבֵד לְפָנָיו הַרְבֵּה לְהַשִּׂיגוֹ. וּבַדָּבָר הַקָּשֶׁה הַהֶכְרֵחַ לְהִתְגּוֹלֵל בְּנַחַת. וּלְהַשִּׂיגוֹ בְּרֹב זְמַן וְעִדָּן. עִם הַתְּשׁוּקָה לְהַשִּׂיגוֹ בִּמְהֵרָה. וְהֵן שְׁנֵי כֹּחוֹת מִתְנַגְּדוֹת. אֲשֶׁר צָרִיךְ הָאָדָם לִנְגֹּעַ בִּשְׁנֵיהֶם. כִּי אִם יֶחְדַּל הַתְּשׁוּקָה תִּתְרַפֶּה הַמְּלָאכָה. וְאִם תֶּחֱזַק הַתְּשׁוּקָה בְּיוֹתֵר לִהְיוֹת אָץ. תִּשְׁבַּת כִּמְעַט הָעֲבוֹדָה וְלֹא תִשָּׂא פְּרִי חָלִילָה. הָאָדָם הַנִּלְבָּב הַמַּשְׁקִיף עַל עַצְמוֹ. יָבִין בִּכְלָל אֵיךְ לְתַוֵּךְ בֵּינֵיהֶם בְּלִי גֶּדֶר מְגֻבָּל.

עֵסֶק הַמִּדּוֹת מֻכְרָח מְאֹד וְצָרִיךְ זְמַן וְעִדָּן לָזֶה (לְמִי אֲשֶׁר בְּטִבְעוֹ אֵינוֹ מְסֻגָּל כָּל כָּךְ) הַפְּרַאקְטִישׁ יוֹרֵנוּ כִּי כִּמְעַט לִמּוּד הַמִּדּוֹת תָּלוּי

1. This letter, like the previous ones, is addressed to the recipient in the third person.

Letter 20

[Your] honor's[1] precious letter from the twenty-second of Shevat reached me safely. I must reply to [your] honor. I have already written that practical experience is the basis for how one makes progress in Mussar. It is impossible to prescribe this precisely, like one can [prescribe] how to progress commercially – especially not when [the individual] is a great person [such as yourself], may there be many like him in Israel. It is particularly difficult – perhaps even likely to fail, God forbid – to write in a way that will pierce the outer layers of an individual's heart.

In general, when it comes to the powers of the human psyche, we cannot simply infer from one thing to another.[2] For the individual, one thing might be easy and something else very difficult to achieve. With respect to the difficult matter, it is necessary to grapple with it calmly, achieving [correction] gradually, over the long term – despite the great yearning to achieve it quickly. These are two opposing forces; a person must be attached to both of them. For if he stops desiring [to achieve], he will grow slack in his work. But if the longing becomes too intense and his acts become hasty, his labors will all but shut down and be fruitless, God forbid. A person who is emotionally invested, who engages in self-reflection, will understand generally how to mediate between these [two], despite the absence of a demarcated boundary [between them].

The business of character [refinement] is very necessary; one needs lots of time for it (if he is not naturally adept at it). Practical

2. Compare Yevamot 109b.

בְּמִלֵּי דְעָלְמָא הַמִּתְנַגֵּד לִפְרִישׁוּת. (אוּלַי זֹאת הַסִּבָּה אֲשֶׁר מֵחִפּוּשׂ הַמִּדּוֹת נִרְפֶּה אֶצְלוֹ הַחִיּוּב מִבְּלִי לֵילֵךְ בָּטֵל כו׳ אֲשֶׁר זָכַר כְּבוֹד תּוֹרָתוֹ בְּמִכְתָּבוֹ).

וְאִם כִּי כָּבֵד לְפָנַי הַדָּבָר לִכְתֹּב לִכְבוֹד תּוֹרָתוֹ. כַּאֲשֶׁר הִזְכַּרְתִּי בְּרֵאשִׁית דְּבָרַי. בְּכָל זֹאת אֲדַבְּרָה בִּקְצָרָה. הַיְסוֹד הַלִּמּוּד וְכַאֲשֶׁר הִזְכַּרְתִּיו בִּהְיוֹתוֹ פֹּה. לָתוּר הַמֶּרְכָּז בִּבְקִיאוּת הַנִּפְלָאָה לְבָרֵר כָּל סְבָרָא מִכָּל דִּבְרֵי חֲכָמֵינוּ זַ״ל וּגְדוֹלֵי הַמְחַבְּרִים. עִם תְּקִיפַת הַדַּעַת. וְגַם הַפְּחִידָה בָּזֶה בְּלִי יְסוֹד וְגָדֵר מְגֻבָּל. וְגַם שְׁמִירַת הַבְּרִיאוּת (בְּלִי הַפְלָגָה רַק לֶאֱכֹל וְלִישֹׁן כָּרָאוּי) וְגַם בְּלִי לַעֲזֹב דַּרְכֵי הָעוֹלָם בִּכְתִיבַת הַתְּשׁוּבוֹת כַּנָּהוּג. (אָכֵן בְּכָל זֹאת עִיּוּן הַדִּין כָּרָאוּי לְדַרְכֵי ד׳ יִתְבָּרַךְ שְׁמוֹ).

גַּם הָעִיּוּן מְעַט בְּמוּסָרֵי הַפְּרִישׁוּת. וְעִיּוּן הַמִּדּוֹת בְּדֶרֶךְ מִלֵּי דְעָלְמָא. הַמִּתְנַגְּדִים זֶה לָזֶה בְּלִי גָּדֵר מְגֻבָּל. אֲרִיכוּת הַזְּמַן תִּתֵּן עֵזָה לִפְנֵי כְּבוֹד תּוֹרָתוֹ אֵיךְ לַהֲקִימָם – לֶחֱזוֹת בְּמִדּוֹת בְּנֵי אָדָם וְדַרְכֵי תַּהֲלוּכוֹתֵיהֶם בְּעַיִן יָפָה. וְלָתוּר עַל מִדּוֹתָיו בִּפְרָט. וְאָז בְּאֹרֶךְ הַזְּמַן יִרְאֶה אֶל מַה יִּפְנֶה יְסוֹד עֲמָלוֹ בְּהַנּוֹגֵעַ לְמִדּוֹת לְפִי הִצְטָרְכוּת הַתּוֹעֶלֶת לְטוֹב וּמֵטִיב. יָשִׂים מְעַט עִיּוּנוֹ כו׳.

וּבִכְלָל יָשִׂים מְעַט עִיּוּנוֹ בְּחָכְמַת תַּהֲלוּכוֹת עִם בְּנֵי אָדָם. בַּמֶּה יְזַכֶּה אֶת אָרְחוֹ לְמַעַן תִּמְצָא יָדוֹ לְהַשְׁפִּיעַ עַל זוּלָתוֹ. הַסִּבּוֹת הַמַּגִּיעוֹת אוֹתוֹ לְמַדְרֵגָה זוֹ. וְהַמְּנִיעוֹת הַמּוֹנְעוֹת אוֹתוֹ מִמֶּנָּה – וְעִם כָּל זֶה הַיְסוֹד הַלִּמּוּד כו׳. אִישׁ עוּל יָמִים הַמְצֻיָּן בְּכִשְׁרוֹנָיו מִבְּנֵי גִילוֹ. הַחוֹבָה עָלָיו לְהִתְחַשֵּׁב לְגֶבֶר בְּגוּבְרִין מִצַּד אֶחָד. לְמַעַן יִמְצָא אֶת לְבָבוֹ לְהַשְׁפִּיעַ לְהוֹעִיל. וּבְיוֹתֵר לְהַחֲזִיק אֶת עַצְמוֹ מִצַּד אַחֵר לִצְעִיר

---

3. Though one major tactic of the Mussar of previous generations was to separate from worldly needs and drives, R. Salanter here stresses the importance of using insights from worldly matters as key guides to Mussar practice.
4. In this letter, R. Salanter explores another of his distinctive themes: the need to combine contradictory drives/tendencies in order to gain the right insight or quality of character. He refers to longing to get it done at once, combined with patience and repetition; to worldliness (exemplified by the practice of writing responsa, an exercise in bringing hypothetical learning to a practical conclusion) combined with asceticism; to self-assertion combined with humility and hesitation.

experience teaches that the study of character traits depends almost entirely on the ways of the world – which stand in opposition to asceticism.[3] (Perhaps this is why [your] pursuit of [improved] character has weakened [your] commitment, although without completely nullifying it, etc., as [your] honor mentioned in [your] letter.)

Even though it is hard for me to write to [your] honor, as I mentioned at the beginning of my words, I will nevertheless speak briefly. The basis [of improvement through Mussar] is to study – as I mentioned to [you] when [you] were here – to explore the area with encyclopedic knowledge, to clarify every rationale from all the words of the Sages, of blessed memory, and the great codifiers, albeit with bold judgment – though here, too, there is no clearly marked boundary [between the drive for encyclopedic knowledge and the drive to express original ideas]. Alongside this, one must preserve health (without excess – rather, eating and drinking properly); and without abandoning the worldly practice of writing responsa, as is customary.[4] (Indeed, with all these [qualifiers], study of the laws [must be done] as is appropriate to the ways of God, blessed be His name.)

Also: in studying a bit of ascetic Mussar and in studying character traits according to the way of worldly matters – [these two components of study] conflict with each other without clear boundaries. The passage of time will have its effect on [your] honor, to show how to uphold all of these [approaches].

Observe the character traits of people and their conduct with a generous eye; probe [your] own character traits in detail. Then, over time, [you] will see where you should direct [your] basic efforts as far as character traits are concerned – according to what is necessary for the goal of being good and doing good; [you] will pay some attention etc.

In general, some of [your] study of the behavioral sciences should be together with people – [to understand] the methods by which [your] approach can successfully influence others, what can cause [you] to achieve this level, and what obstacles prevent [you] from it. And with all this, the basis [of improvement through Mussar] is study…

A young person who is superior to his peers in his talents must be reckoned as a man among men, on the one hand – so he can find the courage to influence effectively – but on the other hand, and even

יָמִים. לְהִתְלַמֵּד לִהְיוֹת מֻכְשָׁר לֶעָתִיד לְהוֹעִיל לָרַבִּים לְפִי הָעֵת וְהַזְּמַן לָכֵן כו׳. וְהָעִקָּר בְּלִי שׁוּם קַפְּדָנוּת. וְכֵן לְמַעֵט בְּדַעְתֵּנוּ מִלַּעֲמֹד עַל דַּעְתּוֹ. וּלְהַרְגִּיל אֶת עַצְמוֹ בְּנַחַת אֲשֶׁר הַזְּמַן תִּתֵּן פִּרְיוֹ בְּעֶזְרַת ה׳.
יְדִידוֹ דּוֹרֵשׁ שְׁלוֹמוֹ יִשְׂרָאֵל.

more so, he should carry himself as a young person, conditioning himself to become prepared to help people in the future, at the right time and conditions. Therefore…

And the main thing is: Avoid any impatience; limit rigidity of thought and insistence on [your] own opinion; and habituate [yourself] gently, as time will bear its fruit, with the help of God...

Your friend, who seeks your peace, Israel

כא

יְדִידַי מַה מְּאֹד נִפְלֵאתִי עֲלֵיכֶם עַל מְנִיעַת מִכְתַּבְכֶם אֵלַי. וְלֹא הוֹדַעְתּוּנִי מְאוּמָה מֵהַלִּמּוּד לְמַעֲשֶׂה. אֲשֶׁר הִטְרַחְתִּי עִמָּכֶם הַרְבֵּה אֵיךְ הוּא אֶצְלְכֶם. וְאַתֶּם יְדַעְתֶּם כִּי לִבִּי הוֹמֶה עַל זֶה. לִתְקֹעַ אֶת הַדָּבָר הַנִּצְרָךְ הַלָּזֶה. הַלִּמּוּד לְמַעֲשֶׂה בְּלֵב יִרְאֵי ד׳. מִכְּבָר דָּרַשְׁתִּי מֵאֵת יְדִידִי ר״ג נ״י. לְהוֹדִיעֵנִי מִזֶּה וְלֹא עָנָנִי מְאוּמָה. עַתָּה הִסְכַּלְתֶּם עֲשׂוֹ. וְכָעֵת בַּקָּשָׁתִי שְׁטוּחָה לִפְנֵיכֶם לַהֲשִׁיבֵנִי בְּפָאסְט הַחוֹזֶרֶת אֶת הַדָּבָר בָּאֵר הֵיטֵב. אוֹדִיעֲכֶם כִּי לְפִי הַנִּרְאֶה נִצְרָךְ לֵידַע לְמִצְוַת הֲשָׁבַת אֲבֵדָה אֵיזֶה הָיָה מִיּוֹרֶה דֵּעָה וְאַצִּיג דָּבָר אֶחָד לְדוּגְמָא כו׳ כו׳.

הוּא הַדָּבָר אֲשֶׁר דִּבַּרְתִּי עִמָּכֶם. שֶׁלִּשְׁמִירַת הַדִּין לִהְיוֹת סוּר מֵרַע. אֲשֶׁר הוּא הַחִיּוּב הַקּוֹדֵם בַּעֲבוֹדַת ה׳. צָרִיךְ לִרְאוֹת לֵידַע מַאי דְּאֶפְשָׁר. וּלְתַקֵּן מַאי דְּאֶפְשָׁר בְּהֶקְדֵּם. עַד אֲשֶׁר לֹא נִלְכַּד בְּחַבְלֵי הַנִּסְיוֹנוֹת. אֲשֶׁר אֲנַחְנוּ מִתְפַּלְּלִים עַל זֶה בְּכָל יוֹם. אֵיךְ נָעֵז פָּנֵינוּ לְבַקֵּשׁ מֵאֵת ד׳. וַאֲנַחְנוּ בְּעַצְמֵנוּ לֹא נִיגַע לְהָסִיר הַמִּכְשׁוֹלוֹת. הַמְיֻעָדִים לִלְמֹד

---

1. Compare Genesis 31:28.
2. *Yoreh De'ah,* lit. "will teach knowledge" (see Is. 28:9), is one of the four sections of *Shulḥan Arukh,* the authoritative code of Jewish law, which includes ritual laws of *kashrut* and family purity, and a range of other laws concerning topics like returning lost articles, charity, mourning, conversion, the land of Israel, honoring parents and teachers, etc.

   This reference to practical law reflects R. Salanter's continuing stress that knowing the law is the key to proper ethical behavior and that, in studying the laws, one should focus on their practical application.

Letter 21

My friends:

I am quite astonished that you held back from writing to me. You have not told me at all about applied [Mussar] study, about which I often bother you [to tell me] how it goes with you. You know my heart yearns to inject this much-needed thing – applied [Mussar] study – in the hearts of those who fear God. Some time ago I asked my friend, R.G., may his light shine, to inform me about this, but he hasn't answered me at all. Now you have acted foolishly.[1] So I lay before you my request: respond to me thoroughly on this matter by return mail. I will tell you: it seems we need to know some halakha from *Yoreh De'ah*[2] in order to perform the mitzva of returning lost articles. I present one matter for example....

This is just as I have spoken to you.[3] As regards observance of the law, to be one who "turns away from evil" – for this is the first duty in the service of God – one must seek to know whatever possible and to correct whatever possible as soon as possible, before we are caught in the coils of temptation. We pray for this every day.[4] How can we dare ask it of God when we ourselves make no effort to remove the obstacles – we who have been charged to "study and teach"[5] so that

---

3. Compare Genesis 42:14.
4. "Lead us not into infraction or sin... nor into temptation..." (the conclusion of the morning blessings; see Berakhot 60b).
5. Avot 4:5 as well as the blessing prior to the recitation of the *Shema* in the morning.

וּלְלַמֵּד לִמּוּד לְמַעֲשֶׂה. אֲשֶׁר זֶה הוּא עִקַּר גְּדֻלַּת הַתַּלְמוּד מִמַּעֲשֶׂה. שֶׁתַּלְמוּד מֵבִיא לִידֵי מַעֲשֶׂה. מֵהָרָאוּי הָיָה לְהַאֲרִיךְ יוֹתֵר. אָכֵן אֲיַחֵל לְמִכְתָּבָם בְּפָּאסְט הַמְּקֻדָּם. דַּקְדְּקוּ בְּמִכְתָּבִי וְתַקְּנוּ הַשְּׁגִיאוֹת שֶׁבּוֹ וִיהְיֶה אֱלֹהִים עִמָּכֶם. כְּנַפְשֵׁיכֶם וּכְנֶפֶשׁ יְדִידְכֶם מְצַפֶּה לְמִכְתָּבָם. יִשְׂרָאֵל בְּהָרַב מהרז"ו נ"י.

the learning is applied in practice? After all, the essential superiority of study over action is that study leads to action.[6] It would be worthwhile to expand on this.

Thus, I look forward to your letter in the earliest post. Read my letter carefully and correct the errors in it. And may God be with you.

> [Act in accordance with the urging of] your soul and the soul of your friend who anticipates your letter.

Israel, son of our rabbi and teacher, R. Zev Wolf, may his light shine.

6. See Kiddushin 40a–b, where the Talmud discusses whether learning or action is superior, and concludes that learning is superior, as it leads to action.

כב

מִכְתַּב כְּבוֹד תּוֹרָתוֹ מִן חֹדֶשׁ דְּנָא הִגִּיעַנִי כָּעֵת. וְהִנְנִי נָחוּץ לִכְתֹּב אֵלָיו כִּמְבֻקָּשָׁתוֹ.

זֶה כָּל הָאָדָם לִהְיוֹת מוֹשֵׁל בְּרוּחוֹ, לְהַטּוֹתָהּ לְחֶפְצוֹ אֶל אֲשֶׁר יִשְׁאַל רוּחַ מַצָּבוֹ – אִם לְעַצֵּב לְהִתְמַרְמֵר עַל עֲבוֹדָתוֹ יִתְבָּרַךְ שְׁמוֹ כִּי חָלְפָה. כִּי בַּמֵּתִים חָפְשִׁי – אִם לִמְנוּחַת הַשְׁקָטַת הַנֶּפֶשׁ, עַל אִישׁ יָשָׁר הוֹלֵךְ לְדַרְכּוֹ וּלְבֵית עוֹלָמוֹ הַנִּצְחִי, אֲשֶׁר זֶה תִּקְוַת כָּל אֱנוֹשׁ עַל פְּנֵי הָאֲדָמָה, וְזֶה פְּרִי תַּכְלִיתוֹ וּמְתוּקָה שְׁנַת הָעוֹבֵד כו׳.

לוּלֵי דִּבְרֵי חֲכָמֵינוּ ז״ל הַחֲזָקִים לְאַשֵּׁר וּלְקַיֵּם אֶת כָּל אֲשֶׁר הוֹרוּנוּ, הָיָה הַדַּעַת נוֹתֵן, לִהְיוֹת כְּצוּר נִצָּב נֶגֶד חֵפֶץ הַטִּבְעִי חַיֵּי אֲשֶׁר הָעוֹלָם הַזֶּה מִלְּהִתְאוֹנֵן עַל פְּרִידַת אָדָם הַנַּעֲלֶה, רְכוּשׁוֹ בְּיָדוֹ – וּמִי

---

1. This letter is R. Salanter's reply to a letter informing him of the death of a good person during a cholera epidemic. R. Salanter seeks to guide his correspondent as to how to deal with the threat of the epidemic, the shock of the untimely death of an innocent good man, and how to handle feelings of grief and loss, especially in light of the doctors' warning that excessive grief can weaken the body's resistance and ability to fight off disease.
2. Compare Ecclesiastes 12:13.
3. Compare Proverbs 16:32, Avot 4:1.
4. Meaning to turn it toward his desired outcome in accordance with the Torah's prescribed good behavior – as against where uncontrolled desire [instinct] could lead him.
5. I.e., premature death cut off a person's service of God before their time.

Letter 22

[Your] honor's letter of this month just reached me, and I feel it is urgent that I write [to you] as [you] requested.[1]

The whole purpose of man[2] is to control his spirit,[3] to divert it by his will[4] to whatever his situation demands. [In this case, someone has died, so there is a choice] whether to direct the spirit toward sadness, to be embittered by [the dead man's loss of] His service, blessed be His name, for it has passed,[5] that is, because "the dead are free" [of the Torah and commandments];[6] or, to direct one's spirit toward calming and relaxing the soul, [by regarding this death as a case of] a good man who is on his way to his eternal rest, which is the aspiration of every human being on the face of the earth. This eternal bliss is the fruit of his purpose; "Sweet is the sleep of the toiler…."[7]

Were it not for the strong words of our Sages, of blessed memory, which confirm and uphold all that we have taught, it would stand to reason that we should stand firm as a rock[8] against the natural desire for a happy life in this world,[9] and we would not complain about the

6. Shabbat 30a: "R. Yoḥanan says: 'The dead are free' (Ps. 88:6) – when a person dies, he becomes free of the Torah and the commandments."
7. Compare Ecclesiastes 5:11. R. Salanter's application is that the person is enjoying the fruits of his labor, i.e., his good deeds, in the next world as he sleeps in death.
8. I.e., we would not mourn at all because earning bliss in the World to Come is our main concern.
9. The natural desire is to focus on life in this world; accordingly, it makes sense to mourn the death of someone who departed with unfulfilled desires. However, the

יוֹדֵעַ אַחֲרִיתוֹ מִלְחַמְתּוֹ אִם הָיָה חַי – אָכֵן אַחַר דִּבְרֵי חֲכָמֵינוּ זַ״ל לְהַלֵּךְ לִמְצֹא דֶּרֶךְ, אֵיךְ לְהָקִים דְּאָגָה וְיָגוֹן בַּלֵּב.

וְלָזֹאת לְכָל עֵת, וּלְכָל חֵפֶץ זְמַן – כָּעֵת אֲשֶׁר הַמַּחֲלָה הַלָּזוֹ נִרְאֲתָה בָּאָרֶץ רַחֲמָנָא לִצְלַן גַּם בְּפֹּה – זֹאת תּוֹרַת הָאָדָם, וְזֶה שֵׂכֶל הַיָּשָׁר, לְבִלִּי לִפְחֹד מִמֶּנָּה מְאוּמָה, כִּי מַה הוּא חַיֵּי הָאָדָם בְּכָל הָאֳפָנִים, כִּי מִי יוֹדֵעַ אִם יִכְשַׁר דַּרְכּוֹ, וְגַם לִשְׁמֹר הַהַנְהָגָה אֶת אֲשֶׁר יוֹרוּנוּ חַכְמֵי הָרוֹפְאִים, אֲשֶׁר לְאוֹר דִּבְרֵיהֶם נֵלֵךְ גַּם עַל פִּי הַדָּת, וּלְהָקִים עַל חַיֵּי עוֹלָם הַזֶּה לְטוֹב וּמֵטִיב.

וְהַנִּסָּיוֹן הוֹרָנוּ בְּיָמִים חוֹלְפִים אֲשֶׁר גָּבְרָה רַחֲמָנָא לִצְלַן הַמַּחֲלָה לִמְאֹד, כִּי כָּל אֲשֶׁר נָשָׂא שִׁכְמוֹ לִסְבֹּל עֹל הַנְהָגַת הָרוֹפְאִים בַּאֲכִילָתוֹ כוּ׳ כְּחָכָם וְלֹא כִּכְסִיל, לֹא נִרְאָה בוֹ נֶגַע וּמַחֲלָה רַחֲמָנָא לִצְלַן, וְלָזֹאת כַּאֲשֶׁר כָּל הַנְהָגַת הַדָּת נִשְׁתַּנָּה עַל פִּי הַדִּין בָּעֵת הַלָּזוֹ – אֵין לְרַבּוֹת בִּמְרִירוּת בַּיָּמִים הַקְּדוֹשִׁים, וְעֵת לִשְׁמֹר וְלַעֲבֹד אֶת ה׳ בְּחֶדְוָה וְהִיא הַמָּעוֹז.

Sages' approach, while emphasizing the reward of the next world, nevertheless takes this world seriously and calls on us to mourn loss of life. (See n. 11.)

10. He acquired wisdom and good deeds that assured his place in the next world.
11. R. Salanter is saying that the rational (i.e., religious) reaction to the death of the righteous should be joy, as he has achieved life's ultimate goal of attaining eternal reward in the next world. This shows yet again that R. Salanter profoundly internalized the centrality of reward and punishment in the next world to life in this world. Nevertheless, one must follow the Sages and train his heart to experience fear and grief. Actually, he is acknowledging that the Sages give greater weight to the significance of this life (or its untimely loss) than he does.
12. Compare Ecclesiastes 3:1–2. R. Salanter is saying that the epidemic has created a time for grief in our life. We also are pained by the untimely loss of life. Nevertheless, we should guide our emotions not to fear the plague.
13. Compare II Samuel 7:19. The verse in II Samuel carries the overtone that this guidance is a gracious, unmerited gift from God.
14. Halakha considers "You shall safeguard your lives very much" (Deut. 4:15) to be a mitzva. Halakha also rules that saving a life overrules all of the Torah's commandments except for three.
15. Literally: bowed his shoulder to bear [the weight of] the doctors' instructions. Compare Genesis 49:15.

departure of a noble man; his possessions are in his hand,[10] and who knows what would be the outcome of his struggle, were he to live on?! However, we must follow the words of the Sages, of blessed memory, to go and find a way to maintain fear and grief in our heart.[11]

Yet, for everything there is an occasion, and for every experience, a time.[12] Now that this plague has appeared in the land, and even here – may the Merciful One save us – this is the teaching that should guide a person,[13] and this is common sense: Do not be afraid of [the disease] at all. For what is human life in any case? Who knows if his [future] path [in life] would have turned out [to be] upright.

Furthermore, we must act in accordance with the wise doctors' instructions – for our religion tells us to walk by the light of their words[14] and thus uphold this life to be good and do good.

Experience also taught us in past days when the plague was rife, may the Merciful One save us, that whoever submitted to the burden of the doctors' orders[15] vis-à-vis diet, etc., wisely, not foolishly, was not affected by plague or disease, may the Merciful One save us.

Thus, since all religious behavior is altered according to halakha itself[16] at this time, one should not be excessively bitter on the holidays. This is the time to observe and serve God in joy, and this will be our strength.[17]

---

16. R. Salanter is saying that one should not view the shift away from mourning and grief as the interference of a "secular" or "outside" approach in halakhic practice. Rather, halakha itself commands us to follow the instructions of physicians. This is in keeping with R. Salanter's leadership during the cholera epidemic in Vilna in 1848. R. Salanter insisted not only on doing life-saving work on Shabbat (and eating on Yom Kippur to protect life), but that all should follow doctors' orders and do anything that promotes health, without trying to minimize medically prescribed halakhic changes or seeking exemptions for religious activities.
17. See Nehemiah 8:10. There is a tension between joy and dread during the Days of Awe. Here, R. Salanter is instructing his disciples to tilt the balance away from dread by alluding to Ezra the Scribe's admonition of those who were weeping on Rosh HaShana that they should prepare festive meals and rejoice, for it is a joyous day. He is also responding to the doctors' instructions that grief and mourning make the individual more vulnerable to illness, while joy strengthens resistance to the plague. The shift of balance from dread to joy is appropriate in a time of plague.

כֵּן אֵין לִדְאֹג וְאֵין לְהִתְאוֹנֵן עַל נֶפֶשׁ יְקָרָה, כִּי נִפְטְרָה מִצָּרָתָהּ חַיֵּי הַהֶבֶל, לָבוֹא לִמְחוֹז דַּרְכָּהּ הַנְּכוֹנָה תְּהֵא נַפְשׁוֹ צְרוּרָה בִּצְרוֹר הַחַיִּים.

יְנַחֵם ד׳ יִתְבָּרַךְ שְׁמוֹ אֶת כְּבוֹד כו׳.

תִּתְבָּרְכוּ בִּרְכַּת מַזָּל טוֹב וּבְרָכָה שְׁנוֹת חַיִּים וְשָׁלוֹם.

Similarly, do not grieve or be upset about the precious soul [of the dead], for it has been freed from the troubles of vain life to go on to the ultimate destination of its journey.[18] May his soul be preserved in the bonds of life.

May God, may His name be blessed, comfort [you] ...

May you be blessed with the blessing of *mazal tov,* and the blessing of years of life and peace.

18. R. Salanter concludes by reasserting his belief that the untimely death of a righteous person means that the person has left the vanities of this life and gone to a desirable eternal reward.

גַּם זֶה מָצָאתִי בִּכְתַב יָדוֹ הַקְּדוֹשָׁה.

כג

בַּגְּמָרָא שַׁבָּת דַּף כ"א, מַאי חֲנֻכָּה דְּתָנוּ רַבָּנָן בְּכ"ה בְּכִסְלֵו יוֹמֵי דַּחֲנֻכָּה כו' נַעֲשָׂה בּוֹ נֵס כו'. לְשָׁנָה אַחֶרֶת קְבָעוּם וַעֲשָׂאוּם יָמִים טוֹבִים בְּהַלֵּל וְהוֹדָאָה עַיֵּן שָׁם. וְיֵשׁ לְהָבִין הָא דְּלֹא עֲשָׂאוֹ גַּם בְּמִשְׁתֶּה כְּמוֹ בְּפוּרִים, הֲלֹא גַּם הָכָא הָיָה נֵס בַּגּוּף. כְּמַאֲמַר הַתְּפִלָּה מָסַרְתָּ גִּבּוֹרִים כו' וְרַבִּים כו'.

הָעִנְיָן יֵשׁ לְהַסְבִּיר בְּהֶקְדֵּם מַאֲמָרָם זַ"ל בַּגְּמָרָא מוֹעֵד קָטָן דַּף כ"ה, מִפְּנֵי מָה בָּנָיו וּבְנוֹתָיו שֶׁל אָדָם מֵתִין כְּשֶׁהֵן קְטַנִּים כו'. מִפְּנֵי שֶׁלֹּא בָּכָה וְהִתְאַבֵּל עַל אָדָם כָּשֵׁר כו'. וְיֵשׁ לְהַסְבִּיר הַמִּדָּה כְּנֶגֶד מִדָּה, בְּהֶקְדֵּם מַאֲמַר בְּיַלְקוּט תְּהִלִּים תש"י.

כְּשֶׁנָּתַן הַקָּדוֹשׁ-בָּרוּךְ-הוּא תּוֹרָה לְיִשְׂרָאֵל הָיָה קוֹלוֹ הוֹלֵךְ כו' וְכָל מַלְכֵי הָעוֹלָם כו' נִתְקַבְּצוּ אֵצֶל בִּלְעָם אָמְרוּ לוֹ מֶה קוֹל הֶהָמוֹן הַזֶּה שֶׁשָּׁמַעְנוּ כו' אָמַר לָהֶם כו' אֶלָּא חֶמְדָּה טוֹבָה יֵשׁ לוֹ בְּבֵית גְּנָזָיו כו' וְנוֹתְנָהּ לְעַמּוֹ שֶׁנֶּאֱמַר ד' עֹז לְעַמּוֹ יִתֵּן. עָנוּ כֻּלָּם וְאָמְרוּ ד' עֹז

1. "*Hallel*" means "praise" and also refers to the series of psalms recited on Ḥanukka and other Jewish holidays.
2. From the *Al HaNissim* ("For the miracles") prayer inserted into the *Amida* prayer and *Birkat HaMazon* during Ḥanukka.

I also found this written by his holy hand.
[R. Isaac Blazer]

Letter 23

The Talmud [states], in Shabbat 21b: "What is Ḥanukka? Our Rabbis taught: On the twenty-fifth of Kislev, the days of Ḥanukka.... A miracle occurred thereon.... The next year they permanently instituted them as holidays with praise[1] and thanksgiving." See further there.

We must understand why they did not institute feasting, as on Purim. After all, here, too, there was a miracle involving the body, as the liturgy states: "You delivered the mighty [to the weak]... the many [to the few]...."[2]

[To understand] this matter, we must first explain [the Sages'] statement in Moed Katan 25a: "Why do a person's sons and daughters die young...? Because he did not weep and mourn at the death of a worthy person."[3] We can explain how this is *quid pro quo* by first citing a statement from *Yalkut* [*Shimoni*], Psalms, 710:

> When the Holy One, blessed be He, gave the Torah to Israel, His voice went forth... and all the kings of the world... gathered around Balaam and asked: What is this mighty noise we have heard...? He said to them... He has a wondrous delight in His treasure house... and He is giving it to His people, as it says: "God

3. The passage continues: "For whoever weeps and mourns over a worthy person is forgiven all his sins, due to the honor he showed the deceased."

כו׳ ד׳ יְבָרֵךְ אֶת עַמּוֹ בַשָּׁלוֹם. לְהַסְבִּיר הַדָּבָר נַקְדִּים מַה שֶּׁבְּפָרָשַׁת רְאֵה בְּחַג הַשָּׁבוּעוֹת מְסַיֵּם וְזָכַרְתָּ כו׳ אֶת הַחֻקִּים הָאֵלֶּה, וְלֹא בְּפֶסַח וְסֻכּוֹת.

וְיֵשׁ לְבָאֵר הָעִנְיָן כִּי נוֹדַע הַפְּלוּגְתָּא בְּעֵרוּבִין דַּף י״ג שֶׁבֵּין בֵּית שַׁמַּאי וּבֵית הִלֵּל. אִם נוֹחַ לוֹ לָאָדָם שֶׁנִּבְרָא יוֹתֵר מִשֶּׁלֹּא נִבְרָא. נִמְנוּ וְגָמְרוּ נוֹחַ לוֹ לָאָדָם שֶׁלֹּא נִבְרָא יוֹתֵר מִשֶּׁנִּבְרָא כו׳. כִּי הֲגַם שֶׁבִּבְרִיאַת הָאָדָם יֵשׁ רֶוַח הַרְבֵּה אִם מַצְדִּיק מַעֲשָׂיו. אָכֵן הַהֶזֵּק מָצוּי לִמְאֹד כַּאֲשֶׁר עֵינֵינוּ רוֹאוֹת כִּי הָרֹב נִכְשָׁלִים בַּעֲבֵרוֹת, וְלָזֹאת לְפִי שֵׂכֶל הָאָדָם נוֹחַ לוֹ לָאָדָם שֶׁלֹּא נִבְרָא כו׳, כֵּן בְּמַתַּן תּוֹרָה הָיָה בְּרִיאָה חֲדָשָׁה, לְקַיֵּם תַּרְיַ״ג מִצְוֹת אֲשֶׁר אֵין עֵרֶךְ לְמַתַּן שְׂכָרָן. אָכֵן לְעֻמַּת זֶה בְּקַבָּלַת הַתּוֹרָה הַהֶזֵּק מָצוּי, לְהֵעָנֵשׁ עַל תּוֹרָה גְּדוֹלָה כָּזֹאת, לָזֹאת הָעוֹבְדֵי כּוֹכָבִים לֹא רָצוּ לְהִכָּנֵס בְּסַכָּנָה, וְרַק יִשְׂרָאֵל הָלְכוּ בְּתֹם, (עַיֵּן שַׁבָּת דַּף פ״ח תֻּמַּת גו׳), לְקַיֵּם רְצוֹן הַשֵּׁם יִתְבָּרַךְ, כְּמוֹ שֶׁהָיָה רְצוֹנוֹ יִתְבָּרַךְ שְׁמוֹ בִּבְרִיאַת הָאָדָם שֶׁהוּא נֶגֶד שִׂכְלֵנוּ כַּנִּזְכָּר לְעֵיל.

וְהִנֵּה הָעֳנָשִׁים הֵמָּה בָּעוֹלָם הַנִּצְחִי וְגַם בָּעוֹלָם הַזֶּה, אֶלָּא שֶׁלְּעָנְשֵׁי עוֹלָם הַזֶּה יֵשׁ תַּקָּנָה כְּמַאֲמָרָם ז״ל בִּפְסָחִים וּבְיַלְקוּט הוֹשֵׁעַ ב׳ תק״כ. גָּדוֹל הַשָּׁלוֹם כו׳ אֵינוֹ יָכוֹל לִשְׁלֹט בָּהֶם כו׳. וְהָעִקָּר מַה שֶּׁפָּחֲדוּ הָעוֹבְדֵי כּוֹכָבִים הוּא מִפֻּרְעָנוּת הָעוֹלָם הַזֶּה, כִּי עוֹלָם הַבָּא אֵינוֹ נִכְנָס בַּלֵּב בִּמְהֵרָה, לָזֹאת כַּאֲשֶׁר שָׁמְעוּ שֶׁקִּבְּלוּ יִשְׂרָאֵל אֶת הַתּוֹרָה, עָנוּ כֻּלָּם ד׳ יְבָרֵךְ אֶת עַמּוֹ בַשָּׁלוֹם, שֶׁיִּנָּצְלוּ מִפֻּרְעָנוּת הָעוֹלָם הַזֶּה.

will give strength to His people" (Ps. 29:11). Then they all replied and said: "God will give strength [to His people], God will bless His people with peace."

To explain this matter, we must preface it with by noting that in the Torah portion of *Re'eh,* [the section dealing] with the festival of Shavuot concludes: "And you shall remember [that you were slaves in the land of Egypt] ... [and you shall keep] these statutes" (Deut. 16:12) – whereas [the sections about] Passover and Sukkot do not [conclude thus].

We can now propose the following idea. There is a well-known argument, in Eiruvin 13b, between the Schools of Shammai and Hillel, about whether a person is better off being created. "They voted and concluded: A person is better off having not been created than having been created...." For although a person stands to gain a great deal if he is righteous in his actions, loss is nevertheless all too common, for, as we see, most people succumb to sin. Thus, human reason dictates that a person is better off not having been created....

Thus, the giving of the Torah was a new creation – [a new opportunity] to uphold 613 mitzvot, whose reward is immeasurable. On the other hand, with receipt of the Torah comes the prevalence of loss and punishment for [violating] this great Torah. Therefore, the idolaters did not want to take on the risk. Only the people of Israel followed with guileless integrity (see Shabbat 88b, "The guileless integrity [of the upright] shall guide them" [Prov. 11:3]), to fulfill the will of God, blessed be He – just as His will to create man contravenes human reason, as noted.

Now, there are punishments in the eternal world and in this world, except that the punishments of this world can rectified, as they, of blessed memory, said in Pesaḥim and in the *Yalkut* [*Shimoni*], Hosea, 2:520: "Great is peace, [for as long as the people of Israel are at peace with each other,] [the enemy] cannot rule over them...." The main thing the idolaters feared was [divine] retribution in this world, because the next world does not enter the heart easily. Therefore, when they heard that Israel accepted the Torah, they all said: "May God bless His people with peace," so that they are saved from retribution in this world.

וְלָזֹאת לְפִי שֵׂכֶל הָאָדָם. אֵין מָקוֹם לִשְׂמֹחַ בְּשָׁבוּעוֹת עַל קַבָּלַת הַתּוֹרָה, וְרַק הוּא חֹק, לָכֵן כְּתִיב בָּהּ וְשָׁמַרְתָּ וְעָשִׂיתָ אֶת הַחֻקִּים כּוּ׳ מַה שֶּׁאֵין כֵּן בְּפֶסַח וְסֻכּוֹת הַשֵּׂכֶל נוֹתֵן לִשְׂמֹחַ עַל הַנֵּס – וּבָזֹאת מַה שֶּׁהָאָדָם רוֹצֶה לִחְיוֹת הִיא רַק תַּאֲוָה גּוּפָנִית, כִּי לְפִי שֵׂכֶל הָאֲמִתִּי נוֹחַ לוֹ לָאָדָם שֶׁלֹּא נִבְרָא, וְיוֹתֵר טוֹב לָמוּת חַס וְשָׁלוֹם לְמַעַן לֹא יְקַלְקֵל עוֹד בַּעֲבֵרוֹת, אָכֵן יֵשׁ מָקוֹם גַּם בַּשֵּׂכֶל לִרְצוֹן הַחַיִּים. לְתַקֵּן הֶעָבָר אֲשֶׁר אֵין זְמַנָּהּ רַק בַּחַיִּים. אָכֵן בְּאָדָם כָּשֵׁר שֶׁלֹּא נִכְשַׁל בַּעֲבֵרוֹת, וְכֵן בִּקְטַנִּים הַמָּוֶת חַס וְחָלִילָה יוֹתֵר טוֹב לְפִי שֵׂכֶל הָאֱנוֹשִׁי.

אָכֵן הַשֵּׁם יִתְבָּרַךְ רוֹצֶה בַּחַיִּים כְּמוֹ שֶׁבָּרָא הָאָדָם, הֲגַם כִּי נוֹחַ לוֹ שֶׁלֹּא נִבְרָא, וְלָזֹאת הַמִּצְוָה לִבְכּוֹת עַל אָדָם כָּשֵׁר, וְזֶהוּ הַמִּדָּה כְּנֶגֶד מִדָּה, כְּשֶׁלֹּא בָּכָה עַל אָדָם כָּשֵׁר, וְהָלַךְ אַחַר שֵׂכֶל הָאֱנוֹשִׁי, בָּנָיו מֵתִים חַס וְחָלִילָה כְּשֶׁהֵם קְטַנִּים לְטוֹב לָהֶם לְפִי שֵׂכֶל הָאֱנוֹשִׁי.

וְהִנֵּה יִסּוּרִים גַּם לְפִי שֵׂכֶל הָאֱנוֹשִׁי אֵינֶנָּה טוֹבָה, כִּי הָאָדָם מְחֻיָּב גַּם בְּיִסּוּרִין עַל שְׁמִירַת הַתּוֹרָה, וְהַנִּסָּיוֹן רַבָּה זֶהוּ מַאֲמָרָם זַ״ל בָּבָא בַּתְרָא דַּף ח׳ רָעָב כּוּ׳ שְׁבִי כּוּ׳ קָשֶׁה כַּנִּזְכָּר לְעֵיל, וְלָזֹאת בְּפוּרִים הַנֵּס לְנַפְשִׁי לְהַמְדַבֵּק שִׂכְלוֹ בַּד׳ יִתְבָּרַךְ שְׁמוֹ, כִּי רְצוֹנוֹ בְּחַיֵּי הָאָדָם, אוֹ הַדָּבֵק בַּגּוּפָנִי, כִּי תַּאֲוַת הַחַיִּים גְּדֵלָה לִמְאֹד, אֲבָל

4. Beginning in the early medieval era, Jewish thinkers have differentiated between "*ḥukkim*" and "*mishpatim*." The former term refers to commandments whose rationales are inaccessible and that seem arbitrary, whereas the latter comports with conventional notions of natural reason, justice, and morality. Here, R. Salanter is categorizing rejoicing on the festival of Shavuot as a *ḥok*, asserting that it is unreasonable to celebrate the giving of the Torah, as most people will fail to live up to its standards, thus incurring divine punishment.
5. On these two festivals, the joy over the miracle of liberation from Egypt is unalloyed by anxiety about new responsibilities and the punishments for failure to meet them.
6. Who are innocent.
7. I.e., when we weep for a worthy person, we show that we are looking at the world from God's view, as it were; from a human standpoint, we should rejoice at the death of the worthy, as the deceased person has successfully navigated this world's minefield of temptation and will now reap eternal reward. However, God created

Thus, according to human reason, it does not make sense to rejoice on Shavuot for receiving the Torah; rather, it is a statute ("*ḥok*"),[4] and hence it is written with regard to it: "And you shall keep these statutes." In contrast, reason dictates that we rejoice over the miracles associated with Passover and Sukkot.[5]

The desire to live is only a bodily instinct, for according to true reason, it would have been better for man to have not been created. It is better to die, God forbid, rather than being further ruined by sin. To be sure, even according to reason [and not only bodily instinct], it can make sense to want to live in order to rectify the past, which can only be done in [this] life. But for a worthy man who never succumbed to sin, and for children,[6] death (God forbid) is better – according to human logic.

However, God, blessed be He, wants life – indeed, He created man even though it is better for man not to have been created. This is why there is a mitzva to weep for a worthy person.[7] And when one does not weep for a worthy person, he shows that he follows human reason [according to which the worthy person is better off dead], and *quid pro quo*, his children die young, God forbid, which, according to human reason, is better for them.

Suffering, [as opposed to death,] is not good even according to human reason, for a person is obligated to keep the Torah even when suffering. This is a terrible trial, as [the Sages] say in Bava Batra 8b:

> "[Such as are for death, to death; and such as are for the sword, to the sword; and such as are for famine, to] famine; [and such as are for captivity, to] captivity" [(Jer. 15:2). And R. Yoḥanan says: The later [a punishment appears] in this verse, the more] severe.

So on Purim, the miracle [was deeply experienced by] the spiritual [person], whose reason adheres to God, blessed be His name, in that he wants humans to live; and by the person who clings to bodily existence, for his yearning for life is very great. But for the average person it was

---

man for life in this world, and from that perspective, the loss of a worthy human life is indeed cause for mourning.

לְהַמְמֻצָּע לֹא הָוֵי נֵס כָּל כָּךְ, זֶהוּ שַׂק וָאֵפֶר יֻצַּע לָרַבִּים דַּיְקָא, לֹא לְכֻלָּם, וְלָזֹאת בְּפוּרִים הַמִּצְוָה בַּמְּגִלָּה הִיא נַפְשִׁי, וּבַמִּשְׁתֶּה הִיא גּוּפָנִי. אֲבָל בַּחֲנֻכָּה רַק לְהַלֵּל, הִיא נַפְשִׁי, כִּי הָיוּ כּוֹבְשִׁים אוֹתָם לַעֲבָדִים כַּנִּזְכָּר לְעֵיל.

8. I.e., the average person, who clings to life neither out of identification with God's will nor from the survival instinct, was not desperate for a miracle.
9. Esther 4:3.

not such a miracle.[8] This is the meaning of "Sackcloth and ashes were put on for the many"[9] – "for the many" but not for all. So on Purim, the mitzva [to read] the scroll [of Esther] is spiritual, and the feast is physical, but on Ḥanukka we have only *Hallel,* the spiritual, for they would have been enslaved [but not killed].[10]

10. On Ḥanukka, there is no commemoration of a bodily miracle because our lives were not threatened. However, even for the average person, there was a spiritual threat of enslavement, and so *Hallel* is recited to mark the miraculous spiritual salvation.

כד

שְׁנֵי מִכְתָּבִים הָאֵלּוּ הֵם מֵרַבּוֹ שֶׁל אדמו"ר זצוק"ל. כְּבוֹד קְדֻשַּׁת הַגָּאוֹן הֶחָסִיד קָדוֹשׁ ה׳ מְכֻבָּד מָרָנָא יוֹסֵף זוּנְדִיל מִסַּאלַאנְט זצוק"ל. אֲשֶׁר כָּתַב מֵעִיר הַקֹּדֶשׁ יְרוּשָׁלַיִם תִּבָּנֶה וְתִכּוֹנֵן בִּמְהֵרָה. לִבְנוֹ יְחִידוֹ אֲשֶׁר נָסַע בִּשְׁלִיחוּת מִצְוָה שֶׁל בִּקּוּר חוֹלִים וּפִקּוּחַ נֶפֶשׁ. בְּעַד אֲחוֹתוֹ אֲשֶׁר הָיְתָה עֲצוּרָה בָּעִיר וִוין.

ב"ה כ"ד כִּסְלֵו תרח"י.

אָמַר הַכּוֹתֵב בְּנִי שָׁלוֹם, שָׁלַחְתִּי לְךָ מְלִיצוֹת כְּמוֹ שֶׁבִּקַּשְׁתָּ, אָמְנָם אַל תִּבְטַח, זֶהוּ רַק שֶׁלֹּא יָבֹא עֶזְרְךָ בְּנֵס נִגְלֶה, אָמְנָם הָעִקָּר לִבְטֹחַ בַּה׳ בְּכָל לְבָבְךָ, וְאֶל בִּינָתְךָ אַל תִּשָּׁעֵן, וְלֹא תַּעֲשֶׂה יוֹתֵר הִשְׁתַּדְּלוּת, שֶׁלֹּא תַּחֲשֹׁב כֹּחִי וְעֹצֶם יָדִי הָיָה לִי לִישׁוּעָה, כְּמוֹ שֶׁכָּתוּב אַל תִּבְטְחוּ בִנְדִיבִים כו׳, אַשְׁרֵי כו׳ שִׂבְרוֹ עַל ה׳, אֲקַוֶּה אֶל ה׳ שֶׁיְּזַדְּמֵן לְךָ מָעוֹת בְּרֶוַח עַל הוֹצָאוֹתֵיכֶם דְּשָׁם וְעַל הוֹצָאוֹת הַחֲזָרָה, הַרְבֵּה סִבּוֹת וּשְׁלוּחִים לַמָּקוֹם, הֵן לְגַלְגֵּל זְכוּת עַל יְדֵי זַכָּאִים, כְּמוֹ שֶׁכָּתוּב בָּבָא בַּתְרָא י׳ הָיָה רַבִּי מֵאִיר אוֹמֵר כו׳, הֵן עַל אֵיזוֹ אֳפָנִים, וְתַחֲזֹר תָּמִיד

1. See Proverbs 3:5.
2. See Deuteronomy 5:17.
3. Rabbi R. Meir says there that God allows the poor to exist so good people will help them and thereby earn reward in the next world.

Letter 24

These two letters were written by the teacher of *our master, teacher, and rabbi* [R. Israel Salanter], *ztvk"l,* his honored holiness, the eminent, pious, honored divine holiness, our master, Joseph Zundel of Salant, *ztvk"l.* He wrote these from the holy city of Jerusalem, may it be rebuilt and renewed speedily in our days, to his only son, who traveled on a mitzva mission of seeing to the needs of the sick (*bikkur ḥolim*) and saving a life (*pikuaḥ nefesh*) on behalf of his sister, who was confined [by illness] in Vienna.

With the help of God. 24 Kislev, 5618 [1857].

Said the writer: Greetings, my son. I sent you the letters of recommendation as you requested. However, do not put faith [in them]. [I wrote them] only so that your success will not be the result of an overt miracle. Nevertheless, the main thing is to trust in God with your whole heart. Do not rely on your own understanding,[1] and do not make too much effort, so that you will not think that "my strength and the might of my hand"[2] were my salvation. As it is written (Ps. 146:3): "Do not put your trust in princes...." "Happy is he... whose hope is in the Lord" (ibid. 5). I hope to God that He will arrange abundant funds for you, for your expenses there and the cost of the return journey. God has many agents and messengers, both for the purpose of accruing merit to the worthy, as it is said in Bava Batra 10[a]: "R. Meir used to say..."[3] and for several other purposes.

פְּסוּקֵי הַהַשְׁגָּחָה וּבִטָּחוֹן וִישׁוּעָה, כְּמוֹ קַוֵּה אֶל ה׳, חִזְקוּ וְאִמְצוּ כוּ׳, עֵינַי תָּמִיד אֶל ה׳ כִּי הוּא יוֹצִיא מֵרֶשֶׁת רַגְלַי וְכַדּוֹמֶה, עֶזְרָה בְצָרוֹת נִמְצָא מְאֹד, וְאָז תֵּלֵךְ לָבֶטַח וּתְשׁוּעַת ה׳ כְּהֶרֶף עַיִן.

כַּיָּדוּעַ שֶׁהַבּוֹרֵא יִתְבָּרַךְ שְׁמוֹ מַשְׁגִּיחַ בְּכָל רֶגַע עַל כָּל אָדָם בִּפְרָטִיּוּת עִנְיָנָיו, וּכְמוֹ שֶׁהָאָדָם פּוֹנֶה לִבּוֹ לַה׳, כֵּן ה׳ פּוֹנֶה לְהַשְׁגִּיחַ עָלָיו כְּמוֹ שֶׁנֶּאֱמַר ה׳ צִלְּךָ, וְאִם פּוֹנֶה יוֹתֵר גַּם ה׳ מַשְׁגִּיחַ עָלָיו יוֹתֵר, כְּמוֹ שֶׁנֶּאֱמַר בַּמִּדְרָשׁ ה׳ צִלְּךָ מַה הַצֵּל הַזֶּה כְּשֶׁאַתָּה מַרְאֶה אוֹתוֹ אֶצְבַּע אַחַת הוּא מַרְאֶה אוֹתְךָ אֶצְבַּע אַחַת, וְאִם כָּל הַיָּד מַרְאֶה כְּנֶגְדְּךָ כָּל הַיָּד, כֵּן הַקָּדוֹשׁ־בָּרוּךְ־הוּא כְּדֶרֶךְ שֶׁבָּא הָאָדָם לִרְאוֹת כָּךְ בָּא לֵרָאוֹת עַיִן נֶפֶשׁ הַחַיִּים, וּכְשֶׁבָּא עֹנֶשׁ עַל הָאָדָם אֵינוֹ יוֹדֵעַ בַּמֶּה לִתְלוֹת תְּחִלָּה, כִּי אָמְרוּ חֲכָמֵינוּ זַ״ל (יוֹמָא ל״ח ב׳) הַשּׁוֹכֵחַ דָּבָר אֶחָד מִתַּלְמוּדוֹ גּוֹרֵם גָּלוּת לְבָנָיו, וּמִכָּל שֶׁכֵּן מִי יֹאמַר זִכִּיתִי לִבִּי שֶׁעֲוֹנוֹתֵינוּ רַבּוּ לְמַעְלָה רֹאשׁ כוּ׳, וּבִפְרָט עַל בִּטּוּל תּוֹרָה, שֶׁאָמְרוּ בִּסְפָרִי כְּשֵׁם שֶׁתַּלְמוּד תּוֹרָה גָּדוֹל כֵּן בִּטּוּל תּוֹרָה גָּדוֹל מִכָּל עֲוֹנוֹת, וְאָמְרוּ גָּלוּת מְכַפֶּרֶת עָוֹן וּבִפְרָט גָּלוּת לִדְפֹּק עַל פִּתְחֵי נְדִיבִים בְּבוּשָׁה וּכְלִמָּה וּבִזָּיוֹן, וְתָשִׂים עַל לִבְּךָ כָּל מַה שֶׁאַתָּה סוֹבֵל יוֹתֵר כְּלִמָּה, הוּא יוֹתֵר כַּפָּרַת עָוֹן.

עַל כֵּן קַבֵּל עָלֶיךָ בְּאַהֲבָה, וּשְׂמַח בָּהֶם יוֹתֵר מֵעַל כָּל הוֹן, כְּמוֹ שֶׁאָמְרוּ בְּרָכוֹת ה׳ יָכוֹל אֲפִלּוּ לֹא קִבְּלָם מֵאַהֲבָה כוּ׳, וְאִם קִבְּלָם מַה שְּׂכָרוֹ יִרְאֶה זֶרַע יַאֲרִיךְ יָמִים כוּ׳, וּבִפְרָט שֶׁאַתָּה הוֹלֵךְ בְּדֶרֶךְ מִצְוָה בִּקּוּר חוֹלִים וּגְמִילוּת חֲסָדִים שֶׁאִי אֶפְשָׁר בְּאַחֵר, וְנֶחְשָׁב לְךָ כְּאִלּוּ

4. This statement appears in Ḥagiga 2a in context of making a festival pilgrimage to the Temple: One comes to the Temple to both see and be seen. Here R. Joseph Zundel uses this statement to bolster a broader theological claim, namely, that God "sees" and watches over a person commensurate to the degree to which that person "sees" and perceives God in all his affairs.

5. R. Chaim of Volozhin's *Nefesh HaḤayim,* first published in Vilna in 1824, several years after the author's death, is the key modern theological treatise of Lithuanian, non-hasidic Judaism. *Inter alia,* the book describes in great detail how prayer, Torah

Constantly review verses about providence, faith, and salvation, like: "Hope to God" (Ps. 27:14), "Be strong and courageous..." (Deut. 31:6), "My eyes are always toward God for He will free my feet from the snare" (Ps. 25:15), and the like. [God's] help in our difficulties is often present. Thus shall you walk securely, and God's salvation comes in the blink of an eye.

As is known, the Creator, blessed be His name, watches at every moment over every person in his particular affairs. The way that a person turns his heart to God, so will God turn and watch over him, as it is written: "The Lord is your shadow" (Ps. 121:5). The more he turns to God, the more God watches over him, as is written in a midrash: "'The Lord is your shadow' – just as this shadow, when you show it one finger, it shows you one finger, and if you show your whole hand then it correspondingly shows the whole hand, so it is with the Holy One, blessed be He. The same manner that a person comes to see, so he comes to be seen."[4] See *Nefesh HaḤayim*.[5]

When punishment comes upon a person, he does not know initially to what to attribute it, for our Sages, of blessed memory, said (Yoma 38b): "One who forgets a thing that he learned causes his children to go into exile." This certainly applies [to us]; "Who can say, 'I have cleansed my heart'"? (Prov. 20:9), "For our iniquities are overwhelming..." (Ezra 9:6), especially the sin of neglecting Torah, for [the Sages] said in *Sifrei*: "Just as the study of Torah is great, so the neglect of Torah is greater than all sins." They also said that exile brings atonement for sin, especially being exiled to knock on the doors of the generous with shame, embarrassment, and degradation. Take to your heart that the more you suffer embarrassment, the more your sins are forgiven.

Therefore, accept [your shame] with love. Rejoice in it more than in any treasure, for [the Sages] said (Berakhot 5a): "I might think [that this applies] even if he does not accept them out of love.... If he does accept them, what will be his reward? 'He will see his offspring; he will live long' (Is. 53:10)." Especially since you are journeying for the mitzva of seeing to the needs of the sick and doing acts of loving-kindness that

---

study, and performance of mitzvot affect the entire world. R. Chaim was a primary disciple of the Vilna Gaon and R. Zundel of Salant's teacher.

אַתָּה מְקַיֵּם וְהָגִיתָ בּוֹ, כְּמוֹ שֶׁאָמְרוּ בְּמוֹעֵד קָטָן ט׳ ב׳ וְנִפְסַק בְּיוֹרֶה דֵעָה רמ״ו סָעִיף ח׳, עַל כֵּן אַל תִּהְיֶה עָצֵב רַק תִּהְיֶה שָׂמֵחַ וְטוֹב לֵב, וּכְשֶׁתּוֹדִיעֵנִי שֶׁאֵין אַתָּה מֵצֵר וְדוֹאֵג רַק שָׂמֵחַ, אָז אֶשְׂמַח גַּם אֲנִי, וְאֵין לָנוּ לְהִשָּׁעֵן אֶלָּא עַל אָבִינוּ שֶׁבַּשָּׁמַיִם, כִּי אִם הוֹגָה וְרִחֵם כְּרֹב חֲסָדָיו, וְלֹא יִזְנַח לְעוֹלָם ה׳, טוֹב ה׳ לְקוֹוָיו, אָבִיךָ זוּנְדִיל מִסַּאלַאנְט.

---

6. The printed version has 246:8, but this is an error. Rema, *Yoreh De'ah* 246:1 cites *Tur* as stating that one who cannot study Torah because of preoccupations is considered

no one else can do. Then this is credited to you as if you are fulfilling, "Meditate upon [the Torah day and night" (Josh. 1:8), as [the Sages] said in Moed Katan 9b, and as codified in *Yoreh De'ah* 246:1.[6]

So do not be sad. Be happy and in good spirits, and when you notify me that you are not feeling distressed and worried, but happy, then I, too, will be happy. We have no one to lean on but our Father in heaven, who "first afflicts, then shows mercy, in His abundant kindness" (Lam. 3:32). "For the Lord does not forsake forever" (ibid. 31), and "The Lord is good to those who trust in Him" (ibid. 25).

Your father, Zundel of Salant

---

to have studied himself if he provides for others who study. See the next letter for a fuller exploration of the cited passage from Moed Katan.

כה

ב״ה כ״ד נִיסָן.

אָמַר הַכּוֹתֵב בְּנִי הִשָּׁמֵר לְךָ פֶּן כְּשֶׁתִּרְאֶה אֲרִיכוּת גָּלוּתְךָ וּבִזְיוֹנוֹתֶיךָ, כֵּיוָן שֶׁנִּצְרָךְ אָדָם לַבְּרִיּוֹת פָּנָיו מִשְׁתַּנּוֹת כִּכְרוּם, וְתִתְחָרֵט בִּלְבָבְךָ, וּמִכָּל שֶׁכֵּן שֶׁלֹּא תוֹצִיא מִפִּיךָ שֶׁאִם הָיִיתִי יוֹדֵעַ זֹאת, לֹא עָשִׂיתִי מִצְוָה זֹאת, כִּי אָמְרוּ רַבּוֹתֵינוּ זַ״ל כְּשֶׁאָדָם מִתְחָרֵט עַל הַמִּצְוָה מְאַבֵּד שְׂכָרוֹ, [יְרוּשַׁלְמִי פֵּאָה פֶּרֶק א׳ עַיֵּן שָׁם] עַיֵּן קִדּוּשִׁין מ׳ ע״ב אָמַר רֵישׁ לָקִישׁ בַּתּוֹהֶא עַל הָרִאשׁוֹנוֹת, זֹאת תִּהְיֶה נֶחָמָתְךָ. (א) שֶׁאַתָּה עוֹסֵק בְּבִקּוּר חוֹלִים וּגְמִילוּת חֲסָדִים שֶׁאִי אֶפְשָׁר בְּאַחֵר, שֶׁעַל זֶה אָמְרוּ בְּמוֹעֵד קָטָן ט׳ ב׳ שֶׁמְּבַטְּלִין תַּלְמוּד תּוֹרָה לַעֲשׂוֹת הַמִּצְוָה, עַיֵּן רַשִׁ״י דִּבּוּר הַמַּתְחִיל חֶפְצוֹ וְתוֹסָפוֹת דִּבּוּר הַמַּתְחִיל כָּאן, וְאִם כֵּן בְּשָׁעָה שֶׁאֵין לְךָ פְּנַאי לִלְמֹד נֶחֱשָׁב לְךָ יוֹתֵר מִלִּמּוּד. (ב) שֶׁהַרְבֵּה בְּנֵי אָדָם הוֹלְכִים בַּדֶּרֶךְ לְמֵרָחוֹק לִסְחוֹרָה, וְאֵינָם חוֹשְׁשִׁים לִטְרָדוֹת הַדֶּרֶךְ וְגֶשֶׁם וְשֶׁלֶג וְקֹר וָחֹם, בִּשְׁבִיל סְפֵק רֶוַח אוֹ הֶפְסֵד, וְאַתָּה שְׂכָרְךָ בְּוַדַּאי קָצוּב מֵרַבּוֹתֵינוּ זַ״ל, כָּל שֶׁהַקָּדוֹשׁ־בָּרוּךְ־הוּא חָפֵץ בּוֹ כוּ׳, וְאִם קִבְּלוֹ מֵאַהֲבָה יִרְאֶה זֶרַע יַאֲרִיךְ יָמִים וְתַלְמוּדוֹ מִתְקַיֵּם בְּיָדוֹ.

וְשָׁמַעְתִּי מִפִּי קָדְשׁוֹ שֶׁל אדמו״ר רשכבה״ג מוהר״ח זַ״ל, אִם

---

1. As described in the previous letter.
2. See Berakhot 6b, which describes how such a person's face turns red and white from shame, so that he resembles a starling, whose feathers shine different colors when the sun shines on them at different angles.

Letter 25

With the help of God, Nissan 24

Said the writer: My son! Beware lest when you see the length of your exile and all your disgrace[1] – when a person becomes dependent on other people, his face changes colors like a starling[2] – you will have regret in your heart. Certainly you should not articulate, "If I had known this [extent of suffering], I would not have done this mitzva." For our Rabbis, of blessed memory, said: When a person regrets a mitzva, he loses its reward [Y. Pe'ah, ch. 1; see ad loc.]. See Kiddushin 40b: "Resh Lakish says: [One loses reward] when he regrets his past [mitzvot]."

This should be your consolation: A) That you are engaged in tending to the needs of the sick and doing acts of loving-kindness that cannot be done by another. Regarding this [the Sages] said in Moed Katan 9b that one puts aside Torah study to do this mitzva. See Rashi s.v. "*ḥeftzo*" and *Tosafot* s.v. "*kan*." Thus, when you have no time to study, it is considered greater than studying for you. B) Many people travel very far for business. They are not concerned about the stresses of the road, rain, snow, cold, or heat for uncertain profit or loss, whereas your reward is set aside for you with certainty. From our Rabbis, of blessed memory (Berakhot 5a): Whomever the Holy One, blessed be He, cherishes....[3] If he accepts it out of love, "He will see his offspring; he will live long" (Is. 53:10), and his learning will endure for him.

I heard from the holy mouth of our master, our teacher, and rabbi, the rabbi of all the Diaspora, our teacher R. Chaim [of Volozhin], of

3. Whomever God cherishes, He crushes with afflictions.

יְבַטֵּל חַס וְשָׁלוֹם דָּבָר אֶחָד מִן הַגְּמָרָא צָרִיךְ לֵיחָרֵב כָּל הָעוֹלָם, וְכָל שֶׁהַגָּלוּת וּבִזְיוֹנוֹת יוֹתֵר, וְהוּא מְקַבֵּל בְּאַהֲבָה בְּיֶתֶר שְׂאֵת וּבְשִׂמְחָה רַבָּה, שְׂכָרוֹ גַּם כֵּן מְרֻבֶּה בְּהַרְבֵּה זֶרַע וּבְיוֹתֵר אֲרִיכוּת יָמִים וְקִיּוּם תַּלְמוּדוֹ.

וְהִנֵּה כֻּלָּם מִתְאַוִּים לִזְכּוֹת לְאֵלּוּ הַשְּׁלֹשָׁה דְּבָרִים, שֶׁזֶּהוּ הַצְלָחַת הָאָדָם בָּזֶה וּבַבָּא, אֲבָל לֹא כָּל אָדָם זוֹכֶה לָזֶה רַק אַחַר יְגִיעוֹת הַרְבֵּה בְּמָמוֹן רַב, וְאֶת אֲשֶׁר יֶאֱהַב ה׳ יוֹכִיחֶנּוּ בְּיִסּוּרִים אוֹ בְּגָלוּת אוֹ בְּבִזְיוֹנוֹת, וּכְשֶׁמְּקַבֵּל בְּאַהֲבָה זוֹכֶה לָזֶה בִּזְמַן מוּעָט.

עַל כֵּן בְּכָל פַּעַם שֶׁיַּעֲלֶה עַל לִבְּךָ אֲרִיכוּת הַגָּלוּת וּסְבִילַת צַעַר וּבִזְיוֹנוֹת, תָּשִׂים עַל לִבְּךָ שֶׁשְּׂכָרְךָ הַרְבֵּה מְאֹד. (ג) כְּשֶׁמְּקַבֵּל בְּאַהֲבָה וְשָׂמֵחַ בָּזֶה עוֹבֵד לְהַבּוֹרֵא יִתְבָּרַךְ שְׁמוֹ, כְּמוֹ שֶׁכָּתַב בְּשֻׁלְחָן עָרוּךְ אֹרַח חַיִּים סִימָן רל״א סָעִיף ג׳ עַיֵּן שָׁם, וּכְשֶׁתָּבֹא לְאֵיזֶה מְקוֹמָן תְּבַקֵּשׁ שֶׁיֵּלְכוּ עֲבוּרְךָ שְׁנֵי אֲנָשִׁים וְיוֹתֵר לֹא תִּשְׁתַּדֵּל, כְּמוֹ שֶׁכָּתַב בְּחוֹבוֹת הַלְּבָבוֹת מִי שֶׁבּוֹטֵחַ בַּה׳ וּבִזוּלָתוֹ אֵין בִּטְחוֹנוֹ שָׁלֵם, וְנֶאֱמַר גֹּל עַל ה׳ דַּרְכֶּךָ וּבְטַח עָלָיו (וְלֹא עָלָיו וְעַל זוּלָתוֹ) וְהוּא יַעֲשֶׂה (וְלֹא זוּלָתוֹ) כְּמוֹ שֶׁנֶּאֱמַר וּמוֹשִׁיעַ אֵין זוּלָתִי.

וְהִנֵּה הָאָדָם יוּכַל לְהַכִּיר יוֹתֵר חַסְדֵי ה׳, אֲשֶׁר עוֹשֶׂה עִמּוֹ בְּכָל פַּעַם, כְּשֶׁהוּא בְּשִׁפְלוּת מִמִּי שֶׁהוּא בִּגְדֻלָּה, כִּי כַּמָּה חֲסָדִים עוֹשֶׂה ה׳ עִמָּנוּ וְעִם בִּתִּי שָׁם וְעִמְּךָ, בְּכָל מִדְרַךְ כַּף רַגְלֶיךָ, לֹא כַּעֲוֹנוֹתֵינוּ גָּמַל עָלֵינוּ, רַק בִּזְכוּת אֲבוֹתֵינוּ וִירוּשָׁלַיִם גָּבַר חֲסָדָיו עָלֵינוּ, עַד הֵנָּה עֲזָרוּנוּ רַחֲמָיו וְלֹא עֲזָבוּנוּ חֲסָדָיו, כִּי הַרְבֵּה אֲשֶׁר בָּאוּ לְמִדָּה זוֹ שֶׁקָּטְנָם עָבִים מִמָּתְנֵינוּ, גְּדוֹלִים וְטוֹבִים מִמֶּנּוּ בְּכָל מִלֵּי דְּמֵיטַב, וְלֹא מְקַבְּלִים אוֹתָם בְּסֵבֶר פָּנִים יָפוֹת כָּל כָּךְ כְּמוֹ שֶׁמְּקַבְּלִים אוֹתְךָ, עַד שֶׁכַּמָּה גְּדוֹלִים וְרַבָּנִים כָּתְבוּ אֵלַי שֶׁהָיָה לָהֶם זְכִיָּה שֶׁרָאוּךָ, וְשָׂמַחְתִּי כִּי מִסְתָמָא יֵשׁ לְךָ מְעַט עֲנָוָה וְשִׁפְלוּת, כְּמוֹ שֶׁנֶּאֱמַר וְלַעֲנָוִים יִתֵּן

4. Therefore, the son can rest assured that his reward is certain to be received.
5. R. Baḥya ibn Pakuda, *Ḥovot HaLevavot*, Gate of Faith, 3:3.
6. See Psalms 103:10.
7. See the *Nishmat* prayer, recited in the morning on Shabbat and festivals.
8. See I Kings 12:10. Rehoboam tells the people that he will outdo his father using this metaphor, which has become a standard expression for expressing superiority.

blessed memory, that if one word of learning is neglected, God forbid, then the whole world should be destroyed.[4] And the greater the exile and disgrace, if he accepts them with love, surpassing courage, and great joy, then the greater is his reward, through having many children, living longer, and retaining his learning.

Everyone wants to have these three things [i.e., children, long life, and learning], for they constitute a person's success in this world and the next, but not everyone attains this, except after great efforts and much money. But the one that God loves He will admonish with afflictions or exile or disgrace, and when he accepts them with love, he attains this success in very little time.

Therefore, whenever you think about the length of the exile, the suffering endured, and the disgrace, think about how your reward will be very great. C) When one accepts [suffering] with love and rejoices in it, he serves the Creator, blessed be His name, as is written in *Shulḥan Arukh, Oraḥ Ḥayim* 231:3; see ad loc. When you get to some place, you should ask that two people go on your behalf, but make no further effort, as it is written in *Ḥovot HaLevavot*:[5] Whoever puts faith in God and in others does not have complete faith. And it says (Ps. 37:5): "Commit your way to God and depend on Him" (and not on Him and another), and He (and no other) will do [what you need], as it says, "There is no savior but Me" (Is. 43:11).

In fact, a person is more able to recognize the kindnesses of God, which He does for him all the time, when he is in a state of lowliness than can one who is in a state of eminence. For God does so many kindnesses for us, for my daughter who is there, and for you, at every step of your way – He did not repay us according to our sins;[6] rather in the merit of our ancestors and of Jerusalem, He increases His kindness to us. To this point, His mercies have helped us, and His kindnesses have not abandoned us.[7] Yet many have found themselves in this predicament whose smallest fingers are thicker than our loins,[8] who are greater and better than us in every beneficial way, yet they are not received with a pleasant countenance as you are received. Several great scholars and rabbis have written to me that it was a privilege to see you. I rejoiced, for presumably you have some humility and self-deprecation, as it is written:

חֵן וְלִפְנֵי כָבוֹד עֲנָוָה, עַל כֵּן בְּהַעֲלוֹת עַל לִבְּךָ צַעַרְךָ וּכְלִמָּתְךָ וְאֹרֶךְ גָּלוּתְךָ תִּתְנַחֵם בָּזֶה וְתִהְיֶה שָׂשׂ וְשָׂמֵחַ, קַוֵּה אֶל ה׳ וְיוֹשַׁע לְךָ בְּכָל עִנְיְנֵיכֶם, הַשְׁלֵךְ עַל ה׳ יְהָבְךָ כו׳. וּתְשׁוּעַת ה׳ כְּהֶרֶף עַיִן, כְּמוֹ שֶׁנֶּאֱמַר רוֹצֶה ה׳ כו׳ אֶת הַמְיַחֲלִים לְחַסְדּוֹ, אָבִיךָ זוּנְדִיל מִסַּלַאנְט.

9. Proverbs 3:34.
10. Ibid. 15:33.
11. Psalms 27:14.
12. Ibid. 55:23.

"To the humble, He will give grace"[9] and "Humility precedes honor."[10] Accordingly, when you think about your pain, your embarrassment, and the duration of your exile, take comfort in this, rejoice, and be happy. "Hope to the Lord"[11] and He will save you in all your matters; "cast your burden on the Lord."[12] God's salvation comes in the blink of an eye,[13] as it is written, "God wants...those who long for his kindness."[14]

Your father, Zundel of Salant

13. This well-known adage, "*Teshuat* (or *yeshuat*) *Hashem keḥeref ayin*," originated in the medieval era.
14. Psalms 147:11.

כו

בַּגְּמָרָא בְּרָכוֹת דַּף י״ח הֵבִיאוּ בָּרַיְתָא וְזֶה לְשׁוֹנָהּ. תַּנְיָא מַעֲשֶׂה בְּחָסִיד אֶחָד שֶׁנָּתַן דִּינָר לְעָנִי בְּעֶרֶב רֹאשׁ הַשָּׁנָה בִּשְׁנַת בַּצֹּרֶת. וְהִקְנִיטַתּוּ אִשְׁתּוֹ וְהָלַךְ וְלָן בְּבֵית הַקְּבָרוֹת. וְשָׁמַע שְׁתֵּי רוּחוֹת שֶׁמְּסַפְּרוֹת זוֹ לָזוֹ כּוּ׳ בּוֹאִי וְנָשׁוּט בָּעוֹלָם כּוּ׳ עַיֵּן שָׁם. הַדָּבָר מַפְלִיא מְאֹד. מַה לְּחָסִיד לָלוּן בַּלַּיְלָה בְּבֵית הַקְּבָרוֹת בִּמְקוֹם טֻמְאָה. וְעַיֵּן בְּמַהַרְשָׁ״א בְּחִדּוּשֵׁי אַגָּדוֹת. שֶׁהֵבִיא שֶׁכְּבָר נִתְקַשָּׁה בָּזֶה בְּסֵפֶר עֵין יַעֲקֹב. וְעַיֵּן שָׁם שֶׁזֶּה הֱבִיאוּ לִשְׁלֹל הַדָּבָר מִפְּשָׁטֵיהּ וְכָתַב שֶׁבְּוַדַּאי הַנָּכוֹן כְּדִבְרֵי הָרִיטְבָ״א שֶׁדָּבָר זֶה הָיָה בַּחֲלוֹם וְהֶאֱרִיךְ בָּזֶה עַיֵּן שָׁם.

אוּלָם שָׁמַעְנוּ מִפֶּה קָדוֹשׁ אדמו״ר הַגָּאוֹן הֶחָסִיד זצוק״ל. שֶׁאָמַר עַל זֶה בֵּאוּר אֲמִתִּי נִפְלָא עַל פִּי דֶּרֶךְ הַמּוּסָר. שֶׁהַמַּעֲשֶׂה הוּא כִּפְשָׁטֵיהּ בְּהָקִיץ. לֹא בְּחָזוֹן וְלֹא בַּחֲלוֹם. כִּי הִנֵּה הַלָּשׁוֹן וְהִקְנִיטַתּוּ אִשְׁתּוֹ.

---

1. A *baraita* (lit. "outside teaching") is a tannaitic teaching that was not included in the Mishna. Talmud frequently quotes *baraitot*.
2. The spirit reported a coming ruinous rain during the planting season. The pious man delayed his planting, and so avoided ruin. Thus, he was rewarded for his generosity.
3. R. Shmuel Edels (1555–1631), a talmudist whose dual commentary on the legal (*Ḥiddushei Halakhot*) and non-legal portions of the Talmud (*Ḥiddushei Aggadot*) is printed in many editions of the Talmud.
4. *Ein Yaakov* is a collection of all the aggadic (non-legal) material in the Talmud. It was compiled by R. Yaakov ibn Ḥaviv in the fifteenth century.

Letter 26

The Talmud, in Berakhot 18b, cites the following *baraita*:[1]

> It was taught: There was an incident wherein a pious man gave a dinar to a pauper on the eve of Rosh HaShana during a year of drought. His wife annoyed him [for his excessive largesse], so he went and slept in the cemetery. He heard two spirits talking with one another.... Let us go and wander in the world..., see ad loc.[2]

This is quite astonishing. Why would a pious man go to sleep at night in the cemetery, a place of impurity? See Maharsha,[3] who writes in *Ḥiddushei Aggadot* that the author of *Ein Yaakov*[4] was likewise troubled by this. See there that this led him to deny the plain meaning of the story and write that the correct approach is certainly that of Ritva,[5] namely, that this whole matter occurred in a dream. He wrote at length on this, see ad loc.

However, we heard an amazing and true explanation from the holy mouth of our eminent and pious master, teacher, and rabbi, [R. Israel Salanter,] *ztvk"l*, in accordance with a Mussar approach. This story happened as straightforwardly told, while the man was fully awake, in neither a vision nor a dream.

5. R. Yom Tov ben Avraham Assevili (1250–1330), a leading sage of Spain who wrote a commentary on the Talmud.

מוֹרֶה בַּעֲלִיל שֶׁהֶחָסִיד הַזֶּה הָיָה לוֹ הֶרְגֵּשׁ. וְנִתְפַּעֵל מִמַּה שֶּׁהִרְגִּיזָה אוֹתוֹ. וְהִרְגִּישׁ בִּלְבָבוֹ צַעַר וּקְפִידָא. אוֹ גַּם כַּעַס עִנְיָנוֹ. וְכַמְבֹאָר בְּשַׁבָּת דַּף ל׳. תָּנוּ רַבָּנָן לְעוֹלָם יְהֵא אָדָם עִנְוְתָן כְּהִלֵּל. וְאַל יְהֵא קַפְּדָן כְּשַׁמַּאי. מַעֲשֶׂה בִּשְׁנֵי בְּנֵי אָדָם שֶׁהִמְרוּ זֶה אֶת זֶה. אָמְרוּ כָּל מִי שֶׁיֵּלֵךְ וְיַקְנִיט אֶת הִלֵּל יִטֹּל אַרְבַּע מֵאוֹת זוּז. אָמַר אֶחָד מֵהֶן אֲנִי אַקְנִיטֶנּוּ כו׳. הָלַךְ וְעָבַר עַל פֶּתַח בֵּיתוֹ. אָמַר מִי כָּאן הִלֵּל מִי כָּאן הִלֵּל כו׳. אָמַר לוֹ אַתָּה הוּא הִלֵּל שֶׁקּוֹרִין אוֹתְךָ נְשִׂיא יִשְׂרָאֵל כו׳ לֹא יִרְבּוּ כְּמוֹתְךָ בְּיִשְׂרָאֵל כו׳. אָמַר לוֹ הֱוֵי זָהִיר בְּרוּחֲךָ. כְּדַאי הוּא הִלֵּל שֶׁתְּאַבֵּד עַל יָדוֹ אַרְבַּע מֵאוֹת זוּז וְאַרְבַּע מֵאוֹת זוּז וְהִלֵּל לֹא יַקְפִּיד עַיֵּן שָׁם. הֲרֵי שֶׁהַלָּשׁוֹן יַקְנִיט הוּא לְהָבִיא לְמִי שֶׁמַּקְנִיטִים אוֹתוֹ לִידֵי קְפִידָא וְכַעַס. אוּלָם לֹא עָלְתָה בְּיַד הָאִישׁ לְהַקְנִיט אֶת הִלֵּל. כִּי הִלֵּל מִגֹּדֶל עִנְוְתָנוּתוֹ לֹא נִתְפַּעֵל כְּלָל מִכָּל דִּבְרֵי נִרְגָּן וּבוּז שֶׁל הָאִישׁ. וְלֹא הִרְגִּישׁ וְלֹא בָּא לִידֵי קְפִידָא כְּלָל.

עַל כָּל פָּנִים בְּכָאן שֶׁאָמְרוּ וְהִקְנִיטַתּוּ אִשְׁתּוֹ. מְבֹאָר בַּעֲלִיל שֶׁהֶחָסִיד נִתְפַּעֵל מִדְּבָרֶיהָ מִמַּה שֶּׁהִקְנִיטָה אוֹתוֹ. וּבָא לִידֵי קְפִידָא אוֹ גַּם כַּעַס. נִמְצָא שֶׁנִּכְשַׁל הֶחָסִיד הַזֶּה בְּרִפְיוֹן מִדַּת הָעֲנָוָה. כִּי אֵין זֶה מִדַּרְכֵי הַחֲסִידִים הָעֲנָוִים וְהַשְּׁפָלִים בְּדַעְתָּן. לִהְיוֹת מַקְנִיטִים וּמַרְגִּיזִים אוֹתָם. כִּי מִדֶּרֶךְ הָעֲנָוָה הָאֲמִתִּית הוּא שֶׁלֹּא לְהַרְגִּישׁ כְּלָל מִשּׁוּם דִּבְרֵי נִרְגָּן וְקִנְטוּר. וְלֹא יָנוּחַ שֵׁבֶט הַקְּפִידָא בְּגוֹרַל הָעֲנָוָה בְּשׁוּם עִנְיָן בָּעוֹלָם. וּכְמוֹ שֶׁסִּפְּרוּ בַּגְּמָרָא עַל הִלֵּל. כִּי מִגֹּדֶל עִנְוְתָנוּתוֹ לֹא הִקְפִּיד עַל הָאִישׁ שֶׁרָצָה לְהַקְנִיט אוֹתוֹ. וְכֵן אָמְרוּ חֲזַ״ל בְּסוֹטָה

6. In this story, Hillel exemplifies the trait of patience. The word used, however, is *anvetan,* which is related to *anava,* which is classically translated as humility, which is how we translated it. Yet *anavah* connotes humility, empathy patience and unpretentiousness.
7. The Talmud records how the man proceeded to repeatedly interrupt Hillel with puerile questions, which Hillel then praised as good questions and answered.
8. A paraphrase of Psalms 125:3.

The language, "His wife annoyed him" ("*hiknitato*") shows clearly that this pious man had an emotional response and was agitated by his wife's pestering him. He experienced pain and took offense in his heart, or possibly this was a matter of anger.

This [i.e., the proposed meaning of "*hiknitato*"] is explained in Shabbat 30b:

> The Rabbis taught: A person should always be humble (*anvetan*)[6] like Hillel and not be strict (*kapdan*) like Shammai. There was an incident with two people who wagered that the first one who would go and annoy (*yaknit*) Hillel would take 400 *zuz*. One of them said: I will annoy him.... He went and passed by the entrance to [Hillel's] house. He said: Who here is Hillel? Who here is Hillel?....[7] Then he asked: Are you Hillel who is called the Prince of Israel? He said to him: Yes. [The man continued and] said to [Hillel: If you are him,] may there not be many like you among Israel. [He said: My son, why? He replied: Because I lost 400 *zuz* because of you.] He said to him: Be cautious of spirit. Hillel is capable of causing you to lose 400 *zuz* and then another 400 *zuz*, yet he will not be offended.

Thus, the term "*yaknit*" means to bring the target of the taunting to a state of offense and rage. But this man was unable to bring Hillel to such a state, because Hillel, given his great humility (*anvetanut*), was not affected in the slightest by all the man's petulance and scorn; he felt nothing and did not take offense at all.

However, here [in Berakhot 18b] it says that his wife annoyed him, so clearly this means that the pious man was emotionally affected by her taunting, and it brought him to take offense or even become angry. It emerges that this pious man failed due to his weakness in the trait of humility (*anava*), for it is not the manner of the pious, who are humble and self-effacing in their demeanor, to be offended or annoyed. For the path of true humility is not to have any emotional response to petulant and taunting words. The rod of offense shall never rest in the place of humility,[8] for any reason, ever, just as they said of Hillel in the Talmud that due to his great humility, he was not offended by the man

דַּף מ׳ אָמַר רַבִּי אֲבָהוּ מֵרֵישׁ הֲוָה אֲמִינָא עִנְוְתָנָא אֲנָא. כֵּיוָן דַּחֲזִינָא לֵיהּ לְרַבִּי אַבָּא דְּמִן עַכּוֹ. דְּאָמַר אִיהוּ חַד טַעֲמָא. וְאָמַר אֲמוֹרֵיהּ חַד טַעֲמָא וְלֹא קָפִיד. אֲמִינָא לָאו עִנְוְתָנָא אֲנָא. הֲרֵי כִּי יְסוֹד הָעֲנָוָה הוּא שֶׁלֹּא לְהַקְפִּיד כְּלָל עַל שׁוּם דָּבָר בָּעוֹלָם.

וְלָזֶה כַּאֲשֶׁר הִרְגִּישׁ הֶחָסִיד שֶׁנִּתְפַּעֵל מִמַּה שֶּׁהִקְנִיטַתּוּ אִשְׁתּוֹ וּבָא לִידֵי קְפִידָא. וְנִכְשַׁל בְּמִדַּת הָעֲנָוָה. רָצָה לַעֲשׂוֹת תְּשׁוּבָה וּלְהַשְׁלִים נַפְשׁוֹ בְּמִדַּת הָעֲנָוָה בְּתַכְלִית. וְהִנֵּה יָדוּעַ כִּי יְסוֹד דַּרְכֵי הַתְּשׁוּבָה הוּא עֲזִיבַת הַחֵטְא וְקַבָּלָה עַל לְהַבָּא. אָמְנָם אֵינוֹ דּוֹמֶה הַתְּשׁוּבָה בְּדַרְכֵי הַמִּדּוֹת. לִשְׁאָר עֲבֵרוֹת וּמִצְוֹת מַעֲשִׂיּוֹת. אֲשֶׁר בְּקַל יוּכַל הָאָדָם לְקַבֵּל עַל עַצְמוֹ לִהְיוֹת זָהִיר בְּמִצְוָה. וְלִפְרֹשׁ מִן הַחֵטְא. לֹא כֵן בְּדַרְכֵי הַמִּדּוֹת. אֲשֶׁר שָׁרְשָׁם הוּא בִּפְנִימִיּוּת הַלֵּב. וְנִדְרַשׁ עַל זֶה עָמָל וְהִתְבּוֹנְנוּת רַב. לַעֲקֹר מִשֹּׁרֶשׁ אֵיזֶה מִדָּה שֶׁאֵינֶנָּה רְצוּיָה.

וְהִנֵּה בְּדַרְכֵי קְנִיַּת הָעֲנָוָה. שָׁנִינוּ בְּאָבוֹת פֶּרֶק ד׳ רַבִּי לְוִיטַס אִישׁ יַבְנֶה אוֹמֵר מְאֹד מְאֹד הֱוֵי שְׁפַל רוּחַ שֶׁתִּקְוַת אֱנוֹשׁ רִמָּה. וְעַיֵּן לְהָרַמְבַּ״ם שָׁם בְּפֵרוּשׁ הַמִּשְׁנָה שֶׁכָּתַב זֶה לְשׁוֹנוֹ. רוֹצֶה לוֹמַר שֶׁאַתָּה צָרִיךְ לְהַכְרִיחַ נַפְשְׁךָ עַד שֶׁתַּרְחִיק מִמֶּנָּה הַגַּאֲוָה. בְּחָשְׁבְךָ בְּאַחֲרִית הַגּוּף וְהוּא שׁוּבוֹ רִמָּה עַיֵּן שָׁם. הֲרֵי שֶׁדֶּרֶךְ קְנִיַּת הָעֲנָוָה הוּא הַהִתְבּוֹנְנוּת בְּאַחֲרִית הָאָדָם. כִּי סוֹפוֹ רִמָּה וְתוֹלֵעָה. וְכֵן כָּתַב בְּסֵפֶר מְסִלַּת יְשָׁרִים פֶּרֶק כ״ג בְּדַרְכֵי קְנִיַּת הָעֲנָוָה. שֶׁהוּא הַהִתְבּוֹנְנוּת עַל עִנְיָנִים שׁוֹנִים כו׳. כִּי בִּהְיוֹת הָאָדָם מִסְתַּכֵּל בִּפְחִיתוּת חָמְרוֹ כו׳. וּכְשֶׁיַּחֲשֹׁב כְּמוֹ כֵן שֶׁבְּסוֹף כָּל גְּדֻלָּתוֹ יָשׁוּב לְעָפָר מַאֲכָל לְתוֹלַעַת.

---

9. In its common usage, an *Amora* is a Sage of the talmudic era, after the era of the Mishna (whose Sages are called *Tanna'im*). R. Abbahu himself was an *Amora* in this sense. There is also a sense in which an *amora* is a "speaker" or "spokesman," a sort of "human microphone" who would repeat the teaching of living, present Sages to larger audiences assembled at the Babylonian academies. These *amora'im* were undoubtedly learned men, but it would have been considered both presumptuous and offensive for an *amora* to alter the teaching of a Sage, especially in his presence.

who was taunting him. Our Sages, of blessed memory, likewise said in Sota (40a):

> R. Abbahu said: At first I would have said that I am humble. Once I saw R. Abba of Akko state an explanation, whereupon his *amora*[9] gave a different explanation, yet he did not take offense, I said that I am not humble.

Thus, we see that the foundation of humility is never to take offense at anything in the world.

Therefore, when the pious man noticed that he was emotionally affected by his wife's taunts, to the extent that he took offense, and thus had failed with respect to the trait of humility, he wanted to repent and perfect his soul to the utmost through the trait of humility. Now, it is well known that the basic path of repentance is abandonment of the sin and resolution about the future. However, repentance with regard to character traits cannot be compared to other sins or practical mitzvot, where a person can easily resolve to be fastidious about a mitzva or to separate from the sin. But this is not the nature of character traits, which are rooted in the inner reaches of the heart. Uprooting an undesirable character trait therefore demands a great deal of effort and contemplation.

In terms of the methods for acquiring humility, we learned in Avot 4:4: "R. Levitas of Yavneh says: Be very lowly of spirit, for the ultimate destiny of man is maggots." And see that Rambam wrote in his *Commentary on the Mishna* there: "That is, you must compel your soul, to the point that you distance it from pride, by contemplating the destiny of the body, which is to return to maggots." We see that the way to acquire humility is to contemplate the ultimate destiny of a person, for his end is maggots and worms. This is also written in *Mesillat Yesharim* (*Path of the Just*), chapter 23, [titled] "On the Methods for Acquiring Humility":

> [One develops humility] through contemplation of various matters.... For when a person scrutinizes the triviality of his material being...and likewise when he considers that after all his greatness, he will return to dust and be food for worms, his pride will

כָּל שֶׁכֵּן שֶׁיִּכָּנַע גְּאוֹנוֹ. כִּי מַה טּוּבוֹ וּמַה גְּדֻלָּתוֹ וְאַחֲרִיתוֹ בּוּשָׁה וּכְלִמָּה עַיֵּן שָׁם.

וְעַל כֵּן הֶחָסִיד הַזֶּה שֶׁנִּכְשַׁל בְּרִפְיוֹן מִדַּת הָעֲנָוָה. וְרָצָה לָשׁוּב בִּתְשׁוּבָה וּלְהַשְׁלִים נַפְשׁוֹ בְּמִדַּת הָעֲנָוָה בְּתַכְלִית. הָיָה עָלָיו לְהִתְבּוֹנֵן בְּדַרְכֵי הַמּוּסָר. בִּפְחִיתוּת וְשִׁפְלוּת הָאָדָם. שֶׁתִּקְוַת אֱנוֹשׁ רִמָּה כַּנִּזְכָּר לְעֵיל. וְהִנֵּה בְּעֵת אַחֵר הָיָה אֶפְשָׁרִיּוֹת לִהְיוֹת עָמֵל בְּדַרְכֵי הִתְבּוֹנְנוּת הַנִּזְכָּר לְעֵיל בְּהֶמְשֵׁךְ זְמַן מָה. אוּלָם כַּאֲשֶׁר הָעֵת הָיָה עֶרֶב רֹאשׁ הַשָּׁנָה. רָצָה לַעֲשׂוֹת תְּשׁוּבָה שְׁלֵמָה וּלְמַהֵר לְהַשְׁלִים נַפְשׁוֹ בְּמִדַּת הָעֲנָוָה. עוֹד בַּלַּיְלָה הַזֶּה. טֶרֶם קוּמוֹ לַבֹּקֶר מִשְׁפָּט בְּיוֹם הַדִּין הַנּוֹרָא. עַל כֵּן רָאָה לְהִשְׁתַּמֵּשׁ בָּאֶמְצָעִים הַיּוֹתֵר חֲזָקִים. לְהַגְבִּיר דַּרְכֵי הַהִתְבּוֹנְנוּת מִשִּׁפְלוּת וּפְחִיתוּת הָאָדָם. שֶׁיַּעֲשֶׂה רֹשֶׁם וְיִפְעַל כָּל עֹז עַל לוּחַ לִבּוֹ.

וְעַל כֵּן הָלַךְ וְלָן בְּבֵית הַקְּבָרוֹת. בֵּית מוֹעֵד לְכָל חַי וְסוֹף כָּל הָאָדָם. אֲשֶׁר שָׁם הוּא מֻכְשָׁר בְּיוֹתֵר לְהִתְפַּעֵל מַהֵר מִדַּרְכֵי הַהִתְבּוֹנְנוּת הַנִּזְכָּר לְעֵיל. שֶׁתִּקְוַת אֱנוֹשׁ רִמָּה וְאַחֲרִיתוֹ בּוּשָׁה וּכְלִמָּה. וְלִקְנוֹת מַהֵר עֲנָוָה וְשִׁפְלוּת הָרוּחַ בְּתַכְלִית. וּמֵעַתָּה לֹא יִפָּלֵא אֵפוֹא מַה שֶׁהָלַךְ וְלָן בְּבֵית הַקְּבָרוֹת. כִּי כָּל מַה שֶׁהָיָה נָחוּץ לָהֶם לַעֲבוֹדַת ד׳ יִתְבָּרַךְ שְׁמוֹ. וּבִפְרָט לְדַרְכֵי הַתְּשׁוּבָה. לֹא יִבָּצֵר מֵהֶם כָּל עֵצָה וְכָל תַּחְבּוּלָה שֶׁבָּעוֹלָם.

> certainly surrender…for what do all his benevolence and greatness mean when his end is shame and disgrace?

Therefore, this pious man, who failed through weakness of the trait of humility and wanted to repent and perfect his soul to the utmost through the trait of humility, had to contemplate the methods of Mussar with respect to the triviality and lowliness of human beings – for the ultimate destiny of man is maggots, as said above. At a different time, it would have been possible to work through the aforementioned methods of contemplation over a period of time. But on the eve of Rosh HaShana, he wanted to do a complete repentance and quickly perfect his soul vis-à-vis the quality of humility – that very night – before he arose in the morning to face his trial on the awesome day of judgment [i.e., Rosh HaShana]. Therefore, he saw fit to use the strongest means to intensify the methods of contemplating the lowliness and triviality of human beings, which would make an impression and powerfully affect the tablet of his heart.

So he went and slept in the cemetery, the appointed meeting place for all the living and the end of every human being. This place is most capable of rapidly affecting the aforementioned methods of contemplation, namely, that the ultimate destiny of a person is maggots and that his end is shame and embarrassment. Thus, one can acquire humility and the utmost lowliness of spirit quickly. It is therefore not astonishing that he went and slept in the cemetery, for whatever [the pious] need in their service of God, blessed be His name, and especially in methods of repentance, they would not deny themselves – not any suggestion or strategy in the world.

כז

בַּגְּמָרָא שַׁבָּת דַּף ל״א זֶה לְשׁוֹנָהּ, אָמַר רָבָא בְּשָׁעָה שֶׁמַּכְנִיסִין אָדָם לַדִּין, אוֹמְרִים לוֹ נָשָׂאתָ וְנָתַתָּ בֶּאֱמוּנָה. קָבַעְתָּ עִתִּים לַתּוֹרָה כוּ׳, צִפִּיתָ לִישׁוּעָה פִּלְפַּלְתָּ בַּחָכְמָה, הֲבַנְתָּ דָּבָר מִתּוֹךְ דָּבָר, וַאֲפִלּוּ הָכִי אִי יִרְאַת ה׳ אוֹצָרוֹ אִין אִי לֹא לֹא, מָשָׁל לְאָדָם שֶׁאָמַר לִשְׁלוּחוֹ. הַעֲלֵה לִי כּוֹר חִטִּים לַעֲלִיָּה, הָלַךְ וְהֶעֱלָה לוֹ, אָמַר לוֹ עֵרַבְתָּ לִי בָּהֶן קַב חֻמְטִין, אָמַר לוֹ לָאו, אָמַר לוֹ מוּטָב אִם לֹא הֶעֱלִיתָה עַד כָּאן לְשׁוֹן הַגְּמָרָא, וּפֵרֵשׁ רַשִׁ״י קַב חֻמְטִין אֶרֶץ מְלֵחָה וּמְשַׁמֶּרֶת אֶת הַפֵּרוֹת מֵהַתְלִיעַ עַיֵּן שָׁם.

וְהִנֵּה לְפִי סִגְנוֹן הַמָּשָׁל שֶׁאָמַר לוֹ מוּטָב אִם לֹא הֶעֱלִיתָ, נִרְאֶה בְּהַנִּמְשָׁל דְּאִם אֵין יִרְאַת ד׳ אוֹצָרוֹ, מוּטָב לוֹ שֶׁלֹּא לָמַד כְּלָל, יִפָּלֵא מְאֹד כִּי לֹא מַשְׁמַע כֵּן בְּכָל הַשַּׁ״ס, וְאַף שֶׁאָמְרוּ חֲכָמֵינוּ זַ״ל בִּבְרָכוֹת דַּף י״ז, דְּכָל הָעוֹשֶׂה שֶׁלֹּא לִשְׁמָהּ נוֹחַ לוֹ שֶׁלֹּא נִבְרָא, כְּבָר פֵּרְשׁוּ

Letter 27

The Talmud in Shabbat 31a states:

> Rava said: When a person is brought in for judgment, they ask him: Were you reliable in your business dealings? Did you set fixed times for Torah study? [Did you engage in procreation?] Did you anticipate redemption? Did you engage in discourse about [the Torah's] wisdom? Did you infer one thing from another? Nevertheless, [beyond all of these], if "fear of the Lord is his storehouse" (Is. 33:6), then yes [he is worthy of ultimate reward], and if not, he is not [worthy]. A parable [to illustrate this]: A person said to his agent: Bring a *kor* of wheat to the upper floor [to store there]. He went and brought it up for him. He said to him: Did you mix in a *kav* of *ḥomtin*? [The agent] answered: No. He said to him: Then it would have been better had you not brought it up.

Rashi explains: A *kav* of *ḥomtin* is salty soil that protects produce from becoming worm-infested.

According to the idiom of the parable, namely, that he said [to his agent], "It would have been better had you not brought [the wheat] up," then the lesson seems to be that without "fear of the Lord is his storehouse," it would have been better if he had never studied Torah. This is astonishing, for there is no such implication anywhere in the Talmud. True, our Sages, of blessed memory, said in Berakhot 17a: "One who [studies Scripture and the Oral Torah] not for their own sake would have

שָׁם הַתּוֹסָפוֹת, דְּהַיְנוּ שֶׁאֵינוֹ לוֹמֵד אֶלָּא לְקַנְטֵר חֲבֵרָיו עַיֵּן שָׁם, וְאַף גַּם זֶה הֲרֵי אָמְרוּ רַק נוֹחַ לוֹ שֶׁלֹּא נִבְרָא וְלֹא בָּא לָעוֹלָם כְּלָל, אוּלָם מֵאַחַר שֶׁנִּבְרָא אֵינוֹ בֶּן חוֹרִין לְהִבָּטֵל מִשּׁוּם מִצְוָה, וְחָלִילָה לוֹמַר כִּי כָּל מִי שֶׁאֵין בּוֹ יִרְאַת שָׁמַיִם, מוּטָב שֶׁלֹּא יִלְמַד כְּלָל.

הִנֵּה בְּמִצְוַת תַּלְמוּד תּוֹרָה יֵשׁ בָּזֶה שְׁנֵי עִנְיָנִים, אֶחָד לִמּוּד הַתּוֹרָה, שֵׁנִי יְדִיעוֹת הַתּוֹרָה, מִצְוַת לִמּוּד הַתּוֹרָה הוּא מִן הַכָּתוּב וְהָגִיתָ בּוֹ יוֹמָם וָלַיְלָה, וּכְמוֹ שֶׁכָּתַב הָרַמְבַּ"ם וְהַטּוּר וְשֻׁלְחָן עָרוּךְ בְּרֵישׁ הִלְכוֹת תַּלְמוּד תּוֹרָה וְזֶה לְשׁוֹנוֹ, כָּל אָדָם מִיִּשְׂרָאֵל חַיָּב בְּתַלְמוּד תּוֹרָה כּוּ' שֶׁנֶּאֱמַר וְהָגִיתָ בּוֹ יוֹמָם וָלַיְלָה עַיֵּן שָׁם, וְהִנֵּה לְמִצְוָה זוֹ שֶׁל לִמּוּד הַתּוֹרָה, כָּל מַה שֶּׁלּוֹמֵד מְקַיֵּם הַמִּצְוַת עֲשֵׂה וְהָגִיתָ בּוֹ יוֹמָם וָלַיְלָה, הֵן מִקְרָא אוֹ מִשְׁנָה גְּמָרָא הֲלָכוֹת וְאַגָּדוֹת שֶׁכֻּלָּן נִתְּנוּ לְמֹשֶׁה מִסִּינַי, וּכְמוֹ שֶׁהֶאֱרִיךְ בָּזֶה בְּסֵפֶר נֶפֶשׁ הַחַיִּים שַׁעַר ד' פֶּרֶק ו' עַיֵּן שָׁם, וְאַף שֶׁלֹּא יוּכַל לִפְסֹק דִּין מִתּוֹךְ מִקְרָא אוֹ מִשְׁנָה וְכָל שֶׁכֵּן מִן אַגָּדָה, בְּכָל זֹאת יוֹצֵא יְדֵי מִצְוַת לִמּוּד הַתּוֹרָה.

אוּלָם הַגֶּדֶר הַשֵּׁנִי בְּמִצְוַת תַּלְמוּד תּוֹרָה, הוּא יְדִיעוֹת הַתּוֹרָה, וְהוּא מַה שֶּׁאָמְרוּ חֲכָמֵינוּ זַ"ל בְּקִדּוּשִׁין דַּף ל', וְשִׁנַּנְתָּם שֶׁיִּהוּ דִּבְרֵי תוֹרָה מְחֻדָּדִים בְּפִיךָ, שֶׁאִם יִשְׁאַל לְךָ אָדָם דָּבָר, אַל תְּגַמְגֵּם וְתֹאמַר לוֹ אֶלָּא אֱמֹר לוֹ מִיָּד, שֶׁנֶּאֱמַר אֱמֹר לַחָכְמָה אֲחֹתִי אָתְּ, וְאוֹמֵר קָשְׁרֵם עַל לוּחַ לִבֶּךָ כּוּ', וְאוֹמֵר חִצֶּיךָ שְׁנוּנִים כּוּ', וּפֵרֵשׁ רַשִׁ"י יִהוּ מְחֻדָּדִים בְּפִיךָ, חֲזֹר עֲלֵיהֶם וּבְדֹק בְּעָמְקָם, שֶׁאִם יִשְׁאָלְךָ אָדָם לֹא תִּצְטָרֵךְ לְגַמְגֵּם כּוּ', אֱמֹר לַחָכְמָה אֲחֹתִי אָתְּ שֶׁתְּהֵא בָּקִי בָּהּ כַּאֲחוֹתְךָ שֶׁאֲסוּרָה לְךָ עַיֵּן שָׁם.

---

1. This explanation appears in Rashi ad loc. as well (s.v. "*haoseh*"). It is not clear why R. Salanter cites the later Tosafists.
2. The three sources cited have slightly different formulations, but all use language that clearly limits the obligation to Jewish men. For instance, Rambam and *Shulḥan Arukh* use the term "*ish*" ("man"). R. Salanter uses the more inclusive language of "*adam*."
3. The verse, cited in full by the Talmud (ad loc.), states: "Bind them on your fingers; write them on the tablet of your heart." R. Salanter misquotes the verse here, though he cites it accurately in the next paragraph.

been better off had he never been created"; the *Tosafot*[1] have explained there that this refers to one who studies Torah only to provoke his colleagues; see ad loc. Moreover, they only said that he would have been better off had he never been created and never come into this world. However, now that he has been created, he is not at liberty to neglect any mitzva. God forbid that we say of someone who has no fear of Heaven that it would be better that he not study Torah at all.

There are two aspects to the mitzva of Torah study: a) studying Torah [i.e., the act itself]; b) knowing the Torah. The commandment to study Torah is derived from the verse "Meditate upon [the Torah] day and night" (Josh. 1:8). As Rambam, *Tur*, and *Shulḥan Arukh* state at the beginning of the Laws of Torah Study: "Every person[2] in Israel is obligated to study Torah... as it is written, 'Meditate upon it day and night'"; see ad loc. When it comes to this mitzva of studying Torah, whatever one studies fulfills the positive commandment of "Meditate upon it day and night," be it Scripture, Mishna, Talmud, halakha, or *aggada*, all of which were given to Moses at Sinai. And this is expounded at length in the *Nefesh HaḤayim* 4:6; see ad loc. Although one cannot reach a conclusion on matters of law based on Scripture or Mishna, and certainly not based on *aggada*, one still fulfills the mitzva of learning Torah.

However, the second dimension of the mitzva of Torah study is knowing the Torah. It is to this that our Sages, of blessed memory, refer in Kiddushin 30a:

> "You shall teach them (*veshinantam*)" (Deut. 6:7) [means] that the words of the Torah shall be honed in your mouth; if someone asks you something, do not stammer a response, but answer at once, as it says: "Say to wisdom, you are my sister" (Prov. 7:4); and it says: "Bind them on the tablet of your heart..." (ibid. 3);[3] [...]and it is said: "Your arrows are sharp..." (Ps. 45:6).

Rashi explains: "'Shall be honed in your mouth' – Review them and delve into their depths, so that if someone asks you, you do not need to stammer.... 'Say to wisdom, you are my sister' – Master it like [you have mastered the law that] your sister is forbidden to you [sexually]"; see ad loc.

יְסוֹד הַמִּצְוָה הַזֹּאת כּוֹלֵל שְׁנֵי פְּרָטִים, אֶחָד הַיְדִיעָה לִרְכֹּשׁ לוֹ הַבְּקִיאוּת בְּכָל חֶלְקֵי הַתּוֹרָה, שֶׁיִּהְיֶה תַּלְמוּדוֹ שָׁגוּר בְּפִיו, שֵׁנִי הוּא הַיְכֹלֶת, לְהִתְחַכֵּם בַּתּוֹרָה לְחַדֵּד הַשֵּׂכֶל לְשַׁנְּנוֹ וּלְהֵישִׁירוֹ שֶׁיּוּכַל לִישָּׂא וְלִיתֵּן בְּמִלְחַמְתָּהּ שֶׁל תּוֹרָה, וְלַעֲקֹר הָרִים בְּפִלְפּוּלוֹ, וּשְׁתֵּי אֵלֶּה כִּנּוּ חֲכָמֵינוּ זַ"ל בְּשֵׁם סִינַי וְעוֹקֵר הָרִים, וְזֶהוּ נִכְלָל גַּם בַּכָּתוּב שֶׁהֵבִיאוּ חֲכָמֵינוּ זַ"ל בַּגְּמָרָא קִדּוּשִׁין הַנִּזְכָּר לְעֵיל, כָּתְבֵם עַל לוּחַ לִבֶּךָ, זֶהוּ יְסוֹד הַבְּקִיאוּת, חִצֶּיךָ שְׁנוּנִים, זֶהוּ הַפִּלְפּוּל וְהַחֲרִיפוּת, וְהִנֵּה לִיסוֹד יְדִיעַת הַתּוֹרָה הוּא דַּוְקָא לִמּוּד הַגְּמָרָא וְהַפּוֹסְקִים, וְאֵינוֹ יוֹצֵא בְּלִמּוּד אַחֵר כַּמּוּבָן, וְגַם סֵדֶר הַלִּמּוּד יִהְיֶה בְּעִנְיָן שֶׁיַּגִּיעַ לְמַטְּרָתוֹ, כִּי לֹא כָּל הַמְּקוֹמוֹת שָׁווֹת, וּכְבָר אָמְרוּ חֲכָמֵינוּ זַ"ל בְּשִׁלְהֵי בָּבָא בַּתְרָא דַּף קע"ה, אָמַר רַבִּי יִשְׁמָעֵאל הָרוֹצֶה שֶׁיַּחְכִּים יַעֲסֹק בְּדִינֵי מָמוֹנוֹת כּוּ' עַיֵּן שָׁם.

תַּכְלִית הַמִּצְוָה שֶׁל יְדִיעַת הַתּוֹרָה, הוּא לֵידַע דִּינֵי הַתּוֹרָה וּמִשְׁפָּטֶיהָ עַל בּוּרְיָן שֶׁיִּהְיֶה לוֹ הֲלָכָה בְּרוּרָה בְּכָל מָקוֹם, אֵיךְ לִשְׁמֹר וּלְקַיֵּם אֶת כָּל הַתּוֹרָה וְהַמִּצְוָה וְעַיֵּן לְהָרַמְבַּ"ם וְהַטּוּר וְשֻׁלְחָן עָרוּךְ בְּהִלְכוֹת תַּלְמוּד תּוֹרָה, וְזֶה לְשׁוֹנוֹ וְחַיָּב לְשַׁלֵּשׁ אֶת זְמַן לְמִידָתוֹ שְׁלִישׁ בַּתּוֹרָה שֶׁבִּכְתָב כּוּ', וּשְׁלִישׁ יָבִין וְיַשְׂכִּיל כּוּ', וְיוֹצִיא דָּבָר מִדָּבָר וִידַמֶּה דָּבָר לְדָבָר כּוּ' עַד שֶׁיֵּדַע כּוּ', וְהֵיאַךְ יוֹצִיא הָאָסוּר וְהַמֻּתָּר כּוּ', וְעִנְיָן זֶה הוּא הַנִּקְרָא גְּמָרָא עַיֵּן שָׁם, וְהִנֵּה כְּכָל אֲשֶׁר יַרְבֶּה לְהִתְחַכֵּם וּלְהִתְעַצֵּם בַּמִּקְצוֹעוֹת הָאֵלּוּ בִּבְקִיאוּת וַחֲרִיפוּת, כֵּן יָבִין וְיַשְׂכִּיל יוֹתֵר בִּידִיעַת מִשְׁפְּטֵי הַתּוֹרָה הֲלָכָה לְמַעֲשֶׂה. לְחַדֵּשׁ דִּינִים מִדַּעְתּוֹ וּלְהַכְרִיעַ בֵּין הַשִּׁיטוֹת, וְסוֹף הַתַּכְלִית הוּא לְהַגִּיעַ

4. As R. Salanter explains in the next paragraph, the purpose of this aspect of Torah study is to know the practical halakha. This, obviously, is achieved by studying the relevant parts of the Talmud and the legal codes.

There are two basic elements of this mitzva [of knowing the Torah]: a) knowledge, the acquisition of proficiency in all parts of the Torah, so that his learning is well rehearsed in his mouth; b) the ability to become wiser through Torah, to sharpen, hone, and arrange the mind so one can thrust and parry in the war of Torah, and uproot mountains with his dialectical thinking.

Our Sages, of blessed memory, called these two [elements] "Sinai" and "uprooter of mountains" [respectively]. These two [elements] are also included in the verses cited by our Sages, of blessed memory, in the passage from Kiddushin cited above: "Write them on the tablet of your heart" refers to the element of proficiency; "Your arrows are sharp" refers to dialectic and acute analytical skills.

Now, the "knowledge of Torah" aspect [of the mitzva of Torah study] is specifically the study of the Talmud and legal codes; one does not fulfill this obligation by studying anything else, of course.[4] Moreover, the order of study should be geared toward achieving this goal, for not all areas [of Torah] are equivalent; our Sages, of blessed memory, have said at the end of Bava Batra (175b): R. Ishmael said: "One who wants to become wiser should study monetary law..."; see ad loc.

The goal of knowing the Torah is to know the Torah's laws and juridical principles thoroughly, so that he has clear rulings for all matters regarding how to observe and uphold the whole of the Torah and commandments. And see Rambam, *Tur*, and *Shulḥan Arukh* in the Laws of Torah Study, where they write:

> One must divide his [study] time into thirds: one third Scripture... one third he should focus on understanding and discern..., deriving one matter from another and comparing one matter to another... until he knows... how to ascertain what is forbidden and what is permitted.... This is what is called "*gemara*."

Now, the wiser, more proficient, and sharper he becomes in these matters, the more understanding and discerning he will be in his knowledge of the laws of the Torah, applied as practical halakha. He will be able to produce novel rulings through his own understanding and decide

לְמַעֲלַת הַהוֹרָאָה בִּבְחִינָה נַעֲלָה, לְהוֹרוֹת הוֹרָאָה לְעַצְמוֹ וְלַאֲחֵרִים, וּכְמוֹ שֶׁאָמְרוּ שֶׁאִם יִשְׁאָלְךָ אָדָם כו'.

וְהִנֵּה יֵשׁ יִרְאֵי ד' טוֹעִין וְחוֹשְׁבִין, כִּי עִקַּר נְחִיצַת שֶׁל יְכֹלֶת הַלִּמּוּד, הוּא רַק לְמִי שֶׁרוֹצֶה לְהַגִּיעַ לְהוֹרָאָה לְהוֹרוֹת הוֹרָאָה לָרַבִּים. אוּלָם מִי שֶׁהוּא בּוֹדֵד בְּמוֹעֲדוֹ, יוּכַל לִהְיוֹת עוֹבֵד אֶת ד' יִתְבָּרַךְ שְׁמוֹ וּלְקַיֵּם אֶת כָּל דִּבְרֵי הַתּוֹרָה וְהַמִּצְוָה, גַּם שֶׁלֹּא יִהְיֶה גָּדוֹל בַּתּוֹרָה כָּל כָּךְ, אוּלָם בֶּאֱמֶת הוּא טָעוּת, כִּי גַּם כָּל אָדָם לְעַצְמוֹ, מִי שֶׁרוֹצֶה לֵילֵךְ בְּדַרְכֵי ד' יִתְבָּרַךְ שְׁמוֹ, וְלָשׂוּם דְּרָכָיו עַל פִּי דֶּרֶךְ הַתּוֹרָה, כָּל מַה שֶּׁיּוֹסִיף דַּעַת וְיִתְחַכֵּם יוֹתֵר, כֵּן יוּכַל לְקַיֵּם הַתּוֹרָה וְהַמִּצְוָה בְּיִתְרוֹן הֶכְשֵׁר. גַּם הָאָדָם לְעַצְמוֹ צָרִיךְ לִהְיוֹת בָּקִי בְּכָל הַתּוֹרָה, וְלִהְיוֹת לוֹ לֵב נָבוֹן וְשֵׂכֶל חָרוּץ, לְמַעַן שֶׁיּוּכַל לִשְׁמֹר וּלְקַיֵּם אֶת הַתּוֹרָה, עַל פִּי גִּדְרֵי מִשְׁפָּטֶיהָ, גַּם חֵלֶק הַתּוֹרָה שֶׁל חֹשֶׁן מִשְׁפָּט וְאֶבֶן הָעֵזֶר צָרִיךְ לִהְיוֹת שְׁגוּרִים בְּפִיו לְעַצְמוֹ לְמַעֲשֶׂה, וְאדמו"ר זצוק"ל הֶרְאָה לָנוּ כַּמָּה דּוּגְמָאוֹת בָּזֶה.

וְכַאֲשֶׁר נַשְׂכִּיל בִּינָה נִמְצָא כִּי יֵשׁ דְּבָרִים שֶׁהֻתַּר לְמַלְאוֹת הַמַּטָּרָה שֶׁל מִצְוַת יְדִיעַת הַתּוֹרָה, מַה שֶּׁלֹּא הָיָה עִנְיָן לְמִצְוַת לִמּוּד הַתּוֹרָה וּכְמוֹ בִּטּוּל הַזְּמַן. כִּי לְשֵׁם יְדִיעוֹת הַתּוֹרָה שֶׁהוּא יְכֹלֶת הַלִּמּוּד, רַשַּׁאי לְבַטֵּל זְמַן לֵילֵךְ מֵעִיר לְעִיר, גַּם לְהַרְחִיק נְדוֹד לְחַפֵּשׂ אַחַר רַב גָּדוֹל לְבַקֵּשׁ תּוֹרָה מִפִּיו, וּלְקַבֵּל מִמֶּנּוּ דַּרְכֵי הַלִּמּוּד וְהָעִיּוּן. וְכֵן לְבַלּוֹת זְמַן עַל עִתּוֹת מְנוּחָה וְשֵׁנָה, מַה שֶּׁנָּחוּץ לוֹ לְפִי טִבְעוֹ. שֶׁיִּהְיֶה אַחַר כָּךְ דַּעְתּוֹ צְלוּלָה עָלָיו בְּיוֹתֵר לְהָבִין וּלְהַשְׂכִּיל בְּעֹמֶק הָעִיּוּן, אֲשֶׁר כָּל זֶה לֹא הָיָה עִנְיָן לְמִצְוַת לִמּוּד הַתּוֹרָה בִּלְבַד כַּמּוּבָן.

וְכֵן גַּם גּוּף הָעִנְיָן שֶׁל הַפִּלְפּוּל וְהַחִדּוּד, הוּא רַק לְשֵׁם יְכֹלֶת הַלִּמּוּד שֶׁל יְדִיעוֹת הַתּוֹרָה, וּכְבָר הִתִּירוּ חֲכָמֵינוּ ז"ל לוֹמַר לִפְעָמִים

---

5. Based on Isaiah 14:31.
6. The section of *Shulḥan Arukh* that deals with jurisprudence, civil law, torts, contracts, and other forms of monetary law.
7. The section of *Shulḥan Arukh* that deals with marriage, divorce, and procreation.
8. As is often the case in *Ohr Yisrael*, R. Isaac Blazer is recording what he heard from R. Salanter.

among [different] opinions. The ultimate purpose is to become a bona fide *posek* (decisor), issuing rulings for himself and others, as they said: "If someone asks you, [you do not need to stammer]...."

There are God-fearing people who err and think that the essential need to be able to study Torah is only for someone who wishes to become a *posek* and issue rulings to the public, but one who is a straggler in the ranks[5] can be a servant of God, blessed be His name, and uphold every word of the Torah and the commandments, even if he is not so great in Torah.

However, in truth, this [view] is a serious error. Even each person [studying only] for himself, if he wants to go in the ways of God, blessed be His name, and to set his course in accordance with the path of the Torah, then any way that he increases his [Torah] knowledge and wisdom, the more capably he can uphold the Torah and the commandments. Even the person who is learning just for himself must become proficient in the whole Torah – to have an understanding heart and an assiduous mind – so that he can observe and uphold the Torah in accordance with and within the parameters of its laws. Even the *Ḥoshen Mishpat*[6] and *Even HaEzer*[7] parts of the Torah must be fluent in his mouth for his own practice. Our master, teacher, and rabbi [R. Israel Salanter,] *ztvk"l*, showed us several examples of this principle [namely, how thorough knowledge of these areas of halakha are essential for individual practice].[8]

As we increase our understanding, we find that there are things that are permitted for fulfilling the objective of the mitzva of knowing the Torah which would not be relevant to the mitzva of studying Torah – for example, wasting time. For the sake of knowing the Torah – that is, [developing] the capacity to study – one may "waste" time traveling from city to city, even wandering far away, in search of a great rabbi from whose mouth he may seek Torah and from whom he can receive methods of study and analysis. Similarly, one may spend time on periods of rest and sleep – as he needs according to his nature – so that afterward his mind will be clearer to understand and discern matters in depth. All this has no connection to the mitzva of simply studying Torah, of course.

This is also the essence of studying with dialectical analysis and to sharpen [the mind]: They are only to improve one's capacity to know Torah. Our Sages, of blessed memory, have even permitted occasionally

לִפְנֵי הַתַּלְמִידִים דָּבָר שֶׁאֵינוֹ לְפִי הָאֱמֶת, כְּדֵי לְחַדֵּד אֶת הַתַּלְמִידִים שֶׁיִּתְּנוּ לֵב לְהָשִׁיב, וְכַמְבֹאָר בְּנִדָּה דַּף מ"ה וְאַף רַבִּי עֲקִיבָא לֹא אֲמָרָהּ אֶלָּא לְחַדֵּד בָּהּ אֶת הַתַּלְמִידִים, וְכָל זֶה אֵינוֹ עִנְיָן לְמִצְוַת לִמּוּד הַתּוֹרָה לְבַד.

וְהִנֵּה עֶצֶם מִצְוַת לִמּוּד הַתּוֹרָה לְבַד, הִיא כִּשְׁאָר כָּל הַמִּצְוֹת, וְאֵין לָהּ יִחוּס כְּלָל לְיִרְאַת ד', כִּי כָּל שָׁעָה וְכָל רֶגַע שֶׁהוּא לוֹמֵד הוּא מְקַיֵּם מִצְוַת עֲשֵׂה שֶׁל וְהָגִיתָ כוּ', וּכְמוֹ שֶׁאֵין יִחוּס לִשְׁאָר מִצְוֹת כְּמוֹ שׁוֹפָר סֻכָּה וְלוּלָב לְיִרְאַת ד' יִתְבָּרַךְ שְׁמוֹ.

אָכֵן לְגֶדֶר הַלִּמּוּד לְמַלְאוֹת הַמִּצְוָה שֶׁל יְדִיעַת הַתּוֹרָה, וְהוּא לְהָבִין וּלְהַשְׂכִּיל וּלְהִשְׁתַּלֵּם בְּחָכְמַת הַתּוֹרָה, אֲשֶׁר הַיְסוֹד בָּהּ לֵידַע מִשְׁפְּטֵי הַתּוֹרָה לְהַגִּיעַ לְמַדְרֵגַת הַהוֹרָאָה, לְהוֹרוֹת בֵּין דָּם לְדָם וּבֵין דִּין לְדִין, לָזֶה מֻכְרָח וְנָחוּץ דַּוְקָא שֶׁיִּהְיֶה יִרְאַת ד' אוֹצָרוֹ, כִּי בְּלֹא יִרְאַת ד' תּוּכַל לִהְיוֹת חָכְמָתוֹ לוֹ לְפוּקָה וּלְמִכְשׁוֹל עָוֹן, הִנֵּה מַה שֶּׁנּוֹגֵעַ לְעַצְמוֹ, כְּבָר אָמְרוּ חֲכָמֵינוּ זַ"ל בְּשַׁבָּת דַּף ל"א כָּל אָדָם שֶׁיֵּשׁ בּוֹ תּוֹרָה וְאֵין בּוֹ יִרְאַת שָׁמַיִם דּוֹמֶה לְגִזְבָּר כוּ' בְּהֵי עָיֵל עַיֵּן שָׁם וּפֵרֵשׁ רַשִׁ"י יִרְאַת שָׁמַיִם דּוֹמָה כוּ', כָּךְ אִם יְרֵא שָׁמַיִם הוּא נַעֲשֶׂה חָרֵד לִשְׁמֹר וְלַעֲשׂוֹת, וְאִם לָאו אֵינוֹ חָשׁ לְתוֹרָתוֹ עַיֵּן שָׁם, וּלְפִי זֶה אִם אֵין יִרְאַת ה' אוֹצָרוֹ, כָּל מַה שֶּׁמַּרְבֶּה לְהִתְחַכֵּם לֵידַע הָאָסוּר וְהַמֻּתָּר וְאֵינוֹ נִזְהָר יִגְדַּל עָנְשׁוֹ.

וּמַה גַּם לְהוֹרוֹת הוֹרָאָה לָרַבִּים, הִנֵּה יִרְאַת ד' מֻכְרָח לוֹ בְּיוֹתֵר, לְמַעַן שֶׁיַּעֲמֹל לְהִשְׁתַּלֵּם כָּל צָרְכּוֹ בְּמִשְׁפַּט הַהוֹרָאָה, אָכֵן בְּלֹא יִרְאַת ד' יוּכַל לִהְיוֹת בִּכְלָל מַה שֶּׁאָמְרוּ חֲכָמֵינוּ זַ"ל בַּגְּמָרָא עֲבוֹדָה זָרָה דַּף י"ט, כִּי רַבִּים חֲלָלִים הִפִּילָה זֶהוּ תַּלְמִיד שֶׁלֹּא הִגִּיעַ לְהוֹרָאָה

9. The first aspect of Torah study highlights the act of studying and can be compared to the performance of any other mitzva. When one is actively studying, he fulfills the mitzva; it hardly matters whether he fears God or whether he retains what he has learned. The second aspect of Torah study, namely, knowing the Torah, focuses on retention and understanding. Thus, taking time off to relax the mind, investing in the search for the right teacher, and exercising the critical faculties are all endeavors

saying something to students that is not quite true in order to sharpen the students, so that they consider the matter and respond. This is clear from Nidda 45a: "R. Akiva did not say this except to sharpen the students with it." None of this has anything to do with the mitzva of simply studying Torah.

Now, the essence of the mitzva of simply studying Torah is like all the other mitzvot. It has no special relationship with the fear of God, for every minute and second that one studies Torah, he fulfills the positive commandment of "Meditate upon it...." This is just like there is no special relationship between other mitzvot, like shofar, sukka, and lulav, and fear of God, blessed be His name.[9]

Indeed, the definition of learning in order to fulfill the mitzva of knowing the Torah is to understand, to discern, and to become complete in wisdom of the Torah. Its essence is to know the laws of the Torah and reach the level of being able to issue rulings, to decide "between blood and blood, between plea and plea" (Deut. 17:8). [To reach this stage] it is necessary and essential that "fear of the Lord is his storehouse," for without fear of God, his wisdom can be "a cause of stumbling and faltering" (I Sam. 25:31) into sin. When it comes to himself, our Sages, of blessed memory, have said in Shabbat 31b: "Anyone who has Torah but does not have fear of Heaven is like a treasurer [who was given the keys to the inner doors but not the keys to the outer doors]. With what will he enter?" Rashi explains there that fear of Heaven resembles [the outer doors, through which one can enter to the inner doors]. Thus, if he fears Heaven, he becomes vigilant about observing and performing [the mitzvot], and if not, he is not concerned about his Torah; see ad loc. Accordingly, if fear of the Lord is not his storehouse, then the more wisdom he acquires to discern between what is forbidden and what is permitted – yet without being cautious in practice – the greater will be his punishment.

When it comes to offering halakhic instructions to the masses, it is all the more critical that he possess fear of God, so that he works hard to become as thorough as necessary to issue rulings. Indeed, without fear of God, he might become part of what our Sages, of blessed memory, said in Avoda Zara 19b: "'For she has cast down many wounded' (Prov. 7:26) – This is referring to a student who has not reached [the

וּמוֹרֶה, וְכֵן צָרִיךְ לִהְיוֹת מִירְאֵי הוֹרָאָה, וּכְמוֹ שֶׁאָמְרוּ חֲכָמֵינוּ ז״ל בְּסַנְהֶדְרִין דַּף ז׳, לְעוֹלָם יִרְאֶה דַּיָּן עַצְמוֹ, כְּאִלּוּ חֶרֶב מֻנַּחַת לוֹ בֵּין יַרְכוֹתָיו, וְגֵיהִנֹּם פְּתוּחָה לוֹ מִתַּחְתָּיו, אִם כֵּן הֲרֵי צָרִיךְ שֶׁיִּהְיֶה פַּחַד אֱלֹקִים לְנֶגֶד עֵינָיו.

וְכֵן לְעִנְיַן מַדְרֵגַת הַהוֹרָאָה צָרִיךְ לִהְיוֹת מְכֻתָּר בִּשְׁלֵמוּת וּמַעֲלוֹת הַמִּדּוֹת, שֶׁיִּהְיֶה מְשֻׁלָּל מִכָּל רָצוֹן וּנְגִיעָה עַצְמִית, וּכְמוֹ שֶׁכָּתַב אדמו״ר זצוק״ל בַּהַקְדָּמָה לְסֵפֶר תְּבוּנָה לְעִנְיַן בַּקָּשַׁת הָאֱמֶת, וְזֶה לְשׁוֹנוֹ. הַטָּהֳרָה – הִיא אֲשֶׁר יְכַנּוּהָ הַחֲכָמִים בְּשֵׁם הַכָּרָה מַדָּעִית, וְחַכְמֵי הַמּוּסָר בְּשֵׁם הִתְפַּשְּׁטוּת הַגַּשְׁמִיּוּת, הַיְנוּ שֶׁיִּהְיֶה הַשֵּׂכֶל בּוֹדֵד בְּלִי הַרְכָּבָתוֹ עִם יֶתֶר כֹּחוֹת הַנְּפָשׁוֹת אֲשֶׁר בְּהָאָדָם, כִּי זוּלַת זֹאת נְטִיַּת כֹּחוֹת הַנַּפְשִׁיּוֹת הֵמָּה מַסָּכִים מַבְדִּילִים בֵּינוֹ לְבֵין הַכָּרַת הָאֱמֶת כּוּ׳ וְהַנְּטִיָּה תְּעַקְּמֶהָ לִצְעֹד בְּדֶרֶךְ עֲקַלְקַלּוֹת.

גַּם כִּי יִהְיֶה שָׁוֶה בְּעֵינָיו, בֵּין אִם כְּבָר הוֹצִיא הַדָּבָר מִפִּיו אוֹ לֹא הוֹצִיא, וְכַאֲשֶׁר הָאָדָם עָלוּל לִשְׁגִיאָה לִפְעָמִים, לֹא יִהְיֶה לוֹ שׁוּם נְגִיעָה וְרָצוֹן לְהִתְאַמֵּץ לַעֲמֹד עַל דַּעְתּוֹ, וּלְהַחֲזִיק אֶת דְּבָרָיו, מֵאַחַר שֶׁכְּבָר הוֹצִיא מִפִּיו, וְלֹא יֵבוֹשׁ לַחֲזֹר מִדְּבָרָיו, וּכְמוֹ שֶׁמָּצִינוּ אֲשֶׁר חֲכָמֵינוּ ז״ל לֹא בּוֹשׁוּ לַחֲזֹר מִדִּבְרֵיהֶם, וְלִדְרֹשׁ בָּרַבִּים בְּרַם דְּבָרִים שֶׁאָמַרְתִּי לִפְנֵיכֶם טָעוּת הֵן בְּיָדִי.

וְכֹה אָמַר אדמו״ר זצוק״ל, מִי לָנוּ גָּדוֹל מִמּוֹרֵנוּ וְרַבֵּנוּ הַגָּאוֹן הֶחָסִיד רשכבה״ג מָרָנָא צְבִי הִירְשׁ בְּרוֹדָא זצוק״ל הגאבד״ק סַאלַאנְט, וְלִפְעָמִים הָיָה פּוֹסֵק שְׁאֵלָה בְּהִלְכוֹת טְרֵפוֹת עַל תַּרְנְגֹלֶת, וְהַשּׁוֹאֵל שָׁב לְבֵיתוֹ עִם הַשְּׁאֵלָה, אִם אַחַר כָּךְ הָיָה נִרְאֶה לִי אֵיזֶה פִּקְפּוּק בְּהוֹרָאָתוֹ, הָיָה מְצַוֶּה לְהָבִיא לְפָנָיו הַשְּׁאֵלָה בַּחֲזָרָה לְעַיֵּן בָּהּ שֵׁנִית.

---

that can enhance one's knowledge of Torah but are not themselves acts of Torah study.

10. See below, Letter 29, p. 179.

11. Laws regarding the internal blemishes and defects that render a slaughtered animal non-kosher.

level where he can render] halakhic rulings, yet issues rulings." Likewise, he should be among those who fear issuing rulings, as our Sages, of blessed memory, said in Sanhedrin 7a: "A judge should always view himself as though there is a sword placed between his thighs and Hell is open below him." Thus we see that fear of God must be before his eyes [when he issues his rulings.]

Likewise, when it comes to being on the level where one may issue rulings, one must be crowned with wholeness and refinement of character, free of all personal desires or biased self-interest. As our master, teacher, and rabbi, [R. Israel Salanter,] *ztvk"l,* wrote in the introduction *to Sefer Tevunah:*[10]

> Purity – this is what scientists call "scientific knowledge" and the Mussar sages call the stripping away of physicality, meaning that the intellect stands alone and is not combined with other human psychic drives. Otherwise, the tendencies of the psychic drives are screens separating him from recognizing the truth. For, even though straight judgment helps [in recognizing the truth], tendencies distort [judgment, leading it] to proceed along crooked paths.

Even when he reaches this stage of equanimity – whether he already uttered [this ruling] or not – and considering that a person is liable to err at times, he should have no self-interest or will to stand by his opinion and hold fast to his words, once he uttered them. He should not be ashamed to retract his words, as we see that our Sages, of blessed memory, were not ashamed to recant and to publicly declare, "The words I said before you were [the result of] an error on my part."

This is what our master, teacher, and rabbi, [R. Israel Salanter,] *ztvk"l,* said: Who is a greater scholar than our teacher and master, the eminent and pious, the leader of the entire Diaspora, our master Zvi Hirsh Braude, *ztvk"l,* the eminent head of the Salant rabbinical court? Sometimes he ruled on a question in the laws of *tereifot*[11] in a chicken and the applicant already returned to his house with the object of the inquiry; if some niggling question about his ruling would occur to him later, he would instruct them to bring the subject of the inquiry back again so he could study the matter a second time.

אָכֵן בְּלֹא יִרְאַת ד׳ וּשְׁלֵמוּת הַמִּדּוֹת. יוּכַל לִהְיוֹת נֶאֱחָז בִּסְבַךְ כַּמָּה קִלְקוּלִים וּמִכְשׁוֹלִים, כִּי כַּמָּה נְגִיעוֹת מִדַּרְכֵי הַמִּדּוֹת יוּכְלוּ לִפְעָמִים לְשַׁחֵד אֶת שִׂכְלוֹ וּלְהַטּוֹתוֹ עֲקַלְקַלּוֹת, וְאִם לִפְעָמִים יִשְׁגֶּה בַּהוֹרָאָה יֵבוֹשׁ מִלַּחֲזֹר בּוֹ, וְיִתְאַמֵּץ לְהַחֲזִיק אֶת דְּבָרָיו, וְלָכוֹף אֶת הָהָר כְּגִיגִית עַל הוֹרָאָתוֹ, וְלִפְעָמִים גַּם אִם יוֹצִיא מִפִּיו בִּלְבַד, יִתְאַמֵּץ לְהַחֲזִיק אֶת דְּבָרָיו. מִבְּלִי לְהוֹדוֹת עַל הָאֱמֶת.

וְכָל זֶה הוּא עָוֹן גָּדוֹל, כִּי הִנֵּה הַתּוֹרָה כֻּלָּהּ הוּא שֶׁל הַקָּדוֹשׁ־בָּרוּךְ־הוּא, וְכָל הֶעָמָל שֶׁיַּעֲמֹל הָאָדָם לִפְסֹק אֵיזֶה דִּין וּמִשְׁפָּט, אוֹ לְהָבִין וּלְהַשְׂכִּיל בְּאֵיזֶה הֲלָכָה, הוּא רַק לֵידַע וּלְהַשְׂכִּיל לְהַשִּׂיג רְצוֹן ד׳ יִתְבָּרַךְ שְׁמוֹ בְּדַרְכֵי תּוֹרָתוֹ, כִּי כָּל הַתּוֹרָה הוּא חָכְמָתוֹ וּרְצוֹנוֹ יִתְבָּרַךְ שְׁמוֹ, אוּלָם אִם אֵיזֶה נְגִיעָה תּוֹלִיךְ אוֹתוֹ שׁוֹלָל, וְיִרְצֶה לְהִתְעוֹת אֶת שִׂכְלוֹ לְהַטּוֹת אוֹתוֹ לְחֶפְצוֹ, לִפְסֹק אֵיזֶה דִּין, אוֹ לְפָרֵשׁ אֵיזֶה הֲלָכָה עַל פִּי דַּעְתּוֹ וּרְצוֹנוֹ, אַף כִּי לִבּוֹ יוֹדֵעַ כִּי הָאֱמֶת אֵינוֹ כֵּן, הֲרֵי הוּא בּוֹדֶה תּוֹרָה חֲדָשָׁה מִשִּׂכְלוֹ, וְהוּא הֵרוּס יְסוֹדֵי הַדָּת רַחֲמָנָא לִצְלַן, וְאֵין לְהַאֲרִיךְ בָּזֶה כַּמּוּבָן. וְכֵן בְּלֹא יִרְאַת ד׳ וּשְׁלֵמוּת הַמִּדּוֹת, יֵבוֹשׁ לְהִתְיַשֵּׁב לִפְעָמִים עִם זוּלָתוֹ בְּאֵיזֶה דִּין וְהוֹרָאָה, וְלִפְעָמִים אַף עִם מִי שֶׁגָּדוֹל מִמֶּנּוּ, וְכֵן יִתְעַצֵּל לִפְעָמִים מִלִּהְיוֹת מָתוּן בַּדִּין וְלִטְרֹחַ לְהַעֲמִיק עַד שֶׁיִּהְיֶה בָּרוּר לוֹ הַדָּבָר.

כְּלָלוֹ שֶׁל דָּבָר כִּי לְמַלְאוֹת הַתַּכְלִית שֶׁל יְדִיעַת הַתּוֹרָה, וְהוּא לֵידַע הֲלָכָה בְּרוּרָה לְהוֹרוֹת לְעַצְמוֹ וְלַאֲחֵרִים, עַל זֶה מֻכְרָח שֶׁיִּהְיֶה יִרְאַת ד׳ אוֹצָרוֹ, וּבְלֹא זֶה יוּכַל לָבֹא לִידֵי כַּמָּה קִלְקוּלִים וּמִכְשׁוֹלִים רַבִּים, וּלְהַחֲרִיב עוֹלָם מָלֵא.

וְהִנֵּה לְעִנְיַן מִצְוַת לִמּוּד הַתּוֹרָה לְקַיֵּם מִצְוַת עֲשֵׂה שֶׁל וְהָגִיתָ כּוּ׳, הַתַּכְלִית הוּא מִיָּד, כִּי בְּכָל שָׁעָה וָרֶגַע שֶׁהוּא לוֹמֵד הוּא מְקַיֵּם מִצְוַת עֲשֵׂה, אוּלָם דַּרְכֵי הַלִּמּוּד לִידִיעַת הַתּוֹרָה, לְמַלְאוֹת הַמִּצְוָה שֶׁל וְשִׁנַּנְתָּם שֶׁיִּהְיֶה דִּבְרֵי תּוֹרָה מְחֻדָּדִים בְּפִיו, וְהוּא לְהִשְׁתַּלֵּם

12. I.e., he forces evidence to fit his ruling. The expression comes from Shabbat 88a.

13. I.e., without delivering a formal written ruling.

Indeed, without fear of God and wholeness of character traits, one can get caught in the thicket of several obstacles and forms of corruption, for several biases that are common within character traits can sometimes "bribe" his reason and turn it crooked. So if sometimes he errs in his ruling, he will be embarrassed to recant it; rather, he will make an effort to reinforce his words and "press the mountain like a barrel"[12] over his ruling. Sometimes, even if he merely uttered [his ruling],[13] he will fortify himself to maintain his position – and not admit the truth.

All [such behavior] is a great sin. For the Torah in its entirety belongs to the Holy One, blessed be He, and all the effort that a person expends to properly decide some law or judgment, or to understand and gain deeper insight into some halakha, is only in order to know and comprehend how to attain the will of God, blessed be His name, by means of His Torah – for the Torah is entirely the wisdom and will of [God], blessed be His name. But if some bias leads him astray, and he wishes to fool his reason, turning it toward his desire, to rule on some law or explain some halakha according to his opinion and will – although in his heart he knows that this is not the true [Torah] – he is, in fact, inventing a new Torah out of his own mind. This wrecks the foundations of the religion, God save us. There is no need to belabor this matter. Similarly, without fear of God and wholeness of character traits, he will be ashamed to come to a joint understanding with another decisor in some law or decision. Sometimes he will hold back even though the other is greater than him. Sometimes he will be slothful and not consider his ruling carefully or not bother penetrate the matter until it becomes clear to him.

The principle of the matter is: To fulfill the objective of knowing the Torah – that is, to know halakha with clarity, to instruct himself and others – it is necessary that "fear of the Lord is his storehouse." Without it, he may encounter many stumbling blocks and forms of corruption, even destroying a whole world.

Now, with respect to the mitzva to study Torah to fulfill the positive commandment of "Meditate [upon it day and night]," the purpose is realized immediately, for every moment he studies, he fulfills the positive commandment. However, the methods of studying in order to know the Torah – to fulfill the commandment "'You shall teach them' – the words of the Torah shall be honed in your mouth," which means becoming

בְּחָכְמַת הַתּוֹרָה, לִרְכֹּשׁ לוֹ יְדִיעוֹת וּלְחַדֵּד הַשֵּׂכֶל שֶׁיּוּכַל לְפַלְפֵּל בְּחָכְמָה וְלֵב נָבוֹן לִסְבָרָא יְשָׁרָה, לֹא בְּשָׁעָה אַחַת יְוָלֵד זֶה הַתַּכְלִית, כִּי אִם בְּהֶמְשֵׁךְ הַזְּמַן בְּהַרְבֵּה יָמִים וְשָׁנִים, וּכְפִי עֲמָלוֹ וִיגִיעָתוֹ כֵּן יַגִּיעַ לַתַּכְלִית הַנִּרְצֶה, נִמְצָא כִּי דַּרְכֵי הַלִּמּוּד וְהֶעָמָל לִידִיעַת הַתּוֹרָה הוּא עַל לְהַבָּא, וְהוּא בְּדִמְיוֹן כְּמִי שֶׁמַּכְנִיס תְּבוּאָה לָאוֹצָר, שֶׁיִּהְיֶה מֻנָּח שָׁם זְמַן רַב, עַד עֵת שֶׁיִּתְיַקֵּר הַתְּבוּאָה וְיִמְצָא פְּרִי רֶוַח הַרְבֵּה, כֵּן הוּא מִי שֶׁעָמֵל בִּידִיעַת הַתּוֹרָה, לֶאֱסֹף וְלִכְנֹס עִנְיַן חָכְמָה וָדַעַת, לְהַכְנִיס בְּאוֹצָרוֹ תָּמִיד, עַד עֵת קֵץ שֶׁיֵּצֵא הַתַּכְלִית.

וּכְבָר נִתְבָּאֵר כִּי הַרְבֵּה דְּבָרִים שֶׁהֻתְּרוּ לְשֵׁם מִצְוָה שֶׁל יְדִיעַת הַתּוֹרָה, מַה שֶּׁלֹּא הָיָה עִנְיָן לְשֵׁם מִצְוַת לִמּוּד הַתּוֹרָה לְבַד, כְּמוֹ יְסוֹד דַּרְכֵי הַפִּלְפּוּל לְחִדּוּדֵי, וְהַרְבֵּה בִּטּוּל הַזְּמַן מַה שֶּׁיּוּכַל לִהְיוֹת מִכֹּחַ דַּרְכֵי יְדִיעַת הַתּוֹרָה כַּנִּזְכָּר לְעֵיל. וְהִנֵּה אִם יִרְאַת ד׳ הִיא אוֹצָרוֹ. הֲרֵי הִגִּיעַ לַתַּכְלִית הַנִּרְצֶה בִּשְׁלֵמוּת, וּכְדַאי הוּא לְפָנָיו כָּל דְּבַר הַפִּלְפּוּל וְהַחִדּוּד וּבִטּוּל הַזְּמַן, וּבְכֵן יְהִי לִבּוֹ שָׂמֵחַ מִכָּל עֲמָלוֹ לְקַיֵּם מִצְוַת וְשִׁנַּנְתָּם, לֵאמֹר לַחָכְמָה אֲחוֹתִי, וְלִהְיוֹת הֲלָכָה כְּמוֹתוֹ, אוּלָם אִם אֵין יִרְאַת ד׳ אוֹצָרוֹ, אַף כִּי הוּא יוֹדֵעַ לְהָבִין וּלְהוֹרוֹת, בְּכָל זֹאת לֹא הִגִּיעַ לַתַּכְלִית הַנִּרְצֶה, כִּי חָכְמָתוֹ תּוּכַל לִהְיוֹת לוֹ לְפוּקָה וּלְמִכְשׁוֹל כַּנִּזְכָּר לְעֵיל, אִם־כֵּן לֹא הָיָה כְּדַאי לְפָנָיו כָּל עֵסֶק הַפִּלְפּוּל וְהַחִדּוּד וּבִטּוּל הַזְּמַן, לִהְיוֹת עוֹקֵר הָרִים בְּפִלְפּוּלוֹ, וְהַלְוַאי הָיָה עוֹסֵק בַּתּוֹרָה תָּמִיד רַק לְקַיֵּם הַמִּצְוַת עֲשֵׂה שֶׁל וְהָגִיתָ כוּ׳.

הוּא מַה שֶּׁאָמְרוּ חֲכָמֵינוּ זַ״ל בְּשָׁעָה שֶׁמַּכְנִיסִין אָדָם לַדִּין, אוֹמְרִים לוֹ קָבַעְתָּ עִתִּים לַתּוֹרָה כוּ׳, פִּלְפַּלְתָּ בַּחָכְמָה הֵבַנְתָּ דָּבָר מִתּוֹךְ דָּבָר, וַאֲפִלּוּ הָכֵי אִי יִרְאַת ד׳ הִיא אוֹצָרוֹ אִין אִי לֹא לֹא מָשָׁל

whole through the wisdom of the Torah, acquiring knowledge and sharpening the intellect so that he can engage in wise discourse, and [acquiring] an understanding heart for straightforward reasoning – this cannot be accomplished all at once, only over a long time of many days and years. In accordance with his effort and toil, he will reach the desired end goal. We find, therefore, that the methods of studying and working in order to know the Torah are oriented toward the future. It can be compared to one who fills the granary with grain – where it will be stored for a long time, until the price rises and he produces much profit. So it is with one who puts great effort into knowing Torah, gathering and collecting wisdom and judgment to continually add to his storehouse – until the very end, when the goal is realized.

It has already been explained that many behaviors were permitted for the sake of knowing the Torah, which would not have been relevant for the sake of only studying Torah – such as the element of dialectic methods to sharpen [the mind] and wasting much time [in ways] that can improve methods for knowing the Torah, as mentioned above. Now, if "fear of the Lord is his storehouse," then he will reach the desired outcome in wholeness – so it was worth all the dialectics and mind sharpening and wasted time. Then his heart should rejoice at all his efforts to fulfill the mitzva "You shall teach them," to "call wisdom his sister," and for halakha to be in accordance with his view. However, if fear of the Lord is not his storehouse, then even if he knows [Torah to the extent that he can] understand and issue rulings, he still has not attained the desired outcome, for his wisdom may be "a cause of stumbling and faltering," as mentioned above. In such a case, all the effort at dialectic and mind sharpening and time wasted to become one who can uproot mountains with his erudition was not worth it. It would have been better that he spent all his time learning Torah constantly, only to fulfill the positive commandment of "Meditate [upon it day and night]."

This is [the meaning of] what our Sages, of blessed memory, said:

> When a person is brought in for judgment, they ask him [...] Did you set times for Torah study?... Did you engage in discourse about [the Torah's] wisdom? Did you infer one thing from another? Nevertheless, if "fear of the Lord is his storehouse,"

כו׳, אָמְנָם לֹא כִּוְּנוּ בָּזֶה עַל עֶצֶם מִצְוַת לִמּוּד הַתּוֹרָה שֶׁל מִצְוַת עֲשֵׂה וְהָגִיתָ כו׳, כִּי אֵין לָהּ יִחוּס עִם יִרְאַת ד׳ כְּמוֹ שֶׁאֵין עִנְיָן לִשְׁאָר מִצְוֹת עִם יִרְאַת ד׳ יִתְבָּרַךְ שְׁמוֹ, אוּלָם זֶה סוֹבֵב עַל הַשְּׁאֵלָה פִּלְפַּלְתָּ בְּחָכְמָה הֲבַנְתָּ דָּבָר מִתּוֹךְ דָּבָר, וְעַל זֶה אוֹמֵר אִי יִרְאַת ד׳ אוֹצָרוֹ אִין אִי לֹא לֹא, כִּי אִם אֵין יִרְאַת ד׳ אוֹצָרוֹ, לֹא הִגִּיעַ לְהַתַּכְלִית, כִּי חָכְמָתוֹ הוּא לוֹ עוֹד לְמִכְשׁוֹל עָוֹן, אִם־כֵּן מוּטָב שֶׁלֹּא פִּלְפֵּל כְּלָל כַּנִּזְכָּר לְעֵיל.

וְעַל זֶה מְכֻוָּן מְאֹד הַמָּשָׁל לְמִי שֶׁאָמַר לִשְׁלוּחוֹ הַעֲלֵה לִי כּוֹר חִטִּים לַעֲלִיָּה, הָלַךְ וְהֶעֱלָה לוֹ, אָמַר לוֹ עֵרַבְתָּ לִי בָּהֶן קַב חֻמְטִין, אָמַר לוֹ לָאו אָמַר לוֹ מוּטָב אִם לֹא הֶעֱלֵיתָ, כִּי הִנֵּה מַה שֶּׁהֶעֱלָה כּוֹר חִטִּים לַעֲלִיָּה, הוּא בְּעַל כָּרְחוֹ לְהַנִּיחַ בָּאוֹצָר עַל זְמַן רַב עַד שֶׁיִּתְיַקֵּר הַתְּבוּאָה אוֹ לִשְׁאָר מַטָּרָה שֶׁיֵּשׁ לוֹ, אוּלָם אִם לֹא עֵרֵב בָּהֶן קַב חֻמְטִין וְאֶפְשָׁר שֶׁהַתְּבוּאָה יַתְלִיעַ. אָמַר מוּטָב שֶׁלֹּא הֶעֱלֵיתָ, וְהָיָה אוֹכֵל אוֹתָם אוֹ מוֹכֵר מִיָּד מִשֶּׁיַּתְלִיעַ הַתְּבוּאָה, וְכֵן הַדָּבָר בְּדַרְכֵי הַלִּמּוּד שֶׁל יְדִיעַת הַתּוֹרָה, לְפַלְפֵּל בְּחָכְמָה וּלְהָבִין דָּבָר מִתּוֹךְ דָּבָר. שֶׁהוּא בְּדִמְיוֹן לְהַכְנִיס לָאוֹצָר עַל לְהַבָּא כַּנִּזְכָּר לְעֵיל, אוּלָם אִי אֵין יִרְאַת ד׳ אוֹצָרוֹ, וְחָכְמָתוֹ תּוּכַל לִהְיוֹת לוֹ לְפוּקָה וּלְמִכְשׁוֹל עָוֹן, אִם־כֵּן מוּטָב הָיָה שֶׁלֹּא פִּלְפֵּל וְלֹא הֵבִין דָּבָר מִתּוֹךְ דָּבָר וְלֹא בִּטֵּל שׁוּם זְמַן לְהַכְנִיס לָאוֹצָר כַּנִּזְכָּר לְעֵיל, רַק הָיָה עוֹסֵק בַּתּוֹרָה תָּמִיד בִּפְשׁוּטֶיהָ, לְקַיֵּם הַמִּצְוַת עֲשֵׂה שֶׁל וְהָגִיתָ אֲשֶׁר הַתַּכְלִית הוּא מִיָּד כַּנִּזְכָּר לְעֵיל.

> then yes [he is worthy of ultimate reward], and if not, he is not [worthy]. A parable…

They are not referring here to the essence of the mitzva to study Torah, the positive commandment of "Meditate [upon it day and night]," for it has no relationship with fear of God, just as there is no connection between other mitzvot and the fear of God, blessed be His name. Rather, this [parable] applies to the questions, "Did you engage in discourse about [the Torah's] wisdom? Did you infer one thing from another?" About this it states, "If 'fear of the Lord is his storehouse,' then yes [he is worthy of ultimate reward], and if not, he is not [worthy]." For if fear of the Lord is not his storehouse, then he never got to the end purpose; his wisdom remains a stumbling block into sin for him. It would have been better that he never engaged in dialectics, as said above.

For this reason, the parable is very precise in being about someone who said to his agent: "Bring a *kor* of wheat to the upper floor." He went and brought it up for him. He said to him: "Did you mix in a *kav* of *ḥomtin*?" [The agent] answered: "No." He said to him: "Then it would have been better had you not brought it up." Perforce, one brings a *kor* of wheat to the upper floor to leave it in the storehouse for a long time, until its price rises or for any other purpose he may have. But if he does not mix [the wheat] with a *kav* of *ḥomtin* it is quite possible that the produce will become infested. So he says, "It would have been better had you not brought it up," for [the owner] would have eaten it or sold it right away, before it becomes infested.

So it is with methods of learning Torah in order to know it, engaging in wise dialectic and inferring one matter from another. This is comparable to bringing produce into the storehouse for the future, as said above. However, if fear of the Lord is not his storehouse, and his wisdom may be for him "a cause of stumbling and faltering," then it would have been better that he never engaged in dialectic, did not infer one matter from another, and did not waste any time trying to bring things into his storehouse, as mentioned above, but instead studied Torah constantly and straightforwardly, to fulfill the positive commandment of "Meditate [upon it day and night]," whose end purpose is realized at once, as mentioned above.

וְזֶהוּ שֶׁשּׁוֹאֲלִין אוֹתוֹ כַּסֵּדֶר, קָבַעְתָּ עִתִּים לַתּוֹרָה, הוּא מִצְוַת לִמּוּד הַתּוֹרָה, פִּלְפַּלְתָּ בַּחָכְמָה הֵבַנְתָּ דָּבָר מִתּוֹךְ דָּבָר, הוּא יְדִיעַת הַתּוֹרָה מֵהַכָּתוּב וְשִׁנַּנְתָּם, וְעַל זֶה אָמַר וַאֲפִלּוּ הָכִי אִי יִרְאַת ד׳ אוֹצָרוֹ אִין אִי לֹא לֹא מָשָׁל לְאָדָם כו׳ כַּנִּזְכָּר לְעֵיל.

This is why they ask him in this order. "Did you set times for Torah study?" This refers to the mitzva of learning Torah. "Did you engage in discourse about [the Torah's] wisdom? Did you infer one thing from another?" These refer to knowing the Torah, from the verse "You shall teach them." It is about this [aspect of Torah study] that it says: "If 'fear of the Lord is his storehouse,' then yes [he is worthy of ultimate reward], and if not, he is not [worthy]. A parable…," as mentioned above.

כח

בַּגְּמָרָא תַּעֲנִית דַּף כ"ה תָּנוּ רַבָּנָן כוּ' שׁוּב מַעֲשֶׂה בְּרַבִּי אֱלִיעֶזֶר שֶׁיָּרַד לִפְנֵי הַתֵּבָה, וְאָמַר עֶשְׂרִים וְאַרְבַּע בְּרָכוֹת וְלֹא נַעֲנָה. יָרַד רַבִּי עֲקִיבָא אַחֲרָיו וְאָמַר אָבִינוּ מַלְכֵּנוּ אֵין לָנוּ מֶלֶךְ אֶלָּא אַתָּה כוּ' וְיָרְדוּ גְשָׁמִים. הָוֵי מְרַנְּנֵי רַבָּנָן. יָצְתָה בַּת קוֹל וְאָמְרָה לֹא מִפְּנֵי שֶׁזֶּה גָּדוֹל מִזֶּה, אֶלָּא שֶׁזֶּה מַעֲבִיר עַל מִדּוֹתָיו, וְזֶה אֵינוֹ מַעֲבִיר עַל מִדּוֹתָיו עַד כָּאן לְשׁוֹן הַגְּמָרָא. וְלִכְאוֹרָה יִפָּלֵא מְאֹד. הֲלֹא הַמִּדָּה הַזֹּאת שֶׁל מַעֲבִיר עַל מִדּוֹתָיו בִּלְבַד, תַּסְפִּיק לְהַגְדִּיל מַעֲלַת רַבִּי עֲקִיבָא עַל רַבִּי אֱלִיעֶזֶר. כִּי יָדוּעַ כַּמָּה גָּדוֹל כֹּחַ הַמִּדָּה הַזֹּאת. עַד שֶׁאָמְרוּ חֲכָמֵינוּ זַ"ל בַּגְּמָרָא רֹאשׁ הַשָּׁנָה דַּף י"ז. כָּל הַמַּעֲבִיר עַל מִדּוֹתָיו מַעֲבִירִין לוֹ עַל כָּל פְּשָׁעָיו. שֶׁנֶּאֱמַר נוֹשֵׂא עָוֹן וְעוֹבֵר עַל פֶּשַׁע כוּ' עַיֵּן שָׁם. וְאֵיךְ אָמְרָה הַבַּת קוֹל לֹא מִפְּנֵי שֶׁזֶּה גָּדוֹל מִזֶּה.

וְשָׁמַעְנוּ מִפֶּה קָדוֹשׁ אדמו"ר קְדוֹשׁ יִשְׂרָאֵל זצוק"ל שֶׁאָמַר לְיַשֵּׁב, כִּי הִנֵּה בַּגְּמָרָא שַׁבָּת דַּף ל' אִיתָא, תָּנוּ רַבָּנָן לְעוֹלָם יְהֵא אָדָם עַנְוְתָן כְּהִלֵּל, וְאַל יְהֵא קַפְּדָן כְּשַׁמַּאי כוּ', וְעַיֵּן שָׁם בַּגְּמָרָא שֶׁסִּפְּרוּ

Letter 28

The Talmud, Taanit 25b [states]:

> The Rabbis taught.... There was another incident involving R. Eliezer who went down [to pray for rain] before the ark. He recited twenty-four blessings but was not answered. R. Akiva went down after him and said: "Our Father, our King, we have no King but You...." And the rains fell. The Sages were murmuring [that R. Akiva was answered while his teacher, R. Eliezer, was not.] A divine voice emerged and said: "It is not that this one [R. Akiva] is greater than that one [R. Eliezer], but that this one is forgiving (*maavir al middotav*) and that one is not forgiving."

At first glance, this is quite amazing. This trait of being forgiving alone is enough to raise R. Akiva's merit above R. Eliezer's! It is known that this trait is very powerful, to the point where our Sages, of blessed memory, said in the Talmud, in Rosh HaShana 17a: "Anyone who is forgiving [of others] has his sins forgiven for him, as it says: '[God] bears iniquity and forgives sin....' (Mic. 7:18);" see further ad loc. But then how could the divine voice say: "It is not because this one is greater than that one"?

We heard, from the holy mouth of our master, teacher, and rabbi, the holy one of Israel, [R. Israel Salanter,] *ztvk"l,* a resolution: The Talmud states in Shabbat 30b: "A person should always be humble (*anvetan*) like Hillel and not be strict (*kapdan*) like Shammai"; see further ad loc.,

כַּמָּה מַעֲשִׂיּוֹת מֵעַנְוְתָנוּתוֹ שֶׁל הִלֵּל וְקַפְּדָנוּתוֹ שֶׁל שַׁמַּאי עַיֵּן שָׁם, וְהִנֵּה הָעוֹלָם חוֹשְׁבִין כִּי מַעֲלָתוֹ שֶׁל הִלֵּל הָיְתָה גְּדוֹלָה יוֹתֵר מִמַּעֲלַת שַׁמַּאי. כַּיָּדוּעַ כַּמָּה מְשֻׁבָּח מִדַּת הָעֲנָוָה. וְכַמָּה גָּרוּעַ מִדַּת הַקַּפְּדָנוּת. וְכַמְבֹאָר בְּכַמָּה מְקוֹמוֹת בַּשַּׁ"ס. וְעַל כֵּן בְּעוֹלָם הָאֱמֶת בְּלִי סָפֵק מַדְרֵגָתוֹ שֶׁל הִלֵּל גְּבוֹהָה יוֹתֵר מִמַּדְרֵגָתוֹ שֶׁל שַׁמַּאי.

אָכֵן בֶּאֱמֶת זֶהוּ טָעוּת. כִּי הִנֵּה לִכְאוֹרָה יֵשׁ לְהִתְפַּלֵּא וּלְהִשְׁתּוֹמֵם עַל סִבַּת קַפְּדָנוּתוֹ שֶׁל שַׁמַּאי. הֲלֹא יָדוּעַ כִּי כָּל בַּעֲלֵי חֲכָמֵינוּ זַ"ל. אַף דּוֹרוֹת הָאַחֲרוֹנִים. וּמַה גַּם דּוֹרוֹת הָרִאשׁוֹנִים הָיוּ דּוֹמִים לְמַלְאֲכֵי הַשָּׁרֵת מַמָּשׁ. וְקִיְּמוּ כָּל הַתּוֹרָה כֻּלָּהּ וְכָל הַמִּדּוֹת טוֹבוֹת שֶׁבָּעוֹלָם, וּמֵעַתָּה מֵאַיִן נוֹלַד סִבַּת קַפְּדָנוּתוֹ שֶׁל שַׁמַּאי. הַאִם מֵאֲשֶׁר הָיָה קַפְּדָן בְּטֶבַע. אוּלָם הֲכִי יִבָּצֵר מִשַּׁמַּאי לִכְבּשׁ אֶת מִדּוֹתָיו וּלְהַטּוֹתָם לְחֶפְצוֹ לְהִשְׁתַּלֵּם בְּמִדַּת הָעֲנָוָה.

אוּלָם בֵּאוּר הָעִנְיָן הוּא. כִּי זֶה הָיְתָה מִסִּבַּת מַחֲלֹקֶת שַׁמַּאי וְהִלֵּל בְּדַרְכֵי עֲבוֹדַת ה' יִתְבָּרַךְ שְׁמוֹ, כִּי כְּמוֹ שֶׁנֶּחְלְקוּ שַׁמַּאי וְהִלֵּל בְּכָל הַתּוֹרָה. כֵּן נֶחְלְקוּ בְּדַרְכֵי הָעֲבוֹדָה. אִם לְהִתְנַהֵג בְּמִדַּת הָעֲנָוָה. אוֹ לִכְבוֹד הַתּוֹרָה צָרִיךְ לְהִתְנַהֵג בְּמִדַּת הַקַּפְּדָנוּת. שַׁמַּאי הָיָה סָבוּר כִּי עַל פִּי דֶּרֶךְ הַתּוֹרָה, צָרִיךְ אָדָם לְהִתְנַהֵג בְּמִדַּת הַקַּפְּדָנוּת לִכְבוֹד הַתּוֹרָה. וְהִלֵּל הָיָה סְבִירָא לֵיהּ כִּי לְעוֹלָם צָרִיךְ אָדָם לְהִתְנַהֵג בְּמִדַּת הָעֲנָוָה. וְכָל אֶחָד הֶחֱזִיק בְּדַעְתּוֹ וְהִתְנַהֵג עַל פִּי שִׁיטָתוֹ. אָמְנָם אִם שַׁמַּאי הָיָה סָבוּר כְּהִלֵּל. שֶׁעַל פִּי הַתּוֹרָה צָרִיךְ אָדָם לְהִתְנַהֵג בְּמִדַּת הָעֲנָוָה. גַּם הוּא הָיָה עָנָו כְּהִלֵּל. וְכֵן אִם הִלֵּל הָיָה סְבִירָא לֵיהּ שֶׁעַל פִּי הַתּוֹרָה צָרִיךְ לְהִתְנַהֵג בְּמִדַּת הַקַּפְּדָנוּת גַּם הוּא הָיָה קַפְּדָן כְּשַׁמַּאי. אַךְ בְּמִקְרֶה נִהְיְתָה הַדָּבָר. כִּי שַׁמַּאי הָיָה סְבִירָא לֵיהּ שֶׁצָּרִיךְ אָדָם לְהִתְנַהֵג בְּמִדַּת הַקַּפְּדָנוּת לִכְבוֹד הַתּוֹרָה. וְהִלֵּל הָיָה סָבוּר לְהִתְנַהֵג בְּמִדַּת הָעֲנָוָה. וְכָל אֶחָד הִתְנַהֵג עַל פִּי שִׁיטָתוֹ כַּנִּזְכָּר לְעֵיל.

where the Talmud tells several stories about Hillel's humility and Shammai's strictness; see further ad loc.

Now, people think that Hillel's merits were greater than Shammai's, for it is well known how praiseworthy is the trait of humility and how bad is the trait of strictness, as explained in many places in the Talmud. Therefore, in the world of truth, Hillel's stature is greater than that of Shammai.

But in truth, this is an error, for, at first glance, Shammai's strictness is surprising, even astonishing! It is well known that all the master Sages, of blessed memory – even of the later generations, so certainly of the earlier generations – were literally like the attending angels. They fulfilled the whole Torah and possessed all the good character traits in the world. If so, what was the motivation for Shammai's strictness? Was it because he was naturally unyielding? If that is true, then would it be beyond Shammai to master his character traits and turn them toward his desire to perfect his quality of humility?

The explanation of this matter is that these differences stem from the disagreement between Shammai and Hillel about how to serve God, blessed be His name. Just as Hillel and Shammai disagreed about matters in every area of the Torah, so too, they disagreed about the proper ways to serve God – whether to conduct oneself according to the virtue of humility or whether, for the honor of Torah, to behave according to the trait of strictness. Shammai thought that the proper Torah path is to behave in accordance with the trait of strictness, for the honor of the Torah; Hillel thought that a person must always behave in accordance with the trait of humility. Each one of them maintained his view and acted accordingly. If Shammai had thought like Hillel that, according to the Torah, a person must behave in accordance with the trait of humility, then he, too, would have been humble like Hillel. Similarly, if Hillel had thought that according to the Torah one must behave strictly, then he would have acted as strictly as Shammai. It was by chance that Shammai maintained that a person must behave in accordance with the trait of strictness, for the honor of the Torah, while Hillel thought that one must behave in accordance with the trait of humility. Each of them acted in accordance with his opinion, as mentioned above.

וְהִנֵּה בִּיבָמוֹת דַּף י"ג פְּלִיגֵי בֵּית שַׁמַּאי וּבֵית הִלֵּל. אִם צָרַת עֶרְוָה מֻתֶּרֶת לְהִתְיַבֵּם. דְּבֵית שַׁמַּאי מַתִּירִין הַצָּרוֹת לָאַחִים וּבֵית הִלֵּל אוֹסְרִין. וּבַגְּמָרָא שָׁם אָמַר שְׁמוּאֵל כִּי עָשׂוּ בֵּית שַׁמַּאי כְּדִבְרֵיהֶם עַיֵּן שָׁם. וְהַיְנוּ שֶׁהָיוּ נוֹהֲגִין לְיַבֵּם צָרַת עֶרְוָה. וְהִנֵּה אֲנַן קָיְמָא לָן הֲלָכָה כְּבֵית הִלֵּל. וּלְפִי זֶה לְפִי הַהֲלָכָה מִי שֶׁמְּיַבֵּם צָרַת עֶרְוָה. הוּא פּוֹגֵעַ בְּאִסּוּר כָּרֵת שֶׁל אֵשֶׁת אָח. וּבָנָיו הֵם מַמְזֵרִים. וְהִנֵּה מוּבָן מֵאֵלָיו. כִּי בְּכָל זֹאת בֵּית שַׁמַּאי עַצְמָם שֶׁעָשׂוּ כְּדִבְרֵיהֶם וְיִבְּמוּ צָרַת עֶרְוָה. לֹא הָיָה לָהֶם שׁוּם עָוֹן כְּלָל. וְלֹא הָיוּ נִדּוֹנִים כְּפוֹגְעִים בְּאִסּוּר עֶרְוָה בְּשׁוֹגֵג. כִּי פְּסַק הַהֲלָכָה שֶׁפָּסְקוּ חֲכָמֵינוּ ז"ל אַחַר כָּךְ כְּבֵית הִלֵּל. לֹא הָיָה שַׁיָּךְ לְבֵית שַׁמַּאי עַצְמָם שֶׁאָמְרוּ הֲלָכָה כְּמוֹתֵנוּ. וְעַל פִּי הַתּוֹרָה הָיוּ צְרִיכִים לִנְהֹג כִּסְבָרָתָם. אָמְנָם לֹא זוֹ בִּלְבַד שֶׁלֹּא הָיָה לָהֶם שׁוּם עִנְיָן מֵעָוֹן שׁוֹגֵג. אָכֵן הִנֵּה בְּלִי סָפֵק אוֹתָן שֶׁעָשׂוּ כְּדִבְרֵיהֶן וְיִבְּמוּ צָרַת עֶרְוָה. עוֹד הִנֵּה שְׂכָרָם אִתָּם, כִּי בְּעוֹלַם הָאֱמֶת הֵם מְקַבְּלִים שָׂכָר בְּעַד מִצְוַת יִבּוּם לְפִי דַּעְתָּם. אָכֵן אַחֲרֵי אֲשֶׁר פָּסְקוּ חֲכָמֵינוּ ז"ל הֲלָכָה בְּכָל מָקוֹם כְּבֵית הִלֵּל. הִנֵּה עַתָּה מִי שֶׁמְּיַבֵּם צָרַת עֶרְוָה חַיָּב כָּרֵת. וְנִדּוֹן בְּגֵיהִנֹּם כְּכָל חַיָּבֵי כְּרֵיתוֹת.

וְכֵן הוּא בְּעִנְיַן הַמַּחֲלֹקֶת שַׁמַּאי וְהִלֵּל. בְּדֶרֶךְ הָעֲבוֹדָה אִם לְהִתְנַהֵג

---

1. Since the laws of levirate marriage (*yibum*) are complex and unfamiliar, we shall clarify the law in dispute. According to Torah law (Deut. 25:5–10), if a man dies childless, one of the deceased's brothers must either marry his widowed sister-in-law or undergo a ceremony called *ḥalitza,* whereby the bond between the widow and her dead husband's brothers is severed. If the widow is forbidden to marry the brothers due to a familial relationship – for instance, if there was only one brother, and the widow is his wife's sister – then the widow never attaches to the brothers in the first place; *yibum* with her is forbidden, and *ḥalitza* is unnecessary.

But what if the deceased brother was married to two women (co-wives or rival wives, recalling that the Torah legitimates polygyny), one of whom is forbidden to the remaining brothers due to a close familial relation? According to the School of Shammai, this prevents the attachment of the related widow to the remaining brothers, but the co-wife, who is not related to the brothers, must undergo either *yibum* or *ḥalitza*. According to the School of Hillel, the exemption of one wife from attachment to the brothers also exempts any co-wives. Thus, even with respect to those co-wives, *yibum* is forbidden, and *ḥalitza* unnecessary.

In Yevamot 13a–b, the Schools of Shammai and Hillel argue: Is it permitted to perform levirate marriage (*yibum*) with the co-wife of a forbidden relative? The School of Shammai permits the co-wives to the brothers, whereas the School of Hillel prohibits.[1] In the discussion there, Shmuel says that the School of Shammai acted in accordance with their views; see further ad loc. That is, they performed *yibum* with co-wives of forbidden relatives. Now, we uphold the established ruling that halakhic practice follows the School of Hillel. According to this ruling, one who performs *yibum* with the co-wife of a forbidden relative would violate the prohibition of having a sexual liaison with the wife of one's [living or dead] brother, a sin punishable by *karet* (excision, an extremely grave punishment). His sons [with this co-wife] would be *mamzerim* [illegitimate].

Yet, it goes without saying that the School of Shammai themselves, who acted in accordance with their own rulings and performed *yibum* with co-wives of forbidden relatives, committed no sin whatsoever. They were not judged to be in violation of consanguinity prohibitions, [even] unintentionally. [This is] because the later halakhic ruling of the Sages, of blessed memory, in accordance with the School of Hillel did not affect the School of Shammai themselves, who said that the halakha was in accordance with them; according to the Torah, they *had* to act in accordance with their view. Not only were they not considered unintentional sinners in any way, there is also no doubt that those who acted in accordance with their view and performed *yibum* with co-wives of forbidden relatives even received their reward; in the world of truth[2] they received reward for having performed, in their opinion, the mitzva of *yibum*. However, once our Sages, of blessed memory, ruled that the halakha follows the School of Hillel everywhere, from that point on, one who performs *yibum* with the co-wife of a forbidden relative is liable for the punishment of *karet* and is condemned in Hell to the same fate as all others liable for *karet*.

The same principle applies to the disagreement between Hillel and Shammai about whether one should serve God through strictness,

2. The divine realm.

בְּקַפְּדָנוּת לִכְבוֹד הַתּוֹרָה. אוֹ לְהִתְנַהֵג בְּמִדַּת הָעֲנָוָה. וְכָל אֶחָד נָהַג כְּפִי שִׁיטָתוֹ. הִנֵּה שַׁמַּאי מְקַבֵּל שָׂכָר בְּעַד קַפְּדָנוּתוֹ. כְּמוֹ שֶׁהִלֵּל מְקַבֵּל שָׂכָר בְּעַד מִדַּת עַנְוְתָנוּתוֹ. אַחֲרֵי כִּי שְׁנֵיהֶם הָיוּ עוֹשִׂין רְצוֹנוֹ שֶׁל מָקוֹם עַל פִּי הַתּוֹרָה. נִמְצָא כִּי מַעֲלָתוֹ שֶׁל הִלֵּל לֹא הָיָה גְּדוֹלָה כְּלָל מִמַּעֲלַת שַׁמַּאי. וְשָׁם בְּעוֹלָם הָאֱמֶת הֵמָּה תְּקוּעִים זֶה אֵצֶל זֶה. וּמִתְעַנְּגִים בְּנֹעַם זִיו הָעֶלְיוֹן כָּל אֶחָד בְּעַד הַנְהָגָתוֹ לְפִי שִׁיטָתוֹ. אָכֵן אַחֲרֵי אֲשֶׁר חֲכָמֵינוּ זַ"ל פָּסְקוּ כְּהִלֵּל. וְאָמְרוּ לְעוֹלָם יְהֵא אָדָם עַנְוְתָן כְּהִלֵּל. וְאַל יְהֵא קַפְּדָן כְּשַׁמַּאי. הִנֵּה עַתָּה מִי שֶׁמִּתְנַהֵג בְּמִדַּת הַקַּפְּדָנוּת. עֲוֹנוֹ גָּדוֹל מְאֹד.

הוּא הַדָּבָר מַה שֶּׁיָּצְתָה בַּת קוֹל וְאָמְרָה לֹא מִפְּנֵי שֶׁזֶּה גָּדוֹל מִזֶּה. אֶלָּא שֶׁזֶּה מַעֲבִיר עַל מִדּוֹתָיו. וְזֶה אֵינוֹ מַעֲבִיר עַל מִדּוֹתָיו. אֲשֶׁר לִכְאוֹרָה יִפָּלֵא מְאֹד. מַה זֶּה בֶּאֱמֶת כִּי רַבִּי אֱלִיעֶזֶר לֹא הָיָה מַעֲבִיר עַל מִדּוֹתָיו. הֲכִי יִפָּלֵא מִמֶּנּוּ לְהַטּוֹת מִדּוֹתָיו לְחֶפְצוֹ וְלִהְיוֹת מַעֲבִיר עַל מִדּוֹתָיו. אוּלָם לְפִי הַנִּזְכָּר לְעֵיל יוּבַן שַׁפִּיר. כִּי הִנֵּה יָדוּעַ כִּי רַבִּי אֱלִיעֶזֶר הָיָה שַׁמּוּתִי הַיְנוּ מִתַּלְמִידֵי שַׁמַּאי. וְהָיָה סְבִירָא לֵיהּ לַהֲלָכָה כְּשַׁמַּאי שֶׁצָּרִיךְ אָדָם לְהִתְנַהֵג בְּמִדַּת הַקַּפְּדָנוּת לִכְבוֹד הַתּוֹרָה. וְעַל כֵּן לֹא הָיָה מַעֲבִיר עַל מִדּוֹתָיו. אוּלָם רַבִּי עֲקִיבָא הָיָה מִתַּלְמִידֵי הִלֵּל. וְהָיָה סְבִירָא לֵיהּ כְּהִלֵּל שֶׁצָּרִיךְ לְהִתְנַהֵג בְּמִדַּת הָעֲנָוָה. וְעַל כֵּן הָיָה מַעֲבִיר עַל מִדּוֹתָיו. נִמְצָא כִּי בֶּאֱמֶת לֹא הָיָה רַבִּי עֲקִיבָא גָּדוֹל מֵרַבִּי אֱלִיעֶזֶר. אַחֲרֵי כִּי כָּל אֶחָד הָיָה מִתְנַהֵג לְפִי שִׁיטָתוֹ כַּאֲשֶׁר נִרְאֶה לוֹ עַל פִּי הַתּוֹרָה.

אָמְנָם מַה שֶּׁאָמְרָה הַבַּת קוֹל. כִּי לְכָךְ לֹא נַעֲנָה רַבִּי אֱלִיעֶזֶר. וְרַבִּי עֲקִיבָא נַעֲנָה וְיָרְדוּ גְּשָׁמִים. מִפְּנֵי שֶׁזֶּה מַעֲבִיר עַל מִדּוֹתָיו. וְזֶה אֵינוֹ מַעֲבִיר עַל מִדּוֹתָיו. הָעִנְיָן הוּא כִּי הִנֵּה יָדוּעַ דַּרְכֵי הַנְהָגַת הַקָּדוֹשׁ־בָּרוּךְ־הוּא עִם בְּרִיּוֹתָיו. לְהִתְנַהֵג עִמָּהֶם מִדָּה כְּנֶגֶד מִדָּה. וּכְמַאֲמָרָם זַ"ל שַׁבָּת דַּף קנ"א כָּל הַמְרַחֵם עַל הַבְּרִיּוֹת מְרַחֲמִין עָלָיו מִן הַשָּׁמַיִם. וְכֵן כָּל הַמַּעֲבִיר עַל מִדּוֹתָיו מַעֲבִירִין לוֹ עַל כָּל פְּשָׁעָיו. וְלָזֹאת לְהִתְפַּלֵּל עַל צָרַת הַצִּבּוּר. וּלְבַקֵּשׁ רַחֲמִים מִלְּפָנָיו יִתְבָּרַךְ שְׁמוֹ לַעֲבֹר עַל פִּשְׁעָם וְלַעֲנוֹת לָהֶם בְּעֵת צָרָתָם. מְסֻגָּל לָזֶה מִי שֶׁהוּא בְּעַצְמוֹ מַעֲבִיר עַל מִדּוֹתָיו. יִתְקַבֵּל תְּפִלָּתוֹ לְרָצוֹן מִדָּה כְּנֶגֶד מִדָּה כַּנִּזְכָּר לְעֵיל.

for the honor of the Torah, or through the trait of humility. Each one acted in accordance with his view. Shammai is rewarded for his strictness just as Hillel gets reward for his humility, since both were doing the will of God in accordance with the Torah. It thus emerges that Hillel's virtue was no greater than Shammai's virtue. There, in the world of truth, they are ensconced alongside one another, enjoying the pleasant radiance of the Most High, each one for acting in accordance with his view. However, now that our Sages, of blessed memory, have ruled in accordance with Hillel and said, "A person should always be humble like Hillel and not be strict like Shammai," one who acts in accordance with the trait of strictness commits a grave sin.

This is why a divine voice emerged and said: "It is not that this one [R. Akiva] is greater than that one [R. Eliezer], but that this one is forgiving and that one is not forgiving." At first glance this is quite astonishing. What does it really mean that R. Eliezer was not forgiving? Was it beyond his capacity to turn his character traits where he willed and become forgiving? According to the above, we can understand this well. It is known that R. Eliezer was a Shammaite, that is, among the disciples of Shammai. He shared Shammai's halakhic view that a person should behave strictly for the sake of the honor of the Torah. This is why he was not forgiving. However, R. Akiva was among the disciples of Hillel. He shared Hillel's opinion that one must act humbly, and so he was forgiving. It emerges that in truth R. Akiva was not greater than R. Eliezer, for each of them acted in accordance with the view that appeared to him to be consistent with the Torah.

As for why the divine voice said that R. Eliezer's prayer was not answered and R. Akiva was answered and the rains fell because this one is forgiving and that one is not, this is the idea: It is known that the Holy One, blessed be He, interacts with His creatures according to a pattern of *quid pro quo*. As [the Sages] said in Shabbat 151b: "Whoever has compassion on creatures is shown compassion by Heaven." Likewise: "Anyone who is forgiving [of others] has his sins forgiven for him." Thus, one who is himself forgiving is better equipped to pray about a communal distress and beseech compassion from God, blessed be His name; his prayers will be willingly accepted, *quid pro quo*, as above.

וְלָזֹאת כַּאֲשֶׁר הִתְפַּלְלוּ עַל הַגְּשָׁמִים. הִנֵּה רַבִּי עֲקִיבָא שֶׁמִּדָּתוֹ הָיָה בְּדֶרֶךְ הִלֵּל לִהְיוֹת מַעֲבִיר עַל מִדּוֹתָיו. עַל כֵּן נַעֲנָה מִן הַשָּׁמַיִם מִדָּה כְּנֶגֶד מִדָּה. אָכֵן רַבִּי אֱלִיעֶזֶר שֶׁמִּדָּתוֹ הָיָה בְּדֶרֶךְ שַׁמַּאי וְלֹא הָיָה מַעֲבִיר עַל מִדּוֹתָיו. אִם אָמְנָם כִּי יְקַבֵּל שָׂכָר הַרְבֵּה גַּם עַל זֶה מַה שֶּׁהוּא עוֹשֶׂה רְצוֹן ה׳ יִתְבָּרַךְ שְׁמוֹ לְפִי שִׁיטָתוֹ. אוּלָם כַּאֲשֶׁר סוֹף סוֹף לְפִי שִׁיטָתוֹ לֹא הָיָה מַעֲבִיר עַל מִדּוֹתָיו. עַל כֵּן אֵין זֶה מִדָּה כְּנֶגֶד מִדָּה לַעֲבֹר עַל פִּשְׁעֵי צִבּוּר וּלְכָךְ לֹא נַעֲנָה. וְזֶה שֶׁאָמְרָה הַבַּת קוֹל לֹא מִפְּנֵי שֶׁזֶּה גָּדוֹל מִזֶּה. אֶלָּא שֶׁזֶּה מַעֲבִיר עַל מִדּוֹתָיו כו׳ לְכָךְ נַעֲנָה מִדָּה כְּנֶגֶד מִדָּה כַּנִּזְכָּר לְעֵיל.

Thus, when they prayed for rain, R. Akiva, whose character, following Hillel, was to be forgiving, was answered from Heaven *quid pro quo*. Whereas, R. Eliezer, whose character, following Shammai, was to be unforgiving – even though he will receive great reward for this, as he is doing the will of God, blessed be His name, according to his own view – ultimately, consistent with his view, he was not forgiving. Therefore, forgiving the sins of the community would not be *quid pro quo*, so he was not answered. This is the meaning of what the divine voice said: "It is not that this one is greater than that one, but that this one is forgiving and that one is not forgiving," as explained above.

Translator's Introduction to Tevunah

In the introduction to this book, we argued that R. Salanter opposed *Haskala* and modernization because he saw that the traditional Jewish religious community and culture would be undermined by exposure to them. Traditional culture had been "hollowed out." Its authority had been self-evident and grounded in conformity, and was thus being undermined by the presence of alternatives. The internalization of values had weakened, and the consciousness of purpose and meaning in observance was absent. Thus, when new ways of life that promised significant economic rewards and political improvement of the Jewish condition appeared in the Tsarist empire, individuals had little in the way of capacity or desire to resist. One might say that all of R. Salanter's educational experiments and strong propagation of Mussar study derived from the central question which he posed to himself: What improvements to religious culture and institutional systems would be necessary for traditional Judaism to maintain its credibility in the presence of modernity and alternative cultural configurations?

Like other champions of traditional Judaism in Eastern Europe, R. Salanter perceived the danger that modernization posed to the inherited way of life. However, unlike others, R. Salanter did not believe that the traditional community could insulate itself from modernity by prohibiting participation in it or by excluding its proponents. He strongly opposed the creation of a government-mandated rabbinical seminary because he believed it would train rabbis who would prioritize modern values and undermine tradition. Other traditional Jewish leaders chose to accommodate the Tsarist decree while fighting to minimize its impact (by marginalizing its graduates). R. Salanter, however, chose to flee Vilna rather than be pressured into joining the seminary faculty by the government. Clearly, he felt that other leaders' policy did not address the primary challenge: developing a Judaism that could hold its own in the face of modernity.

After fleeing Vilna, R. Salanter spent the next nine years in Kovno trying to organize a Mussar movement that would reach out to community leaders and raise the quality of religious life among laypeople. He felt that the laity would constitute the communal power base once modernity became dominant. While he did win disciples and accrue influence in yeshiva circles, his students failed to create a lay Mussar movement that could anchor a modern religious community.

In 1857, R. Salanter left Kovno, traveling mostly westward over the following years and decades. His first stop was East Prussia, a German (and hence more modernized) enclave in Eastern Europe, where he was especially active in the port cities of Memel and Koenigsberg. He spent the last twenty-four years of his life shuttling between Koenigsberg, Berlin, and Paris, with periodic visits to Eastern Europe. This migration pattern shows that R. Salanter believed that he must understand – and confront – modernity where it was already dominant. Only then could he decipher its cultural code, identify its sources of strength, and formulate responses that would enable traditional Judaism to endure in the new cultural environment.

R. Salanter grasped that modern culture thrived on discussion and exchange of views. He therefore concluded that traditional Judaism must articulate its teachings and views to compete for loyalty in the new environment. He intuitively understood the need to cultivate a cohort of rabbis who write for and communicate with the wider public. In 1861–62, R. Salanter created a periodical called *Tevunah* (lit. "Understanding") that published Torah novellae, so that rabbis could begin to share their Torah with a wider audience. This was R. Salanter's way of encouraging important scholars to articulate and disseminate their Torah. Indeed, he recruited a significant number of leading Lithuanian rabbis to write for *Tevunah*. He also wrote articles analyzing the methods of Torah study in Lithuanian yeshivot and explored what is the right way to learn and teach a "Torah of truth." This journal competed with a growing number of *Haskala* periodicals that spread other ideas about proper Torah study and with many other voices of the new culture.

In *Tevunah,* R. Salanter also included articles on Mussar and character development, subjects he believed should be incorporated into the curriculum of every yeshiva alongside the regnant paradigm of exclusive study of classic talmudic literature. *Tevunah* was thus a living model of his vision of Torah study.

Alas, the venture foundered. Printing costs were greater than expected while subscriptions and resources fell short of projections. After publishing twelve issues, R. Salanter ran out of money and had to suspend publication of *Tevunah*. Despite repeated efforts, he never was able to restart it.[1]

There was a silver lining in the dark cloud of this failure. To fill the pages of *Tevunah* and to include a substantial Mussar section, R. Salanter himself wrote three major essays on Mussar and its methods.[2] Each of these essays is far more substantial an articulation of his thinking than anything he had written in his letters to his disciples.

These essays adopt a somewhat homiletic format (like the book of sermons he published in Vilna in the 1840s, *Even Yisrael*); however, these later essays subordinate the sermonic elements to the explication of his theories on Mussar, character building, and human psychology.

1. For more on *Tevunah,* see Etkes, *Salanter,* 261–8.
2. R. Isaac Blazer republished these three essays in *Ohr Yisrael,* with the following note: "Copied from the introduction to *Sefer Tevunah,* with the omission of passages concerning the publication of that book." In the present volume, the paragraphs that R. Blazer omitted at the end of the letter have been reinserted.

The essays, then, represent R. Salanter's most expansive and developed writing. Moreover, he articulates methods of character development in pedagogical and psychological terms. He also offers a theory of how to arrive at truth in Torah through argumentation and discussion, i.e., through the interaction of multiple viewpoints. By arguing back and forth, ideas are clarified, sharpened, and refined into better understanding, which the tradition can then absorb as Torah truth.

Letter 21 of this volume is a landmark in R. Salanter's thought and in nineteenth-century Jewish thought more generally. To the extent that Orthodox thinkers tried to respond to the modernist critique – including the uncovering of historical development and cultural context of Torah ideas – they generally sought to position the Torah and Talmud as being "outside" history. They argued that both Scripture and the Oral Law were directly from God and relatively untouched by human hands. Their exclusively divine origin provides the Torah's claim to authority and irrefutability. Historical circumstances, as well as change and development, were written out of the narrative.

Unfortunately, this approach denied the human elements and cultural contexts of Torah. For those who accepted these claims, the modernist approach could be dismissed. But historical, critical studies identified increasing amounts of human cultural elements in the tradition. Therefore, for many people, Orthodoxy lost the argument for divine authority to the growing body of evidence of human elements and cultural context.

Among Orthodox thinkers, R. Salanter was among a small number who were able to recognize the human elements, the conflicting voices, and the cultural contexts of Torah without going into denial. Yet he articulated how these elements were filtered and clarified in the process of being incorporated into the eternal Torah. We believe that this approach will become even more important as postmodern culture becomes dominant. The "objectification" of Torah and its divinity will become less credible and less relevant in the new cultural context. We daresay that R. Salanter's exploration of the process of hammering out truths of Torah through multiple analyses as well as clashing views and schools of thought will be drawn upon and validated. This promises to be a more credible way of not denying, but rather incorporating, the historical and subjective elements of Torah, without yielding its divinity and its wisdom.

כט

אָבוֹת (פֶּרֶק ב׳ מִשְׁנָה ב׳) וְכָל הָעֲמֵלִים עִם הַצִּבּוּר יִהְיוּ עֲמֵלִים עִמָּהֶם לְשֵׁם שָׁמַיִם. לֹא אָמְרָה הַמִּשְׁנָה יִהְיֶה כַּוָּנָתָם לְשֵׁם שָׁמַיִם. בָּזֹאת נָאוֹת לְבָאֵר כִּי הַתּוֹסָפוֹת בִּבְרָכוֹת (י״ז) הִקְשׁוּ עַל הָא דְּאָמְרִינַן (שָׁם) לָעוֹשִׂים לֹא נֶאֱמַר אֶלָּא לְעוֹשֵׂיהֶם לָעוֹשִׂים לִשְׁמָהּ וְלֹא לָעוֹשִׂים שֶׁלֹּא לִשְׁמָהּ מֵהָא דְּאָמְרִינַן לְעוֹלָם יַעֲסֹק אָדָם בַּתּוֹרָה וּבַמִּצְוֹת אֲפִלּוּ שֶׁלֹּא לִשְׁמָהּ שֶׁמִּתּוֹךְ שֶׁלֹּא לִשְׁמָהּ בָּא לִשְׁמָהּ. וְיֵשׁ לְיַשֵּׁב קֻשְׁיָתָם דְּהִנֵּה בְּכָל מִצְוָה יֵשׁ גְּדָרִים מְגֻבָּלִים בְּאֹפֶן עֲשִׂיָּתָהּ עַל פִּי הַתַּלְמוּד וְהַפּוֹסְקִים וְאִם תֵּצֵא מִגִּדְרָהּ וּגְבוּלָהּ אֵינֶנָּה מִצְוָה – לְפִי עֵרֶךְ יְצִיאָתָהּ מִגְּבוּלָהּ – כְּמַאֲמָרָם זַ״ל (יְרוּשַׁלְמִי הֱבִיאוֹ הָרֹא״שׁ בְּפֶרֶק כָּל שָׁעָה) אֵלֶּה הַמִּצְוֹת אִם עֲשָׂאָן כְּמִצְוָתָן מִצְוָה וְאִם לָאו אֵינָהּ מִצְוָה. וְלִפְעָמִים לֹא יֵלְכוּ אֲחוּזֵי יָד מֶרְכַּז הַנְּטִיָּה עִם גֶּדֶר הָעֲשִׂיָּה עַד אֲשֶׁר תִּוָּלֵד הִתְנַגְּדוּת חֲזָקָה. וְאִם תִּגְבַּר כֹּחַ הַנְּטִיָּה לַעֲשׂוֹת הַמִּצְוָה עַל פִּיהָ אֵינֶנָּה

---

* R. Blazer notes: "Copied from the introduction to *Sefer Tevunah*; things that pertain only to the printing of that book have been omitted."

1. The Talmud is commenting on Psalms 111:10: "The beginning of wisdom is the fear of the Lord – those who practice it (*oseihem*) gain sound understanding."
2. The Talmud continues: "One who practices them for ulterior motives – it would have been better had he not been created."
3. Ad loc., s.v. "haoseh."

Letter 29*

Avot (2:2): "All those who toil for the community should do so for the sake of Heaven." The mishna does not say that "their *intention* should be for the sake of Heaven." There is a fitting explanation for this, as follows.

[The Talmud in] Berakhot (17a) states:[1] "It does not say 'those who practice' ('*osim*') but 'those who practice *them*' ('*oseihem*'). [Reward awaits] those who practice for its sake, not those who practice for ulterior motives."[2] *Tosafot*[3] question this statement in light of the statement: "A person should always engage in Torah and mitzvot, even for ulterior motives, for from ulterior motives he will come to do it for its own sake" (Pesaḥim 50b).

Their question can be resolved as follows. Every mitzva is delimited by the parameters of its proper fulfillment, based on the Talmud and codes. If it strays from the limits and parameters, if the behavior violates this guideline and boundary, it is not a fulfillment of a commandment – to the extent that it has gone beyond the limit. As they, of blessed memory, state (Yerushalmi [Ḥalla 1:5], cited by Rosh in the chapter "*Kol Shaa*" [Pesaḥim 2:18]): "'These are the commandments' (Lev. 27:34): If he performed them as commanded, they are a mitzva; if not, they are not a mitzva."

Sometimes, the focus of one's tendencies is misaligned with the parameters of practice – to the point where they conflict sharply. And if the force of the tendencies prevails so that the mitzva is performed in accordance with it, it is no mitzva. Is it conceivable that a person could

מִצְוָה. הֲיַעֲלֶה עַל הַדַּעַת שֶׁיִּקַּח אָדָם לוּלָב נָאֶה וְגַם יָפֶה לְהִתְגַּדֵּר קֳבָל עִם בְּחֶסְרוֹן הַגֶּדֶר לָכֶם? בְּוַדַּאי עָנְשׁוֹ גָּדוֹל כִּי בִּטֵּל מִצְוַת עֲשֵׂה. וְזֶה מְדַקְדֵּק קְצָת בִּלְשׁוֹן הַגְּמָרָא לְעוֹשֶׂיהָ לֹא נֶאֱמַר אֶלָּא לְעוֹשֵׂיהֶם הַיְנוּ שֶׁיַּעֲשֶׂה הַמִּצְוָה בְּגִדְרָהּ הָאֲמִתִּי. לָעוֹשִׂים לִשְׁמָהּ הַיְנוּ שֶׁעוֹשִׂים בְּזֶה הָאֹפֶן כְּמוֹ שֶׁיַּעֲשֶׂה מִי שֶׁכַּוָּנָתוֹ לְשֵׁם שָׁמַיִם אֲשֶׁר זֹאת מֶרְכָּזוֹ הָעִקָּרִי לְהַשְׁקִיף הֵיטֵב עַל גְּבוּלֵי גֶּדֶר הַמִּצְוָה לְהִלְכוֹתֶיהָ. וְלֹא לָעוֹשִׂים שֶׁלֹּא לִשְׁמָהּ הַיְנוּ שֶׁיִּתְנַהֵג בְּמַעֲשֶׂה עַל פִּי נְטִיָּתוֹ – וְכָל אֲשֶׁר יוֹסִיף הָאָדָם לְנַהֵל מַעֲשָׂיו עַל פִּי נְטִיָּתוֹ כֵּן יִתְרַחֵק הָלְאָה מִבְּחִינַת לִשְׁמָהּ – אָכֵן כַּאֲשֶׁר יַעֲשֶׂה הָאָדָם לְחֹק נִצָּב לְהִתְנַהֵג בְּמַעֲשָׂיו עַל פִּי חֻקִּים וְכָל הָרוּחוֹת שֶׁבָּעוֹלָם לֹא יְזִיזֻנּוּ. אִם כִּי כַּוָּנָתוֹ אֵינֶנָּה לְשֵׁם שָׁמַיִם כָּל אֲשֶׁר יוֹסִיף בְּטִיב מַעֲשָׂיו וְיַחֲזִיק בָּהֶם כֵּן תֶּחֱלַשׁ נְטִיָּתוֹ – בִּהְיוֹת לִפְעָמִים הַמַּעֲשֶׂה תִּתְנַגֵּד לְהַכַּוָּנָה וְתִתְגַּבֵּר עָלֶיהָ – וְיָבוֹא לְלִשְׁמָהּ. וְזֶה מְדַקְדֵּק בִּלְשׁוֹן הַגְּמָרָא לְעוֹלָם יַעֲסֹק אָדָם בַּתּוֹרָה וּבַמִּצְוֹת אֲפִלּוּ שֶׁלֹּא לִשְׁמָהּ שֶׁמִּתּוֹךְ שֶׁלֹּא לִשְׁמָהּ בָּא לִשְׁמָהּ.

כֵּן הַדָּבָר גַּם בְּהֶעָמֵל עִם הַצִּבּוּר. אוּלַי לֹא הֶעֱמִיסָה עָלֵינוּ הַמִּשְׁנָה לִהְיוֹת דַּוְקָא הַכַּוָּנָה רְצוּיָה לְשֵׁם שָׁמַיִם רַק שֶׁהֶעָמָל יִהְיֶה עַל תְּכוּנַת הַמִּתְעַמֵּל לְשֵׁם שָׁמַיִם בְּלִי נְטִיַּת הָרָצוֹן רַק כְּפִי הַנָּאוֹת לַצִּבּוּר כַּדָּת וְכַהֲלָכָה.

---

4. Leviticus 23:40; the Sages derive from here that one fulfills the mitzva only with one's own lulav.

5. R. Salanter is developing a thesis that a person who performs mitzvot in an externally correct fashion may not be fulfilling them at all (or may be committing a sin under the facade of performing a mitzva). This is why Mussar's analysis and self-analysis,

take a nice, beautiful lulav to display before everyone, but [in taking it] not meet the [halakhic] parameter of "unto you"?![4] Certainly his punishment will be great, for he nullified a positive commandment.

This is implied in the language of the Talmud: "It does not say 'those who practice' but 'those who practice *them*,'" meaning, one who performs the mitzva within its true parameters. "Those who practice for its sake" means those who practice in the same manner as one whose intention is for the sake of Heaven, whose primary focus is to observe carefully the boundaries and parameters of the mitzva in all its detailed laws; "not those who practice for ulterior motives" refers to conducting oneself according to his tendencies. The more one behaves according to his tendencies, the further he is from acting "for its sake."[5]

However, when a person makes it a hard-and-fast rule to act in accordance with the law, and all the winds of the world will not move him – even if his intention is not for the sake of Heaven – still, the more he continues in these types of actions and holds fast to them, the more his tendencies will weaken (for, from time to time, the action will conflict with his intention and overcome it), and so he will come to act "for its sake."[6] The language of the Talmud is precise: "A person should always engage in Torah and mitzvot, even for ulterior motives, for from ulterior motives he will come to do it for its own sake."

So it is when one works for the community. Perhaps the Mishna did not impose on us to have the desirable intentions "for the sake of Heaven," but all efforts must be patterned on those who labor for the sake of Heaven, free of the tendencies of the will, and only in accordance with what is appropriate for the community, according to the law and halakha.

---

as well as the study of Mussar texts, is so important in order to prevent a perversion of Torah understanding or practice.

6. Nevertheless, if one can commit to the parameters of proper observance and execute them even when they conflict with his tendencies, it will weaken the control of his tendencies over him and move him closer to acting "for its sake."

וְהַיּוֹתֵר גְּדוֹלָה אֵלַי הִיא בַּקָּשַׁת תּוֹרַת הָאֱמֶת. אֲנִי בַּחֲלוֹמִי בְּעֵת עִסְקִי לְצָרְכֵי הַגּוּף. אֲדַבְּרָה בְּרַעְיוֹנוֹת מְקַשְׁקְשׁוֹת בְּלִי סְדָרִים אֶת אֲשֶׁר נִקְרָה אֶצְלִי מִכְּבָר וְעַל יַד הַבִּקֹּרֶת הַחֲזָקָה אֶסְמֹךְ לְדַבֵּר דִּבְרֵי בֶּטַח כִּי אִם שָׁגִיתִי הַבִּקֹּרֶת תְּיַשֵּׁר דַּרְכִּי – מַה הִיא הָאֱמֶת? לֹא עַל הַפַּשְׁטוּת לְבַדּוֹ יִהְיֶה הָאֱמֶת כִּי הַפַּשְׁטוּת אֵינוֹ אֶלָּא סָעִיף מִדַּרְכֵי הָרְאָיוֹת וְעַל פִּי הָרֹב קֻשְׁיוֹת הַחֲמוּרוֹת הַנּוֹלָדוֹת מֵהַרְכָּבוֹת הַקּוֹדְמוֹת מְשֻׁלָּבוֹת בְּשִׁלּוּב חָזָק (כַּל יִנָּתְקוּ בְּנַקַלָּה כִּי אֵין לְבַקֵּשׁ מוֹפֵת אֲשֶׁר הַקְדָּמוֹתָיו מְשֻׁלָּב לְבַל יִנָּתְקוּ. כְּמוֹ שֶׁכָּתַב הָרַמְבַּ"ן בַּהַקְדָּמָה לְסֵפֶר הַמִּלְחָמוֹת) עוֹמְדִים הָכֵן לִלְחֹם נֶגֶד הַפַּשְׁטוּת וְלַהֲזִיזָהּ. כַּאֲשֶׁר אֲנַחְנוּ רוֹאִים בְּדִבְרֵי הַתַּלְמוּד בְּהָאֳקִימְתּוֹת. וּבְדִבְרֵי רַבּוֹתֵינוּ בַּעֲלֵי הַתּוֹסָפוֹת אֲשֶׁר לְאוֹרָם נֵלֵךְ תָּמִיד. גַּם לֹא בַּחִדּוּשׁ הַקָּצָר יִתָּמֵךְ הָאֱמֶת. כִּי יֵשׁ דָּבָר קָצָר וְהַקְדָּמוֹתָיו מְשֻׁלָּבִים בְּשִׁלּוּב פּוֹרֵחַ בַּאֲוִיר עַד אֲשֶׁר גַּם רֵיחַ הָאֱמֶת אֵין בּוֹ. וְיֵשׁ מַאֲמַר אָרֹךְ וְהַקְדָּמוֹתָיו מְשֻׁלָּבִים בְּשִׁלּוּב נָכוֹן אֲזַי בְּחֶדֶר הָאֱמֶת יָבוֹא. אִם כִּי נִצְרָךְ לְבִקּוּר רַב וּלְחִפּוּשׂ יְתֵרָה בִּהְיוֹת שְׁלִיבוֹתָיו רַבִּים. וְאָז לִפְעָמִים גַּם בְּהִנָּתֵק אַחַת מֵהֵנָּה בְּסֵפֶר הָאֱמֶת בַּל יִכָּתֵב. גַּם לֹא עַל יְדֵי חֵפֶץ הָאָדָם לָתוּר אַחֲרֵי תּוֹרַת הָאֱמֶת יִבָּנֶה הָאֱמֶת

---

7. R. Salanter has made two points in the essay. 1) Performance of a mitzva that is dominated and distorted by the egocentric sins of one's tendencies does not constitute a true fulfillment of that mitzva. This implies the need to study and practice Mussar, so as to identify one's distorting tendencies and to gain greater control over them – in order to perform mitzvot properly. 2) R. Salanter teaches that if, in performing a mitzva, a person steadfastly adheres to the parameters of observance described in the Torah and codes, it can defeat the biases and distortive effects of the egocentric tendencies. Then such a performance will be a true fulfillment of the mitzva.

   R. Israel now turns to the question of how to read the Torah objectively and identify the correct parameters of performance. How can one prevent one's tendencies from distorting, or even undermining or reversing, what the Torah is actually instructing us to do?
8. I.e., the Torah understood as actually communicated by God, when one's understanding of it is not twisted by unconscious drives and needs. One may arrive at true Torah if one can neutralize egocentric bias and not let it distort judgment or even the choice of criteria by which one judges what is true.
9. Compare Genesis 40:16.

Most important to me[7] is to seek the true Torah.[8] In my dream,[9] while working for the needs of the body,[10] I spoke in glittering generalities, without order, ideas that had been inscribed in me for some time. [Now I speak new thoughts which contradict the old truth.] However, through receiving strong criticism from others – on which I depend – I learned to speak confidently – for if I err, criticism will straighten me out.

What is truth? Truth is not based on simplicity[11] alone[12] – for plain meaning is but a branch of the methods for proving assertions, and, for the most part, the difficult questions that arise from the synthesis of strongly linked premises [which are not easily disconnected – for one should not ask for a demonstration whose linked premises cannot be disconnected, as Ramban (Nahmanides) wrote at the beginning of *Milḥamot Hashem*] stand ready to do battle with plain meaning and displace it. We see this in the Talmud in the case of *okimtot*[13] and in the words of our masters, the Tosafists, by whose light we walk always.[14]

Nor is truth supported by a brief, novel interpretation, for there may be a brief articulation whose premises are combined with ephemeral connections which do not even have a whiff of truth. And there are lengthy treatises whose [diverse] premises are combined properly; these enter the realm of truth, though they require much examination and extra investigation[15] because there are so many links. Sometimes, if one of the links is broken, then they cannot be written in the book of truth.

10. In his early study of Torah, he still focused on the body, i.e., external actions and observances. He had not yet grasped the power of "tendencies" and the centrality of psychological forces in shaping judgments as to what the Torah was instructing or the manner in which one interpreted and practiced it.
11. I.e., plain meaning.
12. Compare Deuteronomy 8:3.
13. Qualifications on what initially seemed to be the simple meaning of a text.
14. The Tosafists juxtapose two or more texts whose plain meanings seem contradictory or problematic. To resolve the clash between two texts, the Tosafists often posit subtle distinctions between cases and applications.
15. Arguments and analyses of Torah texts need to be thoroughly examined and criticized. The implication is that if learning is done in a group, the others' insights and criticism will help one to arrive at the truth. Others – especially others who have undergone Mussar analysis and character corrections – will discern things that one does not realize about himself. This will help in arriving at the truth.

לְהָבִיא בְּחַדְרָהּ אֶת אֲשֶׁר יוֹרֶנּוּ שִׂכְלוֹ. וּמִקְרָא מָלֵא דִּבֵּר הַכָּתוּב (מִשְׁלֵי ב׳) אִם תְּבַקְשֶׁנָּה כַכָּסֶף (קָאֵי עַל הַתּוֹרָה כְּהַתְחָלַת הַפְּסוּקִים בְּנִי כוּ׳ וְכַמְבֹאָר בַּיַּלְקוּט בִּמְקוֹמוֹ) וּבְבַקָּשַׁת הַכֶּסֶף אֵין דַּי בְּחֵפֶץ הָאָדָם לְבַד רַק אִם יִמָּצֵא לוֹ הַהֲכָנוֹת הַשַּׁיָּכִים לְבַקָּשָׁתוֹ. כֵּן גַּם בְּבַקָּשַׁת הַתּוֹרָה. וּבְיֶתֶר שְׂאֵת כִּי בַּכֶּסֶף הַיְסוֹד הִיא עֵזֶר אֱלֹקִי. וּבַתּוֹרָה הַיְסוֹד הֲכָנוֹת הָאָדָם (אִם מֵעַצְמוֹ אִם מֵאֲחֵרִים) וְאָז יַזְהִיר עָלָיו גַּם נֹגַהּ עֶלְיוֹן. כִּי לֹא בַשָּׁמַיִם הִיא וְהַתּוֹרָה נְתוּנָה לִבְנֵי אָדָם. אָכֵן לֹא כְּשִׁבְיָהּ הִיא אֶצְלָם לְהִתְנַהֵג בָּהּ כְּחֶפְצָם רַק כְּבַעַל דַּעַת יְשָׁרָה לְהָקִים הַסִּבּוֹת הַטִּבְעִיּוֹת הַמּוֹבִילִים לְהַמְסוּבָּב. הִיא יְדִיעַת הָאֱמֶת. וּבִכְלָל לְבַקָּשַׁת תּוֹרַת הָאֱמֶת שְׁנֵי יְסוֹדוֹת לָהּ. הַיְכֹלֶת בַּטִּבְעִי. וְהַטָּהֳרָה בְּמַחֲשַׁבְתּוֹ – הַיְכֹלֶת – הִיא הַבְּקִיאוּת הַגְּדוֹלָה בְּהַקְדָּמוֹת וְהַתְּבוּנָה הַיְתֵרָה בְּשֵׂכֶל יָשָׁר וְחַד לִבְנוֹת הַרְכָּבוֹת חֲזָקוֹת כִּרְאִי מוּצָק. וְאַחַר הָעִיּוּן הָרַב עַל כָּל הַצְּדָדִים לְבָרֵר הָאֱמֶת. הַטָּהֳרָה – הִיא אֲשֶׁר יְכַנּוּהָ הַחֲכָמִים בְּשֵׁם הַכָּרָה מַדָּעִית וְחַכְמֵי הַמּוּסָר בְּשֵׁם הִתְפַּשְּׁטוּת הַגַּשְׁמִיּוּת הַיְנוּ שֶׁיִּהְיֶה הַשֵּׂכֶל בּוֹדֵד בְּלִי הַרְכָּבָתוֹ עִם יֶתֶר כֹּחוֹת הַנַּפְשׁוֹת אֲשֶׁר בְּהָאָדָם. כִּי זוּלַת נְטִיַּת כֹּחוֹת הַנַּפְשִׁיּוֹת הֵמָּה מָסַכִּים מַבְדִּילִים בֵּינוֹ לְבֵין הַכָּרַת הָאֱמֶת. אֲשֶׁר גַּם שִׁקּוּל דַּעַת הַיָּשָׁר בְּעוֹזְרָהּ. וְהַנְּטִיָּה תְּעַקְּמָהּ לִצְעֹד בְּדֶרֶךְ עֲקַלְקַלּוֹת. מְקוֹר הַיְכֹלֶת – אֶת אֲשֶׁר נֶאֱצַל מִתְּבוּנַת רַבִּים גְּדוֹלִים חִקְרֵי לֵב

---

16. Here, again, is R. Salanter's dialectic guidance. Humans cannot attain perfect rationality and objective knowledge of the Torah. God accepts that fact. This is the implication of giving the Torah to humans. They will mix in some of their subjective needs and distortions. However, God requires humans to try to neutralize the bias and reduce its distorting effects to a minimum.

17. E.g., correct understanding. There's a reasonable relationship between your conclusions and the material in the text. The student of Torah must carefully analyze how one thing leads to the next and determine that this is a reasonable conclusion. Coincidence or superficial resemblance is not adequate. Correct meaning is established by rational analysis and straight, commonsense deduction and analogy.

18. Lit. "a solid mirror."

19. "*Hakara mada'it*"; R. Salanter was apparently aware of the scientific method and was familiar with texts and sources that spoke of it. Its superiority lay in the fact that the empirical method stripped out human subjective needs and distortions and established the truth objectively.

20. "*Hitpashtut hagashmiyut*," meaning, the stripping away of all instincts and drives that come with embodiment. To R. Salanter, this means removing or neutralizing

Nor can truth be built simply by the desire of a person to seek knowledge of truth, bringing into its chamber whatever his reason has taught him. This idea is stated fully in a verse in Scripture (Prov. 2:4): "If you seek it as you do silver…" (this applies to Torah as indicated in the beginning of these verses, "My son…" [Prov. 2:1], and as explained in *Yalkut [Shimoni]* ad loc.). When seeking silver, a person's desire alone is not enough; only if he has prepared himself properly [will he succeed]. The same applies to the seeking of the Torah – and even more so – for when seeking silver, the basis is divine aid, whereas with respect to Torah, the basis is human preparation (by himself or others); only then will the divine light also shine on him.

"For the Torah is not in the heavens" (Deut. 30:12); rather, the Torah is given over to human beings. However, it is not held captivity by them, i.e., to act with it as they see fit; rather, as one who uses straightforward reason[16] to devise causes that naturally lead to the desired effect.[17] This constitutes knowledge of the truth.

In general, there are two fundamental principles in the search for the true Torah: natural ability and purity of thought. Ability means comprehensive mastery of basic premises and additional insight through strong and keen reason to build composites that are strong as cast iron,[18] and after much analysis of all sides of the argument to clarify the truth.

Purity – this is what scientists call "scientific knowledge"[19] and the Mussar sages call the stripping away of physicality,[20] meaning that the intellect stands alone and is not combined[21] with other human psychic drives. Otherwise, the tendencies of the psychic drives are screens separating him from recognizing the truth. For, even though straight judgment helps [in recognizing the truth], tendencies distort [judgment, leading it] to proceed along crooked paths.[22]

---

the self-serving egocentric bias which is embodied in the self so that undistorted reason can grasp the Torah's true meaning.

21. I.e., intermixed and distorted.

22. Hitherto, R. Salanter has presented Mussar learning and character refinement as ancillary activities, and in Letter 6 he stressed that learning Torah itself is the priority activity. Here R. Salanter is saying that without Mussar and character refinement, all the Torah that one studies will become distorted, because straight judgment is twisted by bias. Mussar and self-improvement are thus prerequisites for true understanding of Torah.

כַּאֲשֶׁר הָסְכַּן בִּימֵי חֲכָמֵינוּ ז"ל וְהַקַּדְמוֹנִים רַבּוֹתֵינוּ ז"ל – וִיסוֹד הַטָּהֳרָה – כַּאֲשֶׁר יִשְׁווּ כֹּחוֹת הַנַּפְשִׁית בְּמִשְׁקָל אֶחָד לִשְׁנֵי הַצְּדָדִים. וְהַשֵּׂכֶל יַעֲמֹד נִצָּב בְּאֵין מַכְרִיעַ. וְאָז ד׳ הַטּוֹב לֹא יִמְנַע טוֹב לַהוֹלְכִים בְּתָמִים (בַּהֲכָנָה הַנִּדְרֶשֶׁת) לְהָאִיר עֵינֵיהֶם בְּמָאוֹר תּוֹרָתוֹ. וְאוּלַי נוּכַל לְהַעֲמִיס הַדָּבָר בְּדִבְרֵי חֲכָמֵינוּ ז"ל (סוֹטָה דַּף כ"ב) יְרָא אֶת ד׳ בְּנִי וָמֶלֶךְ עִם שׁוֹנִים אַל תִּתְעָרַב אָמַר רַבִּי יִצְחָק אֵלּוּ שֶׁשּׁוֹנִים הֲלָכוֹת. כִּי מִצְוַת הַתּוֹרָה הִיא. לִשְׁמֹר מִשְׁפְּטֵי הַמֶּלֶךְ גַּם בְּאֵין רוֹאֶה וְאֵין יוֹדֵעַ כְּמַאֲמָרָם ז"ל דִּינָא דְּמַלְכוּתָא דִּינָא. יַעַן כָּל מְקוֹר הָאֱמֶת בְּיָדוֹ בְּתַכְלִית הַשְּׁלֵמוּת. הַיְכֹלֶת וְהַטָּהֳרָה וְעֵזֶר אֱלֹקִי כְּמַאֲמַר הַכָּתוּב לֵב מֶלֶךְ בְּיַד ד׳. כֵּן גַּם בְּיִרְאַת ד׳ הִיא הַתּוֹרָה עַל דֶּרֶךְ אֱמֶת (עַיֵּן בָּבָא בַּתְרָא דַּף ט"ז תָּפֵר יִרְאָה כו׳ בָּרָא לוֹ תּוֹרָה כו׳) יְסוֹדָהּ הַיְכֹלֶת וְהַטָּהֳרָה וְאָז יְסַיְּעֵהוּ הַשֵּׁם יִתְבָּרַךְ מִשָּׁמַיִם. וְעִם שׁוֹנִים אֵלּוּ שֶׁשּׁוֹנִים הֲלָכוֹת בְּלִי תַּלְמוּד אַל תִּתְעָרַב.

אַחַת הִיא אֲשֶׁר חַכְמֵי הַמּוּסָר הִרְחִיקוּהָ מִלָּבוֹא בִּקְהַל יִשְׂרָאֵל הִיא הַפִּלְפּוּל וּלְדַעְתִּי נֶהְפַּךְ הַדָּבָר. הַפִּלְפּוּל הוּא יְסוֹד גָּדוֹל וְחָזָק לְבַקָּשַׁת הָאֱמֶת וְכִמְעַט בִּלְעָדָהּ לֹא תָּקוּם לִשְׁתֵּי עִלּוֹת. הָאַחַת. הַשֵּׂכֶל הָעָמֹק וְהַיָּשָׁר אֲשֶׁר הוּא יְסוֹד הָרָאשִׁי (אַחַר יְסוֹד הָעִקָּר גֹּדֶל הַבְּקִיאוּת) לְמַטְּרַת הָאֱמֶת. הַחוֹב וְהַהֶכְרֵחַ לְהַרְחִיבוֹ לְחַדְּדוֹ וּלְהַיְשִׁירוֹ (אִישׁ לְפִי עֶרְכּוֹ) אֲשֶׁר כִּמְעַט בִּלְתִּי אֶפְשָׁר עַל יְדֵי בְּחִינַת הָאֱמֶת הַמְּגֻבָּל מִכָּל צַד. אָכֵן עַל־יְדֵי הִתְבּוֹנְנוּת בְּפִלְפּוּל הַתּוֹרָה. וּבְיַד הָאָדָם לְהַרְחִיבָהּ כְּחֶפְצוֹ. בְּאֹפֶן שֶׁיֵּלֵךְ עַל דָּבָר הַנָּאֶה וְהַיָּפֶה מְאִירַת עֵינַיִם. תְּיַשֵּׁר וּתְחַדֵּד שֵׂכֶל הָאָדָם וְאָז אִם יִלָּוֶה גֹּדֶל הַבְּקִיאוּת. בְּיָדוֹ

23. Compare Judges 5:16.
24. Gittin 10b et al.
25. The emphasis is in the original, presumably to dispel any possible danger that government censors might interpret the Talmud as saying that teachers of halakha dissent from the king's law.
26. Compare Deuteronomy 23:2–3.
27. Dialectics/casuistry. In his early days, after he became conscious of Mussar and the dangers of egocentricity, R. Salanter also proposed eliminating *pilpul*.
28. Compare Esther 9:1.

The source of ability is in what has been distilled from the understanding of many great searchers,[23] as was customary in the days of our Sages and Rabbis, of blessed memory. And the source of purity is when the psychic forces are in perfect equilibrium between the two sides. Reason will then stand upright, without bias. Then the good God will not deny good to those who go wholeheartedly (with proper preparation) to illuminate their eyes with His Torah.

Perhaps we can attach these words to the words of the Sages, of blessed memory (Sota 22a). "'**Fear God my son, and the king**, and with dissenters (*shonim*) do not get involved' (Prov. 24:21). R. Yitzḥak said: These are those that repeatedly learn (*shonim*) halakhot [without proper study]." **For it is a commandment of the Torah to observe the laws of the king even when no one sees or knows, as they say, "The law of the kingdom is law."[24] For the source of truth is entirely in his hands – ability, purity, and God's assistance. As Scripture says: "The heart of a ruler is in the hand of God"** (Prov. 21:1).[25] So too, through fear of God is the Torah arrived at by the way of truth (see Bava Batra 16a, "'He sewed reverence' [Job 15:4]... [He created the evil urge and] He created Torah [to cure it]...."). The basis is ability and purity – and then God, blessed be He, helps from the Heavens. But "with dissenters" – those who study halakhot without the proper preparation – do not get involved.

One thing that the Mussar sages banished from entering the congregation of Israel[26] is *pilpul*,[27] but in my present view, the opposite is true.[28] *Pilpul* is a great and strong basis for seeking the truth, without which it will not endure. There are two reasons. One: its profound and straight reason, which is the prime basis (after the fundamental principle of encyclopedic knowledge) of getting to the goal of the truth. The necessity of expanding, sharpening, and straightening reason (each person to his level), which is practically impossible by only examining the truth, which is limited, from every angle, [is possible,] however, through pilpulistic study of Torah.[29] It is in each person's power to expand it as he wishes so that it will follow the pleasant and beautiful Torah that illuminates. Thus, human reason will be straightened and

29. Which requires constant revision due to challenges from peers.

(לְפִי עֶרְכּוֹ) לְחַפֵּשׂ הָאֱמֶת. הַשְּׁנִיָּה, הִיא אֲשֶׁר חָזְקָה עָלַי יַד הַנִּסָּיוֹן בְּיַלְדוּתִי בִּהְיוֹתִי אָסוּר בְּלִמּוּד הַמּוּסָר וּמִשְׁפָּטָיו.*

* וְיָצַקְתִּי מַיִם עַל יְדֵי מוֹרִי הָרַב מ׳ יוֹסֵף זוּנְדֶל הַיּוֹשֵׁב בִּירוּשָׁלַיִם תִּבָּנֶה וְתִכּוֹנֵן בִּמְהֵרָה, וְעַד כֹּה לֹא הִגַּעְתִּי לְקַרְסֻלָּיו, הוּא הָיָה סֻלָּם מֻצָּב אַרְצָה טָרוּד בְּרַעְיוֹנֵי הַמִּסְחָר, לְבַקֵּשׁ טַרְפּוֹ כְּדֶרֶךְ בַּעֲלֵי בָּתִּים אֲשֶׁר מִחְיָתָם כָּבֵד לִפְנֵיהֶם, וְרֹאשׁוֹ מַגִּיעַ הַשָּׁמַיְמָה בִּטְרָדָה גְּדוֹלָה מִדַּי לְחַיֵּי נַפְשׁוֹ. מִשְׁפַּט לִמּוּדוֹ הָעִקָּרִי הָיָה בָּעִיּוּן הַנִּצְרָךְ לוֹ לְמַעֲשֶׂה, לָמַד הַגְּמָרָא כו׳ הַבֵּית יוֹסֵף וְכָל הָאַחֲרוֹנִים בְּעִיּוּן, וּבְיוֹתֵר הָעִיּוּן הַגָּדוֹל בְּבֵאוּרֵי הַגְּרָ״א זַ״ל, וּכְשֶׁלָּמַד הַסָּעִיף שֻׁלְחָן עָרוּךְ אוֹ הָעִנְיָן עִם כָּל אֲבִיזְרַיְהוּ, הָיָה הַצִּיּוּר לְפָנָיו כְּמוֹ שֶׁבָּא הַדִּין לְפָנָיו לְמַעֲשֶׂה. וְעִיֵּן וְחָקַר הֵיטֵב מִשְׁפָּטוֹ עַד שֶׁהֶעֱמִידוֹ לִפְסָק נִצָּב, וְאָז חָזַר פְּעָמִים רַבּוֹת עַד שֶׁהָיוּ בְּיָדוֹ כְּמֻנָּח בְּקֻפְסָא, כָּל לִמּוּדוֹ בְּתַנַ״ךְ גְּמָרָא מִדְרָשִׁים זֹהַר הַיְסוֹד לְחַפֵּשׂ יְדִיעַת הַמַּעֲשֶׂה, וְעַל כָּל אֵלֶּה גֹּדֶל הַיְגִיעָה לְיַשֵּׁר הַמִּדּוֹת וּלְחוֹבַת הַלְּבָבוֹת, הֶאֱרַכְתִּי מְעַט בְּמַעֲלַת אָדָם הַגָּדוֹל הַלָּזֶה, (אוֹר עוֹלָם לְפִי הַשְׁעָרָתִי), יַאֲרִיךְ ד׳ יָמָיו וּשְׁנוֹתָיו לְמַעַן יִשְׁמְעוּ הַבַּעֲלֵי בָּתִּים וְיֵלְכוּ בְּאָרְחוֹתָיו. גָּמַרְתִּי בְּדַעְתִּי לָכוֹף יִצְרִי (אֲשֶׁר הִשְׁתּוֹקְקָה לְהַרְאוֹת פִּלְפּוּלִי נֶגֶד בְּנֵי גִילִי).

לַעֲזֹב לְגַמְרֵי דְּבַר הַפִּלְפּוּל וְרַק אֶל הָאֱמֶת יִהְיֶה מַבָּטִי (נַעַר הָיִיתִי מְקוֹם הָאֱמֶת לֹא יָדַעְתִּי כִּי רְחוֹקָה מִמֶּנִּי כִּרְחוֹק מִזְרָח מִמַּעֲרָב) עַל פִּי צִיּוּרִי אָז. הַפַּשְׁטוּת. הַקִּצּוּר. וְהַחֵפֶץ לִדְרֹשׁ הָאֱמֶת. בַּהֲלִיכָתִי בַּמַּצָּב הַלָּזוֹ הַשְׁקָפָתִי בְּעַיִן חוֹדֶרֶת כִּי הַתְּשׁוּקָה לְהַרְאוֹת כֹּחַ שִׂכְלִי פָּרְצָה גְּבוּל הָאֱמֶת וַתַּתְעֶה אֶת שִׂכְלִי לְהַטּוֹת הָאֱמֶת אֶל חֶפְצִי וְהָאֱמֶת בְּרָצוֹן תִּכּוֹנָן. אָז אָמַרְתִּי טוֹב טוֹב לִי לְהַתִּיר לִי בְּאֵין חֲשָׁשׁ וְיִרְאָה לְהִשְׁתַּמֵּשׁ בְּפִלְפּוּלִים (כַּאֲשֶׁר הִתִּירוּ חֲכָמֵינוּ זַ״ל לְחִדּוּדָא) לְמַעַן תִּהְיֶה שִׂכְלִי חָפְשִׁי מִשְּׁבִיַּת הַיֵּצֶר. וְדָל כָּךְ גָּדַל הָרַעְיוֹן הַזֶּה אֶצְלִי עַד

30. Compare Psalms 37:25.
31. Compare Psalms 103:12. See also *Yalkut Shimoni* 1:178 and 631.
32. In other words: the anti-*pilpul*, just-the-plain meaning approach, was driven by egotistical desire (to be superior to those who were showing off their power of *pilpul*). R. Salanter's conclusion is that distortion by the ego is inescapable. Using a method that allowed it full play but critiqued it and corrected it by encouraging expression of a wide range of interpretations was a better method of neutralizing bias than a method that suppressed it and gave the illusion that it was eliminated.
33. His reason was captured by the bias of "simplicity" (plain meaning) and was in its thrall just as much as egotistical scholars are driven to come up with farfetched

honed. Then, if it is accompanied by great mastery, it will be within his power (at his level) to seek out the truth. Two: This is what experience impressed upon me in my youth, when I was bound up in the study of Mussar and its laws.*

* [R. Salanter's footnote:] I served my master (lit. "poured water over my master's hand"), R. Joseph Zundel, who now lives in Jerusalem, may it be built and established speedily in our days. To this day, I have not reached up to the ankles of his feet. He was a "ladder planted on the ground" (Gen. 28:12) – preoccupied with matters of commerce, seeking his food as do other laymen whose livelihood is difficult for them – but his "head reached the heavens" (ibid.), in his extraordinary preoccupation for the life of his soul. His main way of learning was in-depth study for the sake of action. He learned the Talmud, etc., *Beit Yosef*, and all the later codifiers in depth. His greatest intellectual effort was on the explanations of the Vilna Gaon, of blessed memory. When he studied a section of *Shulḥan Arukh* or any matter there with all the commentaries, he would imagine as if the law had come before him in an actual case. He studied and investigated its law properly until he could establish it as a well-founded decision. Then he reviewed it many times until he had it in the bag. In all his studies of Scripture, Talmud, Midrashim, and *Zohar*, the fundamental principle was to seek knowledge of what to do. On top of all this, he made a great effort to improve character and the duties of the heart.

I have gone on somewhat at length on the virtues of this great man (a light of the world, in my assessment). May God give him long life and years, so the laymen may hear and walk in his ways.

I made up my mind to compel my urge (which sought to show off my power of *pilpul* compared to my peers) to abandon entirely this matter of *pilpul* and look only to the truth. (I was young.[30] I had no idea where truth is found. It was as far from me as east is from west.[31]) According to what I imagined then, truth was plain meaning, brevity, and the desire to seek the truth.

As I went along in this state, I saw, with a penetrating eye, that the longing to demonstrate intellectual prowess breached the boundaries of truth and misled my intellect to divert the truth toward my desire – and that "truth" was being established by the underlying, driving will.[32] Then I said: It is far, far, better for me to allow myself to use *pilpulim* without hesitation or fear (as the Sages, of blessed memory, permitted it to sharpen one's mind) so that my reason would not be held captivity by the evil urge.[33] This idea has grown so large in my mind that now I find it hard to

אֲשֶׁר רָחֲקָה נַפְשִׁי לְהַאֲמִין (אִם לֹא לִיחִידֵי סְגֻלָּה) כִּי יִתְיַצֵּב הָאָדָם בְּטָהֳרַת הַשֵּׂכֶל לְבַל יַטֵּהוּ אֶל הָרָצוֹן לֵאמֹר כִּי זֶהוּ שֵׂכֶל מְזֻקָּק. בִּלְתִּי אִם יֵצֵא חָפְשִׁי לְהַגִּיד פִּלְפּוּלִים כִּרְצוֹנוֹ בְּאֵין מַפְרִיעַ.

בְּזֹאת אִם כִּי הַחוֹב פְּרוּשָׁה לִלְמוֹד הַתּוֹרָה גַּם בְּאֵין דֶּרֶךְ מוֹצֵאת לְבַקָּשַׁת הָאֱמֶת וְגַם הָרְשׁוּת נְתוּנָה לְהוֹרוֹת גַּם בְּלִי מַדְרֵגָה הַנִּשָּׂאָה הַלָּזוֹ. בְּכָל זֹאת בְּוַדַּאי הַחוֹב מֻטָּל עַל כָּל לוֹמְדֵי תוֹרָה – וְגַם לְבַעֲלֵי בָתִּים הַקּוֹבְעִים עִתִּים לַתּוֹרָה – לְחַפֵּשׂ גַּם אֶל דְּבַר אֱמֶת כַּמַּטְמוֹנִים וְהָאֱמֶת מֵאַיִן תִּמָּצֵא? הַאִם יִטֹּל נֹאד שֶׁל קֶמַח עַל כְּתֵפוֹ וְיֵלֵךְ אֶל אִישׁ הָאֶשְׁכּוֹל אֲשֶׁר יִקָּבְצוּ בּוֹ כָּל הַמַּעֲלוֹת הַנִּדְרָשׁוֹת לִמְצֹא הָאֱמֶת. כו'.

עוֹד אַחַת אָמַרְתִּי לְהָעִיר בִּדְבַר אֱמֶת הַנּוֹגֵעַ בְּתַהֲלוּכוֹת דַּרְכֵי הַמִּדּוֹת וּסְעִיפֵיהֶם אֲשֶׁר הָאֱמֶת יָקָר מְאֹד לִמְצֹא בָּהֶם לִהְיוֹתָם מֵהַמְפֻרְסָמוֹת נִבְדָּלוֹת מִמֻּשְׂכָּלוֹת אֲשֶׁר גִּדְרָם הָאֲמִתִּי הוּא אֱמֶת וָשֶׁקֶר נִתְלִים בְּשֵׂכֶל פָּשׁוּט חָפְשִׁי מִכָּל כֹּחוֹת הַנַּפְשִׁי (כַּנִּזְכָּר לְעֵיל) לֹא כֵן הַמְפֻרְסָמוֹת בְּגִדְרָם הָאֲמִתִּי טוֹב אוֹ רָע. מְגֻנֶּה אוֹ נָאֶה. אִם כִּי יְסוֹדָם הוּא הַשֵּׂכֶל הַחָפְשִׁי בְּלִי נְטִיַּת צְדָדִי. בְּכָל זֹאת גַּם כֹּחוֹת הַנַּפְשִׁי יִתְּנוּ חֵילָם. בְּאֹפֶן שֶׁיִּהְיֶה אֲסוּרִים בְּמַאֲסַר שֵׂכֶל הַחָפְשִׁי לְבַל יִפְרְצוּ גְּבוּל עֶרְכָּם – בְּזֹאת – פְּנִיַּת הַנְּטִיָּה. רוּחַ מְצוּיָה הִיא לְהַטּוֹת הָאֱמֶת אֶל חֵפֶץ נִקְנֶה לֹא אֶל חֵפֶץ טִבְעִי הַנְּטוּעָה בְּלֵב כָּל אִישׁ יָשָׁר (בִּלְתִּי נִשְׁחָת בְּמִדּוֹתָיו. בְּמַצָּבוֹ הַפְּשׁוּטָה בְּלִי עִנְיָן אוֹ כֹּחַ מוֹשֵׁךְ אוֹ דוֹחֶה) אֲשֶׁר הֵמָּה יְסוֹדוֹת הָרָאשִׁי וְעַל פִּיהֶן יִבְנֶה הַשֵּׂכֶל הֶקֵּשָׁיו בְּהַרְכָּבָתוֹ הַנְּכוֹחָה.

גַּם הַדִּבּוּר בָּהֶם נִבְדָּל מִבַּמֻּשְׂכָּלוֹת אֲשֶׁר כִּמְעַט רֵיחַ רַעְיוֹן אוֹ דִּבּוּר מְלִיצִי פּוֹסֵל בָּהֶם. וּבַמִּדּוֹת נֶהְפַּךְ הוּא כִּמְעַט בִּלְתִּי אֶפְשָׁר

---

pilpulim – but in this case, the bias tricked him into believing that he had freed himself from egocentric bias.

34. It appears that R. Salanter is softening his statements in the previous paragraphs, lest people conclude that if one hasn't studied Mussar, one should not study Torah at all (and certainly not issue halakhic rulings), lest the outcome be distorted.
35. Moral categories.
36. Aesthetic categories.
37. R. Salanter is borrowing a metaphor from Rambam's *Guide for the Perplexed*: before

believe (except possibly for an elite few) that a person can be staunchly pure of reason without being biased by the desire to say that his reason is refined – unless he freely says *pilpulim*, as he wishes, without any hindrance.

True – there is an obligation to study Torah even if no way can be found to seek the truth, and one may issue rulings even without achieving this elevated level.[34] Still, the obligation applies to all who study Torah – and also to laymen who set time aside regularly for Torah – to seek truth as one seeks treasures. And where will truth be found? Will it take a sack of flour on its shoulder and go to the polymath in whom are found all the needed qualifications to find the truth ... ?

One more point I thought to raise about truth, which pertains to the advancement of character traits and its ramifications. Truth is rarely found through them, as they are conventional. In contrast to the rational, which is truly defined as true or false, depending on abstract reason and free of all psychic forces (as described above), the conventional is defined truly as good or evil,[35] ugly or beautiful.[36] Even though their basis is in reason that is free of biases that divert,[37] the psychic forces cannot simply be eliminated, because they, too, contribute, as long as they are restrained by reason so they do not breach the boundaries of their actual value.

Now, the direction set by the tendencies are like a common breeze, diverting the truth toward an acquired desire, not to the natural desire implanted in the heart of a just man (who is not corrupted in his traits; who is in a simple, disinterested state without any attraction or repulsion), which supplies the primary foundational principles; at their direction, reason should build its analogies with correct combinations.

Speaking about these traits is also unlike speaking about the rational, where almost any whiff of imagery or figurative speech disqualifies them. Regarding character traits, it is the opposite; it is almost impossible

---

they ate of the fruit, Adam and Eve knew everything as necessary truths, i.e., true or false. After their consciousness changed, they came to understand the good and the bad, which are conditional truths. In establishing the truth about Torah's laws or text, the operating categories are true and false. In shaping and improving character traits, the operative categories are good and bad (i.e., conditional truth), because the admixture of psychic drives makes it almost impossible to arrive at pure, i.e., necessary truth.

לְהַצִּיגָם וּלְבָאֲרָם בְּלִי רַעְיוֹן בְּדַרְכֵי הַמְּלִיצָה אֲשֶׁר יְסוֹדָם לְהָעִיר כֹּחוֹת נַפְשִׁית הַנִּתְלִים בָּם. וְכָל אֲשֶׁר יוֹסִיף הָאָדָם אֶת כֹּחוֹ (אִם בְּיָדוֹ הִיא) לְהַגְבִּיהַּ עוּף מְלִיצָתוֹ לְבָאֵר הַדָּבָר אֶל נָכוֹן. כֵּן הַטָּעוּת כָּרוּךְ בַּעֲקֵבֶיהָ לְבַל לְכַסּוֹת הַשֶּׁקֶר בִּמְעִיל הַמְּלִיצָה. לָצֵאת מַה טּוֹב לְהַצִּיג לְעֵינֵי הַשֶּׁמֶשׁ חֵלֶק הַדְּרוּשׁ (אֲשֶׁר הִיא דְּבַר הַמְּלִיצָה לָאֵינוֹ רָגִיל בַּחָכְמָה הַלָּזוֹ בִּגְדָרֶיהָ) וְעֵינֵי רַבִּים יְשׁוֹטְטוּ בָּם בְּבִקֹּרֶת נוֹרָאָה לְהִתְנוֹצֵץ בְּמִדּוֹת (כִּמְעַט יְסוֹד הָרָאשִׁי לְנַפְשִׁי וְגוּפָנִי) דְּבַר אֱמֶת לִמְבַקְשֶׁיהָ.

וְהִנְנִי מוֹצֵא עֹז בְּנַפְשִׁי לְבָאֵר עוֹד דָּבָר יָקָר (לְפִי הַשְׁעָרָתִי) הַנּוֹלֶדֶת מֵחִבּוּר דְּבָרִים הַנִּפְרָדִים בַּסֵּפֶר הַלָּזֶה. לְיַשֵּׁר הַמִּדּוֹת וּלְהַרְגִּילָם לַנַּעַר חַד הַשֵּׂכֶל (אֲשֶׁר בִּכְלַל דְּבַר הַמִּדּוֹת נִצְרָךְ לְהַשְׁקָפָה גְּדוֹלָה אֶצְלוֹ לְבַל יַטֵּהוּ גֹּדֶל שִׂכְלוֹ הַמִּדּוֹת אֶל רְצוֹנוֹ) עוֹדֶנּוּ בְּאִבּוֹ טֶרֶם יִנָּגְפוּ רַגְלָיו בְּתַהְפּוּכוֹת הַזְּמַן וְטִרְדוֹתָיו (בְּאֵיזֶה מַצָּב שֶׁיִּהְיֶה) אֲשֶׁר כָּבֵד לִפְנֵי הָאָדָם לְהִתְלַמֵּד וּלְהִתְרַגֵּל בָּהֶם. וְרַק בִּימֵי הַבַּחֲרוּת אָז יְלַמֵּד וְיַרְגִּיל מִדּוֹתָיו בְּמַדְרֵגָה נִפְלָאָה עַד אֲשֶׁר יָבוֹא לְרַגְלֵי הַזְּמַן (לִבּוֹ וְדַעְתּוֹ בַּל עִמּוֹ לְהִתְבּוֹנֵן וּלְהַשְׁקִיף עֲלֵיהֶם) עוֹד יַכּוּ שֹׁרֶשׁ לָשֵׂאת פְּרִי הַצְלָחָה לְהִתְנַהֵג בְּמִדּוֹת יְשָׁרוֹת וְנִדְרָשׁוֹת בְּמִדָּה נִגְבָּלָה לְפִי תְּכוּנָתוֹ וְעִנְיָנוֹ. וְכַאֲשֶׁר הַלִּמּוּד בְּחָכְמַת הַמִּלְחָמָה הוּא בְּדִיּוּק עָצוּם וְנוֹרָא אֲשֶׁר כִּמְעַט בִּלְתִּי אֶפְשָׁר לְהֵעָשׂוֹת כֵּן בְּעֵת הַמִּלְחָמָה. כֵּן הַלִּמּוּד בְּחָכְמַת מִלְחֶמֶת כְּבִישַׁת הַמִּדּוֹת לְהַטּוֹתָם וּלְהַרְגִּילָם בַּדֶּרֶךְ הַנְּכוֹחָה. זֹאת מִשְׁפָּטָם לִלְמֹד וּלְהַרְגִּיל בָּהֶם בְּדִיּוּק נָכוֹן. הֲגַם שֶׁלֹּא יֵלְכוּ בִּשְׁלֵמוּתָם בְּעֵת עִסְקוֹ בְּגַלֵּי יַם הַזְּמַן גַּם כִּי הַדֶּרֶךְ יִהְיֶה צְלֵחָה לְפָנָיו וְאַיֵּה הַחֹמֶר לָשֵׂאת עָלָיו לִמּוּד וְהֶרְגֵּל הַמִּדּוֹת הַיְשָׁרוֹת? עִנְיָנָיו בְּעֵרוּב בְּנֵי אָדָם מְעַטִּים הֵמָּה וְנִקְלִים בְּאֵיכוּתָם.

---

38. R. Salanter has again articulated his "new" method: Bias is unavoidable, so expose it to scrutiny and alternative viewpoints, which correct distortions better than any internal self-correction can. In the case of figurative rhetoric, since the performance of a speech can mask errors, it is important to offer the material in writing or print, a medium that removes this charismatic element.

39. Compare Genesis 33:12, 14.

40. Meaning that in the storms and stresses of life, the theoretically well-trained method

to present them or explain them without some figurative image whose purpose is to awaken the psychic forces attached to them. The more a person puts his strength (if he can) into explaining something properly with soaring rhetoric, the more susceptible to error it becomes, as one can cover error in the garment of imagery. Therefore, it is very good to publish the "*drush*" (that is, the figurative component, for those not familiar with the definition of this art) and let the eyes of many scan it with exacting criticism. Thus, through *middot* (which are the prime basis for the spiritual and material), the truth will shine through for those who seek it.[38]

If I may be so bold, I will explain one more precious thing (in my estimation) that follows from putting together distinct elements of this book. Straighten out and condition the *middot* of an intelligent youth (who, in general, in matters of *middot,* needs extra oversight, lest his abundant intelligence divert his *middot* toward his desires) while he is still budding, before his feet get caught in the vicissitudes and preoccupations of time (whatever state he may be in), which make it difficult for a person to train and condition himself then.

Only in youth can one learn and condition his *middot* to a wonderful degree. So when, with the passage of time he arrives[39] [at older age] (when his heart and mind are not with him to concentrate or observe them), they will continue to strike root and bear the fruits of success – his behaving with proper and needed *middot* – to a degree limited by his nature and situation.

Just like learning the science of war requires tremendous and awesome precision that is practically impossible to learn during actual battle, so it is with learning the science of the war to conquer the *middot* and direct and condition them in the right way. This is their rule: one must study and condition them with correct precision in advance, even though they will not operate completely[40] when he is caught up in the waves of the ocean of time, even if he is on a successful path.

And where is the material that can carry the heavy weight of learning and conditioning proper *middot*? The presentation of interpersonal

---

will not function perfectly but in a flawed manner. Still, by training in advance, it will operate better.

בַּסֵּפֶר הַלָּזֶה לִהְיוֹת שׁוֹאֵל וּמֵשִׁיב כַּמִּשְׁפָּט בְּאֹרַח נְכוֹחָה וּבְדֶרֶךְ אֶרֶץ אֲשֶׁר קָדְמָה לַתּוֹרָה, אֲשֶׁר כִּמְעַט כָּל הַמִּדּוֹת שַׁיָּכִים לָזֶה, חֹמֶר נָאֶה וְגַם יָפֶה הִיא לָחוּל עָלֶיהָ צוּרַת לִמּוּד וְהֶרְגֵּל הַמִּדּוֹת בְּדֶרֶךְ סְלוּלָה.

וְהִנְנִי מְחַלֶּה פְּנֵי גְּדוֹלֵי הַזְּמַן לְכַבְּדֵנִי בְּדִבְרֵיהֶם הַנְּכוֹחִים, וְאַחֲרֵיהֶם גַּם צְעִירֵי הַיָּמִים יִמָּשְׁכוּ - וְיִמְחֲלוּ נָא כְּבוֹד תּוֹרָתָם הַנִּשָּׂאָה לְבָאֵר הֵיטֵב אֵיךְ לְהַצִּיג שְׁמָם בְּסוֹף דִּבְרֵיהֶם לְהִוָּדַע אֶל נָכוֹן מִבֶּטֶן מִי יָצָא הַדָּבָר. וְהִנְנִי לְגַלּוֹת מֵרֹאשׁ (לְבַל אֶהְיֶה כְּגוֹנֵב דַּעַת הַבְּרִיּוֹת) כִּי דְּבָרַי (לְמִעוּט יְדִיעָתִי) יָבוֹאוּ בְּעֵזֶר זוּלָתִי אי״ה.

כַּאֲשֶׁר כָּתַבְתִּי לְכַמָּה גְּדוֹלֵי גְּאוֹנֵי הַזְּמַן, יֵשׁ אֲשֶׁר כִּבְּדוּנִי בְּדִבְרֵיהֶם וְיֵשׁ אֲשֶׁר הִבְטִיחוּ לִשְׁלֹחַ, יָצָאתִי יְדֵי חוֹבַת לְקִיחַת הַתְּעוּדוֹת.

זְכוּת הָעֲמֵלִים עִם הַצִּבּוּר לְשֵׁם שָׁמַיִם - לִשְׁלֹחַ דְּבָרִים נְכוֹחִים - וּזְכוּת אֲבוֹתָם יְסַיְּעָן לְהַגְדִּיל תּוֹרָה וּלְהַאֲדִירָהּ בְּעֶזְרַת ה׳.

וְד׳ יִהְיֶה בְּעֶזְרִי הִנְנִי הַמְדַבֵּר יִשְׂרָאֵל בְּהָרַב מוהר״ר זְאֵב וואלף זללה״ה

41. Here ends the text as published by R. Blazer in *Ohr Yisrael*. Our translation continues until the end of the introduction written by R. Salanter, as actually published in *Tevunah*.

42. Compare Avot 5:7.

43. See Leviticus Rabba 9:3.

44. Lit., "out of whose womb did they come forth." Compare Job 38:29.

experience is very limited and poor in quality.[41] [Therefore,] this book purports to ask and reply[42] as is proper – in the correct path and with "*derekh eretz* (proper behavior), [which] precedes the Torah,"[43] and in which all *middot* are included. This will be good and beautiful material with which to apply a paved path for studying and conditioning *middot*.

So I beg the great Torah sages of this time to honor me with their correct words – followed by the youths – and may [they] deign to explain clearly how to present their names at the end of their essays so it will be accurately known who uttered these words.[44] And let me reveal in advance (so that I may not mislead people) that my essays (because of my scant knowledge) will be written with the help of others,[45] with the help of God.

When I wrote to several great and eminent sages of our time, some honored me with their writings, and some promised to send them. I have fulfilled the obligation of incorporating their documents.

The merit of those who work with the community for the sake of Heaven[46] will accrue to those who send correct writings, and the merit of their fathers will help them to increase Torah and glorify it.

May God help me, I who speak am Israel, son of R. Zev Wolf, may his memory be a blessing and for life in the World to Come.

---

45. It is not clear whether R. Salanter is referring to a student/disciple serving as co-writer or perhaps is crediting the non-Jewish/modern scholars whose writings shaped his ideas about the role of the unconscious forces. That these forces drive reason and judgment in egocentric and biased ways is a prominent feature in all three of R. Salanter's *Tevunah* essays.
46. Compare Avot 2:2, and the opening words of this introduction.

ל

וַיֹּאמֶר יְהוֹשֻׁעַ אֶל בְּנֵי יִשְׂרָאֵל גֹּשׁוּ הֵנָּה וְגוֹ׳ (יְהוֹשֻׁעַ ג׳).

בַּמִּדְרָשׁ (בְּרֵאשִׁית רַבָּה פָּרָשָׁה ה׳). רַב הוּנָא אָמַר זְקָפָן בֵּין שְׁנֵי בַּדֵּי הָאָרוֹן. אָמַר רַב אָחָא בַּר חֲנִינָא סְמָכָן בֵּין שְׁנֵי בַּדֵּי הָאָרוֹן. רַבָּנָן אָמְרֵי צִמְצְמָן בֵּין שְׁנֵי בַּדֵּי הָאָרוֹן. אָמַר לָהֶן יְהוֹשֻׁעַ מִמַּה שֶּׁהֶחֱזִיקוּ אֶתְכֶם שְׁנֵי בַּדֵּי הָאָרוֹן אַתֶּם יוֹדְעִין שֶׁשְּׁכִינָתוֹ שֶׁל הַקָּדוֹשׁ־בָּרוּךְ־הוּא בֵּינֵיכֶם. הָדָא הוּא דִכְתִיב (שָׁם) וַיֹּאמֶר יְהוֹשֻׁעַ בְּזֹאת תֵּדְעוּן כִּי אֵל חַי בְּקִרְבְּכֶם עַד כָּאן.

טֶרֶם נַתְחִיל לְהָפִיחַ רוּחַ פְּנִימִי בְּהַמַּאֲמָר. (גַּם אִם לֹא כִּוְּנוּ לָזֶה רַק שֶׁהָרוּחַ אוּלַי בְּמִישׁוֹר יְנַשֵּׁב). נַבִּיעַ נָא בִּמְעַט אֹמֶר וּדְבָרִים בִּכְלַל תְּכוּנַת דַּרְכֵי בְּנֵי הָאָדָם כִּי נִפְרָדִים הֵמָּה: יֵשׁ אֲשֶׁר תְּכוּנָתוֹ טוֹבָה. מִדּוֹתָיו בְּטִבְעוֹ רְצוּיוֹת. וְיֵשׁ לְהֵפֶךְ. כֵּן גַּם בְּאָדָם פְּרָטִי לִפְעָמִים כֹּחוֹת נַפְשׁוֹ בַּל יֵלְכוּ בְּמִצְעָד שָׁוֶה. אֵיזֶה מֵהֶם יִצְעֲדוּ (בְּאֵין מוֹשֵׁךְ וּמְנַהֵל) בְּאֹרַח נְכוֹחָה. וְאֵיזֶה מֵהֶם יֵלְכוּ דֶּרֶךְ עֲקַלְקַלּוֹת. יִפְרְצוּ לְהַשְׁחִית אִם לֹא יַעַצְרֵם הָאָדָם בְּכֹחַ תְּבוּנָתוֹ.

1. This comment reflects R. Salanter's sophistication as a reader (in light of his exposure to the role of the unconscious forces in a person). Plain meaning (*peshat*) is often not plain meaning. Reason and seemingly rational conclusions are often driven by irrational desires and forces to predetermined (non-rational) conclusions. One can also say that, by 1861, R. Salanter's cultural interpretive context was affected by modern perspectives. He did not interpret this rabbinic text according to its "naive," plain meaning, as did other readers still primarily embedded in traditional culture.

Letter 30

"And Joshua said to the Israelites: 'Come step here'" (Josh. 3:9).

In the Midrash (Genesis Rabba 5:7):

> Rav Huna said: He stood all of them up between the two carrying-poles of the Ark. Said Rav Aḥa bar Ḥanina: He supported them between the two carrying-poles of the Ark. The Rabbis said: He squeezed them between the two carrying-poles of the Ark. Joshua said to them: From the fact that the two carrying-poles of the Ark held all of you, know that the Presence of God is among you. This is as it says: "And Joshua said: *With this*, you will know that the Living God is in your midst (Josh. 3:10)."

Before we begin to breathe inner life into this teaching (even if the Rabbis did not have this in mind, the spirit of this teaching perhaps moves in the same plane),[1] let us express, briefly and succinctly, some generalizations about the character of the ways of human beings, for they are diverse. Some have good character. Their traits are naturally desirable. And some are the opposite. So too, within an individual person, sometimes psychic forces do not march in lockstep. Some march (without a control or guide) in a straight path. Some of them go in twisted paths. They will erupt to do harm if the person does not stop them with the power of his reason.

אַל יֹאמַר הָאָדָם אֶת אֲשֶׁר עָשָׂה הָאֱלֹהִים אֵין לְשַׁנּוֹת וְהוּא יִתְבָּרַךְ הִטְבִּיעַ בִּי כֹּחַ הָרַע וְאֵיךְ אֲקַוֶּה לְעָקְרוֹ מִשֹּׁרֶשׁ. לֹא כֵן הַדָּבָר. כֹּחוֹת הָאָדָם בְּנֵי כְבִישָׁה גַּם חִלּוּף הֵמָּה. כַּאֲשֶׁר עֵינֵינוּ רוֹאוֹת בְּטִבְעֵי בַּעֲלֵי חַיִּים. אֲשֶׁר הָאָדָם רַב חֵילוֹ לְכָבְשָׁם בְּמַאֲסַר רְצוֹנוֹ לְבַל יִרְעוּ וּבַל יַשְׁחִיתוּ. גַּם לַעֲשׂוֹתָם בְּנֵי תַּרְבּוּת לַהֲפֹךְ טִבְעָם וְלַעֲקֹר מִשֹּׁרֶשׁ רֹעַ תְּכוּנָתָם. כֵּן הָאָדָם בְּעַצְמוֹ יֵשׁ לְאֵל יָדוֹ לִכְבֹּשׁ טִבְעוֹ הָרַע לְבַל יֵצֵא לִפְעֻלָּה אָדָם. וְגַם לְשַׁנּוֹת טִבְעוֹ לְטוֹב עַל יְדֵי הַלִּמּוּד וְהַהֶרְגֵּל. (עַיֵּן חֶשְׁבּוֹן הַנֶּפֶשׁ). וּכְמַאֲמַר רַבּוֹתֵינוּ זַ"ל (אָבוֹת פ"ד) אֵיזֶהוּ גִּבּוֹר הַכּוֹבֵשׁ אֶת יִצְרוֹ שֶׁנֶּאֱמַר (מִשְׁלֵי י"ט) טוֹב אֶרֶךְ אַפַּיִם מִגִּבּוֹר וּמוֹשֵׁל בְּרוּחוֹ מִלֹּוֹכֵד עִיר. כִּי גֶּדֶר הַגְּבוּרָה הוּא. לְהִתְקוֹמֵם עַל שֶׁכְּנֶגְדּוֹ בְּחָזְקָה וּבְאֹמֶץ יָד לְכָבְשׁוֹ. וְגֶדֶר לְכִידַת עִיר. הוּא בִּהְיוֹת אַנְשֵׁי הָעִיר סָרִים לְמִשְׁמַעַת לוֹכְדָם בְּאַהֲבָה וְחִבָּה. בַּל יִכְבַּד עֲלֵיהֶם לְמַלְּאוֹת פְּקֻדָּתוֹ. וּבְגִילָה וְרִנָּה יָשִׂישׂוּ לְהָקִים מְזִמָּתוֹ. לָזֹאת הַכּוֹבֵשׁ אֶת יִצְרוֹ. הוּא רַק גִּבּוֹר לְהִתְחַזֵּק לִהְיוֹת עוֹצֵר תַּאֲוָתוֹ. זֶהוּ בְּחִינַת אֶרֶךְ אַף. שֶׁהוּא בַּעַל אַף אַךְ עוֹצְרוֹ לְבַל יִפְרֹץ. וּמִזֶּה לְאַט לְאַט יָבוֹא לִבְחִינַת מוֹשֵׁל בְּרוּחוֹ. שֶׁיִּהְיֶה רוּחַ תַּאֲוָתוֹ מָסוּר בְּיַד שִׂכְלוֹ הַיָּשָׁר לֶאֱהֹב אֶת הַצֶּדֶק בַּל יַחְפֹּץ הֶפְכּוֹ. וְזֶה כָּל הָאָדָם לְשָׁרֵשׁ מִלְּבָבוֹ כָּל תְּכוּנָה וּמִדָּה רָעָה. כִּי כָל עוֹד לֹא נִקָּה מֵחֶלְאָתָם. אַף כִּי יִתְגַּבֵּר עַל יִצְרוֹ פְּעָמִים רַבּוֹת. יִפֹּל בְּרִשְׁתָּם. (עַיֵּן שַׁעֲרֵי קְדֻשָּׁה חֵלֶק א' שַׁעַר ג'). וְזֶה הָיָה מַעֲלַת

2. Compare Ecclesiastes 7:29.
3. Compare Isaiah 11:9.
4. Compare Genesis 31:39.
5. Below R. Salanter describes this as a method of character formation – *kibbush hamiddot* – literally, "conquering the traits." We translate this as the method of repression.
6. Below, R. Salanter describes this as an alternative method of character improvement called *tikkun hamiddot* – literally, "the improvement of traits." We translate this as the method of sublimation.
7. A book whose title literally means "accounting of the soul," published in the early nineteenth century by a moderate *maskil,* Menachem Mendel Lefin of Satanov (1749–1826), which deals with identifying character traits and working on changing them. Lefin's work was influenced by the moral self-improvement program described in *The Autobiography of Benjamin Franklin* (1791).
8. This is a typographical error – the actual location is Proverbs 16:32.

A person should not say: Whatever God has made[2] cannot be changed, and He, blessed be He, imbued this power of evil in me; how can I hope to uproot it completely? This is not so. Human powers can be conquered and changed. Our eyes see this in the nature of animals; a human being is powerful enough to master them in the control of his will, that they not do evil or destroy.[3] He can domesticate them, changing their nature and thoroughly uprooting the evil of their character. So, the human being himself has within his power[4] to conquer his evil nature[5] so that it is not expressed in personal action, and also to change his nature for the better through study and habituation *(hergel)*.[6] (See *Ḥeshbon HaNefesh.*)[7]

And as our Rabbis, of blessed memory, say (Avot 4:1): "Who is [truly] mighty? One who conquers his [evil] urge, as it is said (Prov. 19[8]): 'Better one who is slow to anger than one who is mighty; and one who controls his spirit than one who captures a city.'" For the definition of "might" is to rise up against an opponent and conquer him by force and strength. And the "capture of a city" occurs when the people of the city accede to the dictates of their captor with love and affection, and it is not burdensome for them to fulfill his commands. With joy and festivity, they are happy to carry out his plans.

So the "conqueror of his urge" is only mighty in that he strengthens himself to hold back his desire. This is the state of "slow to anger" – the person has anger, but he holds it back so that it does not break out. From this, little by little, he can arrive at the state of "controls his spirit," i.e., that the spirit of his desire is in the power of his straightforward reason to love righteousness – and not desire its opposite.

This is the whole duty of man:[9] to root out of his heart every bad quality and character trait (*midda*). For as long as he has not been cured of their sickness, even if he overcomes his urge many times, he will eventually fall into its net (see *Shaarei Kedusha,*[10] Part 1, Gate 3). This

9. Compare Ecclesiastes 12:13.
10. R. Chaim Vital (1542–1620, Safed) was a kabbalist and the foremost disciple of R. Isaac Luria (Arizal), a Jewish mystic and the founder of modern Kabbala. R. Vital's *Shaarei Kedusha* (*The Gates of Holiness*) is a manual of proper comport and character for aspiring mystics.

אַבְרָהָם אָבִינוּ עָלָיו הַשָּׁלוֹם שֶׁתִּקֵּן כָּל כֹּחוֹת נַפְשׁוֹ הַנִּלְוִים עִם גּוּפוֹ. כְּמַאֲמָרָם זַ״ל (מִדְרַשׁ רַבָּה סֵדֶר לֶךְ לְךָ פָּרָשָׁה מ״ו) אָמַר הַקָּדוֹשׁ בָּרוּךְ הוּא לְאַבְרָהָם אֵין בְּךָ פְּסֹלֶת אֶלָּא הָעָרְלָה הַעֲבֵר אוֹתָהּ וּבַטֵּל הַמּוּם. הִתְהַלֵּךְ לְפָנַי וֶהְיֵה תָמִים. עַיֵּן שָׁם. וּכְמַאֲמָרָם (שָׁם פָּרָשָׁה י״א) כָּל מַה שֶּׁנִּבְרָא בְּשֵׁשֶׁת יְמֵי בְּרֵאשִׁית צְרִיכִין עֲשִׂיָּה כְּגוֹן הַחַרְדָּל צָרִיךְ לְמָתוֹק כוּ׳ אֲפִלּוּ אָדָם צָרִיךְ תִּקּוּן*

* וּבָזֶה יְבֹאַר הַמִּדְרָשׁ (סֵדֶר נֹחַ פָּרָשָׁה ל׳) אֶת הָאֱלֹהִים הִתְהַלֶּךְ נֹחַ כוּ׳ רַבִּי יְהוּדָה אוֹמֵר מָשָׁל לְמֶלֶךְ שֶׁהָיוּ לוֹ שְׁנֵי בָנִים אֶחָד גָּדוֹל וְאֶחָד קָטָן אָמַר לַקָּטָן הֲלֹךְ עִמִּי וְאָמַר לַגָּדוֹל בֹּא וַהֲלֹךְ לְפָנַי. כָּךְ אַבְרָהָם שֶׁהָיָה כֹּחוֹ יָפֶה (בְּרֵאשִׁית י״ז) הִתְהַלֵּךְ לְפָנַי וֶהְיֵה תָמִים. אֲבָל נֹחַ שֶׁהָיָה כֹּחוֹ רַע. אֶת הָאֱלֹהִים הִתְהַלֶּךְ נֹחַ. כִּי נֹחַ (לְפִי עֶרְכּוֹ) יַעַן לֹא נִצְטַוָּה עַל הַמִּילָה. לֹא הָיָה בְּיָדוֹ לָבוֹא לִבְחִינַת תִּקּוּן אֲמִתִּי רַק בִּבְחִינַת כּוֹבֵשׁ אֶת יִצְרוֹ. וְהוּא בְּעֵזֶר ה׳ יִתְבָּרַךְ. כְּמַאֲמָרָם זַ״ל (סֻכָּה נב:) יִצְרוֹ שֶׁל אָדָם מִתְגַּבֵּר עָלָיו בְּכָל יוֹם וְאִלְמָלֵא הַקָּדוֹשׁ־בָּרוּךְ־הוּא שֶׁעוֹזְרוֹ אֵינוֹ יָכוֹל לוֹ עַיֵּן שָׁם. וְזֶהוּ אֶת הָאֱלֹהִים וְכוּ׳. אֲבָל אַבְרָהָם אַחַר הַעֲבָרַת הַמּוּם נִתְקְנוּ כָּל כֹּחוֹת נַפְשׁוֹ. וּמֵעַצְמוֹ כְּהוֹלֵךְ בֶּחָלִיל שָׂשׂ לִשְׁמֹר דֶּרֶךְ ה׳. זֶהוּ הִתְהַלֵּךְ לְפָנַי.

וְכִדְאִיתָא בְּתָנָא דְּבֵי אֵלִיָּהוּ (פֶּרֶק כ״ה) לְפִיכָךְ הָיִיתִי אוֹמֵר שֶׁכָּל אֶחָד מִיִּשְׂרָאֵל חַיָּב לוֹמַר מָתַי יַגִּיעוּ מַעֲשַׂי לְמַעֲשֵׂי אֲבוֹתַי אַבְרָהָם יִצְחָק וְיַעֲקֹב. וּבָזֶה יְבֹאַר הַמִּדְרָשׁ (שָׁם) עַל הַפָּסוּק (הוֹשֵׁעַ ט׳) כְּבִכּוּרָה בִתְאֵנָה בְּרֵאשִׁיתָהּ רָאִיתִי אֲבוֹתֵיכֶם. אָמַר רַבִּי יוּדָן מַה הַתְּאֵנָה הַזֹּאת אֵין לָהּ פְּסֹלֶת אֶלָּא עָקְצָהּ בִּלְבַד הַעֲבֵר אוֹתָהּ וּבַטֵּל הַמּוּם. כָּךְ אָמַר הַקָּדוֹשׁ־בָּרוּךְ־הוּא לְאַבְרָהָם אֵין בְּךָ פְּסֹלֶת וְכוּ׳. עַד כָּאן לְשׁוֹנוֹ.

וְעַל פִּי מַאֲמַר הַמִּדְרָשׁ (שָׁם פָּרָשָׁה א׳) שִׁשָּׁה דְבָרִים קָדְמוּ לִבְרִיאַת הָעוֹלָם. יֵשׁ מֵהֶם שֶׁנִּבְרְאוּ וְיֵשׁ מֵהֶן שֶׁעָלוּ בְּמַחֲשָׁבָה לְהִבָּרְאוֹת כוּ׳. הָאָבוֹת כוּ׳ עָלוּ בְּמַחֲשָׁבָה לְהִבָּרְאוֹת. הָאָבוֹת מִנַּיִן שֶׁנֶּאֱמַר (הוֹשֵׁעַ

11. How can any individual do as much as Abraham, Isaac, and Jacob? Can they start the Jewish people and religion again? R. Salanter's answer is: "No" – but they can match Abraham in achieving perfection of the urge and removal of inner flaws.

was the virtue of our father Abraham, may peace be upon him, that he sublimated all the psychological drives that came with his body. As they, of blessed memory, said (Genesis Rabba, *Lekh Lekha* 46): "The Holy One, blessed be He, said to Abraham: 'You have only one husk – the foreskin. Remove it and the flaw will be gone.' 'Walk before Me and be whole' (Gen. 17:1)." See further there. And as they said (Genesis Rabba 11): "Everything that was created during the six days of creation needs work; for example, the mustard seed needs to be sweetened... even the human being needs to be perfected."*

* [R. Salanter's footnote:] With this we can explain the Midrash (*Noaḥ* 30): "'Noah walked with God' (Gen. 6:9).... R. Yehuda says: This is analogous to a king who had two sons, one big and one small. He said to the small one: Walk with me. And he said to the big one: Come and walk before me. So Abraham who had great strength – 'Walk before Me and be whole' (Gen. 17:1); but Noah, who had little strength – 'Noah walked with God.'"

Because Noah (in accordance with his capacity) was not commanded to circumcise, he could not reach the stage of true perfection, but only reached the stage of conquering his urge, and even that, only with the help of God, blessed be He. As they, of blessed memory, say (Sukka 52b): "A man's [evil] urge comes on strongly against him every day, and but for the help of the Holy One, blessed be He, he could not cope with it" (see further there). And this is the meaning of "Noah [walked with God]...." However, Abraham, after the flaw was removed, all his psychic forces were perfected. He walked on his own, like one marching with a flute, rejoicing to keep the "way of God" (compare Gen. 18:19). This is (the meaning of God's instruction to Abraham to) "walk before Me."

As is found in *Tanna DeVei Eliyahu* (ch. 25): "Therefore I would say that each person in Israel must say: 'When will my actions reach the level of deeds of my fathers, Abraham, Isaac and Jacob?'"[11] And with this we can explain the midrash (Genesis Rabba 46) on the verse (Hos. 9:10): "'As the first fruit to ripen on a fig tree, so I regarded your fathers'.... R. Yudan says: Just as this fig has no husk except for its stem, take that off and the flaw will be gone, so the Holy One, blessed be He, said to Abraham: 'You have only one husk – the foreskin. Remove it and the flaw will be gone.' 'Walk before Me and be whole' (Gen. 17:1)."

This also fits the midrashic statement (ibid., ch. 1): "Six things preceded the creation of the world. Some were created and some arose in thought to be created.... The patriarchs... arose in thought

ט׳) כַּעֲנָבִים בַּמִּדְבָּר (סֵיפָא דִקְרָא כְּבִכּוּרָה בִתְאֵנָה הַנִּזְכָּר לְעֵיל). וְיֵשׁ לְבָאֵר הַדָּבָר. כִּי נוֹדַע שֶׁבְּמַעֲשֶׂה. הַסִּבָּה קוֹדֶמֶת לְהַמְסוֹבָב. וְהַמְסוֹבָב (הוּא הַתַּכְלִית) הוֹלֵךְ לְרַגְלֵי הַסִּבּוֹת הַקּוֹדְמוֹת לוֹ. אָכֵן בְּמַחֲשָׁבָה הַדָּבָר לְהֶפֶךְ. הַתַּכְלִית קוֹדֵם. וּלְפִיהוּ (לְהַצִּיבוֹ עַל מְכוֹנוֹ) יְסָדְּרוּ הֲכָנוֹת הַסִּבּוֹת לְמֶרְכַּז הַמְסוֹבָב. וְהִנֵּה בְּרִיאַת הַתֵּבֵל (הָאָרֶץ וְכָל אֲשֶׁר עָלֶיהָ. עַיֵּן בַּמְחַבְּרִים מַה שֶּׁדִּבְּרוּ בָּזֶה) תַּכְלִית אָדָם הַשָּׁלֵם יְרֵא אֶת ה׳ וְשׁוֹמֵר מִצְוֹתָיו. כְּמַאֲמַר רַבּוֹתֵינוּ זַ״ל (שַׁבָּת לא:) מַאי כִּי זֶה כָּל הָאָדָם (קֹהֶלֶת י״ב) אָמַר רַבִּי אֶלְעָזָר אָמַר הַקָּדוֹשׁ־בָּרוּךְ־הוּא כָּל הָעוֹלָם כֻּלּוֹ לֹא נִבְרָא אֶלָּא בִּשְׁבִיל זֶה עַיֵּן שָׁם. וּלְפִי מַאֲמַר הַתָּנָא דְּבֵי אֵלִיָּהוּ (הַמּוּבָא לְעֵיל) נִרְאֶה בַּעֲלִיל כִּי מֶרְכַּז הַבְּרִיאָה בַּעֲבוּר הָאָדָם הַמְעֻלֶּה. הַמַּשְׁלִים חִיּוּבוֹ לַעֲלוֹת בְּמַדְרֵגַת הָאָבוֹת.

זֶהוּ מַאֲמַר הַמִּדְרָשׁ הָאָבוֹת עָלוּ בְּמַחֲשָׁבָה לְהִבָּרְאוֹת הַיְנוּ הַתַּכְלִית בִּבְרִיאַת הָעוֹלָם בְּמַחֲשַׁבְתּוֹ יִתְבָּרַךְ (הַקּוֹדֶמֶת לְהַסִּבָּה הִיא בְּרִיאַת הַתֵּבֵל) הִיא מַדְרֵגַת בְּחִינַת הָאָבוֹת.

וְזֶהוּ מַאֲמַר הַמִּדְרָשׁ הַנִּזְכָּר לְעֵיל כְּבִכּוּרָה בִתְאֵנָה בְּרֵאשִׁיתָהּ רָאִיתִי אֲבוֹתֵיכֶם. הַיְנוּ שֶׁהָאָדָם נִבְרָא לְתַכְלִית זוֹ. וְכָל אָדָם בְּיָדוֹ וּבְכֹחוֹ לְתַקֵּן כָּל כֹּחוֹת נַפְשׁוֹ הַמִּשְׁתַּתְּפִים עִם חָמְרוֹ. לְבַד הַחֵלֶק שֶׁנִּצְטַוָּה אַבְרָהָם לְכָרְתוֹ.

אָכֵן בְּמַצַּב תִּקּוּן הַיֵּצֶר. גַּם בְּחִינַת כְּבִישַׁת יִצְרוֹ. בַּל יַרְפֶּה יָדוֹ מֵהַחֲזִיק בָּהּ. כִּי אַף שֶׁנֶּעֱקַר הָרַע מִקִּרְבּוֹ. עוֹד מַעְיָן נִרְפָּשׂ טָמוּן בְּחֶבּוֹ לְהָקִיר מֵימָיו. עַל יְדֵי סִבָּה גְּדוֹלָה הַמְעוֹרְרָתָם לְהִתְגַּלּוֹת מִמַּחֲבוֹאָם לְהִתְפַּשֵּׁט לָצֵאת הַחוּצָה לְהַשְׁחִית. כְּמוֹ הָאִישׁ אֲשֶׁר הִרְגִּיל אֶת עַצְמוֹ

12. I.e., the perfect human, the patriarchs.

13. Here again, R. Salanter, applying his own creative thinking, is re-presenting the practice of Mussar. Earlier, he stressed its importance as a particular behavior intended to increase awareness of God and true reverence. Now he presents Mussar as the way to achieve the universal goal of the Torah (and God's reason for creating the world) – to perfect human character. Each individual is obligated to make himself whole, like Abraham. An oral tradition of the Mussar movement quotes R. Salanter as saying: "The Torah came to make a *mentsch*." This, on one foot, is his summary and his view of the goal of the whole Torah.

to be created. From whence [do we learn this about] the patriarchs? It is said (Hos. 9:10): 'As grapes in the desert…' (this is the end of the aforementioned verse, 'as the first fruit to ripen in a fig tree…')." This can be explained [as follows]: It is known that in action, cause precedes effect. And the effect (which is the goal) follows its preceding causes. However, in thought, the matter is reversed – the goal comes first. In accordance with the goal (and in order attain it), the preceding causes are arranged to arrive at the effect. Now in the creation of the universe (the earth and everything on it – see what the writers have said about this), the goal was the perfect human being, who fears God and observes His commandments. As our Rabbis, of blessed memory, said (Shabbat 31b): "What does 'This is the whole duty of man' (Eccl. 12:13) mean? R. Elazar said: The Holy One, blessed be He, said: The whole world was created solely for the sake of this one."[12] See further there. According to the saying of the *Tanna DeVei Eliyahu* (quoted above), it can be seen clearly that the focus, that is, the goal, of creation is for the sake of the superior human being – the one who fulfills his obligation to rise to the level of the patriarchs.

This is the meaning of the above-quoted midrashic saying: before creation took place, "the patriarchs arose in thought to be created." That is, the goal of creating the world in His thought, blessed be He (which precedes the cause, i.e., the actual creation of the universe), was to generate human beings who reach the level of the patriarchs.

This is the meaning of the above-quoted midrash, "As the first fruit to ripen in a fig tree, so I regarded your fathers," that is, the human was created for this goal. And each person has it in his hands and in his power to sublimate all the psychological drives that are intertwined with his materiality – except for the piece that Abraham was commanded to cut off.[13]

However, even under conditions of "perfecting the urge" [i.e., sublimation], he should not slacken his grip on "conquering his urge" [i.e., repression], for even if the evil is uprooted from within him, there is still a source of pollution buried in him to taint his waters – through an intense stimulus that can arouse them to emerge from hiding, spread out, and destroy. For example: a man conditioned himself with the virtue

בְּמִדַּת הַסַּבְלָנוּת לְבַל יִקְצֹף מְאוּמָה עַל כָּל אֲשֶׁר נַעֲשָׂה נֶגֶד רְצוֹנוֹ וְתוֹעַלְתּוֹ. בְּכָל זֹאת אֵינֶנּוּ בָּטוּחַ בְּדָבָר גָּדוֹל אֲשֶׁר כְּנֶטֶל הַחוֹל יִכְבַּד עָלָיו לְסָבְלוֹ. אִם לֹא יַחְתֹּר בְּעִמְקֵי גָּדְלַת הָעִנְיָן לַהֲרֹס בִּנְיָנוֹ הַטּוֹב אֲשֶׁר קָנָה בַּעֲמָלוֹ. וְאָז נִצְרָךְ לִגְבוּרָה יְתֵרָה לִכְבֹּשׁ תַּאֲוָתוֹ אֲשֶׁר לֹא הֻסְכַּן בָּהּ. (כִּי כְּבָר נֶעֱזַב וְנֶעֱקַר מִקִּרְבּוֹ הֶרְגֵּל הַכְּבִישָׁה בַּמִּדָּה הַלָּזוֹ אֲשֶׁר קָנָה מִלְּפָנִים בְּעֵת הֱיוֹתָהּ אֶצְלוֹ בִּבְחִינַת כְּבִישָׁה. יַעַן לֹא הִשְׁתַּמֵּשׁ בָּהּ זְמַן כַּבִּיר מֵעֵת זָכָה לָהּ בִּבְחִינַת תִּקּוּן). וּמִי יוֹדֵעַ אִם לָעֵת כָּזֹאת יַגִּיעַ לְמִדַּת הַגְּבוּרָה. אֲשֶׁר בִּלְתִּי הַהֶרְגֵּל קָשֶׁה לִקְנוֹתָהּ.

לְזֹאת מַה טּוֹב לָאָדָם אֲשֶׁר מִדּוֹתָיו יְשָׁרִים. לְהַעֲלוֹתָם בְּמַדְרֵגָה נִשְׂגָּבָה בִּבְחִינַת הַכְּבִישָׁה. לְהַרְגִּיל אֶת עַצְמוֹ לַהֲפֹךְ מִדּוֹתָיו בְּחָזְקָה. לְהָאִיר נֵר לְפָנָיו לִימֵי הָרָעָה עֵת הַנִּסָּיוֹן אֲשֶׁר יְרוֹפְפוּ חַס וְשָׁלוֹם עַמּוּדָיו הַטּוֹבִים. וּמַה כָּבֵד לְהָאָדָם לְהִשְׁתַּמֵּשׁ בְּמִדַּת הַגְּבוּרָה לִסְבֹּל עֹל וָצַעַר תְּמִידִי. לְזֹאת יְחַפֵּשׂ הָאָדָם עֵצָה וְתַחְבּוּלָה. אֵיךְ לְתַקֵּן מִדּוֹת וְכֹחוֹת נַפְשׁוֹ אִם מְעַט וְאִם הַרְבֵּה. אֲשֶׁר לְכָל הַפָּחוֹת הַשְׁחָתַת מִדּוֹתָיו מֵרָחוֹק יַעֲמֹדוּ. וְלֹא יִצְטָרֵךְ לְמִדַּת הַגְּבוּרָה כִּי אִם לְעִתִּים רְחוֹקוֹת בְּעֵת הַנִּסָּיוֹן לְפִי מַצָּבוֹ וְעִנְיָנוֹ וּתְכוּנַת נַפְשׁוֹ.

הוּא מַאֲמַר רַבּוֹתֵינוּ ז״ל בְּאָבוֹת (פֶּרֶק ד׳) וּבוֹרֵחַ מִן הָעֲבֵרָה וְכוּ׳. כִּי כָּל אָדָם וְאָדָם מִדּוֹתָיו מִשְׁתַּנּוֹת. וְכָל אֶחָד יִזָּהֵר מְאֹד בְּנַפְשׁוֹ לַחְתֹּר אַחַר אֵיזֶה מִדָּה הָעֲלוּלָה בְּיוֹתֵר לְקַלְקְלוֹ. לַהֲבִיאָהּ מְעַט בִּבְחִינַת תִּקּוּן עַד אֲשֶׁר תִּהְיֶה דַּרְכָּהּ רְחוֹקָה מִמֶּנּוּ. יְסוֹד בְּחִינַת הַתִּקּוּן הוּא בִּדְבָרִים

14. See Esther 4:14.

15. Conquering (repressing, *kevisha*) the urge means resisting one's inclinations. For example: Take the case of careful language. Conquering the evil urge would entail resisting the urge to speak derogatory words about another. (Note: Negative speech typically reflects the speaker's own feelings of inadequacy or being in a low state.) Perfecting the urge (sublimation, *tikkun*) means controlling and redirecting the inclination so that it does not manifest in the desire for evil. In the case of language, this might mean channeling the desire to say something derogatory into a desire to speak positively. In the past, there was a pleasure in belittling the other person. Now, one receives pleasure from building the other up. (Such speech typically reflects the speaker's attaining a state of self-acceptance.) However, R. Salanter warns that even after one reaches the states of sublimation, one must be careful to maintain

of patience, so that he does not get angry at all at anything done against his will or advantage. Still, in an important matter, which weighs upon him heavily as a pile of sand and pains him because it strikes deep, he is not assured that it will not undermine and destroy the good thing he built with so much toil. At such a time, he will need extra strength to conquer this intense desire that he is not accustomed to. (For the habit of "conquering" [repressing] this trait [of anger], which he acquired earlier, when he was at the stage of repression, has already been abandoned and uprooted from within him, for he has not used it for a long time – since he first attained the level of "perfecting" [sublimating]). Who knows if at such a time[14] he will attain the required degree of strength – especially since repression is hard to achieve without heavy conditioning?[15]

So it is good for a person of upright character traits to raise them to a high level from the perspective of repression – to habituate [i.e., condition] himself to reverse his traits forcefully, thereby to light a lamp before him for the "bad days," the time of temptation, when (God forbid) his good foundations will weaken. Nevertheless, since it is hard for a person to use the trait of strength [i.e., repression] and to bear its perpetual yoke and pain, one should seek counsel and strategy to perfect [i.e., sublimate] his character traits and psychological drives, more or less – so that, at least, the corruption of his character traits will be remote, and he will not need the trait of strength except very occasionally, at a time of temptation according to his emotional state, situation, and psychological constitution.[16]

This is the meaning of the statement of our Rabbis, of blessed memory, in Avot (4:2): "Flee from transgression." Each person has different character traits, and so each person should be very cautious and seek the character trait that is most likely to corrupt him and sublimate it so that the path [to corruption] is remote.

---

the ability to repress when necessary. In the example of language, despite having redirected the urge, there are always latent levels of inclination that can be aroused by a personal setback or new pressures in one's life. The evil urge then could come rushing back and must be conquered. At that point, one can only suppress the urge by an act of will.

16. A chart comparing R. Salanter's two methods of altering behavior – repression and sublimation – appears in the final footnote of this chapter.

שֶׁבֵּין אָדָם לַחֲבֵרוֹ אֲשֶׁר עֲלֵיהֶם אֵין יוֹם הַכִּפּוּרִים מְכַפֵּר (יוֹמָא פה:). וּכְמַאֲמַר הַכָּתוּב (שְׁמוּאֵל-ב׳ כ״ד) נִפְּלָה נָא בְּיַד ה׳ כִּי רַבִּים רַחֲמָיו וּבְיַד אָדָם אַל אֶפֹּלָה.

וְזֶה לְשׁוֹן הָרַמְבַּ״ם (בִּשְׁמוֹנָה פְּרָקָיו פֶּרֶק ו׳) אָמְרוּ הַפִּילוֹסוֹפִים שֶׁהַמּוֹשֵׁל בְּנַפְשׁוֹ. אַף עַל פִּי שֶׁעוֹשֶׂה הַמַּעֲשִׂים הַטּוֹבִים וְהַחֲשׁוּבִים. הוּא עוֹשֶׂה אוֹתָם וְהוּא מִתְאַוֶּה אֶל הַפְּעֻלּוֹת הָרָעוֹת וְנִכְסָף אֲלֵיהֶם. וְיִכְבֹּשׁ אֶת יִצְרוֹ כו׳. וְיַעַשׂ הַטּוֹבוֹת וְהוּא מִצְטַעֵר בַּעֲשִׂיָּתָם וְנִזּוֹק. אֲבָל הֶחָסִיד. הוּא נִמְשָׁךְ בִּפְעֻלָּתוֹ אַחַר מַה שֶׁיְּעִירוּהוּ תַּאֲוָתוֹ וּתְכוּנָתוֹ. וְיַעֲשֶׂה הַטּוֹבוֹת וְהוּא מִתְאַוֶּה וְנִכְסָף אֲלֵיהֶם. וּבְהַסְכָּמָה מִן הַפִּילוֹסוֹפִים. שֶׁהֶחָסִיד יוֹתֵר חָשׁוּב וְיוֹתֵר שָׁלֵם מִן הַמּוֹשֵׁל בְּנַפְשׁוֹ. אֲבָל אָמְרוּ שֶׁהַמּוֹשֵׁל בְּנַפְשׁוֹ כְּחָסִיד בְּעִנְיָנִים רַבִּים וְכוּ׳. וּכְבָר אָמַר שְׁלֹמֹה הַמֶּלֶךְ עָלָיו הַשָּׁלוֹם כַּיּוֹצֵא בָּזֶה (מִשְׁלֵי כ״א) נֶפֶשׁ רָשָׁע אִוְּתָה רָע. וְאָמַר בְּשִׂמְחַת הֶחָסִיד בְּמַעֲשֶׂה הַטּוֹב. וְהַצַּעַר מִי שֶׁאֵינוֹ צַדִּיק בַּעֲשִׂיָּתוֹ. זֶה הַמַּאֲמָר (שָׁם) שִׂמְחָה לַצַּדִּיק עֲשׂוֹת מִשְׁפָּט וּמְחִתָּה לְפֹעֲלֵי אָוֶן. זֶה הַנִּרְאֶה מִדִּבְרֵי הַנְּבִיאִים נָאוֹת לְמַה שֶׁזְּכָרוּהוּ הַפִּילוֹסוֹפִים. וְכַאֲשֶׁר חָקַרְנוּ דִּבְרֵי הַחֲכָמִים בְּזֶה הָעִנְיָן. נִמְצָא לָהֶם שֶׁהַמִּתְאַוֶּה לַעֲבֵרוֹת וְנִכְסָף אֲלֵיהֶם הוּא יוֹתֵר חָשׁוּב וְיוֹתֵר שָׁלֵם מֵאֲשֶׁר לֹא יִתְאַוֶּה אֲלֵיהֶם וְלֹא יִצְטַעֵר בְּהַנָּחָתָן וְכוּ׳. וְיוֹתֵר מִזֶּה שֶׁהֵם צִוּוּ לִהְיוֹת הָאָדָם מִתְאַוֶּה לַעֲבֵרוֹת. עַד שֶׁהִזְהִירוּ מִלּוֹמַר שֶׁאֲנִי

17. This is R. Salanter's personal midrash on the verse. Literally, the verse means that King David chooses to have a divine punishment inflicted on him and Israel (for the sin of carrying out an unauthorized census) rather than a human enemy be sent by God to punish them. He trusts that God's mercies will minimize the punishment. An enemy may inflict pain without limit. R. Salanter's midrash is: If the person sins, let it be a failure in the service of God – for God is merciful and quick to forgive. But do not sin against a fellow human being – for that person suffers more than God does from your behavior. That person also possesses less love and compassion than God – so he will be slower to forgive. Note that in the *Iggeret HaMussar*, R. Salanter complained that in Lithuania, pious Jews meticulously observed the commandments to serve God (for example, keeping Jewish dietary laws) but permitted themselves too often to violate the laws governing behavior toward other human beings.

The foundational principle of when to use sublimation is in interpersonal (*bein adam leḥavero*) matters – for which even Yom Kippur cannot atone (Yoma 85b). As the verse says (II Sam. 24:14): "May I fall into the hand of God, for His mercies are many, and not fall into the hand of man."[17]

Rambam wrote (*Shemona Perakim*, ch. 6):[18]

> Philosophers maintain that though the man of self-restraint performs moral and praiseworthy deeds, yet he does them desiring and craving all the while for immoral deeds, but, subduing his passions ... succeeds, though with constant vexation and irritation, in acting morally. The saintly man, however, is guided in his actions by that to which his inclination and disposition prompt him, in consequence of which he acts morally from innate longing and desire. Philosophers unanimously agree that the latter is superior to, and more perfect than, the one who has to curb his passions, although they add that it is possible for such a one to equal the saintly man in many regards....
>
> King Solomon, peace be upon him, entertained the same idea when he said (Prov. 21:10): "The soul of the wicked desires evil," and, in regard to the saintly man's rejoicing in doing good, and the discontent experienced by him, who is not innately righteous, when required to act justly, he says (Prov. 21:15): "It is bliss to the righteous to do justice, but torment to the evil-doer. Thus, what the prophets say [in Proverbs] is in agreement with what the philosophers mention.
>
> When, however, we consult the Rabbis on this subject, it would seem that they consider him who desires iniquity, and craves for it [but does not do it], more praiseworthy and perfect than the one who feels no torment at refraining from evil; and they even go so far as to maintain that the more praiseworthy and perfect a man is, the greater is his desire to commit iniquity, and the more irritation does he feel at having to desist from it.... Furthermore, they command that man should conquer his desires,

18. This translation follows the Gorfinkle translation, available on Sefaria: https://www.sefaria.org/Eight_Chapters.

בְּטִבְעִי לֹא אֶתְאַוֶּה לְזֹאת הָעֲבֵרָה וְאַף עַל פִּי שֶׁלֹּא אָסְרָה הַתּוֹרָה. וְהוּא אָמְרָם. רַבָּן שִׁמְעוֹן בֶּן גַּמְלִיאֵל אוֹמֵר לֹא יֹאמַר אָדָם אִי אֶפְשִׁי לֶאֱכֹל בָּשָׂר בְּחָלָב וְכוּ׳ אֶלָּא אֶפְשִׁי וּמָה אֶעֱשֶׂה אָבִי שֶׁבַּשָּׁמַיִם גָּזַר עָלַי. וּלְפִי הַמּוּבָן מִפְּשׁוּטֵי שְׁנֵי הַמַּאֲמָרִים (רְצוֹנוֹ לוֹמַר מַאֲמַר חֲכָמֵינוּ זַ״ל וּמַאֲמַר הַפִּילוֹסוֹפִים) בִּתְחִלַּת הַמַּחֲשָׁבָה הֵן סוֹתְרִין זֶה אֶת זֶה. וְאֵין הָעִנְיָן כֵּן. אֲבָל שְׁנֵיהֶם אֱמֶת וְאֵין מַחֲלֹקֶת בֵּינֵיהֶם כְּלָל. וְהוּא שֶׁהָרָעוֹת אֲשֶׁר הֵן אֵצֶל הַפִּילוֹסוֹפִים רָעוֹת. אֲשֶׁר אָמְרוּ שֶׁמִּי שֶׁלֹּא יִתְאַוֶּה אֲלֵיהֶן יוֹתֵר חָשׁוּב מִן הַמִּתְאַוֶּה אֲלֵיהֶן וְיִכְבֹּשׁ אֶת יִצְרוֹ מֵהֶן. הֵם הָעִנְיָנִים הַמְפֻרְסָמִים אֵצֶל כָּל בְּנֵי אָדָם שֶׁהֵם רָעוֹת. כִּשְׁפִיכַת דָּמִים וּגְנֵבָה וּגְזֵלָה וְאוֹנָאָה. וּלְהַזִּיק לְמִי שֶׁלֹּא הֵרַע לוֹ. וְלִגְמֹל רַע לַמֵּטִיב לוֹ. וּלְבַזּוֹת אָב וָאֵם. וְכַיּוֹצֵא בְּאֵלּוּ. וְהֵם הַמִּצְוֹת שֶׁאָמְרוּ עֲלֵיהֶם חֲכָמֵינוּ זַ״ל (יוֹמָא סז:) שֶׁאִלּוּ לֹא נִכְתְּבוּ רְאוּיִים הֵם לִיכָּתֵב. וְיִקְרְאוּ אוֹתָן כּוּ׳ מִצְוֹת הַשִּׂכְלִיּוֹת. וְאֵין סָפֵק אֲשֶׁר הַנֶּפֶשׁ אֲשֶׁר תִּשְׁתּוֹקֵק לְדָבָר מֵהֶם וְתִכְסֹף אֵלָיו. שֶׁהִיא חֲסֵרָה. וְשֶׁהַנֶּפֶשׁ הַחֲשׁוּבָה לֹא תִתְאַוֶּה לְאֶחָד מֵאֵלּוּ הָרָעוֹת כְּלָל. וְלֹא תִּצְטַעֵר בְּהִמָּנְעָהּ מֵהֶם. אֲבָל הַדְּבָרִים שֶׁאָמְרוּ עֲלֵיהֶם הַחֲכָמִים שֶׁהַכּוֹבֵשׁ אֶת יִצְרוֹ מֵהֶם הוּא יוֹתֵר חָשׁוּב וּגְמוּלוֹ יוֹתֵר גָּדוֹל. הֵם הַתּוֹרוֹת הַשִּׁמְעִיּוֹת. (רְצוֹנוֹ לוֹמַר הַמִּצְוֹת אֲשֶׁר שָׁמַעְנוּ עַל הַר סִינַי. וְלוּלֵא הַקַּבָּלָה אֵין הַשֵּׂכֶל מְחַיְּבָם). וְזֶה אֱמֶת. שֶׁאִלְמָלֵא הַתּוֹרָה לֹא הָיוּ רָעוֹת כְּלָל. וּמִפְּנֵי זֶה אָמְרוּ. שֶׁצָּרִיךְ הָאָדָם שֶׁיָּנִיחַ נַפְשׁוֹ אוֹהֶבֶת אוֹתָן. וְלֹא יִהְיֶה מוֹנֵעַ מֵהֶם אֶלָּא הַתּוֹרָה. וּבְחֹן חָכְמָתָם עֲלֵיהֶם הַשָּׁלוֹם וּבַמֶּה הִמְשִׁילוּ. שֶׁהֵם לֹא אָמְרוּ

19. Sifra, Parshat Kedoshim 10.

20. This is R. Salanter's parenthetical interjection.

21. This is R. Salanter's parenthetical interjection.

but they forbid one to say, "I, by my nature, do not desire to commit such and such a transgression, even though the Law does not forbid it." R. Simeon ben Gamaliel summed up this thought in the words, "Man should not say, 'I do not want to eat meat together with milk; I do not want to wear clothes made of a mixture of wool and linen; I do not want to enter into an incestuous marriage,' but he should say, 'I do indeed want to, yet I must not, for my father in Heaven has forbidden it.'"[19]

At first blush, by a superficial comparison of the sayings (of the Sages, of blessed memory, and of the philosophers),[20] one might be inclined to say that they contradict one another. Such, however, is not the case. Both are correct and, moreover, are not in disagreement in the least, as the evils which the philosophers term such and of which they say that he who has no longing for them is more to be praised than he who desires them but conquers his passion are things which all people commonly agree are evils, such as the shedding of blood, theft, robbery, fraud, injury to one who has done no harm, ingratitude, contempt for parents, and the like. These proscriptions are called commandments (mitzvot) about which the Rabbis said (Yoma 67b): "If they had not already been written in the Torah, it would be proper to add them." Some... called these rational laws. There is no doubt that a soul which has the desire for, and lusts after, the above-mentioned misdeeds, is imperfect, that a noble soul has absolutely no desire for any such crimes, and experiences no struggle in refraining from them.

When, however, the Rabbis maintain that he who overcomes his desire has more merit and a greater reward (than he who has no temptation), they say so only in reference to laws that are ceremonial prohibitions. (That is, the commandments which we heard at Mount Sinai, and which otherwise our reason would not require.)[21] This is quite true, since, were it not for the Torah, they would not at all be considered transgressions. Therefore, the Rabbis say that man should permit his soul to entertain the natural inclination for these things, but that the Torah alone should restrain him from them. Ponder over the wisdom of these

אַל יֹאמַר אָדָם אִי אֶפְשִׁי לַהֲרֹג נֶפֶשׁ. אִי אֶפְשִׁי לִגְנֹב. אִי אֶפְשִׁי לְכַזֵּב וְכוּ׳. אֲבָל הֵבִיאוּ דְּבָרִים שִׁמְעִיִּים כֻּלָּם. בָּשָׂר בְּחָלָב וּלְבִישַׁת שַׁעַטְנֵז וְכַיּוֹצֵא בָּהֶם וְכוּ׳. עַד כָּאן לְשׁוֹנוֹ.

וְאֵין דִּבְרֵי הָרַמְבַּ"ם סוֹתְרִים לְמַה שֶּׁכָּתַבְנוּ. שֶׁצָּרִיךְ הָאָדָם לְתַקֵּן כָּל כֹּחוֹת נַפְשׁוֹ. כִּי שְׁנֵי מִינֵי תִּקּוּן הֵם. הָאֶחָד שֶׁיִּהְיֶה הָאָדָם מְהַפֵּךְ כֹּחוֹת נַפְשׁוֹ וּמִדּוֹתָיו לְטוֹב. עַד אֲשֶׁר כֹּחַ הָרַע תֵּעָקֵר מִמֶּנּוּ וּבַל יֵרָאֶה וּבַל יִמָּצֵא בְּקִרְבּוֹ כְּלָל. וְלַבְּחִינָה הַלָּזוֹ לֹא יַסְפִּיק לְגֶבֶר לְתַקֵּן רְצוֹנוֹ בִּכְלָל. לִכְסֹף לַטּוֹב וְלִשְׂנֹא אֶת הָרַע. רַק צָרִיךְ הָאָדָם לְחַפֵּשׂ דַּרְכֵי הַתִּקּוּן לְכָל מִדָּה וּלְכָל כֹּחוֹת הַנֶּפֶשׁ בִּפְרָט. זֶהוּ בַּמִּצְוֹת הַשִּׂכְלִיּוֹת אֲשֶׁר בֵּין אָדָם לַחֲבֵרוֹ כְּדִבְרֵי הָרַמְבַּ"ם זַ"ל הַנִּזְכָּר לְעֵיל. הַשֵּׁנִי. הוּא תִּקּוּן רָצוֹן הַכְּלָלִי. לֶאֱהֹב לִשְׁמֹר מוֹצָא פִּי ה׳ יִתְבָּרַךְ בַּמִּצְוֹת הַשִּׁמְעִיּוֹת. וּלְחַפֵּשׂ לְהַקְטִין כֹּחַ הַתַּאֲוָה בְּכָל פְּרָט. עַד אֲשֶׁר כִּמְעַט גֶּדֶר הָאֶפְשִׁי לֶאֱכֹל בָּשָׂר בְּחָלָב. אוֹ הָאִי אֶפְשִׁי לֶאֱכֹל בָּשָׂר בְּחָלָב. לֹא יֶחֱלַק רַק בַּצּוּרִיִּי וְלֹא בַחָמְרִי. בַּשֵּׂכֶל וְלֹא בַחוּשׁ.

וְהַיּוֹתֵר כָּבֵד בִּבְחִינַת הַתִּקּוּן. הוּא בִּדְבַר הַמִּדּוֹת. כִּי זֶה כְּלָל גָּדוֹל בַּמִּדּוֹת. שֶׁרֹב מִדּוֹת הַטּוֹבוֹת. הֵמָּה רַק בַּמֶּה שֶּׁנּוֹגֵעַ לְהָאָדָם בְּעַצְמוֹ. אָכֵן בַּמֶּה שֶּׁנּוֹגֵעַ לַחֲבֵרוֹ. הַחוֹב לְהִשְׁתַּמֵּשׁ בְּכָל עֹז בְּהִפּוּכָהּ. כְּמוֹ לִבְרֹחַ מִן הַכָּבוֹד הִיא מִדָּה יְקָרָה. כְּמַאֲמָרָם זַ"ל (אָבוֹת פֶּרֶק ד׳) כִּי תַּאֲוַת הַכָּבוֹד תּוֹצִיא אֶת הָאָדָם מִן הָעוֹלָם. אָכֵן בַּמֶּה שֶּׁנּוֹגֵעַ לַחֲבֵרוֹ. אָמְרוּ רַבּוֹתֵינוּ זַ"ל (שָׁם) אֵיזֶהוּ מְכֻבָּד הַמְכַבֵּד אֶת הַבְּרִיּוֹת. הַפְּרִישׁוּת אֲשֶׁר הִיא מַעֲלָה נִשְׂגָּבָה לִבְנֵי עֲלִיָּה. הִיא רַק בִּבְחִינַת הָאָדָם לְעַצְמוֹ. אֲבָל בַּמֶּה שֶּׁנּוֹגֵעַ לְתוֹעֶלֶת וַהֲנָאַת חֲבֵרוֹ. הַחוֹב פְּרוּשָׁה לְהִשְׁתַּמֵּשׁ הֶפֶךְ הַפְּרִישׁוּת. לָצֵאת בַּשְּׁוָקִים וּבָרְחוֹבוֹת קִרְיָה. לְחַפֵּשׂ לְמַלְאוֹת טוֹבַת חֲבֵרוֹ. וּמִכָּל שֶׁכֵּן טוֹבַת רַבִּים. הוּא מַאֲמַר רַבּוֹתֵינוּ

22. Compare Pesaḥim 5b; 48a. Compare also Exodus 12:19 and 13:7.

> men of blessed memory manifest in the examples they adduce. They do not declare, "Man should not say, 'I have no desire to kill, to steal and to lie... !'" The instances they cite are all from the ceremonial law, such as partaking of meat and milk together, wearing clothes made of wool and linen, etc.

The words of Rambam do not contradict what we wrote, [namely] that a person must perfect [sublimate] all his psychological drives, for there are two kinds of sublimation. The first is that a person transforms his psychological drives and character traits for the good – until the evil urge is completely uprooted and is neither seen nor found[22] in him at all. To reach this level, it is not enough for a person to sublimate his will in general to long for good and to hate evil. Rather a person must seek out ways to sublimate each character trait and each of the psychological drives specifically. This approach applies to the rational, interpersonal mitzvot, in accordance with the aforementioned words of Rambam, of blessed memory.

The second type of perfection is the sublimation of one's will in general to love to observe the words of blessed God in ceremonial [i.e., non-rational] commandments. One should seek to reduce the power of desire in every detail – until, practically, the sense of "I want to eat meat with milk" and the sense of "I cannot eat meat with milk" are distinguishable only in the abstract, not on the material level – rationally, not instinctively.

The more difficult aspect of sublimation pertains to the character traits, for the general rule of character traits is that good character traits apply only as far as the person himself is concerned, but with regard to one's fellow, the duty is to use the opposite trait with all one's might. For example, fleeing from honor is a rare trait. As the [Sages,] of blessed memory, said (Avot 4:21), the lust for honor shortens a person's life. Yet when it comes to one's fellow, our Rabbis, of blessed memory, said (ibid. 1): "Who is honored? One who honors all human beings." Asceticism is a sublime virtue of the elite, but only with respect to the person himself. When it comes to the benefit and pleasure of his fellow, the duty to use the opposite of asceticism applies. One must go out into the markets and streets of the city for the benefit of his fellow and, all the more so, public benefit.

זַ"ל (מִדְרַשׁ רַבָּה דְּבָרִים פָּרָשָׁה י"א) מַהוּ אִישׁ הָאֱלֹהִים. אָמַר רַבִּי אָבִין מֶחֶצְיוֹ וּלְמַטָּה אִישׁ. מֶחֶצְיוֹ וּלְמַעְלָה אֱלֹהִים. כִּי מֹשֶׁה רַבֵּנוּ. אִם כִּי הָיָה אִישׁ אֱלֹהִים קָדוֹשׁ פָּרוּשׁ מִכָּל מַחֲמַדֵּי תֵּבֵל. בְּכָל זֹאת חֶצְיוֹ הָיָה בְּחִינַת אִישׁ. בַּמֶּה שֶׁנּוֹגֵעַ לְיִשְׂרָאֵל הַתְּלוּיִים עָלָיו. וְכֵן כַּיּוֹצֵא בְּרֹב הַמִּדּוֹת. וּבִפְרָט בַּעֲנָוָה הַגְּדוֹלָה מִכָּל הַמִּדּוֹת. הַחוֹב לְהִשְׁתַּמֵּשׁ בָּהּ עַד קָצֵה הָאַחֲרוֹן. כְּמַאֲמָרָם זַ"ל (סוֹטָה דַּף ה') אָמַר רַב אַחָא בַּר יַעֲקֹב. לֹא מִינָהּ וְלֹא מִקְצָתָהּ. וְכַאֲשֶׁר בֵּאֵר הָרַמְבַּ"ם זַ"ל הַמִּשְׁנָה (שָׁם) מְאֹד מְאֹד הֱוֵי שְׁפַל רוּחַ וְכוּ'. חָלִילָה חָלִילָה לְהִשְׁתַּמֵּשׁ בַּמִּדָּה הַלָּזוֹ עַל חֲבֵרוֹ. לְהַפְחִיתוֹ מִמַּעֲלָתוֹ חַס וְשָׁלוֹם.

הוּא מַאֲמַר הַתּוֹסֶפְתָּא (בְּרָכוֹת פֶּרֶק ד') אַף שָׁאוּל לֹא זָכָה לַמַּלְכוּת אֶלָּא מִפְּנֵי הָעֲנָוָה. שֶׁנֶּאֱמַר (שְׁמוּאֵל-א' ט', ה') פֶּן יֶחְדַּל אָבִי מִן הָאֲתֹנוֹת וְדָאַג לָנוּ. שָׁקַל עַבְדּוֹ בּוֹ. אֲבָל שְׁמוּאֵל אֵינוֹ כֵן אֶלָּא (שָׁם י', ב') נָטַשׁ אָבִיךָ אֶת דִּבְרֵי הָאֲתוֹנוֹת וְדָאַג לָכֶם לֵאמֹר מָה אֶעֱשֶׂה לִבְנִי. כִּי שָׁאוּל עַל עַצְמוֹ הִשְׁתַּמֵּשׁ בְּמִדַּת הָעֲנָוָה לְהַשְׁווֹת הָעֶבֶד לוֹ לְעַצְמוֹ. אֲבָל שְׁמוּאֵל שֶׁהָיָה אַחֵר. וְאֵין מָקוֹם לַעֲנָוָה כְּלָל. אֵיךְ יִשְׁקֹל הָעֶבֶד כְּשָׁאוּל וְלָזֹאת אָמַר כִּי יְסוֹד הַדְּאָגָה "מָה אֶעֱשֶׂה לִבְנִי". הַגָּדוֹל בְּעֶרְכּוֹ הַרְבֵּה יוֹתֵר מֵהָעֶבֶד.

לָזֹאת צָרִיךְ הָאָדָם לַעֲמֹל לַעֲשׂוֹת קִנְיָה בְּנַפְשׁוֹ בְּכָל דָּבָר וְהִפּוּכוֹ, וּלְהַרְגִּיל אֶת נַפְשׁוֹ, אֲשֶׁר בְּעֵת כִּי יִדְרֹשׁ דָּבָר הַנּוֹגֵעַ לְעַצְמוֹ, יִתְעוֹרְרוּ בְּקִרְבּוֹ מִדּוֹת הַנִּדְרָשׁוֹת, וְהַהֵפֶךְ יִהְיֶה שָׁכוּחַ מִנַּפְשׁוֹ, אֲבָל בְּעֵת אֲשֶׁר יִדְרֹשׁ לְטוֹבַת חֲבֵרוֹ, תִּתְעוֹרֵר בְּקִרְבּוֹ הַמִּדָּה בְּהִפּוּכָהּ. וִיסוֹד הַמִּדָּה תִּשָּׁכַח לִשְׁעָתָהּ מִנַּפְשׁוֹ.

---

23. Rambam explains that humility is the one human virtue where we do not seek the golden mean – in the case of humility, between pride and lowliness of spirit. Rather, pursue the extreme of lowliness in spirit (Laws of Moral Dispositions 2:3).
24. Emphasis added.
25. R. Salanter is developing a model of a Mussar disciple as a selfless spiritual hero. When it comes to himself, he is self-abnegating, modest to a fault. But with other people, he honors them by feeding their need for recognition and standing. Though not explicit, the underlying assumption is that the Mussar disciple is reaching out to and dealing with laypeople in this fashion. In the case of dealing with another Mussar

This is [the meaning of] the saying of the Rabbis, of blessed memory (Deuteronomy Rabba 11): "What is [the meaning of the verse that Moses was] 'the man of God'? R. Avin said: His lower half was human; his upper half was divine." For our teacher Moses was a godly man – saintly, removed from the pleasures of the world – yet half of him was human when it came to Israel, who depended on him.

So it is with most character traits, and especially humility, the greatest of all the character traits. The duty is to use it in the extreme, as they, of blessed memory, said (Sota 5a): "R. Aḥa bar Yaakov said: '[Have nothing to do] with [pride], even a bit of it.'" And as Rambam, of blessed memory, explained the mishna [Avot 4:4]: "Be very, very lowly in spirit...."[23] However, you dare not, you dare not, use this trait on a friend, to reduce his importance, God forbid.

This is [the meaning of] the saying of the *Tosefta* (Berakhot, ch. 4): "Saul merited the kingship only because of his humility, as it is said (I Sam. 9:5): 'Lest my father stop worrying about the donkeys and worry about us.' He rated his servant equal to himself. But Samuel did not speak accordingly. Rather [he said] (ibid. 10:2), 'Your father has left the matter of the donkeys and is worrying about [the two of] you, saying: What shall I do about my son?'" Saul, with regard to himself, exercised the trait of humility and compared the servant to himself. However, Samuel was another person, so there was no place for humility; how could he rate the servant as he did Saul? Therefore, he said that the basis of the anxiety was "What shall I do about my son?" – for Saul was much greater in importance than his servant was.

To this end, a person must endeavor to incorporate everything *and its opposite* within his psyche.[24] He should condition his soul so that when he seeks something on his own behalf, the necessary character traits are evoked, and their opposite is forgotten. But when he seeks the benefit of the other, this opposite trait should be aroused in him, and the root trait momentarily forgotten from his soul.[25]

---

disciple, would he seek to have them renounce their ego and be totally selfless, or would they be entitled to recognition and ego-stroking (just as another lay person would)?

Disciples in later generations grappled with this question and took different

אַל יִפֹּל לֵב הָאָדָם וְאַל יִשְׁתּוֹמֵם עַל הַמַּרְאֶה הַלָּזֶה, הֲלֹא אֲנַחְנוּ רוֹאִים תָּמִיד בִּתְכוּנַת נֶפֶשׁ הָאָדָם דָּבָר וְהִפּוּכוֹ, וְהָאָדָם מִשְׁתַּמֵּשׁ בָּהֶם בְּטִבְעוֹ (בְּאֵין מוֹשֵׁךְ וּמְנַהֵל) כָּל דָּבָר בְּעִנְיָנוֹ וּבְשַׁעְתּוֹ, כְּמוֹ הַזִּכָּרוֹן וְהַשִּׁכְחָה וְכַיּוֹצֵא בָּהֶם. כֵּן גַּם בְּכֹחַ הָאָדָם לְהַרְחִיב כֹּחוֹת מִדּוֹת נַפְשׁוֹ. וּלְהִשְׁתַּמֵּשׁ בָּהֶם בְּטִבְעוֹ דָּבָר וְהִפּוּכוֹ, הוּא מַאֲמַר רַבּוֹתֵינוּ זַ"ל (מִדְרַשׁ רַבָּה בְּרֵאשִׁית פָּרָשָׁה י"ד) אִם אֲנִי בּוֹרְאוֹ מִן הָעֶלְיוֹנִים כּוּ' מִן הַתַּחְתּוֹנִים כּוּ' אֶלָּא הֲרֵינִי בּוֹרְאוֹ מֵאֵלּוּ וּמֵאֵלּוּ כִּי הָאָדָם נִבְרָא בַּתְּכוּנָה הַלָּזוֹ, שֶׁיִּהְיֶה בְּכֹחוֹ לְתַקֵּן כֹּחוֹת נַפְשׁוֹ, לִהְיוֹת בַּמֶּה שֶׁנּוֹגֵעַ לְעַצְמוֹ, מְכֻתָּר בְּכָל הַמִּדּוֹת וְהַמַּעֲלוֹת דּוֹמֶה לָעֶלְיוֹנִים, פָּרוּשׁ מִכָּל מַחֲמַדֵּי הַתֵּבֵל, וּבַמֶּה שֶׁנּוֹגֵעַ לַאֲחֵרִים לִהְיוֹת דּוֹמֶה לַתַּחְתּוֹנִים, אִישׁ מַרְגִּישׁ וְיוֹדֵעַ בְּכָל מַחֲמַדֵּי הַתֵּבֵל, לְחַזֵּק יְדֵי רַבִּים וְלִהְיוֹת דַּעְתּוֹ מְעֹרֶבֶת עִמָּהֶם, כְּמַאֲמַר רַבּוֹתֵינוּ זַ"ל (כְּתֻבּוֹת י"ז) לְעוֹלָם תְּהֵא דַּעְתּוֹ שֶׁל אָדָם מְעֹרֶבֶת עִם הַבְּרִיּוֹת.

וּבִכְלָל לְהָאָדָם בִּימֵי עֲלוּמָיו, בְּטֶרֶם נִסָּה לִסְבֹּל עֹל, כָּבֵד לְפָנָיו בְּחִינַת כְּבִישַׁת הַמִּדּוֹת, וּלְעֻמַּת זֶה נָקֵל לְפָנָיו לִמּוּד תִּקּוּן הַמִּדּוֹת, כְּמַאֲמָרָם (אָבוֹת פֶּרֶק ד') הַלּוֹמֵד יֶלֶד לְמָה הוּא דּוֹמֶה לִדְיוֹ כְּתוּבָה עַל נְיָר חָדָשׁ, וּבִימֵי הָעֲמִידָה וְהַזִּקְנָה, אֲשֶׁר כָּבֵד לְהָאָדָם לִמּוּד תִּקּוּן הַמִּדּוֹת, כְּמַאֲמָרָם (שָׁם) וְהַלּוֹמֵד זָקֵן לְמָה הוּא דּוֹמֶה לִדְיוֹ כְּתוּבָה עַל נְיָר מָחוּק, וּבְיוֹתֵר לִבּוֹ בַּל עִמּוֹ מִטִּרְדוֹת הַזְּמַן, אָכֵן הַכְּבִישָׁה לֹא תִּהְיֶה עָלָיו לְמַעֲמָסָה כָּל כָּךְ, בִּהְיוֹתוֹ מֻרְגָּל לִסְבֹּל עֹל לְבַקָּשַׁת טַרְפּוֹ וְהִצְטָרְכִיּוֹתָיו וּמַאֲוַיָּו.

אִי לָזֹאת עֲבוֹדָתוֹ יִתְבָּרַךְ שְׁמוֹ בִּימֵי הַבַּחֲרוּת, בִּבְחִינַת תִּקּוּן

---

paths. Accordingly, some demanded extraordinary selflessness only from themselves as Mussar disciples, while others sought to move both other Mussar disciples and even lay people to extraordinary spiritual standards.

26. Note that in R. Salanter's typology, a typology which runs through much of classical Mussar literature, the heavenly aspect, i.e., the spiritual aspect, of the human renounces the pleasures of this world, including ego satisfaction. The earthly, physical side of humans wants and feels all the delights of the physical world, including ego satisfaction. The Mussarist raises himself to the spiritual level, including renouncing ego satisfaction, but honors and offers these delights to the average person, who

One should not be crestfallen or astonished at this prospect; after all, we constantly see the phenomenon of a trait and its opposite within the human soul, and a person uses them naturally (without being led or guided), each one in its appropriate situation and time – such as memory and forgetfulness and the like. Furthermore, human beings have the capacity to expand the power of their psychological drives and naturally use them for a matter and its opposite. This is [the meaning of] the saying of our Rabbis, of blessed memory (Genesis Rabba 14): "If I create [man] from the heavenly creatures… from the earthly creatures… so I will create him from both." The human being was created with this feature: that he has the power to sublimate his psychological drives, to be, with respect to himself, crowned with all the traits and virtues, like the heavenly creatures, removed from all the delights of the world, but with respect to others, to be like the earthly creatures, a person who senses and knows all the delights of the world,[26] able to give strength to the masses and to empathize with them. As the Rabbis, may they be blessed, said (Ketubbot 17a): "One's mind should always be in sync with mankind's."

In general, when a person is young, before he has had the trial of bearing the yoke, it is very hard for him to repress character traits, but it is easier for him to learn to sublimate his character traits. As they say (Avot 4:20): "He who learns when he is young, to what is it likened? To ink written on new paper." The days of middle and old age, when it is hard for a person to learn sublimation, accords with their saying (ibid.): "And he who learns when he is old, to what is it likened? To ink written on erased [blotted] paper." Moreover, his heart is not in it due to preoccupation with the burdens of life. However, repression is not such a burden for him, since he is conditioned[27] to bear a yoke to seek his food and needs and desires.

Therefore, his service to God, blessed be His name, in the younger years should be in the mode of sublimation of the character traits to

---

enjoys worldly delights. This is in accordance with the Torah's command to treat others with respect.

27. In R. Salanter's use, the term "*murgal*" refers to an intensive conditioning and internalization, to the point where the conditioned emotion or behavior becomes second nature.

הַמִּדּוֹת לַעֲבֹד בְּחֵפֶץ וְשִׂמְחָה, וּבִימֵי הַזִּקְנָה בִּבְחִינַת כְּבִישַׁת הַמִּדּוֹת בְּלִי חֵפֶץ וְרָצוֹן, וְכַאֲשֶׁר יְרַגֵּל הָאָדָם בִּימֵי עֲלוּמָיו לְתַקֵּן מִדּוֹתָיו, לַעֲזֹר וּלְהוֹעִיל לוֹ לִימֵי הַזִּקְנָה (אֲשֶׁר סִבּוֹת מוֹצְאוֹת לְמַרְבֶּה לְחַדֵּשׁ רַע מִדּוֹתָיו כַּנִּזְכָּר לְעֵיל), לְפַנּוֹת לְפָנָיו הַדֶּרֶךְ לִכְבִישַׁת הַמִּדּוֹת, הוּא מַאֲמַר הַכָּתוּב (מִשְׁלֵי כ"ב) חֲנֹךְ לַנַּעַר עַל פִּי דַרְכּוֹ, (הַמְּכַשֵּׁר לְפָנָיו, לְהָסִיר מִמֶּנּוּ אִוַּלְתּוֹ, כְּמַאֲמַר הַכָּתוּב אִוֶּלֶת קְשׁוּרָה וְכוּ', לְמַעַן לֹא תִּהְיֶה הָאִוֶּלֶת לְמָסָךְ מַבְדִּיל, וְלַהֲבִיאוֹ לִבְחִינַת תִּקּוּן הַמִּדּוֹת, וּבְזֹאת) גַּם כִּי יַזְקִין (הֲגַם שֶׁלֹּא תִּהְיֶה אֶצְלוֹ בְּתוֹרַת קְנִיָּה כְּמוֹ שֶׁהָיְתָה בְּעֵת חִנּוּכוֹ, אָכֵן לְכָל הַפָּחוֹת) לֹא יָסוּר מִמֶּנָּה. וּבְקֹהֶלֶת (י"ב) וּזְכֹר אֶת בּוֹרְאֶיךָ בִּימֵי בְּחוּרֹתֶיךָ עַד אֲשֶׁר לֹא יָבֹאוּ יְמֵי הָרָעָה, וְדָרְשׁוּ רַבּוֹתֵינוּ זַ"ל (שַׁבָּת קנא:) אֵלּוּ יְמֵי הַזִּקְנָה וְהִגִּיעוּ שָׁנִים אֲשֶׁר תֹּאמַר אֵין לִי בָּהֶם חֵפֶץ.

אוּלַי נוּכַל לְהַעֲמִיס הַדָּבָר בְּדִבְרֵי חֲכָמֵינוּ זַ"ל (שַׁבָּת סג:) אָמַר רַב הוּנָא מַאי דִּכְתִיב (קֹהֶלֶת י"א) שְׂמַח בָּחוּר בְּיַלְדוּתֶיךָ וִיטִיבְךָ לִבְּךָ בִּימֵי בְחוּרוֹתֶיךָ וְהַלֵּךְ בְּדַרְכֵי לִבְּךָ וּבְמַרְאֵי עֵינֶיךָ וְדָע כִּי עַל כָּל אֵלֶּה יְבִיאֲךָ הָאֱלֹהִים בַּמִּשְׁפָּט, עַד כָּאן (עַד וְדָע כִּי עַל כָּל אֵלֶּה וְגוֹ') דִּבְרֵי יֵצֶר הָרַע, מִכָּאן וְאֵילָךְ דִּבְרֵי יֵצֶר טוֹב, כִּי רַבּוֹתֵינוּ זַ"ל אָמְרוּ (בְּרָכוֹת כ"ד) בְּכָל לְבָבְךָ בִּשְׁנֵי יְצָרֶיךָ בְּיֵצֶר טוֹב וּבְיֵצֶר רָע.

וְיֵשׁ לְבָאֵר הַדָּבָר, כִּי הַמְחַבְּרִים יְכַנּוּ אֶת הַשֵּׂכֶל בְּשֵׁם יֵצֶר טוֹב, וְיֶתֶר כֹּחוֹת נַפְשׁוֹת הָאָדָם בְּשֵׁם יֵצֶר הָרַע (עַיֵּן חוֹבַת הַלְּבָבוֹת שַׁעַר עֲבוֹדַת אֱלֹהִים בִּשְׁאֵלוֹת וּתְשׁוּבוֹת הַשֵּׂכֶל עִם הַנֶּפֶשׁ), בֵּאוּר הַדָּבָר, כִּי הַשֵּׂכֶל לְכָל תַּכְלִית הוּא חוֹקֵר, לֹא יָשִׂים עַיִן בִּינָתוֹ בְּקָרוֹב אֶל מַרְאֵה הַדָּבָר כִּי תַאֲוָה הוּא לָעֵינַיִם, וְלֹא אֶל הֶרְגֵּשׁוֹ כִּי מָתוֹק הוּא

28. Deuteronomy 6:2.

29. Another advantage of the method of sublimation in youth is that one is able to serve God with both urges. The evil urge is being channeled constructively rather than repressed or crushed. Then, the person is serving God with all their desires, both the naturally good ones and the redirected dangerous ones.

30. Baḥya ibn Pakuda, *Duties of the Heart,* a classic of medieval Mussar literature.

31. Compare Genesis 3:6.

serve willingly and joyfully, and in old age, the mode should be repression of character traits, without having to fight as much desire or will. If one is conditioned in his youth to sublimate his character traits, this will be helpful and useful for his old age (as there are many factors that can rekindle the evil of his character traits, as mentioned above), to clear the way to the path of repression. This is the meaning of the verse in Scripture (Prov. 22:6): "Initiate a young man upon his path (the path that is appropriate for him to remove his folly – as Scripture states, 'Folly is settled [in the heart of a youth]…' (Prov. 22:15) – so that the folly is not a screen that impedes him, thus bringing him to the mode of sublimation); thus, even when he is old (although he will not truly control [the urge] as when he was being initiated, at the very least) he will not stray from it." And in Ecclesiastes (12:1): "Remember your Creator in your youth before the bad days come." And our Rabbis, of blessed memory, deduced (Shabbat 151b): "These ['bad days'] are the days of old age, when the years which you say, 'I have no desire for them,' will come."

Perhaps we can read this idea into the words of our Sages, of blessed memory (Shabbat 63b):

> R. Huna said: Why is it written (Eccl. 11:9), "Rejoice, young man, in your childhood, and let your heart be happy in the days of your youth, and follow the ways of your heart and your eyes' delight. But know that on all this, God will bring you to judgment'? Up to this point (up to 'But know that on all this…'), these are the words of the evil urge. The rest of the sentence is the words of the good urge."

As our Rabbis, of blessed memory, said (Berakhot 54a): "'[Serve God] with all your heart'[28] – with both your urges, the good urge and the evil urge."[29]

This must be explained. The writers call reason the "good urge" ("*yetzer tov*") and the other psychological drives are called the "evil urge" ("*yetzer hara*"). (See *Ḥovot HaLevavot*,[30] Gate of the Service of God: ch. 5, on the dialogue of reason and the soul.) This means that reason seeks the ultimate purpose of everything. It does not focus its understanding on the short term, on the appearance of that which is attractive,[31] nor

לַחֵךְ, רַק מֵרָחוֹק הוּא צוֹפֶה אֶל תַּכְלִיתוֹ, אִם יָשָׁר הוּא אָז מֵרֵאשִׁיתוֹ יִשְׁפֹּט הַשֵּׂכֶל עָלָיו לְהַחֲזִיק בּוֹ, וְכֹחוֹת נֶפֶשׁ הָאָדָם, זֶה דַּרְכָּם כֶּסֶל לָמוֹ לַחֲזוֹת מִקָּרוֹב, וְאֵת אֲשֶׁר יִנְעַם לְהַחוּשִׁים יַקְרִיבוּ אֶל נַפְשָׁם, אַף כִּי מָרָה תִּהְיֶה בָּאַחֲרוֹנָה, וְכַאֲשֶׁר כָּל מַעֲשֵׂה הָאָדָם יָבִיא הָאֱלֹהִים בַּמִּשְׁפָּט, אִם טוֹב וְאִם רָע, עַל כֵּן שׁוֹפֵט שֵׂכֶל הַיָּשָׁר לִשְׁמֹר כָּל מוֹצָא פִּי ה׳ זֶהוּ יֵצֶר טוֹב, אָכֵן כֹּחוֹת נֶפֶשׁ הָאָדָם, יִמְשְׁכוּ בְּרִשְׁתָּם אֶת הֶעָרֵב לִשְׁעָתוֹ, גַּם לְהַמְרוֹת נֶגֶד ה׳, זֶהוּ יֵצֶר הָרַע, וּכְשֶׁהָאָדָם בְּמַצַּב כְּבִישַׁת הַמִּדּוֹת וְתַאֲוֹת כֹּחוֹת נַפְשׁוֹ עַל יְדֵי הַשֵּׂכֶל הַמַּכְבִּישָׁם, נִקְרָא עוֹבֵד ה׳ בְּיֵצֶר טוֹב הוּא הַשֵּׂכֶל. וּכְשֶׁהוּא בְּמַצַּב תִּקּוּן הַמִּדּוֹת וְתַאֲוֹת כֹּחוֹת נַפְשׁוֹ, עַד אֲשֶׁר לֹא יַחְפְּצוּ רַק אֶת אֲשֶׁר ה׳ דּוֹרֵשׁ מֵאִתָּם, נִקְרָא עוֹבֵד ה׳ בְּיֵצֶר הָרַע, הֵם כֹּחוֹת הַנַּפְשִׁיּוֹת אֲשֶׁר עַצְמוּתָם לְרַע, וְהָאָדָם תִּקְּנָם לְמַתֵּק מְרִירוּתָם לְהָפְכָם לְטוֹב, זֶהוּ בִּשְׁנֵי יְצָרֶיךָ בְּיֵצֶר טוֹב וּבְיֵצֶר רָע, בִּכְבִישַׁת הַמִּדּוֹת וּבְתִקּוּן הַמִּדּוֹת (כַּנִּזְכָּר לְעֵיל).

וְהָאָדָם בְּבַחֲרוּתוֹ הַיְסוֹד לְחַפֵּשׂ בְּחִינַת תִּקּוּן הַמִּדּוֹת, עַד שֶׁיִּהְיוּ כֹּחוֹת נַפְשׁוֹ נִמְשָׁכִים רַק אֶל הַצֶּדֶק וְהַיֹּשֶׁר, וְאָז הוּא בְּשִׂמְחָה, כְּמַאֲמַר הַכָּתוּב (קֹהֶלֶת י״א) שְׂמַח בָּחוּר בְּיַלְדוּתֶיךָ וְגוֹ׳ וְהַלֵּךְ בְּדַרְכֵי לִבְּךָ וּבְמַרְאֵי עֵינֶיךָ, זֶהוּ לְהִשְׁתַּמֵּשׁ בַּכֹּחוֹת הַנַּפְשִׁיּוֹת אֲשֶׁר דַּרְכָּם לַחֲזוֹת בְּקָרוֹב, וְהוּא מַאֲמָרָם זַ״ל, עַד כָּאן דִּבְרֵי יֵצֶר הָרַע, הַיְנוּ עִנְיַן מַצַּב הָאָדָם בְּעֵת בַּחֲרוּתוֹ, לִרְאוֹת שֶׁיִּהְיוּ מִדּוֹתָיו מְתֻקָּנוֹת וּפְעֻלּוֹתָיו עַל פִּי כֹּחוֹת נַפְשׁוֹ הַמְכֻנִּים בְּשֵׁם יֵצֶר הָרַע, מִכָּאן וָאֵילָךְ יְמֵי הָעֲמִידָה, אֲשֶׁר אָז הַיְסוֹד לַהֲלֹךְ לְרוּחַ הַשֵּׂכֶל הַצּוֹפֶה לְמֵרָחוֹק, וְלִכְבֹּשׁ כֹּחוֹת נַפְשׁוֹ, וְלֵידַע כִּי עַל כָּל אֵלֶּה יְבִיאֲנוּ הָאֱלֹהִים בַּמִּשְׁפָּט, הֵמָּה דִּבְרֵי יֵצֶר טוֹב בְּחִינַת הַשֵּׂכֶל.

אָכֵן בְּנֵי עֲלִיָּה, הֵמָּה אֲשֶׁר גַּם בִּימֵי הָעֲמִידָה וְהַזִּקְנָה רַב חֵילָם

32. Compare Song of Songs 2:3.
33. Compare Psalms 49:14.
34. See Ecclesiastes 11:9.
35. I.e., undistorted.
36. Compare Deuteronomy 8:3.
37. Compare Micah 6:8.

on the sense that something is sweet to the palate.[32] Rather, it looks into the distance, to the ultimate goal. If it is a just outcome, then reason will judge it so from the beginning and uphold it. Yet human emotions – this is their foolish way[33] – see the near term; whatever pleases the senses they bring closer to themselves, even when it will be bitter at the end, when all the human's actions, whether good or evil, will be brought to judgment by God.[34] This is why straight[35] reason decides to observe all of God's decrees[36] and is the *yetzer tov,* while the emotions draw into their net what is immediately pleasant, even when it goes against God. This is the *yetzer hara.*

When a person is in the mode of repressing his character traits and psychological drives, repressed by his reason, he is called one who serves God with his *yetzer tov,* that is, his reason. And when he sublimates his character traits and psychological drives, to the point that they only desire what God asks of them,[37] he is called one who serves God with his *yetzer hara,* that is, the psychological drives whose essence is disposed toward evil, which the person sublimated, sweetening their bitterness and changing them to good. This is "with both your urges, the good urge and the evil urge" – through repression and sublimation (as mentioned).

In his youth, a person's primary efforts should be in the mode of sublimation, to the point where his psychological drives are drawn only to righteousness and uprightness; then he will be joyful, as Scripture says (Eccl. 11:9): "Rejoice, young man, in your childhood… and follow the ways of your heart and your eyes' delight." This means using the psychological drives, which are predisposed to look at the short term. This is what they, of blessed memory, said: "Up to this point, these are the words of the evil urge." That is, a person's concern in his youthful state should be to see to it that his traits are sublimated and his actions in accordance with the psychological drives, called the evil urge. From that point forward is the age of adulthood, when the primary concern is to follow the spirit of reason, which sees the long term, to repress his psychological drives, and to know that God will bring him to judgment for all of this. These are the words of the good urge, the rational mode.

Therefore, those who continue aspiring – those who, even into adulthood and old age, have the vigor to sublimate character traits and

לְתַקֵּן מִדּוֹתֵיהֶם וּתְכוּנַת נַפְשׁוֹתָם, עַד אֲשֶׁר תֵּקַל לָהֶם גַּם עֹל הַזְּמַנִּי (אֲשֶׁר עַל פִּי רֹב גֹּדֶל הַכְּבֵדוּת מֵחֶסְרוֹן תִּקּוּן הַמִּדּוֹת וּתְכוּנַת הַנֶּפֶשׁ) לְחַיֵּי הַגּוּף וְחַיֵּי הַנֶּפֶשׁ, וְאָז אִם לִפְעָמִים לְעִתִּים רְחוֹקוֹת יָבוֹאוּ לְהֶכְרֵחַ בְּחִינַת כְּבִישַׁת הַיֵּצֶר יִכְבַּד הַדָּבָר לִפְנֵיהֶם, יַעַן חָלְפוּ עִדָּן עִדָּנִים אֲשֶׁר לֹא הִשְׁתַּמְּשׁוּ בָּהּ (כַּנִּזְכָּר לְעֵיל).

וּבָזֶה יְבֹאַר מַאֲמַר חֲזַ"ל (מִדְרָשׁ רַבָּה בְּרֵאשִׁית פָּרָשָׁה נ"ט) וַה׳ בֵּרַךְ אֶת אַבְרָהָם בַּכֹּל וְכוּ׳ בַּכֹּל שֶׁהִשְׁלִיטוֹ בְּיִצְרוֹ וְכוּ׳, וַיֹּאמֶר אַבְרָהָם אֶל עַבְדּוֹ וְכוּ׳ הַמֹּשֵׁל בְּכָל אֲשֶׁר לוֹ, שֶׁהָיָה שַׁלִּיט בְּיִצְרוֹ כְּמוֹתוֹ, הַדָּבָר מַפְלִיא לֵאמֹר שֶׁהָיְתָה לֶאֱלִיעֶזֶר הַמַּדְרֵגָה אֲשֶׁר בָּאָה לְאַבְרָהָם בִּבְחִינַת בְּרָכָה, וּלְפִי הַנִּזְכָּר לְעֵיל יֵשׁ לְפָרֵשׁ שֶׁמַּדְרֵגַת אֱלִיעֶזֶר הָיְתָה בְּחִינַת גִּבּוֹר כּוֹבֵשׁ אֶת יִצְרוֹ, כִּי אָמַר שָׁם בַּמִּדְרָשׁ לְהַלָּן, וַיֹּאמֶר אֵלָיו הָעֶבֶד, הָדָא הוּא דִכְתִיב (הוֹשֵׁעַ י"ב) כְּנַעַן בְּיָדוֹ מֹאזְנֵי מִרְמָה לַעֲשֹׁק אָהֵב, כְּנַעַן זֶה אֱלִיעֶזֶר, בְּיָדוֹ מֹאזְנֵי מִרְמָה שֶׁהָיָה יוֹשֵׁב וּמַשְׁקִיל אֶת בִּתּוֹ רְאוּיָה הִיא אוֹ אֵינָהּ רְאוּיָה, לַעֲשֹׁק אָהֵב לַעֲשֹׁק אֲהוּבוֹ שֶׁל עוֹלָם זֶה יִצְחָק, אָמַר אוּלַי לֹא תֹאבֶה הַנַּעֲרָה וְכוּ׳ וְאֶתֵּן לוֹ אֶת בִּתִּי כוּ׳, כִּי מִי שֶׁזָּכָה לְמַעֲלַת תִּקּוּן הַיֵּצֶר, אֵין בְּיָדוֹ כְּלָל עִנְיְנֵי הַיֵּצֶר וְהַשְׁחָתַת הַמִּדּוֹת וְאֵינוֹ אוֹהֲבָם. אָכֵן מִי שֶׁלֹּא בָּא רַק לִבְחִינַת כְּבִישַׁת הַיֵּצֶר, תַּאֲוַת יִצְרוֹ בְּיָדוֹ הִיא וְאוֹהֲבָהּ, אֶלָּא שֶׁכּוֹבְשָׁהּ.

גַּם מִי שֶׁלֹּא בָּא לִבְחִינַת תִּקּוּן הַמִּדּוֹת, הֲגַם שֶׁיְּפַלֵּס דַּרְכּוֹ כְּמַאֲמַר הַכָּתוּב (מִשְׁלֵי ד׳) פַּלֵּס מַעְגַּל רַגְלֶךָ וְכָל דְּרָכֶיךָ יִכֹּנוּ, בְּכָל זֹאת הַטָּעוּת כָּרוּךְ בַּעֲקֵבָיו לִמְאֹד, כִּי תַּאֲוַת כֹּחוֹת הַנַּפְשִׁיּוֹת מַטִּילוֹת אֶרֶס בְּכֹחַ הַשֵּׂכֶל לְעַוֵּר עֵינֵי פִקְחִים.

זֶהוּ מַאֲמַר הַמִּדְרָשׁ, בְּיָדוֹ מֹאזְנֵי מִרְמָה, שֶׁהָיָה יוֹשֵׁב וּמַשְׁקִיל אֶת בִּתּוֹ רְאוּיָה הִיא אוֹ אֵינָהּ רְאוּיָה, כִּי בְּוַדַּאי אֱלִיעֶזֶר שֶׁהָיָה שַׁלִּיט בְּיִצְרוֹ, לֹא יָשִׂים פָּנָיו לְדַבֵּר דִּבּוּר קַל טֶרֶם יִתְיַשֵּׁב וְיִשְׁקֹל בְּדַעְתּוֹ אִם

38. Above, R. Salanter wrote that a key difference between the *yetzer tov* and *yetzer hara*, or between reason and impulse, is that the former is able to set aside short-term desires in favor of long-term objectives, and the latter focuses on the short term. The "burden of temporality" ("*ol hazemani*") thus refers to the effects of those unsublimated impulses that direct attention to short-term desires.

psychological dispositions to the point where the burden of temporality (and usually the heaviness of this burden derives from failure to sublimate character traits and psychological dispositions)[38] upon physical and psychological life is lightened for them – when they occasionally, if infrequently, have to resort to the mode of repression, it will be hard for them, for it will have been a long time since they used this mode (as said above).

With this we can explain the adage of our Sages, of blessed memory (Genesis Rabba 59): "'God blessed Abraham with everything….' (Gen. 24:1) – 'Everything' means He gave him power over his urge…. 'And Abraham said to his servant… who ruled over all that he had' (ibid. 2) [means] 'who ruled his urge as Abraham did.'" It is astonishing to think that Eliezer was at the level that Abraham had achieved only through God's blessing! However, according to what was said above, we can say that Eliezer's level was in the mode of a mighty person who conquers his urge – as the Midrash later states: "'And the servant said to him' (Gen. 24:5) – this refers to the verse (Hos. 12:8): 'Canaan has deceitful scales in his hand to oppress the beloved one.' Canaan – this refers to Eliezer; 'deceitful scales in his hand' means he sat and weighed whether his own daughter is worthy of Isaac or not; 'to oppress the beloved one' means to oppress Isaac, the beloved of the world. He said: 'Perhaps the young woman will not want [to follow me to this land]' (Gen. 24:5)… and I will give him my daughter [instead]…." One who has managed to attain the virtue of sublimation is not tempted by the evil urge or corruption of character traits; he has no affinity for them. But one who has only attained the mode of repression has all the lust of his evil urge. He enjoys it, but he manages to repress it.

Even one who has not reached the level of sublimation, though he may still find his way, as it is said in Scripture (Prov. 4:26): "Lay out the ways of your feet and all your ways will be upright," error still dogs his footsteps. The strong desires of the psychological drives inject their poison into the functioning of his reason, to blind the eyes of the wise.

This is the [meaning of the] Midrash's statement, "'Deceitful scales in his hand' means he sat and weighed whether his own daughter is worthy of Isaac or not." Certainly Eliezer, who was master over his urge, would not consider speaking of even a trivial matter before he con-

כְּשֶׁר הַדָּבָר, אָכֵן מֹאזְנַיִם שֶׁלּוֹ מֹאזְנֵי מִרְמָה הֵמָּה, יַעַן לֹא הָיָה רַק שַׁלִּיט בְּיִצְרוֹ, וְהַשֶּׁקֶר, הוּא הַמִּרְמָה, בְּלִי חֵפֶץ תְּעַטְּרֵהוּ, וְהָאֱמֶת עֲדֶן מֵרָחוֹק תַּעֲמֹד. נִמְצָא לְפִי זֶה. הֲגַם שֶׁבְּכַמּוּת הָיָה אֱלִיעֶזֶר שַׁלִּיט בְּיִצְרוֹ כְּמוֹ אַבְרָהָם, אָכֵן בָּאֵיכוּת גְּדֵלָה בְּחִינַת שְׁלִיטַת הַיֵּצֶר שֶׁל אַבְרָהָם לְמַעְלָה הַרְבֵּה, יַעַן הָיָה בִּבְחִינַת תִּקּוּן הַיֵּצֶר, וְהַכְּבִישָׁה, הִיא הַשְּׁלִיטָה, יָקְרָה לְפָנָיו לִמְאֹד לְמוֹצְאָהּ (כַּנִּזְכָּר לְעֵיל) וּבָאָה לוֹ בִּבְחִינַת בְּרָכָה.

וְהִנֵּה שְׁנֵי מִינֵי תִּקּוּן הַיֵּצֶר הֵמָּה, הָאֶחָד, לְתַקֵּן כֹּחוֹת הַנַּפְשִׁיּוֹת אֲשֶׁר לֹא יִכְסְפוּ רַק הַטּוֹב הַנִּדְרָשׁ עַל פִּי שֵׂכֶל הַיָּשָׁר (אֲשֶׁר לֹא נִשְׁחַת וְנֶאֱסַר תַּחַת כֹּחוֹת נַפְשׁוֹ, אֲשֶׁר עַל פִּי הָרֹב נְטִיָּתָם לְרַע), וְהַשֵּׁנִי, לְהַעֲלוֹתָם לְמַדְרֵגָה נִשָּׂאָה הַגְּבֹהָה לְמַעְלָה מֵאֵת אֲשֶׁר יַקִּיף שֵׂכֶל הָאֱנוֹשִׁי. וְכִמְעַט כָּל יְסוֹד מִדַּת הָעֲנָוָה (הַגְּדוֹלָה מִכֻּלָּן, לְרַבִּי יְהוֹשֻׁעַ בֶּן לֵוִי בְּמַסֶּכֶת עֲבוֹדָה־זָרָה כ:) הִיא בְּחִינָה לְמַעְלָה מִשֵּׂכֶל הָאֱנוֹשִׁי*

* עַיֵּן מַסֶּכֶת דֶּרֶךְ אֶרֶץ זוּטָא (פֶּרֶק ב׳) וְזֶה לְשׁוֹנָם אִם הֲטִיבוֹתָ הַרְבֵּה יִהְיֶה בְּעֵינֶיךָ מְעַט כו׳ וְאִם הֱטִיבְךָ מְעַט יִהְיֶה בְּעֵינֶיךָ הַרְבֵּה, אַל תֹּאמַר בִּשְׁבִיל מַעֲשֵׂי הַהֲגוּנִים כו׳. וְאִם הֲרֵעוֹתָ מְעַט יִהְיֶה בְּעֵינֶיךָ הַרְבֵּה כו׳. אִם הֲרֵעוּךָ הַרְבֵּה יִהְיֶה בְּעֵינֶיךָ מְעַט כו׳ עַיֵּן שָׁם. וְעַיֵּן חוֹבַת הַלְּבָבוֹת שַׁעַר הַכְּנִיעָה פֶּרֶק י׳, וְזֶה לְשׁוֹנוֹ וְשָׁאֲלוּ אֶחָד מִן הַחֲכָמִים בַּמֶּה הָיִיתָ אָדוֹן לְכָל בְּנֵי דוֹרְךָ. אָמַר מִפְּנֵי שֶׁלֹּא פָּגַעְתִּי אֶחָד מֵהֶם שֶׁלֹּא רָאִיתִי לוֹ מַעֲלָה יְתֵרָה עָלַי, כִּי אִם הָיָה יוֹתֵר חָכָם מִמֶּנִּי, הָיִיתִי אוֹמֵר הוּא יְרֵא אֱלֹהִים יוֹתֵר מִמֶּנִּי, לְיִתְרוֹן חָכְמָתוֹ עַל חָכְמָתִי. וְאִם קָטָן מִמֶּנִּי בְּחָכְמָה, אָמַר כִּי חֶשְׁבּוֹנוֹ יִהְיֶה קַל מֵחֶשְׁבּוֹנִי בְּיוֹם הַדִּין, מִפְּנֵי שֶׁאֲנִי עוֹבֵר בְּמֵזִיד וְהוּא עוֹבֵר בְּשׁוֹגֵג. וְאִם יִהְיֶה גָּדוֹל מִמֶּנִּי בְּיָמִים, אָמַר כִּי זְכֻיּוֹתָיו רַבִּים מִזְּכֻיּוֹתַי מִפְּנֵי שֶׁקְּדָמַנִי בָּעוֹלָם, וְאִם יִהְיֶה קָטָן מִמֶּנִּי, אָמַר כִּי עֲוֹנוֹתָיו מְעַטִּים מֵעֲוֹנוֹתַי כו׳. וְאִם יִהְיֶה יוֹתֵר עָשִׁיר מִמֶּנִּי, אָמַר כִּי מָצְאָה יָדוֹ בְּעָשְׁרוֹ לַעֲבֹד הַבּוֹרֵא יוֹתֵר מִמֶּנִּי, וְאִם יִהְיֶה דַּל יוֹתֵר מִמֶּנִּי. אָמַר כִּי הוּא דַּכָּא וְכו׳ וְהוּא טוֹב מִמֶּנִּי, וְלֹא זַזְתִּי כו׳ וּלְהִכָּנַע לָהֶם, עַיֵּן שָׁם. וְאֵין זֹאת דַּרְכֵי הַשֵּׂכֶל הַיָּשָׁר הַמַּשְׁקִיף לְכָל צַד וְנוֹתֵן גִּדְרוֹ שֶׁל כָּל דָּבָר לְפִי עֵרֶךְ אֵיכוּת הַרְכָּבַת כֹּחוֹתָיו, וְלֹא לְהַשְׁקִיף עַל עִנְיָן פְּרָטִי

39. In R. Salanter's interpretation, Eliezer's untamed psychological drives perverted his reason. They sought to convince him that his daughter was worthy of being Isaac's wife. She was not. However, his instinctive desire distorted his reason and made it appear plausible to him that she was a worthy mate for Isaac, admittedly, only if the woman in Abraham's family in Haran were to refuse to marry him.

40. See the previous footnote of this letter for a comparison of R. Salanter's two methods of altering behavior, which we have translated as sublimation and repression.

sidered and resolved that it is worthy. However, his scales were deceitful scales – since he only could rule over his urge. Falsehood – that is, deceit – willy-nilly, still surrounded him, while truth stood afar.[39] We find thus that even though quantitatively, Eliezer could master his urge like Abraham, qualitatively, Abraham's mastery over his urge far surpassed [Eliezer's], because he used the mode of sublimation. Repression, that is, "conquering," was rarely before him (as said above) – it came to him as divine blessing.

Now, there are two types of sublimation:[40] One is to sublimate the psychological drives so that they only yearn for the good demanded by straightforward reason (reason not corrupted and held captive by the psychological drives, which usually incline toward evil). The second is to raise them to a level higher than human reason can comprehend. Almost the entire basis of the virtue of humility (which is the greatest of all character traits according to R. Yehoshua ben Levi in Tractate Avoda Zara 20b) is a mode beyond human reason.*

* [R. Salanter's Footnote:] See Tractate *Derekh Eretz Zuta* (ch. 2):

If you have bestowed much good, let it be as little in your eyes.... If a little good was bestowed upon you, let it be much in your eyes. Do not say, "It is because my actions are deserving".... If you perpetrated a bit of evil, let it be much in your eyes.... If much evil was perpetrated against you, let it be little in your eyes.... (See further there.)

See also *Ḥovot HaLevavot*, Gate of Submission, ch. 10:

They asked one of the Sages: How did you become the master of your peers? He answered: Because I never met one of them in whom I did not see some superior virtue to mine. If he was wiser than me, I said: He is more God-fearing than me, due to his superior wisdom. If he was lesser than me in wisdom, I said that his reckoning will be lesser than mine on the Judgment Day, because I [am like one who] sins willfully and he [is like one who] sins unwittingly. If he is older than me, I say that his merits are greater than mine for he has lived longer. If he is younger than me, I say: His sins are fewer than mine.... If he is richer than me, I say that he found a way to serve God in wealth more than I. If he is poorer than me, I say: He is humble and contrite in spirit...and he is better than me.... I never strayed [from this approach]...[to honor all of them and] to bow to all of them. (See further there.)

This is not the way of straightforward reason, which observes all aspects and defines everything according to an assessment of the quality of its composite powers. Nor is it the way of straightforward reason to observe each specific situation

לְהַעֲלוֹת הַדָּבָר אוֹ לְהַמְעִיטוֹ, וְאֵינָם אֶלָּא רַעְיוֹנוֹת נִשְׂגָּבוֹת מִדַּרְכֵי הַשֵּׂכֶל, אֲשֶׁר מְחַיְּבִים אֲנַחְנוּ לִקְנוֹת מִדּוֹת הָעֲנָוָה הַנִּרְצֵית.

כִּי מֹשֶׁה רַבֵּנוּ עָלָיו הַשָּׁלוֹם הֵעִיד עָלָיו הַכָּתוּב (בַּמִּדְבָּר י"ב) כִּי הָיָה עָנָו מִכָּל הָאָדָם וְכוּ' (וְהוּא עֲנָוָה שֶׁבֵּין אָדָם לַחֲבֵרוֹ כִּסְגְנוֹן הַכָּתוּב), וְהוּא הָיָה גָּדוֹל וְנַעֲלֶה עַל כָּל בְּנֵי דוֹרוֹ. וְאָמְרוּ רַבּוֹתֵינוּ זַ"ל (נִדָּה ל:) וַאֲפִלּוּ הָעוֹלָם כֻּלּוֹ אוֹמְרִים לְךָ צַדִּיק אַתָּה הֱיֵה בְּעֵינֶיךָ כְּרָשָׁע עַיֵּן שָׁם, הַכֹּל דָּבָר שֶׁאֵין הַשֵּׂכֶל מְחַיְּבוֹ. וּמֵאַיִן תּוֹלֵד כָּל אֵלֶּה הֲלֹא כָּל כֹּחַ קְנִיַּת הַמַּדְרֵגוֹת וְהַמַּעֲלוֹת תָּלוּי בְּשֵׂכֶל הָאָדָם, (יִתְרוֹנוֹ עַל בַּעֲלֵי הַחַיִּים אֲשֶׁר אֵין לָמוֹ לְהַעֲלוֹתָם מַעְלָה מֵאֲשֶׁר הָטְבָּעוּ), וְאֵיךְ יַעֲלֶה לְמַעְלָה מִשִּׂכְלוֹ.

אָכֵן נוֹדַע, כִּי שְׁנֵי מִינֵי דִּבּוּר וּמַחֲשָׁבָה הֵמָּה, שִׂכְלִי וְהִתְפַּעֲלִי. בַּשִּׂכְלִי יִשְׁתַּווּ כָּל בְּנֵי הָאָדָם, לֹא כֵן הַהִתְפַּעֲלִי אֵין אָדָם דּוֹמֶה לַחֲבֵרוֹ. גַּם בְּמַצָּב וּתְכוּנָה אַחַת יִפָּרְדוּ, מִסִּבַּת מֶזֶג טִבְעָם הַשּׁוֹנֶה (אִם מִלֵּדָה וְהַקְּנִיָּה מֵאֲחֵרִים בְּהִתְעָרְבוֹ עִמָּהֶם, אוֹ הַהֶרְגֵּל וְהַלִּמּוּד לְיַשֵּׁר כֹּחוֹת הַנֶּפֶשׁ). לָזֹאת גַּם בָּאָדָם הַפְּרָטִי מִפְּאַת הִשְׁתַּנּוּת מִזְגוֹ, גַּם הִתְפַּעֲלִיּוּתוֹ לֹא תִּשְׁוֶה בְּכָל עֵת. וְכָל זֶה הוּא רַק הִשְׁתַּנּוּת דִּמְיוֹנִית בְּהַהִתְפַּעֲלוּת. (לֹא אֲמִתִּית, רַק בְּהַסִּבָּה הַהִשְׁתַּנּוּת אֲמִתִּית), וּמִכָּל שֶׁכֵּן כַּאֲשֶׁר הַמֶּזֶג יִהְיֶה שָׁוֶה בִּשְׁנֵי הָעִתִּים, רַק הָעִנְיָן, הַמְעוֹרֵר אֶת הַהִתְפַּעֲלוּת יִשְׁתַּנֶּה, אֲבָל הַשֵּׂכֶל יִשְׁוֶה בְּכָל עֵת, אֵינֶנּוּ תָּלוּי בְּמֶזֶג וְלֹא בְּעִנְיָן וְדָבָר, לָזֹאת כַּאֲשֶׁר לֹא יִשְׁתַּווּ שְׁנֵי בְּנֵי אָדָם בְּדָבָר שִׂכְלִי, (אִם שֶׁגַּם זֹאת נוֹלַד לָרֹב מִשִּׁנּוּי הַמֶּזֶג וְעִנְיָן מְעוֹרֵר), נֹאמַר שֶׁהָאֶחָד טָעָה, לֹא כֵן בְּהִתְפַּעֲלוּת, שְׁנֵיהֶם כֵּנִים וּנְכוֹחִים בְּהִתְפַּעֲלוּת, לְפִי קִשּׁוּר הַמְּסוֹבָב בְּסִבָּתוֹ, (כִּי זֶה גֶּדֶר אֲמִתַּת הַמְּסוֹבָב בִּהְיוֹת הוֹלֵךְ בְּמִישׁוֹר לְרַגְלֵי סִבָּתוֹ). כֵּן גַּם בְּאָדָם פְּרָטִי, אִם לֹא יִשְׁתַּוֶּה שִׂכְלוֹ בְּאֵיזֶה עִנְיָן בִּשְׁנֵי עִתִּים, נֹאמַר

41. Note that in his interpretation of the trait of humility, R. Salanter argues that the human must use a quality *and its opposite* to attain the right level. Here, the human should use his reason to assess the level of the other and himself. Then he must employ will and desire – beyond all reason – to convince himself of the other's additional greatness and his own shortcomings.

42. I.e., using purely rational thought, based on the same information or assumptions, any two people will arrive at the same conclusion.

> and magnify it or minimize it. Rather, these ideas transcend the ways of reason, which we need in order to attain the desired quality of humility.[41]

Of Moses our teacher, Scripture attests (Num. 12:3): "He was more humble than any other person…." (This refers to interpersonal humility, as is Scripture's style.) He was greater and more refined than everyone in his generation. And the Rabbis said (Nidda 30b): "Even if the whole world tells you, 'You are righteous,' you should see yourself as wicked." See further there. This is something that reason does not require. So what can yield all of this? Isn't the capacity to reach these higher levels and virtues dependent on human reason (and [humanity's] advantage over animals, which have nothing that can raise them above whatever they have by nature)? Then how can one go beyond one's reason?

It is surely known that there are two types of speech and thought: rational and sentimental. With respect to the rational, all humans are the same.[42] This is not so in the arena of sentiment, where no individual is like another. Even under the same circumstances and with the same features, they will diverge, due to their different natural temperaments (whether acquired congenitally, through socialization, or through conditioning and study to train psychological drives). Therefore, even an individual, due to variation in his temperament, will not have the same sentiments at all times. This applies to sentiment that is only imagined. (It is not real; only an [external] factor can produce real variation.) Certainly, then, it applies when the temperament remains the same in both instances but the matter that arouses the sentiment changes. Reason, however, is the same at all times. It does not hinge on temperament, situation, or issue. Therefore, when two people disagree about a rational matter (although this usually grows out of different temperaments and stimuli), we say that one has made a mistake. Not so in matters of sentiment, i.e., emotional knowledge. Both are authentic and justifiable according to the connection of the effect and the cause. (For the measure of the truth of an effect is its following directly in the footsteps of its cause.) The same applies to an individual; if his reasoning is not identical on two different occasions, we can say for certain that he made a mistake one of the times (by juxtaposing contradiction and inconsistency). Not so with emotional understanding. There is no essential contradiction,

שֶׁבְּוַדַּאי בְּפַעַם אַחַת טָעָה (עַל פִּי הֶקֵּשׁ הַסְּתִירָה וְהַחִלּוּף), לֹא כֵן בַּהִתְפַּעֲלוּת, אֵין סְתִירָה בָּהּ בִּבְחִינַת עַצְמוּתָהּ, כִּי שְׁנֵיהֶם אֲמִתִּיִּם, (רַק בִּבְחִינַת סִבָּתָם מֵהַמֶּזֶג אוֹ שִׁנּוּי בְּסִבַּת דָּבָר הַמְעוֹרֵר).

לְפִי זֶה, הַשֵּׂכֶל בְּחִינָה קַיֶּמֶת, לֹא תִּפֹּל תַּחַת הַתְּמוּרָה וְהַחִלּוּף. וְכַאֲשֶׁר יִמְצָא הָאָדָם מוֹפֵת אוֹ רְאָיָה (לְפִי דַּרְכֵי הַחָכְמָה לְמִינֵיהֶם) לְשַׁנּוֹת דְּבַר שֵׂכֶל, נִקְרָא שִׁנּוּי רַק בְּדִמְיוֹן וְלֹא בְּשֵׂכֶל, כִּי הָאֶחָד טָעוּת וְדָבָר בָּטֵל. לֹא כֵן הַהִתְפַּעֲלוּת, הִיא רַק בְּחִינָה לְשַׁעְתָּהּ לְפִי עִנְיָנָהּ.

אוּלַי הוּא בִּכְלַל מַאֲמַר רַבּוֹתֵינוּ ז״ל (שַׁבָּת י׳) רָבָא חֲזֵי לְרַב הַמְנוּנָא דְּקָא מַאֲרִיךְ בִּצְלוֹתָא, אָמַר מַנִּיחִין חַיֵּי עוֹלָם (תּוֹרָה) וְעוֹסְקִין בְּחַיֵּי שָׁעָה. כִּי גֶּדֶר הַתּוֹרָה הוּא, בַּשֵּׂכֶל הַמְּפֻשָּׁט מִכָּל רָצוֹן וְהִתְפַּעֲלוּת הַנֶּפֶשׁ. (כַּמְבֹאָר בַּהַקְדָּמָה לְסֵפֶר הַתְּבוּנָה אֲשֶׁר הוֹצֵאתִי לָאוֹר בִּשְׁנַת תרכ״ב), אֲבָל הַתְּפִלָּה, יְסוֹדָהּ הִתְפַּעֲלוּת הַנֶּפֶשׁ לְשַׁעְתָּהּ, כְּמַאֲמַר רַבּוֹתֵינוּ ז״ל (תַּעֲנִית ב׳) וּלְעָבְדוֹ בְּכָל לְבַבְכֶם, אֵיזוֹ עֲבוֹדָה שֶׁהִיא בַּלֵּב הֱוֵי אוֹמֵר זוֹ תְּפִלָּה, לְזֹאת, הַתְּפִלָּה, הִיא חַיֵּי שָׁעָה, וְהַתּוֹרָה חַיֵּי עוֹלָם בְּחִינָה נִצֶּבֶת.

---

43. This passage and the following represent a remarkable broadening of R. Salanter's conception of how to arrive at correct knowledge and truth. Hitherto, R. Salanter has stressed rational truth and knowledge, which one achieves using straightforward (i.e., undistorted) reason to the maximum extent possible. Thus, one can establish, objectively, what the Torah says, and this becomes the truth and guide to behavior. Much Mussar learning is designed to curb the sentiments and unconscious drives that distort reason and erode the ability to know, objectively, what the Torah actually instructs. Knowing what the Torah wants and internalizing it so that it determines behavior is the key mechanism of proper behavior and avoidance of sin.

However, here R. Salanter affirms that there is a whole realm of knowledge and truth that is arrived at through sentiment. Apparently, emotion and sentiment intuit or subjectively recognize the Torah's message or the truth that one seeks. R. Salanter affirms that the Torah includes such truths. The Torah assumes that humans will use their emotions to arrive at this knowledge. For example, such virtues and behaviors as humility go against straightforward reason, yet are highly valued by the Torah, which expects one to arrive at such knowledge through sentiment.

Sentimental knowledge differs from knowledge arrived at by straightforward reason in that it is more subjective; it may vary from time to time, place to place, and with changes in the individual. Since it is more individuated, their two clashing versions of the truth may both be correct. I.e., each understanding is true for the individual who arrived at it.

for both are true (and the discrepancy arises from changing temperamental causes and stimuli).[43]

Accordingly, it is a fixed element; it cannot be changed or replaced. When a person finds a demonstration or proof (according to the different scientific methods) to alter a matter of reason, it can be called "change" only in our imagination, not from the perspective of reason itself, as the original [thinking] was mistaken and is nullified. Sentiment is not so; it is a temporary, contingent element.[44]

Perhaps this is the meaning of the saying of the Rabbis, of blessed memory (Shabbat 10a): "Rava saw Rav Hamnuna praying at length. He said: 'They set aside eternal life (Torah) to engage in temporal life!?'"[45] Torah, by definition, is abstract reasoning, free of all desire and sentimentality (as explained in the introduction to the volume of *Tevunah* that I published in 1862).[46] Prayer is based on fleeting, sentimental emotion, as the Rabbis, of blessed memory, said (Taanit 2a): "'To serve Him with all your heart': What is the service of the heart? We say it is prayer." Thus, prayer is temporal life and Torah is eternal life, something that endures.[47]

Later in the letter, R. Salanter deals with the dangers of sentimentality: It can lead to distortions in judgment; it can lead to multiple contradictory behaviors and truths; it can easily slip into relativism and self-contained egocentric truths. Since the Torah expects us to use this method, there is no easy escape from these risks. The main corrective R. Salanter comes up with is to pool various individuals' sentimental knowledge, or to have a truth arrived at and reviewed by a range of people. This interaction can reduce individual purely subjective elements and pool them into a kind of consensus truth. The wide range of judgment exercised will tend to exclude extreme distortions. Thus, one ends up with a refined sentimentality that has been filtered, improved, and objectified through the participation of multiple people in arriving at the conclusion.

44. Sentiments can conflict and contradict and remain authentic. Two rational truths which contradict and change cannot both be true; one version must be an error.
45. Prayer is considered an engagement in "temporal life" because it addresses material, contingent needs.
46. Compare Letter 29 above.
47. This reiterates R. Salanter's argument that the only way to know the Torah as truth is to read and study it with abstract reason, free of the unconscious drives and

הֶעָרָה

וּבְכָל זֹאת, הָאָדָם בַּאֲשֶׁר הוּא אָדָם, אִם כִּי בְּיָדוֹ וְכֹחוֹ לְהַפְשִׁיט שִׂכְלוֹ מֵהִתְפַּעֲלוּת כֹּחוֹת נַפְשׁוֹ, עַד אֲשֶׁר יִהְיוּ כֹּחוֹת נַפְשׁוֹ הוֹזִים שׁוֹכְבִים (בְּלִי הִתְעוֹרְרוּת, לְמַעַן לֹא יִפְרְצוּ בַּכֹּחַ הַשִּׂכְלִי לְהַטּוֹתוֹ* בְּכָל זֹאת אָדָם הוּא, וְכֹחוֹת נַפְשׁוֹ בְּקִרְבּוֹ הֵמָּה, אֵין בְּיָדוֹ לְהַפְרִישָׁם מִשִּׂכְלוֹ.

* לָזֹאת הָעִיּוּן בִּדְבַר הַמִּדּוֹת, כִּמְעַט בִּלְתִּי אֶפְשָׁר לְטַהֵר הַשֵּׂכֶל לְגַמְרֵי וּלְהַפְשִׁיטוֹ מִכֹּחוֹת הַנַּפְשִׁיּוֹת, יַעַן כִּי מִתְעוֹרְרִים הֵמָּה מֵהָעִיּוּן וְהַמַּחֲשָׁבָה בָּהֶם, לָזֹאת בְּסוּג הַמְפֻרְסָמוֹת, יָבוֹא דָּבָר שִׂכְלִי מְשֻׁתָּף מְעַט עִם כֹּחוֹת הַנֶּפֶשׁ, גֶּדֶר טוֹב וָרַע. לָכֵן אֵצֶל הַמַּלְאָכִים שֶׁהֵם בִּבְחִינַת שִׂכְלִי בְּלִי שִׁתּוּף עִם כֹּחוֹת הַנֶּפֶשׁ, עַל כֵּן הַכָּרָתָם בְּטוֹב וָרַע בְּסוּג אֱמֶת וָשֶׁקֶר יִכָּנֵס (רָאִיתִי בְּחָפְזָה בַּעֲקֵדַת יִצְחָק שַׁעַר י', וְאוּלַי בָּזֶה סָרָה תְּלוּנָתוֹ, עַיֵּן שָׁם), וְהוּא מַאֲמַר הַכָּתוּב (שְׁמוּאֵל־ב' י"ד, י"ז) כִּי כְּמַלְאַךְ אֱלֹהִים כֵּן אֲדוֹנִי הַמֶּלֶךְ לִשְׁמֹעַ טוֹב וָרַע, וְהוּבָא בַּעֲקֵדַת יִצְחָק שָׁם, כִּי אָמְרוּ רַבּוֹתֵינוּ ז"ל (שַׁבָּת דַּף י') כָּל דַּיָּן שֶׁדָּן דִּין אֱמֶת לַאֲמִתּוֹ וְכוּ'. וְיֵשׁ לְבָאֵר כִּי שְׁבִילֵי הָאֱמֶת הוֹלְכִים אַחֲרֵי דַּרְכֵי הַחָכְמָה לְעִיּוּנִים, אֲשֶׁר נוֹדַע כִּי נֶחֱלָקִים הֵמָּה, יֵשׁ אֲשֶׁר נֶאֱסָרִים בְּמַאֲסַר הַמּוֹפֵת הַבָּרוּר עַל פִּי דַּרְכֵי הֶקֵּשׁ הַהֶגְיוֹנִי, וְיֵשׁ אֲשֶׁר בִּרְאָיוֹת וְהוֹכָחוֹת תִּבָּחֵן אֲמִתָּתָם וְתִתְרַחֵב יְדִיעָתָם לְהוֹצִיא דָּבָר מִדָּבָר, וְיֵשׁ אֲשֶׁר רַק בְּשִׁקּוּל הַדַּעַת הַיְשָׁרָה יְסֹדוֹ. וּבָהֶם יִתְפָּאֵר כָּל אֱנוֹשׁ לֵאמֹר, אָנֹכִי הָרוֹאֶה וְלִי נִגְלוּ תַּעֲלוּמוֹת חָכְמָה, וּבֶאֱמֶת לֹא כֵן הַדָּבָר, הָאִישׁ אֲשֶׁר חָנַן לוֹ ה' יִתְבָּרַךְ דֵּעָה וְהַשֵּׂכֶל לִמְצֹא דַּרְכֵי הַמּוֹפֵת, כֵּן גַּם בְּדַרְכֵי הָרְאָיוֹת יָדָיו רַב לוֹ (בְּלִי לְדַמּוֹת וּלְקָרֵב אֶת הַמְרֻחָקִים) אֲשֶׁר לָזֹאת גַּם שִׁקּוּל דַּעְתּוֹ הִיא הַיְשָׁרָה, וּלְאוֹרוֹ רַבִּים יִמָּשְׁכוּ, וְלֹא רְחוֹקָה הִיא לְהַלְבִּישׁ בָּזֶה שְׁאֵלַת סָבָא דְּבֵי אַתּוּנָא לְרַבִּי יְהוֹשֻׁעַ בֶּן חֲנַנְיָא (בְּכוֹרוֹת דַּף ח' עַמּוּד ב') מְצִיעֲתֵיהּ דְּעָלְמָא הֵיכָא, זְקָפָהּ לְאֶצְבַּעְתֵּיהּ, אֲמַר לוֹ הָכָא, אֲמַר לוֹ וּמִי יֵימַר אִיתוּ אַשְׁלֵי וּמְשָׁחוּ וְכוּ'. כִּי הָרַמְבַּ"ם כָּתַב בְּרֵישׁ הִלְכוֹת דֵּעוֹת. שֶׁצָּרִיךְ הָאָדָם לְהִתְנַהֵג בַּדֶּרֶךְ הַמְּמֻצָּע עַיֵּן שָׁם. וּמִי יַגְבִּיל הַדָּבָר וְאַיֵּה הַחוֹזֶה לֵאמֹר, פֹּה הִיא הַנְּקֻדָּה הָאֶמְצָעִית, לֹא בְּמוֹפֵת וְאַף לֹא בִּרְאָיָה יִוָּדַע הַדָּבָר. כִּי אִם עַל פִּי שִׁקּוּל דַּעַת הַחֲכָמִים לְפִי מְקוֹמוֹ וּשְׁעָתוֹ. זֶהוּ מַאֲמָרָם מְצִיעֲתָא דְּעָלְמָא הֵיכָא, רָצָה לוֹמַר הֵיאַךְ הַדֶּרֶךְ לֵידַע נָתִיב הַמְּמֻצָּע. אֲמַר לוֹ הָכָא, רָצָה לוֹמַר כְּפִי אֲשֶׁר תִּגְזֹר יַד שִׂכְלְכֶם, (יַעַן מַה, יַעַן חָזָק כְּחָכָם לְבָרֵר

---

instinctive needs that distort judgment. Note: When one studies Torah rationally for a second time or more, one may come up with new insights, but they will not contradict what reason objectively understood before. Prayer, by definition, is meant to be an emotional experience, and therefore the experience will change every time.

NOTE

Nevertheless, a person, inasmuch as he is human, even though he has the power and ability to abstract his reason from any desire or sentimentality, to the point where his psychological drives sleep and dream (without being awakened, so that they do not force their way into reason and distort it*), he remains human after all.

* [R. Salanter's footnote:] According to this theory of character traits, it is almost impossible to purify reason entirely and strip it of psychological effects, because they are aroused by thinking about and considering them. Thus, when it comes to conventional matters, reason will be combined, to a degree, with psychological drives, just as with good and evil. This is why, when it comes to angels – rational beings with no admixture of psychological drives – their apprehension of good and evil is in the category of truth and falsehood [i.e., the good, like the true, is determined purely rationally.] (I have seen in passing *Akedat Yitzḥak*, Gate 10; perhaps with this, his objection is removed. See further there.) This is what Scripture says (II Sam. 14:17): "As an angel of God, so is my lord the king, as far as discerning good and evil" (cited in *Akedat Yitzḥak*, ad loc.). For our Rabbis, of blessed memory, said (Shabbat 10a): "Every judge who judges true judgment for the sake of truth [– it is as if he becomes a partner with the Holy One, blessed be He, in the work of creation]." This requires elucidation. The paths of truth follow the methods of science in [different] disciplines, which are known to be distinct. Some [scientific disciplines] are bound to clear demonstration, using the methods of logical deduction; the truth of some is discerned by proofs and demonstrations, but knowledge is then broadened inductively, by understanding one thing from another; and [the truth of] some is based on considered discretion. Everyone boasts of these, saying, "I see it, and the mysteries of wisdom have been revealed only to me." In truth, it is not so. The person whom God has graced with understanding and wisdom to find the ways of demonstration will also have capability in the ways of proof (without comparing and connecting things that are remotely similar) and also be considered in his judgment. Many will be drawn to his illumination.

It is not farfetched to read this idea into the question that the sages of Athens asked of R. Yehoshua ben Ḥananya (Bekhorot 8b): "'Where is the center of the earth?' He held up his finger and said to them: 'Here.' They said to him: 'Who says? [I.e., Prove it.]' He replied, 'Bring ropes and measure….'" For Rambam wrote at the beginning of the Laws of Moral Dispositions [in *Mishneh Torah*] that a person should follow the middle path [i.e., the golden mean]. See further there. But who can demarcate this? Where is the seer who can say: Here is the midpoint? Not by demonstration and not by proof can we know this – only by the considered judgment of the Sages according to the place and time. This is the meaning of their statement: "Where is center of the earth?" That is to say, by what method can one ascertain the middle path? He said to them: "Here." That is to say, it is

הַדְּבָרִים הַנִּתְלִים בְּמוֹפֵת אוֹ בִּרְאָיָה, לָכֵן גַּם בְּאֵלֶּה לָכֶם מִשְׁפַּט הַבְּחִירָה). אָמַר לוֹ וּמִי יֵימַר, כֵּיוָן שֶׁאֵין בְּיָדֵינוּ לְהָבִיא מוֹפֵת עַל מִשְׁפָּטֵנוּ וְהַשְׁעָרוֹתֵינוּ, אָמַר לוֹ אַיְתֵי אַשְׁלֵי וּמְשָׁחוּ. כִּי הַמּוֹפֵת לְבָרֵר הַדָּבָר, כְּמוֹ הַמְּדִידָה לֵידַע כַּמּוּת הַדָּבָר אֲשֶׁר אֵין לִטְעוֹת בָּהּ, וְהוֹאִיל וְאֵין לֵידַע דֶּרֶךְ הַמְמֻצָּע עַל יְדֵי הַמּוֹפֵת, תָּנוּחַ נֶפֶשׁ הָאָדָם בְּשִׁקּוּל דַּעַת הַחֲכָמִים, וְעַל פִּי חָכְמַת דִּבְרֵיהֶם יִתְנַהֵג: וְאוּלַי עַל כַּיּוֹצֵא בָּזֶה אָמְרוּ (אָבוֹת פֶּרֶק ו') בֶּאֱמוּנַת חֲכָמִים, כִּי הַדָּבָר הַתָּלוּי בִּרְאָיָה, מַה הוּא עִנְיַן אֱמוּנָה, הֲלֹא הָרְאָיָה תִּתֵּן צְדָקָה, וְזֶה כְּלָל גָּדוֹל בְּדַרְכֵי הוֹרָאָה לִשְׁמֹר לַעֲשׂוֹת מוֹצָא פִּי גָּדוֹל בְּהוֹרָאָה, בִּבְחִינַת הָרְאָיוֹת וְהוֹכָחוֹת, וּלְבַטֵּל דַּעְתּוֹ נֶגְדּוֹ, אַף אִם דְּבָרָיו רַק מִשִּׁקּוּל הַדַּעַת יֵצְאוּ. וְהוּא מַאֲמַר רַבּוֹתֵינוּ ז"ל (יְרוּשַׁלְמִי פֶּרֶק א' דִּבְרָכוֹת) נָבִיא וְזָקֵן לְמִי הֵן דּוֹמִין, לְמֶלֶךְ שֶׁשּׁוֹלֵחַ פַּלְמַטְרִין (שְׁלוּחִים) שֶׁלּוֹ לַמְּדִינָה, עַל אֶחָד מֵהֶן כָּתַב אִם אֵינוֹ מַרְאֶה לָכֶם חוֹתָם שֶׁלִּי אַל תַּאֲמִינוּ לוֹ, וְעַל אֶחָד מֵהֶם כָּתַב, אַף עַל פִּי שֶׁאֵינוֹ מַרְאֶה לָכֶם חוֹתָם שֶׁלִּי הַאֲמִינוּ לוֹ כו', כָּךְ בְּנָבִיא כְּתִיב וְנָתַן אֵלֶיךָ אוֹת אוֹ מוֹפֵת, בְּרַם הָכָא עַל פִּי הַתּוֹרָה אֲשֶׁר יוֹרוּךָ, עַיֵּן שָׁם. כִּי אוֹת תּוֹרֶה עַל הוֹכָחָה שֶׁיֵּשׁ לְבַעַל דִּין לַחֲלֹק עָלָיו, וּמוֹפֵת (לָרֹב) עַל רְאָיָה מַכְרַעַת. וְהָרַמְבַּ"ם כָּתַב (פֶּרֶק ח' מֵהִלְכוֹת יְסוֹדֵי הַתּוֹרָה) וְזֶה לְשׁוֹנוֹ, מֹשֶׁה רַבֵּנוּ עָלָיו הַשָּׁלוֹם לֹא הֶאֱמִינוּ בוֹ יִשְׂרָאֵל מִפְּנֵי הָאוֹתוֹת שֶׁעָשָׂה, שֶׁהַמַּאֲמִין עַל פִּי הָאוֹתוֹת. יֵשׁ בְּלִבּוֹ דֹּפִי, שֶׁאֶפְשָׁר שֶׁיַּעֲשֶׂה הָאוֹת בְּכִשּׁוּף כו', (וּבַמֶּה הֶאֱמִינוּ בוֹ בְּמַעֲמַד הַר סִינַי שֶׁעֵינֵינוּ רָאוּ וְלֹא זָר וְאָזְנֵינוּ שָׁמְעוּ וְלֹא אַחֵר כו' עַיֵּן שָׁם). אַף עַל פִּי כֵן אוֹת הוּא בְּחִינַת רְאָיָה, וְזֶהוּ לִמְבִינֵי מַדָּע. אֲבָל לְרֹב הָעָם, צָרִיךְ מוֹפֵת, הוּא הוֹכָחָה נִצַּחַת, זֶהוּ וְנָתַן אֵלֶיךָ אוֹת, אוֹ אֲפִלּוּ יִהְיֶה בְּעֵינֶיךָ מוֹפֵת, אַל תִּשְׁמַע לְהַנָּבִיא לַעֲבֹד עֲבוֹדַת אֱלִילִים, אֲבָל בִּשְׁאָר מִצְוֹת תִּשְׁמַע לוֹ גַּם עַל פִּי אוֹת, בִּבְחִינַת הָרְאָיָה, כְּמוֹ שֶׁכָּתַב הָרַמְבַּ"ם שָׁם. בְּרַם הָכָא עַל פִּי הַתּוֹרָה אֲשֶׁר יוֹרוּךָ, גַּם עַל פִּי שִׁקּוּל הַדַּעַת כִּדְאָמְרִינַן (סַנְהֶדְרִין פ"ח) אֲפִלּוּ הוּא אוֹמֵר מִפִּי הַשְּׁמוּעָה וְהֵן אוֹמְרִים כָּךְ הוּא בְּעֵינֵינוּ נֶהֱרָג, עַיֵּן שָׁם. עַל פִּי דַּרְכֵי עִיּוּנֵי הַחָכְמָה, תִּתְיַצֵּב גְּבוּל הָאֱמֶת, בַּל יַעְפִּיל הָאָדָם לַחְתֹּר תָּמִיד בְּדַרְכֵי הַמּוֹפֵת אַחַר הָאֱמֶת, כִּי אִם אֶת אֲשֶׁר נָתַן הָאֱלֹהִים לִבְנֵי אָדָם לַעֲנוֹת וְלַחֲקֹר, הִיא מַטְרַת הָאֱמֶת.

where your reason dictates. (Why is this so? Just as their powers of ascertaining things that hinge on demonstration or proof were strong, so in these matters, the discretionary judgment was rightfully theirs.) They said to him: "Who says so? Since we can't demonstrate our judgment or hypotheses." He said to them: "Bring ropes and measure." Demonstration is for ascertaining something, like measuring to know the quantity of something, which is unmistakable. But since one cannot know the middle path by demonstration, be satisfied with the considered judgment of the Sages, and act in accordance with the wisdom of their words.

Perhaps they similarly said (Avot 6:6) that "trust in the Sages" ("*emunat ḥakhamim*") [is one of the forty-eight ways by which Torah is acquired]. For when a matter depends on proof, what has it got to do with trust? It is justified by the proof. This then is a great principle in the ways of halakhic rulings: One must observe and act according to the utterances of one who is a leading decisor – as though it were proven and demonstrated – and nullify one's own views in the face of his, even if his words grow out of a considered judgment only. And this is the [meaning of the] statement of our Rabbis, of blessed memory (Y. Berakhot 9:1): "A prophet and a sage – to whom can they be compared? To a king who sent two of his messengers to a province. About one of them he writes: 'If he does not show you my seal, don't believe him.' About the other one he writes: 'Even if he doesn't show you my seal, believe him....' It is thus written about the prophet: 'And he shall give you a sign or proof' (Deut. 13:2). But here [with regard to the sage] it is written: 'Go according to the Torah that they teach you' (Deut. 7:11)." See further there. A "sign" ("*ot*") refers to the sort of demonstration with which a litigant can argue. A "proof" ("*mofet*") refers (usually) to a decisive proof. And Rambam writes (ch. 8 of the Laws of the Principles of the Torah [in *Mishneh Torah*]): "Moses our teacher was believed by Israel not because of the signs he performed, for one who believes because of the signs, retains some doubt in his heart, for a sign can be performed with magic....". ("And on what grounds did they trust him? On the grounds of the revelation at Mount Sinai, which our eyes saw, and not a stranger's, and our ears heard and not another's...," cf. ibid.) Nevertheless, a sign ("*ot*") is a type of evidence for those who understand knowledge. But for most people, proof ("*mofet*"), an irrefutable demonstration, is necessary. This is [the meaning of] "He shall give you a sign" – or even if it is a decisive proof in your eyes – do not obey the prophet to worship idolatry. However, when it comes to other commandments, obey him even by a mere sign, which is akin to proof, as Rambam wrote there. However, here, "according to the instruction that [the Sages] instruct you" – even when it comes only from their considered judgment [you must obey]. As we say (Sanhedrin 88a): "Even if [a dissenting elder] claims that his teaching is a received tradition, and [the Sages] say, 'We see the matter otherwise,' [the dissenting elder] is put to death." See further there.

The boundaries of truth are established in accordance with the methods of scientific disciplines. A person should not press forward always to seek truth by means of demonstration. Rather, whatever God gave to men to answer and investigate – that is how to reach the goal of truth. It is called truth; this is its

אֱמֶת תִּקָּרֵא, זֶה שְׁמָהּ וְזֶה זִכְרָהּ. כֵּן גַּם בִּדְבַר הַדִּין, אֲשֶׁר הָאֱמֶת יָקָר לִמְצֹא בָהּ. מִסִּבַּת נְטִיַּת הַדַּעַת לְאַהֲבָה וּלְשִׂנְאָה וְכַיּוֹצֵא הַמְעַוֵּר עֵינֵי פִקְחִים, וְאַף אִם יִשְׁמֹר הָאָדָם דַּרְכּוֹ לְהִזָּהֵר מִכָּל חֲשַׁשׁ נְגִיעַת הַדַּעַת (עַיֵּן כְּתֻבּוֹת דַּף ק"ה עַמּוּד ב'), בְּכָל זֹאת מִי יִתֵּן קַו וּמִשְׁקֹלֶת לְדַרְכֵי הַנְּטִיָּה, הֲלֹא זֶה דֶּרֶךְ כֹּחַ נֶפֶשׁ הָאָדָם לִקְשֹׁר חֶבֶל בְּחֶבֶל, נִימָא בְּנִימָא, הַרְכָּבַת רַעְיוֹנוֹת וַהֲבָלִים הַרְבֵּה, לְהוֹצִיא פְּרִי עָמָל מִבְּלִי אֲשֶׁר יִמְצָא הָאָדָם רֵאשִׁית סִבָּתוֹ. אֲשֶׁר אוּלַי לָזֶה הִזְהִירוּ רַבּוֹתֵינוּ זַ"ל (סַנְהֶדְרִין דַּף ז'), לְעוֹלָם יִרְאֶה דַּיָּן עַצְמוֹ כְּאִלּוּ חֶרֶב מֻנַּחַת לוֹ בֵּין יַרְכוֹתָיו וְגֵיהִנֹּם פְּתוּחָה לוֹ מִתַּחְתָּיו עַיֵּן שָׁם, וְלֹא הִזְהִירוּ כֵּן בְּטַרְפְּתָא (סִפּוּר רַב אָשִׁי הַמֻּזְכָּר שָׁם) יַעַן כִּי בַּדִּין, הַנְּטִיָּה עֲלוּלָה לִמְאֹד. בְּכָל זֹאת אִם יָשִׂים הָאָדָם לִבּוֹ וְנַפְשׁוֹ לְטַהֵר מַחֲשַׁבְתּוֹ עַל פִּי יְדִיעָתוֹ, הִיא הִיא רְדִיפַת הַצֶּדֶק אֲשֶׁר ה' דּוֹרֵשׁ, זֶהוּ לַאֲמִתָּתוֹ (שֶׁל דִּין), מַה שֶּׁהוּא גֶּדֶר הָאֱמֶת אֵצֶל דִּין. וְאוּלַי הוּא מַאֲמַר הַיְרוּשַׁלְמִי (רֵישׁ סַנְהֶדְרִין) רַבִּי יוֹסֵי בֶּן חֲלַפְתָּא אַתּוּן תְּרֵין בַּר נַשׁ מִידוּן קוֹמוֹי, אָמַר לוֹ עַל מְנָת שֶׁתְּדִינֵנוּ דִּין תּוֹרָה אָמַר לוֹן אֲנִי אֵינִי יוֹדֵעַ דִּין תּוֹרָה, עַיֵּן שָׁם. כִּי גֶּדֶר הַתּוֹרָה הוּא בְּחִינַת שֵׂכֶל בְּלִי נְטִיַּת הָרָצוֹן כְּלָל (כַּנִּזְכָּר לְעֵיל), מַה שֶּׁרָחוֹק לְהִמָּצֵא בַּדִּין, כִּי מִי יַעֲרֹךְ נְטִיַּת הַנֶּעְלָמוֹת, לָזֹאת לְהַפְלָגַת יִרְאָתוֹ, חָשַׁשׁ אוּלַי לֹא מִלֵּא חוֹבָתוֹ. וְאוּלַי הַדָּבָר בִּכְלַל מַאֲמַר חֲכָמֵינוּ זַ"ל (סַנְהֶדְרִין ו' עַמּוּד ב') שֶׁמָּא יֹאמַר הַדַּיָּן מַה לִּי בְּצַעַר הַזֶּה, תַּלְמוּד לוֹמַר וְעִמָּכֶם בִּדְבַר הַמִּשְׁפָּט, אֵין לוֹ לַדַּיָּן אֶלָּא מַה שֶּׁעֵינָיו רוֹאוֹת, עַיֵּן שָׁם. כִּי לְאַחַר טָהֳרַת מַחֲשַׁבְתּוֹ, אֵינוֹ בָּטוּחַ אִם לֹא יַד כֹּחוֹת נַפְשׁוֹ בָּאֶמְצַע. וְהוּא מַה שֶּׁעֵינָיו רוֹאוֹת (עַיֵּן לְעֵיל), וְעִמּוֹ הוּא הַמִּשְׁפָּט בְּהַרְכָּבַת כֹּחוֹת נַפְשׁוֹ הַפְּרָטִית. לֹא עַל יְדֵי הַשֵּׂכֶל הַפָּשׁוּט אֲשֶׁר הוּא כְּלָלִי. אָכֵן מִשְׁפְּטֵי הַמֶּלֶךְ בִּהְיוֹתוֹ נַעֲלֶה מִכָּל הָעָם, מִשְׁפָּטָיו בְּגֶדֶר הָאֱמֶת, הַמּוֹפֵת יְבִיאוּ, אֱמֶת הָאֲמִתִּי.

name and its memory. [This is a play on Exodus 3:15.] So it is with judgment, where truth is quite difficult to find because of the tendency of the mind to love and to hate and the like, which blinds the eyes of the wise. And even if a person watches his step to beware of any trace of biased thinking (see Ketubbot 105b), nevertheless, who can measure or weigh the ways of bias? It is the way of human psychological drives to bind one string to another, one rope to another, combining many concepts and vanities, to produce a result without having even found the primary cause. Perhaps this is the intention of the warning of the Rabbis (Sanhedrin 7a): "A judge should always see himself as if a sword is planted between his thighs and hell is opened beneath him"; see further there. Yet they issued no such warning about matters of kosher slaughter of animals (the story of Rav Ashi mentioned there) because in civil judgment, bias is much more likely. [That is, bias is more likely to affect adjudication between litigants than rulings about the ritual status of food items. Apparently, the "tendency of the mind to love and to hate" is more likely to affect judgment between two people, in which one litigant will win at the expense of the other, than rulings about ritual cases.]

Nevertheless, if one sets his heart and soul on purifying his thought to accord with his knowledge, this is the pursuit of righteousness that God demands. This is [the meaning of] "for the sake of truth" [Shabbat 10a, cited above] within judgment; when it comes to judgment, this is the definition of truth. [I.e., when it comes to adjudicating a civil case, true objectivity and certain knowledge is not always possible; however, God demands that we judge "for the sake of truth," working to eliminate biases and refine our thinking so that the judge's sole pursuit is ascertaining the truth of the case.] Perhaps this is also [the meaning of] the saying in the Yerushalmi (at the beginning of Sanhedrin): "Two litigants came before R. Yosei ben Ḥalafta. They said to him: '[Be our judge] on condition that you give us a Torah judgment.' He said to them: 'I do not know Torah judgment.'" See further there. For the definition of "Torah" is the discernment of reason without any bias of the will at all (as mentioned above). This is rarely found in civil judgment, for who can assess the hidden biases? Thus, due to his extreme fear, he worried that he did not fulfill this duty.

Perhaps this idea is also included in the saying of the Sages (Sanhedrin 6b): "Lest the judge say: 'Why do I need this trouble?' The Torah replies: 'And [God is] with you in the matter of judgment' (II Chr. 19:6); the judge can only go by what he sees." See further there. After all the purification of thought, he is never certain that the effects of his psychological drives are not mixed in. This is [the meaning of] "what he sees." Yet "[God is] with you in the matter of judgment," in the makeup of his individual psychological forces, not only through simple reason, which is general [and not individual].

However, when it comes to the king's judgment, since he is above the people, his judgments are within the parameters of truth. They bring demonstrations, the true truth. This is [the meaning of] "As an angel of God, so is my Lord the king, to discern good and evil...." (II Sam. 14:17). For what the people comprehend as "good"

זֶהוּ, כִּי כְּמַלְאַךְ אֱלֹהִים כֵּן אֲדוֹנִי הַמֶּלֶךְ לִשְׁמֹעַ טוֹב וָרַע כוּ׳ (שְׁמוּאֵל ב׳ י״ד, י״ז), כִּי מַה שֶּׁהוּא אֵצֶל הָעָם רַק בְּחִינַת טוֹב, הוּא אֵצֶל הַמֶּלֶךְ בְּחִינַת אֱמֶת, כְּמוֹ אֵצֶל הַמַּלְאָכִים כַּנִּזְכָּר לְעֵיל, עַד כָּאן.

לְזֹאת אֵין בְּיַד הָאָדָם לָבוֹא אֶל שֵׂכֶל אֲמִתִּי הַמְּפֹרָשׁ וּמְבֻדָּל לְגַמְרֵי מִכֹּחוֹת הַנַּפְשִׁיּוֹת, וְהַתּוֹרָה נְתוּנָה לִבְנֵי אָדָם לִשְׁפֹּט בָּהּ עַל פִּי שֵׂכֶל אֱנוֹשִׁי, (בְּטָהֳרַת הָאֶפְשָׁרִית, עַיֵּן בְּכוֹרוֹת (י״ז, ב׳) דְּרַחֲמָנָא אָמַר עֲבֵיד וּבְכָל הֵיכִי דְּמָצֵית לְמֶעְבַּד נִיחָא לֵיהּ), וְעַל פִּי רִבּוּי הָרְאָיוֹת וּמִשְׁקָלָם יִתְבָּרְרוּ הַדְּבָרִים, וּלְאֵיזֶה צַד אֲשֶׁר יִפֹּל עֵרֶךְ הָרְאָיוֹת, אִם מִצַּד הָרִבּוּי אוֹ מִצַּד הַמִּשְׁקָל, שָׁם תִּהְיֶה הַהַכְרָעָה וְכֵן יָקוּם הַדָּבָר.

מִצַּד רִבּוּי הָרְאָיוֹת שָׁוִים כָּל בְּנֵי אָדָם בְּשִׂכְלָם, אִם רַק לֵב מֵבִין לָמוֹ לְהָבִין הָרְאָיוֹת בְּמַתְכֻּנְתָּם. אָכֵן מִצַּד הַמִּשְׁקָל שׁוֹנִים רוּחַ בְּנֵי אָדָם זֶה מִזֶּה, הוּא הוּא שִׁקּוּל הַדַּעַת, אֲשֶׁר דַּעְתָּם שֶׁל בְּנֵי אָדָם נִפְרֶדֶת לְמַרְבֶּה.

וּבִדְבַר מִשְׁקַל הָרְאָיוֹת הָיְתָה הַמַּחֲלֹקֶת שֶׁל בֵּית שַׁמַּאי וּבֵית הִלֵּל. כִּי כָּל אֶחָד מֵהַצְּדָדִים יָדְעוּ כָּל הָרְאָיוֹת הַנִּדְרָשׁוֹת לִדְבַר מַחְלָקְתָּם, בָּאֵר הֵיטֵב. וּמִזֶּה נוֹלְדָה בֵּינֵיהֶם מַחֲלֹקֶת כְּלָלִית עַל הַמַּחֲלֹקֶת בְּעִנְיַן

---

48. [The crux of this footnote by R. Salanter is that statements by our Rabbis, of blessed memory, are not free of any psychological elements, as are the words of Moses or the prophets. Nevertheless, the Rabbis, of blessed memory, achieved a high degree of refinement. Since God affirms judgments reached at this level of refinement, the Sages' statements are deemed true; when one's judgment differs from theirs, one tends to defer to them out of the realization that they achieved purer rational judgments. Furthermore, we follow those qualified judgments even in the face of contradictory demonstrations and proofs.

Note: Just as one is to be modest in making claims about the authority of rabbinic judgment, so one is to be modest in arriving at an understanding of their statements. Here, too, as they do, one should welcome a variety of viewpoints and approaches and try to arrive at a considered judgment of what they are actually saying. This is on the grounds that listening to multiple viewpoints from multiple individuals will make one more likely to avoid the subjective distortions found in each individual view.

Note also that R. Salanter's conclusion, namely, that the king's judgment achieves a level of truth unavailable to common judges, was apparently an attempt to satisfy government censors.]

49. Based on Deuteronomy 19:15, which addresses the laws of weighing testimony.

[which, as noted, is a judgment that incorporates subjective and aesthetic components,] the king perceives as "truth" – in the manner of angels, as mentioned above.[48]

His psychological drives remain within him. He cannot separate them from his reason. Thus, a person cannot achieve true reason, completely removed from and transcending psychological drives, yet the Torah is given to human beings to render judgment in accordance with human reason (in its purest possible form; see Bekhorot [17b]: "The Merciful One said: Do it, and however you manage to do it is acceptable to Him"). By the quantity and quality of proofs, the matter will be clarified. On whichever side the assessment of the proof falls – whether on the side of quantity or quality – that is what he will decide, and so the matter will be established.[49]

As far as the quantity of proofs is concerned, all humans using their reason will arrive at a common conclusion, if only they have an understanding heart to comprehend all the steps of the proofs. However, regarding the quality of proofs, people differ from one another in spirit. This is [the meaning of] "considered judgment" [or "discretion"; "*shikul hadaat*"][50] – regarding which people's opinions often differ.

Assessing the quality of proofs was a central dispute between the School of Shammai and the School of Hillel.[51] Each side was very familiar with all the proofs relevant to their dispute. Out of this grew a

50. Quantity of proofs is an objective measure; once the number of proofs has been determined, there is no rational dispute about which side has more proofs. However, when it comes to assessing the weight of these proofs, there will be significant divergence based on subjective factors unique to each judge – the judge's discretion or "considered judgment." Ideally, each side presents how it weighs the evidence and is attentive to the assessment of the other side, as the divergence in judgment is not the result of ego or prejudice, but is part of the natural variation of human judgment.
51. Dispute first began to proliferate with the Schools of Hillel and Shammai, and so their disputes are paradigmatic within rabbinic literature. R. Salanter asserts that enduring dispute between the schools was not because one side refused to submit to reason and acknowledge its error, and not because the sides were biased by psychological factors. Rather, they disagreed about how to consider evidence and render judgments. Each school came to a different conclusion as to which is the central criterion for reaching a conclusion – quality or quantity. According to R. Salanter, this dispute was not in the realm of strict reason, but in the realm of "discretion," where difference of opinion is expected and justified.

מִשְׁקַל הָרְאָיוֹת, אִם לֵילֵךְ אַחַר הַכַּמּוּת אוֹ אַחַר הָאֵיכוּת. זֶהוּ מַאֲמַר רַבּוֹתֵינוּ זַ״ל (עֵרוּבִין י״ג:) אָמַר רַבִּי אֶלְעָזָר אָמַר שְׁמוּאֵל, שָׁלֹשׁ שָׁנִים נֶחְלְקוּ בֵּית שַׁמַּאי וּבֵית הִלֵּל, הַלָּלוּ אוֹמְרִים הֲלָכָה כְּמוֹתֵנוּ וְהַלָּלוּ אוֹמְרִים הֲלָכָה כְּמוֹתֵנוּ וְכוּ׳. כִּי סְבָרַת בֵּית שַׁמַּאי הָיְתָה לֵילֵךְ אַחַר הָאֵיכוּת, וְהֵם הָיוּ מְחֻדָּדִים טְפֵי, לְפִיכָךְ אָמְרוּ שֶׁהֲלָכָה כְּמוֹתָן, וּסְבָרַת בֵּית הִלֵּל הָיְתָה לֵילֵךְ אַחַר הַכַּמּוּת, וְהֵם הָיוּ הָרֹב.

לֹא לְמַעַן הַחֲזִיק דַּעְתָּם נֶחְלְקוּ שָׁלֹשׁ שָׁנִים, כִּי אִם לְמַעַן הַצֶּדֶק וְהָאֱמֶת בְּטָהֳרַת הַמַּחֲשָׁבָה בְּלִי נְגִיעַת הַדַּעַת כְּלָל. לֹא בִּבְחִינַת כַּוָּנַת הַדַּעַת, רַק בִּבְחִינַת מִקְרֶה נִהְיְתָה הַדָּבָר, אֲשֶׁר בֵּית שַׁמַּאי סָבְרוּ כִּי לָהֶם הַיִּתְרוֹן, וּבֵית הִלֵּל סָבְרוּ לְהֵפֶךְ.

וְיַעַן שֶׁיָּצְאָה בַּת קוֹל וְאָמְרָה שֶׁהֲלָכָה כְּבֵית הִלֵּל, אַלְמָא כַּמּוּת עָדִיף, לָזֹאת פָּסְקוּ הַפּוֹסְקִים דְּמִנְיָן עָדִיף מֵחָכְמָה (עַיֵּן בַּשַּׁ״ךְ יוֹרֶה דֵּעָה סִימָן רמ״ב בְּהַנְהָגַת הוֹרָאַת אִסּוּר וְהֶתֵּר, עַיֵּן שָׁם).

וְאוּלַי לָזֶה יָצְאָה הַבַּת קוֹל וְאָמְרָה, אֵלּוּ וָאֵלּוּ דִּבְרֵי אֱלֹהִים חַיִּים הֵם, וְלֹא דָּבָר חָדָשׁ הוֹדִיעָה הַבַּת קוֹל (כִּי גַּם דֵּעָה הַנִּדְחֵית בִּכְלַל

---

52. Note: In the actual letter, R. Salanter wrote "R. Elazar." He was probably writing from memory.

53. Both schools acknowledged that the School of Shammai had greater mental acuity and that the School of Hillel was greater in number. One who accepts mental acuity and "quality" as the key criterion (as did the School of Shammai) would adopt the rulings of the School of Shammai, and one who accepts larger numbers and "quantity" as the key criterion (as did the School of Hillel) would adopt the rulings of the School of Hillel.

54. That is, they did not shape their arguments to prove that they were right. Rather, both schools were interested in reaching a correct understanding of the Torah.

55. R. Salanter concludes that the differences between the School of Hillel and the School of Shammai were based on legitimate disagreement about non-rational, subjective elements that go into rendering judgment. In this, he inserted himself into a raging polemic; in certain traditional circles, acknowledging such a subjective element was seen as undermining the objective authority of halakha. Therefore, they denied that there was any subjectivity in study of Torah or rendering of halakhic decisions. They held that the human teacher of the Oral Torah was merely a vessel transmitting

meta-dispute about how to weigh evidence within a dispute – [namely,] whether to follow quantity or quality. This is the [meaning of the] saying of our Rabbis, of blessed memory (Eiruvin 13b): "Rabbi [Aba][52] said in the name of Shmuel: For three years the School of Shammai and the School of Hillel argued. These said: The law is according to our view and those said: The law follows our view…." The School of Shammai adopted the view that one should follow quality, and they were sharper, so they said the law was according to them. The School of Hillel adopted the view that one should follow quantity, and they were the majority.[53]

They did not argue for three years merely to uphold their own views – only for the sake of justice and truth through purity of thought without any bias.[54] It was not intentional, but merely accidental, that the School of Shammai thought that they had the advantage, and the School of Hillel thought the opposite.[55]

Since a heavenly voice went forth and stated that the law follows the School of Hillel, it follows that quantity is superior. Therefore, the codifiers have ruled that numbers outweigh wisdom.[56] (See *Shakh* [at the end of *Shulḥan Arukh*:] *Yoreh De'ah* 242, [in his essay on] Procedures for Ruling on What Are Forbidden and Permitted Matters. See further there.)

Perhaps this is why the heavenly voice came out and said: "These and those are the words of the Living God" (Eiruvin 13b). The heavenly voice announced nothing new (for even rejected opinions are part of

---

divine words; the subject had no influence and did not shape the words. In contrast, *maskilim* and reformers emphasized the subjectivity of halakhic disagreement in order to undermine the divine authority of the Oral Torah.

R. Salanter offers a third path, which neither denies subjectivity nor undermines authority. He acknowledges the subjective element ("A person cannot achieve true reason, completely removed from and transcending psychological drives") but asserts that it is a built-in component of the Oral Torah: "Yet the Torah is given to human beings to render judgment in accordance with human reason (in its purest possible form….)." Here R. Salanter states that the rabbis reached a high degree of purity of reason, one that is not distorted by personal bias, which approximates the "true" truth that God imparted through the Torah.

56. A majority of sages outweighs a minority, no matter how brilliant its members.

תּוֹרָה הִיא), כִּי הַתּוֹרָה לֹא בַּשָּׁמַיִם הִיא, וּבְוַדַּאי מְסוּרָה הָיְתָה לְמֹשֶׁה מִסִּינַי וְלֹא שְׁכָחוּהָ, אֶלָּא שֶׁיְּסוֹד הַבַּת קוֹל הָיְתָה, לְמַעַן לֹא יִפֹּל לֵב הָעָם, (בִּרְאוֹתָם כִּי זֶה שָׁלֹשׁ שָׁנִים שֶׁבֵּית שַׁמַּאי מַחֲזִיקִים לֵאמֹר הֲלָכָה כְּדִבְרֵיהֶם כִּי לָהֶם הַיִּתְרוֹן, וּבֵית הִלֵּל לְהֵפֶךְ), פֶּן וְאוּלַי חַס וְשָׁלוֹם נָטוּ אֲשׁוּרֵיהֶם מְעַט מִטָּהֳרַת הַמַּחֲשָׁבָה, וּבָאוּ חַס וְשָׁלוֹם לִקְצַת נְגִיעַת הַדַּעַת. אֲשֶׁר לֹא בְּכְמוֹ אֵלֶּה בָּחַר ה׳ לִמְסֹר תּוֹרָתוֹ, לְהִקָּרֵא תּוֹרַת ה׳ גַּם בַּדֵּעָה הַנִּדְחֵית. לָזֹאת הוֹדִיעָה הַבַּת קוֹל, כִּי מַחְשְׁבוֹתֵיהֶם רְצוּיִים, וּבִבְחִינַת מִקְרֶה הָיָה הַדָּבָר, שֶׁהֶחֱזִיקָה כָּל אַחַת מֵהַחֲבוּרוֹת בְּכָל עֹז, כִּי לְדַעְתָּם הַיִּתְרוֹן. וְלָזֹאת גַּם דִּבְרֵי בֵּית שַׁמַּאי הַנִּדְחֵית דִּבְרֵי אֱלֹהִים חַיִּים הֵן, וְהַהוֹגֶה בְּדִבְרֵיהֶם הוֹגֶה בְּתוֹרַת ה׳ יִתְבָּרַךְ שְׁמוֹ.

הַהוֹדָעָה הַלָּזוֹ פְּרָטִית הִיא, כִּי הַחֲבוּרוֹת כַּוָּנָתָם רְצוּיָה. אֵין בָּזֶה מִשּׁוּם לֹא בַּשָּׁמַיִם הִיא, אֲשֶׁר אֵינֶנָּה רַק בִּכְלָלִי, כְּמוֹ חַטָּאת שֶׁמֵּתוּ בְּעָלֶיהָ וְכַיּוֹצֵא שֶׁהֻזְכַּר בַּגְּמָרָא (תְּמוּרָה ט״ז) אוּלַי הוּא בִּכְלַל מַאֲמַר רַבּוֹתֵינוּ זַ״ל (מִדְרָשׁ רַבָּה קֹהֶלֶת פָּרָשָׁה א׳) אָמְרוּ הֲרֵי כָּל חָכְמָתוֹ שֶׁל שְׁלֹמֹה שֶׁבָּא לֵאמֹר מַה יִּתְרוֹן לָאָדָם בְּכָל עֲמָלוֹ, יָכוֹל אַף בַּעֲמָלָהּ שֶׁל תּוֹרָה חָזְרוּ וְאָמְרוּ לֹא אָמַר בְּכָל עָמָל אֶלָּא בַּעֲמָלוֹ, בַּעֲמָלוֹ (שֶׁל עַצְמוֹ) אֵינוֹ עָמֵל, אֲבָל עָמֵל הוּא בַּעֲמָלָהּ שֶׁל תּוֹרָה כו׳. אָמַר רַבִּי יוּדָן תַּחַת הַשֶּׁמֶשׁ אֵין לוֹ, לְמַעְלָה מִן הַשֶּׁמֶשׁ יֵשׁ לוֹ (עַיֵּן שַׁבָּת ל׳:),

---

57. Deuteronomy 30:12, applied in *Bava Metzia* 59b to mean that once the Torah was given at Sinai, it is in the hands of human beings to determine the law. God's will is ascertained by derivation from past revelation as interpreted and applied by rabbinic learning and reason. R. Salanter is responding to an obvious problem with this passage in Eiruvin: If the Torah is "not in heaven," how could a heavenly voice determine that the halakha follows the School of Hillel? R. Salanter answers that the purpose of the voice was not to decide in favor of the School of Hillel, but to affirm that both schools reached their conclusions with purity of thought, free of personal interests and biases.

58. The Talmud mentions that hundreds of laws were forgotten during the period of mourning for Moses. The people asked figures like Joshua and Phinehas to divine the forgotten laws, but they averred that "it is not in heaven." In these cases, the

Torah), for the Torah "is not in heaven."[57] Certainly, [the principle of majority rule] was given to Moses at Sinai and never forgotten. Rather, the purpose of the heavenly voice was to prevent the people from becoming disheartened (upon seeing that for three years already the School of Shammai held out, saying the law follows their view, for they have the upper hand, while the School of Hillel held the opposite view), lest, God forbid, their self-affirmation deviated somewhat from purity of thought and came, God forbid, to some bias. These are not the kind of people to whom God chose to give over His Torah, and whose rejected views are still called God's Torah. Therefore, the heavenly voice proclaimed that their thoughts are desirable, and it was mere accident that each group held, with all its might, that its view had the upper hand. Therefore, the rejected views of the School of Shammai are nevertheless the words of the Living God, and one who studies their words, studies God's Torah, may His name be blessed.

This message [from heaven] is specifically that the intentions of these fellowships were desirable. This voice from heaven is not a violation of "It is not in the heaven," which applies only to a universal issue, such as in the case of "a sin offering whose owner died,"[58] and similar cases, as mentioned in the Talmud (Temura 16a). Perhaps this [idea that a rejected opinion remains Torah] is included in the saying of our Rabbis, of blessed memory (Ecclesiastes Rabba, ch. 1):

> They said: This is the sum of Solomon's wisdom that he came to assert: "What profit to the human being in all his toil?" (Eccl. 1:3). This might mean even the toil of Torah! They recanted and said: [Solomon] did not say "in all toil" but "in [all] *his* toil." In his toil (for himself), he does not toil [for there is no profit], but he does the toil of Torah [for in this there is profit].... R. Yudan said: "Under the sun" (ibid.) he has no [profit]; "Above the sun" he does. (See Shabbat 30b.)

---

people sought a final answer that would apply throughout the generations, and it is in such cases that the recovery of the laws precludes divine involvement. Ultimately, Othniel ben Kenaz recovered the laws through cognitive effort.

כִּי אָמְרוּ רַבּוֹתֵינוּ זַ"ל (פְּסָחִים נ':) רָבָא רָמִי, כְּתִיב (תְּהִלִּים נ"ז) כִּי גָדֹל עַד שָׁמַיִם חַסְדֶּךָ, וּכְתִיב (שָׁם ק"ח) כִּי גָדוֹל מֵעַל שָׁמַיִם חַסְדֶּךָ, הָא כֵּיצַד, כָּאן בְּעוֹשִׂין לִשְׁמָהּ וְכָאן בְּעוֹשִׂין שֶׁלֹּא לִשְׁמָהּ, וְכִדְרַב יְהוּדָה דְּאָמַר רַב יְהוּדָה אָמַר רַב לְעוֹלָם יַעֲסֹק אָדָם בַּתּוֹרָה וּבַמִּצְוֹת אֲפִלּוּ שֶׁלֹּא לִשְׁמָהּ, שֶׁמִּתּוֹךְ שֶׁלֹּא לִשְׁמָהּ בָּא לִשְׁמָהּ כוּ'. נִמְצָא לְפִי זֶה יֵשׁ לְכַנּוֹת הָעֵסֶק לִשְׁמָהּ, לְמַעְלָה מִן הַשֶּׁמֶשׁ, וְהָעֵסֶק שֶׁלֹּא לִשְׁמָהּ, לְמַטָּה מִן הַשֶּׁמֶשׁ. וּכְשֶׁהָאָדָם מוֹצֵא דְּבַר תּוֹרָה אֲשֶׁר נִתְקַבְּלָה לַהֲלָכָה, לֹא שֶׁלּוֹ הִיא, רַק הִתְגַּלּוּת דָּבָר אֲשֶׁר הָיָה נֶעְלָם עַד כֹּה, אָכֵן אִם לֹא נִתְקַבְּלָה לַהֲלָכָה, וּבְכָל זֹאת תּוֹרַת ה' הִיא וְהַהוֹגֶה בִּדְבָרָיו מְקַבֵּל שָׂכָר, שֶׁלּוֹ הִיא, כִּי הוּא בְּעָמָל הוֹלִיד דָּבָר חָדָשׁ בַּתּוֹרָה מַה שֶּׁלֹּא הָיְתָה מִקֹּדֶם וּבִתְנַאי שֶׁיִּהְיֶה בְּטָהֳרַת הַמַּחֲשָׁבָה בְּלִי נְגִיעַת הַדַּעַת, אֲשֶׁר זֶהוּ הַיְסוֹד שֶׁל לִשְׁמָהּ. זֶהוּ, מַה יִּתְרוֹן (נִצְחִי) בְּכָל עֲמָלוֹ (שֶׁלּוֹ, הוּא הַדָּבָר שֶׁלֹּא נִתְקַבְּלָה לַהֲלָכָה), שֶׁיַּעֲמֹל תַּחַת הַשֶּׁמֶשׁ (שֶׁלֹּא לִשְׁמָהּ), אֲבָל לְמַעְלָה מִן הַשֶּׁמֶשׁ (לִשְׁמָהּ), יִתְרוֹן נִצְחִי הוּא, שֶׁהוֹלִיד דָּבָר בַּתּוֹרָה.

וְאוּלַי הוּא בִּכְלַל הַכָּתוּב (קֹהֶלֶת א') וְאֵין כָּל חָדָשׁ תַּחַת הַשֶּׁמֶשׁ (עַיֵּן פֵּרוּשׁ רַשִׁ"י שָׁם). כִּי כָּל מַה שֶּׁמַּמְצִיא הָאָדָם בַּשֵּׂכֶל, בַּמֶּה שֶּׁלֹּא נִקְרָא תּוֹרַת כוּ', לֹא חֲדָשָׁה בַּשִּׂכְלִי הִיא, רַק בַּחוּשִׁי, כִּי הִיא רַק הִתְגַּלּוּת הַנֶּעְלָם בְּאֹפֶן הַהַרְכָּבָה. כֵּן גַּם בְּתוֹרַת ה' אֲשֶׁר נִתְקַבְּלָה לַהֲלָכָה הִיא הִיא הַתּוֹרָה, וְהָאָדָם הַמַּמְצִיאָהּ אֵינוֹ אֶלָּא מְגַלֶּה הַדָּבָר, וּמַה הוּא הֶחָדָשׁ (הַשִּׂכְלִי), דְּבַר תּוֹרָה אֲשֶׁר לֹא נִתְקַבְּלָה לַהֲלָכָה, וְעַל יְדֵי הָאָדָם הַמַּמְצִיאָהּ נַעֲשֵׂית דְּבַר תּוֹרָה, זֶהוּ אֵין כָּל חָדָשׁ תַּחַת

---

59. A rabbinic halakhic ruling which is accepted as authoritative was always present in the body of revelation. However, it was "hidden," and not known until a particular rabbi articulated it and uncovered this eternal truth. In the case of a halakhic ruling which is not accepted, it was never part of the body of revelation – for if it had been, it would become authoritative. The rejected opinion is a genuine *novum*. It is now absorbed into the corpus of Torah, but it was not there until this person created it.

60. Only innovations that are, on one hand, part of "the Torah of God," and, on the other, not accepted as the halakhic conclusion are true innovations. Torah that is accepted as halakha and discoveries in non-Torah disciplines are not truly novel.

For our Rabbis, of blessed memory, said (Pesaḥim 50b):

> Rava raised a contradiction: It is written (Ps. 57:11): "For Your loving-kindness is great, up to the heavens," and it is written (ibid. 108:5): "For your loving-kindness is great, beyond the heavens." How can this be? Here [Ps. 108:5] [refers to] those who act for its own sake; here [Ps. 57:11] they act for other motives. This follows R. Yehuda's view, for R. Yehuda says in the name of Rav: "A person should always engage in Torah and the commandments even not for its own sake; for in acting for other motives, he will come to do it for its own sake."

Accordingly, we find that engaging in Torah for its own sake should be called "above the sun," and engaging for other motives should be called "under the sun." When a person articulates words of Torah that are accepted as halakha, they are not his; rather, it is the discovery of something that was hidden until now. However, if it was not accepted as halakha, yet it is still the Torah of God, and one who studies its words receives reward, then it is his, for he, by his effort, has created something new in Torah that never existed before.[59] But this is on condition that it was produced with purity of thought, without bias, which is the essence of "for its own sake." This is [the meaning of]: What (eternal) profit in all his toil (*his* work, this refers to a matter not accepted as halakha) that he labors under the sun (i.e., not for its own sake); however, above the sun (i.e., for its own sake) it has eternal profit, for he has given birth to new Torah.

Perhaps this is included in the [meaning of the] verse (Eccl. 1:9): "There is nothing new under the sun." (See Rashis commentary there.) For all that a person produces using the rational faculty, except that which is called the "Torah [of God but has not been accepted as halakha]," is not an innovation of reason, but an emotional innovation, for it is only uncovering something whose manner of synthesis had been lost.[60] So it is with "the Torah of God" that has been accepted as halakha – that is, *the* Torah; the person who produces it is only its discoverer. What is "new" (in the realm of the rational)? Torah that was not accepted as halakha, but which becomes Torah through the person who produces it. This is

הַשֶּׁמֶשׁ (רְצוֹנוֹ לוֹמַר שֶׁלֹּא לִשְׁמָהּ, כִּי גַּם בַּתּוֹרָה אֲשֶׁר נִתְקַבְּלָה לַהֲלָכָה. אִם שֶׁיֵּשׁ לָהּ יֶתֶר שְׂאֵת מֵהַדָּבָר אֲשֶׁר לֹא נִתְקַבְּלָה לַהֲלָכָה בְּכָל זֹאת. חָדָשׁ לֹא נִקְרָאָה. וְגַם אֲשֶׁר לֹא נִתְקַבְּלָה לַהֲלָכָה, אִם הַלִּמּוּד יִהְיֶה שֶׁלֹּא לִשְׁמָהּ, כִּי אֵין לָהּ בְּחִינַת תּוֹרָה), אֲבָל לְמַעְלָה מִן הַשֶּׁמֶשׁ (לִשְׁמָהּ) יֵשׁ וְיֵשׁ חָדָשׁ, הֵמָּה הַדְּבָרִים אֲשֶׁר לֹא הָיוּ בְּגֶדֶר הַתּוֹרָה, וְעַל יְדֵי עֲמַל הָאָדָם. אֲשֶׁר הוֹלִידָם בְּטָהֳרַת מַחֲשַׁבְתּוֹ, בָּאוּ בְּחַדְרֵי הַתּוֹרָה.

הוּא מַאֲמַר הַכָּתוּב (תְּהִלִּים א׳) בְּתוֹרַת ה׳ חֶפְצוֹ וּבְתוֹרָתוֹ יֶהְגֶּה יוֹמָם וָלָיְלָה כוּ׳. כִּי חֵפֶץ וְתַחְבּוּלוֹת הָאָדָם, הוּא לְטַהֵר הַשֵּׂכֶל, לְהַפְשִׁיטוֹ מִכֹּחוֹת הַנַּפְשִׁיּוֹת לָבוֹא לִבְחִינַת שֵׂכֶל אֲמִתִּי, הִיא תּוֹרַת ה׳, וְעִם כָּל זֶה אָדָם הוּא, וּבְתוֹרָתוֹ (שֶׁל עַצְמוֹ) יֶהְגֶּה יוֹמָם וָלַיְלָה. (וִיבֹאַר תֵּבַת ״וּבְתוֹרָתוֹ״ עַל אַשְׁרֵי הָאִישׁ וְכוּ׳ הָאָמוּר קֹדֶם).

וְהוּא מַאֲמַר רַבּוֹתֵינוּ זַ״ל (בְּרָכוֹת ה׳) מִדַּת בָּשָׂר וָדָם אָדָם מוֹכֵר חֵפֶץ לַחֲבֵרוֹ מוֹכֵר עָצֵב וְלוֹקֵחַ שָׂמֵחַ, אֲבָל הַקָּדוֹשׁ־בָּרוּךְ־הוּא אֵינוֹ כֵן, נָתַן לָהֶם תּוֹרָה לִבְנֵי יִשְׂרָאֵל וְשָׂמַח כוּ׳, כִּי הַנְּתִינָה הִיא מֵעֵין גֶּדֶר הַמְּכִירָה, שֶׁכִּמְעַט נִפְרְדָה מִבְּעָלֶיהָ, כִּי הַקָּדוֹשׁ־בָּרוּךְ־הוּא נָתַן הַתּוֹרָה לִבְנֵי אָדָם לִשְׁפֹּט בָּהּ עַל פִּי שֵׂכֶל אֱנוֹשִׁי, לֹא כַּאֲשֶׁר הָיְתָה בְאָמְנָה אִתּוֹ.

* כִּי לֹא בַשָּׁמַיִם הִיא לְגַלּוֹת מַצְפּוּנִים, כִּי אִם אֶת אֲשֶׁר יַחְתֹּר הָאָדָם לָדַעַת עַל פִּי דַּרְכֵי הָרְאָיוֹת, הִיא הִיא תּוֹרַת ה׳ יִתְבָּרַךְ שְׁמוֹ, (עַיֵּן תְּמוּרָה דַּף ט״ז, שְׁלֹשֶׁת אֲלָפִים הֲלָכוֹת נִשְׁתַּכְּחוּ כוּ׳ אָמַר לוֹ לִיהוֹשֻׁעַ שְׁאַל אָמַר לוֹ לֹא בַשָּׁמַיִם הִיא כוּ׳. בְּמַתְנִיתָא תָּנָא אֶלֶף וּשְׁבַע מֵאוֹת קַלִּין וַחֲמוּרִין נִשְׁתַּכְּחוּ כוּ׳ אַף עַל

---

61. The verse (Ps. 1:2) refers to Torah twice: first to "the Torah of God" and then to "his Torah." R. Salanter interprets "his Torah" to mean the Torah of the person studying. Thus, the learner "desires" God's Torah, as He gave it to us, unadulterated and minimally shaped by human factors. However, he inevitably studies "his Torah," the Torah as shaped by his own, human intelligence, and yielding novel insights. It is only by *desiring* the Torah of God that one's innovations are considered, on one hand, "his," and on the other, part of the corpus of "Torah."
62. This paraphrase of Esther 2:20 compares the Torah before it was given to Israel with Esther while still being raised in Mordechai's home. The idea is that before

the meaning of "There is nothing new under the sun" (meaning, [Torah learned] not for its own sake, for Torah that was accepted as halakha, even though it has advantages over something that was not accepted as halakha, it is nevertheless not called "new," and even [Torah] that was not accepted as halakha, if the study was not for its own sake, it is not considered Torah). However, "above the sun" (for its own sake) there certainly is "new." These are the things that were not in the category of Torah, but through the effort of the person who created them with the purity of his thought, have been incorporated into Torah.

This is the [meaning of the] verse (Ps. 1:2): "He desires the Torah of God and studies his Torah day and night...." For the desire and ambition of a person are to purify reason, to strip it of the psychological drives so it can enter the category of true reason – this is "the Torah of God." Yet he is still human, so "he studies his Torah day and night." (The antecedent of "his Torah" [in v. 2] is "Fortunate is the man" [in v. 1], stated immediately prior.)[61]

This is the meaning of the statement of our Rabbis, of blessed memory (Berakhot 5a): "It is characteristic of flesh and blood that when one sells an object to another, the seller is sad [about losing a valuable object] and the buyer rejoices [in gaining the object]. Not so the Holy One, blessed be He. He gave the Torah to Israel and rejoiced...." For a gift is like a sort of sale, in that [the gifted object] is all but detached from the owner, and the Holy One, blessed be He, gave the Torah to human beings so that with it they will judge according to human reason – not as it was when it was under His tutelage.[62]

* [R. Salanter's footnote:] For "it is not in heaven" (Deut. 30:12) where [to understand Torah one would need] to reveal secrets; rather whatever a person strives to know using the methods of proof – this is the Torah of God, blessed be He, itself. (See Temura 16a: "Three thousand rulings were forgotten [when Moses died].... They said to Joshua: 'Ask [for prophetic restoration].' He said to him: 'It is not in heaven....' In a *baraita* it was taught: One thousand and seven hundred *a fortiori* arguments

---

it was given to human beings, the Torah was unaffected by human concerns and psychological impulses. It was understood through pure, divine reason. This recalls Shabbat 88b–89a, wherein the angels wish to keep the Torah in heaven, and Moses must debate them to show that the Torah addresses human needs and concerns.

פִּי כֵן הֶחֱזִירָן עָתְנִיאֵל בֶּן קְנַז, עַיֵּן שָׁם). וְאִם יֵשׁ כֹּחַ לַשָּׁמַיִם לְהַכְרִיעַ בְּדָבָר שֶׁיֵּשׁ בּוֹ מַחְלֹקֶת, תָּלוּי בִּשְׁנֵי הַתֵּרוּצִים שֶׁל הַתּוֹסָפוֹת (בִּיבָמוֹת דַּף י״ד) עַל הָא דְּאָמְרֵי שָׁם. מַאן דְּאָמַר עָשׂוּ (בֵּית שַׁמַּאי כְּדִבְרֵיהֶם) כְּרַבִּי יְהוֹשֻׁעַ דְּאָמַר אֵין מַשְׁגִּיחִין בְּבַת קוֹל. וְכָתְבוּ הַתּוֹסָפוֹת וְזֶה לְשׁוֹנָם, וְאִם תֹּאמַר וּמַאי שְׁנָא דְּלֹא קָיְמָא לָן כְּבַת קוֹל דְּרַבִּי אֱלִיעֶזֶר, אֶלָּא אָמְרִינַן בְּכָל דּוּכְתֵּי דְּשַׁמּוּתִי הוּא וְאֵין הֲלָכָה כְּמוֹתוֹ, וּבְבַת קוֹל דְּבֵית הִלֵּל קָיְמָא לָן הֲלָכָה כְּבֵית הִלֵּל, וְיֵשׁ לוֹמַר מִשּׁוּם דְּבַת קוֹל דְּרַבִּי אֱלִיעֶזֶר לֹא יָצְאָה אֶלָּא לִכְבוֹדוֹ כו׳, אִי נָמֵי בְּהַהִיא בַּת קוֹל שֶׁהָיְתָה כְּנֶגֶד רַבִּים, דְּרַבָּנָן הֲווּ רֻבָּא, וַדַּאי אֵין הֲלָכָה, אֲבָל בְּבַת קוֹל דְּבֵית הִלֵּל, קָיְמָא לָן דַּהֲוֵי בֵּית הִלֵּל רֻבָּא, אֶלָּא דְּבֵית שַׁמַּאי מְחַדְּדֵי טְפֵי עַד כָּאן לְשׁוֹנוֹ. נִמְצָא לְפִי תֵּרוּץ הָרִאשׁוֹן שֶׁל תּוֹסָפוֹת, הַתּוֹרָה בַּשָּׁמַיִם הִיא, אִם רַק אֶחָד בָּעוֹלָם יֹאמַר, הֲגַם שֶׁרַבִּים חוֹלְקִין עָלָיו. אֲבָל לְפִי תֵּרוּץ הַשֵּׁנִי, הִיא רַק בַּשָּׁמַיִם, לָתֵת אֵיזֶה כֹּבֶד בְּמָקוֹם שֶׁכִּמְעַט שְׁנֵי הַמִּשְׁקָלוֹת שָׁוִים, כְּמוֹ, אִם לְצַד אֶחָד רֻבָּא וּלְצַד הַשֵּׁנִי מְחַדְּדֵי, הַשָּׁמַיִם נוֹתְנִים עֹז לְצַד אֶחָד לְהַכְרִיעַ. וּלְרַבִּי יְהוֹשֻׁעַ לֹא בַּשָּׁמַיִם הִיא כְּלָל, אַף לָתֵת אֵיזֶה כֹּבֶד לְצַד אֶחָד. וּלְפִי דְּבָרֵינוּ בְּשֵׂכֶל וְהִתְפַּעֲלוּת, נִרְאֶה בַּעֲלִיל שֶׁהַדָּבָר כֵּן, (וְתִתְיַשֵּׁב קֻשְׁיַת הַתּוֹסָפוֹת שָׁם שֶׁכָּתְבוּ וְזֶה לְשׁוֹנָם, וְאִם תֹּאמַר וְדִלְמָא רַבִּי יְהוֹשֻׁעַ נָמֵי דַּוְקָא הָתָם קָאָמַר דְּאֵין מַשְׁגִּיחִין אֲבָל בְּעָלְמָא לֹא כו׳ עַיֵּן שָׁם), כִּי זֶה דֶּרֶךְ הַשֵּׂכֶל לְהִשָּׁמֵר מִכָּל הִתְפַּעֲלוּת נַפְשִׁיּוּת (כִּדְלְעֵיל), וְכָל אֲשֶׁר יוֹסִיף לְהִתְוַכֵּחַ עִם זוּלָתוֹ בְּדָבָר שִׂכְלִי, כֵּן גַּם הַשְּׁמִירָה רַבָּה לִמְאֹד, לְהִתְרַחֵק מֵהִתְפַּעֲלוּת הָעֲלוּלָה לָבוֹא מִכֹּחַ אַהֲבַת הַנִּצּוּחַ לְכַבּוֹת אוֹר הַשֵּׂכֶל אוֹת הִיא, כִּי הַשֵּׂכֶל לְבַדּוֹ יְהַלֵּךְ מַהֲלָכוֹ, בִּהְיוֹת אֹזֶן הָאָדָם קַשֶּׁבֶת לְקוֹל דִּבְרֵי הָרְאָיָה לְהַחֲזִיק דִּבְרֵי מְנַגְּדוֹ, אַף אִם לֹא תִּהְיֶה מֻכְרַחַת בִּשְׁקִיטַת מְנוּחַת הַנֶּפֶשׁ בְּלִי הִתְפַּעֲלוּת מְאוּמָה, וְאִם יִצְטָרֵךְ לְהִתְפַּעֲלוּת לִדְחוֹת הִתְפַּעֲלוּת הַמְנַגֵּד, יַנִּיחֶנָּה לְאַחַר זְמַן, לְמַעַן הַשֵּׂכֶל יֵלֵךְ בֶּטַח מַהֲלָכוֹ. לָזֹאת כַּאֲשֶׁר אֲנַחְנוּ רוֹאִים בְּרַבִּי יְהוֹשֻׁעַ שֶׁלְּאַחַר כָּל הַוִּכּוּחַ הַגָּדוֹל וְהַנּוֹרָא שֶׁהָיָה לוֹ עִם רַבִּי אֱלִיעֶזֶר, עָמַד עַל רַגְלָיו, (שֶׁזּוֹ הִיא דֶּרֶךְ

63. [See R. Salanter's point above (starting at n. 49) about "considered judgment" ("*shikul hadaat*") as well as our discussion in n. 43. We have seen that R. Salanter offers a third approach, between objectivity and self-interested subjectivity. Here he describes the importance of allowing the expression of multiple or contradictory viewpoints and listening attentively to them. When each listens to the other as openly as possible, without emotionally digging in to defend his own position, they can arrive at "considered judgment" that is relatively free of distortion by psychological factors, even if the parties remain in disagreement.]

were forgotten...but Othniel ben Kenaz recovered them [with cognitive effort]." See further there.)

As to whether the heavens can resolve a dispute, this hinges on the two answers of *Tosafot* (Yevamot 14a). The Gemara there says: "The view that (the School of Shammai) acted (in accordance with their own views) [even after the heavenly voice ruled according to the School of Hillel] follows R. Yehoshua, who says: 'We pay no attention to a heavenly voice.'" *Tosafot* state:

Why do we not follow the heavenly voice [that ruled in favor] of R. Eliezer [*Bava Metzia* 59b] and instead say in all places that he is a Shammaite and the law does not follow his view – yet it is through the heavenly voice [that ruled in favor] of the School of Hillel that we establish that the law follows the view of the School of Hillel!? We can answer: The heavenly voice [that ruled in favor] of R. Eliezer only due to his honor [after he said, "Let it be demonstrated from heaven!" the heavens issued a voice in his honor, not really to rule according to his view].... Alternatively: The halakha certainly does not follow the heavenly voice that went against the majority – for the Rabbis were the majority. However, in the case of the School of Hillel's heavenly voice, we have established that the School of Hillel was the majority, but that the School of Shammai was sharper.

According to the first answer of *Tosafot*, the Torah is still in heaven, even if only one person in the whole world states it, and the majority disagree with him. [Note that in R. Salanter's view, a heavenly voice will not intervene, using the authority of revelation to decide the ruling, if no human being holds that position. It will only speak if at least one individual holds this view.] According to the second answer, it is only still "in heaven" to add weight to it in a case of almost complete stalemate; for instance, when one side has the majority and the other is keener, the heavens strengthen one side in order to tip the scales. But according to R. Yehoshua, it is not in heaven at all – not even to give some extra weight to one side.

According to what we have said about reason and sentiment, we can see clearly that the matter is thus [i.e., that according to R. Yehoshua, the principle that the Torah "is not in heaven" totally negates the weight of a heavenly voice in any context]. (This answers the objection of *Tosafot* where they stated: "Perhaps R. Yehoshua only there said, 'We pay no mind [to a heavenly voice],' but generally he does not hold this view...." See further there.) For it is the way of reason to guard itself from all forms of sentimental [that is, emotion-driven] judgment (as said above). The more one argues with someone else rationally, the more on guard one must be to avoid the emotionality likely to stem from the force of the love of victory, which may snuff out the light of reason.

One sign that reason is proceeding alone according to its path is when a person listens attentively to the evidence that supports the view of his opponent, even if it is not compelling, in a state of calm tranquility, without sentiment. And if he must resort to sentiment to combat the sentiment of the opponent, he should leave it until later, so that reason can proceed securely on its path.[63]

We see this in R. Yehoshua who, after all the great and terrific debate he had with R. Eliezer, stood up on his feet (which is a charismatic mode [that evokes

הִתְפַּעֲלוּת לַמֵּבִין קְצָת דַּרְכָּהּ), וְאָמַר אֵין אָנוּ מַשְׁגִּיחִין בְּבַת קוֹל, שְׁמַע מִינָּהּ שֶׁרַבִּי יְהוֹשֻׁעַ סְבִירָא לֵיהּ כִּי לֹא בַּשָּׁמַיִם הִיא כְּלָל, אַף לֹא לָתֵת אֵיזֶה כֹּבֶד, וְאֵינֶנָּה בִּכְלָל הַתְחָלַת רְאָיָה, לָזֹאת הִשְׁתַּמֵּשׁ בְּהִתְפַּעֲלוּת, לִדְחוֹת הִתְפַּעֲלוּת הַתַּלְמִידִים אֲשֶׁר לֹא זָרַח עֲלֵיהֶן עֲדֶן אוֹר הַשֵּׂכֶל הָאֲמִתִּי, וְזֶה דַּרְכָּם לְהִתְפַּעֵל מִדָּבָר גָּדוֹל הַפַּמּוּת, כְּמוֹ בַּת קוֹל מִשָּׁמַיִם, אִם כִּי לְפִי הָאֵיכוּת לֹא בַּשָּׁמַיִם הִיא כְּלָל, לְדַעַת רַבִּי יְהוֹשֻׁעַ, גַּם לָתֵת אֵיזֶה כֹּבֶד לְהַכְרִיעַ.

(עַיֵּן דְּרָשַׁת הָרַ"ן דְּרוּשׁ ז' עַל הָא דְּמַאן נוֹכַח רַבָּה בַּר נַחְמָנִי, בָּבָא מְצִיעָא דַּף פ"ו).

וּבָזֶה יִתְבָּאֵר עִנְיַן בֵּית שַׁמַּאי וּבֵית הִלֵּל, וּבַל נִשְׁתּוֹמֵם עַל הַמַּרְאֶה, אֵיךְ נוֹלַד הַדָּבָר וּמַה סִּבָּתָהּ, מַדּוּעַ תַּלְמִידֵי בֵּית שַׁמַּאי וּבֵית הִלֵּל יַסְכִּימוּ לָרֹב כָּל חֲבוּרָה לְדֵעָה אַחַת, וּמָה עִנְיַן חֲבוּרָה לָזֶה, כִּי סִבַּת מַחְלָקְתָּם הָיְתָה מִשִּׁנּוּי מֶזֶג כֹּחוֹת נַפְשָׁם, אֲשֶׁר אֵין בְּיַד הָאָדָם לְהַפְרִישָׁם מִשִּׂכְלוֹ (כַּנִּזְכָּר לְעֵיל), וְאֵין לְכָל חוֹקֵר בְּתוֹרַת ה', אֶלָּא מַה שֶּׁעֵינָיו רוֹאוֹת, לְאַחַר הַיְכֹלֶת, וּשְׁמִירַת עֶרְכּוֹ לְבַל יִפָּרֵץ גְּבוּלוֹ, וּבְטָהֳרַת שִׂכְלוֹ לְפִי כֹּחַ הָאֱנוֹשִׁי אֲשֶׁר עַל פִּי רֹב, בְּנֵי הַחֲבוּרָה כֹּחוֹת נַפְשָׁם יִצְעֲדוּ בְּמִצְעָד שָׁוֶה, וְהוּא מַאֲמַר רַבּוֹתֵינוּ זַ"ל אֵלּוּ וָאֵלּוּ דִּבְרֵי אֱלֹהִים חַיִּים הֵם, כִּי אֵין סְתִירָה בַּכֹּחוֹת הַנַּפְשִׁיּוֹת (כַּנִּזְכָּר לְעֵיל), וְאִם כִּי כֹּחוֹת נֶפֶשׁ הָאָדָם יִשְׁתַּנּוּ בְּכָל עֵת, לֹא יִפֹּל שִׁנּוּי בְּדַעַת שֵׂכֶל הָאָדָם (הַמְטַהֵר שִׂכְלוֹ בְּדֶרֶךְ הַיָּשָׁר) מִצַּד כֹּחוֹת נַפְשׁוֹ, כִּי שִׁנּוּי בְּכֹחוֹת הַנֶּפֶשׁ יָבוֹא מִפְּאַת הִתְעוֹרְרוּת עִנְיָן אוֹ רַעְיוֹן מָה.

וְזֹאת תּוֹרַת הָאָדָם וְחוֹבָתוֹ, לַחְתֹּר בְּכָל עֹז לִהְיוֹת כֹּחוֹת נַפְשׁוֹ נָחִים וּשְׁקֵטִים בְּעֵת עִיּוּנוֹ בְּדָבָר שִׂכְלִי, וּבְמַצַּב שְׁקִיטַת הַכֹּחוֹת כִּמְעַט שָׁוִים הֵמָּה בְּכָל עֵת, וּבִפְרָט לָאָדָם הַשָּׁלֵם הַשּׁוֹמֵר נַפְשׁוֹ מֵהִתְעוֹרְרוּת חֲזָקוֹת אֲשֶׁר יַשְׁרִשׁוּ בְּנַפְשׁוֹ כֹּחוֹת עֲלוּלִים לְהִתְחַלֵּף תָּמִיד.

---

64. Hence, each Shammaite and Hillelite came to the same conclusion as their whole fellowship, and their perceptions and conclusions, filtered through their temperaments, are thus legitimate interpretations of "the Torah of God."

65. Eiruvin 13b.

66. I.e., because they reflect the differing temperaments of their articulators, the contradictory conclusions are both nevertheless true.

sentiment], for those who understand its methods a bit) and said: "We pay no mind to a heavenly voice." We learn from this that R. Yehoshua holds the view that "it is not in heaven" at all – not even to give weight to one side. It is not even the beginning of a proof. Therefore, he used sentiment to counter the emotional excitation of the students, upon whom the sublime light of true reason had not yet shined. They were prone to be affected by something of such great magnitude as a heavenly voice – though by qualitative criteria, according to R. Yehoshua, "it is not in heaven," at all, even just to tip the scales.

(See *Derashot HaRan,* Homily 7, which addresses the Talmud's story [*Bava Metzia* 86a] about Rabba bar Naḥmani resolving a dispute between God and the heavenly academy.)

With this, the matter of the School of Shammai and the School of Hillel is explained. We should not be astonished at this sight, at how it came to be and what caused it, at why the majority of the students of the School of Shammai and the School of Hillel agree unanimously within their own group – for why should the group matter in this regard? Rather, the reason for their disagreement was rooted in their different psychological temperaments, which a person cannot distinguish from his intellect (as mentioned above). No one who delves into the "Torah of God" has anything but what his eyes perceive, so after [applying] his ability, maintaining his worth so that he does not breach his limits, purifying his intellect as much as humanly possible, in the main, the psychological forces of members of the same group will march in lockstep.[64] This is the meaning of the statement of our Rabbis, of blessed memory: "These and those are the words of the Living God,"[65] for there are no true contradictions between psychological drives[66] (as mentioned above). Even though a person's psychological drives change all the time, there will be no change of view in the intellect of a person (who purifies his reason in the right way) resulting from psychological drives, for changes in psychological drives come from the stimulus of a new situation or a new idea.

This is the Torah of a human and his obligation: to strive with all his might that his psychological drives be dormant and quieted when he studies an intellectual matter. In this state of quieted forces, [the conclusions of the intellect] will almost always be the same, especially for a wholesome person who protects his psyche from strong stimuli that implant in his psyche drives that are likely to change continually.

וְעַל פִּי זֶה נִרְאֶה מַה שֶּׁאָמְרוּ (עֵרוּבִין ז׳) כִּי לֹא עָבְדִינַן כְּחֻמְרֵי דְּבֵי תְּרֵי הֵיכָא דְּסָתְרֵי אַהֲדָדֵי, כְּגוֹן שִׁדְרָה וְגֻלְגֹּלֶת כוּ׳, אֲבָל הֵיכָא דְּלֹא סָתְרֵי אַהֲדָדֵי עָבְדִינַן, עַיֵּן שָׁם. וְכֵן גַּם בִּתְרֵי קֻלֵּי, הַיְנוּ דַּוְקָא אִם יֵשׁ לְצָרֵף דַּעְתּוֹ (אִם הוּא רָאוּי לְכָךְ) לְהַכְרִיעַ בַּדָּבָר, אֲבָל בִּלְעֲדֵי זֶה הִיא סְתִירָה גְּמוּרָה, לַעֲשׂוֹת לִפְעָמִים כְּבֵית שַׁמַּאי וְלִפְעָמִים כְּבֵית הִלֵּל, כֵּיוָן שֶׁיְּסוֹד מַחְלָקְתָּם נוֹבֵעַ מִסִּבָּה אַחַת, כִּי גַּם מַה שֶּׁאָמְרוּ שָׁם, הָרוֹצֶה לַעֲשׂוֹת כְּדִבְרֵי בֵית שַׁמַּאי עוֹשֶׂה כְּדִבְרֵי בֵית הִלֵּל עוֹשֶׂה, הַיְנוּ דַּוְקָא אִם בְּיָדוֹ לְהַכְרִיעַ, (כַּמְבֹאָר בְּחֹשֶׁן מִשְׁפָּט סִימָן כ״ה סָעִיף ב׳ בַּהַגָּהָ״ה), וְאַל יֹאמַר הָאָדָם אֶפְסֹק כְּמִי שֶׁאֶרְצֶה בְּדָבָר שֶׁיֵּשׁ בּוֹ מַחֲלֹקֶת כוּ׳ עַיֵּן שָׁם. מַה נּוֹרָא הַחִזָּיוֹן הַזֶּה לַמַּעֲמִיק בְּדִבְרֵי רַבּוֹתֵינוּ הַפּוֹסְקִים זַ״ל, לַחְתֹּר וּלְחַפֵּשׂ סִבַּת מַחְלָקְתָּם, וְאֶת אֲשֶׁר מִמְּקוֹר שִׁנּוּי מַצַּב כֹּחוֹת נַפְשׁוֹתָם יָצְאוּ, לְהַכְנִיסָם בִּבְרִית יַחַד בַּל יִפָּרֵדוּ, לַעֲשׂוֹת כְּקֻלֵּי דְּבֵי תְּרֵי, גַּם אִם לֹא יִסְתְּרוּ אַהֲדָדֵי בְּעַצְמוּתָם, אִם לֹא תִמָּצֵא לוֹ הַכְרָעָה אוֹ צֵרוּף דֵּעוֹת אֲחֵרוֹת. (עַד כָּאן הֶעָרָה).

---

67. The Mishna records a dispute between the houses of Hillel and Shammai regarding how much must be missing from a corpse in order for it not to impart ritual impurity to anything under the same roof. In the case of a spine, the School of Shammai maintains that if it is missing two vertebrae, it does not impart impurity, whereas the School of Hillel maintains that even if it is missing only one vertebra, it can no longer impart impurity to anything under the same roof. In the case of a skull, the School of Hillel requires a larger missing piece (large enough to kill a human) than the School of Shammai (the size of a drill hole) to lose the power to impart impurity to the whole tent or house. Thus, there are two cases, one in which the School of Shammai is lenient, and one in which the School of Hillel is lenient. The Talmud then cites Rav Yehuda saying in the name of Shmuel that the two schools hold the same views with respect to determining whether an animal is a *tereifa* (i.e., suffering from a mortal injury and therefore forbidden to eat even if properly slaughtered). However, in this case, the school that adopts the larger size is taking the more *lenient* view. For instance, the school which maintains that a corpse missing one vertebra no longer imparts ritual purity to anything under the same roof – the more lenient view – would also maintain that an animal found to be missing one vertebra is not kosher – the more stringent view. Here, since the two disputes are really one, adopting the stringencies of both schools would be logically inconsistent, a self-contradiction.

Based on this, we can understand what [the Sages] said (Eiruvin 7a): "We do not follow the stringencies of two schools when they contradict one another, as in the case of the spinal column and skull[67] ... but where they do not contradict each other, we may [follow the stringencies of both]." See further there. The same is true with two lenient opinions. However, this applies only if we can add his own opinion (if he is worthy) to decide the matter.[68] Without this, it is a complete contradiction to follow the School of Shammai sometimes and the School of Hillel sometimes – since the basis of their conflicting views flows from one cause.[69] For what [the Sages] said there,[70] "One who wishes to act according to the words of the School of Shammai may; according to the words of the School of Hillel – may," also applies specifically to one who is capable of deciding (as explained in *Ḥoshen Mishpat* 25:2, in [Rema's] gloss). And let a person not say: I will rule according to whomever I please in a matter in which there is a disagreement.... See further there. What an awesome spectacle for one who delves deeply into the words of our Rabbis, the codifiers, of blessed memory, plumbing and seeking the root cause of their disagreement – and those [disagreements] which emerged from their psychological differences are brought together into a covenant; they shall not be divided to follow the leniencies of both, even if they are not in essence contradictory, unless one is capable of deciding or can combine other views.

68. The implication of the Gemara is that if adopting the stringencies or leniencies of the two schools does not create an inherent contradiction, one may do so. R. Salanter qualifies that this applies only to one who is worthy of rendering halakhic decisions and has an independent view on this matter. That is, a person, having studied Torah deeply, may find himself agreeing with the School of Shammai on some issues and the School of Hillel on other issues; this is perfectly legitimate as long as he does not adopt self-contradictory views, and as long as he is worthy of making halakhic decisions.
69. One who is not worthy of rendering independent halakhic positions must rely on the decisions of others. Such a person must consistently follow either the School of Hillel or the School of Shammai, as any mixing and matching would be self-contradictory.
70. Eiruvin 6b.

הַשֵּׂכֶל יְגַלֶּה תַּעֲלוּמוֹת חָכְמָה סִתְרֵי צְפוּנִים, יְעוֹרֵר הַדַּעַת וְהַמְּזִמָּה לַחֲקֹר וְלִשְׁאֹל, וִיבָרֵר דְּבָרִים הַמְסֻפָּקִים. הַהִתְפַּעֲלוּת, יְסוֹדָתָהּ לְפַתֵּחַ טִמְטוּם הַלֵּב, לִשְׁפֹּךְ בָּהּ מֵי תְבוּנָתוֹ, אֵת אֲשֶׁר נוֹדַע לְהָאָדָם, אָכֵן בְּקִרְבּוֹ לֹא בָאָה, בָּזֹאת, כַּאֲשֶׁר לִמּוּד הַיְשָׁרַת דַּרְכֵי הַמִּדּוֹת וְטָהֳרַת כֹּחוֹת הַנַּפְשִׁיּוֹת, נִפְרָדִים הֵמָּה מִלִּמּוּד כָּל תּוֹרָה וְחָכְמָה, יַעַן בָּהֶם הַיְדִיעָה וְאָדָם הַיּוֹדְעָם שְׁנֵי דְּבָרִים הֵמָּה, וְהַיְדִיעוֹת הֵמָּה רַק צְפוּנוֹת בְּקֶרֶב הָאָדָם, וּבָזֶה קָנָה הָאָדָם שְׁלֵמוּתוֹ לְהַנְהִיג דְּרָכָיו עַל פִּי יְדִיעוֹתָיו הַנְּכוֹחוֹת וְהַיְשָׁרוֹת. לֹא כֵן בִּדְבַר הַיְשָׁרַת דַּרְכֵי הַמִּדּוֹת וְטָהֳרַת כֹּחוֹת הַנַּפְשִׁיּוֹת, אֲשֶׁר לֹא עַל פִּי יְדִיעָתָם בִּלְבַד יִחְיֶה הָאָדָם, לְנַהֵל מַעֲשָׂיו בְּמִישׁוֹר דַּרְכֵי לְמוֹדֵיהֶם, אִם לֹא קָנְנוּ הַיְדִיעוֹת בִּלְבָבוֹ. וּקְשׁוּרִים וּצְמוּדִים בְּהָאָדָם יִהְיוּ לַאֲחָדִים. זֶה מִשְׁפַּט לְקִיחָתָם עַל יְדֵי תּוֹרַת הַהִתְפַּעֲלוּת, אֲשֶׁר זֶה דַּרְכָּהּ וְחֵילָהּ לְהַנִּיחַ בְּרָכָה בְּקֶרֶב הָאָדָם, וְגַם אַחַר הִסְתַּלְּקוּתָהּ, לֹא תַעֲלֶה בַּתֹּהוּ וְתֹאבַד, כִּי אִם תַּשְׁאִיר אַחֲרֶיהָ אֵיזֶה עוֹלְלוֹת נִסְפָּחִים אֶל הָאָדָם. וְהָיָה בִּרְבוֹת עֵסֶק הַהִתְפַּעֲלוּת, (וּבִפְרָט בַּסֵּדֶר הַמֻּכְשָׁר לְפִי תְכוּנַת הָאָדָם וּמַצָּבוֹ), כֵּן גַּם הָעוֹלְלוֹת יִתְרַבּוּ וְיִתְחַזְּקוּ לְהָפִיק מֶזֶג הָאָדָם לְטוֹב.

וּבָזֶה יֵשׁ לְבָאֵר הַכָּתוּב (מִשְׁלֵי ב׳) בְּנִי אִם תִּקַּח אֲמָרָי וּמִצְוֹתַי תִּצְפֹּן אִתָּךְ כוּ׳. כִּי נוֹדַע שֶׁתּוֹרַת ה׳ יִתְבָּרַךְ שְׁמוֹ נֶחֱלֶקֶת לִשְׁנֵי סוּגִים כּוֹלְלִים: הָאֶחָד, הֵמָּה מִצְוֹתָיו חֻקָּיו וּמִשְׁפָּטָיו יִתְבָּרַךְ שְׁמוֹ. וְהַשֵּׁנִי, יֶתֶר הַתּוֹרָה, אֲשֶׁר יְסוֹדָהּ לִדְלוֹת מִמַּעֲמַקֵּי צְפוּנִים יֹשֶׁר דַּרְכֵי הַמִּדּוֹת וְטָהֳרַת כֹּחוֹת הַנַּפְשִׁיּוֹת, עַד אֲשֶׁר לֹא יִכְסְפוּ רַק הַטּוֹב בְּעֵינֵי אֱלֹהִים וְאָדָם. זֶהוּ, אִם תִּקַּח אֲמָרָי, הֵמָּה סוּג הַשֵּׁנִי אֲשֶׁר יְסוֹדָם שֶׁיִּקְנֶה הָאָדָם

71. After an extensive excursus, R. Salanter returns to his exploration of the differences between using reason and sentiment to ascertain the truth of Torah.

72. Sentiment – what we would call emotion, feeling, excitement, etc. – is the vehicle by which one internalizes one's rational knowledge and enables it to affect character. In this passage, R. Salanter describes the process and method, *hitpaalut* (or "*hispailus*" in the pronunciation of the Mussar yeshivot), by which one attains emotional knowledge, wherein the acquired knowledge becomes part of the learners' core being and can thus shape their character and psyche.

73. Compare Deuteronomy 8:3.

Reason discovers the mysteries of wisdom, the hidden secrets.[71] It arouses the mind and the initiative to inquire and question, and it clarifies uncertain matters. The fundamental [purpose] of sentiment[72] is to break through the stultification of the heart, to pour into it the waters of his understanding – that which a person knows but has not yet internalized. Thus, the study of straightening the ways of the character traits and of the purification of the psychological drives is different from the study of all Torah and wisdom. In the latter, the knowledge and the person who knows it are two different things. The knowledge is merely stored inside a person. A person achieves wholeness by guiding his ways according to his upright and undistorted knowledge.

Not so in the matter of straightening out the ways of the character traits and purification of the psychological drives. A person cannot live by knowing them alone,[73] guiding his actions to align with what he learned, unless this knowledge has nestled into his heart; they are connected and joined to the person, becoming as one. This is the principle of their acquisition through the Torah of sentiment. This is its path and its strength, to have a blessed effect internally in the person.[74] Even after [the emotional excitation] has passed, it does not evaporate into nothingness and get lost. Rather, it leaves behind at least some unripe growth attached to the person, so when the effort through sentiment is increased (particularly in a systematic way, prepared according to the nature of the person and his condition), the immature growth increases and strengthens, affecting the temperament of the person positively.

With this we can explain the verse (Prov. 2:1): "My son, if you will take my sayings and store my commandments with you…." It is known that the Torah of God, blessed be His name, can be divided into two broad types: The first consists of His (blessed be His name) commandments, decrees, and laws. The second is the rest of the Torah, whose fundamental purpose is to draw up, from the hidden depths, the integrity of the virtuous paths and the purification of psychological drives until they long only for what is good in the eyes of God and man. Thus: "If you will take my sayings" – these are the second type, whose

74. Compare Isaiah 19:24.

דַּרְכֵי לְמוֹדֵיהֶם בְּדֶרֶךְ קִנְיָן, שֶׁיִּהְיֶה הוּא וְהֵם דָּבָר אֶחָד, וּמִצְוֹתַי תִּצְפֹּן אִתָּךְ, הֵמָּה סוּג הָאֶחָד, אֲשֶׁר הֵמָּה רַק בְּדֶרֶךְ יְדִיעָה לְהַצְפִּינָם בְּקִרְבּוֹ (כַּנִּזְכָּר לְעֵיל).

הַשֵּׂכֶל, זֶה כֹּחוֹ וּמַעֲלָתוֹ לְהִתְפַּשֵּׁט עַל כָּל גְּדוֹתָיו לְהִתְהַלֵּךְ בִּרְחָבָה, לְחַפֵּשׂ וּלְבַקֵּר עַל כָּל צִדֵּי צְדָדִים. לֹא כֵן הַהִתְפַּעֲלוּת, זֶה דַּרְכָּם לְקַוֵּץ כָּל כֹּחוֹת נַפְשׁוֹ, אֶל הַדָּבָר אֲשֶׁר עָלָיו יוֹרֶה זִקֵּי הַהִתְפַּעֲלוּת, עַד אֲשֶׁר כִּמְעַט כָּל יֶתֶר כֹּחוֹת נַפְשׁוֹ שְׁכוּחִים וְנִכְבִּים לִשְׁעָתוֹ, לְפִי עֵרֶךְ חֹזֶק הַהִתְפַּעֲלוּת.

כֵּן גַּם בִּפְנִימִיּוּת נֶפֶשׁ הָאָדָם וּמַחֲבוֹאֶיהָ, אֲשֶׁר הַכֹּחוֹת הַמְשֻׁרָשִׁים בָּהּ, הֵמָּה הַצִּירִים הַחֲזָקִים אֲשֶׁר עֲלֵיהֶם תִּסּוֹב דֶּלֶת מַעֲשֵׂי הָאָדָם וּמַאֲוָיָו (כַּאֲשֶׁר בֵּאַרְנוּ לְעֵיל), גַּם שָׁמָּה תָּנוּחַ כֹּחַ הַהִתְפַּעֲלוּת (אִם שֶׁכִּמְעַט אֵינוֹ נִכָּר וְאֵינוֹ נִרְגָּשׁ), לְהַגְבִּיר כֹּחַ אֶחָד, עַד אֲשֶׁר יֶתֶר הַכֹּחוֹת נִדְחִים מִלְּפָנָיו, וְכִמְעַט נִכְבִּים הֵמָּה (עַד לְעֵת מְצוֹא, בְּבוֹא עֲלֵיהֶם רוּחַ הִתְעוֹרְרוּת לַהֲקִיצָם שֶׁיִּתְפַּשְּׁטוּ, אָז יֵרָאוּ וְנוֹדְעוּ). לָזֹאת, אֵין לְהִתְפַּלֵּא עַל הַמִּתְגָּאֶה עַל בְּנֵי גִילוֹ, עִם גֹּדֶל חֶסְרוֹנוֹתָיו וְקַטְנוּת עֶרְכּוֹ, אֵיךְ נִהְיְתָה, כִּי מֵאַהֲבַת הָאָדָם שִׁבְחוֹ, הִיא הִיא הִתְפַּעֲלוּתוֹ, לְהַגְבִּיר כֹּחַ שִׁבְחוֹ, לִדְחוֹת כֹּחַ חֶסְרוֹנוֹתָיו וּלְכַבּוֹתָם כָּלִיל מֵהֶרְגֵּשׁ נַפְשׁוֹ. גַּם תַּאֲוַת הַיִּתְרוֹן עַל זוּלָתוֹ, מְקָרֵב אֶל נַפְשׁוֹ בְּהִתְפַּעֲלוּתוֹ אֶת חֶסְרוֹן חֲבֵרוֹ, וְנִגְבַּר כֹּחוֹ לְהַדְעִיךְ כֹּחַ הֶרְגֵּשׁ מַעֲלַת חֲבֵרוֹ, וּמְמַלֵּא הַהֶרְגֵּשׁ בְּנַפְשׁוֹ, רַק שֶׁבַח עַצְמוֹ וְחֶסְרוֹן זוּלָתוֹ. וּבָזֶה הַגַּאֲוָה מְלֵאָה כָּל בָּתֵּי נַפְשׁוֹ בְּלִי הֶרְגֵּשׁ. כֵּן הָאָדָם, רַב חֵילוֹ לְהַגְדִּיל הִתְפַּעֲלוּת בְּנַפְשׁוֹ עַל חֶסְרוֹנוֹתָיו, עַד אֲשֶׁר יִדָּחוּ מִלִּפְנֵיהֶם כֹּחַ שִׁבְחוֹ וִיכַבּוּ אֶת הַהֶרְגֵּשׁ בְּנַפְשׁוֹ, וְכָל אֲשֶׁר תּוֹסִיף הַהִתְפַּעֲלוּת תֵּת כֹּחַ בְּחֶסְרוֹנוֹתָיו, כֵּן לְעֻמַּת

75. The plain meaning of the Hebrew *tikaḥ*, which appears in the first part of the verse, is "take"; R. Salanter interprets the verse according to a different sense of the work *tikaḥ*, namely, to buy or acquire, and relates it to those "sayings" of God that must be internalized.

76. See Letter 6.

77. Note that in this letter, R. Salanter has shifted the role of sentiment in learning from a general Mussar method that can be used in all areas so that the learning can have

fundamental purpose is for a person to acquire their ways of learning as a possession,[75] such that he and they will be one. "And store my commandments with you" – these are the first type, which are merely stored within him as information (as mentioned above).

The power and superiority of reason is [expressed] in its overflowing all its banks and spreading out, seeking and investigating every last aspect. Not so sentiment; its manner is to focus all his psychological force on the object at which sentiment shoots its arrows, to where practically all his other psychological drives are temporarily forgotten and extinguished, depending on the magnitude of the sentiment.

So it is deep within the human psyche and its hidden alleys; the forces rooted therein are the strong hinges on which the door of a person's actions and desires swings (as we explained above).[76] There, too, the force of sentiment will alight (even though it is barely discernible and not felt) to intensify one force, until the rest of the psychological forces are pushed aside by it and they are almost snuffed out (until the opportune moment, when a spirit of arousal comes upon them to awaken them to spread out – then they are seen and known).[77] So one should not be surprised that someone might take pride in himself over his peers despite his great shortcomings and little value: for a person's love of being praised – this is his sentimentality – amplifies the power of such praise and pushes aside the power of his [awareness of] his shortcomings, completely eliminating them from his conscious perception. Likewise, one's lust for superiority over the other disposes his psyche, in its state of sentimental agitation, to [perceive] his friend's shortcomings. Its power is amplified, crushing his ability to perceive his friend's qualities. Consequently, he consciously perceives only his own praiseworthiness and the shortcomings of the other. Thus, pride fills all the chambers of his soul, unnoticed.

By the same token, a person is perfectly capable of amplifying his sentimental agitation about his own shortcomings, until they push aside the force of his [love of] praise and extinguish it from his conscious perception; the more his sentiments strengthen his [awareness

---

a greater impact and be internalized, to a technique used primarily in character development.

זֶה שָׁכֹחַ יִשָּׁכַח מִמֶּנּוּ הֶרְגֵּשׁ מַעֲלוֹתָיו. זֹאת תּוֹרַת דַּרְכֵי קְנִיַּת הָעֲנָוָה וְזֶה מִשְׁפָּטָהּ בִּכְלָל.

וּבָזֶה יִתְבָּאֵר מַאֲמַר רַבּוֹתֵינוּ זַ״ל (בְּרָכוֹת לב:) הֲתִשְׁכַּח אִשָּׁה עוּלָהּ, אָמַר הַקָּדוֹשׁ־בָּרוּךְ־הוּא כְּלוּם אֶשְׁכַּח עוֹלוֹת אֵילִים וּפִטְרֵי רְחָמִים שֶׁהִקְרַבְתְּ לְפָנַי בַּמִּדְבָּר, אָמְרָה לְפָנָיו רִבּוֹנוֹ שֶׁל עוֹלָם הוֹאִיל וְאֵין שִׁכְחָה לִפְנֵי כִסֵּא כְבוֹדֶךָ, שֶׁמָּא לֹא תִשְׁכַּח לִי מַעֲשֵׂה הָעֵגֶל, אָמַר לָהּ גַּם אֵלֶּה תִשְׁכַּחְנָה כוּ׳ עַיֵּן שָׁם. כִּי יָדוּעַ, שֶׁמִּדּוֹתָיו שֶׁל הַקָּדוֹשׁ־בָּרוּךְ־הוּא מִדָּה כְּנֶגֶד מִדָּה, (בְּשִׂכְלִי וְלֹא בְדִמְיוֹנִי, בְּאֵיכוּת וְלֹא בְכַמּוּת), וּכְשֶׁהָאָדָם אוֹחֵז דַּרְכֵי הַצֶּדֶק לְפַקֵּחַ וּלְהִתְעַמֵּל שֶׁיִּשְׁכַּח מַעֲלוֹתָיו, גַּם הַקָּדוֹשׁ־בָּרוּךְ־הוּא כִּבְיָכוֹל גּוֹמֵל חַסְדּוֹ לִשְׁכֹּחַ חֶסְרוֹנוֹתָיו. אָכֵן צִדְקַת מַעֲשָׂיו הַטּוֹבִים נִזְכָּרִים לְפָנָיו יִתְבָּרַךְ, מִפְּנֵי שֶׁהָאָדָם זוֹכֵר פְּחִיתוּתוֹ. זֶהוּ (לְפִי הַדְּרָשׁ הֲתִשְׁכַּח אִשָּׁה עוּלָהּ, כַּאֲשֶׁר תִּשְׁכַּח כְּנֶסֶת יִשְׂרָאֵל עוֹלוֹת אֵילִים שֶׁהִקְרִיבָה בַּמִּדְבָּר, הַנּוֹבֵעַ מִתִּגְבֹּרֶת הַהִתְפַּעֲלוּת לִזְכֹּר מַעֲשֵׂה הָעֵגֶל), גַּם אֵלֶּה תִשְׁכַּחְנָה, כִּבְיָכוֹל הַקָּדוֹשׁ־בָּרוּךְ־הוּא שׁוֹכֵחַ מַעֲשֵׂה הָעֵגֶל וְזוֹכֵר הָעוֹלוֹת, זֶהוּ שֶׁאָמַר הַקָּדוֹשׁ־בָּרוּךְ־הוּא כְּלוּם אֶשְׁכַּח עוֹלוֹת אֵילִים וּפִטְרֵי רְחָמִים וְכוּ׳.

כֵּן גַּם בְּכָל דַּרְכֵי תִּקּוּן הַמִּדּוֹת, אִם יִשְׁתַּמֵּשׁ הָאָדָם בְּתוֹרַת לִמּוּד הַהִתְפַּעֲלוּת אֲשֶׁר יַשְׁאִירוּ בְּרָכָה בְּקִרְבּוֹ (כַּנִּזְכָּר לְעֵיל), לְהַשְׁרִישׁ הִתְפַּעֲלוּת צְפוּנוֹת בִּלְבָבוֹ וְיֶעֶבְתוּ הַרְבֵּה (מֵרִבּוּי הַלִּמּוּד וְהָעֵסֶק בְּסֵדֶר נָכוֹן לְפִי תְכוּנָתוֹ), עַד אֲשֶׁר יִתְאַחֲדוּ בְּהָאָדָם וְיִתְקְעוּ יָתֵד נֶאֱמָן לְטֶבַע קַיָּם עַל יְדֵי רִבּוּי הַהֶרְגֵּל בְּהִתְנַהֲגוּתָם בְּפֹעַל, (כַּמְבֹאָר בְּדִבְרֵי הָרַמְבַּ״ם בְּהִלְכוֹת דֵּעוֹת), אָז אֵין עֲרֹךְ לְגֹדֶר עֲלִיָּתָם הַגָּבֹהַּ

78. Isaiah 49:15.

79. Compare *Zikhronot*/Remembrances section of the Rosh HaShana *Musaf* prayer.

80. The continuation of Isaiah 49:15.

of] his shortcomings, the more his sense of superiority is forgotten. This is the Torah of how to acquire humility, and this is its general principle.

This explains the adage of our Rabbis, of blessed memory (Berakhot 32b): "'Can a woman forget her nursing child (*ulah*)? [Would she not have mercy (*meraḥem*) the child of her womb?]'[78] The Holy One, blessed be He, said: 'Can I forget the burnt offerings (*olot*) of rams and firstborns (*pitrei reḥem*) that you brought before Me in the desert?' [The community of Israel] said: 'Since there is no forgetting before Your Throne of Glory,[79] perhaps You will never forget the making of the [golden] calf?' He replied: 'Even these will be forgotten....'[80]" See further there.

It is known that the Holy One, blessed be He, metes out [reward and punishment] *quid pro quo* (rationally, not imaginatively; qualitatively, not quantitatively). When a person clings to the ways of righteousness, self-analyzing and struggling to forget his own virtues, then the Holy One, blessed be He, as it were, returns his loving-kindness and forgets his shortcomings. The righteousness of his good deeds is remembered before Him, blessed be He, because the person remembers his own defectiveness.

This is (according to the midrash on "Can a woman forget her nursing child?" – when the community of Israel forgets the burnt offerings of rams they brought in the desert, which stemmed from the increase of their sentimental agitation to remember the deed of the Golden Calf), the meaning of "even these will be forgotten." The Holy One, blessed be He, as it were, forgets the making of the Golden Calf and remembers the burnt offerings. Thus: "The Holy One, blessed be He, said: 'Can I forget the burnt offerings of rams and firstborns ... ?'"

So it is with all the processes of sublimation: If a person uses the method of training the sentiments, which will result in his being blessed (as mentioned above) to imbue sentiment into the hidden recesses of the heart, they will grow more robust (as a result of increased study and engaging in it in the right order, according to his own nature), to the point that they will be joined together in the person and form a steady anchor within one's existing nature through repeated conditioning of behavior (as explained in *Mishneh Torah,* Laws of Moral Dispositions). Then there is no limit to the boundaries of their ascent beyond human

לְמַעְלָה מִשֵּׂכֶל אֱנוֹשִׁי, כִּשְׁאָר תְּכוּנַת טִבְעֵי מִזְגֵי הָאָדָם, אֲשֶׁר לֹא יַקִּיפָם הַשֵּׂכֶל, וּבָזֶה רוּחַ הָאָדָם עוֹלָה לְמַעְלָה. כֵּן תֵּרֵד חַס וְשָׁלוֹם לְמַטָּה, עַד אֲשֶׁר לֹא תַּרְגִּישׁ בְּרָעָתָהּ, מֵרִבּוּי הִתְפַּעֲלוּת הַתַּאֲוָה, אֲשֶׁר תַּשְׁאִיר שָׁרְשָׁהּ לְעַוֵּת נֶפֶשׁ מִטָּהֳרָהּ. לָזֹאת, כַּאֲשֶׁר יִתֵּן הָאָדָם אֶל לִבּוֹ לַחְפֹּץ חַיִּים (חַיֵּי הַשֵּׂכֶל, כִּי כָּל חַי מַרְגִּישׁ), זֹאת יַעֲשֶׂה, יִלְמַד מַאַמְרֵי חֲכָמֵינוּ זַ״ל הַמְדַבְּרִים מִכִּשְׁרוֹן הַמִּדּוֹת וְחַיֵּי הַנִּצְחִי, וְיַחֲזֹר עֲלֵיהֶם כַּמָּה פְּעָמִים לְהִתְפַּעֵל בִּשְׁעָתָם.

אַל יִפֹּל לִבּוֹ בִּרְאוֹתוֹ כִּי לֹא נִשְׁאַר שׁוּם רֹשֶׁם בִּלְבָבוֹ, וְיֵדַע נֶאֱמָנָה, כִּי הִתְפַּעֲלוּתוֹ לֹא עָלְתָה בַּתֹּהוּ, רַק הִנִּיחָה בְּרָכָה בִּלְתִּי נִרְגֶּשֶׁת לְחוּשֵׁי בָּשָׂר, עַד אֲשֶׁר יִרְבּוּ, וְאָז יַכּוּ שֹׁרֶשׁ לְהוֹצִיא פְּרִי צֶדֶק, וְכַאֲשֶׁר רְסִיסֵי מַיִם, אִם יֵרְדוּ טִיף טִיף עַל הָאֶבֶן יָמִים וְשָׁנִים הַרְבֵּה, יִשְׁחָקוּהָ, אִם שֶׁבַּטִּפָּה הָרִאשׁוֹנָה לֹא הָיָה נִרְאֶה וְנִרְגָּשׁ, כֵּן מַאַמְרֵי חֲכָמֵינוּ זַ״ל עַל לֵב הָאֶבֶן, יַהֲפֹךְ בָּם לְמַרְבֶּה, וִיפַלְּחוּ לְבָבוֹ.

אוּלַי הוּא מַאֲמַר חֲכָמֵינוּ זַ״ל (אָבוֹת דְּרַבִּי נָתָן פֶּרֶק ו׳) וְזֶה לְשׁוֹנָם: מֶה הָיְתָה תְּחִלָּתוֹ שֶׁל רַבִּי עֲקִיבָא, אָמְרוּ בֶּן אַרְבָּעִים שָׁנָה הָיָה וְלֹא שָׁנָה כְּלוּם, פַּעַם אַחַת הָיָה עוֹמֵד עַל פִּי הַבְּאֵר, אָמַר מִי חָקַק אֶבֶן זוֹ, אָמְרוּ לוֹ הַמַּיִם שֶׁתָּדִיר נוֹפְלִים עָלֶיהָ בְּכָל יוֹם, אָמְרוּ לוֹ, עֲקִיבָא, אִי אַתָּה קוֹרֵא אֲבָנִים שָׁחֲקוּ מַיִם. מִיָּד הָיָה דָּן רַבִּי עֲקִיבָא קַל וָחֹמֶר בְּעַצְמוֹ, מָה רַךְ פָּסַל אֶת הַקָּשֶׁה, דִּבְרֵי תּוֹרָה שֶׁקָּשָׁה כַּבַּרְזֶל, עַל אַחַת כַּמָּה וְכַמָּה שֶׁיְּחַקְקוּ אֶת לִבִּי שֶׁהוּא בָּשָׂר וָדָם, מִיָּד חָזַר לִלְמֹד תּוֹרָה כו׳ עַיֵּן שָׁם. כִּי רַבִּי עֲקִיבָא בִּרְאוֹתוֹ בִּתְחִלַּת לִמּוּדוֹ, שֶׁאֵינוֹ מוֹצֵא הֶרְגֵּשׁ בְּנַפְשׁוֹ, וַיַּכֵּהוּ לְבָבוֹ לֵאמֹר: לַשָּׁוְא יִתְעַמֵּל (כִּי אִם אֵין יִרְאָה אֵין חָכְמָה), לַתֹּהוּ וָהֶבֶל יְכַלֶּה כֹּחוֹ חַס וְחָלִילָה. אָכֵן בִּרְאוֹתוֹ, כִּי אֲבָנִים שָׁחֲקוּ מַיִם, אִם כִּי לֹא נִרְגַּשׁ בַּתְּחִלָּה, אָזַר עֹז וּגְבוּרָה לְחַזֵּק אֶת נַפְשׁוֹ, כִּי טוֹב אַחֲרִית דָּבָר מֵרֵאשִׁיתוֹ.

---

81. Compare Ecclesiastes 3:21.

82. But only humans can exercise reason.

83. I.e., a positive effect.

84. I.e., prepare it for cultivation.

85. Compare Ecclesiastes 7:8.

reason – just as with the other qualities of the nature of human temperaments, which reason cannot encompass. Thus, the human spirit is raised up,[81] and so it can also sink down, God forbid, to the extent that it does not sense its own wickedness, because of the repeated excitation of lust, which will sink roots that corrupt a soul from its purity. So, when a person commits himself to desire life (the life of reason, for every living thing feels[82]), he should do the following: He should learn sayings of our Sages, of blessed memory, which deal with training the character traits and with eternal life, and go over them several times so that they affect his sentiments in that moment.

One should not be disheartened when he sees that no impression is left in his heart. He should know with certainty that his *hitpaalut* [his sentimental affectation] was not fruitless; rather, it left blessing[83] that cannot be discerned by the physical senses until they grow, at which point they strike roots to bring forth righteous fruit. As drops of water, if they fall drop by drop on a stone for many days and years, will wear a stone away – even though in the first drop this was neither seen nor felt – so the sayings of the Sages, of blessed memory, will affect a heart of stone. One should constantly turn them over, and they will plow his heart.[84]

Perhaps this is the meaning of the saying of our Sages, of blessed memory (*Avot DeRabbi Natan*, ch. 6): "What was the origin of R. Akiva? They said: He was forty years old and had not studied at all. Once he was standing by a well. He said: 'Who hollowed out this stone?' They said to him: 'The water that continually falls on it each day.' They said to him: 'Akiva, have you not read [the Scriptural verse], "The stones worn down by water" [Job 14:19]?' Immediately, R. Akiva reasoned *a fortiori*: If the soft [water] carved out the hard [stone], then the words of Torah, which are as hard as iron, will certainly impress themselves on my heart, which is only flesh and blood! He immediately returned to study Torah...." See further there. For R. Akiva, at the beginning of his studies [when he was young], saw that his soul was not affected, his heart tormented him, saying: You toil in vain (for if there is no reverence, there is no wisdom). You will use up your strength on vanity and fruitlessness. However, when he saw "the stones worn down by water," even though the impression was not initially discernible – he girded up his might and courage to strengthen his soul, for "the end of the matter is better than its beginning."[85]

מַה יָּחִיל לֵב הָאָדָם, פַּלָּצוּת תֹּאחֲזֵנוּ, בְּהִתְבּוֹנְנֵנוּ, פֶּן חַס וְשָׁלוֹם נִתְקְעוּ מוֹרָשֵׁי לְבָבוֹ וְנִתְבַּטֵּל הֶרְגֵּשׁוֹ, אַף גַּם בְּדָבָר אֶחָד, אֲשֶׁר יוֹדֵעַ לְמַעְלָה, כִּי הוּא בְּגֶדֶר אֵינוֹ עוֹשֶׂה תְּשׁוּבָה כִּי בְּנַפְשׁוֹ הוּא חַס וְשָׁלוֹם, וּכְמַאֲמַר רַבּוֹתֵינוּ זַ"ל (יַלְקוּט יְחֶזְקֵאל י"ח) שָׁאֲלוּ לַנְּבוּאָה חוֹטֵא מַה הוּא עָנְשׁוֹ, אָמְרָה לָהֶם הַנֶּפֶשׁ הַחוֹטֵאת הִיא תָמוּת וְכוּ', שָׁאֲלוּ לְהַקָּדוֹשׁ־בָּרוּךְ־הוּא, חוֹטֵא מַה עָנְשׁוֹ, אָמַר לָהֶם, יַעֲשֶׂה תְשׁוּבָה וְיִתְכַּפֵּר לוֹ כוּ' עַיֵּן שָׁם. וּכְאָמְרָם זַ"ל (נִדָּה ע:) כָּתוּב אֶחָד אוֹמֵר (יְחֶזְקֵאל י"ח), כִּי לֹא אֶחְפֹּץ בְּמוֹת הַמֵּת, וְכָתוּב אֶחָד אוֹמֵר (שְׁמוּאֵל־א' ב'), כִּי חָפֵץ ה' לַהֲמִיתָם, כָּאן בְּעוֹשִׂין תְּשׁוּבָה כָּאן בְּשֶׁאֵין עוֹשִׂין תְּשׁוּבָה. וּבִפְרָט טְרוּדֵי הַזְּמַן עֲמוּסֵי הַתְּלָאָה, הָעֲלוּלִים מְאֹד לַעֲבֵרוֹת נִשָּׂאוֹת וּבַל יַרְגִּישׁוּ מְאוּמָה, וּבִפְרָט בֵּין אָדָם לַחֲבֵרוֹ, קִנְאָה, שִׂנְאָה, לָשׁוֹן הָרַע, הַלְבָּנַת פָּנִים וּמִרְמַת הָעֵסֶק עַל כֻּלָּנָה, אֲשֶׁר לְבַקֵּשׁ אֹמֶץ הַחַיִּים, מֵהַיָּאוּת וְהַיָּשָׁר לַעֲשׂוֹת כְּנֶגְדָּם מִצְוֹת וּדְבָרִים טוֹבִים אֲשֶׁר יַכְרִיעוּ בְּמִשְׁקָלָם, וּמַה יַּעֲשֶׂה קָשֶׁה יוֹם. אַחַת הִיא מְלָאכָה קַלָּה, אֵינֶנָּה דּוֹרֶשֶׁת דַּעַת צְלוּלָה וְלֹא זְמַן אָרֹךְ, לַחֲזֹר עַל מוּסְרֵי הַחֲכָמִים כַּמָּה פְּעָמִים, עַד אֲשֶׁר תִּתְעוֹרֵר הִתְפַּעֲלוּת בְּנַפְשׁוֹ לִשְׁעָתָהּ, וְאִם גַּם לֹא תִתֵּן פִּרְיָהּ בָּרִאשׁוֹנָה לְהֵיטִיב דַּרְכֵי גֶבֶר, בְּכָל זֹאת בְּסֵפֶר הַחַיִּים יֵחָשֵׁב, בִּהְיוֹתוֹ חַי מַרְגִּישׁ, וּלְכָל אֲשֶׁר יְחֻבַּר אֶל הַחַיִּים יֵשׁ בִּטָּחוֹן, וּבִכְלָל עוֹשֵׂי תְּשׁוּבָה יִמָּנֶה.

וּבָזֶה יֵשׁ לְבָאֵר הַכָּתוּב (יְחֶזְקֵאל ל"ג) בְּאָמְרִי לָרָשָׁע מוֹת תָּמוּת

---

86. Elsewhere (see for example, Letter 7), R. Salanter generalizes that people who sin become hardened and lose sensitivity. Thus, shaking off sin and then repenting is not just necessary to avoid being punished by God as one who cannot repent, as expressed here, but also shunning evil and turning to good constitutes a reclaiming of zest for life and the revival of emotional life.

87. "*Bitaḥon*"; he can trust that he won't be struck dead as a sinner incapable of repentance.

88. R. Salanter believes that people who sin and slip into this unthinking, ongoing, bad pattern lose the capacity for feeling. The habitual sinner, as it were, is "punished" by a loss of feeling and of awareness. That is why he tends to end up in the category of one who will never repent. In turn, his inability to repent evokes a heavenly judgment that he deserves to die. The challenge (and the opportunity) of the sinner is

How the heart of man will tremble, how terror will seize him, when he considers that, God forbid, the nerves of his heart are severed and his capacity for sentiment has been nullified, if it is known above in Heaven that he is in the category of one who cannot repent – even if in only one matter – and his soul is condemned, God forbid. As our Rabbis, of blessed memory, say (*Yalkut*, Ezekiel 18): "They asked prophecy: 'What is the punishment of the sinner?' She answered: 'The soul that sins shall die….' [Ezek. 18:20]. They asked the Holy One, blessed be He: 'What is the punishment of the sinner?' He said to them: 'Let him repent and be forgiven….'" See further there. And they, of blessed memory, said (Nidda 70b): "One verse (Ezek. 18:32) says: 'For I do not desire the death of the [sinner] who dies,' and another verse says (I Sam. 2:25): 'For the Lord sought to put them to death.' [Isn't this a contradiction? No. Rather,] this [Ezek. 18:20] deals with those who repent, and that [I Sam. 2:25] deals with those who do not repent."

Particularly those preoccupied with daily life, burdened by tribulation, are very prone to terrible sins while feeling nothing, especially interpersonal sins: envy, hatred, slander, shaming, and above all cheating in business.[86] One must seek the vitality of life from what is proper and correct to offset these tendencies through mitzvot and good deeds that outweigh them. But what shall a working person do?

There is one simple activity, which does not require a clear mind nor a lot of time: to go over Mussar sayings of the Sages repeatedly, until it temporarily awakens sentiment within his soul. Even if it does not bear fruit initially to improve the person's ways, he will still be considered in the book of the living – since he is still alive and feeling. And as long as he is connected to life, there is security,[87] and he is counted among those who have the ability to repent.[88]

With this we can explain the verses (Ezek. 33:8–11):

---

to keep feeling and self-awareness alive, so even though he is in a bad pattern, he is able – maybe even likely – to repent, change, and improve. As R. Salanter said below, the human never loses the free will to change from evil to good, but once he loses his feeling and self-awareness, he is much more likely to sink hopelessly into patterns of wickedness.

וְלֹא דִבַּרְתָּ לְהַזְהִיר רָשָׁע מִדַּרְכּוֹ הוּא רָשָׁע בַּעֲוֹנוֹ יָמוּת וְגוֹ׳, וְאַתָּה כִּי הִזְהַרְתָּ רָשָׁע מִדַּרְכּוֹ לָשׁוּב מִמֶּנָּה וְלֹא שָׁב מִדַּרְכּוֹ הוּא בַּעֲוֹנוֹ יָמוּת וְגוֹ׳, וְאַתָּה בֶן אָדָם אֱמֹר אֶל בֵּית יִשְׂרָאֵל כֵּן אֲמַרְתֶּם לֵאמֹר כִּי פְשָׁעֵינוּ וְחַטֹּאתֵינוּ עָלֵינוּ וּבָם אֲנַחְנוּ נְמַקִּים וְאֵיךְ נִחְיֶה. אֱמֹר אֲלֵיהֶם חַי אָנִי וְגוֹ׳ אִם אֶחְפֹּץ בְּמוֹת הָרָשָׁע כִּי אִם בְּשׁוּב רָשָׁע מִדַּרְכּוֹ וְחָיָה שׁוּבוּ שׁוּבוּ מִדַּרְכֵיכֶם הָרָעִים כוּ׳, כִּי פֻּרְעָנִיּוֹת בָּאָה עַל הָאָדָם עַל יְדֵי שְׁתֵּי בְּחִינוֹת. הָאַחַת אִם נִתְמַלְּאָה סְאָתוֹ, כְּמַאֲמַר רַבּוֹתֵינוּ זַ״ל (סוֹטָה ט׳) אֵין הַקָּדוֹשׁ־בָּרוּךְ־הוּא נִפְרָע מִן הָאָדָם עַד שֶׁתִּתְמַלֵּא סְאָתוֹ עַיֵּן שָׁם, וְאָז נִקְרָא רָשָׁע (לִפְנֵי הַמָּקוֹם כְּמוֹ שֶׁבֵּאֵר הָרַ״ן בְּרֹאשׁ הַשָּׁנָה (טז:), עַל הָא דִּשְׁלֹשָׁה סְפָרִים נִפְתָּחִים כוּ׳, רְשָׁעִים כוּ׳, דְּהַיְנוּ רְשָׁעִים בְּדִין זֶה, עַיֵּן שָׁם), הַשֵּׁנִי אִם יֵשׁ לוֹ חֵטְא, אֲשֶׁר הוּא בְּדִין שָׁמַיִם בִּבְחִינַת אֵין עוֹשֶׂה תְּשׁוּבָה, בִּבְחִינַת שִׂכְלִי לְפִי הַקִּשּׁוּר הַמְסוּבָבִים בְּסִבָּתָם.

כִּי כָּל הַדְּבָרִים הַנַּעֲשִׂים תַּחַת הַשֶּׁמֶשׁ נוֹפְלִים תַּחַת שְׁנֵי סוּגִים כּוֹלְלִים: הָאֶחָד בְּחִינָה הַטִּבְעִית, אֲשֶׁר הִיא בְּחִינָה הַשִּׂכְלִית, כָּל מְסוּבָב נוֹלַד מִסִּבָּתוֹ, וְהַסִּבָּה מִסִּבָּה אַחֶרֶת, עַד בּוֹא הַדָּבָר לַבְּחִינָה. הַשֵּׁנִי וְהוּא מְסוּבָב הַבָּא בִּלְתִּי סִבָּה קוֹדֶמֶת (רַק כֵּן גָּזְרָה חָכְמָתוֹ יִתְבָּרַךְ, וְכֵן גַּם בְּחִינָה הַנִּסִּיִּית, אֲשֶׁר הִיא לְמַעְלָה מִשֵּׂכֶל אֱנוֹשִׁי).

כֵּן גַּם הַיְדִיעוֹת שְׁנֵי מִינִים הֵמָּה. הָאֶחָד יְדִיעָה מֻחְלֶטֶת שֶׁאֵינֶנָּה נוֹפֶלֶת תַּחַת הַשִּׁנּוּי וְהַתְּמוּרָה. הַשֵּׁנִי יְדִיעָה שִׂכְלִית לְפִי קִשּׁוּר הַדְּבָרִים, מִסִּבָּה לִמְסוּבָב, וְהַמְסוּבָב נַעֲשֶׂה סִבָּה לִמְסוּבָב אַחֵר, וְכֹה יִתְגַּלְגֵּל הַדָּבָר עַד בּוֹא אֶל הַמְסוּבָב הָאַחֲרוֹן. הַיְדִיעָה הַזֹּאת נוֹפֶלֶת תַּחַת הַתְּמוּרָה, כִּי לִפְעָמִים תֵּצֵא דָבָר מִבְּלִי סִבָּה, אַף אִם סִבָּתָהּ מְנַגַּדְתָּהּ (הַנִּקְרֵאת בְּחִינָה נִסִּיִּית). הַיְדִיעָה הָאַחַת אֵינֶנָּה בְּגֶדֶר אֱנוֹשִׁי,

89. Seeing the propensity of his addiction to his sin and the weakness of his counter-urges or influences, Heaven judges that he will never repent.

> When I [God] say to the wicked man, "You shall die" – and you have not spoken to warn the wicked man away from his ways – then that wicked man will die for his sin, [but I will hold you responsible for his life].... But if you have warned the wicked man to turn from his way and he did not turn from it, then he will die for his sin [and you will have saved your life].... And you, son of man, say to the House of Israel: You have spoken, saying: "Our sins and transgressions [weigh heavily] upon us, and we pine away in them; how shall we live?" Say to them: "As I [God] live...do I desire the death of the wicked? Rather let the wicked one turn from his way and live. Return, return from your wicked ways...."

For retribution comes to a person in two ways. One is if he has filled up his measure, as our Rabbis, of blessed memory, say (Sota 9a): "The Holy One, blessed be He, does not exact retribution from a person until his measure is filled." See further there. Then he is called wicked (before God, as Ran explained the notion, in Rosh HaShana [16b], that "three books are opened...the book of the wicked...," that is, "wicked" with respect to this law; see further there). The second is if he has a sin which, in Heaven's judgment, places him in the category of one who cannot repent – from a rational perspective, according to the chain of cause and effect.[89]

All things done under the sun fall into two general categories. One is the natural, which follows rational criteria: each effect is a product of its cause, and each cause has its cause, until the matter is thoroughly examined. The second is when the effect comes without a preceding cause (only because God's wisdom, blessed be He, has decreed it – this is also the category of the miraculous, which is beyond human reason).

There are likewise two types of knowledge. One is absolute knowledge, which is subject to neither change nor replacement. The second is rational knowledge, arrived at by the chain of matters, from cause to effect, which in turn becomes the cause of another effect, and so the matter goes until reaching the final effect. This kind of knowledge is subject to change, for sometimes, something emerges without a cause, and even in opposition to its causes (this is the category of the

(אִם לֹא עַל יְדֵי בְּחִינַת הַנְּבוּאָה). גַּם בַּיְדִיעָה הַשֵּׁנִית, קָצְרָה יַד אֱנוֹשׁ לָבוֹא עַד תַּכְלִיתָהּ, מִפְּאַת חֶסְרוֹן יְדִיעָתוֹ. מִכָּל עִנְיָנֵי הַסִּבּוֹת הַנּוֹגְעִים אֶל הַדָּבָר הַמְעֻתָּד לָצֵאת לַפֹּעַל, לָזֹאת רָזָה בִּינַת אֱנוֹשׁ לָבוֹא בִּידִיעָה שִׂכְלִית לִשְׁלֵמוּתָהּ.

כֵּן בִּבְחִירַת אֱנוֹשׁ, בְּאֵיזֶה דֶּרֶךְ יִתְהַלֵּךְ אִם לְטוֹב אוֹ לְרַע, יֶשְׁנָן שְׁתֵּי בְּחִינוֹת: הָאַחַת בְּחִירָה שִׂכְלִית בְּקִשּׁוּר הַמְּסוֹבָב בְּסִבָּה, לְרַע, לְפֶתַח הַתַּאֲוָה כְּפִי אֲשֶׁר תַּטֵּהוּ דַּרְכָּהּ לְהַלְאָה אִם יְמַלֵּא חֶפְצָהּ, לְטוֹב לְפִי תַּהֲלוּכוֹת דַּרְכֵי לִמּוּד תּוֹרַת ה׳ וְחָכְמַת מוּסָרוֹ לְהִתְנַהֵג בִּדְרָכָיו. הַשְּׁנִיָּה בְּחִינָה פְּשׁוּטָה מֵרַע לְטוֹב וּלְהֶפֶךְ חַס וְשָׁלוֹם, כִּי בְּכָל עֵת וּזְמַן הָאָדָם עוֹמֵד בִּבְחִירָתוֹ בְּאֵין מוֹנֵעַ. גַּם הַיְדִיעָה בִּבְחִירַת הָאָדָם נֶחֱלֶקֶת לִשְׁנֵי מִינִים.

הָאַחַת יְדִיעָה מֻחְלֶטֶת, אֲשֶׁר אֵין לְהַעֲלוֹת עַל הַדַּעַת, אֵיךְ לֹא תִּהְיֶה סְתִירָה לְהַבְּחִירָה, (כַּאֲשֶׁר בֵּאֵר הָרַמְבַּ״ם בְּפֶרֶק ה׳ מֵהִלְכוֹת תְּשׁוּבָה). הַשְּׁנִיָּה יְדִיעָה שִׂכְלִית, לְפִי הַנְהָגַת הָאָדָם, טִבְעוֹ וְעִנְיָנוֹ, לְפִי קִשּׁוּר הַמְּסוֹבָבִים בְּסִבָּתָם אֶל נָכוֹן, אֲשֶׁר בְּהַיְדִיעָה הַלָּזוֹ מַנְהִיג הַקָּדוֹשׁ־בָּרוּךְ־הוּא אֶת עוֹלָמוֹ לְטוֹב (דַּוְקָא, לֹא לְרַע, כִּי אֵין הַקָּדוֹשׁ־בָּרוּךְ־הוּא דָּן אֶת הָאָדָם אֶלָּא בְּשָׁעָה שֶׁהוּא עוֹמֵד בָּהּ, כַּמְבֹאָר בִּירוּשַׁלְמִי (רֹאשׁ הַשָּׁנָה פֶּרֶק א׳), אֲבָל לְטוֹבָה הַקָּדוֹשׁ־בָּרוּךְ־הוּא נוֹתֵן בְּהַקָּפָה, כְּמַאֲמַר רַבּוֹתֵינוּ ז״ל (יַלְקוּט אִיּוֹב מ״א) מִי הִקְדִּימַנִי וַאֲשַׁלֵּם כּוּ׳, מִי מָל לְפָנַי עַד שֶׁלֹּא נָתַתִּי לוֹ בֵּן, מִי עָשָׂה צִיצִית עַד שֶׁלֹּא נָתַתִּי לוֹ טַלִּית כּוּ׳, עַיֵּן שָׁם).

וּבָזֶה יֵשׁ לְבָאֵר הַכָּתוּב (דְּבָרִים י״א) אֶת הַבְּרָכָה אֲשֶׁר תִּשְׁמְעוּ כּוּ׳, בְּהַקָּפָה, לְמַעַן תִּשְׁמְעוּ וְתַעֲשׂוּ הַטּוֹב בְּבִרְכָתִי, וְהַקְּלָלָה אִם לֹא

---

90. I.e., foreknowledge of human choice.

91. ... for everything under the heavens is Mine."

92. In judging whether a person is evil, God judges the person as of this moment, without factoring in any future wrongs, which God alone knows are coming. In judging whether a person is good, however, God factors in future good behaviors by this person. That is God's way in the world. God gives life and good to people before they have earned it or given back.

miraculous). The first kind of absolute knowledge is not within human capacity (unless it be through the category of prophecy). Even in the second kind of knowledge, it is beyond human capability to arrive at its ultimate end, because of the limits of human capacity to know all the causes that pertain to the eventual effect. In this respect, human understanding is too frail to arrive at complete rational knowledge.

Likewise with regard to human choice – the way one goes, whether to good or to evil – there are two categories. One is rational choice, predicated on the chain of cause and effect. If [the choice is] toward evil, into the maw of lust, it is in keeping with how its methods incline him to itself in order to fulfill its wishes; if toward good, it follows the procedures of the ways of study of God's Torah and the wisdom of His Mussar, to behave in God's ways. The second category is simply choosing to go from evil to good, or the reverse, God forbid. For in every moment and occasion a person retains his capacity to choose with no impediment.

God's knowledge of human choice is also divided into two kinds. The first is absolute knowledge,[90] and one cannot grasp how such knowledge would not contradict free choice (as Rambam explains in chapter 5 of the Laws of Repentance). The second is rational knowledge, based on a person's behavior, nature, and situation, and on properly linking cause and effect. It is with this latter knowledge that God governs His world for good (specifically for good, and not for evil, for the Holy One, blessed be He, does not judge a person except in that moment in which he stands; as explained in the Yerushalmi [Rosh HaShana, ch, 1]. For good, however, the Holy One, blessed be He, extends credit, as our Rabbis, of blessed memory, say [*Yalkut*, Job ch. 41]: "'Who has a prior claim on Me that I will pay...[91]' [Job 41:3] – Who practiced circumcision even before I had given him a son? Who made fringes before I gave him a four-cornered garment?..."; see further there).[92]

With this we can explain the verse (Deut. 11:27): "The blessing on condition that you listen ... ." I give you the blessing on credit, so that you then listen and do the good with My blessing. "The curse, [I give you only] if you do not listen..." (ibid. 11:28) – and not before then.

תִּשְׁמְעוּ וְגוֹ׳, לֹא מִקֹּדֶם. גַּם יֵשׁ לְבָאֵר מַאֲמַר חֲכָמֵינוּ זַ״ל (פְּסָחִים קי״א) הוֹדוּ לַה׳ כִּי טוֹב, הוֹדוּ לְמִי שֶׁגּוֹבֶה חוֹבָתוֹ שֶׁל אָדָם בְּטוֹבָתוֹ, עָשִׁיר בְּשׁוֹרוֹ עָנִי בְּשֵׂיוֹ כוּ׳, כִּי בִּרְכַּת הָאָדָם בִּגְלַל שְׁנֵי דְבָרִים: הָאַחַת, עֲבוּר הַטּוֹב שֶׁעָשָׂה וְהַקָּדוֹשׁ־בָּרוּךְ־הוּא שִׁלֵּם שְׂכָרוֹ, אֲשֶׁר לֹא נִקְרָא (בְּהַשְׁקָפָה בִּלְתִּי מְדֻיֶּקֶת) טוֹבַת ה׳, רַק שֶׁל הָאָדָם הִיא, כְּשָׂכִיר אֲשֶׁר יְקַוֶּה פָּעֳלוֹ, וּמַה הִיא הַטּוֹבָה הַפְּשׁוּטָה וְנִגְלֵית, הִיא הַבְּחִינָה הַשְּׁנִיָּה, מַה שֶּׁנּוֹתֵן הַקָּדוֹשׁ־בָּרוּךְ־הוּא מִקֹּדֶם, לְמַעַן יַעֲשֶׂה הָאָדָם הַטּוֹב בְּבִרְכָתוֹ. וְכַאֲשֶׁר הָאָדָם נֶעֱנָשׁ בְּמָמוֹנוֹ, אֲשֶׁר קָנָה בִּשְׂכַר עֲמַל כִּשְׁרוֹן מַעֲשָׂיו, דִּין וּמִשְׁפָּט נָכוֹן הוּא לִגְבּוֹת חוֹבָתוֹ בָּזֶה, וּמַה הוּא הַחֶסֶד הָאֲמִתִּי, שֶׁגּוֹבֶה חוֹבָתוֹ שֶׁל אָדָם בְּטוֹבָתוֹ, בְּהַמָּמוֹן שֶׁבָּא לוֹ מֵאֵת ה׳ יִתְבָּרַךְ, בִּבְחִינַת טוֹבָה, לְמַעַן יַעֲשֶׂה הַיָּשָׁר וְהַצֶּדֶק, וְהָאָדָם סִלֵּף דַּרְכּוֹ, וְלֹא נִתְקַיְּמָה מַחֲשַׁבְתּוֹ יִתְבָּרַךְ כִּבְיָכוֹל, וְאָז בַּדִּין שֶׁיִּטֹּל הַקָּדוֹשׁ־בָּרוּךְ־הוּא מָמוֹנוֹ, כִּי לֹא עַל מְנָת כֵּן נָתַן לוֹ הַקָּדוֹשׁ־בָּרוּךְ־הוּא הַמָּמוֹן לְהָאָדָם, גַּם לֹא יְנֻכֶּה לְהָאָדָם מֵחוֹבָתוֹ. וְיֵשׁ לְהוֹדוֹת לַה׳ עַל הַחֶסֶד הַלָּזֶה, אֲשֶׁר גַּם בְּלָקְחוֹ מֵהָאָדָם הַמָּמוֹן שֶׁבָּא לוֹ מִטּוֹבָתוֹ יִתְבָּרַךְ, גּוֹבֶה חוֹבָתוֹ בָּהֶם.

בַּמֶּה יִבָּדְלוּ הַהַקָּפוֹת הָרְאוּיוֹת לָתֵת לִבְנֵי אָדָם מֵאֵת ה׳ יִתְבָּרַךְ, אִם לֹא בִּבְחִינַת יְדִיעָה שִׂכְלִית, מִי הוּא הַבָּטוּחַ, אֲשֶׁר מֵהַיָּאוּת לִמְסֹר לוֹ הַקָּפָה, (אִם שֶׁלִּפְעָמִים נִשְׁתַּנֶּה הַדָּבָר כַּנִּזְכָּר לְעֵיל, כִּי בִּבְחִינַת יְדִיעָה מֻחְלֶטֶת, אֵין הַקָּדוֹשׁ־בָּרוּךְ־הוּא מַנְהִיג עוֹלָמוֹ הַתָּלוּי בִּבְחִירַת אֱנוֹשׁ, וְדָבָר אֵין לָהּ עִם יְדִיעָה מֻחְלֶטֶת).

וּבָזֶה צָדְקוּ דִּבְרֵי הַיְרוּשַׁלְמִי (רֹאשׁ הַשָּׁנָה פֶּרֶק א׳) שְׁלֹשָׁה פִּנְקָסִין הֵם כוּ׳, שֶׁל בֵּינוֹנִים כְּבָר נִתַּן לָהֶם עֲשָׂרָה יְמֵי תְשׁוּבָה שֶׁל

93. Psalms 106:11 and elsewhere.

94. It is not goodness, but justice.

95. Not the person's own, i.e., the first type, which he earned by his own efforts.

96. Here again, R. Salanter uses the logic of business to make an ethical point. God, as it were, must decide which people are worthy of His investment and can be trusted to repay His "goodness" with proper conduct, justice, and righteousness. This decision must be rational, based on what can be expected of this person. Even though, at some level, God knows what the person will ultimately do, He nevertheless governs the

We can also explain the saying of our Sages, of blessed memory (Pesaḥim 118a): "'Give thanks to the Lord; for He is good'[93] – give thanks to Him who collects a person's debts according to the good given him; a rich man with his ox, a poor man with his lamb...." Blessing comes to a man for two reasons. One, for the good he has done, the Holy One, blessed be He, pays his reward. This should not be called God's goodness (as we do if we do not view it precisely). This bounty belongs to the human being. This is like a case of an employee who expects and receives pay for his labor.[94] So what is plain and obvious good? This is the second type, wherein the Holy One, blessed be He, gives in advance, so that a person will do good with His blessing. When a person is punished by means of the money he obtained by toil and the skill of his actions, it is proper justice and lawful to collect debt from this. But what is true loving-kindness from God? That He collects man's debt from His goodness, from the money granted to a person from God, blessed be He, as an unearned goodness, so that he will perform upright and just deeds with it. Yet if the person distorted their path, and God's plan, as it were, was not carried out, it is just for the Holy One, blessed be He, to take back His money – He did not give it to him for these evil purposes – and at the same time, it will not detract from what the person is due. Thus, one should thank God for this loving-kindness, that even when taking back from the person the money given to him by God's goodness,[95] God lets his debt be paid off with this money.

How can we distinguish which credit is appropriately extended to human beings by God, blessed be He, if not by means of rational knowledge[96] [to determine] who can be trusted and to whom is it appropriate to extend credit? (This is so even though sometimes things change, as said above, because God does not govern His world, which hinges on human choice, from the perspective of absolute knowledge; absolute knowledge thus has no bearing on this.)

The correctness of the Yerushalmi (Rosh HaShana, ch. 1) is thus evident: "There are three record books.... Those in between [the righ-

---

world according to the principle of human free choice, not of divine foreknowledge. The decision is therefore based on rational criteria – who is likely to be worthy of God's goodness.

בֵּין רֹאשׁ הַשָּׁנָה לְיוֹם הַכִּפּוּרִים, אִם עָשׂוּ תְּשׁוּבָה נִכְתָּבִין עִם הַצַּדִּיקִים וְאִם לָאו נִכְתָּבִים עִם הָרְשָׁעִים כוּ׳, רַבִּי חֲנַנְיָא חַבְרוֹן דְּרַבָּנָן בָּעֵי, וְאֵין הַקָּדוֹשׁ־בָּרוּךְ־הוּא רוֹאֶה אֶת הַנּוֹלָד, וְלָא שְׁמִיעַ דְּאָמַר רַבִּי סִימוֹן בְּשֵׁם רַבִּי יְהוֹשֻׁעַ בֶּן לֵוִי אֵין הַקָּדוֹשׁ־בָּרוּךְ־הוּא דָּן אֶת הָאָדָם אֶלָּא בְּשָׁעָה שֶׁהוּא עוֹמֵד בָּהּ, (הַמַּאֲמָר אֲשֶׁר הִזְכַּרְנוּ לְעֵיל) עַיֵּן שָׁם. אֲשֶׁר מְאֹד הַדָּבָר מַפְלִיא לֵאמֹר, שֶׁהַיְרוּשַׁלְמִי יִשְׁאַל בִּדְבַר יְדִיעָה וּבְחִירָה, אֲשֶׁר נִלְאָה שֵׂכֶל אֱנוֹשִׁי בִּכְלָל לַחְתֹּר אַחֲרָיו כְּדִבְרֵי הָרַמְבַּ"ם הַנִּזְכָּר לְעֵיל. וִיבֹאָרָה עַל עִנְיָן פְּרָטִי, אָכֵן שְׁאֵלַת הַיְרוּשַׁלְמִי הִיא עַל יְדִיעָה הַשִּׂכְלִית אֲשֶׁר עַל פִּיהָ מַנְהִיג הַקָּדוֹשׁ־בָּרוּךְ־הוּא אֶת עוֹלָמוֹ.

כֵּן גַּם בְּעִנְיַן עוֹשִׂין תְּשׁוּבָה וְאֵינָם עוֹשִׂין תְּשׁוּבָה, הוּא עַל פִּי בְּחִינַת יְדִיעָה שִׂכְלִית, אִם הָאָדָם עַל פִּי יְדִיעָה הַשִּׂכְלִית מֻכְשָׁר לִתְשׁוּבָה, אֲזַי הַקָּדוֹשׁ־בָּרוּךְ־הוּא מַאֲרִיךְ אַפּוֹ וּמַמְתִּין עַל תְּשׁוּבָתוֹ וָחַי, וְאִם עַל פִּי יְדִיעָה שִׂכְלִית אֵינוֹ מֻכְשָׁר לִתְשׁוּבָה, (אִם כִּי מִכָּל מָקוֹם בִּבְחִירָתוֹ לַעֲשׂוֹת תְּשׁוּבָה), אֲזַי חַס וְחָלִילָה חָפֵץ לַהֲמִיתוֹ, אִם לֹא יִהְיֶה לְהָאָדָם זְכוּת מַכְרִיעַ לְחַיִּים. וּמַה הוּא הַיְסוֹד שֶׁיִּהְיֶה הָאָדָם מֻכְשָׁר לִתְשׁוּבָה, הוּא הַהֶרְגֵּשׁ שֶׁיִּהְיֶה חַי מַרְגִּישׁ בְּחֶסְרוֹנוֹ, וְאָז הַתִּקְוָה שֶׁיִּתְעוֹרֵר לִתְשׁוּבָה, אֲבָל אִם אֵין הֶרְגֵּשׁ, הַתְּשׁוּבָה מֵאַיִן תִּוָּלֵד, אָכֵן זֶהוּ דַּוְקָא כְּשֶׁנִּכְבָּה לְגַמְרֵי הַהֶרְגֵּשׁ מִנַּפְשׁוֹ, עַד אֲשֶׁר לֹא יִתְפָּעֵל מִתּוֹכָחָה וְהִתְעוֹרְרוּת זוּלָתוֹ, כִּי אָז אֵינוֹ בְּגֶדֶר עוֹשֶׂה תְּשׁוּבָה כְּלָל, כֵּיוָן שֶׁגַּם אַחֵר אֵין בְּכֹחוֹ לְעוֹרְרוֹ מִתַּרְדֵּמַת אִוַּלְתּוֹ.

וּבָזֶה יֵשׁ לְבָאֵר אֲשֶׁר נִרְמָז בַּכָּתוּב, יִשּׁוּב הַגְּמָרָא כָּאן בְּעוֹשִׂין תְּשׁוּבָה (יְחֶזְקֵאל י"ח) כִּי לֹא אֶחְפֹּץ בְּמוֹת הַמֵּת וְהָשִׁיבוּ, (הֱיוּ מֻכְשָׁרִים לִתְשׁוּבָה, וְלַמֶּרְכָּז הַלָּזוּ) וִחְיוּ (כִּי אֵין תְּשׁוּבָה לְאַחַר מִיתָה), כָּאן

---

97. I.e., it would be strange for the Yerushalmi to ask such a profound question, which touches on the foundations of theology, in context of a relatively technical discussion about the repentance of "those in between" during the Ten Days of Repentance.
98. I.e., judging a person from current behaviors and the normal process of cause and effect.
99. Excitement is contagious, so a source of one's emotion is the emotion of those around him.

teous and the wicked] have been given the Ten Days of Repentance between Rosh HaShana and Yom Kippur. If they repented, they are inscribed with the righteous. If not, they are inscribed with the wicked.... R. Ḥananya, friend of the Rabbis, asked: 'Doesn't God see what is going to happen?' But he (R. Ḥananya) had not heard what R. Shimon said in the name of R. Yehoshua ben Levi: 'The Holy One, blessed be He, judges a person only as he is in that moment.'" (We cited this saying above.) See further there.

It would be very surprising to say that the Yerushalmi is asking about the matter of foreknowledge and free choice, a matter which is beyond human reason in general to grasp, according to the aforementioned words of Rambam, and explaining it with respect to a specific matter.[97] Rather, the Yerushalmi's question is about rational [non-absolute] knowledge,[98] in accordance with which God governs the world.

The matter of "those who can repent and those who cannot repent" is judged by the same criterion: rational knowledge. If a person is, by rational calculation, capable of repentance, then the Holy One, blessed be He, is patient, waits for his repentance, and he lives. If by rational calculation, he is not capable of repentance (even though he always retains the free choice to repent) then, God forbid, He wants to put him to death – unless that person has some merit that tilts the scale to life. And what is the basis of a person being capable of repentance? It is the sense that he is alive, aware of his shortcomings. Then there is hope that he will awaken to repentance. But if there is no such sense, whence will repentance come? However, [this death sentence is decreed] only if this sense is completely extinguished in his psyche – to the point where he is not stirred by chastisement or by the arousal of another.[99] Then he is not in the category of "one who can repent" at all – since even another does not have the power to awaken him from the deep slumber of his folly.

With this we can explain the allusion of the verse according to the Talmud's resolution (Nidda 70b): "This verse (Ezek. 18:32): 'For I do not desire the death of the person, [declares the Lord God – but rather return (i.e., be capable of repentance in this area) and live (for there is no repentance after death)],' deals with those who repent, and

בְּשֶׁאֵין עוֹשִׂין תְּשׁוּבָה (שְׁמוּאֵל־א׳ ב׳) וְלֹא שָׁמְעוּ לְקוֹל אֲבִיהֶם כִּי חָפֵץ ה׳ לַהֲמִיתָם, כֵּיוָן שֶׁלֹּא הִתְעוֹרְרוּ לְקוֹל תּוֹכַחַת עֵלִי, אֲשֶׁר הָיָה גְּדוֹל הַדּוֹר, מִמֵּילָא לֹא הָיוּ בְּגֶדֶר עוֹשִׂין תְּשׁוּבָה.

זֶהוּ בְּאָמְרִי לָרָשָׁע כוּ׳ וְלֹא דִבַּרְתָּ לְהַזְהִיר רָשָׁע מִדַּרְכּוֹ, (וְאָז הוּא עֲדַיִן בְּגֶדֶר עוֹשֶׂה תְּשׁוּבָה, כִּי אוּלַי יִתְעוֹרֵר מִתּוֹכָחָה), וְלֹא יָמוּת, רַק אִם נִתְמַלְּאָה סְאָתוֹ אֲשֶׁר נִקְרָא רָשָׁע, אֲזַי הוּא רָשָׁע בַּעֲוֹנוֹ יָמוּת כוּ׳, וְאַתָּה כִּי הִזְהַרְתָּ רָשָׁע מִדַּרְכּוֹ לָשׁוּב מִמֶּנָּה וְלֹא שָׁב מִדַּרְכּוֹ, (לֹא נִתְפַּעֵל מִתּוֹכַחְתְּךָ, כִּי אִם הָיָה נִתְפַּעֵל וּמַרְגִּישׁ בְּחֶסְרוֹנוֹ הָיָה נִקְרָא שָׁב מִדַּרְכּוֹ, כִּי מִלְּפָנִים לֹא הִרְגִּישׁ בְּרָעָתוֹ, וְלָזֹאת הוּא בְּגֶדֶר אֵין עוֹשֶׂה תְּשׁוּבָה, אֲזַי) הוּא בַּעֲוֹנוֹ יָמוּת, הֲגַם שֶׁלֹּא נִתְמַלְּאָה סְאָתוֹ, וְלֹא נִקְרָא רָשָׁע, (כִּי הוּא מִשְׁפָּט כְּלָלִי לְמִי שֶׁיֵּשׁ בְּיָדוֹ עָוֹן וְאֵינוֹ בִּבְחִינַת עוֹשֶׂה תְּשׁוּבָה), בְּכָל זֹאת יָמוּת מִסִּבַּת עֲוֹנוֹ, יַעַן עַל פִּי יְדִיעָה שִׂכְלִית לֹא יָבוֹא לִתְשׁוּבָה, כֵּיוָן שֶׁאֵינוֹ מִתְעוֹרֵר גַּם מִתּוֹכָחָה. וּמַה

100. Elsewhere (see for example, Letter 7), R. Salanter generalizes that people who sin become hardened and lose emotional engagement in living. Thus, shaking off sin and then repenting is not just necessary to avoid being punished by God for being one who cannot repent, as expressed here. Rather the act of shunning evil and turning to good constitutes a reclaiming of zest for life and the revival of emotional engagement in living.

101. Wisdom sayings of the rabbis that arouse conscience or stimulate spiritual consciousness, such as "Envy, lust, and excessive honor-seeking shorten a person's life" (Pirkei Avot 4:21).

102. R. Salanter believes that people who sin and slip into this unthinking, ongoing, bad pattern lose the capacity for feeling. The habitual sinner, as it were, is "punished" by a loss of feeling and of awareness. That is why he tends to end up in the category of one who will never repent. In turn, his inability to repent evokes a heavenly judgment that he deserves to die. The challenge (and the opportunity) of the sinner is to keep feeling and self-awareness alive, so even though he is in a bad pattern, he is able – maybe even likely – to repent, change, and improve. As R. Salanter said below, a human being never loses the free will to change from evil to good, but once he loses his feeling and self-awareness, he is much more likely to sink hopelessly into the evil patterns.

that verse (I Sam. 2:25): 'And they did not listen to their father's voice [for the Lord sought to put them to death'] deals with those who do not repent." [Since they did not respond to the words of chastisement of Eli, who was the greatest of the generation, they were consequently not in the category of those who can repent.]

Particularly those preoccupied with daily life, burdened by tribulation, who are prone to commit great sins and not feel anything[100] – in particular, in matters between man and man: jealousy, hatred, speaking evil, shaming, and cheating in business above all – we have to seek out strength from life, from what is proper and correct, to offset these tendencies with good deeds and good actions which will outweigh [the bad behaviors]. But what shall a person who must struggle every day do?

There is one easy skill, which does not require a completely clear mind, nor does it require a lot of time – it is to go over Mussar sayings of the Sages[101] repeatedly, until he arouses excitation in his soul at that moment. Even if it does not bear fruit initially to improve the person's ways, he will still be considered in the book of the living – since he is still alive and feeling. And as long as he is connected to life, there is security, and he is counted among those who have the ability to repent.[102]

This is the meaning of (Ezek. 33:8–9): "When I say to the wicked person.... And you have not spoken to warn the wicked man away from his ways" (then he would still be in the category of one who can repent, for perhaps he would have responded to chastisement), "then he will not die," unless his measure is filled and he is judged a wicked man. "Then he, the wicked man, will die for his sins.... But if you have warned the wicked person to turn from his way and he did not turn from it" (he was not moved by your chastisement; for if he were moved and conscious of his shortcomings he would be called "one who turns from his way" because before your chastisement he was not conscious of his wickedness. Therefore, now he is in the category of "one who cannot repent," and), then "he will die for his sin" – even if his measure is not filled and he is not yet considered wicked (for this general condemnation [of being deemed wicked] is for one who sins and is not in the category of "one who can repent"), still he will die by cause of his sin. We know by rational knowledge that he will not repent since he does not respond even to

הִיא רְפוּאָתוֹ, הִיא, הִתְחַדְּשׁוּת הַהֶרְגֵּשׁ לְעוֹרֵר הַדְּאָגָה וְהַיָּגוֹן וְיִכָּנֵס בְּגֶדֶר עוֹשֶׂה תְּשׁוּבָה וִיחְיֶה.

זֶהוּ, וְאַתָּה בֶן אָדָם אֱמֹר אֶל בֵּית יִשְׂרָאֵל (בְּדֶרֶךְ סִבָּה וּמְסוּבָּב) כֵּן אֲמַרְתֶּם לֵאמֹר, כִּי פְשָׁעֵינוּ וְחַטֹּאתֵינוּ עָלֵינוּ, וּבָם אֲנַחְנוּ נְמַקִּים, וְאֵיךְ נִחְיֶה, (בְּזֹאת הֵמָּה בְּגֶדֶר עוֹשִׂין תְּשׁוּבָה כֵּיוָן שֶׁהֵן מַרְגִּישִׁים וְדוֹאֲגִים, לְזֹאת הִיא הַסִּבָּה לְהַמְסוּבָּב הַלָּזֶה, אֲשֶׁר) אֱמֹר אֲלֵיהֶם וְגוֹ׳ כִּי אִם בְּשׁוּב רָשָׁע מִדַּרְכּוֹ וְחָיָה. (וְאִם כִּי עֲדַיִן הוּא רַק הַתְחָלַת הַהִתְעוֹרְרוּת לִתְשׁוּבָה מִכָּל־מָקוֹם נִקְרְאוּ עוֹשִׂין תְּשׁוּבָה, כֵּיוָן שֶׁהֵמָּה מְכֻשָּׁרִים בְּסִבַּת הֶרְגֵּשָׁם, שֶׁיָּבוֹאוּ לְאַט לְאַט לִבְחִינַת עוֹשִׂין תְּשׁוּבָה כַּהֹגֶן, זֶהוּ) שׁוּבוּ שׁוּבוּ מִדַּרְכֵיכֶם הָרָעִים וְכוּ׳.

הַיּוֹצֵא מִכְּלַל דְּבָרֵינוּ, כִּי הַמַּדְרֵגוֹת בַּעֲבוֹדָתוֹ יִתְבָּרַךְ. שָׁלֹשׁ הֵן בְּמִסְפָּר: הָאֶחָד הוּא הַפֶּתַח וְהַהַתְחָלָה, הוּא הַהֶרְגֵּשׁ, שֶׁיִּהְיֶה הָאָדָם לוֹמֵד מַאַמְרֵי חֲכָמֵינוּ זַ״ל וּמוּסְרֵי הַחֲכָמִים, לַחֲזֹר עֲלֵיהֶם כַּמָּה וְכַמָּה פְּעָמִים, עַד אֲשֶׁר יִתְפַּעֵל, וְיַרְגִּישׁ בְּנַפְשׁוֹ חֶסְרוֹנוֹ, וּמִזֶּה יָבוֹא לַמַּדְרֵגָה הַשְּׁנִיָּה הִיא כְּבִישַׁת הַיֵּצֶר. וְהַשְּׁלִישִׁית הִיא תִּקּוּן הַיֵּצֶר, שֶׁיִּהְיֶה הָאָדָם עָלֵז וְשָׂשׂ לַעֲבוֹדָתוֹ יִתְבָּרַךְ. וְהַתַּבְלִין לְהַיֵּצֶר, לְבַל יִהְיֶה שָׂטָן לְכָל שְׁלֹשֶׁת הַמַּדְרֵגוֹת, הִיא הַתּוֹרָה, כְּמַאֲמָרָם זַ״ל (קִדּוּשִׁין ל:) בָּרָאתִי יֵצֶר הָרָע בָּרָאתִי לוֹ תּוֹרָה תַּבְלִין, אֲשֶׁר אוּלַי לָזֶה נִגְדְּרָה הַתּוֹרָה בְּשָׁלֹשׁ בְּחִינוֹת: הָאַחַת, חוֹמָה (בָּבָא בַּתְרָא ז:, חוֹמָה זוֹ תּוֹרָה) הַיְנוּ לָאָדָם הַשָּׁלֵם בְּמַעֲלָתוֹ בְּמַדְרֵגַת תִּקּוּן הַיֵּצֶר, הַתּוֹרָה חוֹמָה לוֹ מִסָּבִיב, לְהָגֵן עָלָיו מִסִּבּוֹת גְּדוֹלוֹת מִחוּצָה, לְבַל יָרֵעוּ וּבַל יַשְׁחִיתוּ נַפְשׁוֹ הַזַּכָּה. הַשְּׁנִיָּה רְפוּאָה (קִדּוּשִׁין ל׳, וְשַׂמְתֶּם סַם תָּם כוּ׳, מָשָׁל לְאָדָם שֶׁהִכָּה אֶת בְּנוֹ מַכָּה גְּדוֹלָה וְהִנִּיחַ לוֹ רְטִיָּה עַל גַּבֵּי מַכָּתוֹ כוּ׳, כָּךְ הַקָּדוֹשׁ־

---

103. R. Salanter is teaching us another effect of *hitpaalut*, namely, chanting particularly evocative texts with enthusiasm. Earlier he stressed using this method to affect the unconscious. Here he teaches that it also awakens one's emotional awareness of one's sins and future punishments, thus undoing the routinization and the loss of feeling that are caused by sinning.

104. The word for "antidote" is "*tavlin*," which literally means "seasoning," something that removes a foul taste.

chastisement. What is his cure? It is renewal of emotional awareness to awaken anxiety and anguish – so that he will enter the category of "one who can repent," and he will live.

This is the meaning of (Ezek. 33:10): "Son of man, say to the House of Israel" (in the manner of cause and effect) "you have spoken, saying: Our sins and transgressions are upon us, and we pine away in them. How shall we live?" (In this they are in the category of "those who can repent," since they are emotionally conscious and are worried. This is the cause of the following effect, that) "say to them…let the wicked one turn from his way and live." (Even though it is just the beginning of the awakening to repentance, still they are called "those who can repent." Since they are capable because of their emotional awareness, they will come little by little into the category of those who repent properly. This is the meaning of) "Return, return from your wicked ways…."

It emerges from all of this discussion that there are three levels of serving God, blessed be He: One – the opening and the beginning is sentimental. One studies sayings of our Sages, of blessed memory, and chastisements of the wise men, reviewing them over and over again, until he is affected and senses, within his psyche, his shortcomings.[103] From this he comes to the second level: repression of the urge. The third [level] is sublimation of the urge, wherein one is joyful and happy to serve Him, blessed be He.

The antidote for the evil urge, so that it is not a hindrance to all three levels, is the Torah. As they, of blessed memory, said (Kiddushin 30b): "I created their evil urge; I created the Torah as its antidote."[104]

Perhaps this is why Torah is described in three ways. First, as a fortified wall (Bava Batra 7b: "'Wall' [Song. 8:10] refers to Torah"). Meaning, to the person who is completely virtuous and entirely sublimated his urge, the Torah is a wall that fortifies him, protecting from intense external causes so that they not do harm or corrupt[105] his pure soul.

Second, as medicine (Kiddushin 30b: "'And you shall place' ['*vesamtem*' – Deut. 11:18] refers to a 'perfect cure' ['*sam tam*']. This is likened to a person who struck his son and caused a large wound, so he

105. Compare Isaiah 11:9.

בָּרוּךְ־הוּא אָמַר לָהֶם לְיִשְׂרָאֵל בָּרָאתִי לָהֶם יֵצֶר הָרַע וּבָרָאתִי לוֹ תּוֹרָה תַּבְלִין כו׳ עַיֵּן שָׁם). הַיְנוּ לְמִי שֶׁהוּא בְּמַדְרֵגַת כּוֹבֵשׁ אֶת יִצְרוֹ, אֲשֶׁר הוּא חוֹלֶה אַמִּיץ, כִּי תִּגְבֹּרֶת יִצְרוֹ בְּקִרְבּוֹ, הַתּוֹרָה בְּעֶזְרָתוֹ לַעֲמֹד נֶגֶד יִצְרוֹ. הַשְּׁלִישִׁית חַיִּים (עֲבוֹדָה־זָרָה ג׳, אַף בְּנֵי אָדָם כֵּיוָן שֶׁפּוֹרְשִׁין מִן הַתּוֹרָה מִיָּד מֵתִים), הַיְנוּ לְמִי שֶׁהוּא בְּמַדְרֵגַת הַהֶרְגֵּשׁ, הַתּוֹרָה שׁוֹמַרְתּוּ לְבַל יְאַבֵּד הֶרְגֵּשׁוֹ, וִיהְיֶה חַס וְשָׁלוֹם כְּמֵת שֶׁאֵינוֹ מַרְגִּישׁ.

הוּא מַאֲמַר הַמִּדְרָשׁ אֲשֶׁר הִצַּגְנוּ בְּפֶתַח דְּבָרֵינוּ, כִּי כְּשֶׁהָיוּ יִשְׂרָאֵל בַּמִּדְבָּר, אָמְרוּ חֲכָמֵינוּ זַ״ל (יוֹמָא עד:) מִפְּנֵי מָה לֹא הָיָה יוֹרֵד הַמָּן פַּעַם אַחַת בְּשָׁנָה כו׳, וְאַף כָּךְ יִשְׂרָאֵל מִי שֶׁיֵּשׁ לוֹ אַרְבָּעָה וַחֲמִשָּׁה בָּנִים הָיָה דּוֹאֵג וְאוֹמֵר שֶׁמָּא לְמָחָר אֵין הַמָּן יוֹרֵד וְנִמְצְאוּ בְּנֵיהֶם וּבְנוֹתֵיהֶם מֵתִים בָּרָעָב, וְנִמְצְאוּ כָּל יִשְׂרָאֵל מְכַוְּנִים אֶת לִבָּם לַאֲבִיהֶם שֶׁבַּשָּׁמַיִם, עַיֵּן שָׁם. וְכַאֲשֶׁר כִּמְעַט כָּל בְּנֵי אָדָם תְּלוּיִים זֶה בָּזֶה, לְזֹאת, כַּאֲשֶׁר הָיְתָה סִבָּה נוֹרָאָה לִשְׁמִירַת מַדְרֵגַת בַּעֲלֵי הַהֶרְגֵּשׁ, אֲזַי גַּם בַּעֲלֵי הַכְּבִישָׁה וְהַתִּקּוּן עָמְדוּ בְּמַצָּבָם בֶּטַח. אֲבָל כְּשֶׁהִתְחִילוּ לִיכָּנֵס לָאָרֶץ אֲשֶׁר זֶה יִפְנֶה לְכַרְמוֹ וְזֶה לְזֵיתוֹ, הַחֲשָׁשָׁא קְרוֹבָה, פֶּן יְרַקֵּד חַס וְחָלִילָה הַשָּׂטָן בֵּינֵיהֶם לְהַפְרִיעָם מֵעֲבוֹדָתוֹ יִתְבָּרַךְ.

לְזֹאת הֶרְאָם הַקָּדוֹשׁ־בָּרוּךְ־הוּא, כִּי הָאָרוֹן הוּא הַמָּגֵן לְכָל הַמַּדְרֵגוֹת. רַב הוּנָא אָמַר זְקָפָן בֵּין שְׁנֵי בַּדֵּי הָאָרוֹן, וְהָאָרוֹן חוֹמָה לָהֶם. הוּא לְמַדְרֵגַת תִּקּוּן הַיֵּצֶר. אָמַר רַב אָחָא בַּר חֲנִינָא סְמָכָן בֵּין שְׁנֵי בַּדֵּי הָאָרוֹן. וְהָאָרוֹן תּוֹמְכָם לְכוֹבְשֵׁי הַיֵּצֶר לְבַל יִפְּלוּ תַּחְתָּיו. רַבָּנָן אָמְרֵי צִמְצְמָן בֵּין שְׁנֵי בַּדֵּי הָאָרוֹן. וְהָאָרוֹן הוּא קִיּוּמָהּ שֶׁל מַדְרֵגַת הַהֶרְגֵּשׁ, לְמַעַן לֹא תֹּאבַד הֶרְגֵּשָׁם, וְיִתְבַּטֵּל קִיּוּמָם לַעֲבוֹדָתוֹ יִתְבָּרַךְ, כִּי אִם חַס וְשָׁלוֹם אֵין הֶרְגֵּשׁ (הַפֶּתַח וְהַהַתְחָלָה) הָעֲבוֹדָה מֵאַיִן תָּבוֹא.

---

106. Note: The printed text erroneously cites Yoma 74b.
107. I.e., when people receive food in daily doses, they become conditioned to sense their dependence on God and petition Him for sustenance every day.
108. I.e., they will focus on themselves as sources of sustenance, and not God.

put a bandage on his wound.... So the Holy One, blessed be He, said to Israel: I created their evil urge; I created the Torah as its antidote..."; see further there). This refers to one who represses his urge, who is therefore very sick, because his intensified urge is within him. The Torah helps him to stand up to his urge.

Third, as life (Avoda Zara 3a: "So too, human beings, when they separate from the Torah, they die at once"). This refers to the person who is still in the sentimental stage. The Torah keeps him from losing feeling and becoming, God forbid, like a corpse that has no feeling.

This is the meaning of the midrash [Genesis Rabba 5:7] we presented at the beginning of our words, for when Israel was in the wilderness, our Sages, of blessed memory, say (Yoma 76a[106]): "'Why didn't the manna come down...once a year [instead of every day]?'... So too Israel; one who had four or five children worried and said, 'Maybe tomorrow the manna will not descend and consequently their sons and daughters will die of hunger.' Consequently, all of Israel directed their hearts to their Father in Heaven [every day]...."[107] See further there. When almost all people are interconnected, then as there was an overwhelming reason for those in a state of knowing by sentiment to maintain their level, those at the stages of repression and sublimation remained secure at their levels as well. However, once they began to enter the land, and one turned to his vineyard and the next to his olive tree, there was a great concern lest the Hinderer ("*Satan*"), God forbid, dance among them and disrupt their service of God, blessed be He.[108]

Therefore, the Holy One, blessed be He, showed them that the Ark protects people at every level: "Rav Huna said: He stood all of them up between the two carrying-poles of the Ark." The Ark was like a wall protecting them. This refers to those at the level of sublimating the urge.

"Said Rav Aḥa bar Ḥanina: He supported them between the two carrying-poles of the Ark." The Ark formed a support for those who repress their urge, protecting them from falling.

"The Rabbis said: He squeezed them between the two carrying-poles of the Ark." The Ark sustains the person in the state of good by sentiment so that he does not lose feeling, which would erase his existence with respect to serving God – for if, God forbid, there is no feeling (the opening and the beginning), from where will the service come?

וְכַאֲשֶׁר שְׁתֵּי בְּחִינוֹת בַּעֲבוֹדָתוֹ יִתְבָּרַךְ, הָאַחַת לְעָבְדוֹ בְּלִי הִתְבּוֹנְנוּת שִׂכְלִית, רַק בִּתְמִימוּת, לִשְׁמֹר דְּבַר ה׳ וְלַהֲלֹךְ בִּדְרָכָיו, כִּשְׁרוֹן הַמִּדּוֹת וְאַהֲבַת חֶסֶד, וְעַל פִּי בְּחִינָה הַלָּזוֹ, אֵין מָקוֹם לִגְדֹּר מַצַּב מַדְרֵגַת הָאָדָם בַּעֲבוֹדָתוֹ יִתְבָּרַךְ, כִּי עַל יְדֵי רוּחַ קַל, מְהֵרָה תָּעוּף חַס וְחָלִילָה כָּל טוּב דְּרָכָיו, כִּי מִי יַעַצְרֵם. הַשֵּׁנִית הִיא הָעִקָּרִית, בְּהִתְבּוֹנְנוּת שִׂכְלִית, לְפִי דַּרְכֵי תַּהֲלוּכוֹת הָעֲבוֹדָה וּמַצַּב תְּכוּנַת הָאָדָם, לִקְבֹּעַ לְהָעֲבוֹדָה יָתֵד נֶאֱמָן אֲשֶׁר כָּל רוּחוֹת שֶׁבָּעוֹלָם לֹא יְזִיזוּ אוֹתוֹ מִמְּקוֹמוֹ, וּמִי יוֹדֵעַ אִם הִשְׁלִים הָאָדָם דַּרְכֵי שִׂכְלוֹ בַּעֲבוֹדָתוֹ יִתְבָּרַךְ, אֲשֶׁר עַל פִּי יְדִיעָה שִׂכְלִית תְּגַדֵּר מַצַּב יְדִיעָתוֹ, הֲלֹא ה׳ יִתְבָּרַךְ.

גַּם בְּהַנְהָגַת הַקָּדוֹשׁ־בָּרוּךְ־הוּא אֶת עוֹלָמוֹ, שְׁתֵּי בְּחִינוֹת. הָאַחַת מַהֲלָךְ הַטִּבְעִי מִקִּשּׁוּר הַמְּסוּבָּב בְּסִבָּה, אֲשֶׁר הָאָדָם עָלוּל לִטְעוֹת וְלֵאמֹר, שֶׁכֹּחוֹ וְעֹצֶם יָדוֹ עָשָׂה לוֹ אֶת הַחַיִל. וְאֵין הַדָּבָר כֵּן, כִּי הַקָּדוֹשׁ־בָּרוּךְ־הוּא נוֹתֵן לְהָאָדָם כֹּחַ לַעֲשׂוֹת חָיִל, וּמַזְמִין לוֹ הַסִּבּוֹת אֲשֶׁר יוֹצִיאוּ הַמְּסוּבָּבִים לְפָעֳלָם. הַשֵּׁנִית דָּבָר הַנִּסִּי, מְסוּבָּב בְּלִי סִבָּה, וְעַיִן בְּעַיִן יִרְאֶה הָאָדָם, כִּי יַד ה׳ עָשְׂתָה זֹאת. הַבְּחִינָה הַלָּזוֹ נִקְרֵאת שְׁכִינָה בָּאָרֶץ (עַיֵּן דִּבְרֵי הָרַמְבַּ״ם עַל אוֹדוֹת שֹׁרֶשׁ שַׁבָּן בְּסִפְרוֹ מוֹרֶה נְבוּכִים). וְכָל זֶה בַּסִּבָּה הַחוּשִׁית.*

* כָּל דָּבָר הַיּוֹצֵא לַפֹּעַל, שְׁתֵּי סִבּוֹת לוֹ: הָאֶחָד סִבָּה הַחוּשִׁית, הַשֵּׁנִי סִבָּה הַשִּׂכְלִית, אוֹ לְאֵיזֶה תַּכְלִית, אוֹ לִגְמוּל וָעֹנֶשׁ. הָאָרֶץ כַּאֲשֶׁר תּוֹצִיא צִמְחָהּ. סִבָּה הַחוּשִׁית, הֵמָּה הַחֲרִישָׁה וְהַזְּרִיעָה. סִבָּה הַשִּׂכְלִית, הִיא אֲשֶׁר בַּעֲבוּרָהּ יִתְעוֹרֵר הָאָדָם לַעֲבֹד אַדְמָתוֹ, אִם לְתַכְלִית לְמַעַן יִתְעַנֵּג מִטּוּב פִּרְיָהּ, אוֹ לְהַרְוִיחַ מָמוֹן וְכַיּוֹצֵא, וְהַסִּבָּה הַשִּׂכְלִית הָאֲמִתִּית, הִיא הַשְׁגָּחָה הָעֶלְיוֹנָה, אֲשֶׁר גָּזְרָה יְצִיאַת הַדָּבָר לַפֹּעַל, אֲשֶׁר בִּהְיוֹתָהּ בָּאָה בִּגְלַל מַעֲשֵׂי הָאָדָם, לְפָנָיו יִתְבָּרַךְ, אֲזַי הָאָדָם בִּבְחִינַת הַסִּבָּה הָאֲמִתִּית. וּבָזֶה יֵשׁ לְבָאֵר הַכָּתוּב (אֵיכָה ג׳) מִי זֶה אָמַר וַתֶּהִי ה׳ לֹא צִוָּה, מִפִּי עֶלְיוֹן לֹא תֵצֵא הָרָעוֹת וְהַטּוֹב, מַה יִּתְאוֹנֵן אָדָם חָי גֶּבֶר עַל חֲטָאָיו, נַחְפְּשָׂה דְרָכֵינוּ וְנַחְקֹרָה וְנָשׁוּבָה עַד ה׳, נִשָּׂא לְבָבֵנוּ אֶל כַּפַּיִם אֶל אֵל בַּשָּׁמָיִם. כִּי

109. I.e., a slight negative stimulus.

110. R. Salanter again warns that unthinking religious observance is vulnerable to both negative inner motives and external forces.

111. Compare Deuteronomy 8:17.

112. Compare Isaiah 52:8.

There are two modes of His service, blessed be He: One – to serve Him without rational contemplation, simply and naively keeping God's word, walking in His ways, according to the nature of his character, and loving-kindness. In this mode, there is no way to ascertain the level of the state of one's service of God, blessed be He, for with a light wind,[109] all the goodness of his ways may fly away swiftly, for what would hold them back?[110]

The second [mode], which is primary, is through rational contemplation, according to the steps by which service proceeds and the condition of the person's nature, establishing service of God upon a secure foundation, which all the winds of the world cannot budge. And who knows if the person has perfected his rational methods in His service, blessed be He, so that the state of his knowledge can be ascertained through rational knowledge? Only God, blessed be He.

There are also two modes of how God governs His world. The first is through natural processes, the linking of effect to cause, which can lead a person to erroneously think that his might and the strength of his hand have achieved everything for him.[111] Yet it is not so, for the Holy One, blessed be He, gives a person the power to achieve and arranges for him the causes that will produce the resulting effects.

The second [mode] is the miraculous, the uncaused effect, which a person sees, with his own eye, was done by the hand of God.[112] This mode is called the Divine Presence ("*Shekhina*") on earth. (See what Rambam writes about the root *sh-kh-n* in his *Guide to the Perplexed* 1:5.) All this pertains to tangible causes.*

* [R. Salanter's footnote:] Everything that is actualized has two causes: the first is a tangible cause and the second a rational cause – either to some end, or to reward and punish. When the earth produces vegetation, the tangible cause is plowing and planting, and the rational cause, that which motivates a person to cultivate his land, is to enjoy the bounty of its fruit, to profit, or the like. The true rational cause is Higher Providence, which decreed that this outcome actualize. When this decree comes as a result of human actions before Him, blessed be He, the human being is the true cause. With this we can explain the verses (Lam. 3:37–41):

> Whose decree was ever fulfilled, unless the Lord commanded it? Evil and good do not come from the mouth of the Most High. Why should a living person complain, or a man over his sins? Let us search and examine our ways and return to God. Let us lift our hearts with our hands to God in heaven.

בַּהַשְׁקָפָה הָרִאשׁוֹנָה, יִטְעֶה הָאָדָם לֵאמֹר, כִּי הוּא בְּעַצְמוֹ מְנַהֵל עִנְיָנָיו אִם לְטוֹב אוֹ לְמוּטָב, אֲשֶׁר הָאֱמֶת אֵינוֹ כֵן, כִּי הַכֹּל מִשָּׁמַיִם, (עַיֵּן כְּתֻבּוֹת דַּף ל׳ חוּץ מִצִּנִּים וּפַחִים, וּבַתּוֹסָפוֹת שָׁם), זֶהוּ, מִי זֶה אָמַר וַתֶּהִי ה׳ לֹא צִוָּה, בְּכָל זֹאת, מַה הוּא הַצִּיר אֲשֶׁר עָלָיו תִּסֹּב דֶּלֶת הַהַשְׁגָּחָה הָעֶלְיוֹנָה, הֲלֹא מַעֲשֵׂי הָאָדָם, וְעַל פִּי דְּרָכָיו תָּחוּל עָלָיו הַהַשְׁגָּחָה, וְהוּא הוּא הַסִּבָּה הָרִאשׁוֹנָה לִיצִיאַת עִנְיָנָיו לַפֹּעַל, זֶהוּ מִפִּי עֶלְיוֹן לֹא תֵצֵא הָרָעוֹת וְהַטּוֹב. לָזֹאת עַל כָּל מִקְרֶה וּפֶגַע רַע בַּל יִתְלוֹנֵן הָאָדָם, לֹא עַל הַנְהָגָתוֹ הַגּוּפָנִית כִּי בְּרַע הוּא, (כְּפִי אֲשֶׁר יִטְעֶה הָאָדָם בְּהַשְׁקָפָה רִאשׁוֹנָה), וְגַם לֹא עַל ה׳ יִתְבָּרַךְ, כִּי אִם עַל הַנְהָגָתוֹ הַנַּפְשִׁית, (יְסוֹד הַסִּבָּה הָרִאשׁוֹנָה), זֶהוּ מַה יִּתְאוֹנֵן אָדָם חָי, גֶּבֶר עַל חֲטָאָיו. לָזֹאת, לְתַקֵּן רֹעַ מַזָּלוֹ לֹא יוֹעִילוּ לוֹ לְהֵיטִיב מַצָּבוֹ הַגּוּפָנִי. וְגַם אֵין מֵהַיָּאוּת לִדְפֹּק בָּרִאשׁוֹנָה לִשְׁפֹּךְ שִׂיחַ לְפָנָיו יִתְבָּרַךְ, כִּי אִם לְתַקֵּן הַסִּבָּה הָרִאשׁוֹנָה, הִיא, לְהֵיטִיב דַּרְכֵי נַפְשׁוֹ, כְּמַאֲמַר רַבּוֹתֵינוּ זַ״ל (בְּרָכוֹת ה׳) אִם רוֹאֶה אָדָם שֶׁיִּסּוּרִין בָּאִין עָלָיו יְפַשְׁפֵּשׁ בְּמַעֲשָׂיו שֶׁנֶּאֱמַר (שָׁם) נַחְפְּשָׂה דְרָכֵינוּ כו׳ עַיֵּן שָׁם, וְאָז נִשָּׂא לְבָבֵנוּ אֶל כַּפַּיִם אֶל אֵל בַּשָּׁמָיִם.

אֲבָל בַּשִּׂכְלִי נֶהְפַּךְ הַדָּבָר, עֶשֶׂר יָדוֹת בַּסִּבָּה הַשִּׂכְלִית, לַנִּסִּי מִבַּטִּבְעִי, כִּי מַדּוּעַ יְשַׁדֵּד הַקָּדוֹשׁ־בָּרוּךְ־הוּא הַנְהָגָתוֹ הַסְּדוּרָה, אִם לֹא תִּהְיֶה סִבָּה גְּדוֹלָה שִׂכְלִית, אֲשֶׁר בַּעֲבוּרָהּ יַעֲלֶה הָאָדָם הַגְבֵּהַּ לְמַעְלָה מֵהַנְהָגָה הַטִּבְעִית, אֲשֶׁר לְפִי מִדָּתוֹ שֶׁל הַקָּדוֹשׁ־בָּרוּךְ־הוּא, מִדָּה כְּנֶגֶד מִדָּה, נִרְאֶה בַּעֲלִיל, כִּי יְסוֹד הַסִּבָּה הִיא, בִּהְיוֹת הָאָדָם מַשְׁלִים שִׂכְלוֹ לַעֲבוֹדָתוֹ יִתְבָּרַךְ, וּבַשֵּׂכֶל יְנַהֵל דְּרָכָיו, כֵּן גַּם הוּא יִתְבָּרַךְ מִתְנַהֵג עִמּוֹ בִּבְחִינָה אֲשֶׁר יְסוֹדָהּ סִבָּה שִׂכְלִית.

הִיא מַעֲלַת אַבְרָהָם אָבִינוּ עָלָיו הַשָּׁלוֹם, אֲשֶׁר עֲבוֹדָתוֹ לֹא הָיְתָה רַק מִשִּׂכְלוֹ, (כִּי לֹא הָיְתָה לוֹ סִבָּה אַחֶרֶת לֹא מֵהוֹרָיו וְלֹא מִמְּסוֹבְבָיו), לָזֹאת הֶעֱלָהוּ הַקָּדוֹשׁ־בָּרוּךְ־הוּא לְמַעְלָה מִכִּפַּת הָרָקִיעַ (מִדְרָשׁ רַבָּה בְּרֵאשִׁית מ״ד), הַכִּנּוּי לְדַרְכֵי הַטְּבָעִים.

לָזֹאת כַּאֲשֶׁר הֶחֱזִיק אוֹתָם הָאָרוֹן בִּבְחִינוֹת מִתְחַלְּפוֹת, נוֹדַע, כִּי כָּל אֶחָד הִשְׁלִים בְּחִינָתוֹ בְּגֶדֶר הַשִּׂכְלִי. עַל כֵּן אָמַר לָהֶם יְהוֹשֻׁעַ, מִמַּה שֶּׁהֶחֱזִיקוּ שְׁנֵי בַּדֵּי הָאָרוֹן אֶתְכֶם, אַתֶּם יוֹדְעִין שֶׁשְּׁכִינָתוֹ שֶׁל

At first glance, a person errs by thinking that he himself guides his own affairs, for better or worse, which is not true, for all is from Heaven (see Ketubbot 30a – except for colds and fevers; and see *Tosafot* ad loc.). This is the meaning of "Whose decree was ever fulfilled, unless the Lord commanded it?" Nevertheless, what is the hinge on which the door of Higher Providence turns? It is the deeds of human beings. According to his own ways, Providence will apply to him, so he is the prime cause that his matters be carried out. This is the meaning of "Evil and good do not come from the mouth of the Most High." Therefore, a person should not complain about any bad occurrence or setback – neither about his physical behavior being at fault (in accordance with his error at first glance), nor about God, blessed be He – except about his own spiritual behavior (the basis of the primary cause). This is the meaning of "Why should a living person complain, or a man over his sins?"

Thus, he will not improve his bad fortune by improving his physical situation. Nor is it right to charge straight to pouring out his prayer before Him, blessed be He. Further, the first thing is to improve the prime cause, that is, to better the ways of his soul, as our Rabbis, of blessed memory, say (Berakhot 5a): "If a person sees that suffering comes upon him, let him search his actions, as it is said (Lam. ibid.): 'Let us search our ways....'" See further there. Then, "Let us lift our hearts with our hands to God in heaven."

However, when it comes to the rational, the matter is reversed. Rational causes are present tenfold in the miraculous over the natural, for why would God override His regular governance without a powerful rational cause, for which a person is raised above the natural order of governance? According to God's meting out [reward and punishment] *quid pro quo*, it seems clear that the basis for this [rational] cause is that inasmuch as a person has perfected his rational faculty to serve God and behave according to reason, God, blessed be He, acts toward this person in the mode based on rational cause.

This was the virtue of our patriarch Abraham, peace be upon him. His service was through nothing but reason (for it had no other cause – neither from his parents nor from his environment), so the Holy One, blessed be He, "lifted him up above the dome of the heavens" (Genesis Rabba 44) – a euphemism for "above the natural processes."

Thus, when the Ark supported them through different modes, it became known that each person perfected the rational aspect of their mode. Therefore, Joshua said to them: From the fact that the staves of the Ark upheld you, you know that God's *Shekhina* is amongst you,

הַקָּדוֹשׁ־בָּרוּךְ־הוּא בֵּינֵיכֶם. לְהַנְהִיג אֶתְכֶם בַּדֶּרֶךְ הַנִּסִּית, מְסוּבָב מִסִּבָּה שִׂכְלִית, בִּהְיוֹתְכֶם עוֹבְדֵי ה׳ יִתְבָּרַךְ בִּבְחִינַת שִׂכְלִי, כַּנִּזְכָּר לְעֵיל.

governing you with miracles effected by rational causes, for you are servants of God, blessed be He, in the rational mode, as mentioned.

EDITORS' SUMMARY OF LETTER 30

In this essay, R. Salanter calls for reworking character traits, developing strong spiritual discipline, and working on changing one's nature, so that it identifies with and loves that which the Torah defines as good. R. Salanter encourages the reader by saying that this will not be so difficult, for "human capacities are subject to control and to change." Just as humans can train animals, so they can train themselves and change their own character through learning and habituation.

This essay describes the power of the unconscious, which often determines behavior and frequently overrides or distorts reason. There are two methods for controlling the unconscious: repression and sublimation. Repression is harder when one is younger (because the drives are very powerful and hard to curb) and sublimation (i.e., redirecting the energy to good) is easier. When one is older, the situation reverses: repression is easier (because the drives and instincts have been dulled by life experience), while sublimation is more difficult. The following chart summarizes key differences between these two methods:

Tikkun (Sublimation)	*Kibbush* (Repression)
a. It is best to start with sublimation at a young age. b. The advantage of sublimation is that one is not conflicting head-on with the worst drives, which are strongest when young. One is redirecting them. c. When sublimation starts at a young age, there is less conflict and pain in the process of doing good. The disadvantage is that it may not be up to handling a major crisis or problem due to some powerful temptation or eruption.	a. Repression works better when you are old. Life has battered you and you have learned self-control and to live with both frustration and defeat. b. The drawback of repression is that if one starts too young, there will be constant pain and pushback from the instincts. This inner conflict will be hard to handle. c. In repression, all the bad instincts are in full power, so deep down, any choice of good is not as committed and heart-felt as when it comes out of sublimation.

d. The advantage of *Tikkun* is that one is whole-hearted in doing the good. Therefore, one can serve God with both one's good urge (reason) and one's evil urge (desires and instincts). e. In the end, the choice of good in sublimation is purer, more complete, and more dependable.	d. Repression, no matter how successful, leaves one vulnerable to the untamed, subconscious forces which remain. These forces may erupt. They may also strike back by corrupting reasoning and convincing people that their desired outcomes are legitimate by the standard of reason. e. Nevertheless, one should not give up the practice and training of repression because one may need it in a major crisis moment.

On one hand, reason is the most important tool that humans have to establish truth or to make judgments, but in reality, humans are highly subjective. No one can achieve pure rationality. Instincts are so strong that they distort reason. One may try to curb or neutralize instincts, giving him a greater capacity to tame these unconscious forces through reason and through Torah and Mussar study.

God accepts that the inescapable human subjectivity will color and even distort one's reading of the Torah. This is the true meaning of the verse "It [the Torah] is not in the Heavens [anymore]" (Deut. 30:12), i.e., it is no longer pure heavenly revelation – it has an admixture of human elements, including distortions. Still, although God accepts some admixture of "impurity," God requires that humans refine their reason to the extent possible, so that they can read the Torah more objectively and understand it more accurately.

There are three levels of working on oneself to fulfill the service of God: (a) staying awake or alive emotionally, or arousing oneself from a deadened emotional state, where one does not care (this spiritual apathy and emotional deadness is brought on by continuous or habitual sinning); (b) repression (i.e., willed control of behavior, and a choice to not sin out of desire to live up to the Torah); and (c) sublimation (i.e., conscious and emotional redirection of feelings so that the instincts identify with the good as defined by the Torah, and the person willingly and even joyfully does the good).

If a person no longer experiences emotion or sentiment, God considers that person unable to repent. If God concludes that a person is a "hopeless case," then God is ready to end that person's life now. R. Salanter tells us that *hitpaalut* – arousal of the sentiments and emotions – is the key to reviving consciousness and keeping emotions alive, thus avoiding such a fate.

לא

בְּסַנְהֶדְרִין (ע"א) בֵּן סוֹרֵר וּמוֹרֶה לֹא הָיָה וְלֹא עָתִיד לִהְיוֹת. וְלָמָּה נִכְתַּב דְּרֹשׁ וְקַבֵּל שָׂכָר. הַתְּמִיהַ גְּדוֹלָה מְאֹד. הַאִם אֵין דַּי בִּשְׁאָר חֶלְקֵי הַתּוֹרָה אַף אִם אֶלֶף שָׁנִים יִחְיֶה הָאָדָם. לִדְרֹשׁ בָּהֶם לְקַבֵּל שָׂכָר.

בַּיַּלְקוּט (שְׁמִינִי תקכ"א) וְכִי מָה רָאוּ יִשְׂרָאֵל לְהָבִיא יוֹתֵר מֵאַהֲרֹן. אֶלָּא אָמַר לָהֶם. אַתֶּם יֵשׁ בְּיֶדְכֶם בַּתְּחִלָּה. וַיִּשְׁחֲטוּ שְׂעִיר עִזִּים. וְיֵשׁ בְּיֶדְכֶם בַּסּוֹף. עָשׂוּ לָהֶם וְכוּ'. גַּם כֵּן מֻפְלָא מְאֹד. הֲלֹא גַּם אַהֲרֹן הָיָה לוֹ בַּתְּחִלָּה וְגַם בַּסּוֹף, כְּמַאֲמַר הַכָּתוּב (דְּבָרִים ט') וּבְאַהֲרֹן הִתְאַנַּף וְגוֹ'.

בְּסַנְהֶדְרִין (כז:) וְהַכְּתִיב (שְׁמוֹת ל"ד) פּוֹקֵד עֲוֹן אָבוֹת וְגוֹ' כְּשֶׁאוֹחֲזִין מַעֲשֵׂה אֲבוֹתֵיהֶם וְכוּ'. וְהַדַּעַת נוֹתֵן. כִּי זֶה רַק בְּאֹפֶן אֲשֶׁר אֵיכוּת מַעֲשֵׂי הַבָּנִים שָׁוִים בְּעֶרְכָּם עִם מַעֲשֵׂי הָאָבוֹת. לֹא

---

1. See Deuteronomy 21:18–21.
2. At the dedication of the Tabernacle, Aaron was instructed to bring a young calf for a sin offering, and a ram for a burnt offering. The Israelites were instructed to bring a kid goat for a sin offering, a calf and a lamb for a burnt offering, and a bullock and a ram for a peace offering. See Leviticus 9:2–4.
3. See Genesis 37:31. The "sin on the hands" of the Israelite tribes is the sale of Joseph and the cover-up of the crime.
4. See Exodus 32:8. The sin of the desert generation of the Israelites was making the Golden Calf.

Letter 31

Sanhedrin 71a [states]: "The case of the 'rebellious son'[1] never was and never will be. Why then is it written in Scripture? To expound it and receive the reward [of study]." This is very surprising. Isn't there enough material in the other parts of the Torah – even if a person were to live a thousand years – to study and receive reward?

Yalkut Shimoni (*Shemini*, 521) [states]: "Why did [the people of] Israel see fit to bring more [sacrifices to the dedication of the Tabernacle] than Aaron?[2] Because he said to them: You have [sin] on your hands from the beginning – 'And they slaughtered a kid goat'[3] – and you have [sin] on your hands at the end – 'They have made for themselves a molten calf....'"[4] This is also quite astonishing. Did not Aaron, too, have a share in sin at the beginning and at the end,[5] as Scripture says (Deut. 9:20): "The Lord was angered at Aaron..."?[6]

Sanhedrin (27b) states: "Is it not written (Ex. 34:7), 'He visits the sins of the fathers on children...'?[7] This is when they perpetuate the acts of their fathers...." It stands to reason that this holds true only when the quality of the acts of the children is equivalent to the acts of the fathers,

5. Aaron agreed to make an idol and asked the Israelites to give their jewelry of gold (Ex. 32:2). Aaron then made the Golden Calf (ibid. 32:4).
6. Moses had to pray that Aaron be forgiven for his role in making the Golden Calf.
7. Deuteronomy 24:15 states that each person is responsible for his own sin, but the verse in Exodus implies that children are punished for the sins of their forebears.

כַּאֲשֶׁר מַעֲשֵׂי הָאָבוֹת הָיוּ עֲוֹנוֹת גְּדוֹלִים בְּאֵיכוּת עֶרְכָּם מִמַּעֲשֵׂי עֲוֹן הַבָּנִים. וְאָמְרִינַן בְּיוֹמָא (סז:) אֶת מִשְׁפָּטַי תַּעֲשׂוּ. דְּבָרִים שֶׁאִלְמָלֵי לֹא נִכְתְּבוּ דִּין הוּא שֶׁיִּכָּתְבוּ, וְאֵלּוּ הֵן עֲבוֹדַת אֱלִילִים כו׳. אֶת חֻקֹּתַי תִּשְׁמְרוּ. דְּבָרִים שֶׁהַשָּׂטָן מֵשִׁיב עֲלֵיהֶם כו׳. (יַעַן אֵין לְחִיּוּבָם מָבוֹא בְּשֵׂכֶל אֱנוֹשִׁי. רַק אֲנִי ה׳ חֲקַקְתִּים כו׳). וְהַדַּעַת נוֹתֵן. כִּי אֵיכוּת עֲוֹן הַמִּשְׁפָּט תַּעֲלֶה לְמַעְלָה נֶגֶד אֵיכוּת עֲוֹן הַחֻקִּים. וְאָמְרִינַן (שָׁם פה:) אָמְרָה תּוֹרָה חַלֵּל עָלָיו שַׁבָּת אַחַת כְּדֵי שֶׁיִּשְׁמֹר שַׁבָּתוֹת הַרְבֵּה. נִמְצָא לְפִי זֶה. הֲגַם שֶׁעֲוֹן עֲבוֹדַת אֱלִילִים הוּא מִשְׁפָּט (כְּמַאֲמַר הַגְּמָרָא הַנִּזְכָּר לְעֵיל). אָכֵן מַה שֶּׁהִזְהִירָה הַתּוֹרָה לָמוּת עַל עֲבוֹדַת אֱלִילִים. הִיא חֻקָּה. וְאָמְרִינַן בְּסַנְהֶדְרִין (ז׳) וַיַּרְא אַהֲרֹן כו׳. מָה רָאָה אַהֲרֹן. רָאָה חוּר שֶׁזָּבוּחַ לְפָנָיו. אָמַר אִי לֹא שַׁמְעָנָא לְהוּ הַשְׁתָּא עָבְדִי לִי כְּדַעֲבַדוּ בְּחוּר. וּמִיקַיָּם בִּי (אֵיכָה ב׳) אִם יֵהָרֵג בְּמִקְדַּשׁ ה׳ כֹּהֵן וְנָבִיא כו׳. נִמְצָא הָיָה עֲוֹן אַהֲרֹן חֹק. וְלֹא הָיָה בִּבְחִינַת אוֹחֵז מַעֲשֵׂה אָבוֹת (אֲשֶׁר יִפָּקְדוּ עָלָיו עֲוֹנוֹתֵיהֶם). נֶגֶד וַיִּשְׁחֲטוּ שְׂעִיר עִזִּים כו׳. שֶׁהָיָה עֲוֹן מִשְׁפָּט.

וּבָזֶה יֵשׁ לְבָאֵר הַכָּתוּב (וַיִּקְרָא י״ח) אֶת מִשְׁפָּטַי תַּעֲשׂוּ וְאֶת חֻקּוֹתַי תִּשְׁמְרוּ כו׳. אֲשֶׁר יֵשׁ לָשׂוּם לֵב עַל הַשִּׁנּוּי בַּפָּסוּק הַזֶּה. לְהַזְהִיר מִשְׁפָּט בִּבְחִינַת חִיּוּב. וְחֹק בִּבְחִינַת שְׁלִילָה (עַיֵּן מְנָחוֹת ל״ו: הַשָּׁמֵר דַּעֲשֵׂה כו׳). גַּם שִׁנּוּי הַפְּסוּקִים. בַּפָּסוּק הָרִאשׁוֹן מִשְׁפָּט בַּתְּחִלָּה

---

8. R. Salanter continues to apply his principle that particular acts of mitzva or sin may be externally alike yet weighed differently for each person. The more difficult the act, the greater reward in doing a good deed and the lesser the punishment for the sin. The easier it is to act, the lesser the reward for doing a good deed and the greater the punishment for the sin (because it would have been easy to refrain from the act).
9. Yoma ibid.
10. When our reason sees the need for a law, it is easier to observe. In the Talmud's formulation, Satan does not urge us to question the need for such a law. This follows R. Salanter's line of reasoning that laws that we find more compelling are easier to keep, and, correspondingly, one gets less reward for keeping them and more punishment for violating them.
11. The Talmud reasons that it is permissible to violate the Sabbath to save a life on the grounds that the person thus saved will observe the Sabbath for the rest of his life,

not when the acts of the fathers were qualitatively greater sins than the sinful acts of the children.[8]

And we say in Yoma (67b): "'My *mishpatim* (laws), you shall do' (Lev. 18:4) – this refers to matters that, had they not been written, should have been written. They are: idolatry, murder.... 'My *ḥukkim* (statutes), you shall observe' – refers to matters which Satan questions..." (because their obligation has no entry in human reason – only "I the Lord have decreed them..."[9]). It stands to reason that transgression against *mishpat* is qualitatively worse than the transgression of a *ḥok*.[10]

And we say (ibid. 85b): "The Torah said: Violate one Sabbath for his sake so that he will be able to observe many Sabbaths."[11] Accordingly, though the sin of idolatry is a *mishpat* (per the aforementioned passage from the Talmud), the Torah's instruction to die rather than perform idolatry is a *ḥok*.[12]

And we say in Sanhedrin (7a): "'And Aaron saw...' (Ex. 32:5). What did Aaron see? He saw Hur slaughtered before his eyes. He said: If I don't obey them now, they will do to me what they did to Hur.[13] In me will be fulfilled (Lam. 2:20): 'Alas, in the Temple of the Lord, priest and prophet will be killed....'"

It follows that Aaron transgressed a *ḥok*, and he was not in the same category as one "who perpetuates the acts of his fathers" (on whom punishment is visited for the fathers' sins) with respect to [the sin of] "they slaughtered a kid goat...," which transgressed a *mishpat*.

With this we can explain the verse [Leviticus 18:4] "My *mishpatim*, you shall do, and My *ḥukkim*, you shall observe...." Note the change in this verse: The admonition with respect to *mishpatim* is positive, and with respect to *ḥukkim* is negative (see Menaḥot 36b: the term "[be careful to] observe" in connection with a positive commandment [is

---

so it is a "net gain" for Sabbath observance. Torah, judging rationally, does not ask the individual to die rather than violate the Sabbath.

12. Rationally, one could argue: Should I not perform idolatry this one time so that I may continue to serve God for the rest of my life?

13. According to the midrash, the Israelites first asked Hur (Moses and Aaron's companion, and, according to Sanhedrin 69b, their nephew) to make them a Golden Calf. When he refused, they slaughtered him.

וְאַחַר כָּךְ חֹק. וּבַפָּסוּק הַשֵּׁנִי (שָׁם) וּשְׁמַרְתֶּם אֶת חֻקּוֹתַי וְאֶת מִשְׁפָּטַי. בַּתְּחִלָּה חֹק וְאַחַר כָּךְ מִשְׁפָּט. כִּי הָרַמְבַּ"ם כָּתַב (הִלְכוֹת תְּשׁוּבָה פֶּרֶק ג') וְזֶה לְשׁוֹנוֹ. כָּל אֶחָד וְאֶחָד מִבְּנֵי הָאָדָם יֵשׁ לוֹ זְכֻיּוֹת וַעֲוֹנוֹת. מִי שֶׁזְּכֻיּוֹתָיו יְתֵרוֹת עַל עֲוֹנוֹתָיו צַדִּיק. וּמִי שֶׁעֲוֹנוֹתָיו יְתֵרוֹת עַל זְכֻיּוֹתָיו רָשָׁע. מֶחֱצָה עַל מֶחֱצָה בֵּינוֹנִי כוּ'. וְשִׁקּוּל זֶה אֵינוֹ לְפִי מִנְיַן הַזְּכֻיּוֹת וְהָעֲוֹנוֹת אֶלָּא לְפִי גָּדְלָם. יֵשׁ זְכוּת שֶׁהִיא כְּנֶגֶד כַּמָּה עֲוֹנוֹת. שֶׁנֶּאֱמַר (מְלָכִים-א' י"ד) יַעַן נִמְצָא בוֹ דָּבָר טוֹב. וְיֵשׁ עָוֹן שֶׁהוּא כְּנֶגֶד כַּמָּה זְכֻיּוֹת. שֶׁנֶּאֱמַר (קֹהֶלֶת ט', י"ח). וְחוֹטֶא אֶחָד יְאַבֵּד טוֹבָה הַרְבֵּה. וְאֵין שׁוֹקְלִין אֶלָּא בְּדַעְתּוֹ שֶׁל אֵל דֵּעוֹת. וְהוּא הַיּוֹדֵעַ הֵאִיךְ עוֹרְכִין הַזְּכֻיּוֹת כְּנֶגֶד הָעֲוֹנוֹת. עַד כָּאן לְשׁוֹנוֹ. וְאִם כִּי בְּוַדַּאי יֶשְׁנָם סִבּוֹת רַבּוֹת הַמַּגְדִּילוֹת עֶרֶךְ הַזְּכֻיּוֹת וְהָעֲוֹנוֹת. לֹא נֶחְדַּל לְבָאֵר בָּזֶה אֵיזוֹ בְּחִינָה. וְהוּא. כִּי רַבּוֹת מַחֲשָׁבוֹת בְּלֶב אִישׁ. הַשָּׂם לִבּוֹ אֶל דְּרָכָיו וְיוֹדֵעַ כִּי בְּיָדוֹ עָוֹן אֲשֶׁר חָטָא לְמַרְבֶּה. (כָּל יִנָּזֵר מִמֶּנָּה לְפִי דַּעְתּוֹ) הַמְדַמֵּית לְבַל לְסַלְסֵל בְּמַאַמְרֵי רַבּוֹתֵינוּ ז"ל הַמְדַבְּרִים בָּהּ. כִּי מוּטָב שֶׁיִּהְיֶה שׁוֹגֵג. כְּמַאֲמָרָם ז"ל (מִדְרָשׁ רַבָּה דְּבָרִים פָּרָשַׁת תָּבוֹא) כָּל מִי שֶׁלָּמַד תּוֹרָה וְאֵינוֹ מְקַיֵּם אוֹתָהּ עָנְשׁוֹ חָמוּר מִמִּי שֶׁלֹּא לָמַד כָּל עִקָּר. עַיֵּן שָׁם. לֹא זֹאת דֶּרֶךְ ה'. לַעֲטֹף הָרָשָׁע בְּמְעִיל הַצֶּדֶק. וּכְמַאֲמַר הַכָּתוּב (תְּהִלִּים צ') תָּשֵׁב אֱנוֹשׁ עַד דַּכָּא. וְדָרְשׁוּ רַבּוֹתֵינוּ ז"ל. עַד דִּכְדּוּכָהּ שֶׁל נֶפֶשׁ. וַתֹּאמֶר שׁוּבוּ בְּנֵי אָדָם כוּ'. בַּמֶּה יִוָּשַׁע הָאָדָם לְסַעֵף פֹּארָה

---

14. According to the passage in Menaḥot, the term "do" ("*taasu*") connotes a positive commandment, whereas the term "observe" ("*tishmoru*") connotes a negative commandment.

15. See Proverbs 19:21. R. Salanter interprets this to mean that, as the psychology of the individual varies, there will be different weight to similar deeds based on the individual's difficulty (or ease) in doing the act.

16. Compare Beitza 30a.

17. God does not want us to assume that we cannot stop sinning and consequently delude ourselves and avoid studying rabbinic texts in the vain hope that we will be considered unintentional sinners because we are ignorant. Rather, God wants us to fully recognize our sinfulness so we can then change and repent. Facing up to our addiction to the sin is important, despite the possible risk of falling into despondency.

18. Y. Ḥagiga 9b:1 expounds the verse and cites the story of Elisha ben Avuya, who recognized his sin and as a result fell into despair, telling R. Meir that he was so

equivalent to a negative commandment] ...).[14] Note also the change of order in the verses. In the first verse (Lev. 18:4), *mishpat* precedes *ḥok*, but in the next verse, "You shall observe My *ḥukkim* and *mishpatim*" – first *ḥukkim*, then *mishpatim*.

For Rambam wrote (Laws of Repentance 3:1–2):

> Each and every human being has merits and sins. One whose merits exceed his sins is a righteous man. One whose sins exceed his merits is a wicked person. If they are half and half, he is an in between person .... This weighing is not by number of merits and sins but by their magnitude. A merit can equal several sins, as it is said (I Kings 14:13): "For something good was found in him." And a sin can equal several merits, as it is said (Eccl. 9:12): "One sinner destroys much good." And the judging is done only by the mind of the Divine Intellect. He is the One who knows how the merits are assessed as compared to the sins.

Although there are certainly many causes that increase the weight of merits and sins, we shall not hold back from explaining a particular aspect of this matter, viz., "Many are the thoughts in the heart of man."[15] One who pays attention to his own practices knows that he commits a certain sin frequently. (He cannot desist from it, he thinks) in his imagination, and so he does not embrace the sayings of our Rabbis, of blessed memory, which discuss it, thinking that "it is better to do it unintentionally."[16] As they, of blessed memory, said (Deuteronomy Rabba, *Ki Tavo*): "Whoever learned Torah and does not fulfill it, his punishment is more severe than one who never learned it at all." See further there.

This is not the way of God, to put the cloak of righteousness back on the wicked.[17] As the verse says (Ps. 90:3): "You bring a person to dust (*daka*)." The Rabbis, of blessed memory, expounded: "to despondency (*dikhdukh*) of the soul." And the verse continues: "And you say to mankind, return ...."[18]

---

ensnared in his sins that it was too late for repentance. R. Meir (using Psalms 90:3 for support) told him that it is never too late, and that even mired in the deepest sin, God wanted him to return and be accepted. In other words, one should know

הַלָּזוֹ וְאַיֵּה הַמַּעֲרָצָה. זֹאת יָשִׁיב אֶל לִבּוֹ. לֵאמֹר: הֲלֹא כָּל דָּבָר יִתְחַלֵּק עַל פִּי הַפְּעֻלָּה וְעַל פִּי הַפּוֹעֵל.

מִצַּד הַפְּעֻלָּה. יִתְחַלֵּק כָּל דָּבָר טוֹב לְפִי הִתְפַּשְּׁטוּת פִּרְיוֹ. לְעֻמָּתוֹ יֹאמַר בָּרוּךְ לְהָעוֹשֶׂה. וְכָל אֲשֶׁר יוֹסִיף תֵּת כֹּחוֹ. (אִם כִּי סָר כֹּחַ מְיַסְּדוֹ). כֵּן יוֹסִיף שְׂכָרוֹ. וּכְמַאֲמָרָם זַ"ל (קִדּוּשִׁין מ') הַזְּכוּת יֵשׁ לָהּ קֶרֶן וְיֵשׁ לָהּ פֵּרוֹת כּוּ'. עֲבֵרָה יֵשׁ לָהּ קֶרֶן וְאֵין לָהּ פֵּרוֹת. וְאֶלָּא מָה אֲנִי מְקַיֵּם (מִשְׁלֵי א') וְיֹאכְלוּ מִפְּרִי דַרְכָּם וּמִמֹּעֲצֹתֵיהֶם יִשְׂבָּעוּ. עֲבֵרָה שֶׁעוֹשָׂה פֵּרוֹת יֵשׁ לָהּ פֵּרוֹת. שֶׁאֵין עוֹשָׂה פֵּרוֹת אֵין לָהּ פֵּרוֹת כּוּ' עַד כָּאן. לָזֹאת בְּוַדַּאי בְּמִדָּה טוֹבָה (הַמְּרֻבָּה מִמִּדַּת פֻּרְעָנִיּוֹת). הָעוֹשָׂה פֵּרוֹת יִגְדַּל פִּרְיָהּ לְמַעְלָה לְמַעְלָה.

* עַל פִּי הַדְּבָרִים הָאֵלּוּ נוּכַל לְיַשֵּׁב קֻשְׁיַת הַתּוֹסָפוֹת (שַׁבָּת נ"ה) עַל הָא דְּאָמְרִינַן שָׁם מ"ש תָּיו (שֶׁאָמַר הַקָּדוֹשׁ־בָּרוּךְ־הוּא לְגַבְרִיאֵל לֵךְ וּרְשֹׁם עַל מִצְחָן שֶׁל צַדִּיקִים תָּיו שֶׁל דְּיוֹ וְכוּ'), רַב אָמַר תָּיו תִּחְיֶה תָּיו תָּמוּת, וּשְׁמוּאֵל אָמַר תַּמָּה זְכוּת אָבוֹת, וְכֵן רַבִּי יְהוֹשֻׁעַ בֶּן לֵוִי וְרַבִּי יוֹחָנָן אָמְרוּ הָתָם אֵימָתַי תַּמָּה זְכוּת אָבוֹת כּוּ', וַאֲנַן מַזְכִּירִין זְכוּת אָבוֹת עַיֵּן שָׁם. וּלְפִי הַנִּזְכַּר לְעֵיל יֵשׁ לְפָרֵשׁ דִּשְׁתֵּי בְּחִינוֹת בַּדָּבָר. הָאַחַת הִיא זְכוּת אָבוֹת מִמַּעֲשֵׂיהֶם הַנּוֹרָאִים, אֲשֶׁר נִפְסְקוּ בְּהִסְתַּלְּקוּתָם, וְזֹהַר זְכֻיּוֹתָם מִתְנוֹצֵץ לְתוֹלְדוֹתָם בִּבְחִינָה קַיֶּמֶת וּקְצוּבָה, וּפְלִיגֵי אֲמוֹרָאֵי אֵימָתַי גְּבוּל זְמַנָּם. הַשְּׁנִיָּה הִיא זְכוּת אָבוֹת הַנּוֹלֶדֶת מִמַּעֲשֵׂי הַבָּנִים, כִּי הָאָבוֹת הֵמָּה יְסוֹד וְשֹׁרֶשׁ אֲמִתִּי לְכָל מַעֲשֶׂה טוֹב אֲשֶׁר יַעֲשׂוּ הַבָּאִים אַחֲרֵיהֶם, וּזְכוּתָם עוֹשָׂה פֵּרוֹת בִּתְמִידִי בְּלִי גְּבוּל וְקִצְבָּה. וּבִבְחִינָה זוֹ אִי אֶפְשָׁר לִהְיוֹת תַּמָּה זְכוּת אָבוֹת, כִּי לֹא אַלְמָן יִשְׂרָאֵל, וּבְכָל דּוֹר וָדוֹר נִמְצְאוּ אֲנָשִׁים צַדִּיקִים. וְגַם פּוֹשְׁעֵי יִשְׂרָאֵל מְלֵאִים מִצְוֹת כָּרִמּוֹן. וְאַהֲנֵי מַעֲשֵׂיהֶם שֶׁל הָאָבוֹת, לָשֵׂאת פְּרִי וּלְגַדֵּל פֶּרַח זְכֻיּוֹתָם. וּכְדְאָמְרִינַן בַּעֲרָכִין (דַּף ט"ז) עַל שִׁבְעָה דְּבָרִים נְגָעִים בָּאִים, עַל לָשׁוֹן הָרַע וְכוּ', אִינִי וְהָא אָמַר רַבִּי עֲנָנִי בַּר שָׂשׂוֹן לָמָּה נִסְמְכָה פָּרָשַׁת בִּגְדֵי כְהֻנָּה

the full extent of his sins – even at the risk of falling into despair – for even in the moment of being totally in the grip of the sin, God is still saying, "Return to Me, and I will accept you."

19. I.e., cut off the branch of sin from the tree. Compare Isaiah 10:33.
20. Compare Lamentations 3:21.
21. I.e., as an action continues to have an effect, even if the person who performed the action has passed away, reward continues to accrue to that person.

How can a person be rescued to lop off the bough of sin?[19] Where is the terror to motivate turning? He should take this to his heart,[20] saying: Each deed is defined by its action and its actor.

From the perspective of the action, every good deed can be classified in accordance with the extent of its effects, in the face of which one will say that the actor should be blessed. The more the action continues to exert force (even if the originating force has departed), the more his reward increases.[21] As they, of blessed memory, say (Kiddushin 40a): "A merit has principal and dividends (*perot*).... A sin has principal but no dividends. And how do I reconcile this with (Prov. 1:31), 'They shall eat the fruit (*perot*) of their ways and have their fill of their counsels'? A sin which produces fruit has an effect; one that has no fruits has no further effect." Thus, it is certain that by the principle of benevolence (which is greater than the principle of retribution), a good deed which bears fruits will continue to produce greater and greater fruits.*

* [R. Salanter's footnote:] On the basis of these words, we can resolve the objection of *Tosafot* (Shabbat 55a) about what is said: "Why specifically *tav*? (Why did the Holy One, blessed be He, tell Gabriel: Go and inscribe on the forehead of the righteous man a *tav* in ink?... [compare Ezek. 9:4]). Rav says: *Tav* stands for *tiḥyeh* (you shall live); *tav* stands for *tamut* (you shall die). Shmuel says: *Tav* stands for *tama zekhut avot* (the merits of the fathers have been used up). R. Yehoshua ben Levi and R. Yoḥanan likewise said there: When were the merits of the fathers used up?... We still mention the merits of the fathers [in our prayers]!?" See further there. According to our words above, we can answer: There are two aspects in this matter. One is the merits of the fathers because of their awesome deeds, which stopped upon their death, but the radiance of which shines for their descendants in permanent and measured fashion. The *Amora'im* disagree as to when their time of effectiveness reached its limit.

The second is the merits of the fathers which are born from the deeds of the children. For the fathers are the true basis and root of all the good deeds which those who follow them do. These merits bear fruit continually, without limit or end. In this category, it is impossible for the merits of the fathers to be used up. "For Israel is not left bereft" [lit. "widower." See Jer. 51:5], and in each generation righteous men were found; even the sinners of Israel "are as full of good deeds as a pomegranate [is full of seeds]" [compare Eiruvin 19a].

The deeds of the fathers are efficacious to bear fruit and grow blossoms of merit. As we say in Arakhin (16a):

"For seven actions, plagues come: for speaking evil of others.... How is this? Did not R. Anani bar Sason say: 'Why is the portion dealing with the priestly

לְפָרָשַׁת קָרְבָּנוֹת, לוֹמַר לְךָ מַה קָּרְבָּנוֹת מְכַפְּרִין אַף בִּגְדֵי כְהֻנָּה מְכַפְּרִין כו', מְעִיל מְכַפֵּר עַל לָשׁוֹן הָרַע כו', לָא קַשְׁיָא הָא דְּאַהֲנוּ מַעֲשָׂיו הָא דְּלָא אַהֲנוּ מַעֲשָׂיו, אִי אַהֲנוּ מַעֲשָׂיו אַתּוּ נְגָעִים עֲלֵיהּ אִי לָא אַהֲנוּ מַעֲשָׂיו מְעִיל מְכַפֵּר עַיֵּן שָׁם. וְאִם כִּי דִּבּוּר לָשׁוֹן הָרַע שָׁוֶה בִּשְׁנֵיהֶם, בְּכָל זֹאת הַמֶּרְחָק רַב בֵּינֵיהֶם בְּעִנְיַן הַתּוֹלָדָה הַנּוֹלֶדֶת מִמֵּילָא, לִהְיוֹת אַהֲנֵי מַעֲשָׂיו לְהַגְדִּיל כֹּחוֹ לְהִצְטָרֵךְ כַּפָּרָה יְתֵרָה. כֵּן גַּם בִּבְחִינַת הַטּוֹב, אִי אַהֲנוּ מַעֲשָׂיו, לִהְיוֹת נוֹשֵׂא פְּרִי תְנוּבָה, יִגְדַּל מַעֲשֵׂה שָׁרְשׁוֹ לְהוֹסִיף זְכוּת, וְלָכֵן אֲנַחְנוּ מַזְכִּירִים תָּמִיד זְכוּת אָבוֹת, הַמִּתְעוֹרֶרֶת עַל יְדֵי מַעֲשֵׂה הַתּוֹלָדוֹת בַּל תִּפָּסֵק לְעוֹלָם.

וְכֵן כָּל דָּבָר רַע יִתְחַלֵּק לְפִי הִתְפַּשְּׁטוּת פִּרְיוֹ. וְכָל אֲשֶׁר יוֹסִיף תֵּת כֹּחוֹ לְגַדֵּל פְּרִי רֹאשׁ. כֵּן יִגְדַּל גְּרִיעוּת עֶרְכּוֹ וְיִכְבַּד עָנְשׁוֹ. וּפְעָמִים רַבּוֹת יִנְצֹר הָאָדָם אָרְחוֹ. לִכְבֹּשׁ תַּאֲוָתוֹ בְּלִי גְבוּרָה. כַּאֲשֶׁר יִרְאֶה בַּעֲלִיל אֵיךְ מַעֲשָׂיו נִפְרְצוּ לְהַשְׁחִית. כְּזוֹרֵק חֵץ אֲשֶׁר אֵין לַהֲשִׁיב. אִם לֹא נִכְבָּה מִנַּפְשׁוֹ חִיּוּבָהּ הַנּוֹלֶדֶת מִסִּלְסוּל הַרְבֵּה בְּדִבְרֵי רַבּוֹתֵינוּ זַ"ל. וְאֵיךְ יַעֲשֶׂה הָאָדָם שֶׁקֶר בְּנַפְשׁוֹ בַּתְּמוּרָה הַלָּזוֹ. לִהְיוֹת שׁוֹגֵג. (אֲשֶׁר רַק שׁוֹגֵג דִּמְיוֹנִי הוּא, כִּי שִׁגְגַת הַתַּלְמוּד עוֹלָה זָדוֹן. כִּדְאָמְרִינַן בְּבָבָא מְצִיעָא לג:) בַּבְּחִינָה הַנְּמוּכָה. מִלִּהְיוֹת מְרֻחָק מִן הָעֲבֵרָה בַּבְּחִינָה הַגְּבוֹהָה לְמַעְלָה הַרְבֵּה.

מִצַּד הַפּוֹעֵל. יִתְחַלֵּק כָּל דָּבָר טוֹב. בְּאֵיכוּת עֲשִׂיָּתוֹ לְפִי צַעַר קִיּוּמוֹ, כְּמַאֲמָרָם זַ"ל (אָבוֹת פֶּרֶק ה') לְפוּם צַעֲרָא אַגְרָא. וְכֵן כָּל דָּבָר רַע. יִתְחַלֵּק בְּאֵיכוּת צַעַר שְׁמִירָתוֹ. וְכָל אֲשֶׁר יוֹסִיף צַעֲרוֹ כֵּן יִמְעַט בְּחִינָתוֹ. כִּדְאָמְרִינַן (מְנָחוֹת מג:) תַּנְיָא הָיָה רַבִּי מֵאִיר אוֹמֵר גָּדוֹל עָנְשׁוֹ שֶׁל לָבָן יוֹתֵר מֵעָנְשׁוֹ שֶׁל תְּכֵלֶת. מָשָׁל לְמָה הַדָּבָר דּוֹמֶה

---

22. Lit. "path."
23. R. Salanter here makes another case for the need of Mussar analysis and the evaluation of all behaviors and their motivations. The weight (reward and punishment) of an act varies widely, depending on its spread or aftereffects. After analyzing beforehand, one will make extra efforts to do the right thing and not do the wrong thing.
24. And therefore, an unintentional sinner.
25. Instead of trying to minimize guilt and punishment by making himself ignorant of the law in the vain hope of being considered an unintentional sinner, he should face the full extent of the sin (and his proneness to commit it) and repent at the fullest level.

> vestments in proximity with the portion dealing with sacrifices? To tell you that as sacrifices atone for sins, so the priestly vestments atone.... The priestly cloak atones for speaking evil....' [How can there ever be a plague for speaking evil if the priestly cloak atones for speaking evil?] There is no problem: here is a case where his actions were efficacious; here is a case where his actions had no effect. If his actions have an effect, then a plague comes because of it. [Since they spread evil, they outstripped the power of the cloak to atone.] If his actions had no effects, then the cloak atones for it."
>
> Even though the act of speaking evil was the same in both cases, the gap between them is great because of the effect that comes from it. If his words have an effect, he needs much more atonement. It is the same with the category of the good. If his deed has effects, bearing fruit, then his deed continues to add merits. Therefore, we always mention the merits of the fathers – which is continually awakened by the deeds of the descendants and will never ever end.

So too, each evil action can be distinguished according to the spread of its effects. The more the action continues to have effects by growing bitter fruit, the more its negative quality will grow and its punishment increase.

Many times, a person will guard his behavior[22] and repress his strong desire, without a heroic effort, when he sees clearly how his actions break through [controls] and do damage;[23] it is like shooting an arrow which cannot be recalled. [He can do this] as long as he does not snuff out the awareness of the obligation in his soul – which awareness grows out of much fine combing through the words of the Rabbis, of blessed memory. And how can a person lie to himself in his soul with this substitution, claiming to be an unaware sinner[24] in the lowest category of sin (this is only an illusory "unawareness" – for erroneous action growing out of not having studied is considered like a deliberate sin, as we say in Bava Metzia 33b), instead of making the effort to stay far from the transgression in the highest category?[25]

From the perspective of the human actor: the value of each good deed can be classified in accordance with the effort of observing it. As they, of blessed memory, said (Avot 5:23): "According to the pain [of the effort] is the reward." Each evil deed also can be classified in quality according to the pain of the effort of observing it. The more the effort, the lesser the category of guilt. As we say (Menaḥot 43b): "It was taught: R. Meir used to say: 'Greater is the punishment for [not wearing] the white [*tzizit*] string than the punishment for [not wearing] the sky-blue

לְמֶלֶךְ בָּשָׂר וָדָם שֶׁאָמַר לִשְׁנֵי עֲבָדָיו לְאֶחָד אָמַר הָבֵא לִי חוֹתָם שֶׁל טִיט וּלְאֶחָד אָמַר הָבֵא לִי חוֹתָם שֶׁל זָהָב וּפָשְׁעוּ שְׁנֵיהֶם וְלֹא הֵבִיאוּ אֵיזֶה מֵהֶן עָנְשׁוֹ יוֹתֵר גָּדוֹל. הֱוֵי אוֹמֵר זֶה שֶׁאָמַר לוֹ הָבֵא לִי חוֹתָם שֶׁל טִיט וְלֹא הֵבִיא. עַד כָּאן.

אִי לָזֹאת. זֹאת תּוֹרַת הָאָדָם לְפַקֵּחַ עַל כָּל דְּרָכָיו. לְבַל יִפֹּל בְּרֶשֶׁת הַיֵּאוּשׁ. כִּי כָּל עוֹד אֲשֶׁר עֵינָיו פְּקוּחוֹת לְהַרְגִּישׁ בְּרָעָתוֹ. בְּלִי סָפֵק. בְּאֵין תַּאֲוָה מוֹצֵאת יִשְׁמֹר דַּרְכּוֹ וְיִנָּצֵל מֵחֵלֶק הַיּוֹתֵר גָּדוֹל. וּמִי פֶּתִי יֶאֱהַב פְּתָיוּת כָּזוֹ. לְהִתְבָּרֵךְ בִּלְבָבוֹ לֵאמֹר. הֲלֹא טוֹב לִי לִסְתֹּם עֵין בִּינָתִי. לְמַעַן הַקְטִין הָעֵרֶךְ בִּהְיוֹתִי שׁוֹגֵג בַּחֵלֶק הַקָּטָן. וְיַעֲזֹב שְׁמִירָתָהּ בַּחֵלֶק הַיּוֹתֵר גָּדוֹל.

הֵן הֵמָּה דִּבְרֵי הָרַמְבַּ"ם הַנִּזְכָּרִים לְעֵיל. כִּי אֵין בְּיַד הָאָדָם לֵידַע הִשְׁתַּלְשְׁלוּת הַדְּבָרִים. לְבָרֵר עֵרֶךְ הַמִּצְוֹת וְהָעֲוֹנוֹת עַל פִּי הִתְפַּשְּׁטוּתָם. וְכֵן עֵרֶךְ צַעַר קִיּוּם וּשְׁמִירַת הַתּוֹרָה וְהַמִּצְוָה. כִּי כֹּחוֹת נֶפֶשׁ הָאָדָם, יֵלְכוּ מֵהַקּוֹדֵם אֶל הַמְאֻחָר. מֵעִמְקֵי שָׁרְשֵׁי הַלֵּב אֶל הִתְגַּלּוּתָם. וְסִבּוֹת הַחִיצוֹנִיּוֹת מוֹצְאוֹת לְמַרְבֶּה, לְהַרְחִיב וּלְגַלּוֹת אֵיזֶה כֹּחַ אֲשֶׁר יִגָּרַע חֶלְקוֹ (נֶגֶד יֶתֶר הַכֹּחוֹת) בְּשָׁרְשׁוֹ. לְזֹאת הָאָדָם הַמַּשְׁקִיף בְּעֵין בִּינָתוֹ מֵהַמְאֻחָר אֶל הַקּוֹדֵם, יִשְׁגֶּה הַרְבֵּה בְּשָׁפְטוֹ עַל שָׁרְשֵׁי הַכֹּחוֹת הַמּוֹלִידִים צַעַר וָעֹנֶג. וְכָל עוֹד אֲשֶׁר כֹּחַ נַפְשׁוֹ מִסְתַּתֵּר בְּשָׁרְשׁוֹ מִתְחַבֵּא מִבִּינַת אֱנוֹשׁ. כֵּן יוֹסִיף לִירוֹת חִצָּיו לְפָעֳלַת אָדָם. עַל כֵּן אֵין בְּיַד הָאָדָם לִמְצֹא אֶל נָכוֹן מַצָּב וְעֵרֶךְ צַעַר קִיּוּם וּשְׁמִירַת תּוֹרַת ה' יִתְבָּרַךְ שְׁמוֹ. וְהוּא לְבַדּוֹ יוֹדֵעַ עֶרְכָּם עַל אֲמִתּוּתָם. כְּמַאֲמָרָם זַ"ל (אָבוֹת פֶּרֶק ד') הוּא הַמֵּבִין.

26. For it would have been an easier matter for him to do.
27. Compare Deuteronomy 29:18.
28. There are certain psychic drives that are, by nature, weak, but are magnified and strengthened by environmental factors.
29. If a person attempts to understand his root motivations deductively, proceeding from their external manifestations to conclusions about his psychological make-up, he will necessarily err, because environmental factors affect the manifestation of those psychic forces, magnifying some at the expense of others.

[string].' A parable: To what is this comparable? To a flesh-and-blood king who instructs two servants. To one he said: 'Bring me a clay seal'; to the other he said: 'Bring me a gold seal.' Both transgressed and brought nothing. Which one's punishment will be greater? You can be sure that the one to whom he said, 'Bring me a clay seal,' and who did not bring it."[26]

This, therefore, is the essential human doctrine: One must monitor all his actions so that he does not fall into the net of despair. For as long as his eyes are open to sensing his own wickedness, then, without a doubt, as long as the objective of his strong evil desire is not easily available, he will watch his step and will be saved from the greater part of sin. And what fool loves such foolishness as to smugly think,[27] "Better that I close my mind's eye, so as to minimize the magnitude [of the sin] by being unintentional vis-à-vis the smaller part [of sin]," for he abandons all safeguards against the greater part!?

These are the very words of Rambam cited above. It is not in a person's hands to know how things will develop – that is, to ascertain the magnitude of mitzvot and sins according to their effects. The same is true of the magnitude of the effort to uphold and observe the Torah and the commandments. For the psychic forces of the human being proceed from the prior to the subsequent, [i.e., inductively,] from the deepest roots of the heart to their manifestation. And there are many external factors that expand and manifest some internal force which, at its root, is weak (in contrast with other forces).[28] Therefore, a person who looks with his mind's eye from the subsequent to the prior will err greatly in judging the roots of the forces which give rise to pain and pleasure.[29] Moreover, as long as his psychic force, hidden in its roots, is obscured from human intelligence, it will continue to shoot its arrows[30] into the person's actions.

Thus, it is impossible for a person to ascertain accurately the extent and the value of the pain of upholding and observing God's Torah, blessed be He. God alone knows their true value, as they, of blessed memory, said (Avot 4:22): "God [alone] understands."

---

30. I.e., drive.

וּבִכְלַל שְׁתֵּי מַדְרֵגוֹת בִּזְכִיּוֹת וַעֲוֹנוֹת. בְּחִיּוּב וּשְׁלִילָה. וְאֶת אֲשֶׁר יָבוֹא בַּמַּדְרֵגָה הַנִּשָּׂאָה בִּבְחִינַת חִיּוּב לְקַבָּלַת הַשָּׂכָר. כֵּן גַּם לְעֻמָּתוֹ יָבוֹא בַּמַּדְרֵגָה הַנְּמוּכָה בִּבְחִינַת הַשְּׁלִילָה לְקַבָּלַת הָעֹנֶשׁ. וְאֶת אֲשֶׁר יָבוֹא בַּמַּדְרֵגָה הַנְּמוּכָה בִּבְחִינַת חִיּוּב לְקַבָּלַת הַשָּׂכָר. כֵּן יָבוֹא לְעֻמָּתוֹ בַּמַּדְרֵגָה הַגְּבוֹהָה לְקַבָּלַת הָעֹנֶשׁ בִּבְחִינַת שְׁלִילָה. לָכֵן עֲשִׂיַּת הַמִּשְׁפָּט (בְּחִינַת חִיּוּב) וּשְׁמִירַת הַחֹק (בְּחִינַת שְׁלִילָה) בְּמֵתָר וְקַו אֶחָד יָבוֹאוּ.

וְהִנֵּה הַמִּשְׁפָּט. מַדְרֵגָה הָאַחַת. וּמַדְרֵגָה הַשְּׁנִיָּה הִיא הַחֹק. הוּא מַאֲמַר הַכָּתוּב (וַיִּקְרָא י״ח) אֶת מִשְׁפָּטַי תַּעֲשׂוּ וְאֶת חֻקּוֹתַי תִּשְׁמְרוּ. כְּסֵדֶר הַמַּדְרֵגוֹת. אָכֵן כָּל אֶחָד הָעִנְיָנִים לְפִי צוּרָתָם בְּעֶרְכָּם. וּבְהַהַנְהָגָה הַדָּבָר כִּמְעַט לְהֵפֶךְ. הַחֻקִּים הֵמָּה הַשְּׁלִיבוֹת לַעֲלוֹת בָּהֶם אֶל סֻלָּמֵי הַמִּשְׁפָּטִים. וּבִפְרָט בִּדְבַר הַמִּדּוֹת. מִשְׁפָּטִים הֵמָּה. וְכָל עֲמַל הָאָדָם לֹא יוֹעִיל לְתַקְּנָם וּלְיַשְּׁרָם בְּגִדְרָם הַנְּכוֹחָה. אִם לֹא יָשִׂים פָּנָיו אֶל שֵׂכֶל הָאֱנוֹשִׁי. לֶאֱהֹב אֶת הַיַּשְׁרוּת וְלִשְׂנֹא אֶת הַמְעֻקָּלוּת בְּטִבְעוֹ (גַּם בְּלִי אַזְהָרַת הַתּוֹרָה). עַל יְדֵי הִתְבּוֹנְנוּת רַבָּה בְּדַרְכֵי שֵׂכֶל אֱנוֹשִׁי כִּי אָדָם הוּא.

הֲיוֹעִיל לְאִישׁ עָלוּל לְרַגְזָנוּת יְתֵרָה עַל יְדֵי הִתְעוֹרְרוּת קְטַנָּה הַמְעִירַתּוּ. גַּם אִם יַחֲזֹר הַרְבֵּה פְּעָמִים בְּמַאֲמַר רַבּוֹתֵינוּ זַ״ל (נְדָרִים כ״ב) כָּל הַכּוֹעֵס כָּל מִינֵי גֵיהִנֹּם שׁוֹלְטִין בּוֹ כו׳. עַד אֲשֶׁר הַמַּאֲמָר יָאִיר תָּמִיד מוּל פָּנָיו. בְּכָל זֹאת כַּאֲשֶׁר תַּעֲלֶה עָלָיו רוּחַ הָרַגְזָנוּת. לִבּוֹ בַּל עִמּוֹ וְנֶהְפַּךְ אָז לְאִישׁ אַחֵר. קַל מְהֵרָה יַגְבִּיהוּ עוּף מִמֶּנּוּ כָּל צִיּוּרָיו הַיָּפִים אֲשֶׁר קָנָה בַּעֲמָלוֹ. וְאֵין רְפוּאָה לוֹ. בִּלְתִּי אִם יָשִׂים עֵין בִּינָתוֹ לַחְתֹּר בְּמַעֲמַקֵּי שָׁרְשֵׁי לְבָבוֹ. מַה הֵמָּה הַכֹּחוֹת הַכְּלָלִיּוֹת אֶצְלוֹ. הָעֲלוּלִים לְהִתָּפֵשׂ בְּהִתְעוֹרְרוּת קְטַנָּה מִחוּצָה לָהֶם. וְלִשְׁפֹּךְ עֲלֵיהֶם מֵי תְּבוּנָתוֹ. לְכַבּוֹתָם מְעַט שֶׁלֹּא יֵלְכוּ כָּל כָּךְ בְּחִפָּזוֹן עָצוּם. עַד אֲשֶׁר יִהְיֶה בְּכֹחוֹ לִהְיוֹת אִישׁ עוֹצֵר בְּרוּחוֹ.

---

31. I.e., the easier it is to refrain from doing something, the harder it is to do, and vice versa. Thus, fulfilling a difficult obligation will accrue greater reward, and reciprocally, negating that obligation will incur less punishment.
32. They can be judged side by side, as one is the mirror of the other.
33. See Job 5:7.
34. Casual consideration and superficial analysis are not enough. Given the power of

In general, there are two levels in merits and sins: fulfillment and nuillification. That which accrues greater reward for fulfillment will, reciprocally, accrue a lower level of punishment for nullification, and that which is at the lower level of reward for fulfillment will reciprocally accrue a higher level of punishment for nullification.[31] Therefore, "doing *mishpatim*" (the aspect of fulfillment) and "observing *ḥukkim*" (the aspect of nullification) operate along the same line.[32]

Mishpat is one level, and the second level is *ḥok*. This is what Scripture states (Lev. 18:4): "My *mishpatim*, you shall do, and My *ḥukkim* (statutes), you shall observe" follows the order of the levels. Indeed, each of these matters is weighted in accordance with its form. However, when it comes to behavior, the matter is virtually reversed. The *ḥukkim* are the rungs on which one ascends the ladder of *mishpatim*. And especially when it comes to human character traits, which are *mishpatim*, all of a person's efforts will not succeed in perfecting them or straightening them out within their given parameters unless one turns to human reason: naturally loving integrity and hating distortions (even absent the Torah's admonitions) by means of much contemplation of the paths of human reason – for he is a human.

Will it help a person prone to excessive anger – the slightest provocation arouses it – even if he often reviews the statement of the Rabbis, of blessed memory (Nedarim 22a): "He who gets angry, all sorts of hell will take him over…," until the statement shines before his face constantly? In any case, when the spirit of anger overcomes him, his heart will not be with him, and he will become a different person. All the lovely images that he acquired through his effort will quickly and easily fly away.[33] There is no cure for him unless he focuses his mind's eye on penetrating the deepest roots of his heart. What are the general forces in him which are prone to be caught up even by a slight external provocation? He then should pour over them the waters of his understanding to extinguish them a bit, so that they do not ignite with such powerful swiftness.[34] Ultimately he will become one who can restrain his spirit.[35]

---

unconscious forces, one must analyze and penetrate deeply (using Mussar tactics) to really affect behavior.

35. Compare Proverbs 16:32.

אָכֵן מֵאַיִן תָּבוֹא לָאָדָם הַתְּבוּנָה. וּמַה תְּעוֹרְרֵהוּ לָכוּף תַּאֲוָתוֹ הַחָפְשִׁית. לְהֵאָסֵר תַּחַת עָמָל כִּשְׁרוֹן הַמִּדּוֹת כִּי רַב הוּא. הַיְסוֹד הָרָאשִׁי. הוּא הַחֹק. מִצְוַת תּוֹרַת ה׳. כִּי הַכַּעַס עֲבֵרָה חֲמוּרָה הִיא. וְכָל מִינֵי גֵיהִנֹּם שׁוֹלְטִין בְּהַכּוֹעֵס. הַדְּאָגָה הַלָּזוּ (לְפִי עֶרְכָּהּ) בְּכֹחָהּ לְלַטֵּשׁ שֵׂכֶל הָאָדָם (לְפִי מַצָּבוֹ) בְּהִתְבּוֹנְנוֹ אֵת אֲשֶׁר לֹא יְשֹׁעַר בִּתְחִלָּתוֹ. כַּאֲשֶׁר אֲנַחְנוּ רוֹאִים תָּמִיד בְּעִנְיְנֵי הַמִּסְחָר. אֲשֶׁר עַל יְדֵי הַדְּאָגָה וְהַהֶכְרֵחַ יַעֲלֶה שֵׂכֶל הָאָדָם לִבְחִינָה נִשְׂגָּבָה מְאֹד אֲשֶׁר יְשֹׁעַר. וְכֵן כִּמְעַט בְּכָל הַמִּדּוֹת. הַפֶּתַח לְהִכָּנֵס בָּהֶם. הוּא הַחֹק. מִצְוַת תּוֹרַת ה׳. כִּי מִדָּה רָעָה עֲבֵרָה נִשְׂגָּבָה הִיא. כַּאֲשֶׁר חֲכָמֵינוּ ז״ל הִפְלִיגוּ בְּעָנְשָׁם. וּמִדָּה טוֹבָה מִצְוָה גְּדוֹלָה הִיא. כַּאֲשֶׁר חֲכָמֵינוּ ז״ל הֶאֱרִיכוּ בְּמַעֲלָתָם. וְלָזֹאת. לְפִי רֹב פִּרְיָם יָבוֹא לְהִתְבּוֹנְנוּת הַשִּׂכְלִית. עַד אֲשֶׁר יִתְקְנוּ וְיָבוֹאוּ לִבְחִינַת מִשְׁפָּט. גִּדְרָם הָאֲמִתִּי. הוּא מַאֲמַר הַכָּתוּב הַשֵּׁנִי (וַיִּקְרָא י״ח) וּשְׁמַרְתֶּם אֶת חֻקֹּתַי (בָּרִאשׁוֹנָה. וּמֵהֶם) וְאֶת מִשְׁפָּטַי תַּעֲשׂוּ וְגוֹ׳.

וְכֵן בִּדְבַר שְׁמִירַת חֻקֵּי הַמְּדִינָה. אִם כִּי בְּסוּגֵי הַמִּשְׁפָּט יָבוֹאוּ. וְשֵׂכֶל הָאָדָם שׁוֹפֵט לְשָׁמְרָם בִּשְׁלֵמוּת בְּאֵין מִגְרַעַת. גַּם בְּאֵין רוֹאֶה. בְּכָל זֹאת. גַּם בְּחִינַת הַחֹק. הִיא מִצְוַת תּוֹרַת ה׳. מֵהַכָּתוּב וְהַקַּבָּלָה. הַמַּזְהִירִים בְּכָל עֹז. לַאֲשֶׁר וּלְקַיֵּם כְּכָל הַיּוֹצֵא מֵהַמֶּמְשָׁלָה יָרוּם הוֹדָהּ. הִיא תִּתֵּן חֵילָהּ לְמַכְבִּיר. לְגָרֵשׁ כָּל חוֹחֵי הַתַּאֲוָה לְמַעַן יָאִירוּ עֵינֵי הַשֵּׂכֶל. לִהְיוֹתוֹ רוֹאֶה הָאֱמֶת לַאֲמִתּוֹ. לֶאֱהֹב אֶת מוֹשְׁלֵי הַמְּדִינָה. וְלִמְסֹר נַפְשׁוֹ לְמַלְאוֹת תַּפְקִידָם.

עַתָּה נָשׁוּב לִרְאוֹת בְּמִצְוַת לִמּוּד הַתּוֹרָה מַה הִיא. חֹק אוֹ מִשְׁפָּט. הַדַּעַת נוֹתֵן כִּי גַּם לִמּוּד תּוֹרַת הַחֹק. לְמִשְׁפָּט יֵחָשֵׁב. כִּדְאָמְרִינַן בַּגְּמָרָא (בָּבָא קַמָּא י״ז) וְכָבוֹד עָשׂוּ לוֹ בְּמוֹתוֹ. זֶה חִזְקִיָּה מֶלֶךְ

---

36. As the saying goes, necessity is the mother of invention.

37. It becomes a quality which reason persuades him is right or wrong. He is not just driven by knowing that it is a decree of the Torah. Put another way: developing good character traits becomes a commandment so compelling that we feel that if it were not written, it should have been written.

Yet, from where will the understanding come to the person? What will arouse him to restrain his unbridled desire, so that it is reined in by the effort of training his character traits? There is so much to do.

The fundamental principle is the *ḥok*, the commandment of God's Torah, not to get angry. For anger is a grave transgression, and all sorts of hell will take over the one who gets angry. This anxiety (according to its degree) can sharpen a person's reason (in accordance with his condition) as he contemplates what he could not have imagined at first.[36] As we see in matters of business: out of anxiety and necessity, a person's reason reaches a quality far beyond what he could have imagined.

So it is with practically all the character traits: the entree to them is *ḥok*, a commandment of God's Torah. For a bad character trait is a great transgression, as our Sages, of blessed memory, went far in describing their punishments. And a good character trait is a great mitzva, which our Sages, of blessed memory, praised at length. Thus, in accordance with their many effects, he will come to rational contemplation – until they are improved and reach the quality of *mishpat*, their true category.[37] This is the meaning of the second verse (Lev. 18:5): "And you will observe my *ḥukkim*" (first, and from them) "and my *mishpatim* . . . ."

The same applies to observing the laws of the state. While these are types of *mishpatim*, and human reason judges to observe them completely, without diminution, even when no one sees, there is still an aspect of *ḥok*. It is the commandment of God's Torah, from Scripture and tradition, which vigorously admonishes us to affirm and uphold all that issues forth from the government, may its glory increase. This will have the mighty effect of driving out all the thorns of strong desire so that the eyes of reason will be illuminated, to truly see the truth, to love the rulers of the state, and to give his life to obey their orders.[38]

Let us now return to see what is the nature of the mitzva of studying Torah. Is it *ḥok* or *mishpat*? It stands to reason that even learning the *ḥok* aspect of the Torah should be considered a *mishpat*, as we say in the Talmud (Bava Kamma 17a): "'And they did great honor to

38. Presumably, this effusive language is meant to assure government censors that R. Salanter and all those who study Mussar are totally devoted to the observance of the general society's laws.

יְהוּדָה. שֶׁהִנִּיחוּ סֵפֶר תּוֹרָה עַל מִטָּתוֹ וְאָמְרוּ קִיֵּם זֶה מַה שֶּׁכָּתוּב בָּזֶה. וְהָאִידְנָא כו׳ אֲפִלּוּ קִיֵּם אָמְרִינַן לָמַד לֹא אָמְרִינַן. וְהָאָמַר מָר גָּדוֹל לִמּוּד הַתּוֹרָה שֶׁהַלִּמּוּד מֵבִיא לִידֵי מַעֲשֶׂה כו׳. וְכָתְבוּ הַתּוֹסָפוֹת. וְאוֹמֵר רַבֵּנוּ תָּם דְּהָכִי פֵּרוּשׁוֹ. וְהָא אָמַר מָר שֶׁהַלִּמּוּד מֵבִיא לִידֵי מַעֲשֶׂה. וְכֵיוָן שֶׁאָנוּ אוֹמְרִים קִיֵּם הֲרֵי אָנוּ אוֹמְרִים שֶׁלָּמַד. דְּאִי לֹא לָמַד אֵיךְ קִיֵּם. שֶׁהַלִּמּוּד מֵבִיא לִידֵי מַעֲשֶׂה. עַד כָּאן לְשׁוֹנוֹ. הֲרֵי אַף שֶׁהַקִּיּוּם יִהְיֶה חֹק. מִכָּל מָקוֹם חִיּוּב הַלִּמּוּד. הוּא מִשְׁפָּט אֲשֶׁר יְחַיְּבֶנּוּ שֵׂכֶל הָאֱנוֹשִׁי. דְּאִם לֹא יִלְמַד אֵיךְ יְקַיֵּם.

אָכֵן גַּם מִגֶּדֶר הַחֹק. בַּל יֵצֵא אַף לִמּוּד תּוֹרַת הַמִּשְׁפָּט. כִּי הַלִּמּוּד בְּעַצְמוֹ מִצְוָה הִיא. אַף אִם לֹא הָיְתָה מְבִיאָה לִידֵי מַעֲשֶׂה. כְּמוֹ שֶׁמִּצְוָה לִדְרֹשׁ בְּבֵן סוֹרֵר וּמוֹרֶה. (לְמַאן דְּאָמַר לֹא עָתִיד לִהְיוֹת). וְהַשֵּׂכֶל הָאֱנוֹשִׁי מְנַגְּדָהּ. רַק אֲנִי ה׳ חֲקַקְתִּים. וְכֵן בְּכָל חֶלְקֵי הַתּוֹרָה בְּלִמּוּדָהּ. גַּם מִצְוָה חֻקִּית בָּהּ. אֲשֶׁר אֵין לְהִתְחַלֵּק רַק בְּמַחֲשָׁבָה.

וְאוּלַי לָזֶה רָמְזָה הַמִּשְׁנָה (אָבוֹת פֶּרֶק ד׳) וְהַלּוֹמֵד עַל מְנָת לַעֲשׂוֹת וְכוּ׳. וְלֹא אָמַר הַלּוֹמֵד בִּכְדֵי לַעֲשׂוֹת. כִּי הַלִּמּוּד בְּעַצְמוֹ. טוֹב שֶׁיִּהְיֶה בְּמַחֲשָׁבָה הַחֻקִּית. (אַף אִם לֹא הָיָה נִצְמָח מִמֶּנָּה הַמַּעֲשֶׂה). כִּי הִיא בְּחִינָה נִשָּׂאָה מִלִּמּוּד הַמִּשְׁפָּטִי. אָכֵן בִּתְנַאי שֶׁתּוֹלֵד הַמַּעֲשֶׂה מִמֶּנָּה. עַל כֵּן דְּבַר הַלִּמּוּד יִתְנַהֵל בְּאֹפֶן שֶׁיִּתְקַיֵּם הַתְּנַאי. הַיְנוּ לְהַשִּׂיג בְּרֹאשׁ הַבְּקִיאוּת וְהַחֲרִיפוּת (אִישׁ אִישׁ לְפִי עֶרְכּוֹ). לִהְיוֹת כְּלִי מֻכְשָׁר לִלְמֹד עַל פִּי תְּנַאי הַנִּדְרָשׁ. הוּא חֵפֶץ הַמַּעֲשֶׂה.

וּבִדְבָרֵינוּ אֵלֶּה. יֵאִירוּ דִּבְרֵי רַבּוֹתֵינוּ זַ״ל (נְדָרִים פ״א) הַיְנוּ לֹא שָׁמְעוּ בְּקוֹלִי הַיְנוּ לֹא הָלְכוּ בָם. אָמַר רַב יְהוּדָה אָמַר רַב שֶׁאֵין מְבָרְכִין בַּתּוֹרָה תְּחִלָּה כו׳. וּפֵרְשׁוּ. שֶׁלֹּא בֵּרְכוּ בִּרְכַּת הַתּוֹרָה כְּשֶׁהֵן

---

39. So why is studying Torah a greater and rarer compliment than fulfilling it?
40. Compare Yoma 67b.
41. It is harder to commit to mastering those parts of the Torah (such as *ben sorer umoreh*, the "wayward and rebellious son") that have no real-world application, so the reward is greater. Although studying Torah law appears to be rationally compelling for one who is willing to live by the Torah, it is important that some element of Torah study be "*ḥok*" – performed solely for the reason that God commanded us to (whether or not it can be acted upon or shape our lives).

him at his death' (II Chr. 32:33) – this refers to King Hezekiah of Judah. They put a Torah scroll on his coffin and said: 'This one fulfilled what is written in this one.' And nowadays... even if we say, 'He fulfilled,' we do not say, 'He studied.' But did the Master not state: 'Great is the study of Torah, for study leads to action...'?"[39] *Tosafot* stated: "And Rabbenu Tam says that this is the explanation: 'Did the Master not say that study leads to action?' Since we say, 'He fulfilled,' we imply that he studied, for if he did not study, how did he fulfill, if study leads to action?" Thus, even if fulfillment is a *ḥok,* the obligation to study is *mishpat,* something that reason dictates that we undertake, for if one does not study, how can he fulfill?

However, even the study of the *mishpat* aspect of the Torah should not be removed from the category of *ḥok,* for study is itself a mitzva even when it does not lead to action. Just as it is a mitzva to study the case of the "rebellious son" (according to the view that it will never actually occur), and even when human reason opposes it, except that "I, God, legislated this"[40] – so too there is a *ḥok* aspect in the study of every part of Torah, which we can never separate off, except in theory.

Perhaps the Mishna alludes to this (Avot 4:5): "One who studies [Torah] with the condition of (*al menat*) performance...." It did not say: "One who studies to be able to (*bikhedei*) perform," for it is good that the study itself be in the mode of *ḥok* (even if no action can come out of it), for it is a higher level than Torah study as *mishpat.*[41] Indeed, it is on condition that it is able to produce action. Therefore, study takes place in a manner that fulfills this condition, namely, to intellectually attain the mastery and sharpness (each person according to his level) to be a finely calibrated instrument of learning, according to the requisite condition – the desire to act.

With these words of ours, we can illuminate the words of our Rabbis, of blessed memory (Nedarim 81a): "'They did not listen to My voice' is the same as 'They did not follow it' [Jer. 9:12].[42] R. Yehuda said in the name of Rav: ['This means that] they do not bless on the Torah

42. The verse in Jeremiah states: "They did not listen to My voice and they did not follow it." The Talmud is asking about this apparent redundancy.

מַשְׁכִּימִין לִלְמֹד תּוֹרָה. עַיֵּן שָׁם. אֲשֶׁר כָּל אֱנוֹשׁ יִתְפַּלֵּא עַל הַתַּאֲוָה הַזָּרָה הַזֹּאת. לְבִלְתִּי הֱיוֹת עָצֵל בְּלִמּוּד הַתּוֹרָה הַמַּתֶּשֶׁת כֹּחוֹ שֶׁל אָדָם. רַק שֶׁלֹּא לְבָרֵךְ עָלֶיהָ בִּתְחִלָּתָהּ. (וְהָרַ"ן כָּתַב בְּשֵׁם הָרַב רַבֵּנוּ יוֹנָה זַ"ל. עוֹסְקִין הָיוּ בַּתּוֹרָה תָּמִיד. וְלֹא הָיוּ מְבָרְכִין בַּתּוֹרָה תְּחִלָּה. כְּלוֹמַר שֶׁלֹּא הָיְתָה הַתּוֹרָה חֲשׁוּבָה בְּעֵינֵיהֶם כָּל כָּךְ שֶׁיְּהֵא רָאוּי לְבָרֵךְ עָלֶיהָ. שֶׁלֹּא הָיוּ עוֹסְקִין בָּהּ לִשְׁמָהּ. וּמִתּוֹךְ כָּךְ הָיוּ מְזַלְזְלִין בְּבִרְכָה. עַד כָּאן לְשׁוֹנוֹ. וְהַדָּבָר תָּמוּהַּ מְאֹד. לֵאמֹר שֶׁמִּתּוֹךְ כָּךְ יְזַלְזְלוּ בְּבִרְכַּת הַתּוֹרָה. אֲשֶׁר הִיא מִדְּאוֹרָיְתָא. בְּאֵין כָּל תַּאֲוָה לְהַפְרִיעָהּ).

וְאָמְנָם לְפִי מַה שֶּׁבֵּאַרְנוּ. יֵשׁ לְפָרֵשׁ דְּאָמְרִינַן (מְנָחוֹת מב:) כָּל מִצְוָה דַּעֲשִׂיָּתָהּ גְּמַר מִצְוָה כְּגוֹן מִילָה כּו' צָרִיךְ לְבָרֵךְ. וְכָל מִצְוָה דַּעֲשִׂיָּתָהּ לָאו גְּמַר מִצְוָה כְּגוֹן תְּפִלִּין. (עֲשִׂיָּתָן לֹא זוֹ הִיא גְּמַר מִצְוָתָן עַד שֶׁיִּקְשְׁרֵם). אֵינוֹ צָרִיךְ לְבָרֵךְ כּו' עַיֵּן שָׁם. עַל כֵּן לְפִי זֶה עַל מִצְוַת לִמּוּד תּוֹרָה הַמִּשְׁפָּטִי. אֵינוֹ צָרִיךְ לְבָרֵךְ. דַּעֲשִׂיָּתָהּ הַיְנוּ הַלִּמּוּד. לָאו גְּמַר מִצְוָה הִיא (עַד שֶׁקִּיֵּם אֶת אֲשֶׁר הוּא לוֹמֵד). כִּי כָּל עִנְיַן הַמִּצְוָה הוּא. לִלְמֹד בִּכְדֵי לֵידַע הַמַּעֲשֶׂה. וִיסוֹד בִּרְכַּת הַתּוֹרָה הֻנְּחָה עַל מִצְוַת לִמּוּד הַתּוֹרָה בִּבְחִינַת חֹק. הַיְנוּ שֶׁהַלִּמּוּד בְּעַצְמוֹ מִצְוָה. אִי לָזֹאת יוּכַל הֱיוֹת כִּי שָׁלְטָה עֲלֵיהֶם הַתַּאֲוָה. שֶׁלֹּא רָצוּ רַק לִלְמֹד בְּגֶדֶר הַמִּשְׁפָּט. יַעַן הַשֵּׂכֶל הָאֱנוֹשִׁי מְחַיְּבוֹ. אֲבָל לִלְמֹד בִּבְחִינַת חֹק. לִהְיוֹת שֶׁהַשֵּׂכֶל מְנַגְּדוֹ וְהַיֵּצֶר מֵשִׁיב עָלָיו. גָּעֲלָה נַפְשָׁם. לְזֹאת אַף שֶׁעָסְקוּ בַּתּוֹרָה. הָיְתָה כַּוָּנָתָם רַק בְּתוֹר בְּחִינַת מִשְׁפָּט. וְלֹא הָיָה גְּמַר מִצְוָה וְלֹא בֵּרְכוּ עָלֶיהָ.

נִמְצָא לְפִי זֶה. שְׂכַר לִמּוּד הַתּוֹרָה אֵינָהּ רַק בִּבְחִינַת מִשְׁפָּט. הַמִּשְׁתַּתֵּף עִמָּהּ גַּם בְּתוֹר בְּחִינַת חֹק. בְּכַוָּנָתָהּ הָרְצוּיָה.

הוּא הַמַּאֲמָר אֲשֶׁר הִצַּבְנוּ בְּפֶתַח דְּבָרֵינוּ (סַנְהֶדְרִין ע"א) בֵּן סוֹרֵר

43. R. Nissim maintains that they studied Torah for ulterior motives, and therefore did not respect it enough to make a blessing first.

first…'" The commentators explain this to mean that they did not recite the blessing over the Torah when they arose early to study Torah; *cf.* ibid.

Everyone should be astonished by this strange impulse – not to be derelict in studying Torah, which exhausts a person's strength, but not to recite a blessing over it beforehand! (R. Nissim wrote in the name of R. Jonah of Girona, of blessed memory: "They studied Torah constantly, but they did not recite the blessing over the Torah first. That is, the Torah was not so important to them that they deemed it worthy of reciting a blessing over it. They did not study it for its own sake[43] – and because of this they belittled the blessing." This is most puzzling: to say that because of not studying Torah for its own sake, they would belittle the blessing over the Torah, which is a biblical commandment? Why would they do this absent any impulse to interfere with [the blessing]?)

However, we can explain this based on what we have ascertained: It is said (Menaḥot 42b): "Any mitzva whose performance completes the mitzva, such as circumcision…one must bless over it. Any mitzva whose performance does not complete the mitzva, such as tefillin (making them does not complete the mitzva; rather, only when they have been bound), it is not necessary to recite a blessing…." See further there.

Accordingly, there is no need to recite a blessing on the mitzva of studying Torah as *mishpat*, for its performance – the study itself – is not the completion of the mitzva (not until he fulfills what he studied). The whole idea of the mitzva is to study in order to know what to do. But the premise of the blessing over the Torah was placed on the *ḥok* aspect of the mitzva of Torah study – that is, the study is itself a mitzva.

It is possible, therefore, that they were governed by the impulse to study only as *mishpat* – for human reason demands this – but the *ḥok* aspect of study, which the intellect rejects and the evil urge questions, was repugnant to them. Thus, although they engaged in Torah study, their intention was only qua the *mishpat* aspect. [This study of Torah] was not the completion of a mitzva, so they did not recite a blessing over it.

We thus find that the reward for learning Torah is not only for the *mishpat* aspect; one who combines it with the *ḥok* aspect as well fulfills it with its proper intention.

This is the meaning of the statement that we placed in our opening remarks, "The matter of the rebellious son never was and never will

וּמוֹרֶה לֹא הָיָה וְלֹא עָתִיד לִהְיוֹת. וְלָמָּה נִכְתַּב דְּרֹשׁ וְקַבֵּל שָׂכָר. הַיְנוּ שָׂכָר עַל בְּחִינַת חֹק לְבַדָּהּ. הַנַּעֲלָה בְּמַדְרֵגָתָהּ (כְּבְחִינָה הַלָּזוֹ. אִם כִּי נִגְרַעַת בְּעֶרְכָּהּ. יַעַן אֵינָהּ מְבִיאָה לִידֵי מַעֲשֶׂה כו'. עַיֵּן קִדּוּשִׁין מ: נַעֲנוּ כֻּלָּם כו') מִשְּׁאָר חֶלְקֵי הַתּוֹרָה. אֲשֶׁר יְסוֹדָתָם הִיא בְּחִינַת מִשְׁפָּט.

be. Why then is it written [in Scripture]? To study it and receive the reward" (Sanhedrin 71a). That is, the reward is for the *ḥok* aspect [of Torah study] alone, which is at a higher level (in this respect, although it is of lesser value in that does not lead to action.... See Kiddushin 40b, "They all responded...") than the other parts of Torah, whose basis is the *mishpat* aspect.

אגרת המוסר

הָאָדָם חָפְשִׁי בְּדִמְיוֹנוֹ, וְאָסוּר בְּמֻשְׂכָּלוֹ. דִּמְיוֹנוֹ מוֹלִיכוֹ שׁוֹבָב בְּדֶרֶךְ לִבּוֹ רְצוֹנוֹ, בַּל יֵחַת מֵהֶעָתִיד הַוַּדַּאי, עֵת יִפְקֹד ה׳ עַל כָּל מִפְעָלָיו, וּבִשְׁפָטִים קָשִׁים יְוַסֵּר, בַּל יִלָּכֵד זָר בִּגְלָלוֹ, הוּא לְבַדּוֹ יִשָּׂא פְּרִי חֶטְאוֹ, אֶחָד הוּא, עוֹשֵׂה הָעֲבֵרוֹת וְהַנֶּעֱנָשׁ. מָרָה הִיא, בַּל יֹאמַר הָאָדָם זֶה חֳלִי וְאֶשָּׂאֶנּוּ.

פִּגְעֵי הַתֵּבֵל מְצַעֲרִים הֵמָּה, לְמַכְבִּיר, מוּל עָנְשֵׁי הָעֲבֵרוֹת; תִּגְעַל נֶפֶשׁ הָאָדָם לְמַדַּי, יוֹם לְשָׁנָה יֵחָשֵׁב. אוֹי לַדִּמְיוֹן, אוֹיֵב הָרַע הַלָּזֶה, מִיָּדֵינוּ הוּא, בְּכֹחֵנוּ לְהַרְחִיקוֹ. בְּתִתֵּנוּ אֹזֶן קַשֶּׁבֶת אֶל הַשֵּׂכֶל, לְהַשְׂכִּיל עַל דְּבַר אֱמֶת, לַחֲשֹׁב שְׂכַר עֲבֵרָה נֶגֶד הֶפְסֵדָהּ; וּמַה נַּעֲשֶׂה, הַדִּמְיוֹן נַחַל שׁוֹטֵף, וְהַשֵּׂכֶל יִטְבַּע, אִם לֹא נוֹלִיכֶנּוּ בָּאֳנִיָּה, הִיא רִגְשַׁת הַנֶּפֶשׁ וְסַעֲרַת הָרוּחַ.

---

* *Iggeret HaMussar* (*The Letter on Mussar*) was first printed as an appendix to the 1858 edition of R. Moses Cordovero's sixteenth-century kabbalistic Mussar book *Tomer Devora*, published by R. Salanter in Koenigsberg, the year after he arrived from Kovno. This is the first piece written by R. Salanter for publication, in which he presents his rationale for the study of Mussar as an important requirement for every person.

1. One who lives according to his imagination is unbridled and instinctive, whereas one who lives according to the dictates of reason exercises restraint and recognizes boundaries.

2. Compare Isaiah 27:1.

*Iggeret HaMussar: The Letter on Mussar**

The human being is free in his imagination but fettered by his reason.[1] His imagination leads him, undisciplined, on the path his heart desires. He acts without fear of the inevitable future, when God will hold him accountable[2] for all his activities, and he will be chastised with harsh judgments. No one else will be held accountable in his stead. He alone will bear the fruit of his sin. The one who commits the sin is the one who is punished. It is a bitter fate. Let the person not say: This is my affliction and I will bear it.[3]

The misfortunes of the world cause pain but are enormously outstripped by the punishment for sins. The person's soul will feel utter revulsion. Each day of suffering will be experienced like a year. Woe to our imagination, this evil enemy.[4] He is the product of our hands. We have the power to distance him by giving an attentive ear to reason, to be intelligent about recognizing this truth, to calculate the reward of a sin against its loss.[5] What can we do? The imagination is a constantly flowing river, and reason will be inundated unless we guide it in a boat – the sentiments of the soul and the tempestuousness of the spirit.[6]

3. Compare Jeremiah 10:19. He should not be complacent about the possibility of punishment, for it will exceed his capacity to bear it.
4. Compare Esther 7:6.
5. I.e., punishment. See Avot 2:1.
6. I.e., fear of God and of punishment.

בְּכָל הַדְּבָרִים וְהָעִנְיָנִים יֵשׁ כְּלָל וּפְרָט, (אוֹ סוּגִי וּמִינִי וְאִישִׁי, אִם אֵין כְּלָל אֵין פְּרָט, כִּי אֵין בַּפְּרָט אֶלָּא מַה שֶּׁבַּכְּלָל, אָכֵן יֵשׁ כְּלָל אַף בְּאֵין פְּרָט מוֹצֵאת. אִי לָזֹאת, רֵאשִׁית כָּל דָּבָר הוּא הַכְּלָל, וּמִמֶּנּוּ הַפְּרָטִים יִמָּשְׁכוּ.

עַתָּה נַשְׁקִיף נָא בַּעֲבוֹדָתֵנוּ הַמְחֻיֶּבֶת לְבוֹרְאֵנוּ יִתְבָּרַךְ, הֲלֹא דָבָר הוּא, מַה הוּא הַכְּלָל אֲשֶׁר מִמֶּנּוּ נִשְׁאַב הַפְּרָטִים.

בְּלִי דַּעַת וּבְלִי תְּבוּנָה, נַכִּיר, שֶׁהָאֱמוּנָה הַמְרַחֶפֶת בָּנוּ, שֶׁהָאֱלֹהִים שׁוֹפֵט הוּא, לָתֵת לְאִישׁ כִּפְרִי מַעֲלָלוֹ, (אִם רַע וָמַר דַּרְכּוֹ יְוֻסַּר בַּעֲנָשִׁים רָעִים, אִם בָּעוֹלָם הַזֶּה, אוֹ בָּעוֹלָם הַבָּא עוֹלָם הַנִּצְחִי, בַּל יֵדַע אֱנוֹשׁ עֶרְכָּהּ, עַד כַּמָּה תִּגְדַּל לְמַעְלָה רֹאשׁ בְּאֵיכוּת וּבְכַמּוּת. וְאִם זַךְ וְאִם יָשָׁר פָּעֳלוֹ, לְעֻמָּתוֹ בָּרוּךְ יֹאמַר, בְּתַעֲנוּגִים נִשָּׂאִים בָּעוֹלָם הַזֶּה, וּבְיוֹתֵר בָּעוֹלָם הַבָּא, בְּעֵדֶן נִפְלָא לְמַעְלָה הַרְבֵּה מִשֵּׂכֶל וְהֶרְגֵּשׁ אֱנוֹשִׁי), הִיא רֵאשִׁית מִצְעָדֵנוּ לַעֲבוֹדָתוֹ יִתְבָּרַךְ.

הוּא מַאֲמַר חֲכָמֵינוּ ז״ל (מַכּוֹת כד:) בָּא חֲבַקּוּק וְהֶעֱמִידָן עַל אַחַת, וְצַדִּיק בֶּאֱמוּנָתוֹ יִחְיֶה וְכוּ׳, וּמַאֲמַר חֲכָמֵינוּ ז״ל (בָּבָא בַּתְרָא עח.) עַל כֵּן יֹאמְרוּ הַמֹּשְׁלִים בֹּאוּ חֶשְׁבּוֹן כוּ׳, הֶפְסֵד מִצְוָה כְּנֶגֶד שְׂכָרָהּ וּשְׂכַר עֲבֵרָה כְּנֶגֶד הֶפְסֵדָהּ.

אָכֵן לְמוֹרֶת רוּחַ וְדַאֲבוֹן לֵב, כֹּחַ הַכְּלָלִי הַזֶּה, רַק מִסְתַּתֵּר בָּנוּ, נֶחְבָּא בְּמַצְפּוּנֵי הַלֵּב בַּל יֵרָאֶה הַחוּצָה, אִם לֹא נָשִׂים לֵב לְשַׁדֵּד אַדְמַת לְבָבֵנוּ בְּהַרְחָבַת רַעְיוֹנֵי הַמּוּסָר. אִי לָזֹאת גַּם הַכֹּחַ הַכְּלָלִי הַלָּזֶה בַּל יִשְׁלַח פֹּארוֹתָיו עַל הָאֵבָרִים לְאָסְרָם בְּמַאֲסַר הַיִּרְאָה. וּמִזֶּה הַכְּלָל לֹא יִמָּשְׁכוּ הַפְּרָטִים, לְהִשָּׁמֵר מֵהָעֲבֵרוֹת הַמִּתְרַגְּשׁוֹת. וְנִכְשָׁלִים אֲנַחְנוּ בְּכָל עֵת בַּעֲבֵרוֹת רָמוֹת עַד שָׁמַיִם יַגִּיעוּ, בְּחֶטְאֵי הַלָּשׁוֹן בְּאֵין מַעֲצוֹר

7. Compare Deuteronomy 32:47.
8. Compare Ezekiel 3:12–13 and the *Kedusha* prayer in the Ashkenazic liturgy.
9. In addition to being a place name in Transjordan, the word "*ḥeshbon*" can also mean "calculation" or "introspection."

In all matters and topics there is a general rule and specific detail (or types and kinds and individuals). If there is no general rule, there is no specific detail, for there is nothing in the specific that is not in the general, whereas there is a general principle even if there is no detail present. Therefore, the first step is to find the general principle; from it the details will extend.

Now let us look into our mandatory service of our blessed Creator, for this is an important matter.[7] What is the general principle from which we can draw out the details?

Even without considered judgment and without understanding, we recognize that the faith that hovers within us – that God judges, giving each person the fruits of his actions. (If his way is wicked and bitter, he will be punished with terrible punishment whether in this world, or in the World to Come, the eternal world; a mortal can scarcely know the extent of its overwhelming magnitude, both quantitative and qualitative. And if his actions are pure and straight, he will be called "blessed"[8] with sublime enjoyments in this world and even greater ones in the next world, in wondrous Eden, which is far beyond human reason and sensation.) This understanding constitutes our first steps in our worship of Him, may He be blessed.

This is [the meaning of] the dictum of our Sages, of blessed memory (Makkot 24b): "Habakkuk came and established [all of the commandments] on one [principle]: 'The righteous one shall live by his faith' (Hab. 2:4)"; and the saying of our Sages, of blessed memory (Bava Batra 78a): "'Therefore the rulers shall say: Come to Heshbon' (Num. 21:27),[9] [i.e., calculate] the cost of a mitzva against its benefit and the benefit of a sin against its cost."

Truly, to our chagrin and regret, this universal force [i.e., recognition that there is ultimate judgment,] is only latent within us, concealed in the inner recesses of the heart and not outwardly visible – unless we take care to till the soil of our heart by expanding on the concepts of Mussar. Without this, even this universal force will not extend its tendrils to the limbs, to bind them within the grasp of reverence. From this general principle, no specific ramifications will be drawn to safeguard against looming sins. So we constantly stumble into sins that tower unto the heavens: with sins of speech in the absence of a brake on our

לְרוּחֵנוּ, וּבְעִסְקֵי מַשָּׂא וּמַתָּן לְמַכְבִּיר, וּבִטּוּל תּוֹרָה עַל כְּלָנָה. וּבִכְלָל, בְּכָל הָאֵבָרִים כִּמְעַט אֵין בָּמוֹ מְתוֹם, לַמִּתְבּוֹנֵן הֵיטֵב אִישׁ לְפִי עֶרְכּוֹ, שֶׁכָּל הַגָּדוֹל מֵחֲבֵרוֹ יִצְרוֹ גָּדוֹל מִמֶּנּוּ (סֻכָּה נ״ב), וְנִכְשָׁל בַּעֲבֵרוֹת נִשָּׂאוֹת וְרָמוֹת, אֲשֶׁר אִם גַּם לְחֶשְׁכַת לְבָבֵנוּ כְּסוּמִים נֶחְשַׁבְנוּ, אֵין רוֹאֶה גָּדְלָם (נֶגֶד עֲבֵרוֹת הֶהָמוֹן). רַק אִם נַשְׁקִיפֵם עַל יְדֵי כְּלִי הַמַּחֲזֶה (הַמַּגְדֶּלֶת דָּבָר גָּדוֹל לִמְאֹד, הַנִּרְאֶה לְחֻלְשַׁת רְאוּתֵנוּ כְּקָטָן, כְּמוֹ הַכּוֹכָבִים אֲשֶׁר גָּדְלָם יוֹתֵר מִכַּדּוּר הָאָרֶץ, וְנִרְאִים כִּנְקֻדּוֹת קְטַנּוֹת, וְעַל יְדֵי כְּלִי הַמַּחֲזֶה נִרְאִים יוֹתֵר גְּדוֹלִים מְעַט, וּבֶאֱמֶת אֵין עֲרֹךְ לְגָדְלָם. כֵּן הַדָּבָר הַזֶּה), הוּא הַשֵּׂכֶל הַנָּכוֹן, עַל פִּי הַתּוֹרָה הַנֶּאֱמָנָה, נִמְצָא אוֹתָם חֲמוּרִים הַרְבֵּה בְּאֵיכוּתָם בְּיֶתֶר שְׂאֵת וְיֶתֶר עֹז.

הוּא הַדָּבָר אֲשֶׁר נוּכַל לְהַעֲמִיס בְּדִבְרֵי רַבּוֹתֵינוּ זַ״ל (יוֹמָא ט:) מִקְדָּשׁ רִאשׁוֹן מִפְּנֵי מָה חָרַב, מִפְּנֵי שְׁלֹשָׁה דְּבָרִים שֶׁהָיוּ בּוֹ עֲבוֹדָה זָרָה גִּלּוּי עֲרָיוֹת וּשְׁפִיכוּת דָּמִים, אֲבָל מִקְדָּשׁ שֵׁנִי שֶׁהָיוּ עוֹסְקִין בַּתּוֹרָה וּבְמִצְוֹת וּגְמִילוּת חֲסָדִים מִפְּנֵי מָה חָרַב מִפְּנֵי שֶׁהָיְתָה בּוֹ שִׂנְאַת חִנָּם, רַבִּי יוֹחָנָן וְרַבִּי אֶלְיעֶזֶר דְּאָמְרֵי תַּרְוַיְהוּ רִאשׁוֹנִים שֶׁנִּתְגַּלָּה עֲוֹנָם נִתְגַּלָּה קִצָּם, אַחֲרוֹנִים שֶׁלֹּא נִתְגַּלָּה עֲוֹנָם לֹא נִתְגַּלָּה קִצָּם (הָעִנְיָן שֶׁנִּתְגַּלָּה עֲוֹנָם שֶׁל הָרִאשׁוֹנִים, לִהְיוֹתָן עֲבֵרוֹת חֲמוּרוֹת לְעֵין הָרוֹאֶה בְּאֵין פְּנוֹת אֶל הַבִּינָה, אֲבָל עֲוֹנוֹת הָאַחֲרוֹנִים בַּל יֵרָאוּ רַק לַמִּתְבּוֹנֵן הֵיטֵב הָדֵק גֹּדֶל חָמְרָם לְמַעְלָה לְמַעְלָה לְהַפְלֵא, מִסְתַּעֲפוֹת לִפְרָטֵי חֲטָאִים עֲצוּמִים בְּאֵין מַעֲצוֹר רַחֲמָנָא לִצְלַן) כו׳, וְשָׁאֲלוּ שָׁם אֲמוֹרָאֵי, רִאשׁוֹנִים עֲדִיפֵי אוֹ אַחֲרוֹנִים עֲדִיפֵי, וְהֵשִׁיבוּ, תְּנוּ עֵינֵיכֶם בַּבִּירָה שֶׁחָזְרָה לָרִאשׁוֹנִים וְלֹא חָזְרָה לָאַחֲרוֹנִים. הוּא הַדָּבָר אֲשֶׁר דִּבַּרְנוּ לְמַעְלָה, כִּי הַגָּדוֹל מֵחֲבֵרוֹ, (כְּמוֹ בְּבַיִת שֵׁנִי שֶׁהָיוּ עוֹסְקִין בַּתּוֹרָה וְכוּ׳) יִצְרוֹ גָּדוֹל, וּמַכְשִׁילוֹ בַּחֲטָאִים עֲצוּמִים, נוֹדְעוּ לַמַּשְׂכִּיל עַל דְּבַר אֱמֶת גֹּדֶל אֵיכוּתָם לְהָרַע.

10. I.e., impulse.
11. Compare Isaiah 1:6.
12. That is, correct reason functions in this case as a telescope, restoring large things to their proper proportion.

spirit;[10] and even to a greater extent in business matters; and most of all, in neglect of Torah study.

In general, almost in all the limbs, "[from head to toe] there is not a [morally] sound [spot],"[11] [according] to one who analyzes carefully, each according to his own ability, for "one who is greater than his friend has a greater evil urge than him" (Sukka 52a) and falls into high and mighty sins. When it comes to seeing the darkness in our own heart, we are like blind people. No one sees their magnitude (compared to the sins of the masses). Only if we observe them through a telescope (which magnifies to a very large degree things that seem small to us due to our weak sight – like stars, which are larger than Earth but seem like small dots; through a telescope they appear a bit larger – but in truth, they are inestimably large. So it is in this matter) – that is, with correct reason, in accordance the trusted Torah[12] – will we find them to be far more severe in character, with greater scope and force.[13]

This is something we can attribute to the words of our Rabbis, of blessed memory (Yoma 9b): "Why was the First Temple destroyed? Because of three things that existed there: idolatry, sexual perversion, and bloodshed. But the Second Temple in which they occupied themselves with Torah, good deeds, and acts of loving-kindness – why was it destroyed? Because there was baseless hatred. R. Yoḥanan and R. Eliezer both say: Those first ones [who lived in First Temple times] – their sins were revealed and the end [of their exile] was revealed. Those who lived later [i.e., in Second Temple times], their sin was not revealed, so the end [of their exile] was not revealed…." (The meaning of the matter is that the sins of the First Temple were revealed and open, known to be grave sins in the eyes of observers without even turning to contemplate, but the later sins were not visible except to one who closely scrutinized their great severity and astonishing magnitude, manifesting in the specific of terrible sins with nothing to check them, may God save us.)

The *Amora'im* then ask: Who was better, the earlier or later? They answered: Look at the Temple – which was restored after the first but not after the second. This is what we said above: The one who is greater than his friend (like in the Second Temple, when they were occupied with Torah…) – his evil urge is greater, leading him to terrible sins, the magnitude of whose evil is known only to one who is wise enough to grasp the truth.

עַתָּה, בְּכָל הָאֳפָנִים אֲשֶׁר יִתְיַצֵּב הָאָדָם, מַה יַּעֲשֶׂה, יוֹם הַמָּוֶת מִכֹּל מְכֻסֶּה, פִּתְאוֹם יָבוֹא, וְהָאֱלֹהִים יִפְקֹד אֶת כָּל מַעֲשֶׂה אֲשֶׁר עָשָׂה מִסְפַּר מִפְקַד יְמֵי חַיָּיו, אַחַת מֵהֶן לֹא נֶעְדָּרָה, וּמַר מִמָּוֶת תִּהְיֶה הָאַחֲרִית בְּאֵין מָנוֹס וּמִפְלָט לְהִנָּצֵל. הוּא מַאֲמַר הַכָּתוּב (קֹהֶלֶת ט׳, ד׳) כִּי מִי אֲשֶׁר יְחֻבַּר אֶל כָּל הַחַיִּים יֵשׁ בִּטָּחוֹן, כִּי לְכֶלֶב חַי (כִּדְרָשַׁת רַבּוֹתֵינוּ זַ״ל) הוּא טוֹב מִן הָאַרְיֵה הַמֵּת, כִּדְרָשַׁת רַבּוֹתֵינוּ זַ״ל (בַּיַּלְקוּט בִּמְקוֹמוֹ), שֶׁכָּל זְמַן שֶׁאָדָם חַי יֵשׁ לוֹ בִּטָּחוֹן וְתִקְוָה לַעֲשׂוֹת תְּשׁוּבָה וְכֵיוָן שֶׁמֵּת אָבְדָה תִקְוָתוֹ כו׳.

אִי לָזֹאת, כָּל עוֹד נִשְׁמָתֵנוּ בְּקִרְבֵּנוּ, נְמַהֵר נָחִישָׁה לְפַלֵּס דַּרְכֵּנוּ לְטוֹב, אָכֵן עַל יְדֵי אֶבֶן הַנֶּגֶף יָרַט הַדֶּרֶךְ לְנֶגְדֵּנוּ. לֹא נֶחֱרַד מִיּוֹם הַמִּיתָה גַּם אִם בְּפִינוּ נַזְכִּירֵהוּ, כְּמַאֲמַר רַבּוֹתֵינוּ זַ״ל (שַׁבָּת לא:) שֶׁמָּא תֹּאמַר שִׁכְחָה הִיא כו׳, גַּם אִם עֵינֵינוּ רוֹאוֹת מִיתַת בְּנֵי אָדָם כָּמוֹנוּ, לֹא תִתֵּן עֹז בְּנַפְשֵׁנוּ לָשׁוּב בְּכָל לֵב לְבוֹרְאֵנוּ, אֲשֶׁר לַסּוֹף נָבוֹא לְפָנָיו לְמִשְׁפָּט וְיִתְוַכַּח עִמָּנוּ עַל כָּל רֹעַ מִפְעָלֵינוּ, הֵפֶךְ מַאֲמַר הַכָּתוּב (קֹהֶלֶת ז׳, ב׳) טוֹב לָלֶכֶת אֶל בֵּית אֵבֶל מִלֶּכֶת אֶל בֵּית הַמִּשְׁתֶּה בַּאֲשֶׁר הוּא סוֹף כָּל הָאָדָם וְהַחַי יִתֵּן אֶל לִבּוֹ. אֵין זֹאת, כִּי אִם רִבּוּי הָעֲוֹנוֹת שֶׁטִּמְטְמוּ לִבֵּנוּ וַיְהִי לְאֶבֶן, כִּדְרָשַׁת חֲכָמֵינוּ זַ״ל (יוֹמָא ל״ט) עַל הַפָּסוּק (וַיִּקְרָא י״א) וְלֹא תִטַּמְּאוּ בָּהֶם וְנִטְמֵתֶם בָּם אַל תִּקְרֵי וְנִטְמֵאתֶם אֶלָּא וְנִטַּמְטֶם כו׳. וְלָכֵן גַּם עֲוֹנוֹתֵינוּ נִסְתָּרִים מִלְּפָנֵינוּ, וְלֹא נַרְגִּישׁ בָּהֶם בִּמְהֵרָה, כְּמַאֲמַר רַבּוֹתֵינוּ זַ״ל (קִדּוּשִׁין מ׳) כֵּיוָן שֶׁעָבַר אָדָם עֲבֵרָה וְשָׁנָה כו׳ נַעֲשֵׂית לוֹ כְּהֶתֵּר, וְהֵן מְסַבְּבִים אוֹתָנוּ לְיוֹם הַדִּין, כְּמַאֲמַר רַבּוֹתֵינוּ זַ״ל (עֲבוֹדָה־זָרָה י״ח) עֲוֹנוֹת שֶׁאָדָם דָּשׁ בַּעֲקֵבָיו כו׳ הֵן מְסַבְּבִין כו׳. עַתָּה הַאִם אָבְדָה תִקְוָתֵנוּ חַס וְחָלִילָה, אֵין מָזוֹר לָנוּ חָלִילָה.

13. Compare Genesis 49:3.

14. Compare Isaiah 40:26.

15. Compare Numbers 22:32.

16. The wicked have not forgotten the day of death; they know their end will come yet they stay on their evil course.

17. "You shall not make yourselves unclean with them and thus become unclean."

18. See Ezekiel 37:11.

Now, in whatever circumstances in which a person is situated, what shall he do? The day of death is hidden from everyone. It will come suddenly, and God will remember every act he did in accordance with the number of the recorded days of his life. Not one of them is omitted.[14] This end will be more bitter than death with no escape or refuge to save him. This is what the verse states (Eccl. 9:4): "For he who is reckoned among the living can be secure; for a live dog is better than a dead lion." As interpreted by our Rabbis, of blessed memory (in the *Yalkut* on that verse), as long as a person is alive, he has the security and hope that he can repent, but once he dies, his hope is lost....

In light of this, as long as our soul is still in us, we should quickly hasten to set our course toward the good. However, there is an obstacle blocking the road to us.[15] We do not tremble at the day of death, even if we pay lip service to it. As our Rabbis, of blessed memory, say (Shabbat 31b): "Lest you think it is a matter of their [evil men] forgetting [the day of death]..."[16] Even if our eyes see the death of a person just like us, it does not embolden our souls to return to our Creator with a full heart – notwithstanding that in the end we will come before Him for judgment and He will contend with us on all our evil activities. This [indifference to our death] is the opposite of Scripture's statement (Eccl. 7:2): "It is better to go to a house of mourning than go to a house of festivity, for this death is the end of every man and the one who lives should take it to heart."

This is only because our many sins have dulled our heart and turned it into stone. As our Sages, of blessed memory, expound (Yoma 39a), on the verse (Lev. 11:43): "'*Velo tit'amu vahem, venitmeitem bam*';[17] do not read *venitmeitem* [you shall become unclean], but *venitamtem* [you shall become dulled]...." Therefore, even our sins are hidden from us and we do not feel them readily. As our Rabbis, of blessed memory, say (Kiddushin 40a): "Once a person does a sin and then repeats it... it becomes [in his mind] as if [the act is] permitted." Yet these bad acts beset us on the day of judgment. As our Rabbis, of blessed memory, say (Avoda Zara 18a): "Sins that a person tramples underfoot...beset him [on the day of judgment]...." So have we lost hope,[18] God forbid? Is there no healing for us,[19] God forbid?

---

19. Compare Jeremiah 30:13.

אַחַת הִיא מְצָאנוּ, חָכְמָה וְאֵינָהּ מְלָאכָה, נָשִׂיחַ נָא מְעַט וְיִרְוַח לָנוּ.

נָשִׂימָה לֵב לְהִתְבּוֹנֵן בְּעִנְיַן הָעֲבֵרוֹת, וְנִרְאֶה כִּי שְׁתַּיִם הֵנָּה בְּסוּגֵיהֶם: הָאַחַת, נוֹבַעַת מֵהַתַּאֲוָה הַנִּפְרָצָה, לֶאֱהֹב הֶעָרֵב לְשַׁעְתּוֹ, לִבְלִי הַשְׁקִיף הַנּוֹלָד, אִם כִּי מָרָה תִּהְיֶה בָּאַחֲרוֹנָה. נִמְצָא דּוּגְמָתָהּ מַה גַּם בְּעִנְיְנֵי הָעוֹלָם, הָאִישׁ הַסָּכָל, וּבִפְרָט הַחוֹלֶה לְחָלְשַׁת שִׂכְלוֹ, יֹאהַב לַחֲטֹף לֶאֱכֹל אֶת הֶעָרֵב לְחִכּוֹ, וְיִשְׁכַּח כִּי זֶה יְבִיאֶנּוּ לְמַחֲלָה נִפְרָצָה. לְכָךְ אָמְרוּ רַבּוֹתֵינוּ זַ"ל (אָבוֹת) אֵיזֶה חָכָם הָרוֹאֶה אֶת הַנּוֹלָד, הוּא מַאֲמַר רַבּוֹתֵינוּ זַ"ל (סוֹטָה ג') אֵין אָדָם עוֹבֵר עֲבֵרָה אֶלָּא אִם כֵּן נִכְנְסָה בּוֹ רוּחַ שְׁטוּת. וְזֶה כָּל עֲמַל הָאָדָם לַעֲבוֹדָתוֹ יִתְבָּרַךְ, לַחֲשֹׁב וּלְהִתְבּוֹנֵן בְּיִרְאַת ה' בְּפַחַד עָנְשׁוֹ עַל יְדֵי סִפְרֵי הַמּוּסָר וְאַגָּדוֹת חֲכָמֵינוּ זַ"ל, עַד אֲשֶׁר בְּאָזְנָיו יִשְׁמַע כִּמְעַט בְּעֵינָיו יִרְאֶה הָעֹנֶשׁ הַגָּדוֹל בְּכַמּוּת וְאֵיכוּת נִצָּב לְנֶגֶד עֵינָיו, כְּמַאֲמַר רַבּוֹתֵינוּ זַ"ל (סַנְהֶדְרִין ז') לְעוֹלָם יִרְאֶה דַּיָּן, (לִהְיוֹתוֹ עָלוּל לְהִכָּשֵׁל, וְהוּא הַדִּין כָּל אָדָם. לְהִשָּׁמֵר מִפֶּגַע רַע מֵעֲבֵרוֹת הַחֲמוּרוֹת) כְּאִלּוּ כּוּ' גֵּיהִנֹּם פְּתוּחָה לוֹ מִתַּחְתָּיו. וְאִם כֹּה יַעֲשֶׂה הָאָדָם וּלְבָבוֹ יָבִין, וָשָׁב וְרָפָא לוֹ.

אָכֵן רַבָּה רָעַת הָאָדָם בָּאָרֶץ, אֵין דּוֹרֵשׁ בְּצֶדֶק וְאֵין מַשְׂכִּיל בְּיִרְאַת ה', לִקְבֹּעַ עִתִּים סְדוּרוֹת בַּעֲמַל הַיִּרְאָה, לִדְלוֹת מֵי תְּבוּנָה מֵהָאֱמוּנָה הַנֶּחְבָּאָה וּמִסְתֶּרֶת בְּמַחֲבוֹאֵי הַלֵּב, לְהַרְחִיבָהּ וּלְסַעֲדָהּ, לָתֵת לָהּ תֹּקֶף וָעֹז, לָשִׂים הַמִּשְׂרָה עַל שִׁכְמָהּ, לִמְשֹׁל עַל הָאֵבָרִים לְבַל יִפְרְצוּ גְּדֵרָהּ וְכַתּוֹרָה יַעֲשׂוּ. זֶהוּ הַסּוּג הַשֵּׁנִי. דּוּגְמַת זֶה הַדָּבָר לֹא מָצָאנוּ בְּעִנְיְנֵי הָעוֹלָם, אֵין אִישׁ שֶׁצָּרוֹת מְרַחֲפוֹת מִמּוּל פָּנָיו, אֲשֶׁר לֹא

20. I.e., it does not require highly developed skill.
21. "*Taava*" (lust, desire) is an elemental drive that seeks its own fulfillment and is oblivious to rational or moral considerations.
22. Non-legal, ethical literature of the Rabbis.
23. Isaiah 6:10.
24. And with one misstep, he may fall in.
25. See Isaiah 6:10.
26. See Genesis 6:5

Only one [remedy] have we found. It is a science, not a craft.[20] Let us discuss it a bit and it will be profitable for us.

Let us pay attention and analyze the matter of sins. We will see that there are two types. One stems from unbridled lust,[21] loving what is immediately gratifying without paying heed to the outcome – even though that will be very bitter ultimately. We find its analogue in worldly matters as well. A fool, and especially one whose weak intellect renders him ill, loves to grab and eat that which is pleasant to his palate, forgetting that this will often make him sick. On this our Rabbis, of blessed memory, said: "Who is wise? One who sees what will develop" (Avot 4:1).

This is also the meaning of the saying of our Rabbis, of blessed memory (Sota 3a): "A person does not sin unless a spirit of foolishness enters into him." This is a person's primary labor in His service, may He be blessed: to think and consider the reverence of God and the fear of His punishment by means of the Mussar books and the aggadot[22] of our Sages, of blessed memory, to the point that he hears it with his own ears and virtually sees it with his own eyes[23] – the quantitatively and qualitatively great punishment standing before him. As our Rabbis, of blessed memory, say (Sanhedrin 7a): "At all times, a judge should see (given his likelihood to err; the same applies to every person vis-à-vis safeguarding against serious harm from grave sins) as if… hell is open below him."[24] If a person acts this way and his heart truly understands, he will repent and be healed.[25]

Indeed, man's wickedness on the earth is great.[26] No one seeks righteousness, and no one is truly enlightened through the fear of God,[27] setting aside fixed times to work on the fear of God, drawing out waters of understanding from the concealed faith that is hiding in the inner recesses of the heart, to broaden it and sustain it and to give it force and strength, to place on its shoulders the authority[28] to govern the external limbs that they not breach its fences but act in accordance with the Torah.

This, then, is the second type of transgression. It has no analogue in worldly matters; there is no person who, when faced with burden-

27. Compare Psalms 14:2.

יִקַּח לוֹ עֵת לַחֲשֹׁב מַחֲשָׁבוֹת לְהִנָּצֵל מֵהֶן. אִי לָזֹאת, גַּם אֵין הַתַּאֲוָה סִבָּתָהּ, פְּלִיאָה הִיא הָעֲבֵרָה הַלָּזוֹ, וְזֶה שְׁמָהּ פִּלְאִי, לִבְלִי שׂוּם עַל לֵב לְהִתְבּוֹנֵן בְּיִרְאַת ה׳ וּבְמוּסַר עָנְשׁוֹ, עֲבֵרוֹת כָּאֵלּוּ לֹא יוּכְלוּ הֱיוֹת מִסּוּג הָרִאשׁוֹן, יַעַן אֵין דַּי בְּהַתַּאֲוָה לִהְיוֹת סִבָּתָן, רַק הֵן מֵרוּחָנִיּוּת הַטֻּמְאָה הַמְלַפֶּפֶת אֶת הָאָדָם לְהַחֲטִיאוֹ, וּבְיוֹתֵר בְּחֶטְאֵי הַדִּבּוּר, כִּי מַה יִּתְרוֹן לְבַעַל הַלָּשׁוֹן, כְּמַאֲמַר רַבּוֹתֵינוּ זַ״ל (עֲרָכִין ט״ו) עַיֵּן שָׁם.

בָּזֹאת מָצָאנוּ פֵּשֶׁר דָּבָר בֵּין הַשִּׁיטוֹת, בְּעִנְיַן יֵצֶר הָרַע וְיֵצֶר טוֹב מַה הֵמָּה, הַשִּׁיטָה הָאַחַת הִיא הַשִּׁיטָה הַנּוֹדַעַת, כִּי יֵצֶר הָרַע, הוּא כֹּחַ הַטֻּמְאָה בָּאָדָם הַמּוֹבִילוֹ לַפְּשָׁעִים, וְיֵצֶר הַטּוֹב הוּא כֹּחַ הַקְּדֻשָּׁה בָּאָדָם הַמּוֹבִילוֹ לַטּוֹב. הִיא שִׁיטַת רֹב הַמְחַבְּרִים הַגְּדוֹלִים. וְהַשִּׁיטָה הַשְּׁנִיָּה הִיא, שֶׁיֵּצֶר הָרַע הוּא כֹּחַ תַּאֲוַת הָאָדָם, הַמַּשְׁקֶפֶת אֶל כָּל דָּבָר הֶעָרֵב לִשְׁעָתוֹ, אוֹתוֹ תַּאַסְפֵהוּ אֶל בֵּיתָהּ וּבוֹ תִּדְבַּק לְאַהֲבָה, וְיֵצֶר טוֹב הוּא הַשֵּׂכֶל הַיָּשָׁר הַצּוֹפֶה וּמַבִּיט לְהַנּוֹלָד, הוּא פַּחַד יִרְאַת ה׳ יִתְבָּרַךְ שְׁמוֹ וּמִשְׁפָּטָיו הָרָעִים לְמַרְבֶּה. וּבוֹחֵר בַּדָּבָר הַמּוֹעִיל, לִכְבֹּשׁ הַתַּאֲוָה, לְמַעַן יִתְעַדֵּן בָּאַחֲרוֹנָה בְּעֹנֶג נִפְלָא, אֲשֶׁר אֵין דֵּי בָּאֵר יְקָרַת תִּפְאַרְתָּהּ. בַּאֲשֶׁר אֲנַחְנוּ רוֹאִים בְּכָל עֵת עִנְיְנֵי הָאָדָם מִתְחַלְּפִים, כָּל אֶחָד נִדְבָּק יוֹתֵר לַעֲבֵרָה אַחֶרֶת, יֵשׁ אֲשֶׁר חַטָּאתָם תִּגְדַּל יוֹתֵר בְּבִטּוּל תּוֹרָה מִמַּשָּׂא וּמַתָּן בֶּאֱמוּנָה וּנְתִינַת צְדָקָה וְיֵשׁ לְהֶפֶךְ, וְכֵן בְּכָל הָעֲבֵרוֹת אֵין אָדָם דּוֹמֶה לַחֲבֵרוֹ. וְאִלּוּ הָיָה הַיֵּצֶר הָרַע רַק כֹּחַ הַטֻּמְאָה הַמְפַתֵּהוּ, מַדּוּעַ לֹא

28. Compare Isaiah 9:5.

29. Such sinful behavior comes as a surprise, because it reflects an unexpected heedlessness, disregarding any consequences or punishment.

30. Based on Judges 13:18.

31. Identification of two types of sin.

32. In the Talmud and most of the classic medieval books of Mussar, the good urge and the evil urge are personified and externalized. It is as if a distinct good entity and a distinct evil entity exist within the person (but are not the person), constantly motivating the individual on to good or bad behaviors.

33. Salanter's pun, based on Isaiah 40:16, switches the ע to an א in "אֵין דֵּי בָּעֵר". Just as there, there is not enough wood in the Lebanon forest to set a significant fire compared to the infinity of God, so here the imagination cannot adequately describe the eternal rewards and pleasures in the World to Come.

ing troubles, would not take time to think about how to escape them. Moreover, it is not caused by lust. This sin is dumbfounding (*pelia*),[29] and its name is unknowable (*peli*),[30] for [in committing the sin] the sinner does not pay attention to and consider his punishment through fear of God and Mussar. Such sins cannot be of the first type, for desire is not strong enough to be their cause. Rather, they stem from the spiritual impurity that coils around a person to cause him to sin. And especially in sins of speech, "for what benefit is there to the one who speaks evil?," as stated by our Rabbis, of blessed memory (Arakhin 15b). See further there.

With this,[31] we can reconcile between two views about what the evil urge and good urge are. One view, which is well known, is that the evil urge is the force of impurity within a person, which leads him to transgressions, and the good urge is the force of holiness in the person that leads him to do good. This is the view of most major writers.[32] The second view is that the evil urge is the force of desire in a person, which focuses temporarily on whatever is pleasant, which it takes home and lovingly clings to. The good urge is straightforward reason, which anticipates and looks to the future – that is, to the fear of God, blessed be His name, and His truly terrible judgments. It chooses the more beneficial action – suppressing desire – so that it is ultimately sublimated in wondrous pleasure, of which there can be no adequate parsing[33] of its precious splendor.[34]

For we see that human situations change at every moment, with each person clinging to a different sin. Some sin more in neglect of Torah than in not following honest business practices or not giving charity, and with others, it is just the opposite. This is true for all transgressions; each person is different. Now, were the evil urge just a force of impurity that tempts him, why would it not wrap its coils around all

34. A paraphrase of Esther 1:4. This second view, that the struggle between the "urges" is in fact a conflict between desire and reason, is R. Salanter's own theory (although in his modesty he does not identify himself as the originator). It is striking that he has moved from a medieval, dualist portrait of human psychology (the conflict between multiple distinct urges) to a more unified conception of human psychology, driven by conflict between emotions/instincts and reason.

תְּלַפֵּף אֶת כָּל בְּנֵי אָדָם בְּשָׁוֶה (אִם לֹא נַשְׁקִיף עַל שָׁרְשֵׁיהֶם לְמַעְלָה).
אָמְנָם אִם נֹאמַר כִּי הַיֵּצֶר הָרַע הוּא כֹּחַ הַתַּאֲוָה. הַדָּבָר נָכוֹן, כִּי תַּאֲוַת הָאָדָם תְּלוּיָה בְּמִזְגּוֹ (לֵידָתוֹ וְהַרְכָּבָתוֹ שְׁעָתוֹ וְעִנְיָנָיו), וּמִזְגֵי בְּנֵי אָדָם מִתְחַלְּפִים, לָזֹאת גַּם עֲוֹנוֹתֵיהֶם מִתְחַלְּפִים. אָכֵן גַּם בָּזֶה לֹא יִתָּכֵן, הֲלֹא עֵינֵינוּ רוֹאוֹת בְּנֵי אָדָם עוֹשִׂים עֲבֵרוֹת עֲצוּמוֹת, שֶׁאֵין תַּאֲוָתָם גּוֹרֶמֶת לָהֶם כָּל כָּךְ. וְלִפְעָמִים הַתַּאֲוָה מְנַגַּדְתָּהּ, כְּמוֹ, הָאָדָם הֶחָפֵץ וּמִשְׁתּוֹקֵק הַרְבֵּה אֶל הַכָּבוֹד הַמְּדֻמֶּה, וּבִכְבוֹד מִצְוָה תִּגְעַל נַפְשׁוֹ וְכַיּוֹצֵא בָּזֶה, אֵין זֹאת, כִּי אִם רוּחַ הַטֻּמְאָה הַמְבַלְבְּלוֹ לְהָרֵעַ גַּם נֶגֶד תְּשׁוּקָתוֹ הַהֶבְלִית.

מִזֶּה נִרְאֶה בַּעֲלִיל. כִּי שְׁתֵּי הַשִּׁיטוֹת נְכוֹנוֹת. הַיֵּצֶר הָרַע, הוּא כֹּחַ הַתַּאֲוָה, וְגַם יֵשׁ בּוֹ רוּחַ הַטֻּמְאָה. וְכֵן יֵצֶר הַטּוֹב, הוּא הַשֵּׂכֶל הַנָּכוֹן (שֶׁלֹּא נִתְקַלְקֵל עַל יְדֵי הָעֲבֵרוֹת וְהַתַּאֲווֹת) הָרוֹאֶה אֶת הַנּוֹלָד, וְגַם יֵשׁ רוּחַ הַקֹּדֶשׁ בָּאָדָם.

וְהִנֵּה בִּשְׁנֵי הַצְּדָדִים, יֶשְׁנוֹ בָּאָדָם גַּשְׁמִי וְרוּחָנִי, כְּעִנְיַן בְּרִיאַת הָאָדָם עַצְמוֹ גּוּפָנִי וְנַפְשִׁי. הַגּוּפָנִי נִרְאֶה לְעֵין בָּשָׂר, וְהַנַּפְשִׁי נוֹדַע מִפְּעֻלּוֹת וְעִנְיְנֵי הַגּוּף. תַּחְבּוּלוֹת הָאָדָם וּמְזִמּוֹתָיו לְהַחֲזִיק הַנֶּפֶשׁ בַּגּוּף, הֵמָּה רַק בַּגּוּף לְבַדּוֹ, לְתָמְכוֹ בַּאֲכִילוֹת טוֹבוֹת וּבִשְׁמִירוֹת מְעֻלּוֹת מִכָּל נֶזֶק וּפֶגַע רַע, וּבָזֶה יְשַׁמֵּר נַפְשׁוֹ בְּגוּפוֹ, אֵין מָבוֹא בַּטִּבְעִי (עַל פִּי רוּחָנִיּוּת, לְפִי הָאֱמֶת, עִקַּר שְׁמִירַת הַנֶּפֶשׁ בַּגּוּף תָּלוּי רַק בְּנַפְשׁוֹ, לְפִי עֲבוֹדָתָם לְבוֹרְאָהּ יִתְבָּרַךְ שְׁמוֹ). לַעֲשׂוֹת תַּחְבּוּלָה בַּנֶּפֶשׁ לְהַחֲזִיקָהּ בַּגּוּף. כִּי אֵין רוֹאָהּ וְאֵין מַרְגִּישָׁהּ לְבַדָּהּ, וּמַה יַּעֲשֶׂה בָּהּ.

---

35. "Above" is R. Salanter's depiction of the varied inner drives of people, which conceivably could filter or modify the effects of the force of impurity from person to person. R. Salanter is conceding that his argument that a spirit of impurity would affect all people the same way is only partially convincing. There might be variations in response to the spirit of impurity due to differences in other inner forces between one individual and another.

Nevertheless, underlying this analysis is R. Salanter's focus on the inner psychological forces of humans as the key motivators of behaviors. Also present is R. Salanter's stress on the uniqueness of each person, with the implication that God judges – and rewards and punishes – each person differently even for seemingly identical actions. This "modern" emphasis on individual differences became a *leitmotif* of R. Salanter's writings throughout out his career. Similarly, the role of unconscious forces as the primary driver of human behavior dominates his later writings.

human beings in the same manner? (This analysis holds if we don't look at their roots above.)[35]

However, if we say that the evil urge is the force of desire, then it is true that a person's lust is a function of his temperament (his birth, his make-up, his condition at the time, and his circumstances). Since human temperaments change, so their transgressions change.

Yet even this explanation is not so plausible. With our own eyes we see people commit terrible sins that are not really caused by lust. Sometimes, they run counter to their desires. For example, a person might want and long greatly for imaginary honor, yet his soul will despise the true honor of doing a mitzva – and the like. The only explanation is that the spirit of impurity confuses him and leads him to evil – even against the opposition of his vain desire.

From all this we see clearly that both views are correct. The evil urge is the force of lust, but it also has a spirit of impurity. Similarly, the good urge is the force of straightforward reason (that has not been corrupted by sins and desires), which anticipates the future, and it is also the human spirit of sanctity.

According to both views, every person has physical and spiritual aspects, just as the actual creation of the human being was both physical and spiritual.[36] The physical aspect is visible to carnal eyes, and the spiritual is discerned through the actions and involvements of the body.[37] The strategies and ploys by which a person keeps the soul in the body are only done with the body – sustaining it by eating good foods and with strong protections against all damage or harm. He thus keeps his soul in his body. There is no natural way (although by spiritual standards, in truth, keeping the soul in the body hinges only on the soul, on its service to its Creator, blessed be His name) to perform any operation on the soul to keep it in the body, for no one can see or sense it on its own, so what can he do with it?

---

36. This seems to refer to the Genesis narrative of the creation of human beings, in which God forms the first human from the dust of the earth (representing the physical body) and then infuses the spirit of life (*nishmat ḥayim*) into him (see Gen. 2:7). In the Torah, the human being is seen as a body/soul unity.
37. The movements of the limbs and the cognitive activities of the mind both suggest an inner force or self which is operating in the body.

כֵּן בַּעֲבוֹדַת ה׳ יִתְבָּרַךְ שְׁמוֹ, עִקַּר הַתַּחְבּוּלָה לְהַחֲזִיק אֶת הַיֵּצֶר טוֹב לְפִי שְׁתֵּי הַשִּׁיטוֹת. הֱיוֹתוֹ כֹּחַ הַקְּדֻשָּׁה וְהַשֵּׂכֶל הַנָּכוֹן (אֲשֶׁר לֹא נִתְקַלְקֵל), וְלִדְחוֹת אֶת הַיֵּצֶר הָרַע הוּא כֹּחַ הַטֻּמְאָה וְהַתַּאֲוָה. תָּלוּי בִּבְחִינָה הַגּוּפָנִית, לְהַאֲכִילֵהוּ מַאֲכָלִים טוֹבִים, הֵמָּה הִתְבּוֹנְנוּת הַיִּרְאָה וְהַמּוּסָר הַנּוֹבְעִים מֵהַתּוֹרָה הַטְּהוֹרָה.

הוּא מַאֲמַר רַבּוֹתֵינוּ זַ״ל (בָּבָא בַּתְרָא ט״ז) בִּקֵּשׁ אִיּוֹב לִפְטֹר אֶת כָּל הָעוֹלָם כֻּלּוֹ מִן הַדִּין. אָמַר לְפָנָיו רִבּוֹנוֹ שֶׁל עוֹלָם בָּרָאתָ שׁוֹר פַּרְסוֹתָיו סְדוּקוֹת בָּרָאתָ חֲמוֹר פַּרְסוֹתָיו קְלוּטוֹת, בָּרָאתָ גַּן עֵדֶן בָּרָאתָ גֵּיהִנֹּם, בָּרָאתָ צַדִּיקִים בָּרָאתָ רְשָׁעִים, מִי מְעַכֵּב עַל יָדֶךָ, וּמַאי אַהַדְרוּ לֵיהּ חַבְרֵיהּ דְּאִיּוֹב (אִיּוֹב ט״ו) אַף אַתָּה תָּפֵר יִרְאָה וְתִגְרַע שִׂיחָה לִפְנֵי אֵל, בָּרָא הַקָּדוֹשׁ־בָּרוּךְ־הוּא יֵצֶר הָרַע בָּרָא לוֹ תּוֹרָה תַּבְלִין כּוּ׳. בָּזֶה הוֹרוּנוּ חֲכָמֵינוּ זַ״ל, כִּי תַּבְלִין שֶׁל תּוֹרָה, הִיא הַיִּרְאָה הַנּוֹבַעַת מִמֶּנָּה, כְּמַאֲמַר הַכָּתוּב (הַנִּזְכָּר לְעֵיל) תָּפֵר יִרְאָה, וְהִיא בְּחִינָה גַּשְׁמִית, מוּבֶנֶת לְעֵינֵי בָּשָׂר, סִבַּת רְפוּאָתָהּ לְחֹלִי הַנֶּפֶשׁ, אִם יָשִׂים הָאָדָם לִבּוֹ וְנַפְשׁוֹ אֶל יִרְאַת הַתּוֹרָה. אִם בִּכְלָל, לֵידַע וּלְהָבִין מֵהַתּוֹרָה, כִּי לְכָל עֲבֵרָה יֵשׁ עֹנֶשׁ עָצוּם וְנוֹרָא, וּלְכָל מִצְוָה יֵשׁ שָׂכָר נַעֲלֶה מְאֹד. אִם בִּפְרָט, וְהוּא הָעִקָּר, לִלְמֹד תּוֹרַת כָּל עֲבֵרָה וַעֲבֵרָה לְבַדָּהּ, לְגַאֲוָה תּוֹרַת הַגַּאֲוָה, לְמַשָּׂא וּמַתָּן בֶּאֱמוּנָה חֶלְקֵי הַתּוֹרָה אֲשֶׁר לָעִנְיָנִים שֶׁבֵּין אָדָם לַחֲבֵרוֹ בְּעִסְקֵי הָעוֹלָם וְכַדּוֹמֶה, וְכֵן לְכָל מִצְוָה וּלְכָל עֲבֵרָה אֶת תּוֹרָתָהּ.

---

38. Since there is no counterforce and no one can unmake what God has made, the righteous and the wicked are both created by God. Both act in accordance with their God-given nature – and no one is guilty or is to be punished.
39. You undermine the fear of punishment which keeps people on the path of Torah. Furthermore, there is no point to prayer if all our behaviors are determined by our nature, implanted in us by God.
40. Lit. spice or seasoning. This imagery evokes the idea that just as a spice removes the bitter taste out of food, so does the Torah remove the bitter effect of the *yetzer hara* (evil urge).
41. Human behavior is not determined. Humans have free will and God gave them the Torah to equip them to fight the evil urge and guide them to live the good life.
42. In this letter, R. Salanter shifts his understanding of the evil urge from being a

So it is with the service of God, blessed be His name. The main strategy to support the good urge according to both views – that it is the force of sanctity and proper reason (that has not been corrupted) – and to push away the evil urge – the force of impurity and lust – hinges on the physical aspect. It must be fed good foods, namely, contemplation of reverence and Mussar that emanate from the pure Torah.

This is the saying of our Rabbis, of blessed memory (Bava Batra 16a): "Job sought to exonerate the whole world from [divine] judgments. He said before Him: 'Master of the Universe! You created the ox with split hooves; you created the donkey with whole hooves. You created the Garden of Eden [i.e., heaven]. You created Gehenna [i.e., hell]. You created righteous people. You created wicked people. Who can hold You back?'[38] What did Job's friends respond to him? 'You undermine fear and reduce prayer before God' (Job 15:4).[39] [True,] the Holy One, blessed be He, created the evil urge but He also created the Torah as an antidote[40] for it...."[41] With this, our Sages, of blessed memory, taught us that the antidote of Torah is the reverence that stems from it, as the verse says (mentioned above): "You undermine fear." This verse captures the physical aspect [of healing the evil urge], in ways discernible by carnal eyes. The cause of healing of the spiritually ill is that a person turns his heart and soul to the reverence of the Torah. [This is done] in general, through knowing and understanding from the Torah that for every sin there is a powerful and terrible punishment, and for each mitzva there is a sublime reward. [This is done] in specific detail, which is primary, through studying the Torah of each sin and transgression individually. For pride, [he studies] the Torah of pride; for honesty in business matters, the parts of the Torah that deal with interpersonal situations and worldly matters; and so forth, to the Torah of every mitzva and every sin.[42]

---

generalized external evil force that takes over the person toward being an internal force (which operates deeply and differently in every person). Similarly, he refines the "cure" of sin from general Torah study, which repels the outside force, to study of the specific Torah and halakhot of the sins one is tempted to commit. This individualized study is more likely to affect the individual's distinct inclinations toward sin. Of course, *yira* – increasing reverence through the direct study of the reward and punishment for each sin – is most likely to stop bad behavior.

הַנִּשְׂגָּב וְהָעִקָּר בְּשִׁמּוּשׁ רְפוּאוֹת הַתּוֹרָה לְתַחֲלוּאֵי הַיֵּצֶר, הוּא לִלְמֹד בְּעֹז וְעִיּוּן עָמֹק הֵיטֵב, דִּינֵי הָעֲבֵרָה עַצְמָהּ, הַהֲלָכָה עִם כָּל סְעִיפֶיהָ. כִּי עֵינֵינוּ הָרוֹאוֹת הַרְבֵּה מֵהָעֲבֵרוֹת אֲשֶׁר הָאָדָם נִמְנָע מֵהֶם בְּטֶבַע, וְלֹא יַעֲבֹר עֲלֵיהֶם אַף גַּם בְּעֵת אֲשֶׁר יְלַחֲצֵנּוּ לָזֶה אֵיזֶה דָּבָר, וְיֶשְׁנָם עֲבֵרוֹת חֲמוּרוֹת מֵאֵלּוּ, וְהָאָדָם הַזֶּה בְּעַצְמוֹ יַעֲבֹר עֲלֵיהֶם בְּנָקֵל. דֶּרֶךְ מָשָׁל, חֵלֶק גָּדוֹל מֵאַחֵינוּ בְּנֵי יִשְׂרָאֵל כִּמְעַט רֻבָּם כְּכֻלָּם לֹא יֹאכְלוּ, בְּלִי נְטִילַת יָדַיִם חָלִילָה, אַף גַּם בְּעֵת אֲשֶׁר יִרְעֲבוּ וְיִצְטַעֲרוּ הַרְבֵּה. וּבְלָשׁוֹן הָרַע הַחֲמוּרָה, בְּנָקֵל יַעַבְרוּ עָלֶיהָ גַּם בְּלִי תַּאֲוָה גְּדוֹלָה. וְעַתָּה הִנְנוּ רוֹאִים כִּי עִקַּר הַשְּׁמִירָה מֵהָעֲבֵרָה הִיא, רַק לַעֲשׂוֹת אֶת הַהֶרְגֵּל (הַשִּׁמּוּר) טֶבַע אֵצֶל הָאָדָם, עַל כֵּן אַף אִם יִתְאַמֵּץ הָאָדָם הַלָּזֶה לָלֶכֶת בְּדַרְכֵי הַמּוּסָר, לְיַגֵּעַ עַצְמוֹ בְּהַשְּׁמִירָה מִלָּשׁוֹן הָרַע עִם כָּל חוּשָׁיו וְרַעְיוֹנָיו כַּיָּאוּת, בְּכָל זֹאת, כָּל עוֹד שֶׁלֹּא נִתְחַלֵּף טִבְעוֹ וְהֶרְגֵּלוֹ בָּזֶה שֶׁלֹּא יִהְיֶה לוֹ שׁוּם חֵפֶץ טִבְעִי לְסַפֵּר לָשׁוֹן הָרַע, יוֹתֵר יַעֲבֹר בְּנָקֵל עַל לָשׁוֹן הָרַע מֵאֲשֶׁר יֹאכַל בְּלִי נְטִילַת יָדַיִם חָלִילָה. וְכֵן הוּא הָעִנְיָן בְּכָל מִינֵי עֲבֵרוֹת, הַכֹּל לְפִי הָאָדָם וְהַזְּמַן וְהַמָּחוֹז, כִּי גַּם לֹא כָּל הַמְּחוֹזוֹת שָׁוִים בָּזֶה, כִּי אִם מִתְחַלְּפִים בְּעִנְיָנָם, כָּל מָחוֹז יֵשׁ לוֹ עֲבֵרוֹת אֲחֵרוֹת אֲשֶׁר יִשָּׁמֵר אֶצְלָם בְּנָקֵל וּמְרֻחָק מֵהֶם בְּטֶבַע. וְזֹאת הֲלֹא יָדוּעַ, כִּי הִשְׁתַּנּוּת הַטֶּבַע תִּוָּלֵד רַק מִלִּמּוּד וְהֶרְגֵּל רַב, וְלָכֵן הַיְסוֹד הָעִקָּרִי וְהָעַמּוּד הַנָּכוֹן, לְהָכִין אֶת עַצְמוֹ לִשְׁמִירָה מֵהָעֲבֵרוֹת וַעֲשִׂיַּת הַמִּצְוֹת, הוּא רַק הַלִּמּוּד הָרַב בַּהֲלָכָה זוֹ הַנּוֹגַעַת לַעֲבֵרָה זוֹ אוֹ לְמִצְוָה זוֹ, וּבִפְרָט בְּעִיּוּן הָדֵק הֵיטֵב, כִּי זֶה הַלִּמּוּד עוֹשֶׂה קִנְיָן חָזָק בַּנֶּפֶשׁ, לִהְיוֹת הָעֲבֵרָה מְרֻחֶקֶת מִמֶּנּוּ בְּטֶבַע.

כַּדּוֹמֶה בִּמְחוֹזוֹתֵינוּ אֵלּוּ, תְּהִלָּה לָאֵל אִסּוּרֵי נְבֵלוֹת וּטְרֵפוֹת וְדוֹמֵיהֶם מֻטְבָּעִים בְּנַפְשׁוֹת הַיִּשְׂרְאֵלִי, עַד אֲשֶׁר לֹא יִצְטָרֵךְ שׁוּם אִישׁ לְאַכֵּף טִבְעוֹ וְתַאֲוָתוֹ לְהִתְרַחֵק מֵהֶם, כִּי הֵמָּה לוֹ לְזָרָא. הֲלֹא לֹא יַעֲלֶה חָלִילָה עַל לֵב שׁוּם אֶחָד מִמּוֹכְרֵי בָּשָׂר כָּשֵׁר, לְהִתְרַפּוֹת מִלִּדְרֹשׁ

43. I.e., saying words which demean another.

44. The image is borrowed from the preparation of the incense, in which the priestly preparer would grind the ingredients into the finest powder.

The highest and primary aspect of using the Torah's remedies for the sicknesses of the urge is to study, with vigor and penetrating analysis, the laws of the sin itself – its halakha in all its detail. For we see with our own eyes many sins from which a person naturally refrains, even when under duress, while the very same person will commit more severe sins. For example, the greater part – the vast majority – of our fellow Jews will not eat without first ritually washing their hands, God forbid, even when they are hungry and feeling great discomfort. Yet when it comes to the much more serious sin of evil speech,[43] they will casually transgress, even without much appetite for it.

Now we see that the main safeguard against this sin is simply to make the habit (of refraining) second nature in the person. Thus, even if a person makes a strong effort to go in the ways of Mussar, to wear himself out guarding against speaking evil, with all his senses and ideas properly attuned to this goal, even so, as long as he has not changed his nature and his habituation so that he has no natural desire to speak evil, he will more easily violate the law of evil speech than he would eat without ritually washing his hands, God forbid. The matter is the same in all manner of transgressions; it is all according to the person, the timing, and the locale. For not all locales are the same in this respect; rather they vary in different matters. Each locale has different transgressions that are easily and naturally avoided, as it is against their nature. This is also well known: changing one's nature results from a great deal of training and habituation. Therefore, the essential foundation and the right pillar to prepare himself to keep from sins and to do mitzvot is only a lot of learning of the halakha that relates to this sin or this mitzva, especially with close attention to the finest details,[44] for such learning establishes a strong impression in the soul and renders the sin naturally distant from him.

Similarly, in our locales, praise God, the prohibitions against [eating] carcasses, improperly slaughtered animals, and the like [i.e., non-kosher foods] are deeply rooted in the Jewish soul, to the point that no one needs to force his nature and appetite to distance himself from them, for they are repulsive to him. It would not occur, God forbid, to any seller of kosher meat to fail to consult a local rabbinic authority[45] when

45. Heb. "*moreh tzedek.*"

אֵצֶל הַמּוֹרֶה צֶדֶק, בְּמָצְאוֹ שׁוּם דָּבָר שֶׁיֵּשׁ בּוֹ חֲשַׁשׁ טְרֵפוֹת בָּאֵבָרִים הַפְּנִימִים, עִם הֱיוֹת לוֹ לִפְעָמִים בְּעִנְיָן כָּזֶה הֶפְסֵד מְרֻבֶּה, מוֹרָא שָׁמַיִם עָלָיו בְּטִבְעוֹ וְהֶרְגֵּלוֹ, חָלִילָה לוֹ מֵרֶשַׁע, לְהַכְשִׁיל אֶת יִשְׂרָאֵל.

וְאוּלָם בַּעֲוֹנוֹתֵינוּ הָרַבִּים, בְּמַשָּׂא וּמַתָּן הוּא בְּהֵפֶךְ, רֹב בְּנֵי אָדָם לֹא יִדְרְשׁוּ עַל חֲשַׁשׁ גָּזֵל וְעֹשֶׁק מֵעַצְמָם. טֶרֶם יִתְבָּעֵנוּ חֲבֵרוֹ, וּמֵהֶם אֲשֶׁר גַּם אַחַר הַתְּבִיעָה יַעֲשֶׂה תַּחְבּוּלוֹת מִרְמָה אוֹ יָעַז. וַהֲלֹא בַּתּוֹרָה הַכֹּל שָׁוֶה, זֶה לֹא תַעֲשֶׂה וְזֶה לֹא תַעֲשֶׂה, כְּפִי עִנְיַן הַתּוֹרָה וּמִשְׁפָּטֶיהָ, וּבָשָׂר בַּשָּׂדֶה טְרֵפָה לֹא תֹאכֵלוּ, לֹא תֹאכְלוּ כָל נְבֵלָה, אוֹ לֹא תַעֲשֹׁק אֶת רֵעֲךָ, וְלֹא תִגְזֹל, וְדוֹמֵיהֶם. וּכְמוֹ שֶׁהֻטְבַּע בְּנֶפֶשׁ הַיִּשְׂרְאֵלִי, שֶׁכָּל מִינֵי טְרֵפוֹת שָׁוִים אֶצְלוֹ, וְכָל אֲשֶׁר יוֹרֶה הַמּוֹרֶה כִּי הוּא טְרֵפָה מְרֻחָק אֶצְלוֹ וְכַתּוֹרָה יַעֲשֶׂה, כֵּן בְּמָמוֹן, הֲלֹא כָל מַה שֶּׁעַל פִּי הַתּוֹרָה שַׁיָּךְ לַחֲבֵרוֹ הָוֵי גָּזֵל וְעוֹבֵר בְּלֹא תִגְזֹל. וַאֲנַחְנוּ רוֹאִים שֶׁבַּעֲוֹנוֹתֵינוּ הָרַבִּים אֲפִלּוּ הַלּוֹמְדִים וְכִמְעַט גַּם הַיְרֵאִים, אֵינָם נִזְהָרִים כָּרָאוּי בְּלֹא תַעֲשֶׂה הַלָּזוּ, אֲשֶׁר יוֹם הַכִּפּוּרִים וְגַם הַמִּיתָה אֵינָם מְכַפְּרִים עָלֶיהָ.

אָכֵן אִם יָשִׂים הָאָדָם לִבּוֹ וְנַפְשׁוֹ, לִלְמֹד הַהֲלָכוֹת הַשַּׁיָּכוֹת לְמָמוֹן בְּעִיּוּן, גְּמָרָא וּפוֹסְקִים אִישׁ לְפִי עֶרְכּוֹ, וּבִפְרָט אִם הַמֶּרְכָּז יִהְיֶה עַל תְּכוּנַת אִסּוּר וְהֶתֵּר, לֵידַע אֵיךְ לְהִשְׁתַּמֵּר מִגָּזֵל, (אַף אִם לֹא יְקַיֵּם בַּתְּחִלָּה, כִּי הַתַּאֲוָה רַבָּה בָּזֶה, וְגַם רָחוֹק הַדָּבָר מֵהֶרְגֵּל הַמְּדִינִי), מָה רַב כֹּחָהּ לְהַשְׁרִישׁ לְאַט לְאַט קִנְיָן רַב בַּנֶּפֶשׁ, עַד אֲשֶׁר יִהְיֶה שָׁוֶה בְּעֵינָיו שְׁאֵלוֹת אִסּוּר וְהֶתֵּר וּשְׁאֵלוֹת הַשַּׁיָּכוֹת לְמָמוֹן. כֵּן אִם הָאָדָם נִכְשַׁל רַחֲמָנָא לִצְלַן בַּעֲבֵרָה אֲשֶׁר אֵין הָעוֹלָם רְגִילִין בָּהּ, כְּמוֹ בְּנִאוּף וְכַיּוֹצֵא, כְּמַאֲמָרָם ז״ל מִעוּטָן בַּעֲרָיוֹת, וְתָקַף עָלָיו יִצְרוֹ שֶׁנַּעֲשָׂה לוֹ כְּהֶתֵּר רַחֲמָנָא לִצְלַן, עִקַּר רְפוּאָתוֹ (לְבַד הִתְבּוֹנְנוּת הַיִּרְאָה וְהַמּוּסָר מֵאַגָּדוֹת וּמִדְרְשֵׁי חֲכָמֵינוּ ז״ל וְסִפְרֵי מוּסָר הַשַּׁיָּכִים לָזֶה), הוּא לִמּוּד

46. Exodus 22:30, referring, per the Sages, to improperly slaughtered meat.
47. Deuteronomy 14:21, referring, per the Sages, to unslaughtered carcasses.
48. Leviticus 19:13.
49. See Mishna Yoma 8:9. For interpersonal sins, one must appease the wronged party.
50. A veiled reference to the corruption of the Tsarist state.
51. See Bava Batra 165a.

he finds something in the internal organs that he suspects renders [the meat] *treif*, even though, sometimes, this would cause him a substantial financial loss. The fear of Heaven is upon him, both in his nature and by habit. Wickedness, causing Jews to stumble, is unthinkable to him.

However, due to our many sins, in business matters the situation is just the opposite. Most people will not inquire on their own about suspected theft or exploitation, until they are sued by another. Some of them, even after suit is brought, will resort to deceitful strategies or will brazenly deny. Yet in the Torah, all such sins are equal. Both [forbidden foods] and [stealing] are prohibitions, subject to the Torah and its laws: "You must not eat meat torn by beasts in the field";[46] "You shall not eat any carcass";[47] "You shall not defraud your fellow. You shall not steal";[48] and the like. Just as it has been implanted in the Jewish soul that all forms of *treif* are the same to him, and whatever the rabbi decides is non-kosher is repulsive to him, and he will act as instructed, so too with regard to money, whatever, according to the Torah, belongs to his fellow, is stolen and in violation of "You shall not steal." Yet we see that, due to our many sins, even students of Torah and nearly even those who fear God are not properly careful about this prohibition – which is not atoned for by Yom Kippur or even death.[49]

However if a person commits his heart and soul to learning monetary halakhot in depth, from the Talmud and codes, each according to his ability, and especially if the focus is on the character of the permitted and the prohibited, in order to know how to guard against stealing (even if he does not uphold these laws at first, for desire is great, and this is very far from official habits),[50] it has the power to slowly make a deep impression in the soul, to the point where questions of prohibited and permitted foods will be the same in his eyes as questions concerning financial matters.

So it is even if a person stumbles – God save us – in a sin which the masses do not commit regularly, such as adultery and the like – as they, of blessed memory, said: Only a minority [commits] sexual transgressions[51] – but his evil urge so overwhelmed him that it became as if it were permitted, God save us. The main remedy (aside from contemplation of reverence and Mussar from the aggadot and midrashim of our Sages, of blessed memory, and the relevant Mussar books) is the

הַהֲלָכוֹת הַשַּׁיָּכִים לָזֶה בְּעִיּוּן, וּבִפְרָט עַל מְנַת לַעֲשׂוֹת, זֹאת תִּתֵּן פְּרִיָּהּ לְאַט לְאַט, לָתֵת עֹז בַּנֶּפֶשׁ לְהִשָּׁמֵר מְעַט מִשְּׁאוֹל תַּחְתִּית, לְכָל הַפָּחוֹת מִלַּעֲשׂוֹת אֶת הָעֲבֵרָה בִּבְחִינַת לְהַכְעִיס.*

* בִּתְחִלָּתָהּ יִשְׁתַּמֵּשׁ בַּמֶּה שֶׁאֵין יִצְרוֹ תּוֹקְפוֹ לָזֶה, כִּדְאַשְׁכְּחָן בַּגְּמָרָא (חֻלִּין ד׳) בִּמוּמָר לְתֵאָבוֹן, שֶׁהֶחָמֵץ שֶׁהָיָה בְּבֵיתוֹ בְּפֶסַח וְעָבַר עַל בַּל יֵרָאֶה, מַחֲלִיפָהּ אַחַר הַפֶּסַח לְהָקֵל הָאִסּוּר (כְּפֵרוּשׁ רַשִׁ״י שָׁם), וְסָמְכִינַן עַל זֶה דְּוַדַּאי עוֹשֶׂה כֵּן. וְאֵיךְ לֹא נֵבוֹשׁ וּלְבָבֵנוּ בַּל יִמַּס כַּמַּיִם, בִּרְאוֹתֵנוּ שִׁפְלוּת נַפְשֵׁנוּ נֶגֶד דּוֹרוֹת הָרִאשׁוֹנִים, שֶׁהַמּוּמָר לְפָנִים, אֲשֶׁר הֶחֱזִיק חָמֵץ בְּפֶסַח בְּבֵיתוֹ, הָיְתָה לוֹ קְנִיָּה טִבְעִית לְהָקֵל אִסּוּרוֹ בְּהַדָּבָר הַהוּא, בַּמֶּה שֶׁאֵין לוֹ תַּאֲוָה. וּבְדוֹרוֹתֵינוּ בַּעֲוֹנוֹתֵינוּ הָרַבִּים אֲנַחְנוּ נוֹפְלִים בְּגֶדֶר לְהַכְעִיס, בַּעֲבֵרוֹת אֲשֶׁר הֻרְגַּלְנוּ, לֹא נָשִׂים לֵב, לְהַחֲלִיף תַּאֲוָתֵנוּ בָּהֶם לְהָקֵל הָאִסּוּר, וְרָעָתֵנוּ רַבָּה כְּדִין מוּמָר לְהַכְעִיס רַחֲמָנָא לִצְּלַן. וְרוֹאִים אֲנַחְנוּ אֲשֶׁר גַּם לְדִינָא נִשְׁתַּנָּה בִּזְמַן הַזֶּה, כְּמוֹ שֶׁכָּתַב הַבַּ״ח (יוֹרֶה דֵּעָה סִימָן ב׳ סְעִיף קָטָן ב׳) וְזֶה לְשׁוֹנוֹ: מוּמָר אוֹכֵל נְבֵלוֹת לְתֵאָבוֹן, וְנִרְאֶה דְּעַכְשָׁו בִּזְמַנֵּנוּ, מִי שֶׁהוּא חָשׁוּד לֶאֱכֹל נְבֵלוֹת לְתֵאָבוֹן, אֵין אוֹכְלִין מִמֶּנּוּ שׁוּם דְּבַר מַאֲכָל, שֶׁיֵּשׁ לָחוּשׁ בּוֹ חֲשַׁשׁ אִסּוּר לְשׁוּם דָּבָר שֶׁבִּקְדֻשָּׁה, (רְצוֹנוֹ לוֹמַר שֶׁחָשׁוּד הוּא לַעֲשׂוֹת אַף שֶׁלֹּא לְתֵאָבוֹן, אַף עַל פִּי שֶׁלְּפָנֵינוּ לֹא הֻחְזַק אֶלָּא לֶאֱכֹל לְתֵאָבוֹן), וּמִכָּל שֶׁכֵּן שֶׁלֹּא לִיתֵּן לוֹ סַכִּין בָּדוּק לִשְׁחֹט וְלֶאֱכֹל מִשְּׁחִיטָתוֹ (שֶׁהָיָה מֻתָּר מִדִּינָא דִּגְמָרָא), וּמִי שֶׁעוֹשֶׂה דָּבָר זֶה, מוּמָר יֵחָשֵׁב לְכָל הַתּוֹרָה כֻּלָּהּ.

עַד אֲשֶׁר תּוּכַל תֵּת כֹּחָהּ, עַל יְדֵי עֵסֶק רַב בַּהֲלָכוֹת הַשַּׁיָּכִים לְהָעֲבֵרוֹת הָרְגִילוֹת, לִקְנוֹת טֶבַע אַחֵר, לְבַל יַעֲלֶה עַל לֵב לַעֲבֹר עֲלֵיהֶם גַּם אִם יִכְבַּד הַדָּבָר.

וְהִנֵּה בְּתַבְלִין הַתּוֹרָה לַיֵּצֶר הָרָע, יֵשׁ עוֹד בְּחִינָה רוּחָנִית, (שֶׁהַשֵּׂכֶל וְחוּשֵׁי הָאָדָם נִלְאוּ לְהַכִּיר סִבָּתָהּ), הוּא מַאֲמַר חֲכָמֵינוּ זַ״ל (סוֹטָה כ״א) תּוֹרָה בְּעִדָּנָא דְּעָסִיק בָּהּ מַצְלָא כו׳. וְאֵין חִלּוּק בְּאֵיזֶה

52. "*Lehakh'is*," lit. "to cause anger," sinning to spite God.

in-depth study of the halakhot relevant to this matter, especially with intent to practice them. This will bear fruit slowly, empowering the soul to save itself somewhat from the depths of the Underworld, or at least from committing the sin out of spite.[52*]

* [R. Salanter's footnote:] He should start by dealing with sins where his evil urge is less aggressively pushing him. As we find in the Talmud (Ḥullin 4a–b) with regard to one who sins impulsively, any *ḥametz* he had in his house during Passover, with which he violated the law of owning *ḥametz*, he exchanges it with other leaven after Passover in order to reduce the level of prohibition (as Rashi explains ad loc.). We rely upon the presumption that he will definitely do this. [Since he will exchange it, we can assume that any leaven which he sells to us is not prohibited for our use.]

So how can we not feel shame and our hearts not melt as water when we see the lowliness of our souls compared to earlier generations? In olden times, one who kept *ḥametz* in his house during Passover nevertheless adopted the habit of reducing the level of prohibition in that matter where there is no appetite for the forbidden food [i.e., *ḥametz* that had been owned by a Jew on Passover, which is prohibited after the holiday but, in terms of appetite, is no different from permissible *ḥametz*]. But in our generations, due to our many sins, we fall into the category of "sinners out of spite" vis-à-vis the sins to which we have become habituated. We do not bother to replace the object of our appetites [with permitted foods] in order to minimize the prohibition. Our wickedness is great, like that of a sinner out of spite, may God save us.

Consequently, the halakha has adapted accordingly, as *Bayit Ḥadash* (*Yoreh De'ah* 2:2) states: "A violator who eats the flesh of carcasses out of appetite – it seems that now, in our times, we eat no food that is provided by a violator who eats the flesh of carcasses out of appetite, for we should suspect him of providing prohibited food in any situation requiring holy [i.e., kosher] food. [This is to say that he is suspected of sinning even when there is no appetite.] All the more so, one cannot give such a person a tested knife to slaughter so we can eat from his slaughter [which is permitted under talmudic law]. Anyone who does this is considered as one who violates all the laws of the Torah.

Eventually, it will empower him, through much engagement with the halakhot of typical transgressions, to adopt a different nature, so that he will not even consider violating these norms, even when it is burdensome.

There is another, spiritual aspect of the Torah as the "antidote" to the evil urge (whose efficacy cannot be discerned by reason and human senses). This is the statement of our Sages, of blessed memory (Sota 21a): "Torah – when you study it, [protects you] and saves you [from

דִּבְרֵי תּוֹרָה שֶׁיִּהְיֶה עִסְקוֹ, תַּצִּילֶנּוּ מֵחֵטְא, אִם יַעֲסֹק בְּעִנְיַן שׁוֹר שֶׁנָּגַח אֶת הַפָּרָה וְכַיּוֹצֵא, תַּצִּילֶנּוּ, גַּם מִלָּשׁוֹן הָרַע וְכַיּוֹצֵא, הֲגַם כִּי אֵינָם שַׁיָּכִים זֶה לָזֶה, רַק רוּחָנִיּוּת הַתּוֹרָה תִּשְׁמְרֶנּוּ.

וְהִנֵּה אִם נַשְׁקִיף בְּעַיִן חוֹדֶרֶת נִרְאֶה, כִּי תַּחְבּוּלוֹתֵינוּ לְמֶרְכַּז רְפוּאַת הַיֵּצֶר הָרַע, הֵמָּה רַק בַּבְּחִינָה הַגַּשְׁמִית, הִיא הִתְבּוֹנְנוּת הַיִּרְאָה וְלִמּוּד הַהֲלָכוֹת כַּנִּזְכָּר לְעֵיל. כִּי הָרְפוּאָה הַשְּׁנִיָּה, הִיא בְּחִינָה הָרוּחָנִית, בָּאָה מִמֵּילָא, וְעַל כֵּן תִּקָּרֵא רְפוּאָה מִקְרִית, כִּי מִצְוַת לִמּוּד הַתּוֹרָה, הִיא מִצְוַת עֲשֵׂה בִּפְנֵי עַצְמָהּ, תְּלוּיָה בִּגְדָרָהּ הַמְבֹאָר בְּהִלְכוֹת תַּלְמוּד תּוֹרָה, אֵיךְ לְהִתְנַהֵג בָּהּ נֶגֶד עִנְיְנֵי הָעוֹלָם, אֵין נַפְקָא מִינָּהּ בְּהַנְהָגָתָהּ, אֵיךְ יִצְרוֹ שֶׁל אָדָם מִתְגַּבֵּר עָלָיו, אִם מְעַט וְאִם הַרְבֵּה, וְהָאָדָם צָרִיךְ לִלְמֹד תָּמִיד לְקַיֵּם מִצְוַת תַּלְמוּד תּוֹרָה כָּרָאוּי, גַּם אִם אֵין יִצְרוֹ מִתְגַּבֵּר עָלָיו, (עַיֵּן דְּבָרֵינוּ בְּמַאֲמָרֵנוּ הַקּוֹדֵם). וְאֵין בְּיָדוֹ לִלְמֹד יוֹתֵר מֵחִיּוּבוֹ, וּכְשֶׁיְּקַיֵּם מִצְוַת תַּלְמוּד תּוֹרָה כָּרָאוּי, מִמֵּילָא נִמְשַׁךְ רְפוּאָתָהּ הָרוּחָנִית לְיִצְרוֹ, עַל אֵיזֶה אֹפֶן שֶׁהוּא.

אָכֵן בְּחִינָה הַגַּשְׁמִית, הִיא הַהִתְבּוֹנְנוּת בְּיִרְאַת ה׳ וְלִמּוּד הַהֲלָכוֹת, הִיא רְפוּאָה עַצְמִית, וְהָאָדָם צָרִיךְ לְהִתְנַהֵג בָּהּ, כְּדֶרֶךְ רְפוּאַת חוֹלִי הַגּוּף, אֲשֶׁר לְפִי עֵרֶךְ הַמַּחֲלָה כֵּן עֵרֶךְ הָרְפוּאָה בְּכַמּוּת וּבְאֵיכוּת, כֵּן בְּחֹלִי הַנֶּפֶשׁ הָרְפוּאָה הַלָּזוֹ תִּתְיַסֵּד לְפִי עֵרֶךְ הַמַּחֲלָה, כָּל עוֹד אֲשֶׁר יִצְרוֹ יִתְקֹף עָלָיו כֵּן הַהֶכְרֵחַ לְהוֹסִיף בְּהִתְבּוֹנְנוּת הַיִּרְאָה וְלִמּוּד הַהֲלָכוֹת כַּנִּזְכָּר לְעֵיל. וְאִם לֹא יִשְׁתַּמֵּשׁ הָאָדָם בָּרְפוּאָה הַגַּשְׁמִית, אֲזַי גַּם הָרוּחָנִית הִיא לִמּוּד הַתּוֹרָה, לֹא תִּתֵּן כֹּחָהּ כָּל כָּךְ לַיֵּצֶר הָרַע הָרוּחָנִי, כִּתְכוּנַת בְּרִיאַת הָאָדָם, אֲשֶׁר פְּעֻלַּת הָרוּחָנִית, הִיא הַנֶּפֶשׁ, תָּלוּי בִּבְחִינַת הַגּוּף, כַּנִּזְכָּר לְעֵיל.

---

53. Torah study in general, not necessarily halakhot connected with the specific sin.

54. There is no logical connection between the studied text and the sin; the healing effect is consequent to Torah study.

55. This may be an editorial reference inserted by R. Blazer to Letter 31, which addresses the importance of learning Torah. In R. Blazer's editorial judgement, he placed *Iggeret HaMussar* immediately after Letter 31, even though chronologically it was written much earlier.

56. R. Salanter may be polemicizing against those who argue that one should learn Torah

the evil urge]...." It makes no difference what Torah texts he is occupied with – it saves him from sin. If he studies the topic of an ox that gores a cow and the like, it will save him from evil speech and the like. Even though there is no connection between these topics, the spirituality of the Torah will protect him.

Now, if we look with a penetrating eye, we will see that our strategies focused on remedies against the evil urge are only in the physical dimension, namely, contemplation of reverence and study of halakhot, as mentioned above. For the second type of remedy,[53] the spiritual dimension, emerges of its own accord,[54] and is therefore called a coincidental remedy. For Torah study, a positive mitzva in its own right, hinges on its parameters, as defined by the halakhot of Torah study regarding how to practice it vis-à-vis worldly affairs. There is no difference in the practice [of Torah study] whether a person's urge overwhelms him a lot or a little; a person must study constantly in order to fulfill the mitzva of Torah study properly, even if his urge is not overwhelming (see our preceding essay[55]). And [even if his evil urge is overwhelming], he is not required to learn more than his obligation. When he upholds the mitzva of learning Torah properly, its spiritual remedies are extended, as a matter of consequence, to his urge, somehow.[56]

Thus, the physical dimension, namely, contemplation of fear and of God and study of halakhot, is a self-evident remedy. A person should practice as though healing a physical illness; according to the extent of the illness, so should be the strength of the remedy, quantitatively and qualitatively. So with illnesses of the soul, the remedy should be based on the severity of the illness. To the extent that his urge overwhelms him, it is necessary for him to increase his contemplation of fear and learning of the halakhot, as mentioned above. If a person does not use the physical remedies, then the spiritual remedy, that is, learning Torah, will not be so powerful against the spiritual evil urge. This accords with the pattern of human creation: affecting the spiritual, that is, the soul, hinges on the physical dimension, as mentioned above.

---

and not Mussar. They would be claiming that learning Torah reduces the evil urge and prevents sin. R. Salanter acknowledges this effect, although he has no rationale for it, but still insists that learning Torah is not enough.

וְהִנֵּה הָאוֹיֵב הָאוֹרֵב לְהָאָדָם, הוּא הַיֵּצֶר הָרַע, הַפּוֹעֵל בּוֹ, לָשׂוּם לִבּוֹ לְאֶבֶן, לְבַל יַרְגִּישׁ אֶת חֲטָאָיו הָעֲצוּמִים, לִבְלִי יִרְאֶה חֶסְרוֹנוֹ, וְיָדָיו בַּל תַּעֲשֶׂינָה תּוּשִׁיָּה, לְהִתְבּוֹנֵן בְּיִרְאַת ה׳, לְבַקֵּשׁ רִפְאוּת תְּעָלָה, הִיא רְפוּאָה הַגַּשְׁמִית.

לְזֹאת יָשִׂים הָאָדָם אֶל לִבּוֹ, לְזַכּוֹת אֶת הָרַבִּים, לְעוֹרְרָם לְהִתְבּוֹנְנוּת הַיִּרְאָה וְהַמּוּסָר. כִּי עֵינֵי הָאָדָם פְּקוּחוֹת עַל אֲחֵרִים לָדַעַת וּלְהַכִּיר אֶת חֶסְרוֹנוֹתֵיהֶם, וְכִי נִצְרָכִים הֵמָּה לְמוּסָר לְמַרְבֶּה. כֵּן יַחֲזִיק בְּכָל עֹז בַּלִּמּוּד הַמּוּסָרִי, לְמַעַן יְשׁוֹטְטוּ בּוֹ רַבִּים וְתִרְבֶּה יִרְאַת ה׳ וּזְכוּת הָרַבִּים תִּהְיֶה תְּלוּיָה בּוֹ. וּמִמֵּילָא לְאַט לְאַט לִמּוּד הַמּוּסָר יַדְרִיכֵהוּ בִּנְתִיב הַצֶּדֶק, וְהִיא רְפוּאָה גַּשְׁמִית וְגַם רוּחָנִית, כְּמַאֲמַר חֲכָמֵינוּ ז״ל (יוֹמָא פ״ז) כָּל הַמְזַכֶּה אֶת הָרַבִּים אֵין חֵטְא בָּא עַל יָדוֹ.

וּמַה מְּאֹד תִּגְדַּל מִצְוָה הַלָּזוֹ בְּעֵינֵי הָאָדָם, לָשׂוּם לִבּוֹ וְנַפְשׁוֹ, לְהַדְרִיךְ בְּנֵי אָדָם לְלִמּוּד הַמּוּסָר, לְהַצִּיל נַפְשָׁם מִשְּׁאוֹל תַּחְתִּית. וּכְמַאֲמַר רַבּוֹתֵינוּ ז״ל (שַׁבָּת קנ״א) כָּל הַמְרַחֵם עַל הַבְּרִיּוֹת מְרַחֲמִין עָלָיו מִן הַשָּׁמַיִם, וְאֵין לְךָ רַחֲמָנוּת גְּדוֹלָה מִלְּהַזְכִּיר וּלְעוֹרֵר בְּנֵי אָדָם לְלִמּוּד הַיִּרְאָה, כִּי אָז בְּעֵינֵיהֶם יִרְאוּ, וְאָזְנֵיהֶם יִשְׁמְעוּ, וּלְבָבָם יָבִינוּ גֹּדֶל הַמִּכְשֵׁלָה אֲשֶׁר לִפְנֵיהֶם, וְיִנָּהֲמוּ עַל אַחֲרִיתָם. לָשׁוּב אֶל ה׳ יִתְבָּרַךְ, לִהְיוֹת סָר מֵרַע וְעוֹשֶׂה טוֹב, אִם מְעַט וְאִם הַרְבֵּה. הָאָדָם הַמְעוֹרֵר לָזֶה, יִהְיֶה לוֹ חֵלֶק נָכוֹן בְּכָל אֲשֶׁר יִוָּלֵד מִזֶּה, לְהִתְעַדֵּן בְּעֵדֶן נִצְחִי אֲשֶׁר עַיִן לֹא רָאָתְהוּ. נִלְאֶה שֵׂכֶל אֱנוֹשִׁי לְהַקִּיף וּלְהַכִּיר הֵיטֵב כַּמּוּת וְאֵיכוּת מִצְוַת הָרַבִּים, אֲשֶׁר תְּלוּיָה לְהָאָדָם מִדָּבָר הַנִּקְלֶה הַלָּזֶה. הֶעָמָל מְעַט וְהַשָּׂכָר הַרְבֵּה בְּאֵין עֵרֶךְ וְשִׁעוּר, לָזֹאת יָשִׂים הָאָדָם עֵינוֹ וְכֹחַ שִׂכְלוֹ לְהַדָּבָר הַגָּדוֹל הַלָּזֶה, אִם בַּעַל נֶפֶשׁ הוּא.

בעזהי״ת

57. Compare Isaiah 64:3.
58. Compare Psalms 34:15.
59. See Isaiah 64:3.

Lo! The enemy who ambushes the person, that is, the evil urge, operates within him to turn his heart to stone, that he not feel the enormity of his sins, that he not see his faults, and that his hands not act wisely to contemplate fear of God and seek effective remedies, that is, physical remedies.

Therefore, a person should set his heart on bringing benefit to the masses by arousing them to contemplate reverence and Mussar, for human eyes are more open to knowing and recognizing the faults of others, and [to know] that they have a great need for Mussar. Then, he should uphold the study of Mussar with all his strength, so that many may engage in it, increasing fear of God. The public benefit will thus be attributed to him. Consequently, bit by bit, Mussar study will guide him in the path of righteousness. This is both a physical and spiritual remedy, in accordance with the statement of our Sages, of blessed memory (Yoma 87a): "Whoever brings benefit to the masses, no sin will come to his hand."

How great must this mitzva appear in a person's eyes to set his heart and soul to guiding people to the study of Mussar and thus save their souls from the Underworld. As our Rabbis, of blessed memory, stated (Shabbat 151b): "Whoever has mercy on [God's] creatures, Heaven will have mercy on him." There is no greater compassion than to remind and arouse people to the study of fear of God, for then they will see with their own eyes, hear with their own ears,[57] and understand in their hearts the great stumbling block before them. Then they will sigh about their end and turn to God, may He be blessed. They will turn from evil and do good,[58] whether a little or a lot. A person who thus inspires others will receive the proper portion of whatever comes out of this and will enjoy eternal pleasure, which no mortal eye has ever seen.[59] Human intelligence is unable to encompass or recognize correctly the quantity and quality of [the reward for] a mitzva for the benefit of the masses, which will attach to a person as a result of this seemingly easy matter. The effort is small, but the reward great, beyond our ability to value or measure. Thus, one should apply his eye and the force of his intellect to this great thing, if he is spiritually sensitive.

With God's help

מאמר בענין חיזוק לומדי תוה"ק

מִכְּבוֹד אַדְמוֹ"ר הַגָּאוֹן הָאֲמִתִּי פְּאֵר דוֹרֵנוּ רשכבה"ג
מָרָן יִשְׂרָאֵל מִסַּלַאנְט ז"ל

שָׁלוֹם רָב לְאֹהֲבֵי תוֹרָתֶךָ וְאֵין לָמוֹ מִכְשׁוֹל (תהלים קיט).
נִדָּחָה קָרְאוּ לָךְ צִיּוֹן (שְׁעָרִים הַמְצֻיָּנִים בַּהֲלָכָה)
הִיא דֹּרֵשׁ אֵין לָהּ מִכְּלָל דְּבָעֵי דְּרִישָׁה (רֹאשׁ הַשָּׁנָה ל, א)

אִיתָא בְּסֻכָּה (נב, ב) יִצְרוֹ שֶׁל אָדָם מִתְגַּבֵּר עָלָיו בְּכָל יוֹם כו' וְאִלְמָלֵא הַקָּדוֹשׁ בָּרוּךְ הוּא שֶׁעוֹזֵר לוֹ אֵינוֹ יָכוֹל לוֹ, עַיֵּן שָׁם. וְהִנֵּה אַחֲרֵי אֲשֶׁר נוֹדַע כִּי הַיֵּצֶר הָרַע לֹא נִבְרָא רַק לְטוֹבַת הָאָדָם כְּדֵי שֶׁיְּנַצְּחוֹ וִיקַבֵּל שְׂכָרוֹ, וְאִם יִמָּשֵׁךְ אַחַר יִצְרוֹ מִמֵּילָא יְקַבֵּל עָנְשׁוֹ, וְאִם כֵּן הֲלֹא יִפָּלֵא לְאֵיזֶה תַּכְלִית בָּרָא הַקָּדוֹשׁ בָּרוּךְ הוּא אֶת הָאָדָם עַל זֶה הָאֹפֶן אֲשֶׁר לֹא יִהְיֶה הַכֹּחַ בְּיָדוֹ לְנַצֵּחַ אֶת יִצְרוֹ הָרַע בִּלְתִּי עֵזֶר מֵעִם ה'. וּמַדּוּעַ נָתַן הַקָּדוֹשׁ בָּרוּךְ הוּא כֹּחַ וְעֹז כָּזֶה לְהַיֵּצֶר הָרַע עַד כִּי לֹא יָכוֹל הָאָדָם לְבַדּוֹ לְנַצְּחוֹ כִּי אִם בְּעֵזֶר הַקָּדוֹשׁ בָּרוּךְ הוּא.

אָמְנָם יְבֹאַר כִּי כַּאֲשֶׁר חָקְרוּ חוֹקְרֵי נֶפֶשׁ הָאָדָם וּמָצְאוּ כִּי יֵשׁ בְּנֶפֶשׁ הָאָדָם שְׁנֵי מִינֵי כֹּחוֹת חִיצוֹנִיּוֹת וּפְנִימִיּוֹת, לְמָשָׁל כַּאֲשֶׁר נַתְחִיל

* This essay was first published in *Etz Peri* (Vilna, 1880), a booklet containing the present essay and the "Letter on Mussar" that also appears in the present volume.

*An Essay on Strengthening Those Who Learn Our Holy Torah**

[The Talmud] states (Sukka 52b): "A man's [evil] urge comes on strongly against him every day.... But for the help of the Holy One, blessed be He, he could not cope with it." See further ad loc. Now, it is known that the evil urge was created only for the person's benefit – so that he may defeat it and receive his reward. But if he is drawn after his [evil] urge, he will, in consequence, receive his punishment. If so, is [the Talmud's statement] not puzzling? To what end did God create people such that they do not have the strength to defeat the evil urge without God's help? And why did God give such power and strength to the evil urge, such that a person cannot defeat it alone, but only with God's help?

This will indeed be elucidated. When psychologists studied the human psyche, they found that it contains two types of powers: external (conscious) and internal (subconscious and unconscious). For example,

---

The publisher of the essay notes in a postscript that it was not written by R. Salanter himself. Rather, the publisher, at R. Salanter's request, developed it out of a shorthand, Yiddish version of the essay. The publisher then apologizes for any misinterpretations of R. Salanter's intent.

The anonymous publisher/ghostwriter has been identified as R. Eliezer Schulwitz (1848–1931), a disciple of R. Salanter in Memel who founded the Mussar yeshiva in Lomza, Poland, and its branch in Petah Tikva.

לִלְמֹד אָלֶ״ף בֵּי״ת אוֹ שָׂפָה אַחַת אֲשֶׁר לֹא נֵדַע, כַּמָּה תִּכְבַּד עָלֵינוּ עַד אֲשֶׁר נֵדַע הָאוֹתִיּוֹת, וְאַחַר זֶה לְחַבְּרָם עִם תְּנוּעוֹת לְתֵבָה, וּלְצָרֵף כָּל הַתֵּבוֹת לְמִשְׁפָּט שָׁלֵם (צו וויסין איין גאנצין זאץ). אָמְנָם אַחַר כָּךְ כַּאֲשֶׁר הֻרְגַּלְנוּ בְּהַשָּׂפָה בְּהַחִיצוֹנִיּוֹת, אָז נוּכַל כִּמְעַט בְּהֶרֶף עַיִן לִרְאוֹת וּלְהָבִין מִשְׁפָּטִים רַבִּים כְּאֶחָד וּכְלֵי הַדִּבּוּר מוֹצִאִים מֵעַצְמָם הַדְּבָרִים כְּרֶגַע לְמַעֲנֵהוּ, מִבְּלִי שֶׁיֵּדַע הָאָדָם אֵיכָכָה נַעֲשׂוּ, כִּי יִתְהַוּוּ בְּהָאָדָם בִּפְנִימִיּוּתוֹ הִתְקַשְּׁרוּת מִשְׁפָּטִים רַבִּים, וְיוֹצְאִים כְּרֶגַע מִבְּלִי אֲשֶׁר יֵדַע הָאָדָם בְּעַצְמוֹ, אָמְנָם הֵמָּה בְּהָאָדָם בְּמַצָּב כֵּהִים (גאנץ דונקעל) וְרַק עַל יְדֵי הִתְעוֹרְרוּת קַלָּה מֵהָאָדָם יֵצְאוּ וְיִתְרָאוּ לְפָנֵינוּ בְּרוּרִים וּנְכוֹחִים. כֵּן בְּמִדּוֹת הָאָדָם, בְּהַכֹּחוֹת הַפּוֹעֲלִים עָלָיו יֶשְׁנָם גַּם כֵּן שְׁנַיִם, חִיצוֹנִיּוֹת וּפְנִימִיּוֹת, כֵּהוֹת וּבְרוּרוֹת.

וְיָדוּעַ כִּי הַפְּנִימִיּוֹת יִפְעֲלוּ פְּעֻלָּתָם עַל הָאָדָם יוֹתֵר מֵהַחִיצוֹנִיּוֹת כַּאֲשֶׁר נִרְאֶה בְּחוּשׁ, לְמָשָׁל אִם יֵשׁ לוֹ לְאִישׁ תַּלְמִיד אָהוּב וְחָבִיב לוֹ כְּבָבַת עֵינוֹ וַיַּעֲשֶׂה טוֹבוֹת עִמּוֹ, וְיֵשׁ לְהָאִישׁ הַזֶּה גַּם בֵּן, אָמְנָם יִשְׂנָאֵהוּ תַּכְלִית שִׂנְאָה, וְיֵרָאֶה לוֹ בְּפֹעַל שִׂנְאָתוֹ אֵלָיו. וְהִנֵּה קָרָה כַּאֲשֶׁר נָפַל שֵׁנָה עַל הָאִישׁ הַזֶּה וְעַל עַפְעַפָּיו תְּנוּמָה, וְהִנֵּה אֵשׁ יָצָא מֵאֵת ה׳ וַתֹּאחַז בְּבֵית הַבֵּן גַּם בְּבֵית הַתַּלְמִיד וּשְׁנֵיהֶם בְּסַכָּנָה, וְנִעוֹרֵר פִּתְאוֹם אֶת הָאִישׁ לְהָחִישׁ לְעֶזְרָה, לְהַצִּיל מִן הַדְּלֵקָה גַּם הַבֵּן גַּם הַתַּלְמִיד, נִרְאֶה כִּי יָרוּץ עַד מְהֵרָה לְהַצִּיל בְּנוֹ לָרִאשׁוֹנָה, יַעַן מָה? יַעַן בִּפְנִימִיּוּתוֹ בְּטִבְעוֹ קָמָה הָאַהֲבָה לִבְנוֹ הַשָּׂנָאוּי לוֹ יוֹתֵר מֵאַהֲבָה שֶׁאוֹהֵב לְתַלְמִידוֹ עַל יְדֵי כֹּחוֹתָיו הַחִיצוֹנִים. וְלָכֵן כַּאֲשֶׁר נְעוֹרֵר הָאִישׁ מִשְּׁנָתוֹ אֲשֶׁר אָז גַּם כֹּחוֹתָיו הַחִיצוֹנִים נָמוּ שְׁנָתוֹ, אָז חִישׁ קַל יִתְעוֹרְרוּ כֹּחוֹתָיו הַפְּנִימִיּוֹת וְיִתְבָּרְרוּ וְיִתְגַּבְּרוּ עַל הַחִיצוֹנִיּוֹת וְיָרוּץ לְהַצִּיל אֶת בְּנוֹ לָרִאשׁוֹנָה.

וְהִנֵּה עִקַּר מִלְחֶמֶת הַיֵּצֶר הִיא לְהַגְבִּיר יִרְאַת ה׳ בִּלְבָבוֹ נֶגֶד תַּאֲוַת הַיֵּצֶר, וּכְפִי גֹּדֶל הַתַּאֲוָה כֵּן עָלָיו לְהַגְדִּיל יִרְאָתוֹ יוֹתֵר לְהַכְנִיעַ הַיֵּצֶר בָּזֶה. וְנִסְיוֹן הָעֲקֵדָה שֶׁל אַבְרָהָם אָבִינוּ הָיָה נִסָּיוֹן גָּדוֹל לְהִתְגַּבֵּר עַל הַתַּאֲוָה הַפְּנִימִית בְּטֶבַע אַהֲבַת הַבֵּן, וְעַל זֶה אָמַר הַכָּתוּב (בְּרֵאשִׁית

---

1. As explained in Letter 6, R. Salanter uses "the state of darkness" ("*matzav kakehe*") or "*dunkel*" to refer to processes that occur reflexively and subconsciously.
2. Based on Leviticus 9:24.

when we begin to learn the alphabet or an unfamiliar language, it is so difficult for us to become familiar with the letters, then to combine them with vowels [in the case of unvowelized languages like Hebrew] into words and join all the words into a complete sentence. But later, once we have gotten used to the language by means of the external [conscious] processes, we can, in barely the blink of an eye, see and understand many other sentences at once. And our speech organs automatically and instantly find the appropriate words of response, without the person consciously knowing how these [sentences] were generated. For the linking of many sentences occurs internally, within the person, yet they can be expressed in an instant, without the person's knowledge. Rather, they were in a "state of darkness" (unconscious knowledge) within the person,[1] and with the barest stimulation of the person, they emerge and appear before us clearly and demonstrably. So it is with human character traits. There are two kinds of forces [or drives] that affect him: external and internal, conscious and unconscious, "dark" and "clear."

It is known that inner [unconscious drives] affect a person more than external [conscious desires]. We can illustrate this with an example: Let us say a person has a beloved, precious student, the apple of his eye, whom he showers with favor. And this man also has a son whom he hates utterly and to whom he demonstrates his hatred. Now, it happened that while this man slept, and while slumber was upon his eyes, a fire went forth from before God[2] and engulfed the house of the son as well as the house of the disciple, endangering both. The man awakens suddenly and rushes to help, to save both the son and the student from the fire. We will see that he will run swiftly to save his son first. Why? Because deep down, he unconsciously and naturally harbors love for the son he despises, more than he loves his student consciously. Therefore, when the man awakens from his sleep – when his consciousness slept as well – then his unconscious drives quickly awaken, attain clarity, and overcome his conscious drives; thus, he runs to save his son first.

Now, the essence of the battle with the [evil] urge is to strengthen the reverence of God in one's heart, to counter the desires of the urge. The greater the desires, the more he must increase his reverence of God to overcome the urge thereby. The great trial of the Binding of Isaac was for Abraham to overcome the natural, reflexive love for a son. Of this

כב) עַתָּה יָדַעְתִּי כִּי יְרֵא אֱלֹקִים אַתָּה וְלֹא חָשַׂכְתָּ אֶת בִּנְךָ אֶת יְחִידְךָ מִמֶּנִּי.

אָכֵן מְבֹאָר בְּדִבְרֵי הַיַּלְקוּט (פ׳ וַיֵּרָא עַל הַפָּסוּק וַיָּשֶׂם אֹתוֹ עַל הַמִּזְבֵּחַ), וְזֶה לְשׁוֹנוֹ, הָיוּ דְּמָעוֹת מְנַשְּׁרוֹת וְנוֹפְלוֹת מֵעֵינֵי אַבְרָהָם עַד שֶׁהָיְתָה קוֹמָתוֹ מְשׁוֹטֶטֶת בִּדְמָעוֹת. וְשָׁם אִיתָא, הַקָּדוֹשׁ בָּרוּךְ הוּא רוֹאֶה אֶת הָאָב מַעֲקִיד בְּכָל לֵב. וְלִכְאוֹרָה הַמַּאֲמָרִים סוֹתְרִים זֶה אֶת זֶה, כִּי אַחֲרֵי אֲשֶׁר הָיָה מַעֲקִיד בְּכָל לֵב, אֵיךְ יוּכַל לִהְיוֹת כִּי יִזְּלוּ כָּל כָּךְ דְּמָעוֹת מֵעֵינָיו, אָמְנָם לְפִי דְּבָרֵינוּ צָדְקוּ יַחְדָּיו, כִּי מַה שֶּׁאָמַר הַיַּלְקוּט מַעֲקִיד בְּכָל לֵב, זֶהוּ בְּכֹחוֹתָיו הַחִיצוֹנִים אֲשֶׁר הָיוּ בְּאַבְרָהָם בְּמַדְרֵגָה הַיּוֹתֵר נַעֲלָה לְהִתְגַּבֵּר עַל הַפְּנִימִיִּים בְּמַעֲשֶׂה. אֲבָל הַדְּמָעוֹת בִּכְלַל תְּכוּנַת הָאָדָם, וּמִזֶּה נִרְאֶה בַּעֲלִיל כִּי גַּם בְּאַבְרָהָם אָבִינוּ אֲשֶׁר מִי לָנוּ גָּדוֹל בְּיִרְאָתוֹ וְצִדְקָתוֹ, עִם כָּל זֶה פָּעֲלוּ הַכֹּחוֹת הַפְּנִימִיּוֹת עָלָיו פְּעֻלָּה עַזָּה, לְהוֹרִיד דְּמָעוֹת, אַף כִּי הַמַּעֲשֶׂה הָיָה בִּשְׁלֵמוּת גָּדוֹל וְעָשָׂה בְּלֵב שָׁלֵם, גַּם בְּשִׂמְחָה כַּמְבֹאָר בַּמִּדְרָשׁ.

וְהִנֵּה הַיִּרְאָה בִּכְלָל אֵינֶנָּה נְטוּעָה בְּטֶבַע הָאָדָם, אַךְ כָּל אָדָם יֵשׁ בְּכֹחוֹ לְהָבִין וּלְהַשְׂכִּיל לְתַקֵּן אֶת עַצְמוֹ וּלְהַגְבִּיר יִרְאָתוֹ עַל תַּאֲוָתוֹ בְּמַדְרֵגָה גָּבֹהַּ וּכְמוֹ שֶׁאָמְרוּ חֲזַ״ל בְּתָנָא דְּבֵי אֵלִיָּהוּ ׳חַיָּב אָדָם לוֹמַר מָתַי אַגִּיעַ לְמַעֲשֵׂי אֲבוֹתַי אַבְרָהָם וְיִצְחָק כו׳׳, כִּי כָּל אִישׁ יֵשׁ בְּכֹחוֹ לְהַעֲלוֹת אֶת יִרְאָתוֹ גָּבֹהַּ לְמַעְלָה מִן הַתַּאֲוָה כְּמוֹ בְּעִנְיַן הָעֲקֵדָה. אָמְנָם עַל פִּי רֹב אֵין הַיִּרְאָה מְתֻקֶּנֶת תָּמִיד בְּמַדְרֵגָה עֶלְיוֹנָה, אֲשֶׁר יִהְיֶה בְּכֹחָהּ לְהַגְבִּיר חֲיָלִים תָּמִיד נֶגֶד הַתַּאֲוָה הַיּוֹתֵר גְּדוֹלָה. וְרַק כַּאֲשֶׁר יַרְגִּישׁ וְיִרְאֶה הָאָדָם מֵרֹאשׁ, אֲשֶׁר מְמַשְׁמֵשׁ וּבָא לְפָנָיו נִסָּיוֹן כָּבֵד, אֲשֶׁר עַל יָדוֹ אוּלַי יִכָּשֵׁל בַּעֲבֵרָה, אוֹ יָבוֹא לִידֵי בִּטּוּל מִצְוָה, אָז מֻכְרָח הוּא לְבַקֵּשׁ תַּחְבּוּלָה וְעֵצָה מֵרֹאשׁ לְהַגְבִּיר הַיִּרְאָה כָּל כָּךְ, עַד שֶׁיִּהְיֶה לִבּוֹ בָּטוּחַ כִּי תְּנַצֵּחַ יִרְאָתוֹ אֶת תַּאֲוָתוֹ.

וְהִנֵּה נֶגֶד כֹּחוֹת הַחִיצוֹנִיּוֹת, וְגַם הַמְּעַט אֲשֶׁר יוּכַל לְשַׁעֵר עַל כֹּחוֹת הַפְּנִימִיּוֹת, יְכֹלֶת בְּיַד הָאָדָם לָבוֹא חֶשְׁבּוֹן וְלָדַעַת עַד כַּמָּה

---

3. A two-part midrashic compilation redacted in the tenth century CE and including materials from earlier periods. The two parts are called "*Rabba*" ("large") and "*Zuta*" ("small") based on their relative sizes.

Scripture says: "Now I know that you fear God, since you have not withheld your son, your favored one, from Me" (Gen. 22:12).

This is explained in the words of the *Yalkut* [*Shimoni* 101] (on the verse "He laid him on the altar" [Gen. 22:9]): "Tears were running down and falling from Abraham's eyes, until his whole body swam in tears." And there it also says: "The Holy One, blessed be He, saw the father binding his son with his whole heart." At first glance, these two statements contradict each other. If he was wholeheartedly binding, how could so many tears be running from his eyes? However, based on what we have said, the descriptions can both be correct. When the *Yalkut* states that he was "binding his son with his whole heart," this was with his conscious drives. In Abraham, they were developed to the highest level, to overcome unconscious drives through action. But the tears that flowed came from the unconscious, whose effects are stronger than any human trait. Therefore, we see clearly that even in our patriarch Abraham – and who was more God-fearing and charitable than him? – was still affected strongly by unconscious drives, causing him to shed many tears even though his actions were perfect and wholehearted, and even joyful, as the midrash [*Yalkut Shimoni*, ad loc.] explains.

In general, reverence [of God] is not embedded in human nature. Yet every person has the ability to understand and discern how to improve himself and increase his reverence so it far outweighs his desires. As our Sages, of blessed memory, said in *Tanna DeVei Eliyahu* [*Rabba*] (25:1):[3] "Every person must say, 'When will my deeds approximate the deeds of my ancestors, Abraham, Isaac, and Jacob?...'" Each person has the capacity to raise his reverence to a level beyond his desires, as in the case of the Binding of Isaac. However, for the most part, reverence is not developed to the highest level, where it has the capacity to intensify its strength and always overcome the greatest desires. Only when a person has a premonition that a grave trial looms before him – one that may cause him to stumble into sin or neglect a mitzva – will he be compelled to seek out counsel and strategies in advance, and to intensify his reverence so much that he is certain that his reverence will vanquish his desire.

When it comes to confronting conscious [desires], as well as the little he can estimate [about the proclivities] of his unconscious, one can calculate and know the extent to which he must gather up his

יִתְאַזֵּר עֹז לְהַגְבִּיר הַיִּרְאָה עַל הַתַּאֲוָה, אֲבָל מַה יַּעֲשֶׂה הָאָדָם עִם אֵלֶּה כֹּחוֹתָיו הַפְּנִימִיּוֹת אֲשֶׁר אֵינֶנּוּ יוֹדֵעַ מֵהֶם, וּבִלְתִּי מַרְגִּישׁ אוֹתָם, כִּי אוּלַי יֵשׁ בְּכֹחָם לִמְשֹׁל עָלָיו הַרְבֵּה, יוֹתֵר מִן הַחִצוֹנִיּוֹת. אִי לָזֹאת בָּאוּ חֲזַ"ל בְּדִבְרֵיהֶם הַקְּדוֹשִׁים לְהָשִׁיב נִחוּמִים לְהָאִישׁ הַמִּתְאַמֵּץ לְתַקֵּן כֹּחוֹתָיו הַחִיצוֹנִיּוֹת לְבַל יִפֹּל לִבּוֹ, אוּלַי יִפֹּל בְּרֶשֶׁת הַיֵּצֶר לְרַגְלֵי כֹּחוֹתָיו הַפְּנִימִיּוֹת, לָכֵן הוֹדִיעוּ חֲזַ"ל כִּי הַקָּדוֹשׁ בָּרוּךְ הוּא יִהְיֶה עוֹזֵר לוֹ. וְכַאֲשֶׁר יַעֲשֶׂה הָאָדָם אֶת שֶׁלּוֹ, לְהַשְׁלִים וּלְתַקֵּן הַחִיצוֹנִיּוֹת שֶׁלּוֹ, יִשְׁלַח ה' עֶזְרוֹ מִקֹּדֶשׁ לְתַקֵּן וּלְהַגְבִּיר נֶגֶד הַכֹּחוֹת הַפְּנִימִיּוֹת בְּיִרְאַת ה' כָּל הַיּוֹם.

וְיוֹצֵא לָנוּ מִדְּבָרֵינוּ אֵלֶּה כִּי לֹא נִבְרָא הָאָדָם לְתַקֵּן אֶת כֹּחוֹתָיו הַפְּנִימִיּוֹת בִּשְׁלֵמוּת גָּמוּר, וְרַק רֵאשִׁית הִשְׁתַּדְּלוּתוֹ צָרִיךְ לִהְיוֹת לְתַקֵּן הַחִיצוֹנִיּוֹת בְּתַכְלִית הַשְּׁלֵמוּת, עַד אֲשֶׁר יִפְעֲלוּ פְּעֻלָּה חֲזָקָה גַּם עַל הַפְּנִימִיּוֹת, וְאָז יַעֲזֹר לוֹ הַקָּדוֹשׁ בָּרוּךְ הוּא לְנַצֵּחַ אֶת יִצְרוֹ אַף אִם בְּעַצְמוֹ לֹא עָלָה בְּיָדוֹ לְתַקֵּן אֶת פְּנִימִיּוּתוֹ בִּשְׁלֵמוּת.

וְהִנֵּה בָּאָדָם יֵשׁ שְׁנֵי מִינֵי כֹּחוֹת, יֵשׁ כֹּחוֹת אֲשֶׁר הֵמָּה בְּכָל הָאָדָם כְּמוֹ תַּאֲוַת הָאֲכִילָה וְאַהֲבַת הַבָּנִים אַךְ אֵינָם שָׁוִים בְּכָל הָאָדָם בְּרַב אוֹ בִּמְעַט. וְיֵשׁ כֹּחוֹת אֲשֶׁר אֵינָם בְּכָל הָאָדָם, וְיֵשׁ אֶחָד אֲשֶׁר יִמְצְאוּ בוֹ הַכֹּחַ גָּדוֹל מְאוֹד, וְיֵשׁ אֶחָד אֲשֶׁר לֹא יִמְצְאוּ בוֹ מְאוּמָה מֵהַכֹּחוֹת הָהֵם. כְּמוֹ לְמָשָׁל אַהֲבַת הַמָּמוֹן. יֵשׁ אָדָם אֲשֶׁר אוֹהֵב כֶּסֶף לֹא בַּעֲבוּר הַתַּכְלִית אֲשֶׁר יַשִּׂג מֵהֶם לִקְנוֹת לוֹ כָּל צְרָכָיו, כִּי אִם יֶאֱהַב הַכֶּסֶף בְּעֶצֶם, וְהַבְּחִינָה לָזֶה כִּי אַף כַּאֲשֶׁר צָבַר כְּעָפָר כֶּסֶף לֹא יוֹצִיאֵם אַךְ לְצֹרֶךְ דְּבָרִים הַהֶכְרֵחִיִּים לוֹ מְאֹד וְלֹא לְשׁוּם תַּעֲנוּג. וְיֵשׁ אָדָם אֲשֶׁר עֶצֶם הַמָּמוֹן לֹא יֶאֱהַב כְּלָל וְהַבְּחִינָה הוּא לְהֵפֶךְ, כִּי אַף אִם לֹא מָצָא יָדוֹ עֹשֶׁר, בְּכָל זֶה גַּם עַל כָּל תַּעֲנוּג קָטָן לֹא יְקַמֵּץ מָמוֹנוֹ וְיוֹצִיא כַּסְפּוֹ, וְכָכָה יִמְצָא גַּם בִּשְׁאָרֵי כֹּחוֹת הַנֶּפֶשׁ, כְּמוֹ הַקִּנְאָה, שִׂנְאָה, נִצָּחוֹן וְדוֹמֵיהֶם. וְלָכֵן מִמַּעֲשֵׂה אַבְרָהָם אָבִינוּ נוּכַל לִשְׁפֹּט רַק עַל כֹּחוֹת הַנֶּפֶשׁ אֵלֶּה נִמְצָאִים בְּכָל הָאָדָם כְּאַהֲבַת הַבָּנִים, אֲשֶׁר אֵלֶּה גַּם בְּהַצַּדִּיק כְּאַבְרָהָם לֹא יָכְלוּ הַפְּנִימִיּוֹת לִהְיוֹת מְתֻקָּנִים בְּתַכְלִית גָּדוֹל.

4. Based on Psalms 20:3.

strength to intensify his reverence so that it outweighs desire. But what can a person do with the unconscious drives about which he does not know and which he does not sense? Perhaps they have the power to rule over him definitively, more than the conscious drives. For this reason, our Sages, of blessed memory, came with their holy teachings to console the person who exerts himself to improve his consciousness, so that he does not become downhearted over the possibility that he will fall into the net of the evil urge because of his unconscious drives. So our Sages, of blessed memory, tell him that the Holy One, blessed be He, will help him. When a person does his part, perfecting and repairing his consciousness, God will send him help from the sanctuary[4] to repair and intensify, each day, the opposition to the unconscious drives, through reverence of God.

It follows from these words that a person was not created to improve his unconscious to complete perfection. Rather, his first efforts must be to improve his consciousness to the utmost perfection, to the extent that it has a strong effect on the unconscious as well. And then the Holy One, blessed be He, will help him vanquish the [evil] urge even if he has not managed on his own to repair his unconscious completely.

Now, within every person there are two kinds of forces [or drives]. There are drives that are common to every person – the appetite for food, the love of children – though they are not of the same magnitude in every person; and there are drives that not everyone has. The same drive may be very strong in one person and completely absent in another. For example, there is love of money. There are people who love money not as a means to the end of affording and buying one's needs; rather, they love money itself. The litmus test for this is whether even once one has accumulated money like dirt, he does not spend it except on absolute necessities, never for pleasure. Then there are people who do not love money itself at all. The litmus test for them is the opposite: even if they have no wealth, they do not close their fists even to the smallest pleasures, but rather spend on them. The same applies to the other psychological drives, like jealousy, hatred, the drive to win and the like. Thus, from Abraham's actions we can only judge those psychological drives found in every person, like love of children. With regard to these drives, even in the righteous Abraham, the unconscious drives cannot be improved to a large extent.

אָמְנָם בְּכֹחוֹת הַנֶּפֶשׁ אֵלֶּה אֲשֶׁר יֶשְׁנָם אַךְ בִּקְצָת בְּנֵי אָדָם וּבִקְצָתָם אֵינָם, בְּאֵלֶּה הַכֹּחוֹת אַף בְּמִי שֶׁיֵּשׁ לוֹ הַכֹּחוֹת הָאֵלֶּה מִלֵּדָה, יָכוֹל הָאָדָם הַנַּעֲלֶה בְּצִדְקָתוֹ עַל יְדֵי הַתּוֹרָה וְהַיִּרְאָה לְשַׁנּוֹת הַפְּנִימִיּוֹת מִן הַקָּצֶה אֶל הַקָּצֶה. [וּבָזֶה יְבֹאַר אוּלַי דִּבְרֵי הַגְּמָרָא בְּחֻלִּין (ה, ב) הַצַּדִּיקִים אֵין הַקָּדוֹשׁ בָּרוּךְ הוּא מֵבִיא תַּקָּלָה עַל יָדָם, וְכָתְבוּ הַתּוֹס׳ שָׁם, דְּזֶהוּ דַּוְקָא בְּמִידֵי דַּאֲכִילָה וְלָא בְּמִידֵי אַחֲרִינֵי, וְהַטַּעַם הוּא לְפִי זֶה יַעַן עִנְיַן תַּאֲוַת אֲכִילָה הוּא דָּבָר הַשָּׁוֶה לְכָל נֶפֶשׁ, וּבַכֹּחוֹת הַכּוֹלְלִים אֶת כָּל בְּנֵי הָאָדָם אֵין בְּכֹחַ הָאָדָם לְתַקֵּן אֶת הַפְּנִימִיּוֹת בִּשְׁלֵמוּת, וְדֶרֶךְ הַשְּׁגִיאָה לָבוֹא רַק בַּפְּנִימִיּוֹת אֲשֶׁר בָּהֶם רַק לְהַקָּדוֹשׁ בָּרוּךְ הוּא לִהְיוֹת בְּעֶזְרוֹ, עַל כֵּן הֶעֱמִיד וְיָסַד הַקָּדוֹשׁ בָּרוּךְ הוּא שֶׁאִם הָאָדָם הוּא צַדִּיק בֶּאֱמֶת לֹא יִקְרֶה לְפָנָיו שְׁגִיאָה מֵהַפְּנִימִיּוֹת, אֲבָל בְּעִנְיָנִים אֲחֵרִים אֲשֶׁר יֵשׁ בְּכֹחַ הָאָדָם לְשַׁנּוֹתָם בִּשְׁלֵמוּת מוּטָל עַל הָאָדָם לְתַקֵּן בְּעַצְמוֹ אִם גַּם לֹא יִהְיֶה נֶעֱזָר מֵאֵת הַקָּדוֹשׁ בָּרוּךְ הוּא, עַל כֵּן יוּכַל לָבוֹא שְׁגִיאָה גַּם לְהַצַּדִּיק כָּל זְמַן שֶׁהַפְּנִימִיּוֹת לֹא נִתְקְנוּ בִּשְׁלֵמוּת.]

וְיַעַן לָנוּ לָדַעַת, כִּי הַכֹּחוֹת הַפְּנִימִיּוֹת וְהַחִיצוֹנִיּוֹת נִבְדָּלִים הֵמָּה אֵצֶל בְּנֵי אָדָם, לִפְעָמִים יִהְיֶה בְּאָדָם אֶחָד הַחִיצוֹנִיּוֹת טוֹבוֹת מְאֹד וְהַפְּנִימִיּוֹת רָעוֹת מְאֹד וְלִפְעָמִים לְהֵפֶךְ, כִּי הִנֵּה הַחִיצוֹנִיּוֹת עִקַּר יְסוֹדָם הָרָאשִׁי הוּא הַחִנּוּךְ - הָאִישׁ אֲשֶׁר נִתְגַּדֵּל וְנִתְחַנֵּךְ אֵצֶל הוֹרִים וּמוֹרִים יְשָׁרִים יִרְאֵי חֵטְא, וּבַמָּקוֹם אֲשֶׁר גַּם אֲנָשָׁיו יִרְאֵי חֵטְא הֵמָּה עַל יְדֵי זֶה נַעֲשׂוּ גַּם הַחִיצוֹנִיּוֹת שֶׁלּוֹ עַל דֶּרֶךְ הַמּוּסָר וְהַצֶּדֶק, אָמְנָם הַפְּנִימִיּוֹת שֶׁלּוֹ יְכוֹלִים לִהְיוֹת עוֹד בְּרַע, יַעַן הֵמָּה בּוֹ מִלֵּדָה וְכָל זְמַן אֲשֶׁר הַחִיצוֹנִיּוֹת שֶׁלּוֹ הַטּוֹבִים עוֹד לֹא פָּעֲלוּ פְּעֻלָּה רַבָּה עֲלֵיהֶם לְהֵטִיבָם יִשָּׁאֲרוּ עַל תְּכוּנָתָם הָרָע. וְלִפְעָמִים יִהְיֶה בְּהֵפֶךְ אֲשֶׁר הַחִיצוֹנִיּוֹת יִהְיוּ רָעוֹת מְאֹד עַל יְדֵי חִנּוּךְ הוֹרִים וּמוֹרִים פּוֹרְעֵי מוּסָר וְעַל יְדֵי הִתְחַבְּרוּת לַאֲנָשִׁים רָעִים, אָמְנָם הַפְּנִימִיּוֹת שֶׁלּוֹ יוּכְלוּ לִהְיוֹת טוֹבִים מְאֹד מִתּוֹלַדְתּוֹ.

עַל כֵּן נִרְאֶה לִפְעָמִים אִישׁ אֲשֶׁר הָיָה יְרֵא אֱלֹקִים גָּדוֹל וְעַל יְדֵי

However, with regard to those psychological drives that some people possess and others do not – with regard to such drives, even for one in whom such drives are innate, a person who has become sublimely righteous can, through Torah and reverence, change his inner [unconscious] self, from one extreme to the other. (Perhaps this can explain the words of the Talmud in Ḥullin 5b: "The Holy One, blessed be He, does not bring about flawed behaviors at the hand of the righteous." *Tosafot* state there that this [principle] applies only to matters of food, but not to other matters. The reason for this, according to what we have suggested, is that the appetite for food is common to everybody, and when it comes to drives that are shared by all people, an individual is incapable of completely repairing his unconscious. His mistakes are likely to occur only through the unconscious, and there, only the Holy One, blessed be He, can help. Therefore, Holy One, blessed be He, ordained and set down that if a person is truly righteous, no errors stemming from the unconscious will happen to him. However, with respect to other matters, which a person has the capacity to change to perfection, a person has the duty to repair them himself, even if he is not helped by the Holy One, blessed be He. Therefore, a flawed behavior can occur even at the hand of a righteous person, as long as he has not completely fixed his unconscious.)

We ought to understand that the unconscious and conscious drives remain distinct within a person. Sometimes an individual person can have very good conscious drives but very bad unconscious drives. Sometimes, the opposite is true. This is because conscious drives are based primarily on education; if a person was raised and educated by honest parents and teachers who fear sin, and in a place whose inhabitants fear sin, then his consciousness will be shaped in the way of Mussar and righteousness. Nevertheless, his unconscious drives may still be wicked, because they were this way from his birth, and as long as his good conscious drives have not greatly affected them for the better, they will retain their evil nature. And sometimes the situation is just the opposite: His conscious drives are very bad because he was educated by immoral parents and teachers and became socially attached to wicked people. Yet his unconscious drives can be very good innately. That is why we sometimes encounter a person who was greatly God-fearing,

סִבָּה חֲזָקָה אֲשֶׁר פָּעֲלָה עָלָיו בְּנָקֵל נִתְהַפֵּךְ לְרַע, יַעַן כִּי הַפְּנִימִיּוֹת שֶׁלּוֹ הָיוּ רָעִים, וְהַסִּבָּה הַחֲזָקָה עוֹרְרָה אוֹתָם עַד כִּי עָלוּ בְּמִשְׁקָל גָּבֹהַּ עַל הַחִיצוֹנִיּוֹת הַטּוֹבִים וְהֶחֱלִיפוּ אוֹתָם מִן הַקָּצֶה אֶל הַקָּצֶה. וְכֵן לִפְעָמִים לְהֵפֶךְ יִהְיֶה הָאָדָם רַע מְאֹד בְּהַחִיצוֹנִיּוֹת, וְעַל יְדֵי סִבָּה יֵהָפֵךְ לִירֵא חֵטְא, יַעַן הַפְּנִימִיּוֹת הָיוּ טוֹבִים, לָכֵן עוֹרְרָה הַסִּבָּה אוֹתָם וְנִתְגַּבְּרוּ עַל הַחִיצוֹנִיּוֹת.

וְאֶת הַדְּבָרִים הָאֵלֶּה נוּכַל לְרַמֵּז אוּלַי בְּהַכָּתוּב (הוֹשֵׁעַ יג) כְּדַבֵּר אֶפְרַיִם רְתֵת נָשָׂא הוּא בְּיִשְׂרָאֵל וַיֶּאְשַׁם בַּבַּעַל וַיָּמֹת, וְהִנֵּה אָמְרוּ חֲזַ"ל בַּגְּמָרָא סַנְהֶדְרִין (קא, ב) מִפְּנֵי מָה זָכָה יָרָבְעָם לַמַּלְכוּת מִפְּנֵי שֶׁהוֹכִיחַ אֶת שְׁלֹמֹה, וּבַמִּדְרָשׁ שְׁמִינִי (פי"ב) אִיתָא, בְּשָׁעָה שֶׁהוֹכִיחַ אֶת שְׁלֹמֹה, אָמַר לוֹ הַקָּדוֹשׁ בָּרוּךְ הוּא לָמָּה אַתָּה מוֹכִיחוֹ נָשִׂיא הוּא בְּיִשְׂרָאֵל, חַיֶּיךָ שֶׁאֲנִי מַטְעִימְךָ מִשְּׂרָרוּתוֹ, וְאֵין אַתָּה יָכוֹל לַעֲמֹד בָּהּ. וְלִכְאוֹרָה הַמַּאֲמָר הַזֶּה סוֹתֵר דִּבְרֵי הַגְּמָרָא, שֶׁחָשַׁב אֶת תּוֹכַחְתּוֹ לִשְׁלֹמֹה לְמַעֲלָה וְלִזְכוּת, וְהַמִּדְרָשׁ חוֹשֵׁב זֹאת לְחִסָּרוֹן וּלְחוֹב.

אַךְ יְבֹאַר כִּי הַחִיצוֹנִיּוֹת שֶׁל יָרָבְעָם הָיוּ טוֹבִים וּבְמַדְרֵגָה נַעֲלָה, וְכַמְּבֹאָר בְּסַנְהֶדְרִין (קב) תּוֹרָתוֹ שֶׁל יָרָבְעָם לֹא הָיָה בָּהּ שׁוּם דֹּפִי, אֲבָל פְּנִימִיּוּתוֹ הָיָה רַע מְאֹד, וּכְדְאִיתָא בַּיַּלְקוּט (מְלָכִים א׳ יב) עַל פָּסוּק וַיֹּאמֶר יָרָבְעָם בְּלִבּוֹ, כֶּסֶף סִיגִים מְצֻפֶּה עַל חָרֶשׂ שְׂפָתַיִם דֹּלְקִים וְלֶב רָע כו׳, לְמָה הוּא דוֹמֶה, לְמֶלְיָר שֶׁמִּבַּחוּץ הָיָה שֶׁל זָהָב וּמַרְגָּלִיּוֹת קְבוּעוֹת בּוֹ, אֶלָּא מִבִּפְנִים הָיָה שֶׁל חֶרֶשׂ, כָּךְ וכו׳ וַיֹּאמֶר בְּלִבּוֹ, עַיֵּן שָׁם, וְנִרְאֶה בָּרוּר כִּי הַחִיצוֹנִיּוֹת שֶׁלּוֹ הָיוּ טוֹבִים וְהַפְּנִימִיּוֹת רָעִים, וְעַל יְדֵי הַסִּבָּה אֲשֶׁר נַעֲשָׂה מֶלֶךְ פָּעַל עַל הַפְּנִימִיּוֹת כִּי עָלוּ עַל הַחִיצוֹנִיּוֹת וְהִשְׁחִיתוּ אוֹתוֹ.

וְהִנֵּה בְּהַתּוֹכָחָה שֶׁהוֹכִיחַ יָרָבְעָם אֶת שְׁלֹמֹה הָיָה יָרָבְעָם בְּסַכָּנָה, אַף כִּי אִיתָא בַּמִּדְרָשׁ שָׁם הִכְנִיס אֶלֶף מִשִּׁבְטוֹ וְהוֹכִיחוֹ, עִם כָּל זֶה הָיָה בְּהָעִנְיָן סַכָּנוֹת נְפָשׁוֹת, אֲשֶׁר עַל פִּי דִּין מִשּׁוּם מִצְוַת תּוֹכָחָה אֵין

5. It is a mitzva to correct a sinner, but most people fear to chastise a king.
6. By committing *lèse-majesté.*

but when some powerful cause affected him, he turned evil rather easily – because his unconscious drives were evil all along. The powerful stimulus awakened them to the point where they outweighed the good conscious drives and replaced them with their diametric opposites. Sometimes the opposite is the case; a person is very wicked in terms of his conscious drives, but some stimulus will cause him to become one who fears sin, because his unconscious drives are good. The stimulus awakened them, and they overcame the conscious drives.

There is perhaps an allusion to these words in the verse "When Ephraim spoke piety, he was exalted in Israel; but he incurred guilt through Baal, and so he died" (Hos. 13:1). Now, the Sages, of blessed memory, said in the Talmud in Sanhedrin (101b): "Why did Jeroboam merit kingship? Because he chastised Solomon."[5] Yet the midrash on [*Parashat*] *Shemini* ([Leviticus Rabba] 12) says: "When [Jeroboam] chastised Solomon, the Holy One, blessed be He, said to him: 'Why are you chastising him? He is a leader in Israel! By your life, I will give you a taste of his power, and you will not be able to withstand its [temptations].'" At first glance, this teaching contradicts the words of the Talmud, which considered [Jeroboam's] rebuke of Solomon to be a virtue and a merit, whereas the midrash considers it a shortcoming and a demerit.

However, there is an explanation: Jeroboam's conscious drives were good and exceedingly refined, as explained in Sanhedrin (102a): "There was no imperfection in Jeroboam's Torah." But deep down, he was very wicked, as stated in *Yalkut* [*Shimoni*] (I Kings 12[:26, 198]): "'Jeroboam said [...in] his heart' – 'Burning lips and a wicked heart are like an earthenware dish covered with silver dross' [Prov. 26:23]. This can be compared to a vessel that was gold on the outside, with precious stones embedded in it, but was earthenware on the inside. Thus was... 'Jeroboam said in his heart.'" See further there. It seems clear that his conscious drives were good and his unconscious drives were wicked. Being made king was the cause that affected his unconscious, which overcame his conscious drives and corrupted him. Now, when Jeroboam chastised Solomon, he endangered himself.[6] Even though it says in the midrash there [Leviticus Rabba 12] that he brought along a thousand people of his tribe and chastised [Solomon], he was still risking his life. According to halakha, one should not give one's life to fulfill the

לִמְסֹר נַפְשׁוֹ עֲבוּרָהּ אָמְנָם לִפְעָמִים יַעֲשֶׂה חָסִיד מִפְעָל כָּזֶה, מִקִּנְאַת חֲסִידוּתוֹ וּבְהִתְפַּעֲלוּת הַנֶּפֶשׁ, כַּאֲשֶׁר יִרְאֶה מַעֲשִׂים לַמְרוֹת רְצוֹן קוֹנוֹ תִּתְלַהֵב נַפְשׁוֹ, לִמְחוֹת בְּעוֹבְרֵי עֲבֵרָה וְיִשְׁכַּח הַסַּכָּנָה אֲשֶׁר לְנֶגֶד עֵינָיו עַל יְדֵי זֶה, אַךְ הִתְפַּעֲלוּת כָּזֶה לֹא תּוּכַל לָבֹא בְּאִישׁ אֲשֶׁר יֵדַע בְּנַפְשׁוֹ כִּי גַּם הוּא אֵינֶנּוּ צַדִּיק וְתוֹכַחְתּוֹ יִהְיֶה עָלָיו, עָוֹן אֲשֶׁר גַּם הוּא אֵינֶנּוּ נָקִי, וְאֵיךְ יָכוֹל לְהוֹכִיחַ אֶת חֲבֵרוֹ, וְלָכֵן כַּאֲשֶׁר יָרָבְעָם לֹא הָיָה טוֹב בִּפְנִימִיּוּתוֹ כְּמוֹ שֶׁאָמַרְנוּ לְעֵיל, לָכֵן יַחֲשֹׁב הַמִּדְרָשׁ לוֹ לְחוֹב עַל אֲשֶׁר הוֹכִיחוֹ אַף כִּי בְּעֶצֶם הַתּוֹכָחָה הָיָה זְכוּת.

וְהַמַּאֲמָרִים אֵינָם סוֹתְרִים, כִּי מִדָּתוֹ שֶׁל הַקָּדוֹשׁ בָּרוּךְ הוּא שֶׁבְּמָקוֹם שֶׁדָּנִין אֶת הָאָדָם שָׁם מַזְכִּירִין גַּם צִדְקוֹתָיו כַּמְבֹאָר בִּיבָמוֹת (עח, ב) קָא תָּבַע אֶל שָׁאוּל שֶׁלֹּא נִסְפַּד כַּהֲלָכָה וְקָא תָּבַע עַל אֲשֶׁר הֵמִית הַגִּבְעוֹנִים, אִין דְּאָמַר רֵישׁ לָקִישׁ מַאי דִּכְתִיב כוּ׳ אֲשֶׁר מִשְׁפָּטוֹ פָּעֳלוֹ כַּאֲשֶׁר מִשְׁפָּטוֹ שָׁם פָּעֳלוֹ, וּפֵרֵשׁ רַשִׁ״י בְּמָקוֹם שֶׁדָּנִים הָאָדָם שָׁם מַזְכִּירִין פֹּעַל צִדְקוֹתָיו עַיֵּן שָׁם. וּלְפִי זֶה אִם יַעֲשֶׂה אָדָם דָּבָר אֶחָד, אֲשֶׁר עַל יְדֵי הַחִיצוֹנִיּוּת הוּא טוֹב וְעַל יְדֵי הַפְּנִימִיּוּת אֵינֶנּוּ טוֹב, מַעֲנִישִׁים עַל הָרַע הַנִּמְצָא בָּזֶה, וְנוֹתְנִים שָׂכָר עַל הַטּוֹב. וְכַאֲשֶׁר בְּיָרָבְעָם נִמְצְאוּ שְׁתֵּי אֵלֶּה כְּמוֹ שֶׁבֵּאַרְנוּ, לָכֵן עַל יְדֵי זְכוּת הַתּוֹכָחָה שֶׁבָּאָה מִן הַחִיצוֹנִיּוּת זָכָה לַמַּלְכוּת, וִיבֹאַר זֹאת בַּמִּקְרָא כְּדַבֵּר אֶפְרַיִם רְתֵת, שֶׁהוּא הַתּוֹכָחָה לִשְׁלֹמֹה (כַּמְבֹאָר בַּמִּדְרָשׁ שָׁם) זָכָה בָּזֶה ״כִּי נָשָׂא הוּא בְּיִשְׂרָאֵל״ וְזָכָה לִמְלוּכָה, אֲבָל יַעַן הָיָה אֶצְלוֹ כָּל כָּךְ הִתְפַּעֲלוּת הַנֶּפֶשׁ, עַד אֲשֶׁר לֹא הִבִּיט אֶל פְּנִימִיּוּתוֹ, אֵיךְ גַּם הוּא אֵינֶנּוּ נָקִי, וְגַם לֹא רָאָה לְתַקֵּן אֶת הַפְּנִימִיּוּת שֶׁלּוֹ לְטוֹב, גָּרְמָה לוֹ

---

7. There was a drought in Israel as punishment for sin. King David consulted the *Urim VeTumim* to learn the cause of the drought, and it indicated: "It is for Saul, and for the bloody house, because he put to death the Gibeonites" (I Sam. 21:1). The Talmud (Yevamot 78b) explains that this refers to two matters: "'For Saul' – because he was not eulogized properly; 'and for the bloody house, because he put to death the Gibeonites.'"

8. There is no explicit mention of Saul killing Gibeonites. The Talmud, earlier in this passage, explains that by killing the priests of Nob, who sheltered David during his flight from Saul, he destroyed the Gibeonites' source of livelihood and was thus responsible for their deaths as well. Furthermore, there were seven Gibeonites among those killed in Nob.

mitzva of chastisement. But sometimes a pious person will undertake such action out of zealous piety and an agitated spirit. When he sees actions that violate the will of his Creator, his soul becomes inflamed to protest against sinners, and so he forgets the danger it places him in. Yet such agitation cannot enter a person who knows deep down that he is not righteous either and that his chastisement will be about a sin from which he is not free – for how can he chastise his fellow? Therefore, since Jeroboam was unconsciously wicked, as we said above, the midrash considers his chastisement of Solomon a discredit, even though, in essence, the chastisement was a meritorious act. The two accounts do not contradict each other, for the quality of the Holy One, blessed be He, is that when a person is judged, his righteous deeds are mentioned as well, as explained in Yevamot (78b):[7]

> [God] demands [retribution] "for Saul" because he was not eulogized properly and He demands [retribution] "because he put to death the Gibeonites"?[8] [I.e., Israel was punished for Saul's deeds and also because of their failure to honor him properly?] Yes. As Resh Lakish said: What is the meaning of the verse (Zeph. 2:3): "Seek the Lord all you humble of the earth, who have performed [*paalu*] His judgment [*mishpato*]"? Where there is judgment, [i.e., where a person stands trial,] the deeds he performed (*paalo*) are [mentioned].

Rashi explains: "When a person is judged, they mention the charitable deeds that he performed." See further there. Accordingly, if someone does a single deed that is outwardly good but inwardly not good, the wickedness therein is punished, while the good therein is rewarded. Since both of these are found in Jeroboam, as we explained, by virtue of his chastisement that stemmed from conscious motives he merited kingship. This is illuminated by the verse "When Ephraim spoke piety" – this refers (as explained in the midrash [Leviticus Rabba 12]) to his chastisement of Solomon – he merited that "he was exalted in Israel" and earned the kingship. But since he was so agitated that he did not scrutinize his unconscious [and understand] that he, too, was not innocent, and he, too, did not seek to improve his unconscious, his elevation to leadership

הַסִּבָּה מֵהַנְּשִׂיאוּת שֶׁלּוֹ לְעוֹרֵר אֶת רֹעַ הַפְּנִימִיּוֹת לַעֲלוֹת וּלְהִתְגַּבֵּר עַל הַחִיצוֹנִיּוֹת לְהָפְכָם לְרַע, עַד כִּי בָּא לִידֵי "וַיֶּאְשַׁם בַּבַּעַל" וגו'.

וּנְבָאֵר עוֹד דִּבְרֵי הַגְּמָרָא בְּסֻכָּה (נב, א), צַדִּיקִים נִדְמֶה לָהֶם כְּהַר גָּבֹהַּ וּרְשָׁעִים נִדְמֶה לָהֶם כְּחוּט הַשַּׂעֲרָה כו'. צַדִּיקִים בּוֹכִים וְאוֹמְרִים הָאֵיךְ יָכֹלְנוּ לִכְבֹּשׁ הַר גָּבֹהַּ כָּזֶה, וּרְשָׁעִים בּוֹכִים וְאוֹמְרִים הָאֵיךְ לֹא יָכֹלְנוּ לִכְבֹּשׁ אֶת חוּט הַשַּׂעֲרָה הַזֶּה. וּלְהָבִין דִּבְרֵיהֶם נַקְדִּים מַה שֶּׁכָּתוּב (שָׁם) כָּל הַגָּדוֹל מֵחֲבֵרוֹ יִצְרוֹ גָּדוֹל מִמֶּנּוּ, וְלִכְאוֹרָה אָנוּ רוֹאִים כִּי מִי שֶׁהוּא יְרֵא אֱלֹקִים וְצַדִּיק חֶפְצוֹ תָּמִיד לְהִצְטַדֵּק יוֹתֵר, וְאִם כֵּן אֵפוֹא הֲלֹא הַיֵּצֶר הָרַע קָטָן אֶצְלוֹ.

אָמְנָם יִתְבָּאֵר כִּי בְּאָדָם אֲשֶׁר אֵינֶנּוּ יָרֵא יִרְאֶה הַיֵּצֶר רֵאשִׁית לוֹ לְהִתְדַּבֵּק אֶל הַחִיצוֹנִיּוֹת לְקַלְקְלָם וּמִן הַפְּנִימִיּוֹת יַנִּיחַ יָדוֹ, וּכְמוֹ שֶׁכָּתוּב בְּמִדְרָשׁ הָרְשָׁעִים מְלֵאִים חֲרָטוֹת, וְסִבַּת הַדָּבָר, יַעַן כִּי הַחִיצוֹנִיּוֹת לֹא יִתְגַּבְּרוּ וְיִמְשְׁלוּ עַל הָאָדָם רַק בְּעֵת אֲשֶׁר הַתַּאֲוָה לְנֶגֶד עֵינָיו כְּמַאֲמָרָם "הָעַיִן רוֹאָה וְהַלֵּב חוֹמֵד", וְלָכֵן כַּאֲשֶׁר תַּעֲבֹר הַתַּאֲוָה מִנֶּגֶד עֵינָיו וְהַחִיצוֹנִיּוֹת יִתְקָרְרוּ, אָז יִתְעוֹרְרוּ הַפְּנִימִיּוֹת אֲשֶׁר לֹא נִשְׁחֲתוּ עֲדֶנָה, וִיבִיאוּהוּ לִידֵי חֲרָטָה עַד כִּי יִרְצֶה לַעֲזֹב מַעֲשֵׂה הַחִיצוֹנִיּוֹת. אֲבָל בָּאִישׁ הַיָּרֵא, הַחִיצוֹנִיּוֹת הֵמָּה טוֹבִים מְאֹד, לָכֵן יִרְאֶה הַיֵּצֶר רֵאשִׁית לוֹ אַךְ לִפְעֹל פְּעֻלָּתוֹ עַל הַפְּנִימִיּוֹת, וְכָל מַה שֶּׁהוּא צַדִּיק יוֹתֵר יַחֲדֹר עָמֹק בִּפְנִימִיּוּתוֹ לְמַעַן אֲשֶׁר לֹא יַרְגִּישׁ בּוֹ וּבִפְעֻלּוֹתָיו אֲשֶׁר יִפְעַל עָלָיו לְרָע. אַךְ הָאִישׁ הַיָּרֵא בְּתַכְלִית הַשְּׁלֵמוּת, יִתְעַמֵּל וְיִתְאַמֵּץ עַל יְדֵי הַחִיצוֹנִיּוֹת הַטּוֹבִים שֶׁלּוֹ וּבְיוֹתֵר בְּעֶצֶם וְרִאשׁוֹנָה עַל יְדֵי סְגֻלַּת הַתּוֹרָה לַהֲפֹךְ מִשֹּׁרֶשׁ אֶת יֵצֶר הָרָע הַשּׁוֹכֵן בִּפְנִימִיּוּתוֹ, וּלְתַקֵּן אֶת הַפְּנִימִיּוֹת, אָמְנָם כָּבֵד יוֹתֵר עַל הָאָדָם, וְזֶה הַכַּוָּנָה אֲשֶׁר לְהָרָשָׁע

9. Based on Deuteronomy 33:21.
10. This saying is common in rabbinic ethical treatises, but its evident source (as indicated by Abarbanel in his commentary on Gen. 23 and I Sam. 13) is Aristotle's *Nicomachean Ethics* 9.4.10.
11. Numbers Rabba 10:2 (cited in Rashi on Num. 15:39).

became the catalyst that aroused his inner wickedness to surge and overcome his conscious drives, turning them wicked. And so, ultimately, "he incurred guilt through Baal…."

Let us further explain the words of the Gemara in Sukka (52a):

> To the righteous [the sight of the slain evil urge] will appear as a huge mountain; to the wicked, it will appear as a strand of hair…. The righteous will weep and say: "How were we able to overcome such a high mountain?" The wicked will weep and say: "How is it that we could not overcome something the size of a strand of hair?"

To understand their words, let us first understand their statement (ibid.): "One who is greater than his friend has a greater evil urge than him." At first glance, we see that one who fears God and is righteous wants to become more righteous constantly. This being the case, isn't the evil urge within him small? This is explained as follows: Within a person who has no fear of God, the urge will see fit to begin[9] by attaching to the conscious drives, to corrupt them, and will leave the unconscious aside. This is as they say in the midrash, "The wicked are full of regrets."[10] The reason for this is that the conscious drives do not overwhelm and govern a person unless the object of their desire is before him, as [the Sages] say: "The eye sees and the heart desires."[11] So when the object of desire passes from before his eyes and the conscious drives are cooled off, the unconscious drives, which have not yet been corrupted, will be awakened and bring him to regret – to the point that he wishes to abandon the actions of the conscious drives. However, in a [God-]fearing person, the conscious drives are very good. Therefore, the urge will see fit to begin working only on the unconscious drives. The more righteous he is, the deeper it will dig into his unconscious, so that he does not sense it or the actions it takes to turn him to evil. But the person who has fear of God in complete fashion will work hard and will train himself with his good conscious drives, and first and foremost with the special power of the Torah tear up, by the roots, the evil urge that dwells in his unconscious, to repair the unconscious. However, this is much harder for a person. This is the intent of [the statement] that to the wicked, the

נִדְמֶה הַיֵּצֶר כְּחוּט הַשַּׂעֲרָה, יַעַן כִּי פְּנִימִיּוּתוֹ לֹא הָיְתָה נִשְׁחֲתָה כָּל כָּךְ, וְעַל יְדֵי חֶשְׁבּוֹן מוּעָט וְעַל יְדֵי לִמּוּד הַתּוֹרָה וְהַמּוּסָרִי הָיָה יָכוֹל לְעוֹרֵר וּלְגַבֵּר אֶת הַפְּנִימִיּוּת אֲשֶׁר יַעֲלוּ עַל הַחִיצוֹנִיּוּת וְיַהַפְכוּ גַּם אוֹתָם לְטוֹב, אֲבָל לְהַצַּדִּיק אֲשֶׁר פְּנִימִיּוּתוֹ הַשְׁחִית הַיֵּצֶר וְאַךְ הוּא בִּפְעֻלָּתוֹ הַגְּדוֹלָה עַל יְדֵי הַחִיצוֹנִיּוּת הַטּוֹבִים עָלְתָה בְּיָדוֹ לְהַגְבִּיר עַל הַפְּנִימִיּוּת וּלְתַקְּנָם, לָכֵן נִדְמֶה לוֹ כְּהַר גָּבֹהַּ, וְהָבֵן.

וְהִנֵּה מִמּוֹצָא כָּל הַדְּבָרִים הָאֲמוּרִים לְעֵיל, יוֹצֵא לָנוּ לָדַעַת אַחֲרֵי אֲשֶׁר בָּאָדָם יוּכַל לְהִמָּצֵא דָּבָר אֲשֶׁר בְּהַחִיצוֹנִיּוּת יִהְיֶה טוֹב מְאֹד, אֲבָל פְּנִימִיּוּת יִהְיוּ נִשְׁחָתִים, וְעַל יְדֵי הִתְעוֹרְרוּת מְעַט אוֹ הִשְׁתַּנּוּת שׁוֹנוֹת (פארשידענע אומשטענדין) יוּכְלוּ הַפְּנִימִיּוּת לְהִתְעוֹרֵר עַד אֲשֶׁר יַגְבִּירוּ לְשַׁנּוֹת הַחִיצוֹנִיּוּת [וְלָכֵן מְחוּבַת הָאָדָם אִם יַחְפֹּץ לַעֲשׂוֹת דָּבָר בְּתַכְלִית הַשְּׁלֵמוּת, אִם יִרְאֶה מֵרֹאשׁ אֲשֶׁר יוּכַל לָבוֹא אַךְ לִידֵי מְנִיעָה קַלָּה, יִפְחַד וְיַעֲשֶׂה תַּחְבּוּלוֹת לְהִלָּחֵם עִם יִצְרוֹ, אַחֲרֵי אֲשֶׁר לֹא יוּכַל לָדַעַת כָּל הַדְּבָרִים הַקְּטַנִּים אֲשֶׁר יוּכְלוּ לִפְעֹל לְרָעָה בְּהַפְּנִימִיּוּת], וְהָאָדָם יֵשׁ לוֹ יְדִיעָה אַךְ בְּהַחִיצוֹנִיּוּת וְלֹא בַּפְּנִימִיּוּת, וְעִקַּר הַכְּבֵדוֹת וְהַקַּלּוֹת בָּאָדָם תְּלוּיוֹת רַק בִּפְנִימִיּוּתָיו.

וּלְפִי זֶה יוּכַל לִהְיוֹת אִם יַעֲשֶׂה הָאָדָם שְׁתֵּי מִצְוֹת, הָאַחַת הָיְתָה כְּבֵדָה בְּהַחִיצוֹנִיּוּת וְהַשְּׁנִיָּה אַף כִּי קַלָּה הָיְתָה בְּהַחִיצוֹנִיּוּת אֲבָל בַּפְּנִימִיּוּת אֲשֶׁר לֹא יַרְגִּישׁ בָּהּ הָאָדָם הָיְתָה כְּבֵדָה מְאֹד. וְהִנֵּה לְפִי הַשְׁקָפָה תִּהְיֶה הַמִּצְוָה הַכְּבֵדָה בְּהַחִיצוֹנִיּוּת גְּדוֹלָה מֵהַשְּׁנִיָּה (הַכְּבֵדָה בַּפְּנִימִיּוּת), אֲבָל הַקָּדוֹשׁ בָּרוּךְ הוּא יַחְשֹׁב לִפְעָמִים אֶת הַשְּׁנִיָּה גְּדוֹלָה, יַעַן הוּא יוֹדֵעַ אֶת הַפְּנִימִיּוּת כַּנִּזְכָּר לְעֵיל. וּכְמוֹ כֵן בַּעֲבֵרוֹת אִם יַעֲשֶׂה הָאָדָם שְׁתֵּי עֲבֵרוֹת הָאַחַת לְפִי הַחִיצוֹנִיּוּת הָיְתָה כְּבֵדָה אֲבָל לְפִי הַפְּנִימִיּוּת הָיְתָה קַלָּה וְהַשְּׁנִיָּה לְהֵפֶךְ לְפִי הַפְּנִימִיּוּת הָיְתָה כְּבֵדָה וּלְפִי הַחִיצוֹנִיּוּת הָיְתָה קַלָּה, וּמַה שֶּׁהָעֲבֵרָה כְּבֵדָה לְהִשָּׁמֵר מִמֶּנָּה נֶחְשֶׁבֶת לִפְנֵי הַקָּדוֹשׁ בָּרוּךְ הוּא לַעֲבֵרָה קַלָּה וּמַה שֶּׁהִיא קַלָּה לְהִשָּׁמֵר מִמֶּנָּה נֶחְשֶׁבֶת לַחֲמוּרָה, וְלָכֵן כַּאֲשֶׁר יַחְשֹׁב ה׳ אֶת הַמִּצְוָה כְּפִי

evil urge appears to be like a strand of hair – because his unconscious was not so corrupted, with a little introspection and study of Torah and Mussar, he could have aroused and strengthened his unconscious to master his conscious and turn it to the good. But for the righteous person, whose unconscious was corrupted by the evil urge, only by great effort, through his good conscious drives, could he manage to overcome his unconscious and repair it. Therefore it appears to him as like a big mountain. Understand.

Now, the upshot of all the things said above is that we now know that since there can be something very good in a person at the conscious level but his unconscious drives are corrupted, by a minor stimulus or variation in circumstances, the unconscious can be aroused to the point of strengthening itself and changing the conscious drives. (Therefore, a person has the duty, if he wants to do something at the highest standard of perfection, that if he sees at the beginning that he can come to a minor obstacle, he should fear this outcome and develop strategies to fight his urge – since he cannot know all the little factors that can work for evil in his unconscious.)

Now, a person has knowledge of his conscious drives, but not the unconscious. Yet the weightiness (difficulty) and lightness (ease) of someone [doing a mitzva or sin] hinges, in the main, only on his unconscious drives. Accordingly, it is possible that a person does two mitzvot, one was difficult at the conscious level but the second, though easy to do at the conscious level, was very difficult at the unconscious level, which a person does not sense. At first glance, the mitzva that was difficult at the conscious level is greater than the second (which was more difficult at the unconscious level). But the Holy One, blessed be He, sometimes will judge the second to be greater, for only He knows the unconscious, as mentioned before.

It is the same with sins. If a person does two sins, one that is more difficult at the conscious level but easier at the unconscious level, and the second that is the opposite; at the unconscious level it is more difficult, but at the conscious level is easier. The harder sin to abstain from is considered by the Holy One, blessed be He, to be a lesser violation, and the easier sin to abstain from is considered to be a graver violation. Just as God assesses the mitzva by its difficulty and ease of performance, so

כְּבֵדוּתָהּ וְקַלּוּתָהּ, כְּמוֹ כֵן יַחְשֹׁב אֶת הָעֲבֵרָה הַכְּבֵדָה לְהִשָּׁמֵר מִמֶּנָּה מִצַּד הַפְּנִימִיּוּת לְקַלָּה וכו׳.

וְהִנֵּה שִׁקּוּל הַמִּצְוֹת וְהָעֲבֵרוֹת, כְּבָר כָּתַב הָרַמְבַּ״ם בְּהִלְכוֹת תְּשׁוּבָה (פ״ג הל״ב), וְזֶה לְשׁוֹנוֹ, וְשִׁקּוּל זֶה אֵינוֹ לְפִי מִנְיַן הַזְּכִיּוֹת וְהָעֲוֹנוֹת אֶלָּא לְפִי גָּדְלָן, יֵשׁ זְכוּת שֶׁהוּא כְּנֶגֶד כַּמָּה עֲוֹנוֹת וכו׳ וְיֵשׁ עָוֹן שֶׁהוּא כְּנֶגֶד כַּמָּה זְכִיּוֹת וכו׳ וְאֵין שׁוֹקְלִין אֶלָּא בְּדַעְתּוֹ שֶׁל (הַקָּדוֹשׁ בָּרוּךְ הוּא) אֵל דֵּעוֹת. וְהוּא הַיּוֹדֵעַ אֵיךְ עוֹרְכִין הַזְּכִיּוֹת כְּנֶגֶד הָעֲוֹנוֹת, עַיֵּן שָׁם. וְהִנֵּה הַשִּׁקּוּל הַזֶּה מוּבָן כִּי תָּלוּי לְפִי כֹּבֶד שְׁמִירַת הַתּוֹרָה וְהַמִּצְוֹת, וּלְפִי כֹּבֶד זְהִירַת עֲשִׂיַּת הָעֲבֵרָה כְּמַאֲמַר הַמִּשְׁנָה (אָבוֹת ספ״ה) לְפוּם צַעֲרָא אַגְרָא, וּבַעֲבֵרָה הוּא לְהֵפֶךְ כִּי כָּל מַה שֶּׁהִיא כְּבֵדָה לְהִשָּׁמֵר מִמֶּנָּה [אִם אָמְנָם אַף לְפִי הָאֹפֶן הַיּוֹתֵר כָּבֵד, עִם כָּל זֶה נֶחְשֶׁבֶת לַעֲבֵרָה וִיקַבֵּל עָנְשׁוֹ], לְעֻמַּת הָעֲבֵרָה הַקַּלָּה לְהִשָּׁמֵר מִמֶּנָּה נֶחְשֶׁבֶת עֲבֵרָה קַלָּה (פִיעל גרינגער) וּכְמַאֲמַר חֲזַ״ל מְנָחוֹת (מב) גָּדוֹל עָנְשׁוֹ שֶׁל לָבָן יוֹתֵר מֵעָנְשׁוֹ שֶׁל תְּכֵלֶת, מָשָׁל לְמֶלֶךְ בָּשָׂר וָדָם שֶׁאָמַר לִשְׁנֵי עֲבָדָיו, לְאֶחָד אָמַר הָבֵא לִי חוֹתָם שֶׁל טִיט, וּלְאֶחָד אָמַר הָבֵא לִי חוֹתָם שֶׁל זָהָב וּפָשְׁעוּ שְׁנֵיהֶם וְלֹא הֵבִיאוּ. אֵיזֶה מֵהֶם עָנְשׁוֹ מְרֻבֶּה, הֱוֵי אוֹמֵר זֶה שֶׁאָמַר לוֹ הָבֵא לִי חוֹתָם שֶׁל טִיט וְלֹא הֵבִיא, עַד כָּאן.

וְהִנֵּה לְפִי מִשְׁפְּטֵי ה׳ הַצַּדִּיקִים, לִפְעָמִים אַף כִּי יִהְיֶה צִדְקַת הַצַּדִּיק רַבָּה אַךְ יֵשׁ לוֹ מְעַט עֲוֹנוֹת, יַעֲנִישׁ לוֹ הַקָּדוֹשׁ בָּרוּךְ הוּא בָּעוֹלָם הַזֶּה, אוֹ לְהֵפֶךְ כַּאֲשֶׁר יִהְיֶה רִשְׁעַת הָאָדָם רַבָּה, אַךְ יֵשׁ לוֹ

12. Avot 5:23.

13. This passage is discussed in Letters 7 and 8 as well. See further there.

He considers the sin that is harder to abstain from at the unconscious level to be a lesser violation, etc.

When it comes to the weighing of mitzvot and sins, Rambam wrote in the Laws of Repentance (3:2):

> This weighing is not [simply] by the quantity of merits and sins, but according to their magnitude. One merit can outweigh several sins ... and there are sins that outweigh several merits .... The weighing is only according to the judgment of the God of Understanding, who knows how to assess merits against sins.

See further there.

It is understood that this weighing hinges on the difficulty of observing the Torah and mitzvot and on the difficulty of abstention from committing the sin, as said in the Mishna: "According to the pain [of the effort] is the reward."[12] With regard to sins, the opposite is true. The more difficult it is to abstain (let it be clear that even the most difficult sin to avoid is still considered a transgression, for which he will receive his due punishment), in contrast to a sin that is easier to resist, it is considered a lesser transgression. This is as the Sages, of blessed memory, said in Menaḥot (43b):

> Greater is the punishment for [not wearing] the white [*tzizit*] string than the punishment for [not wearing] the sky-blue [string]. A parable: To what is this comparable? To a flesh-and-blood king who instructs two servants. To one he said: "Bring me a clay seal"; to the other he said: "Bring me a gold seal." Both transgressed and brought nothing. Which one's punishment will be greater? You can be sure that the one to whom he said, "Bring me a clay seal," and who did not bring it.[13]

See further there.

Now, according to God's righteous judgments, sometimes, even if the righteousness of the righteous person is great, if he has a few sins, the Holy One, blessed be He, will punish him in this world. Conversely,

מְעַט תּוֹרָה וּמִצְוֹת, יִקַּח חֶלְקוֹ בָּעוֹלָם הַזֶּה כְּדֵי לְקַבֵּל שְׂכָרוֹ, וּכְמוֹ שֶׁאָמְרוּ חֲזַ"ל בְּקִדּוּשִׁין (מ, ב), לָמָּה צַדִּיקִים נִמְשָׁלִים בָּעוֹלָם הַזֶּה - לְאִילָן שֶׁכֻּלּוֹ עוֹמֵד בִּמְקוֹם טָהֳרָה וְנוֹפוֹ נוֹטֶה לִמְקוֹם טֻמְאָה, נִקְצַץ נוֹפוֹ כֻּלּוֹ עוֹמֵד בִּמְקוֹם טָהֳרָה. כָּךְ הַקָּדוֹשׁ בָּרוּךְ הוּא מֵבִיא יִסּוּרִים עַל הַצַּדִּיקִים בָּעוֹלָם הַזֶּה כְּדֵי שֶׁיִּרְשׁוּ הָעוֹלָם הַבָּא וְכוּ'. וּלְמָה רְשָׁעִים דּוֹמִים בָּעוֹלָם הַזֶּה - לְאִילָן שֶׁכֻּלּוֹ עוֹמֵד בִּמְקוֹם טֻמְאָה וְנוֹפוֹ נוֹטֶה לִמְקוֹם טָהֳרָה נִקְצַץ נוֹפוֹ כֻּלּוֹ עוֹמֵד בִּמְקוֹם טֻמְאָה. כָּךְ הַקָּדוֹשׁ בָּרוּךְ הוּא מַשְׁפִּיעַ לָהֶם טוֹבָה לָרְשָׁעִים בָּעוֹלָם הַזֶּה כְּדֵי לְטָרְדָן וּלְהוֹרִידָן לַמַּדְרֵגָה הַתַּחְתּוֹנָה. וְהִנֵּה כַּאֲשֶׁר הִגִּידוּ חֲזַ"ל (סוֹטָה ח, ב) כִּי הַקָּדוֹשׁ בָּרוּךְ הוּא מְשַׁלֵּם מִדָּה כְּנֶגֶד מִדָּה, נִמְצָא עַל פִּי דֶּרֶךְ זֶה אִם אָדָם אַחַר עָשָׂה מִצְוָה הַנֶּחֱשֶׁבֶת לִפְנֵי הַקָּדוֹשׁ בָּרוּךְ הוּא לְרֹבוֹ זְכֻיּוֹת, וְיֵשׁ בְּהַדָּבָר הַזֶּה מִעוּט עֲוֹנוֹת, אָז יְיַסֵּר אוֹתוֹ הַקָּדוֹשׁ בָּרוּךְ הוּא מִדָּה כְּנֶגֶד מִדָּה. וְאִם עָשָׂה עֲבֵרָה אֲשֶׁר נֶעֶרְכֶת לִפְנֵי הַקָּדוֹשׁ בָּרוּךְ הוּא לְרֻבָּהּ עֲוֹנוֹת וּבְהַדָּבָר הַזֶּה יֵשׁ לוֹ מִעוּט זְכֻיּוֹת, יִתֵּן לוֹ שְׂכָרוֹ בָּעוֹלָם הַזֶּה מִדָּה כְּנֶגֶד מִדָּה. וְיוּבַן עַל פִּי זֶה לָמָּה יוּטַב לָאָדָם בְּדָבָר אֶחָד וְיֵרַע לוֹ בְּדָבָר אֶחָד. וְיָכוֹל לִהְיוֹת שֶׁזֶּהוּ כַּוָּנַת רַשִׁ"י (בְּרָכוֹת ה, א) אִם רוֹאֶה אָדָם שֶׁיִּסּוּרִים בָּאִים עָלָיו יְפַשְׁפֵּשׁ בְּמַעֲשָׂיו, פִּשְׁפֵּשׁ וְלֹא מָצָא יִתְלֶה בְּבִטּוּל תּוֹרָה וְכוּ'. וּפֵרֵשׁ רַשִׁ"י זַ"ל, פִּשְׁפֵּשׁ וְלֹא מָצָא עֲבֵרָה בְּיָדוֹ שֶׁבִּשְׁבִילָהּ רְאוּיִן יִסּוּרִים הַלָּלוּ לָבוֹא עָלָיו, הַיְנוּ שֶׁלֹּא מָצָא עֲבֵרָה בְּיָדוֹ שֶׁיִּהְיוּ הַיִּסּוּרִים מִדָּה כְּנֶגֶד מִדָּה (עַיֵּן נֶפֶשׁ הַחַיִּים שַׁעַר ד' פכ"ט).

אַךְ לְהָאָדָם יִכְבַּד עָלָיו לֵדְעָה הַנְהָגַת הַקָּדוֹשׁ בָּרוּךְ הוּא מִדָּה כְּנֶגֶד

when a person's wickedness is great but he has a little Torah and mitzvot, he will obtain his share of reward in this world. This is as the Sages, of blessed memory, said in Kiddushin (40b):

> Why are the righteous compared in this world to a tree standing entirely in a place of purity while its foliage extends over a place of impurity? For if its foliage is cut, it stands entirely in the place of purity. Likewise, the Holy One, blessed be He, brings suffering on the righteous in this world, so they will inherit the next world.... And why are the wicked compared in this world to a tree standing entirely in a place of impurity while its foliage extends over a place of purity? For if its foliage is cut, it stands entirely in the place of impurity. Likewise, the Holy One, blessed be He, showers goodness on the wicked in this world, in order to burden them and bring them down to the lowest level [of the next world].

Now, as the Sages, of blessed memory, have told us (Sota 8b), God metes out reward and punishment *quid pro quo*. Accordingly, we find that if a person did a mitzva that the Holy One, blessed be He, deems to be primarily meritorious, but the matter also contains a minority component of transgression, then God will inflict suffering, *quid pro quo*. And if he commits a sin that the Holy One, blessed be He, deems to be primarily transgressive but with a meritorious minority component, God will give him his reward in this world, *quid pro quo*. With this we can understand how just one matter can determine that things will be good for a person, and one matter can determine that a person will experience misfortune.

Perhaps this is Rashi's intent [in his comments on the following passage from the Talmud]: "If a person sees that suffering is being visited upon him, he should search through his actions. If he searched and did not find [the sin that caused his suffering], he should attribute it to neglect of Torah [study]...." (Berakhot 5a). Rashi, of blessed memory, explains: "'If he searched and did not find' – a sin for which this suffering is *quid pro quo*." (See *Nefesh HaḤayim* 4:29.) But it is difficult for a person to know God's administration [of the world in accordance with the principle of] *quid pro quo*, especially in light of our words that [reward

מִדָּה, וּבְיוֹתֵר לְפִי דְּבָרֵינוּ שֶׁתָּלוּי לְפִי הַכְּבֵדוּת אֲשֶׁר אֵין בְּיַד הָאָדָם לֵידַע עַל בֻּרְיוֹ וּכְמוֹ שֶׁכָּתַבְנוּ לְעֵיל.

וְנַשְׂכִּיל לְהִתְבּוֹנֵן לַאֲשֶׁר יָדוּעַ כִּי ה׳ יָסַד הַכֹּל שֶׁתִּתְנַהֵג עַל פִּי חֻקֵּי הַטֶּבַע שֶׁחָקַק הַשֵּׁם יִתְבָּרַךְ, וְחַיֵּי הָאָדָם וּמוֹתוֹ, בְּרִיאוּתוֹ וְחָלְיוֹ, עָשְׁרוֹ וְעָנְיוֹ, וְכֵן שְׁאָרֵי הַדְּבָרִים אֲשֶׁר לוֹ הַכֹּל עַל פִּי מַהֲלָךְ הַטִּבְעִי וְלִפְעָמִים נִסְתָּרָה דַּרְכֵי הַטֶּבַע אֲשֶׁר אֵין בְּכֹחַ חָכְמַת חֲכָמִים וּבִינַת נְבוֹנִים לַהֲכִינָם מֵרֹאשׁ כְּמוֹ כִּי יָמוּת הָאָדָם הַבָּרִיא פִּתְאֹם אֲשֶׁר נֶעֶלְמָה הַסִּבָּה עַל פִּי הַטֶּבַע אַף מִגְּדוֹלֵי הָרוֹפְאִים וְכֵן לְהֶפֶךְ, וְגַם זֶה הוּא יָכוֹל לִהְיוֹת עַל פִּי מַהֲלָךְ טִבְעִי נִסְתָּר וְלֹא עַל פִּי נִסִּי, כִּי אָמְנָם נֵס נִגְלֶה יָכוֹל לִהְיוֹת אַךְ אֵצֶל צַדִּיק מְצֻיָּן מְצִיָּן בְּעֵת וּבְדוֹר צַדִּיק (אִין אַיין פרומט צייט) אֲשֶׁר הַנִּסִּים הָיוּ מְצוּיִים אוֹ אֵצֶל רָשָׁע מְצֻיָּן בְּעֵת הַנְהוּגָה בְּנִסִּים (ע׳ רַמְבַּ״ן), וְכֵן נִרְאֶה גַּם כֵּן אֲשֶׁר הֶעָנִי יִהְיֶה עָשִׁיר עַל פִּי סִבּוֹת וְעִנְיָנִים אֲשֶׁר אֵין בְּיַד הָאָדָם לְחָשְׁבָם מֵרֹאשׁ, וְכֵן יִהְיֶה הֶעָשִׁיר לְעָנִי עַל פִּי סִבּוֹת בִּלְתִּי מְרֻגָּלוֹת, וְגַם זֶה מַהֲלָךְ הַטִּבְעִי. אַךְ מַהֲלָךְ הַטִּבְעִי הַבִּלְתִּי מְרֻגָּל אֵינוֹ מָצוּי כָּל כָּךְ, עַל כֵּן מֻכְרָח הָאָדָם בְּכָל עִנְיָנָיו לְבַקֵּשׁ תַּחְבּוּלוֹת בְּעִנְיָנָיו לְפִי מַהֲלָךְ הַטִּבְעִי הַמְּרֻגָּל אַף כִּי יָבִין אֲשֶׁר תַּחְבּוּלוֹת יוּכְלוּ לְהִתְהַפֵּךְ וּלְהִשְׁתַּנּוֹת כְּמַאֲמַר הַכָּתוּב לֹא לַחֲכָמִים לֶחֶם וְלֹא לִנְבֹנִים עֹשֶׁר, וְהָאָדָם יוּכַל אַךְ לְהִתְבּוֹנֵן וְלִרְאוֹת אֲשֶׁר כָּל מַעֲשָׂיו וּמִסְחָרָיו יִהְיוּ קְרוֹבִים לְשָׂכָר וּרְחוֹקִים מֵהֶפְסֵד לְפִי הַנִּרְאֶה, אַף כִּי אֵינֶנּוּ בָּטוּחַ בָּזֶה.

וְיֵשׁ הַנְהָגָה שְׁנִיָּה עַל פִּי חֻקֵּי הַתּוֹרָה, כִּי כְּפֹעַל אָדָם בַּתּוֹרָה וּמִצְוָה יְשֻׁלַּם לוֹ בָּעוֹלָם הַזֶּה בְּכָל עִנְיָנָיו, וְלִפְעָמִים יִהְיֶה לָאָדָם רֹב זְכֻיּוֹת וּמִעוּט עֲוֹנוֹת עַל כֵּן רַע לוֹ בָּעוֹלָם הַזֶּה כְּדֵי שֶׁיָּבוֹא עַל כָּל שְׂכָרוֹ בָּעוֹלָם הַבָּא, וְלִפְעָמִים רֹב עֲוֹנוֹת וּמִעוּט זְכֻיּוֹת יִיטַב לוֹ בָּעוֹלָם הַזֶּה כְּדֵי לְקַבֵּל שְׂכָרוֹ, וּכְמוֹ שֶׁכָּתוּב בְּקִדּוּשִׁין הנ״ל.

וְעוֹד לָנוּ לָדַעַת כִּי יְסוֹד הַנְהָגַת הַקָּדוֹשׁ בָּרוּךְ הוּא עִם רֹב בְּנֵי

14. Deuteronomy 11:13-14: "If you will listen to My commandments...I will give the early rain and later rain in its proper time...." Ramban comments: "Know that miracles are done only to the completely righteous or the completely evil. But for the average person the natural process operates...."

and punishment] depend on the degree of difficulty, which, as I wrote above, a person cannot fully know.

It would be wise for us to consider carefully that which *is* known – namely, that God created the world to be governed according to the laws of nature that He, God, decreed. Human life and death, health and sickness, wealth and poverty, and everything else that appertains to a person occur in accordance with the natural process. Sometimes nature's ways are hidden, so that neither the wisdom of the wise nor the understanding of the sages can predict it – for example, when a healthy person suddenly dies and the natural cause is hidden, even from the greatest of doctors. Or when the opposite happens. This, too, may be in accordance with a mysterious natural process and not miraculous, for overt miracles can happen to an outstanding righteous person in a righteous era and generation when miracles were frequent – or to an egregiously wicked person during a time that is guided by miracles (see Ramban).[14] It would also seem that a poor person becomes rich due to causes and factors that a person cannot calculate in advance, and a rich person likewise becomes poor due to extraordinary factors; this, too, is a natural process. However, an extraordinary natural process is infrequent, so a person must seek out strategies pertaining to his affairs in accordance with the ordinary natural process – even as he understands that these strategies may be upended or reversed. As the verse says: "The wise do not [always] get bread nor do the intelligent [always] get wealth" [Eccl. 9:11]. All the person can do is see to it that his deeds and transactions are likely to yield profit and stay far from loss as far as can be seen, although there is no guarantee.

But there is a second mode of governance – in accordance with the laws of the Torah [as opposed to the laws of nature], that in accordance with a person's actions for Torah and mitzvot he will be compensated in all his affairs in this world. Sometimes a person will have mostly merits but a minority component of sin, in which case he suffers evil in this world so that he obtains his due reward in the next world. And sometimes a majority of sin and a minority of merits means that he will have it good in this world, so that he receives his reward [for good deeds] – as stated in Kiddushin 40b, mentioned above. We must also know that the basis for the conduct of the Holy One, blessed be He,

אָדָם (זוּלַת הַמְעַטִים מִבְּנֵי הָעֲלִיָּה הַנֶּחֱשָׁבִים לְפָנָיו לְצַדִּיקִים גְּמוּרִים) נִקְשַׁר מַהֲלַךְ הַתּוֹרָה עִם מַהֲלַךְ הַטִּבְעִי בְּיַחַד, וְלָכֵן אִם הָאָדָם אֲשֶׁר עַל פִּי מַהֲלָךְ הַטִּבְעִי הַתְּמִידִית צָרִיךְ לִהְיוֹת עָשִׁיר, אַךְ נִמְצָא לָזֶה מְנִיעָה עַל פִּי מַהֲלַךְ הַתּוֹרָה כִּי אָז יְשַׁנֶּה הַקָּדוֹשׁ בָּרוּךְ הוּא אֶת מַהֲלָכוֹ הַטִּבְעִי וִישַׁנֶּה בְּמַהֲלָךְ טִבְעִי אַחֵר וְהָאָדָם לֹא יַרְגִּישׁ וְלֹא יֵדַע אִם יָצָא מִסֵּדֶר הַנְהָגָתוֹ הַתְּמִידִית, וְכֵן לְהֶפֶךְ לִפְעָמִים הָאָדָם לְפִי מַהֲלָךְ הַטִּבְעִי הַתְּמִידִית צָרִיךְ לִהְיוֹת עָנִי, אָכֵן עַל פִּי מַהֲלַךְ הַתּוֹרָה צָרִיךְ לִהְיוֹת עָשִׁיר, יְשַׁנֶּה וְיַחֲלִיף הַקָּדוֹשׁ בָּרוּךְ הוּא אֶת מַהֲלָךְ הַטִּבְעִי הַתְּמִידִי הָרַע, לְמַהֲלָךְ טִבְעִי אַחֵר הַטּוֹב וְגַם אָז לֹא יַכִּיר הָאָדָם הַשִּׁנּוּי בְּמַהֲלָכוֹ הָרָגִיל, וְכֵן יִהְיֶה בִּכְלַל עִנְיְנֵי הָאָדָם הֵן לְטוֹב הֵן לְהֶפֶךְ.

וִיבֹאַר אוּלַי בָּזֶה דִּבְרֵי הַגְּמָרָא (גִּטִּין סח, ב) אֲשֶׁר שָׁאַל בְּנָיָהוּ אֶת הָאַשְׁמְדַאי וּמַאי טַעְמָא כִּי חֲזֵיתֵיהּ לְהַהוּא רַוְיָא דְּקָטָעֵי בְּאוֹרְחָא אַסֻּקְתֵּהּ לְאוֹרְחָא, אָמַר, מַכְרִיזֵי עֲלֵהּ בָּרָקִיעַ דְּרָשָׁע גָּמוּר הוּא וְעָבְדִי לֵהּ נִיחָא נַפְשֵׁהּ כִּי הֵיכִי דְּלֵיכוֹל לֵיהּ לְעָלְמָא, אֲשֶׁר לִכְאוֹרָה יִפָּלֵא הַדָּבָר מְאֹד, וְכִי בִּשְׁבִיל דָּבָר קָטָן כָּזֶה אֲשֶׁר הֶעֱלָהוּ עַל אֵם הַדֶּרֶךְ יֹאכַל אֶת עוֹלָמוֹ, אוּלָם לְפִי דְּבָרֵינוּ יוּכַל לִהְיוֹת כִּי לְפִי מַהֲלַךְ הַטֶּבַע שֶׁל הַשִּׁכּוֹר הָיָה נֶאֱבַד בְּדַרְכּוֹ אֲשֶׁר תָּעָה בָּהּ, אַךְ הַקָּדוֹשׁ בָּרוּךְ הוּא שָׁלַח לוֹ מַהֲלַךְ טֶבַע אַחֵר אֲשֶׁר לֹא נִכָּר לְהָאָדָם וְהֶעֱלָהוּ לְאֵם הַדֶּרֶךְ לְבַל יֹאבַד דֶּרֶךְ וְנִכָּה לוֹ עַל יְדֵי זֶה מִזְּכֻיּוֹתָיו לָעוֹלָם הַבָּא.

עַל כָּל הַדְּבָרִים הָאֲמוּרִים, יֵשׁ אָמְנָם לְהָאָדָם אִישׁ אִישׁ לְפִי מַצָּבוֹ וְעִנְיָנוֹ לִדְאֹג וְלִפְחֹד, פֶּן יְנֻכֶּה לוֹ מִשְּׂכָרוֹ לָעוֹלָם הַבָּא, אַחֲרֵי אֲשֶׁר לֹא יוּכַל הָאָדָם לָדַעַת אֶת מַהֲלָכוֹ הַטִּבְעִי הַתְּמִידִי אֵיךְ וּמָה הוּא וְאוּלַי עַל פִּי מַהֲלָכוֹ הַטִּבְעִי הָיָה רַע לוֹ יוֹתֵר מֵאֲשֶׁר הוּא עַתָּה וּבִמְעַט הַטּוֹבָה אֲשֶׁר לוֹ יוֹתֵר מִכְּפִי מַהֲלָכוֹ הַטִּבְעִי יָכוֹל לִהְיוֹת כִּי יְנֻכּוּ לוֹ מִשְּׂכָרוֹ לָעוֹלָם הַבָּא. וְגַם אִם יִרְאֶה הָאָדָם אֶת עַצְמוֹ שֶׁהוּא מָלֵא תּוֹרָה

15. A member of King Solomon's court and general in Solomon's army.
16. The "king of demons" who, according to this passage in the Talmud, exiled Solomon and posed as king of Israel in his stead. Solomon eventually reclaimed his throne.

toward most people – excluding the elite few whom He considers to be completely righteous – is to link together the process [of governance] that accords with the Torah and the process [of governance] that accords with nature. Therefore, if a person, according to the constant natural process, should be rich, but there is an obstacle to this according to the Torah process, then the Holy One, blessed be He, will alter the natural process and replace it with a different natural process. The person will not feel or know if there was deviation from the constant natural process. The same is true of the opposite case; sometimes a person should be poor according to the constant natural process, but according to the Torah process, he should be rich. In this case, the Holy One, blessed be He, will alter and replace the constant natural process, which produces a bad outcome, with a different, benevolent natural process. In this case, too, the person will not discern the change to the regular process. So it is in all human affairs, be it for good or the opposite.

Perhaps this can illuminate the words of the Talmud in Gittin (68b), wherein Benayahu[15] asked Ashmedai:[16] "'Why, when you saw a drunkard lost on the road, did you bring him to the [correct] road?' [Ashmedai] answered: 'They proclaimed about him in heaven that he is a completely wicked person, and I did good for him so that he uses up his [reward in the next] world.'" It seems quite astonishing that for something so minor as getting directions to the main road he uses up his reward in the next world! However, according to our words, it may well be that the natural process for the drunkard was to get lost on the path where he strayed, but the Holy One, blessed be He, sent him a different natural process, which the person did not recognize. This restored him onto the main road, so that he never lost his way, but it deducted from his merits in the next world.

With regard to all the matters discussed, every individual – each according to his condition and affairs – should be concerned and afraid lest there be deductions from his reward in the next world, since a person cannot know what the constant natural process is and how it applies to him. Perhaps according to the natural process things would be worse for him than they are at present, and the small amount of good that he enjoys beyond the natural process might be deducted from his reward in the next world. And even if a person sees himself as being full of Torah

וּמִצְוֹת וּמַצָּבוֹ בָּעוֹלָם הַזֶּה שָׁפֵל מְאֹד, בְּכָל זֹאת אֵין בְּיָדוֹ לִשְׁפֹּט כִּי מַצָּבוֹ בָּעוֹלָם הַזֶּה הוּא לְכַפָּרָה עַל עֲוֹנֹתָיו, כִּי אוּלַי שׁוֹגֶה הוּא בְּכחוֹתָיו הַפְּנִימִיִּים, וּלְפִיהֶן הוּא אוּלַי רֻבּוֹ עֲוֹנוֹת וכנ״ל, וּבַמַּהֲלָךְ הַטִּבְעִי שֶׁלּוֹ אוּלַי הוּא בְּגֶדֶר שָׁפֵל הַרְבֵּה יוֹתֵר מִמַּצָּבוֹ אֲשֶׁר הוּא עוֹמֵד בּוֹ, וְלָכֵן גַּם לְאִישׁ כָּזֶה יֵשׁ לְפַחֵד אוּלַי מְנַכִּין לוֹ מִזְּכִיּוֹתָיו לָעוֹלָם הַבָּא.

לְזֹאת הָעֵצָה הַיְעוּצָה לָזֶה, שֶׁיִּרְאֶה הָאָדָם לְבַקֵּשׁ אֶמְצָעִיִּים וְיִתְאַמֵּץ שֶׁהוּא בְּכָל פְּעֻלּוֹתָיו וְקִנְיָנָיו יוֹעִילוּ שֶׁיִּהְיוּ לוֹ לְעֵזֶר לַעֲבוֹדַת הַבּוֹרֵא (וְהַיְסוֹד וְהָעִקָּר בַּעֲבוֹדָתוֹ יִהְיֶה רַק לְמַעַן שְׁמוֹ יִתְעַלֶּה), וְעַל יְדֵי זֶה גַּם הֲנָאוֹתָיו וּצְרָכָיו אֲשֶׁר יִשְׁתַּמֵּשׁ בְּעָשְׁרוֹ וְקִנְיָנָיו לֹא יְנֻכֶּה לוֹ עֲבוּרָם מִן עוֹלָם הַבָּא, כִּי דַּעַת לְנָבוֹן נָקֵל. לְמָשָׁל אִם עָשִׁיר יַדְלִיק נֵרוֹ וְכַיּוֹצֵא בָּזֶה לְמַעֲנוֹ וְהֶעָנִי יֵהָנֶה גַּם הוּא לְאוֹרוֹ, הֲיִתָּכֵן כִּי יִדְרֹשׁ הֶעָשִׁיר מֵהֶעָנִי שֶׁיְּשַׁלֵּם לוֹ עֲבוּר הֲנָאָתוֹ. כְּמוֹ כֵן, אִם יַעֲשֶׂה הָאָדָם עִנְיָן אֲשֶׁר הוּא יָקָר וְנִכְבָּד בְּעֶרְכּוֹ לִפְנֵי הַשֵּׁם יִתְבָּרַךְ, וּכְדַאי לוֹ כִּבְיָכוֹל אֲשֶׁר הָאָדָם הַזֶּה יִחְיֶה לְפָנָיו, וְיֵיטִיב לוֹ גַּם בְּכָל עִנְיָנָיו, מִמֵּילָא לֹא יְנֻכֶּה לוֹ עֲבוּר זֶה מִשְּׂכָרוֹ בָּעוֹלָם הַבָּא.

וְזֶהוּ אוּלַי בֵּאוּר הַגְּמָרָא בְּקִדּוּשִׁין (מ, ב), לְעוֹלָם יִרְאֶה אָדָם עַצְמוֹ כְּאִלּוּ חֶצְיוֹ חַיָּב וְחֶצְיוֹ זַכַּאי. עָשָׂה מִצְוָה אַחַת, אַשְׁרֵי לוֹ שֶׁהִכְרִיעַ עַצְמוֹ לְכַף זְכוּת, עָבַר עֲבֵרָה אַחַת, אוֹי לוֹ שֶׁהִכְרִיעַ אֶת עַצְמוֹ לְכַף חוֹבָה כו׳, עַיֵּן שָׁם. וְהִנֵּה חֲזַ״ל חָשְׁבוּ מַחֲשָׁבוֹת בָּזֶה לְעוֹרֵר אֶת הָאָדָם אֶל הַמִּצְוָה וְלִמְנֹעַ מִן הָעֲבֵרָה, כִּי יַחְשֹׁב בִּלְבָבוֹ כִּי עַל יְדֵי מִצְוָה זוֹ יִהְיֶה רֻבּוֹ זְכֻיּוֹת וְעַל עֲבֵרָה זוֹ הֲלֹא יִהְיֶה רֻבּוֹ עֲוֹנוֹת, וְלִכְאוֹרָה אַחֲרֵי שֶׁאָמְרוּ חֲזַ״ל בְּקִדּוּשִׁין (שָׁם) כִּי רֻבּוֹ זְכֻיּוֹת יֵעָנֵשׁ עַל מְעַט עֲוֹנוֹת

and mitzvot, and his condition in this world is very lowly, still he cannot conclude that his [lowly] condition in this world is an atonement for his sins, for perhaps he is mistaken about his unconscious drives, and, measured by them, his sins may be the majority, as mentioned above. Thus, according to his natural process, perhaps his circumstances should be much poorer than they actually are. Therefore, even this person should be concerned about deductions from the merits he has accrued for the next world.

Therefore, the advice offered for this is for a person to see fit to seek means and make efforts that all his actions and possessions effectively aid him in serving the Creator. (The essence and foundation of serving Him should be only for the sake of His name, may it be elevated.) In this way, then even his pleasures and needs for which he uses his wealth and possessions will not cause deductions from his [reward in] the next world. It is easy to clarify this to the wise; for example, if a rich man lights a candle or the like for his own use, but a pauper also benefits from its light, is it possible that the rich man would demand that the pauper pay him for the benefit he drew? Similarly, if a person undertakes something that is precious and dear in God's eyes, and this person is worthy of living in God's presence, as it were, and [God] brings benefit to all his endeavors, nothing will be deducted on account of this from his reward in the next world.

Perhaps this is the Talmud's meaning in Kiddushin (40b):

> A person should always view himself as equally balanced between guilty and exonerated. If he does one mitzva, he is fortunate, because he has tilted himself to the side of merit. If he does one sin, woe to him, for he has tilted himself to the side of guilt....

See further there.

The Sages, of blessed memory, conceived this to inspire a person toward a mitzva and prevent a transgression, for he will think to himself that through this one mitzva he will be mostly meritorious and through this one sin he will be mostly sinful. At first glance, [this is puzzling]: The Sages, of blessed memory, have said in Kiddushin (ibid.) that when one has mostly merits, he will be punished in this world for his

שֶׁלּוֹ בָּעוֹלָם הַזֶּה וְרֻבּוֹ עֲוֹנוֹת יְקַבֵּל שְׂכָרוֹ בָּעוֹלָם הַזֶּה, וְיָדוּעַ כִּי אַךְ מְעַטִּים הֵמָּה הַמַּשְׂכִּילִים שֵׂכֶל טוֹב לַה׳, לָתֵת הַיִּתְרוֹן לְהִשְׁתַּדֵּל בְּיֶתֶר שְׂאֵת וְעֹז בְּעִנְיְנֵי עוֹלָם הַבָּא מֵאֲשֶׁר יִשְׁתַּדְּלוּ בְּעִנְיְנֵי עוֹלָם הַזֶּה, אָמְנָם רַבִּים מֵהֲמוֹן עַם הָעוֹלָם הַזֶּה אֲשֶׁר לִפְנֵיהֶם יָקָר מְאֹד בְּעֵינֵיהֶם וּמִשְׁתַּדְּלִים בְּעִנְיְנֵי עוֹלָם הַזֶּה הַרְבֵּה יוֹתֵר מֵעִנְיְנֵי עוֹלָם הַבָּא, אִם כֵּן זֹאת הָעֵצָה הֲלֹא תְּרַפֶּה יָדֵם עוֹד מֵעֲבוֹדַת ה׳ בְּאָמְרָם הֲלֹא טוֹב לָנוּ לִהְיוֹת רֻבּוֹ עֲוֹנוֹת וְנִירַשׁ עוֹלָם הַזֶּה מִלִּהְיוֹת רֹב זְכֻיּוֹת וּלְקַבֵּל עֹנֶשׁ בָּעוֹלָם הַזֶּה.

אָכֵן עַל פִּי דְּבָרֵינוּ הַקּוֹדְמִים יְבֹאַר כִּי מוּדַעַת זֹאת אֲשֶׁר בְּכָל דָּבָר אָזְלִינַן בָּתַר רֻבָּא וְכַאֲשֶׁר יִהְיֶה לְהָאָדָם רֹב זְכֻיּוֹת אָז יִתְחַשֵּׁב כִּי הוּא שֶׁל הַקָּדוֹשׁ בָּרוּךְ הוּא, כַּאֲשֶׁר יָדוּעַ הַמַּאֲמָר (אַף כִּי אֵין בְּרוּחַ בִּינָתֵנוּ לַהֲבִינוֹ עַל בֻּרְיוֹ) "עֲבוֹדָה צֹרֶךְ גָּבוֹהַּ", וְכָל עִנְיְנֵי טוֹבוֹת הָעוֹלָם הַזֶּה אֲשֶׁר יַשִּׂיג הָאָדָם הַזֶּה יָכוֹל לִהְיוֹת לְתוֹעֶלֶת לְהַגְדִּיל בָּם עֲבוֹדַת ה׳, עַל כֵּן בְּאִישׁ כָּזֶה אַף אִם הַמַּהֲלָךְ הַטִּבְעִי שֶׁלּוֹ הוּא בְּמַצָּב רַע מְאֹד בָּעוֹלָם הַזֶּה יְכוֹנֵן הַקָּדוֹשׁ בָּרוּךְ הוּא אֶת הַמַּהֲלָךְ הַטִּבְעִי לְפָנָיו עַל צַד הַיּוֹתֵר טוֹב, אִם אַךְ לֹא יִהְיֶה בְּיָדוֹ עֲבֵרָה גְּדוֹלָה אֲשֶׁר יִהְיֶה בְּכֹחָהּ לְהַכְרִיעַ אוֹתוֹ לְרָעָה. - אוּלָם אִם יִהְיֶה לָאָדָם רֻבּוֹ עֲוֹנוֹת, אָז יִחְיֶה עַל חֶשְׁבּוֹן עַצְמוֹ וְאִם גַּם יִהְיֶה לוֹ הַרְבֵּה תּוֹרָה וּמִצְוֹת לֹא יִהְיֶה שָׁוֶה לְהָאָדָם אֲשֶׁר הוּא רֻבּוֹ זְכֻיּוֹת וְחוֹסֶה בְּצֵל הַקָּדוֹשׁ בָּרוּךְ הוּא וְחַי עַל חֶשְׁבּוֹן הַשֵּׁם יִתְבָּרַךְ, לָכֵן נְכוֹנָה הִיא הָעֵצָה אֲשֶׁר אָמְרוּ לְהִשְׁתַּדֵּל בְּכָל מִצְוָה לְמַעַן אוּלַי תַּכְרִיעַ הַמִּצְוָה אוֹתוֹ לְרֻבּוֹ זְכֻיּוֹת וְאָז יִיטַב לוֹ מִמֵּילָא גַּם בָּעוֹלָם הַזֶּה, וְגַם יִזָּהֵר מִן הָעֲבֵרָה לְמַעַן לֹא יָבוֹא לִידֵי רֻבּוֹ עֲוֹנוֹת, וְאָז אִם לְפִי מַהֲלָךְ הַטִּבְעִי נְכוֹנִים לוֹ רָעוֹת וּפִגְעֵי הַתֵּבֵל יְהִי רַע לוֹ בְּהֶחְלֵט, וּמְעַט הַמִּצְוֹת אֲשֶׁר יֵשׁ לוֹ לֹא יַסְפִּיקוּ לְשַׁנּוֹת עֲבוּרוֹ

17. II Chronicles 30:22.
18. An idea that appears in talmudic and midrashic literature, and further developed in kabbalistic literature, that God, as it were, "needs" the worship and service of human beings.

few sins, and one who has mostly sins will get his reward [for his few merits] in this world. And it is known that very few understand that "all good is to God"[17] and thus prioritize working with extra energy and strength on matters related to the next world over their efforts relating to affairs of this world; rather, with most of the masses, this world, which is right in front of them, is very precious to them, and their efforts for matters of this world are much greater than for matters of the next world. If so, then this advice [i.e., to imagine oneself as hanging in the balance] will weaken their efforts from the service of God, as they will say, "It is better for us to be mostly sinful so that we inherit this world than to be mostly meritorious and receive punishment in this world."

However, according to our previous words, we can explain: This awareness, namely, that we always follow the majority, means that when a person has mostly merits, then he will be considered one of God's. There is a well-known statement (though our understanding is not able to fully comprehend it), "Service is a need of the Most High."[18] Thus, all the successes that a person achieves in this world can be used to enhance the service of God. Therefore, for such a person whom the natural process would put into terrible circumstances in this world, God will steer his natural process in the best possible way – unless he has a terrible sin that would tilt him to the side of evil. However, if the person is mostly sinful, then he will live at his own expense. And even if he has a lot of Torah and mitzvot, he will not equal a person who has mostly merits, is sheltered in the shadow of the Holy One, blessed be He,[19] and lives on the account of Hashem, the Blessed. Hence, the advice that [the Sages] gave to make an effort for every mitzva, so that mitzva can perhaps tilt him to the side of being mostly meritorious, then it will be well with him in this world as well. He will also be careful not to sin, so that he not come to be mostly sinful. For then, if the course of the natural process has evil and misfortune in store for him, then it will definitely be bad for him. The few mitzvot that he has will not be enough to change

19. See Psalms 91:1.

אֶת מַהֲלָכוֹ הַטִּבְעִי, וְגַם הַמְּעַט אֲשֶׁר יְקַבֵּל בָּעוֹלָם הַזֶּה לְצֹרֶךְ מְזוֹנוֹתָיו וְהִצְטָרְכֻיּוֹתָיו הַהֶכְרֵחִיִּים יֹאכְלֵם רַק בִּשְׂכַר מִצְוֹתָיו הַמּוּעָטִים.

וּבִדְבָרֵינוּ אֵלֶּה נוּכַל לְבָאֵר דִּבְרֵי הַגְּמָרָא רֹאשׁ הַשָּׁנָה (טז, ב) ג׳ סְפָרִים נִפְתָּחִים בְּרֹאשׁ הַשָּׁנָה, אֶחָד שֶׁל רְשָׁעִים גְּמוּרִים, וְאֶחָד שֶׁל צַדִּיקִים גְּמוּרִים, וְאֶחָד שֶׁל בֵּינוֹנִים. צַדִּיקִים גְּמוּרִים נִכְתָּבִים וְנֶחְתָּמִים לְאַלְתַּר לְחַיִּים, רְשָׁעִים גְּמוּרִים נִכְתָּבִים וְנֶחְתָּמִים לְאַלְתַּר לְמִיתָה. בֵּינוֹנִים תְּלוּיִם וְעוֹמְדִים מֵרֹאשׁ הַשָּׁנָה עַד יוֹם הַכִּפּוּרִים, זָכוּ - נִכְתָּבִים לְחַיִּים, לֹא זָכוּ כו׳. וְהִנֵּה כְּבָר נִתְקַשּׁוּ הַקַּדְמוֹנִים בָּזֶה כִּי הֲלֹא אֲנַחְנוּ רוֹאִים בְּחוּשׁ, רְשָׁעִים גְּמוּרִים אֲשֶׁר חָיוּ יִחְיוּ, וְנוֹסָף עוֹד יֵשׁ לְהַקְשׁוֹת עַל פִּי דִּבְרֵי הַתּוֹס׳ שָׁם ד״ה וְנֶחְתָּמִים, שֶׁכָּתְבוּ, שֶׁמַּה שֶּׁיִּקְרָא פֹּה הַגְּמָרָא רְשָׁעִים גְּמוּרִים הוּא לְמִי שֶׁעֲוֹנֹתָיו מְרֻבִּים אֲבָל גַּם זְכֻיּוֹת יֵשׁ לוֹ, אִם כֵּן אֵיךְ אָמְרוּ כִּי הָרָשָׁע נִכְתָּב לְאַלְתַּר לְמִיתָה, הֲלֹא הוּא צָרִיךְ לִחְיוֹת לְמַעַן יְקַבֵּל שְׂכַר זְכֻיּוֹתָיו בָּעוֹלָם הַזֶּה, כַּמְּבֹאָר בְּקִדּוּשִׁין הנ״ל. וְדֹחַק לוֹמַר כִּי הַגְּמָרָא מַיְרֵי בְּרָשָׁע אֲשֶׁר כְּבָר קִבֵּל שְׂכָרוֹ מִזְּכֻיּוֹתָיו.

אָמְנָם עַל פִּי דְּבָרֵינוּ נוּכַל לְבָאֵר דִּבְרֵי הַגְּמָרָא עַל נָכוֹן, בְּהֶקְדֵּם עוֹד דִּבְרֵי הַגְּמָרָא בְּרָכוֹת (ד, א) רַבִּי יַעֲקֹב בַּר אִידִי רָמֵי, כְּתִיב וְהִנֵּה אָנֹכִי עִמָּךְ וּשְׁמַרְתִּיךָ בְּכֹל אֲשֶׁר תֵּלֵךְ, וּכְתִיב וַיִּירָא יַעֲקֹב מְאֹד, וּמְשַׁנֵּי, אָמַר שֶׁמָּא יִגְרֹם הַחֵטְא. וְנִרְאֶה מִזֶּה כִּי גַּם בְּדָבָר אֲשֶׁר יַבְטִיחַ ה׳ בְּהֶחְלֵט יוּכַל לְהִשְׁתַּנּוֹת עַל יְדֵי חֵטְא, וְשָׁם (ז, א) אָמַר רַבִּי יוֹחָנָן

the natural process for him. And the little that he receives in this world for his sustenance and basic necessities will consume the reward of his few mitzvot.

With these words, we can explain the words of the Talmud in Rosh HaShana (16b):

> Three books are opened on Rosh HaShana: one of the completely wicked, one of the completely righteous, and one of those who are in the middle. The completely righteous are immediately inscribed in and sealed for life. The completely wicked are immediately inscribed in and sealed for death. Those in the middle stand suspended from Rosh HaShana to Yom Kippur. If they merit it, they are inscribed for life. If they do not merit [they are inscribed for death].

Now, our predecessors already struggled with this statement, for we see with our own eyes completely wicked people who live on. In addition, we can ask in accordance with *Tosafot* ad loc. (s.v. "*veneḥtamim*"), who wrote that what the Talmud calls "completely wicked" here refers to one whose sins are more numerous, though he does have merits. If so, how could they say that the wicked person is immediately inscribed for death? He needs to live on to receive his reward for his good deeds in this world, as explained in aforementioned talmudic passage from Kiddushin. It would be too contrived to answer that the Talmud refers to a wicked person who already received reward for his good deeds.

According to our words, we can explain this talmudic passage correctly, prefacing it with the words of the Talmud in Berakhot (4a):

> R. Yaakov bar Idi poses a contradiction: It is written, "I will be with you and I will guard you wherever you go" (Gen. 28:8), and it is written, "And Jacob feared greatly" (ibid. 32:15). [Why would Jacob be afraid if God promised to protect him? The Talmud] answers: He said: Perhaps sin will cause [my downfall].

We see from this that even something that God promised definitely can be altered by sin. Yet it says there (Berakhot 7a): "R. Yoḥanan said in

מִשּׁוּם רַבִּי יוֹסֵי, כָּל דִּבּוּר וְדִבּוּר שֶׁיָּצָא מִפִּי הַקָּדוֹשׁ בָּרוּךְ הוּא לְטוֹבָה אַף עַל תְּנַאי לֹא חָזַר בּוֹ כו׳, עַיֵּן שָׁם, וְאֵיךְ יַתְאִימוּ שְׁנֵי הַמַּאֲמָרִים הָאֵלֶּה? אֲבָל הָעִנְיָן הוּא כָּךְ, כִּי הִנֵּה יָדוּעַ אֲשֶׁר יִסּוּרִים מְכַפְּרִים עָוֹן, וְהִנֵּה נַחְקֹר אֵיזֶה יִסּוּרִים מְכַפְּרִים עָוֹן, לְמָשָׁל הַיִּסּוּרִים אֲשֶׁר יְסַבְּבוּ אֶת בַּעַל הַתַּאֲוָה בַּאֲשֶׁר אֵין בְּיָדוֹ לְמַלֹּאות תַּאֲוָתוֹ יַעַן כִּי נַפְשׁוֹ לֹא תִשְׂבַּע תַּאֲווֹת, אַף כִּי לְאִישׁ כָּזֶה לֹא טוֹב לוֹ בְּחַיָּיו, עִם כָּל זֶה לֹא נוּכַל לְחָשְׁבָם לְיִסּוּרִין, אַךְ אֵלֶּה יוּכְלוּ לְהֵחָשֵׁב לְיִסּוּרִין אִם לְפִי מַהֲלָךְ הַטִּבְעִי שֶׁלּוֹ הִתְעַתֵּד לְטוֹב, וְהַקָּדוֹשׁ בָּרוּךְ הוּא שִׁנָּה אוֹתוֹ לְרַע, זֶהוּ יִסּוּרִין שֶׁמְּכַפְּרִים עָוֹן, אֲבָל אִם לְפִי מַהֲלָךְ הַטִּבְעִי שֶׁלּוֹ הִתְעַתֵּד לְרַע הַמַּצָּב, וְאֵין לוֹ זְכִיּוֹת מִדָּה כְּנֶגֶד מִדָּה אֲשֶׁר יְשַׁנֶּה עַל יָדָם מַצָּבוֹ לְטוֹב, וְהַקָּדוֹשׁ בָּרוּךְ הוּא לֹא שִׁנָּה מַצָּבוֹ לְטוֹב, לֹא יִתְחַשְּׁבוּ הָרָעוֹת הַבָּאִים עָלָיו עַל פִּי מַהֲלָכוֹ הַטִּבְעִי לְיִסּוּרִים שֶׁמְּכַפְּרִים, כִּי אִם לֹא יַרְוִיחַ הָאָדָם לֹא יִתֵּן לוֹ הַשֵּׁם יִתְבָּרֵךְ בְּחִנָּם.

אָמְנָם לִפְעָמִים יָכוֹל לִהְיוֹת גַּם בְּאָדָם אֲשֶׁר לֹא הוּכַן לְטוֹב וְהַקָּדוֹשׁ בָּרוּךְ הוּא הִשְׁפִּיעַ לוֹ טוֹב לֹא בִּזְכוּתוֹ אַךְ לְמַעַן יוּכַל לַעֲבֹד אוֹתוֹ, וְאַחַר כָּךְ אִם הָאָדָם לֹא מִלֵּא אַחַר רְצוֹן ה׳, וְהַקָּדוֹשׁ בָּרוּךְ הוּא יִקַּח מִמֶּנּוּ הַטּוֹב אֲשֶׁר נָתַן לוֹ, גַּם אֵלֶּה יוּכְלוּ לְהֵחָשֵׁב לְיִסּוּרִים אֲשֶׁר יְכַפְּרוּ עָוֹן, אַחֲרֵי אֲשֶׁר כְּבָר הָיָה בְּיָדוֹ טוּבוֹ וְנִלְקַח מִמֶּנּוּ. וְכִי זֶה הַהֶבְדֵּל בֵּין הַטּוֹבוֹת אֲשֶׁר יָבוֹאוּ עַל הָאָדָם בָּעוֹלָם הַזֶּה וּבֵין הָרָעוֹת, הָרָעוֹת לֹא יִשְׁלַח ה׳ עַל הָאָדָם טֶרֶם יֶחֱטָא, אַף אִם יוֹדֵעַ ה׳ אֲשֶׁר יֶחֱטָא אַחַר כָּךְ (בִּידִיעַת הַבּוֹרֵא אֵין לָנוּ לְדַבֵּר כְּמוֹ שֶׁכָּתַב הָרַמְבַּ״ם בְּהִלְכוֹת תְּשׁוּבָה, כִּי הַיְּדִיעָה הִיא רַק בַּשֵּׂכֶל הָאֱלֹקִית, כַּאֲשֶׁר יִתְנַהֵג הָאָדָם, אֲבָל הַבְּחִירָה הִיא בְּהָאָדָם), כְּמוֹ שֶׁכָּתוּב בַּגְּמָרָא רֹאשׁ הַשָּׁנָה (יז, ב), אֵין דָּנִין אֶת הָאָדָם אֶלָּא לְפִי מַעֲשָׂיו שֶׁל אוֹתָהּ שָׁעָה, עַיֵּן רַשִׁ״י שָׁם, אֲבָל הַטּוֹבוֹת יִתֵּן ה׳ לְהָאָדָם מִקֹּדֶם, אַף אִם לֹא הִצְטַדֵּק עֲדֶנָה וְכַאֲשֶׁר אָמְרוּ בַּמִּדְרָשׁ עַל הַפָּסוּק מִי הִקְדִּימַנִי וַאֲשַׁלֵּם מִי מָל לְפָנַי עַד

---

20. I.e., suffering that atones.
21. Leviticus Rabba 27:2.

the name of R. Yosei: Every word for good that God utters, even if said conditionally, God will not renege...." See further there. How do we reconcile these two sayings? This is explained as follows. It is known that suffering atones for sin. But let us examine what kind of suffering atones for sin. Take, for example, the suffering that enwraps a lustful person in that he is prevented from satisfying his lust – for his soul's lusts will never be satisfied. Even though this person is not having a good life, this can nevertheless not be considered suffering.[20] It can only be considered [atoning] suffering if his natural course destines him for good, but the Holy One, blessed be He, changes it for the worse. This suffering atones for sins. But if according to his natural process he was destined for a bad situation, and he has no merits which, *quid pro quo*, can improve his condition, and the Holy One, blessed be He, did not change his condition for the better, then the bad things that befall him according to the natural course are not considered suffering that atones. If a person does not earn it, then God will not bestow it on him gratis.

Moreover, sometimes there can be a person who was not destined for good [by natural processes], but the Holy One, blessed be He, still bestows good on him – not by his own merit, but in order that he can better serve [God]. Later, if the person does not follow the will of God, then the Holy One, blessed be He, will take away the good that He gave him. This, too, cannot be considered suffering that atones for sin, since he already had his good, and it was taken away from him.

This [i.e., the idea of reward that stimulates improvement] is the difference between the goodness that comes to a person in this world and the evil [that comes upon him]; God will not visit evil on a person before he actually sins – even if God knows that he will sin afterward. (We will not discuss God's foreknowledge, as Rambam wrote in the Laws of Repentance [5:5] that such knowledge is only within the divine intelligence as to how the person will behave, but the choice remains with the person.) As stated in the Talmud in Rosh HaShana (16b): "A person is only judged by his action as of that moment." See Rashi ad loc.

But God may bestow goodness on a person in advance, even if he has not yet become righteous. As said in the midrash on the verse "Who has a claim on me from before that I should repay him?" (Job 41:3) – Who performs a circumcision before Me before I give him a

שֶׁלֹּא נָתַתִּי לוֹ בֵּן וְכוּ׳, עַיֵּן שָׁם. וְעַל דֶּרֶךְ זֶה יוּכַל לִהְיוֹת כַּוָּנַת הַפָּסוּק דְּבָרִים (יח, כז) אֶת הַבְּרָכָה אֲשֶׁר תִּשְׁמְעוּ וְגוֹ׳. יַעַן לֹא יְוַסֵּר הָאָדָם רַק אִם כְּבָר עָשָׂה רָעָה. וְאֶפְשָׁר כִּי זֹאת הִיא מְלִיצַת הַגְּמָרָא (פְּסָחִים קיח, א) הוֹדוּ לַה׳ כִּי טוֹב, הוֹדוּ לַה׳ שֶׁגּוֹבֶה חוֹבָתוֹ שֶׁל אָדָם בְּטוֹבָתוֹ, עָשִׁיר בְּשׁוֹרוֹ, עָנִי בְּשֵׂיוֹ וכו׳. וּפֵרֵשׁ רַשְׁבָּ״ם שָׁם, מַפְסִיד מָמוֹנוֹ וּמְכַפֵּר עַל גּוּפוֹ, וְלִכְאוֹרָה מָה הִיא הָרְבוּתָא, דְּאֵין זֶה חֶסֶד גָּדוֹל אִם יְוַסֵּר הָאָדָם בְּמָמוֹנוֹ אִישׁ אִישׁ לְפִי עֶרְכּוֹ. אָכֵן לְפִי דְּבָרֵינוּ יְבֹאַר כִּי אִם הִשִּׂיג הָאָדָם טוֹבָתוֹ מֵהַקָּדוֹשׁ בָּרוּךְ הוּא בִּשְׂכָרוֹ עֲבוּר מַעֲשָׂיו הַטּוֹבִים וְאַחַר כָּךְ יִקַּח הַקָּדוֹשׁ בָּרוּךְ הוּא אֶת טוֹבָתוֹ מִמֶּנּוּ, נָכוֹן הַדָּבָר כִּי זֶהוּ יִסּוּרִין הַמְכַפְּרִים. אֲבָל אִם עוֹד לֹא הִרְוִיחַ הָאָדָם אֶת עָשְׁרוֹ עַל פִּי מַעֲשָׂיו, רַק הַקָּדוֹשׁ בָּרוּךְ הוּא עָשָׂה עִמּוֹ טוֹבָה וְנָתַן לוֹ מִקֹּדֶם וכנ״ל, וְהָאִישׁ הַזֶּה לֹא מִלֵּא אַחַר חֶפְצוֹ שֶׁל הַקָּדוֹשׁ בָּרוּךְ הוּא, וְאִם יִקַּח מִמֶּנּוּ הַקָּדוֹשׁ בָּרוּךְ הוּא טוֹבָתוֹ, גַּם זֶה נֶחְשָׁב לְיִסּוּרִין הַמְכַפְּרִין, זֶהוּ הָרְבוּתָא וְזֶה שֶׁכָּתוּב בַּגְּמָרָא הוֹדוּ לַה׳ שֶׁגּוֹבֶה חוֹבָתוֹ בְּטוֹבָתוֹ רוֹצֶה לוֹמַר עִם הַטּוֹבָה אֲשֶׁר נָתַן לוֹ רַק בְּטוֹבָתוֹ שֶׁל הַקָּדוֹשׁ בָּרוּךְ הוּא.

וְיוֹצֵא לָנוּ מִדְּבָרֵינוּ אֲשֶׁר אִם הָיָה לָאָדָם דְּבַר מָה מֵאֵת ה׳ וְאַחַר כָּךְ יִקַּח מִמֶּנּוּ, יֵחָשֵׁב זֹאת לְיִסּוּרִין שֶׁמְּכַפְּרִין, וְגַם אִם מַגִּיעַ לוֹ עַל פִּי מַעֲשָׂיו וְלֹא יִתֵּן לוֹ, גַּם זֶה נֶחְשָׁב לְיִסּוּרִין. אֲבָל אִם אֵין מַגִּיעַ לוֹ לֹא עַל פִּי מַהֲלָךְ טִבְעִי וְלֹא עַל פִּי מַעֲשָׂיו, וְלֹא נָתַן לוֹ, זֶה בְּוַדַּאי לֹא יֵחָשְׁבוּ לְיִסּוּרִין.

וּלְפִי זֶה הָיָה נִרְאֶה לוֹמַר לִכְאוֹרָה, שֶׁאִם יַבְטִיחַ הַקָּדוֹשׁ בָּרוּךְ הוּא טוֹב לָאָדָם עַל תְּנַאי כְּמוֹ בְּמֹשֶׁה שֶׁהִבְטִיחַ לוֹ ה׳ וְאֶעֱשֶׂה אוֹתְךָ לְגוֹי עָצוּם, בִּתְנַאי אִם יִהְיֶה חַס וְשָׁלוֹם כְּלָיָה לְיִשְׂרָאֵל, הֲלֹא הַדִּין שֶׁבְּאִם

son…? See further there.[21] This may be the meaning of the verse in Deuteronomy (11:27): "The blessing: that you will listen…" [This implies that] God sends His blessings first, in the hope that this will inspire the person to do mitzvot. But when it comes to the curse, it says: "If you will not listen…" (ibid. 11:28). A person will not be chastened unless he has already done wrong. This may be the meaning of the Talmud's poetic statement: "'Give thanks to God for He is good' (Ps. 136:1). Thank God, who collects His debt from a person from what is bountiful for him: the ox of a wealthy person, the sheep of a poor person…." (Pesaḥim 118a). Rashbam explains: "He loses his money, but this atones for his body [which is spared suffering]." At first glance, it is hard to understand what this adds, for it is no great kindness that a person is chastened through [losing] his money, each person according to their net worth. However, according to our words, it is understandable; if a person received his bounty from the Holy One, blessed be He, as a reward for his good deeds, and then the Holy One, blessed be He, takes the bounty from him, it is proper, for this is the suffering that atones. But if the person did not yet earn his wealth by his actions, but rather the Holy One, blessed be He, did him a favor and gave him an advance, as mentioned above, whereupon the person did not fulfill the will of the Holy One, blessed be He, then if the Holy One, blessed be He, takes away his bounty, this, too, is considered suffering that atones. This is the added meaning, and this is what the Talmud means by "Thank God, who collects His debt from a person from what is bountiful for him" – that is, from the bounty that was given to him purely out of God's goodness.

It emerges from our words that if a person received something from God that is later taken away, it is considered suffering that atones. Even if he deserves it by virtue of his actions but it is not granted to him, this is also considered suffering [that atones]. But if he does not deserve it, not according to the natural process and not by virtue of his actions, and it was not given to him, this is certainly not considered suffering [that atones]. Accordingly, it seems, at first glance, that if the Holy One, blessed be He, conditionally promises goodness to a person, as with Moses when God promised to make him "a great and mighty nation" (Deut. 9:14) on condition that, God forbid, the Jewish people be wiped out, then the obtaining principle is that if the con-

לֹא יְקַיֵּם הַתְּנַאי לֹא יְחֻיַּב לוֹ הַקָּדוֹשׁ בָּרוּךְ הוּא לְקַיֵּם הַבְטָחָתוֹ, וְאִם כֵּן אִם לֹא הִשִּׂיג הַטּוֹבָה הֲלֹא לֹא יֵחָשְׁבוּ לְיִסּוּרִין אֲשֶׁר יְכַפְּרוּ עֲוֹנֹתָיו, לָזֹאת הוֹדִיעוּ לָנוּ חֲזַ"ל מִדָּתוֹ שֶׁל הַקָּדוֹשׁ בָּרוּךְ הוּא, כִּי אַף אִם יַבְטִיחַ עַל תְּנַאי הִיא כְּמוֹ הַבְטָחָה בְּלֹא תְּנַאי, וְאַף אִם לֹא יְקֻיַּם הַתְּנַאי, לֹא יַחֲזֹר בּוֹ הַקָּדוֹשׁ בָּרוּךְ הוּא, וּמַגִּיעַ לוֹ הַטּוֹבָה מֵהַקָּדוֹשׁ בָּרוּךְ הוּא, אֲבָל יָכוֹל לִהְיוֹת כִּי לֹא יַשִּׂיג הָאָדָם הַטּוֹבָה, אַךְ יַרְוִיחַ כִּי עַל יְדֵי זֶה יִהְיֶה לוֹ לְכַפָּרַת עָוֹן. אֲבָל אִם הָיָה כְּפִי הַסְּבָרָא אֲשֶׁר אֵין מַגִּיעַ לוֹ, אָז לֹא הָיָה נֶחְשָׁב לְיִסּוּרִין אֲשֶׁר יְכַפְּרוּ עֲוֹנֹתָיו. וְהִנֵּה מִטֶּבַע הָאָדָם אִם יָבִין אֲשֶׁר יוּכְלוּ לָבוֹא עָלָיו יִסּוּרִין, אַף כִּי יֵדַע אֲשֶׁר בָּהֶם יְכֻפְּרוּ עֲוֹנֹתָיו, עִם כָּל זֶה יִרָא וְיִפְחַד וְיֵרַע לוֹ אַף אִם הוּא צַדִּיק גָּדוֹל, וְלָכֵן שַׁפִּיר אָמְרוּ בַּגְּמָרָא וַיִּירָא יַעֲקֹב מְאֹד, אַף כִּי הִבְטִיחַ לוֹ הַקָּדוֹשׁ בָּרוּךְ הוּא וְהִנֵּה אָנֹכִי עִמָּךְ וּשְׁמַרְתִּיךָ, בְּכָל זֶה הָיָה יָרֵא שֶׁמָּא יִגְרֹם הַחֵטְא.

וְעַל פִּי דְּבָרֵינוּ אֵלֶּה יוּכַל לִהְיוֹת חֶשְׁבּוֹן הָאָדָם בְּעוֹלָמוֹ עַל זֶה הָאֹפֶן, כִּי אִם יִהְיֶה לָאָדָם דָּבָר טוֹב אוֹ לְהֵפֶךְ, כַּאֲשֶׁר נִגְזַר עָלָיו מֵאֵת הַבּוֹרֵא בְּעֵת לֵדָתוֹ כְּמַאֲמַר חֲזַ"ל (נִדָּה טז, ב) אֲשֶׁר מֵעֵת הַתְחָלַת הֲוָיַת הָאָדָם נִגְזַר עָלָיו אִם יִהְיֶה עָשִׁיר אוֹ עָנִי, (אֲשֶׁר הוּא בֶּאֱמֶת יְסוֹד וְאֶבֶן הַפִּנָּה לְמַהֲלָכוֹ הַטִּבְעִי וּמַצָּבוֹ בָּעוֹלָם הָרָאוּי לִגְזֹר עָלָיו בְּעֵת לֵדָתוֹ) יֵרָאֶה לְפִי הַשְׁעָרַת הַדֵּעַת, כִּי הָאָדָם אֲשֶׁר נִגְזַר עָלָיו עֲשִׁירוּת, אִם לֹא יַעֲשֶׂה אֵיזֶה עֲבֵרָה אֲשֶׁר עֲבוּרָהּ רָאוּי לִקַּח מִמֶּנּוּ עָשְׁרוֹ, אָז לֹא יְנֻכּוּ לוֹ עֲבוּר עָשְׁרוֹ מִשְּׂכָרוֹ בְּעוֹלָם הַבָּא, וְאִם יִקַּח הַקָּדוֹשׁ בָּרוּךְ הוּא אֶת עָשְׁרוֹ מִמֶּנּוּ, יִתְחַשְּׁבוּ לוֹ לְיִסּוּרִים וִיכֻפְּרוּ עֲוֹנֹתָיו. וְעַל הָאָדָם אֲשֶׁר נִגְזַר עָלָיו כִּי יִהְיֶה עָנִי, וְהָעֲנִיּוּת בָּאָה לוֹ בְּמַהֲלָכוֹ הַטִּבְעִי, וְאֵין לוֹ זְכוּת גָּדוֹל אֲשֶׁר יוֹעִיל לוֹ לְהִתְעַשֵּׁר, אָז לֹא יֵחָשֵׁב לוֹ עֲנִיּוּתוֹ לְיִסּוּרִין גְּמוּרִים לְכַפֵּר בָּהֶם עֲוֹנֹתָיו, וְאִם יִתֵּן לוֹ ה' עֲשִׁירוּת יְנֻכּוּ לוֹ עַל יְדֵי זֶה מִן הָעוֹלָם הַבָּא.

dition is not met, then the Holy One, blessed be He, is not required to keep His promise. In such a case, if the goodness was not attained, this is not considered suffering that atones for his sins. Therefore, the Sages, of blessed memory, informed us of God's attribute, namely, that even if He promises conditionally, the Holy One, blessed be He, will not renege, and the person is owed that goodness by the Holy One, blessed be He. However, it is possible that the person does not attain the goodness, but still profits in that through this [withholding of goodness] his sins are atoned. But according to the logic that he is not deserving [if the condition is not met], this would not be considered suffering that atones for his sins. It is human nature that if one understands that suffering may be visited upon him, even if he knows that it will atone for his sins, he will still be afraid and be in a bad state, even if he is a great righteous person. Therefore, the Talmud understandably states that "Jacob feared greatly"; even though the Holy One, blessed be He, promised him "I will be with you and I will guard you," still he was afraid lest his sins cause [his demise].

According to what we have said, the accounting of a person in his world can be undertaken in the following manner: If a person has a good thing, or the opposite, as decreed for him at birth by the Creator – as the Sages, of blessed memory, say in Nidda (16b) that at the beginning of a person's existence it is decreed upon him if he will be rich or poor (and this is actually the basis and the cornerstone of his natural course and situation in the world, as is proper to decree on him at his birth) – it would appear, according to a reasonable assessment, that a person on whom was decreed wealth, if he does not do some sin for which his wealth deserves to be taken away, then nothing will be deducted from his reward in the next world on account of his wealth. And if the Holy One, blessed be He, takes away his wealth, then it will be considered suffering that atones for his sins. As for the person on whom it is decreed to be poor, whose poverty is in accordance with his natural course, and who has no great merit which will make him worthy of wealth – his poverty is not considered definitive suffering that atones for his sins. If the Holy One, blessed be He, then gives him wealth, this will be deducted from his [portion in] the next world.

וְעַל פִּי דְּבָרֵינוּ אֵלֶּה נָבִין מַה שֶּׁכָּתוּב בִּיבָמוֹת (מט, ב) עַל פָּסוּק אֶת מִסְפַּר יָמֶיךָ אֲמַלֵּא, וּפֵרֵשׁ רַשִׁ"י שָׁם שָׁנִים שֶׁפּוֹסְקִים לָאָדָם בִּשְׁעַת לֵדָתוֹ זָכָה מַשְׁלִימִין לוֹ. אֵין הַפֵּרוּשׁ זָכָה אִם הָיָה לוֹ זְכוּת, אַךְ הַפֵּרוּשׁ הוּא שֶׁלֹּא הָיָה לוֹ אֵיזֶה מְנִיעָה לְהַחַיִּים, אָז בְּוַדַּאי יִחְיֶה כַּנַּ"ל, אֲבָל מַה שֶּׁאָמְרָה הַגְּמָרָא וַחֲכָמִים אוֹמְרִים זָכָה מוֹסִיפִין לוֹ, שָׁם יִהְיֶה הַפֵּרוּשׁ זָכָה שֶׁעָשָׂה אֵיזֶה זְכוּת אֲשֶׁר בַּעֲבוּרוֹ יוֹסִיפוּ לוֹ.

כְּלַל הַדָּבָר בַּמֶּה שֶׁכָּתַבְנוּ, כִּי מַה שֶּׁיִּהְיֶה לְהָאָדָם מֵהַקָּדוֹשׁ בָּרוּךְ הוּא הַחַיִּים וְהַבְּרִיאוּת וְכָל הָאֶמְצָעִיִּים לַחַיִּים, אִם הֵמָּה מוֹעִילִים וּמְסַיְּעִים לוֹ לַעֲבוֹדַת הַשֵּׁם יִתְבָּרַךְ, אָז כָּל אָשְׁרוֹ וְטוּבוֹ נוּכַל לוֹמַר אֲשֶׁר הֵמָּה מַגִּיעִים לוֹ מֵהַקָּדוֹשׁ בָּרוּךְ הוּא, וְלֹא יְנַכּוּ לוֹ עֲבוּרָם מֵעוֹלָם הַבָּא, כְּמוֹ שֶׁכָּתַבְנוּ לְעֵיל. אֲבָל אִם נִגְזַר עַל הָאָדָם מֵעֵת לֵדָתוֹ לִהְיוֹת עָנִי וְאֵין לוֹ זְכוּת מִדָּה כְּנֶגֶד מִדָּה לְהִתְעַשֵּׁר, וְיִשָּׁאֵר לְכָל יְמֵי עָנִי רָעִים, לְפִי הַשְׁעָרוֹת הַדַּעַת לֹא יֵחָשְׁבוּ לוֹ הָעֲנִיּוּת לְיִסּוּרִין לְכַפֵּר עָוֹן, וְאִם יִקְרֶה אֲשֶׁר יִתְעַשֵּׁר מְעַט אָז יְנַכּוּ לוֹ מֵהָעוֹלָם הַבָּא. עַל כֵּן כָּל אִישׁ וְאִישׁ לְפִי מַצָּבוֹ, אַף בַּמַּצָּב הַיּוֹתֵר שָׁפֵל, אִם גַּם לֹא שָׁמֵן חֶלְקוֹ בַּחַיִּים וְהַהַצְלָחָה לֹא הֵאִירָה לוֹ פָּנֶיהָ מֵעוֹלָם, בְּכָל זֶה יֵשׁ לוֹ לִפְחֹד וְלִדְאֹג שֶׁמָּא מְנַכִּין לוֹ מֵעוֹלָם הַבָּא, כִּי אוּלַי מִצַּד גְּזֵרַת לֵדָתוֹ הָיָה רָאוּי לִהְיוֹת מַצָּבוֹ יוֹתֵר רַע וְהַמְעַט אֲשֶׁר יֵשׁ לוֹ הוּא רַק עֲבוּר זְכֻיּוֹתָיו אֲשֶׁר יִגָּרַע בָּזֶה חֶלְקוֹ מֵעוֹלָם הַבָּא. וּמַה גַּם לְפִי מַה שֶּׁכָּתוּב בְּנִדָּה (ל"א, א) מַאי דִּכְתִיב עוֹשֶׂה נִפְלָאוֹת (גְּדוֹלוֹת) לְבַדּוֹ, אֲפִלּוּ בַּעַל הַנֵּס אֵינוֹ מַכִּיר בְּנִסּוֹ, הַיְנוּ שֶׁהָאָדָם אֵינוֹ יוֹדֵעַ מַה שֶּׁשְּׁמָרוֹ הַקָּדוֹשׁ בָּרוּךְ הוּא מִן הַפֻּרְעָנִיּוֹת, וְאִם כֵּן אִי אֶפְשָׁר לְהָאָדָם לֵדַע כַּמָּה מְנַכִּין לוֹ מֵעוֹלָם הַבָּא, כֵּיוָן שֶׁאֵינוֹ יוֹדֵעַ כַּמָּה הֵמָּה הַנִּסִּים שֶׁעוֹשֶׂה לוֹ הַקָּדוֹשׁ בָּרוּךְ הוּא.

22. See Proverbs 15:15.

Accordingly, we can understand what is said in Yevamot (50a) on the verse "The number of your days I [God] will fill out" (Ex. 23:26). Rashi explains there: "The number of years allocated to a person at birth – if he is worthy, they are given to him in full." The meaning of "he is worthy" is not that he had merit. Rather, the meaning is that he had nothing that would prevent him from living [his whole life]. This is certainly in accordance with what we said earlier. But regarding what the Talmud said (ibid.): "And the Sages say: If he is worthy, years are added to his life," the meaning of "he is worthy" is that he had some merit for which years were added to his life.

The general principle of what we have said is that what a person has from the Holy One, blessed be He – life, health, and the means of living – if they help and enable him to serve God, then we can say that all his well-being and bounty are deservedly given to him by the Holy One, blessed be He, and nothing will be deducted from [his share in] the next world on their account, as we said above. But if it was decreed on someone at birth to be poor, and he has no merit to make him wealthy *quid pro quo*, so that, by reasonable estimate, he will remain in dire poverty for all his days,[22] then the poverty will not be considered suffering that atones for sin. Then, if it so happens that he becomes a bit richer, there will be deductions from his [reward in] the next world.

Therefore, each person, according to his circumstances, even if he is in the most degraded condition, even if he never lived in luxury and never met with success, he should still be afraid and concerned that perhaps deductions are being made from his [share in] the next world, for perhaps, according to the decree at his birth, his circumstances should have been even worse, and the little that he has is due to his merits, which will diminish his share in the next world. Moreover, according to what [the Sages] said in Nidda (31a), that according to one view, "[God] does wondrous thing alone" (Ps. 72:18) means that "even the beneficiary of a miracle is not aware of the miracle," i.e., the person does not know the extent to which God has protected him from misfortune, it follows that a person cannot know how much is being deducted from his [share in] the next world, since he does not know how many miracles the Holy One, blessed be He, has done for him.

וּבִדְבָרֵינוּ אֵלֶּה נוּכַל לְבָאֵר הַגְּמָרָא בְּרֹאשׁ הַשָּׁנָה שֶׁהֵבֵאנוּ לְעֵיל עַל דֶּרֶךְ זֶה, "צַדִּיקִים" רוֹצֶה לוֹמַר אֲשֶׁר הֵמָּה רֻבָּם זְכֻיּוֹת, וְאִם הֵמָּה רֻבָּם זְכֻיּוֹת, אָז הֵם בְּעֵסֶק הַקָּדוֹשׁ בָּרוּךְ הוּא "נִכְתָּבִים לְחַיִּים" רוֹצֶה לוֹמַר הֵמָּה יִתְיַחֲסוּ לַחַיִּים, כִּי צְרִיכִים הֵם לִחְיוֹת עַל פִּי דֶּרֶךְ הַטֶּבַע. וְגַם כָּל הַדְּבָרִים הַנִּדְרָשִׁים לְצָרְכֵי הַחַיִּים הֵמָּה בִּכְלַל לְחַיִּים כְּדִבְרֵי הָרַמְבַּ"ן בְּשַׁעַר הַגְּמוּל, אֲשֶׁר בְּתֵבַת לְחַיִּים נִכְלָל כָּל הִצְטָרְכוּת הַחַיִּים, וְכַאֲשֶׁר יִחְיֶה הָאָדָם הַזֶּה וְיִהְיֶה לוֹ גַּם צָרְכֵי הַחַיִּים לֹא יְנַכּוּ לוֹ מְאוּמָה עֲבוּרָם מֵעוֹלָם הַבָּא, וְאִם יִקְרֶה לוֹ אַחַר זֶה דְּבַר מָה לְרַע, אָז יִתְחַשֵּׁב לְיִסּוּרִים אֲשֶׁר יְכַפְּרוּ עֲוֹנוֹתָיו, "וּרְשָׁעִים" דְּהַיְנוּ שֶׁהֵם רֻבָּם עֲוֹנוֹת "נִכְתָּבִים לְמִיתָה", רוֹצֶה לוֹמַר הֵם מִדֶּרֶךְ הַטֶּבַע אֵין רָאוּי לִהְיוֹת לָהֶם דְּבַר מָה לְמִחְיָתָם, וְאִם יִהְיֶה לָהֶם דְּבַר מָה, אָז מְנַכִּין לָהֶם מִזְּכֻיּוֹתֵיהֶם.

וְאֶת דְּבָרֵינוּ אֵלֶּה נוּכַל גַּם לְבָאֵר עַל פִּי פֵּרוּשׁ הָרִאשׁוֹנִים שֶׁפֵּרְשׁוּ שֶׁ"צַדִּיקִים" הַכַּוָּנָה שֶׁהֵם צַדִּיקִים בְּדִינָם שֶׁל רֹאשׁ הַשָּׁנָה, אַף כִּי יָכוֹל לִהְיוֹת שֶׁאֵינָם רֻבָּם זְכֻיּוֹת (עַיֵּן בָּרַ"ן) כִּי בֶּאֱמֶת שֶׁיִּקָּרֵא אָדָם צַדִּיק עַל פִּי רֹב זְכֻיּוֹת הוּא דָּבָר כָּבֵד מְאֹד, וְאֵינוֹ מָצוּי כָּל כָּךְ. אֲבָל לִהְיוֹת צַדִּיק רַק עַל הַמִּשְׁפָּט בְּרֹאשׁ הַשָּׁנָה, אֲשֶׁר יִהְיֶה דִּינוֹ כִּי צָרִיךְ הוּא לִחְיוֹת וְלִהְיוֹת לוֹ כָּל הַנִּדְרָשׁ לְחַיִּים, גַּם מִבַּלְעֲדֵי זְכוּת גָּדוֹל אֲשֶׁר יְנַכּוּ לוֹ מֵעוֹלָם הַבָּא, נָקֵל הַדָּבָר גַּם בְּיָמִים אֵלֶּה כַּאֲשֶׁר נָשִׂים עַיִן עַל מַעֲמַד דּוֹרֵנוּ זֶה, וְנָשׁוּב נִרְאֶה לָקַחַת מוּסָר.

וְהִנֵּה כַּאֲשֶׁר נַשְׁקִיף בְּהַשְׁקָפָה נְכוֹנָה עַל מַצַּב הַמּוּסָרִי שֶׁל עַמֵּנוּ בְּיָמֵינוּ אֵלֶּה, הִנֵּה בִּמְעַט הִתְבּוֹנְנוּת נוּכַל לִרְאוֹת כִּי יֵשׁ הֶבְדֵּל גָּדוֹל לְרֹב בְּנֵי עַמֵּנוּ בֵּין הַיָּמִים שֶׁעָבְרוּ לְיָמִים אֵלֶּה אֲשֶׁר אֲנַחְנוּ חַיִּים כְּהַיּוֹם. בְּיָמִים שֶׁעָבְרוּ הָיְתָה עֲבוֹדַת ה' הַפִּנָּה הַיּוֹתֵר נִכְבָּדָה בְּחַיֵּי אִישׁ הַיִּשְׂרְאֵלִי, וְיָדַעְנוּ כִּי כָּל אִישׁ וְאִישׁ אַף אִם הוּא בְּעַצְמוֹ לֹא עָלָה בְּיָדוֹ לִהְיוֹת בְּמַעֲלָה רָמָה בַּעֲבוֹדַת ה', אֲבָל עַל בָּנָיו שָׂם לִבּוֹ וְנַפְשׁוֹ לְהַדְרִיכָם בְּדֶרֶךְ יְשָׁרָה וְלַהֲכִינָם לִהְיוֹת מֻכְשָׁרִים לַעֲבוֹדַת ה' וְלוֹמְדֵי תּוֹרָתוֹ. וְלָכֵן אָז לֹא הָיָה לְהָאָדָם לִפְחֹד כָּךְ כָּךְ עַל מַצָּבוֹ כִּי חַיָּיו וְכָל

23. Ramban, *Shaar HaGemul* (*The Gate of Recompense*) (Jerusalem: Mossad Harav Kook, 1964), 264–5.

With these words of ours, we can explain the Talmud's aforementioned passage in Rosh HaShana (16b) as follows: The righteous – those who have mostly merits – since they have mostly merits, they are part of the project of the Holy One, blessed be He. They are "inscribed for life," i.e., they will be linked to life, for according to the natural state of things, they must live. Furthermore, everything required by life's needs is included in [the inscription] "for life" – as Ramban wrote in *Shaar HaGemul*,[23] "for life" includes all of life's needs. When such a person lives and has all that he needs for living, nothing will be deducted on this account from his [share in] the next world. If something bad occurs to him afterward, it will be considered suffering that atones for his sins. "The wicked" – i.e., those who have mostly sins – "are inscribed for death." That is, by nature, they are not worthy of having anything for sustenance, so if they do have something, it will be deducted from their merits.

We can also explain our words in accordance with the medieval commentators who interpreted "the righteous" to refer to those who are exonerated in their trial at Rosh HaShana, even if they might not have mostly merits (see [the commentary of] Rabbenu Nissim [ad loc.]). In truth, it is very difficult and quite rare for a person to be called righteous on account of having mostly merits. But to be deemed righteous [and exonerated] only with respect to the trial of Rosh HaShana – such that his verdict is that he shall live and have all that is needed for living even without such an abundance of merit that will be deducted from his [share in] the next world – is relatively easy [to achieve], even nowadays, considering the status of our generation. We will return to scrutinize and draw lessons from this.

When we gaze with clear vision upon the ethical condition of our people in these days, with just a bit of reflection we can see that for most of our people, there is a great difference between bygone days and these days, as we live today. In olden times, the service of God was the most honored cornerstone in the life of a Jewish person. We knew that each person – even one who did not personally achieve great heights in the service of God – would still set his heart and soul on his children, to guide them on the straight path and to prepare them to be capable of serving God and studying His Torah. Then, a person did not have to be so afraid about his situation, as his condition in life and his life needs

הִצְטָרְכוּתוֹ לַחַיִּים הָיְתָה עַל חֶשְׁבּוֹן הַבּוֹרֵא יִתְבָּרַךְ שְׁמוֹ. כִּי עַל יְדֵי זֶה יִהְיֶה בְּיָדוֹ לְגַדֵּל וּלְחַנֵּךְ אֶת בָּנָיו לַעֲבוֹדָתוֹ. אֲבָל בְּיָמֵינוּ בִּגְבוּלֵינוּ לְהֵפֶךְ הַדָּבָר בַּעֲוֹנוֹתֵינוּ הָרַבִּים, כִּי הַתְּשׁוּקָה וְהַכֶּסֶף לְגַדֵּל וּלְהַדְרִיךְ אֶת הַבָּנִים בַּתּוֹרָה וַעֲבוֹדַת ה׳ נִתְמַעֲטָה וְקַלָּה מְאֹד מִתְּשׁוּקַת כֶּסֶף הָאָבוֹת בְּעַצְמָם בַּעֲבוֹדַת ה׳, וְאַף הָאָבוֹת אֲשֶׁר דֶּרֶךְ הַתּוֹרָה וְיִרְאָה יָקָר בְּעֵינֵיהֶם, יַעֲלִימוּ עֵינֵיהֶם מִבְּנֵיהֶם, וְלֹא יָשִׂימוּ אֶל לִבָּם לְהַדְרִיכָם וּלְהַיְשִׁירָם לַעֲבוֹדַת ה׳ יִתְבָּרַךְ שְׁמוֹ. וְאִם כֵּן הֲלֹא יִחְיֶה הָאָדָם רַק עַל חֶשְׁבּוֹן עַצְמוֹ.

אָמְנָם בְּכָל זֶה גַּם בְּיָמֵינוּ אֵלֶּה, יֶשְׁנָם עִנְיָנִים גְּדוֹלִים וְרָמִים אֲשֶׁר כָּל אִישׁ וְאִישׁ לְפִי עֶרְכּוֹ יוּכַל לְהַשִּׂיג עַל יָדָם כִּי יִחְיֶה לְמַעַן הַבּוֹרֵא יִתְבָּרַךְ שְׁמוֹ. וְחַיָּיו וְכָל מַחְסוֹרָיו הַמִּצְטָרְכִים לְהַחַיִּים יִהְיֶה עַל חֶשְׁבּוֹן הַקָּדוֹשׁ בָּרוּךְ הוּא. וְהוּא זֶה שֶׁכָּל אִישׁ לְפִי עֶרְכּוֹ יָשִׂים כָּל מַעְיָנוֹ לְפִי שִׂכְלוֹ וְכֹחוֹ לְהִשְׁתַּדֵּל בְּכָל עֹז לְחַזֵּק אֶת עֲבוֹדַת ה׳ יִתְבָּרַךְ שְׁמוֹ, אֲשֶׁר בַּיָּמִים מִלְּפָנִים לֹא כָּל אָדָם הָיָה בְּיָדוֹ לַעֲשׂוֹת כָּזֹאת כִּי אִם צַדִּיק גְּדוֹל הַדּוֹר, לֹא כֵן בְּיָמֵינוּ נִרְאֶה בְּחוּשׁ אֲשֶׁר כָּל אָדָם רָאוּי וּמְכֻשָּׁר לָזֶה.

וְנַצִּיג דָּבָר אֶחָד לְמָשָׁל. נוֹדָע לַכֹּל כִּי לִמּוּד הַתּוֹרָה הִיא עוֹלָה עַל כֹּל, כְּמַאֲמָרָם "תַּלְמוּד תּוֹרָה כְּנֶגֶד כֻּלָּם", וְהִיא נִשְׁמַת חַיֵּי הָאֻמָּה הַיִּשְׂרְאֵלִית וְקִיּוּמָהּ בְּכָל עֵת. וּמַדְרֵגָה הַיּוֹתֵר גְּדוֹלָה בְּלִמּוּד הַתּוֹרָה הִיא לִלְמֹד לָדַעַת לְהוֹרוֹת הוֹרָאָה בְּיִשְׂרָאֵל כַּדָּת וְכַהֲלָכָה עַל פִּי הַגְּמָרָא וְהַפּוֹסְקִים מִבְּלִי שֶׁיִּצְטָרֵךְ לְחַפֵּשׂ בְּפִסְקֵי הָאַחֲרוֹנִים. וְהִנֵּה אַךְ בְּיָמֵינוּ נִמְצָאִים עוֹד צְעִירֵי יָמִים בִּתְכוּנוֹת נַעֲלִים, בְּשִׂכְלָם הַמָּהִיר וּבְבִינָתָם הַיְשָׁרָה, בְּלִמּוּדָם, אֲשֶׁר מְכֻשָּׁרִים הֵמָּה אֲשֶׁר מֵהֶם תֵּצֵא תוֹרָה וְהוֹרָאָה בְּיִשְׂרָאֵל, אֲבָל מַרְבִּיתָם לֹא עֲשִׁירִים הֵמָּה, וְחֶבְלָם לֹא נָפַל בַּנְּעִימִים עֲלֵי חָלֶד, כְּמַאֲמָרָם "הִזָּהֲרוּ בִּבְנֵי עֲנִיִּים שֶׁמֵּהֶם תֵּצֵא תוֹרָה", וְלָכֵן אַף כִּי תְּשׁוּקַת הַתּוֹרָה תְּמַלֵּא אֶת כָּל לְבָבָם וּבְכָל עֹז וְאֹמֶץ יָשׁוּחוּ וְיָשׁוּטוּ בֵּין מִשְׁבְּרֵי וְגַלֵּי מִקְרֵי הַתֵּבֵל, לַעֲבֹר אָרְחוֹת דַּרְכָּם אֶל מְחוֹז חֶפְצָם, לָשׂוּם מִשְׁכָּנָם בְּאֹהֶל הַתּוֹרָה וְלַהֲגוֹת

24. Based on Psalms 16:6.

were provided from the account of the Creator, blessed be He, for with these means he could raise and educate his children to serve Him.

But in our days, in our locales, the matter is reversed, due to our many sins. The longing and yearning to raise and guide children toward Torah and service of God has diminished and is less weighty even than the longing and yearning of the parents for their own service of God. Even parents in whose eyes the way of Torah and fear of God is precious will turn a blind eye to their children and will not attend to guiding and setting them on a straight path to serving God, blessed be His name. Therefore, a person lives only from his own account. Nevertheless, even in our days, there are great and weighty matters that each individual, according to his own level, can achieve and thereby live for the sake of the Creator, blessed be His name. Then, his life and all he needs in life will be from the account of the Holy One, blessed be He. That is, each person, according to his level, should concentrate all his strength and intellectual effort toward strengthening the service of God, blessed be His name. In bygone times, not everyone could do this – only a righteous leader of the generation. This is not so in our time; we actually see that every single person is worthy and capable of this.

Let us present one example: Everyone knows that studying Torah surpasses all [mitzvot], as [the Sages] said: "Torah study equals them all" (Mishna Pe'ah 1:1). It is the animating spirit of the Jewish nation and sustains its existence at all times. Now, the highest level of Torah study is to learn to know and issue proper halakhic instruction in Israel, based on the Talmud and the legal codes, without having to search the rulings of later authorities.

In our times, there are still young people with superior talents, quick intelligence, and clear understanding in their learning, who are qualified and from whom Torah and instruction will go out among Israel. However, most of them are not wealthy. Pleasant portions have not been bequeathed to them on earth.[24] It is as [the Sages] said: "Be attentive to the children of the poor, for from them shall come forth Torah" (Nedarim 81a). Therefore, the desire for Torah fills their hearts completely, and with great effort and strength they swim and float between the breakers and waves of worldly events, and they stay the course to their desired destination – to dwell in the tent of the Torah

בָּהּ, בְּכָל זֶה לֹא יַעַצְרוּ כֹּחַ לְהַתְמִיד יָמִים רַבִּים בְּלִמּוּדָם, כִּי סוֹף סוֹף תִּגְבַּר עֲלֵיהֶם דַּאֲגַת מִחְיָתָם וּמִחְיַת אַנְשֵׁי בֵיתָם. כִּי לֹא כַּיָּמִים מִלְּפָנִים, הַיָּמִים הָאֵלֶּה לָנוּ. צָרְכֵי הַחַיִּים נִתְרַבּוּ בְּיָמֵינוּ, וְהַפַּרְנָסָה נִתְמַעֲטָה, וְגַם מַעְיְנֵי הַפַּרְנָסָה אֲשֶׁר שָׁאֲבוּ לָהֶם לוֹמְדֵי תּוֹרָה דָּלְלוּ וְחָרְבוּ בְּיָמֵינוּ, כִּי בְּיָמִים שֶׁעָבְרוּ, הַצָּעִיר לְיָמִים אֲשֶׁר הִשְׁלִים חֹק לִמּוּדוֹ, וּכְבָר מָצְאָה יָדוֹ לְהוֹרוֹת וְלָדוּן, טֶרֶם מָצָא מָקוֹם לְכַהֵן בָּהּ בְּתוֹר מוֹרֵה הוֹרָאָה, וְגַם מִי אֲשֶׁר לֹא הִשְׁלִים עֲדֶנָה חֹק לִמּוּדוֹ לְהוֹרוֹת, בֶּטַח הָיָה יָכוֹל גַּם כֵּן לָלֶכֶת בְּדַרְכּוֹ הָלְאָה לְהַשְׁלִים חָקּוֹ, כִּי נָקֵל הָיָה לָהֶם לִמְצֹא מִחְיָתָם וְצָרְכֵיהֶם, בַּאֲשֶׁר כְּבוֹד הַתּוֹרָה הָיָה גָּדוֹל בַּיָּמִים הָהֵם וּבַעֲלֵי בָתִּים עֲשִׁירִים אֲשֶׁר הָיוּ לָהֶם בָּנִים אֲשֶׁר רָאוּ בָהֶם אוֹתוֹת כִּשָׁרוֹן אֲשֶׁר יַצְלִיחוּ וְיַעֲשׂוּ פְּרִי בְּלִמּוּד הַתּוֹרָה פִּזְּרוּ כֶּסֶף רַב עֲלֵיהֶם וְשָׂכְרוּ לָהֶם מוֹרִים מֻבְהָקִים כָּאֵלֶּה אֲשֶׁר הִשִּׂיגוּ עֲבוּר לִמּוּדָם שָׂכָר רַב וְהֶעָמָל וְהַזְּמַן לָזֶה הָיוּ מְעַט, וּמִזֶּה הָיָה מְקוֹם מוֹצָא לְפַרְנָסָתָם, וְיֶתֶר הָעֵת הֶאֱצִילוּ לְמִשְׁמֶרֶת תּוֹרָתָם.

אֲבָל לֹא כֵן בְּיָמֵינוּ אֵלֶּה אֲשֶׁר לִמּוּדֵי חֹל נִפְרָץ בֵּין בָּנֵינוּ בְּמִדָּה נִפְרָזָה, וְהַתּוֹרָה יָרְדָה מִכְּבוֹדָהּ, וְהַתְּשׁוּקָה לְלִמּוּד הַתּוֹרָה נִתְמַעֲטָה גַּם מִן הָאָבוֹת גַּם מִן הַבָּנִים הֲלֹא נִגְרַע הַסִּבָּה, וּמִמֵּילָא נִתְמַעֵט הַמְּסֻבָּב, וּמֵאַיִן יָבוֹא עֵזֶר לְאֵלֶּה הַשְּׂרִידִים הַיּוֹשְׁבִים לִפְנֵי ה׳ וְהוֹגִים בַּתּוֹרָה יוֹמָם וָלַיְלָה, וְאִם לֹא יִמְצְאוּ מַשְׁעֵן כֶּסֶף לְמוֹצָא פַּרְנָסָתָם אָז חַס וְשָׁלוֹם כָּל טָרְחָם וַעֲמָלָם יַעֲלוּ בַתֹּהוּ, וְהִיא אֲבֵדָה שֶׁאֵין לָהּ תַּשְׁלוּמִין, וּבְזֶה הָאֹפֶן הֲלֹא יִמְעֲטוּ וְיָשֹׁחוּ דּוֹרְשֵׁי הַתּוֹרָה וְהַהוֹגִים בָּהּ וְאָז הֲלֹא יִמּוֹט חַס וְשָׁלוֹם הָעַמּוּד הָרִאשׁוֹן אֲשֶׁר הָעוֹלָם עוֹמֵד עָלָיו. וּבִלְתִּי הַתּוֹרָה כְּאַיִן וּכְאֶפֶס נֶחְשָׁב חַיֵּי אִישׁ הַיִּשְׂרְאֵלִי, כִּי מַצָּבוֹ הַחָמְרִי וְהַמּוּסָרִי נִיסַד אַךְ עַל אַדְנֵי הַתּוֹרָה. וְאַחֲרֵי אֲשֶׁר אֲנַחְנוּ רוֹאִים כִּי הַתּוֹרָה הוֹלֶכֶת וְדַלָּה יוֹם יוֹם מִלּוֹמְדֶיהָ, אִם כֵּן אֵפוֹא מַה יִּהְיֶה מִבָּנֵינוּ אַחֲרֵינוּ בְּדוֹר יָבוֹא, הֲלֹא יִתְנַגְּפוּ רַגְלֵיהֶם בְּהִכָּשְׁלָם בְּדַרְכֵי הַתּוֹרָה בְּאֵין מוֹרֶה וּמְנַהֵל לָהֶם, וּבַחֲשֵׁכָה יִתְהַלְּכוּ בְּאֵין מִי אֲשֶׁר יָאִיר

25. See Avot 1:2: "The world stands on three things: on Torah, on divine service, and on acts of loving-kindness."

26. Based on Jeremiah 13:16.

and to study it intensely – still, they are incapable of sustaining this for long in their studies. In the end, the concern for their livelihood and sustenance for their households will overcome them. For our time is not like the days before us. The needs for living have increased in our days, and income has diminished. The wellsprings of livelihood from which students of Torah drew have thinned out and dried up in our times. In past times, a young person who finished his course of studies and could already issue instruction and serve as a judge even before finding a place to serve as a decisor of halakha, as well as someone who had not yet finished his course of study to become a decisor, could continue forward and finish the course of study because it was easy for them to find a livelihood and meet their needs; since the prestige of Torah was great in those days, rich lay people who had sons in whom they saw signs of talent that they would succeed and bring forth fruit in studying Torah would spend a lot of money on them, hiring highly qualified tutors for them. Thus, for their studies, [the tutors] received good wages without investing a great deal of time and effort. This offered an opportunity to make a living while setting aside their remaining time to Torah study.

This is not the case in our days, when secular studies are excessively common among our sons, the Torah has lost its prestige, and the yearning to study Torah has diminished, among parents and children. Then if the cause has been removed, then the effect diminishes on its own, so from where will help come to these remnants who sit before God and meditate upon the Torah day and night? If they will not find financial support to sustain them, then, God forbid, all their effort and hard work will yield nothing. This would be an irreplaceable loss.

This is how those who seek Torah and study it deeply will diminish and decline, and then, the first pillar on which the world stands,[25] God forbid, will collapse. Without Torah, the life of a Jewish person is considered like zero, worthless, for his material and moral condition is based only upon the foundation of Torah. And now that we see that the Torah is being stripped each day from those who study it, what, indeed, will become of our children after us, in the next generation? Their feet will stumble[26] as they stagger along the paths of Torah, without the aid of any teacher or guide. They will walk in darkness, without anyone to

לָהֶם אֶת הַדֶּרֶךְ בְּאוֹר הַתּוֹרָה, וְאֵין מִי אֲשֶׁר יוֹרֶה דָּת וְדִין, וְאִם כֵּן כָּל אִישׁ יָשָׁר הוֹלֵךְ וְזִיק אַהֲבַת עַמּוֹ וְתוֹרָתוֹ עוֹד לֹא נִכְבָּה מִקֶּרֶב לִבּוֹ, יָבִין אֵיךְ נָחוּץ לָנוּ לְמַהֵר לְתַקֵּן אֶת הַפִּרְצָה הַזּוֹ אֲשֶׁר תּוּכַל לִהְיוֹת לְפֶרֶץ רָחָב בְּחוֹמַת הַדָּת. וְהַתִּקּוּן לָזֶה לְחַזֵּק אָשְׁיוֹתֶיהָ לְבַל יִמּוֹטוּ לֹא נִפְלֵאת וְלֹא רְחוֹקָה הִיא מֵאִתָּנוּ, וּבְנָקֵל נוּכַל לַעֲשׂוֹתָהּ אִם אַךְ כָּל אִישׁ אֲשֶׁר נָגַע יִרְאַת ה׳ בְּלִבּוֹ יְשַׁחֵד מִכֹּחוֹ וּמָמוֹנוֹ לָתֵת סַעַד לְאֵלֶּה הַלּוֹמְדִים צְעִירֵי הַיָּמִים אֲשֶׁר הִקְדִּישׁוּ אֶת עַצְמָם וְאֶת חֶלְקָם בַּחַיִּים אַךְ לִלְמוֹד הַתּוֹרָה לְמַעַן אֲשֶׁר יוּכְלוּ לִלְמֹד בְּאֵין מַפְרִיעַ, אִם יִהְיֶה לָהֶם מִחְיָתָם, וְיָדָם תִּמְצָא לְשַׁלֵּחַ מָה גַּם לִבְנֵי בֵּיתָם.

וְלַדָּבָר הַזֶּה נִצְרָךְ אַךְ מַעֲשִׂים, וְכָל אִישׁ לְפִי מַדְרֵגָתוֹ מֻכְשָׁר לִהְיוֹת מַעֲשֶׂה אִם אָמְנָם אִישׁ רַם הַמַּעֲלָה מֻכְשָׁר יוֹתֵר לִהְיוֹת מְעַשֶּׂה, אֲבָל בַּדָּבָר הַזֶּה אֲשֶׁר כָּל אִישׁ יָבִין כִּי נָחוּץ הוּא בְּיָמֵינוּ, יוּכַל כָּל אִישׁ לִהְיוֹת מְעוֹרֵר וּמְעַשֶּׂה בַּדָּבָר, וְגָדוֹל הַמְעַשֶּׂה יוֹתֵר מִן הָעוֹשֶׂה כַּמְבֹאָר בְּבָבָא בַּתְרָא, וְהָאִישׁ אֲשֶׁר יִתְאַמֵּץ בְּמִצְוָה רַבָּה כָּזוֹ אֲשֶׁר שָׁרָשֶׁיהָ עַל מַבּוּעֵי הַתּוֹרָה לַעֲשׂוֹת עָנָף וּלְהַגְדִּיל פְּרִי בְּכֶרֶם הַתּוֹרָה עָלָיו יְקֻיַּם הַמִּקְרָא עֵץ חַיִּים הִיא לַמַּחֲזִיקִים בָּהּ וְגוֹ׳.

וְאִיתָא בְּגִטִּין (ס, א), אָמַר ר׳ יוֹחָנָן, לֹא כָּרַת הַקָּדוֹשׁ בָּרוּךְ הוּא בְּרִית עִם יִשְׂרָאֵל אֶלָּא בִּשְׁבִיל תּוֹרָה שֶׁבְּעַל פֶּה, שֶׁנֶּאֱמַר עַל פִּי הַדְּבָרִים הָאֵלֶּה כָּרַתִּי אִתְּךָ בְּרִית, עַיֵּן שָׁם. וּלְהַסְבִּיר הָעִנְיָן מַדּוּעַ דַּוְקָא בִּשְׁבִיל תּוֹרָה שֶׁבְּעַל פֶּה וְלֹא בִּשְׁבִיל תּוֹרָה שֶׁבִּכְתָב, נוּכַל לוֹמַר כִּי הַמִּדְרָשׁ יַחְקֹר אִם יִשְׂרָאֵל נִבְרְאוּ בִּשְׁבִיל הַתּוֹרָה, אוֹ הַתּוֹרָה בִּשְׁבִיל יִשְׂרָאֵל, וּמַסְקָנַת הַמִּדְרָשׁ כִּי הַתּוֹרָה בִּשְׁבִיל יִשְׂרָאֵל. אֲבָל בָּזֶה יֵשׁ שְׁתֵּי בְּחִינוֹת, הַיְסוֹד הָאֲמִתִּי הוּא, כִּי הָעִקָּר נָתַן הַקָּדוֹשׁ בָּרוּךְ הוּא הַתּוֹרָה בִּשְׁבִיל יִשְׂרָאֵל. אֲבָל זֶהוּ רַק אִם יִשְׂרָאֵל עוֹמְדִים בְּמַדְרֵגָה עֶלְיוֹנָה

27. Based on Deuteronomy 29:11.
28. At a low spiritual and moral level.

illuminate their path with the light of the Torah. There will be no one to instruct [in matters of] law and halakha.

Therefore, every person who walks straight and in whose heart the spark of love for his people and his Torah has not been extinguished will understand how important it is for us to swiftly repair this breach, which can become a broad rupture in the fortress of the faith. The remedy for all this – to strengthen the foundations so that they do not collapse – is neither beyond us nor remote.[27] We can easily accomplish it, if only every person whose heart has been touched by fear of God would set aside some of his strength and money to give support to those young students who have devoted themselves and their lot in life exclusively to study of Torah, so they can study without distraction, for they will have a livelihood and can even send something to their family members. To accomplish this, we need people who elicit action in others. Every person, according to his standing, can elicit others. It is true that a person of high standing is better able to elicit action from others, but with respect to this matter, which every person will understand to be especially needed in our time, every person can inspire and elicit action in others. "Greater is the one who elicits action than the doer of the deed," as explained in Bava Batra (9a). A person who makes an extra effort for this great mitzva, the roots of which draw from the flowing streams of the Torah and which will create a new branch to raise fruits in the vineyard of Torah, will be a fulfillment of the verse "It is a tree of life to those who hold onto it" (Prov. 3:18).

The Talmud states in Gittin (60b): "R. Yoḥanan said: The Holy One, blessed be He, established a covenant with Israel only for the sake of the Oral Torah, as it is written: 'On the basis of (lit. by the *mouth* of) these words I established a covenant with you' (Ex. 34:27)." See further there. To explain why it was specifically for the sake of the Oral Torah and not for the sake of the Written Torah, we can say that the midrash is exploring whether Israel was created for the sake of the Torah or the Torah for the sake of Israel. The midrash concludes that the Torah is for the sake of Israel. But there are two dimensions to this; the true principle is that the Holy One, blessed be He, essentially gave the Torah for the sake of Israel. However, this obtains only if Israel stands at the highest

אַךְ אִם הֵם בְּהִפּוּךְ חַס וְשָׁלוֹם, אָז הוּא יִשְׂרָאֵל בִּשְׁבִיל הַתּוֹרָה. וְיֵשׁ לָנוּ לוֹמַר בִּשְׁבִיל זֶה יָסַד הַקָּדוֹשׁ בָּרוּךְ הוּא שֶׁתִּהְיֶה הַבְּחִינָה 'עֲבוֹדָה צֹרֶךְ גָּבוֹהַּ', הַיְנוּ שֶׁהָעֲבוֹדָה תִּהְיֶה מְצִיאוּת בִּפְנֵי עַצְמָהּ כְּדֵי שֶׁיִּהְיֶה קִיּוּם לְיִשְׂרָאֵל, כִּי עֲבוֹדָה בִּלְתִּי אֶפְשָׁר לִהְיוֹת בְּלִי יִשְׂרָאֵל, כִּדְאִיתָא שַׁבָּת (ל, א) בַּמֵּתִים חָפְשִׁי, כֵּיוָן שֶׁמֵּת אָדָם נַעֲשֶׂה חָפְשִׁי מִן הַתּוֹרָה וּמִן הַמִּצְוֹת. נִמְצָא לְפִי זֶה הַבְּחִינָה הָוֵי יִשְׂרָאֵל בִּשְׁבִיל הַתּוֹרָה.

וְאִיתָא בְּמַסֶּכֶת קִדּוּשִׁין (סו, א) כַּאֲשֶׁר אָמַר אֱלִיעֶזֶר בֶּן פּוֹעֵרָה לְיַנַּאי הַמֶּלֶךְ לְאַבֵּד חַכְמֵי יִשְׂרָאֵל, אֲמַר לֵיהּ, וְתוֹרָה מַה תְּהֵא עָלֶיהָ? הֲרֵי כְּרוּכָה וּמֻנַּחַת בְּקֶרֶן זָוִית כָּל הָרוֹצֶה לִלְמֹד יָבוֹא וְיִלְמֹד, תֵּנַח תּוֹרָה שֶׁבִּכְתָב, תּוֹרָה שֶׁבְּעַל פֶּה מַאי אִכָּא לְמֵימַר? עַיֵּן שָׁם. נִמְצָא מְבֹאָר מִזֶּה כִּי אֹפֶן הַבְּחִינָה שֶׁאָמַרְנוּ יִשְׂרָאֵל בִּשְׁבִיל הַתּוֹרָה, הוּא רַק בִּשְׁבִיל תּוֹרָה שֶׁבְּעַל פֶּה כִּי הַתּוֹרָה שֶׁבִּכְתָב הֲלֹא אֶפְשָׁר לִהְיוֹת כְּרוּכָה וּמֻנַּחַת עַד יָבוֹא מִי שֶׁרָאוּי לָהּ וְיִלְמֹד.

וְהִנֵּה אֵימָתַי צְרִיכִים יִשְׂרָאֵל לִכְרִיתוּת בְּרִית, הוּא רַק כְּשֶׁאֵין יִשְׂרָאֵל בַּמַּדְרֵגָה הָעֶלְיוֹנָה וְאָז הוּא יִשְׂרָאֵל בִּשְׁבִיל הַתּוֹרָה וְלָכֵן קָאָמַר הַגְּמָרָא לֹא כָּרַת הַקָּדוֹשׁ בָּרוּךְ הוּא בְּרִית עִם יִשְׂרָאֵל (הַיְנוּ בְּעֵת שֶׁהֵם בְּמַדְרֵגָה פְּחוּתָה שֶׁצְּרִיכִים לִכְרִיתוּת בְּרִית) אֶלָּא בִּשְׁבִיל תּוֹרָה שֶׁבְּעַל פֶּה שֶׁצְּרִיכָה לִהְיוֹת אִישׁ מִפִּי אִישׁ, וְלָכֵן אִי אֶפְשָׁר בִּלְתִּי יִשְׂרָאֵל.

וְאִיתָא בִּתְמוּרָה (טז, א), ג' אֲלָפִים הֲלָכוֹת נִשְׁתַּכְּחוּ בִּימֵי אֶבְלוֹ שֶׁל מֹשֶׁה, וְאַף עַל פִּי כֵן הֶחֱזִירָן עָתְנִיאֵל בֶּן קְנַז בְּפִלְפּוּלוֹ. רוֹאִים אָנוּ מִזֶּה כִּי לִפְעָמִים יִמָּצֵא אִישׁ חָכָם מְאֹד נַעֲלֶה שֶׁיָּכוֹל לֵידַע בְּפִלְפּוּלוֹ כָּל תּוֹרָה שֶׁבְּעַל פֶּה מֵעַצְמוֹ, אֲבָל כָּל זֶה הוּא רַק בִּכְלַל תּוֹרָה שֶׁבְּעַל פֶּה, אֲבָל לֹא בַּהֲלָכָה לְמֹשֶׁה מִסִּינַי, אֲשֶׁר הֵם אֵינָם תַּחַת גֶּדֶר הַשֵּׂכֶל וְאִי אֶפְשָׁר לָדַעַת אוֹתָם כִּי אִם אִישׁ מִפִּי אִישׁ. וְזֶה אֶפְשָׁר כַּוָּנַת הַגְּמָרָא (סוֹף נִדָּה) כָּל הַשּׁוֹנֶה הֲלָכוֹת בְּכָל יוֹם מֻבְטָח לוֹ שֶׁהוּא בֶּן עוֹלָם הַבָּא, כִּי אָמְנָם יָדוּעַ אֲשֶׁר גַּם פּוֹשְׁעֵי יִשְׂרָאֵל מְלֵאִים מִצְוֹת כָּרִמּוֹן, וְכֻלָּם

level. If they are, God forbid, at the opposite pole,[28] then Israel is created for the sake of the Torah.

We may say further that this is why the Holy One, blessed be He, ordained the dimension of "divine service is a need of the Most High," that is, that the divine service should be an entity unto itself so that the existence of Israel will be assured – for there can be no divine service without Israel. As the Talmud states in Shabbat (30a): "The dead are free" (Ps. 88:6) – once a person dies he is free of Torah and mitzvot. We thus find that, according to this dimension, "Israel is for the sake of the Torah." In Kiddushin (66a) we find that when Eliezer ben Po'eyrah told King Jannaeus to wipe out the sages of Israel, [the king] said to him: What will become of the Torah? [He answered:] The Torah is rolled up and lies in a corner; let all who wish to study come and study. [The king challenged this:] This is fine for the Written Torah; but what can we say about the Oral Torah? See further there.

From this we see clearly that the dimension we discussed, that Israel exists for the sake of the Torah, applies only for the sake of the Oral Torah – for the Written Torah can be rolled up and placed in a corner until someone worthy of it comes and studies it. So when does Israel need to establish a covenant? Only when Israel is not at the highest level; then it is "Israel for the sake of the Torah." Therefore, the Gemara says: "The Holy One, blessed be He, established a covenant with Israel (that is, when they are at a lower level and need to enter a covenant) only for the sake of the Oral Torah, which must be [transmitted] from person to person. Therefore, this is impossible without Israel."

It is stated in Temura (15b): "Three thousand halakhot were forgotten during the days of mourning for Moses; nevertheless, Othniel ben Kenaz recovered them through his analysis." We see from this that sometimes there can be a superior sage who is able to know on his own, through analysis, the whole Oral Torah. But this can only apply to the Oral Torah, not to halakhot given to Moses at Sinai, which do not fall into the parameters of reason, so they can only be known by person-to-person [transmission].

This may be the meaning of the Gemara (at the end of Nidda): "Whoever studies halakhot every day is assured a place in the next world." Now, it is known that even Israel's sinners are full of mitzvot as a

יֵשׁ לָהֶם חֵלֶק לָעוֹלָם הַבָּא, רַק כָּל הַפַּחַד עַל חֶלְקוֹ בָּעוֹלָם הַבָּא, הוּא שֶׁמָּא מְנַכִּין לוֹ מִזְּכִיּוֹתָיו בַּעֲבוּר טוֹבָתוֹ בָּעוֹלָם הַזֶּה. וּבְיוֹתֵר שֶׁמָּא מְנַכִּין לוֹ עַל אֲשֶׁר שְׁמָרוֹ הַקָּדוֹשׁ בָּרוּךְ הוּא מֵהַפֻּרְעָנוּת אֲשֶׁר הָיוּ מִתְרַגְּשׁוֹת עָלָיו כִּדְבָרֵינוּ לְעֵיל. אֲבָל הַשּׁוֹנֶה הֲלָכוֹת בְּכָל יוֹם אֲשֶׁר הִיא הַמַּטָּרָה אֲשֶׁר הַתּוֹרָה לֹא תִשְׁתַּכַּח וְלֹא תֹאבַד חַס וְשָׁלוֹם, לָכֵן כַּאֲשֶׁר הַקָּדוֹשׁ בָּרוּךְ הוּא מְשַׁלֵּם לְהָאָדָם מִדָּה כְּנֶגֶד מִדָּה, מְשַׁמְּרוֹ הַקָּדוֹשׁ בָּרוּךְ הוּא מֵהַפֻּרְעָנוּת שֶׁלֹּא יֹאבְדוּ בְּרִיאוּתוֹ וְקִנְיָנוֹ. מִמֵּילָא נִשְׁאַר לוֹ הַתּוֹרָה וְהַמַּעֲשִׂים טוֹבִים לָעוֹלָם הַבָּא. וְלָכֵן קָאָמְרָה הַגְּמָרָא מֻבְטָח לוֹ שֶׁהוּא בֶּן הָעוֹלָם הַבָּא.

וּכְמוֹ כֵן הַמַּחֲזִיק יְדֵי הַלּוֹמְדִים אֲשֶׁר יָדָם רַב לָהֶם בְּלִמּוּד הַתּוֹרָה שֶׁיִּהְיֶה לָהֶם מִשְׁעָן נָכוֹן לִבְנֵי בֵּיתָם לִשְׁלֹחַ לָהֶם עַל פַּרְנָסָתָם אֲשֶׁר עַל יְדֵי זֶה לֹא יֵלֵךְ חַס וְשָׁלוֹם לְאִבּוּד יְגִיעָתָם בְּלִמּוּדָם עַל יְדֵי טִרְדַּת פַּרְנָסָתָם, הָעוֹשֶׂה וְהַמְעַשֶּׂה לַתַּכְלִית הַזֶּה יָכוֹל לְקַוּוֹת כִּי הַקָּדוֹשׁ בָּרוּךְ הוּא יַצִּילוֹ מִכָּל הַפֻּרְעָנִיּוֹת. וְגַם בִּשְׁבִיל שֶׁעַל יָדוֹ יִהְיֶה בְּיַד הַלּוֹמֵד לַעֲלוֹת לְמַעְלָה יוֹתֵר בְּלִמּוּדוֹ וְיַעֲשֶׂה פְּרִי לְהַגְדִּיל תּוֹרָה וּלְהַאֲדִירָהּ, יָכוֹל הַתּוֹמֵךְ וְהַמְסַיֵּעַ לְקַוּוֹת כִּי הַשֵּׁם יִתְבָּרַךְ יַצְלִיחוֹ בְּטוּב וְעֹשֶׁר בָּעוֹלָם הַזֶּה, וְלֹא יְנַכּוּ לוֹ מֵעוֹלָם הַבָּא. כִּי הֲלֹא בִּפְעֻלָּתוֹ וְהִשְׁתַּדְּלוּתוֹ כּוֹנֵן וְהֵקִים דָּבָר יָקָר וְנִכְבָּד לִפְנֵי הַשֵּׁם יִתְבָּרַךְ אֲשֶׁר חֶפְצוֹ כִּי יַחֲזִיקוּ בְּלוֹמְדֵי תּוֹרָה עַד כִּי יֻכְשְׁרוּ לִהְיוֹת מוֹרֵי הוֹרָאָה בְּיִשְׂרָאֵל, וְכְדַאי הוּא לְהַשֵּׁם יִתְבָּרַךְ כִּי יְחַיֶּה וְחַיָּיו וְכָל מַחְסוֹרָיו הוּא עַל חֶשְׁבּוֹן הַקָּדוֹשׁ בָּרוּךְ הוּא.

וְהִנֵּה לְפִי מַה שֶּׁכָּתַבְנוּ לְעֵיל בִּבְחִינַת לִהְיוֹת צַדִּיק אֶל הַמִּשְׁפָּט שֶׁל רֹאשׁ הַשָּׁנָה, הִנֵּה בַּיָּמִים מִלְּפָנִים הָיָה נָקֵל לִהְיוֹת בִּבְחִינַת צַדִּיק אֶל הַמִּשְׁפָּט שֶׁל רֹאשׁ הַשָּׁנָה, עַל יְדֵי גִּדּוּל בָּנִים לַתּוֹרָה. אוֹ אַף אִם לֹא הָיוּ לוֹ בָּנִים, נָקֵל הָיָה לוֹ לְהַשִּׂיג לִסְמֹךְ וְלַעֲזֹר לְבָנִים אֲחֵרִים

---

29. That is, since, by reviewing halakhot daily, this person ensures that the Torah endures, God will reward him *quid pro quo* by ensuring that he endures, i.e., by preserving his health and livelihood.

30. A paraphrase of Isaiah 42:21.

pomegranate [is full of seeds; see Eiruvin 19a], and they all have a share in the next world [per Mishna Sanhedrin 10:1]. The sole fear regarding one's share in the next world is that there are deductions [from it] on account of the good he receives in this world. Even more so [he is concerned] that there are deductions from his merits because the Holy One, blessed be He, protected him from calamities that would have befallen him, as we explained above. However, one who "studies halakhot every day," whose goal is that the Torah not be forgotten or lost, God forbid, when the Holy One, blessed be He, repays a person *quid pro quo*, the Holy One, blessed be He, [also] protects him from calamities – that he not lose his health or his possessions.[29] Consequently, his Torah and good deeds remain his in the next world. Thus, the Gemara says, he "is assured a place in the next world."

Similarly, one who strengthens the hands of the scholars who have accomplished much Torah study, so that they have steady support to send to their households for their sustenance – and thus, their efforts in their studies will not, God forbid, be wasted on account of the burden of making a livelihood – [as well as] one who acts and elicits action in others to these ends can hope that the Holy One, blessed be He, will save him from all calamities. Moreover, since, thanks to him, the scholar can achieve higher levels in his studies, producing fruit that will magnify and glorify the Torah,[30] the supporter and giver of aid can hope that Hashem, the Blessed, will bring him success with all the goodness and success of this world, without deducting from [his share in] the next world. After all, through his activities and advocacy he has founded and established something precious and honored before Hashem, the Blessed, in that his desire is to support students of Torah until they are prepared to be issuers of halakhic instruction in Israel. Therefore, it is worthwhile for Hashem, the Blessed, to sustain him, and for his life and all his needs to be on the account of the Holy One, blessed be He.

According to what I wrote above, on being deemed righteous with respect to the trial of Rosh HaShana: In bygone days it was easy to be deemed righteous in the trial of Rosh HaShana – by raising children [devoted] to Torah. Even if he had no children, it was easy for him to attain by supporting and aiding the children of others, so that

אֲשֶׁר יְגַדְּלוּ עַל בִּרְכֵּי הַתּוֹרָה וִילַמְּדוּ אוֹתָהּ, כֵּן גַּם בְּיָמֵינוּ אַף כִּי לֹא בְנָקֵל יוּכַל הָאָדָם לְהַדְרִיךְ אֶת בָּנָיו כְּחֶפְצוֹ, בְּכָל זֶה יֵשׁ גַּם עַתָּה אֹפֶן אֲשֶׁר כָּל אִישׁ יָכוֹל לִזְכּוֹת עַל יָדוֹ, בְּזֶה אֲשֶׁר יִתֵּן עֵזֶר וְסַעַד לְאֵלֶּה אֲשֶׁר כְּבָר גָּדְלוּ בַּתּוֹרָה לְמַעַן יוּכְלוּ לְהַחֲזִיק בְּמָעֻזָּם וּלְהִשְׁתַּלֵּם עוֹד יוֹתֵר, אֲשֶׁר הַדָּבָר הַזֶּה הוּא מֵהַדְּבָרִים הָעוֹמְדִים בְּרוּמוֹ שֶׁל עוֹלָם, וּמִפְעָל יָקָר הוּא לִפְנֵי הַשֵּׁם יִתְבָּרַךְ, אֲשֶׁר עַל יְדֵי זֶה יֵצֵא מִשְׁפָּטוֹ לַטּוֹב בְּיוֹם הַדִּין וְיִכָּתֵב לְחַיִּים.

וְהִנֵּה אַף כִּי מוּבָן אֲשֶׁר עִקַּר הַנְהָגַת הַבּוֹרֵא אֶת הָעוֹלָם בְּיָמֵינוּ אֵלֶּה, הוּא בַּמַּהֲלָךְ הַטִּבְעִי, וּמַהֲלַךְ הַתּוֹרָה אֵינוֹ נִרְגָּשׁ עוֹד בְּיָמֵינוּ, בְּכָל זֹאת יָדַעְנוּ וּמְקֻבָּל בְּיָדֵינוּ, כִּי קִיּוּם הָעוֹלָם הֵן בְּרוּחָנִיּוּת הֵן בְּגַשְׁמִיּוּת הוּא עַל יְדֵי תּוֹרָתָן שֶׁל תַּלְמִידֵי חֲכָמִים, וּכְמַאֲמָרָם בְּסַנְהֶדְרִין (צט, ב) אֶפִּיקוֹרֶס כְּגוֹן מַאן? אָמַר רַב יוֹסֵף כְּגוֹן הָנֵי דְּאָמְרִי מַאי אַהֲנֵי לָן רַבָּנָן, לְדִידְהוּ קָרוּ, לְדִידְהוּ תָּנוּ וכו׳, וְכָל אֶחָד וְאֶחָד צָרִיךְ לְהַאֲמִין כִּי הָעוֹלָם אֵינוֹ מִתְקַיֵּם אַךְ עַל יְדֵי תּוֹרָתָם, וְאַף שֶׁאֵינוֹ נִרְאֶה לְעֵין הַחוּשׁ הַהֶבְדֵּל בֵּין הַמָּקוֹם אֲשֶׁר יִמָּצְאוּ הַרְבֵּה תַּלְמִידֵי חֲכָמִים הַהוֹגִים בַּתּוֹרָה וּבֵין הַמָּקוֹם אֲשֶׁר מְעַטִּים הֵמָּה. אֲבָל יֵשׁ הֶפְרֵשׁ גָּדוֹל לָעוֹלָם הַנִּצְחִי וְהַקַּיָּם כַּנַּ״ל, כִּי רַק בָּעוֹלָם הַנִּסִּיִּי נִכָּר עֹנֶשׁ הַחוֹטֵא וּבָעוֹלָם הַטִּבְעִי אֵינוֹ נִכָּר, וְהָעִקָּר לָעוֹלָם הַנִּצְחִי וְהַקַּיָּם. וּבִמְעַט הִתְבּוֹנְנוּת נוּכַל לְהָבִין אֲשֶׁר לְפִי הַשֵּׂכֶל הַמַּטָּרָה לְתוֹעֶלֶת מַצָּב הַנִּצְחִי הִיא יוֹתֵר הֶכְרֵחִית וְעִקָּרִית מִמַּטְּרָתוֹ לְמַצָּבוֹ בָּעוֹלָם הַזֶּה בְּעֵת אֲשֶׁר עַצְמוּתוֹ הוּא נַפְשׁוֹ בְּהִתְקַשְּׁרוּת עִם הַגּוּף, כִּי הֲלֹא הַהִתְקַשְּׁרוּת הַזֹּאת מֻכְרָח לְהִנָּתֵק וּלְהִפָּרֵד בְּכָל אָדָם, וְאַךְ עַצְמוּתוֹ לֹא תִּכְלֶה וְלֹא תֵּאָפֵס רַק תִּשָּׁאֵר בְּהֶרְגֵּשׁ שָׁלֵם, וְאוּלַי עוֹד בְּהֶרְגֵּשׁ יוֹתֵר גָּדוֹל וְחָזָק, לְהַרְגִּישׁ

---

31. In this letter, R. Salanter described two processes by which God governs the world: the natural process, meaning, the laws of nature, and the Torah process, in which good is rewarded and evil punished. Here he acknowledges, strikingly, that the Torah process is hidden, and people's actions are determined by the natural process that is discernible to them. Unlike the pre-modern world, in which the supernatural consequences of human moral action was palpable, R. Salanter acknowledges the "disenchantment" and secularization of the modern, post-Enlightenment world.

they grow up in the lap of Torah and study it. It is the same in our time; even though it is not easy for a person to guide his children as he wishes, there is nevertheless still a way whereby any person can earn merit: by giving help and support to those who have already matured in Torah, so that they can stay strong in their fortress and improve even more. This is one of those things that is the highest priority, a precious project in the eyes of Hashem, the Blessed. Through it, the person will be judged favorably on the day of judgment and be inscribed for life.

Even though it is understood that the primary way that the Creator governs the world nowadays is by the natural process, and the Torah's process is no longer discernible nowadays,[31] we still know and have received as a tradition that the world is sustained, both spiritually and materially, by the Torah of the disciples of the sages. As they say in Sanhedrin (99b): "What is an example of an *epikorus*? R. Yosef says: Those who say, 'Of what benefit are the Rabbis to us? They read Bible for their own benefit and they teach [Mishna] for their own benefit....'" Thus, everyone must believe that the world is sustained solely by their Torah.[32] Even though there is no palpable difference between a place where there are many scholars studying Torah and a place where there are only a few, there is a big difference vis-à-vis the eternal, enduring world, as mentioned above, for only in the world of miracles is the punishment of the sinner discernible; it is not discernible in the natural world – yet the eternal, enduring world is primary. With a bit of contemplation on this, we can understand that, rationally, the goal of benefiting our eternal condition is more necessary and essential than the goal of improving our condition in this world, while one's self, which is his soul, is tethered to the body. For this tether [between body and soul] will necessarily break and separate in every person [when they die]. But the self will not come to an end [with death] and will not be wiped out. Rather, it will remain completely sensate – perhaps it will even have greater, more intense feeling, in

32. This axiom, that the world is quite literally sustained by Torah study, is a major element of R. Chaim of Volozhin's *Nefesh HaḤayim* and consequently of the ethos of the Lithuanian yeshivot.

אֶת הַנֹּעַם וְהַתַּעֲנוּג הַנִּצְחִי וְאֶת הָעֹנֶשׁ וְהַצַּעַר הַמַּר אֲשֶׁר יַשִּׂיגֵנוּ לְפִי מִדַּת הַדִּין בְּהַעֲוֹתוֹ אֶת דַּרְכּוֹ.

וְאִם בְּמַצַּב הָאָדָם בָּעוֹלָם הַזֶּה הַכָּלֶה וְנִפְסָד רוֹאִים אָנוּ אֵיךְ יַעֲמֹל הָאָדָם מְאֹד לְהִשָּׁמֵר וְלִמְנֹעַ שֶׁלֹּא תַּשִּׂיגֵנוּ צַעַר וְיִסּוּרִים וְיִרְדֹּף בְּכָל מַאֲמַצֵּי כֹּחוֹ לְהַשִּׂיג טוֹב וְאֹשֶׁר וְחַיִּים נְעִימִים, אֵיךְ אִם כֵּן רָאוּי וְנָכוֹן יוֹתֵר לְהָאָדָם, לְפִי הַבִּינָה הַיְשָׁרָה (אִם אַךְ לֹא הִטְבִּיעַ אֶת בִּינָתוֹ בִּמְצוּלַת הַתַּאֲוָה לָלֶכֶת אַחַר טִבְעוֹ), לִדְאֹג וְלַעֲמֹל עֲבוּר מַצָּבוֹ הַנִּצְחִי, אֲשֶׁר אֵין בְּיַד הָאָדָם לָדַעַת אֵיךְ גָּדוֹל וְחָזָק וּמַתְמִיד יִהְיֶה הָעֹנֶשׁ וְהַצַּעַר עֲבוּר עֲבֵרָה, וּמַה גַּם אֶת הַשָּׂכָר וְהָעֹנֶג הָרַב בְּאֵין שִׁעוּר וּבְלִי הֶפְסֵק אֲשֶׁר יַגִּיעַ לוֹ עֲבוּר תּוֹרָה וּמַעֲשִׂים טוֹבִים. וְהַדֶּרֶךְ הַמּוֹבִיל לָאֹשֶׁר הַנִּצְחִי הוּא אַךְ לָלֶכֶת בְּדֶרֶךְ הַתּוֹרָה וְלַעֲשׂוֹת כָּל מַעֲשָׂיו אַךְ לְמַלֹּאות רְצוֹן הַבּוֹרֵא יִתְבָּרַךְ שְׁמוֹ. וְהָעֲבוֹדָה הַמְּעֻלָּה הוּא לַעֲבֹד אֶת הַבּוֹרֵא יִתְבָּרַךְ שֶׁלֹּא עַל מְנָת לְקַבֵּל פְּרָס. כִּי לָאִישׁ הָעוֹבֵד בְּאֹפֶן זֶה יִצְדַּק עָלָיו בֶּאֱמֶת שֵׁם "עוֹבֵד אֱלֹקִים". אֲבָל הָעוֹבֵד עַל מְנָת לְקַבֵּל פְּרָס שְׁמוֹ הָאֲמִתִּי הוּא "עוֹבֵד אֶת עַצְמוֹ".

וְהִנֵּה לְבַקֵּשׁ תַּחְבּוּלוֹת לָאָדָם הַבֵּינוֹנִי שֶׁיִּהְיֶה גַּם לוֹ חֵלֶק מְעַט בַּעֲבוֹדָה הַמְּעֻלָּה הַזֹּאת לִהְיוֹת עוֹבֵד שֶׁלֹּא עַל מְנָת לְקַבֵּל פְּרָס, הֲלֹא יָדַעְנוּ כִּי הַתַּאֲוָה חֲזָקָה מְאֹד וְהָאָדָם מֻכְרָח לַעֲמֹל הַרְבֵּה עַל יְדֵי יִרְאַת הָעֹנֶשׁ וְתִקְוַת קַבָּלַת שָׂכָר עַד אֲשֶׁר יַטֶּה אֶת עַצְמוֹ לְהִשָּׁמֵר מִן הָעֲבֵרוֹת וְלַעֲשׂוֹת מַעֲשִׂים טוֹבִים. וּלְהָבִין לִהְיוֹת עוֹבֵד שֶׁלֹּא עַל מְנָת לְקַבֵּל פְּרָס אֵין תְּבוּנָה לוֹ. וְאַף כִּי יָדַעְנוּ שֶׁ'הָעֲבוֹדָה צֹרֶךְ גָּבֹהַּ', אֲשֶׁר הַמְכֻוָּן מִזֶּה הוּא כִּי הַבּוֹרֵא יָסַד אֲשֶׁר כָּל בְּרִיּוֹתָיו יִתְנַהֲגוּ עַל פִּי מַעֲשֵׂיהֶם בַּעֲבוֹדָתָם, וְאִם יִהְיֶה הָאָדָם יָרֵא וְצַדִּיק, אָז הוּא נוֹתֵן כִּבְיָכוֹל עֹז וְתַעֲצוּמוֹת לְהַבּוֹרֵא יִתְבָּרַךְ לְהַשְׁפִּיעַ שֶׁפַע בְּרָכָה וְטוֹב לִבְרִיּוֹתָיו אֲשֶׁר אַךְ זֶה חֶפְצוֹ וּרְצוֹנוֹ, אֲבָל הָעִנְיָן הַזֶּה נְבַטֵּא אַךְ בִּשְׂפָתֵינוּ, אֲבָל בִּינָתֵנוּ קְצָרָה מֵהָבִין זֶה.

אָמְנָם לִפְעָמִים יֵשׁ מִצְוָה אֲשֶׁר הַתַּאֲוָה שֶׁתַּפְרִיעַ אֶת הָאָדָם מֵעֲשׂוֹת הַמִּצְוָה הִיא קַלָּה וַחֲלוּשָׁה, אֲשֶׁר אֵין מֵהַצֹּרֶךְ לָזֶה הִתְבּוֹנְנוּת בְּשָׂכָר

33. See Avot 1:2.

order to sense the sweetness of eternal pleasure and the punishment and bitter pain that will grasp him in accordance with divine judgment, if he has distorted his path.

If we can see how a person toils mightily to prevent and protect against being overtaken by pain and suffering in this fleeting, ephemeral world, pursuing the attainment of goodness, happiness, and a pleasant life with all his strength, then, according to straightforward reason, it is all the more proper and right for a person (as long as he has not drowned his intelligence in the muck of desire, to follow his nature) to be concerned and to work hard for his eternal condition. For a person can never know how strong, intense, and continuous will be the punishment and pain for a sin, not to mention the immeasurably great and unceasing reward and pleasure that will come to him for Torah and good deeds.

The way that leads to eternal bliss is simply to walk in the way of Torah and do every deed only to fulfill the will of the Creator, blessed be His name. The highest level of service is to serve the Creator, the Blessed, not for the sake of getting a reward.[33] One who serves in this way will justifiably bear the name of "servant of God," whereas one who serves for the sake of reward deserves the label "servant of himself."

We need to seek out strategies whereby the average person can have a small part in this higher service, to be a servant not for the sake of reward. We know that desire is very powerful, and a person must work intensively, by means of fear of punishment and hope for reward, until he inclines himself to refrain from sin and to do good deeds. He lacks the understanding how to be a servant [of God] not for the sake of reward. And even though we know that "service is a need of the Most High," which means that the Creator ordained that all His creatures act, in all their conduct, in their service [of God], and if a person is God-fearing and righteous then he, as it were, gives strength and power to the Creator, the Blessed, to pour blessing and goodness on His creatures, which is His sole desires and will – we nevertheless articulate this idea with our lips only. Our intelligence is too limited to grasp this.

However, sometimes there is a mitzva, and the lust that distracts the person from doing the mitzva is so mild and weak that one need not contemplate reward and punishment. This mitzva is the root that gives

וְעֹנֶשׁ, וְגַם הִיא שֹׁרֶשׁ לַעֲשׂוֹת עָנָף וְלָשֵׂאת פְּרִי לְהַגְדִּיל תּוֹרָה וַעֲבוֹדָתוֹ יִתְבָּרַךְ. מִצְוָה כָּזוֹ נָקֵל לַעֲשׂוֹתָהּ שֶׁלֹּא עַל מְנָת לְקַבֵּל פְּרָס כִּי בָּזֶה יִרְאֶה הָאָדָם אֵיךְ בִּפְעֻלָּתוֹ נִתְמַלֵּא רְצוֹן הַקָּדוֹשׁ בָּרוּךְ הוּא אֲשֶׁר יִרְצֶה שֶׁעַל יְדֵי הָאָדָם תִּתְחַזֵּק תּוֹרָתוֹ.

וְהִנֵּה עַתָּה בִּזְמַנֵּנוּ וּבִגְבוּלֵנוּ נִמְצָא מִצְוָה כָּזוֹ אֲשֶׁר כָּל אָדָם יָכוֹל לִזְכּוֹת בָּהּ וְלַעֲשׂוֹתָהּ בְּנָקֵל שֶׁלֹּא עַל מְנָת לְקַבֵּל פְּרָס כַּאֲשֶׁר כְּבָר כָּתַבְנוּ כִּי לִמּוּד הַתּוֹרָה הִיא עוֹלָה עַל כֹּל וְיָקָר מְאֹד לִפְנֵי הַקָּדוֹשׁ בָּרוּךְ הוּא. וְהִנֵּה בְּיָמֵינוּ בַּעֲוֹנוֹתֵינוּ הָרַבִּים הֻשְׁפַּל מְאֹד קֶרֶן הַתּוֹרָה וְלוֹמְדֶיהָ יִמָּעֲטוּ יוֹם יוֹם, וְגַם הַמְעַטִּים הַמִּתְחַזְּקִים עוֹד לְהַחֲזִיק בְּמָעֹז הַתּוֹרָה וְהוֹגִים בִּשְׁקִידָה, לֹא יוּכְלוּ לְהַחֲזִיק מַעֲמָדָם בָּהּ מִפְּנֵי הַזְּמַן אֲשֶׁר שִׁנָּה פְּנֵי תֵּבֵל וּמַעַיְנֵי הַפַּרְנָסָה אֲשֶׁר הָיוּ מִלְּפָנִים נִהְיָה עַתָּה לְמָקוֹר אַכְזָב כִּדְבָרֵינוּ לְעֵיל, וְלָכֵן מַה מְּאֹד נָקֵל הוּא לְהָבִין לְכָל אִישׁ יָשָׁר הוֹלֵךְ, כִּי הָעֵת הַזֹּאת דּוֹרֶשֶׁת מֵאִתָּנוּ אֲשֶׁר נְמַהֵר לְהַחֲזִיק בְּיַד הַלּוֹמְדִים כָּל אִישׁ וְאִישׁ כַּאֲשֶׁר תִּמְצָא יָדוֹ, לְמַעַן לֹא תָפוּג תּוֹרָה חַס וְשָׁלוֹם. וּבָזֶה יִתְמַלֵּא רְצוֹן הַבּוֹרֵא יִתְבָּרַךְ וְיִתְקַיֵּם בָּנוּ שָׁלוֹם רָב לְאֹהֲבֵי תּוֹרָתֶךָ וְאֵין לָמוֹ מִכְשׁוֹל. וְנִזְכֶּה לְרַב טוּב הַצָּפוּן לַצַּדִּיקִים בְּעוֹלָם שֶׁכֻּלּוֹ טוֹב.

rise to branches and bears fruit to increase Torah and service of [God], the Blessed. This mitzva is easy to do not for the sake of reward, for here a person sees how his actions fulfill the will of the Holy One, blessed be He, who wants that His Torah be strengthened by human actions.

Now, in our time and within our borders, there is such a mitzva that everyone can merit and can easily do, not for the sake of reward. As we already wrote, study of Torah is greater than all other [mitzvot]. It is very precious in the eyes of the Holy One, blessed be He. In our time, due to our many sins, the glory of the Torah has been brought low, and its students decline in numbers day by day. Even the few who still exert themselves to strengthen the fortress of Torah and study with great dedication will not be able to keep this up due to the times, which have changed the face of the world; the wellsprings of livelihood that once existed have become dried up, unreliable sources, as we said above.

It is therefore easy for any upstanding person to understand that the times demand that we hasten to support the scholars, each person according to his ability, so that the Torah does not grow faint, God forbid. In this, the will of the Creator the Blessed will be fulfilled, and we will become the fulfillment [of the verse] "Abundant peace to those who love Your Torah and there will be no stumbling block among them" (Ps. 119:165). We will merit the great bounty set aside for the righteous in the [next] world which is entirely good.

Afterword: My Personal Encounter with Mussar, and Looking Ahead

Justin Pines

My earliest memory of being in a relationship with Hashem is as a small child, at the top of the stairs in my childhood home in New Jersey, praying to Hashem to help me make it down the stairs safely. It wasn't that I was scared of the stairs, as much as I felt that absolutely everything depended on Hashem, and that Hashem was deeply present in and invested in my life. In retrospect, I imagine much of my relationship with God was seeded by being around my father, Alan Pines, and my maternal grandfather, Murray Pantirer, *zt"l*, both of whom embodied *yirat shamayim*, reverence of God, in their behavior and life choices.

Through my teenage years, I became more and more interested and invested in the Jewish way of life. I dreamt that one day I would be a filmmaker who embedded Jewish lessons in films seen by the masses. Judaism had so much to offer, and I wanted to help get the word out.

At the University of Pennsylvania, I began to understand other rigorous systems of thought – capitalism, psychology, philosophy, democracy, communications – more deeply, and I noticed how they informed our lives. I became convinced that there were deeply powerful and constructive ideas coming out of these fields, but with the caveat that most of the people and companies trying to encourage or even convince me to make certain choices were driven by economic or personal interests, so I couldn't give them my full trust. On the other hand, I felt that Judaism – its divinely inspired eternal conversation and goals – was generally driven by making ourselves better people and the world a better place in partnership with God, despite some serious human blind spots.

I ultimately decided that whenever making a decision about anything, big or small – how to eat, how to dress, what to do with my time, how to have friendships, how to relate to money – I would consider the other, "secular" ideas, but that Judaism would always have a seat in the boardroom of my mind; but to be able to look to Judaism for advice, I felt I needed to learn more Torah.

I decided to spend a year in Israel at the Pardes Institute to accomplish "knowing Judaism" before I returning to my career path at law school. I quickly discovered that the more Torah I learned, the more I realized how much Torah there was still to learn, and that this was truly a lifelong endeavor. And I was late to the game. (Looking back, I also now realize that we must be careful not to substitute learning Torah for our relationship with the Divine, as that can create barriers between us and God.)

At Harvard Law School, I remember struggling to get excited about reading American legal cases that were a mere thirty years old, written by humans, and influenced by political views and economic interests,[1] when Jewish discourse was divinely inspired and spanned millennia.

Throughout my studies, and afterward, when I joined the corporate law firm of Paul, Weiss, Rifkind, Wharton & Garrison LLP, I noticed that many of my Jewishly invested friends and I often compartmentalized our Judaism. Judaism was less of a way of life and more of a hobby, with varying degrees of interest. Thus, a sign of a healthy Jewish life might be something we do with our families on the weekends, before or after work, or even during our lunch break. Though the importance of observing overtly Jewish rituals such as celebrating Shabbat, studying Jewish

1. I have since come to appreciate that building a society that reflects any system of values is no easy task.

texts, or praying should not be understated and is vital to our survival, it didn't feel like enough, whether participating once a year or every day.

I came to believe and still believe that we must bring our Jewish lens and values into every aspect of our daily existence. There is great value in a unifying purpose and overarching values to guide us through our lives, and I wanted to do my part in helping the Jewish community to look to Judaism for that guidance, as I felt it would enrich our lives, infuse every moment with a higher purpose, and allow us to build a better world together.

I ultimately decided to leave my law firm and to study more Torah so that I could be in a position to guide laypeople toward bringing a Jewish lens and values to their lives. I went to Machon Shlomo in Har Nof and then to Yeshivat Chovevei Torah (YCT).

I also became a Wexner Graduate Fellow. The application process forced me to lay out my vision, and sharing that vision with the other fellows helped me to face hard questions. As I heard about their missions – everything from fighting race and gender inequality and violence, to Israel education, to interfaith relations, to facilitating better end-of-life experiences, to building worship communities – I pushed the idea that having a holy mission is not enough; we have to do it in a holy way. How do we ensure that we fight systemic race inequality without losing sight of how to treat individual people along the way? And my colleagues pushed me as well: Could I rigorously clarify what it means to lead with "Jewish values"? What's a "Jewish lens"? How do we know if and when we are doing something in a Jewish way? How do we make sure we aren't so focused on working on embodying Jewish values that we forget to address the suffering beyond our local proximity? These questions stuck with me as I continued my Torah learning.

And then I discovered Mussar. I had seen R. Shlomo Wolbe's *Alei Shor* at other students' *mekomot*[2] in yeshiva, and I heard R. Yisroel Shaw teach from *Alei Shor* at a Shabbat meal in Har Nof. It piqued my interest, but I didn't have a guide. One of my Wexner colleagues, Jenn Weinstock, introduced me to R. David Jaffe, who had brought Mussar

2. A regular seat or "place" in the *beit midrash*, where students often leave books they are studying.

to Gann Academy and also employed Mussar in his social justice work. R. Jaffe suggested I read Alan Morinis's *Everyday Holiness*[3] as an English introduction to Mussar, and we simultaneously began a *ḥavruta* in the second volume of *Alei Shor*.[4]

I realized there was a whole field – a whole movement! – within Judaism focused on clarifying Jewish goals and values, and then how to close the gap – how to turn these ideas from cognitive descriptions to a way of living in all areas of life.

R. Jaffe taught me two of the foundational tools, or *yesodot*,[5] of modern Mussar practice: R. Wolbe's chapter on "*hitlamdut*" (the learner's stance, or priming oneself to learn from everyone) in volume 2 of *Alei Shor*, and R. Eliyahu Dessler's essay "*Nekudat HaBeḥira*" ("*The Choice Point*").[6] He then guided me as we studied the different *middot*, and I formed my own Mussar practice. Based on the model offered in *Alei Shor*, as we studied each *midda*, he would help me to choose a daily practice, or *kabbala*, that would help me to cultivate the *midda* in my practice, such as "greet my partner at the door with a smile," or "learn something from a stranger." In addition, building off of R. Salanter's idea of *hispailus* (*hitpaalut*), we would choose a focus phrase for me to review and repeat with emotional intensity on a daily basis, such as (in Hebrew for me) "The world is built through kindness," or "My order testifies to my will."[7]

---

3. *Everyday Holiness*, in my opinion, continues to be the best introduction to Mussar for English-speaking audiences. It includes both an overview of character traits and models for practicing Mussar.
4. *Alei Shor*, available only in Hebrew, is by far both the most mind-blowing and practical Mussar work written since the Holocaust.
5. I also was blessed to have a *ḥavruta* in the second volume of *Alei Shor* with R. Matisyahu Rosenblum, of blessed memory, my *rebbe* at Machon Shlomo. His method of studying Torah and Mussar continues to inspire me each day, including the way he collected *yesodot* in his life and learning.
6. This idea is developed in R. Dessler's *Mikhtav MeEliyahu* as well as in its English edition, *Strive for Truth*. See R. Jaffe's book, *Changing the World from the Inside Out: A Jewish Approach to Personal and Social Change* (2016), where he develops these two *yesodot*.
7. As someone who is drawn to music, I would often try to find songs that contained relevant focus phrases, which I would listen to or dance to. I have also had students

Once I made my way through most of the *middot*, the next step was to join a *vaad*. At YCT, a group of us created a mini-*ḥabura* around the study of *Alei Shor*. We would study the *middot*, take on practices, and then check in on a weekly basis. This was not quite a *vaad*, but it was a step in the direction of creating a community with support and accountability.

Once I had better familiarity with the different *middot*, R. Jaffe taught me how to customize my practice by clarifying the challenges I was facing on my path, and then picking which *middot* to focus on and which practices to employ to help me grow in those areas.[8]

Around the same time that I was growing in Mussar, I also encountered R. Greenberg for the first time in a serious way, through his *shiur* at YCT. Whereas Mussar had given me the tools to really focus on how to move through the world, Rav Yitz provided me with the theological foundation which clarified the ultimate goal and gave meaning to why I practice Mussar. He taught me that every human being is created in God's image (*betzelem Elokim*) and showed me how this means that every human being is unique and of infinite and equal value; he showed me how every mitzva is ultimately about choosing and elevating life; and

---

who turned focus phrases into works of art or wrote their own music as focus phrases, as ways to bring the ideas into their subconscious.

8. As a recent example, while working at home during the COVID-19 pandemic, I was struggling with being present with both my work and my family. I found that during the *ḥagim* (Jewish holidays), Rosh HaShana and Sukkot, I was laser-focused on being present with my family and creating a sense of meaning and purpose around each holiday, in line with the vision set out by R. Greenberg in *The Jewish Way*. However, once I returned to my "day job," I was laser-focused on the many tasks I had, to the point that my mind would be at work even while I was spending time with my family. R. Jaffe suggested I focus on the combination of *seder* (order), *savlanut* (patience), and *bitaḥon* (trust in God). I needed to arrange my life in a way that made appropriate time for both my family and work; I needed to be patient with myself and acknowledge that I could not do everything I wanted to for my family or for work immediately; and I needed to trust in God that if I kept focusing on treating everyone in my family and work as created in God's image, without worrying about how quickly I accomplished everything, then I would travel along the path at home and at work to where I needed to be. I now focus on this three-*midda* "recipe" on a daily basis, and it allows me to return to center when I fall off the path.

he reminded me that we are partners with God in this work – that we are in a covenantal relationship.[9]

I then set out on a path to try to first live a life which reflected the values of Rav Yitz and Rav Wolbe, and also to bring those ideas to others, with R. Jaffe and my *ḥevre* from YCT as my *ḥavrutot*. I began to lead Mussar *vaadim* in various settings – campus, young adult, lay leaders, and social justice organizations.

As I received *semikha,* a family friend named Gail Propp introduced me to the then Head of School at Ramaz in New York, R. Eric Grossman. R. Grossman recognized that *menschlichkeit* was a core value at Ramaz, but that there was no clear-cut educational strategy as to how they were trying to build *mentschen.*[10] So he brought me on as *Mashgiaḥ Ruḥani* (Director of Character Development) of the middle school.

A listening tour of parents, board members, administration, faculty, and students confirmed excitement about this project, and that success would require an intervention across the whole ecosystem, so that parents, faculty, and students could create a common language around character development.

Working off of R. Jaffe's strategy at Gann Academy, and using the teachings of Rav Yitz and Rav Wolbe, I created a curriculum for parents, students, and faculty, including foundational ideas such as *tzelem Elokim, hitlamdut,* and *beḥirah,* as well as specific *middot.* We learned that: a) the material felt very relevant across all groups; b) parents were particularly eager to participate in these conversations when they were framed as how to parent your children around character development; and c) students loved a space to talk about how to improve their *middot* that was self-driven and encouraged them to take ownership. It is difficult to measure

9. For more of R. Greenberg's theology, see *The Jewish Way* (1993) and *The Triumph of Life* (forthcoming), among his other essays and publications. Interestingly, while I was attending these classes, I had no idea of Rav Yitz's connection to Mussar.

10. I would imagine that this is true of many schools. Parents depend on schools to do this, and schools depend on parents. I would advise that building character starts in the home, and school should be a place to develop scaffolding: from theological understandings of why and how to be a *mensch* to practical assignments around how to develop those skills. Both parents and schools need help in this area.

growth on a communal scale,[11] but one indicator was the way in which much of the common language around Mussar entered the ecosystem, for example, when administrators used a Mussar lens to frame an idea in front of parents or students, or when I would see a family on Shabbat and they would share that a term like "*beḥira* point" had become part of their household language, including among their children who were not in the middle school.

While I was at Ramaz, I also had the life-altering privilege to work closely with R. Greenberg – helping with writing projects, including the book in your hands, and developing a non-profit venture. My brain exploded every time he shared his ideas and his Torah, and I worried about the burden of receiving so much wisdom and how to capture it. Was it possible to record everything? But the moments that will stick with me forever are how he and Rabbanit Blu hosted my wife (then-fiancée) Tali and me for dinner; how he handled a fender bender with a stranger; how he spoke with his children and grandchildren on the phone; how he approached his *avoda* (service) with both *zerizut* (enthusiasm) and *simḥa* (joy); how he ate lunch; even how he responded when Rabbanit Blu bought him the wrong button-down shirts. Though I already knew that he modeled how to truly live a life reflective of Torah values before I stepped foot in his home, I was able to witness this up close, answering the very question I had been seeking to answer for so many years.

In my current role as Director of Youth and Young Adult Initiatives at the Shalom Hartman Institute of North America, in some ways my journey has come full circle. My job is not to teach Mussar – I work with teens and key professional and lay leaders in school, camp, and teen spaces mostly around key questions of North American Jewish identity as it relates to Israel. Instead, I am trying to bring a Mussar lens to the work and those around me – explicitly through offering a *vaad* and running a *teshuva* workshop, but also implicitly by employing Mussar methodologies in my pedagogy and my day-to-day encounters with others. In

11. On an individual level, Mussar practitioners use the tool of *ḥeshbon hanefesh*, an accounting of the soul, popularized by R. Menachem Mendel Lefin in his book of the same name published in the early nineteenth century.

other words, I am trying to navigate how to bring Jewish values to each moment of my life, and trying to give others the same tools.

For millennia, the Jewish tradition has sought to clarify how to live a life in covenant with God, in God's image, through our rich Written and Oral Torah. Rav Yisrael Salanter, *zt"l*, taught us that clarifying our ethical ideals and the nuances of morality and holiness is simply not enough. How is it that we know not to lose our temper, yet we lose our temper? How can we know that every human is created in God's image, yet fail as individuals and as a society to treat them that way? How can we close the gap between how we are and how we know we ought to be?

The Mussar movement shifts our focus from exclusively thinking about *what* we are doing to prioritizing *how* we are doing it. We are reminded that there are no shortcuts to *tikkun olam* (perfecting the world) which ignore *tikkun middot* (perfecting our character). And we discover that we enhance our *avodat Hashem* (service of God) not by choosing a holy path, but by constantly striving to make our path holy.

This is not only our covenantal charge, in partnership with the Creator of the World, but it is also based in science and rational thinking. The strongest indicator of a happy life is not wealth, power, or fame. Nor is it choosing to dedicate one's life to feeding the hungry and clothing those in need. The key to a happy life is healthy relationships.[12] And Mussar is not self-help in the Western sense. Nor is it living alone on a mountain top. Mussar is about helping us to build stronger, healthier, and holier relationships with God, the people created in His image, the world around us, and ourselves.

Self-improvement has become a major industry in our time. Whether it's a child doing math homework or an executive taking a professional development course, we spend countless time and money trying to prepare for big moments. I can now go online and pay to learn how to shoot a basketball off the dribble, how to evolve a brand, or how

12. See the now famous Harvard Study of Adult Development (www.adultdevelopmentstudy.org/).

to prepare fried branzino with Thai chili lettuce cups from the people at the very top of these industries.

Yet we often don't prepare for the moments that matter most. I can spend hours researching and finding the best piano teacher for my young child, and rush her to and from lessons, but have I put any time or money into how I want to act when she needs my help getting her ready to leave? Have I practiced and prepared for how to spend the car ride with her? We think the goal is for her to be a better piano player (for self-esteem, creative output, independence, work ethic, fun, career, the college resume), and we often set aside the more important goal of building a healthy relationship with our children, in God's image. We spend hours ordering groceries and preparing food, or debating which restaurant to choose – yet how much do we invest in how we want to be at dinner?

R. Salanter called for Mussar Houses as places to help those who know the path to then close the gap between how they are and how they ought to be. With exponential innovation in both technology and education, how might we create a model for today?[13]

Furthermore, per R. Greenberg's introduction, Rav Salanter recognized that we needed to adapt and respond to modernity if the Jewish way is to continue to be internalized in the coming generations. His approaches ring true today as much as they did then, if not more:

> We must change the emphasis so that Jews view Judaism's *bein adam leḥavero* approach as just as important as *ben adam laMakom* and not outsource our ethical behavior to secular society.
>
> Our religious practice should not depend on social conformity, but instead be based on a deep, internalized connection with Hashem.
>
> Judaism must be able to compellingly compete in the marketplace of values, ideas, and ways of life.

These are the seeds planted by Rav Salanter, and it is our hope that by providing a new translation and commentary to *Ohr Yisrael* and other

13. See the appendices for a list of organizations and resources related to Mussar.

writing, we will make the light of *Ohr Yisrael* accessible to more people. As we grow the Mussar movement, we should also face the next set of questions: How might we apply this thinking to the rise of the Digital Age and as our lives become more and more virtual? How might we employ a Jewish lens and Jewish values as we build these new worlds?

I close with a Mussar meditation intended to enable readers of this book to "taste" the method – and perhaps even to start on their own path of exploring a conscious life of spiritual/ethical development in every aspect of life. Our meditation begins with the first paragraph of the *Shema*:

> Hear, O Israel! The Lord is our God, the Lord is One. You shall love the Lord your God with all your heart and with all your soul and with all your might. These words with which I command you today shall be on your hearts. And you shall teach them to your children; and you shall speak about them when you are sitting in your home and when you are walking along the path, when you lie down and when you get up. Bind them as a sign on your hand and let them serve as a symbol on your forehead; inscribe them on the doorposts of your house and on your gates. (Deut. 6:4–9)

The opening declaration of "*Shema Yisrael*" ("Hear, O Israel"), and the ensuing "*Ve'ahavta*" ("You shall love") paragraph, make up one of the most well-known prayers in Judaism, if not the most well-known, across denominations. But what does it mean to "hear" that God is one? How can we be commanded to love God with all our heart and all our soul and all our might? The Torah provides the answer: To truly hear that God is one, to truly love God with all our heart and all our soul and all our might, "these words which I command you today [must] be on your hearts." How do you inscribe something onto your heart? How do you close the gap between something being an external idea, and something being deeply woven into the very fabric of your being? You teach it to your children. You talk about it when you are sitting and when you are walking; it is the last thing you speak about before you go to sleep, and the first thing you speak about when you wake up. You put a reminder on your hand, another on your forehead. You write it at the entrance to every room in your house and at your gate. (See *Yalkut Shimoni* 839 and *Alei Shor*, vol. 2, 27–28.)

This is Mussar. Step 1: Learn the *yesod,* the foundational Torah idea. Step 2: Inscribe the *yesod* onto our hearts by developing support practices; discuss; teach; designate times during the day to bring our focus back; create physical reminders. This is how we move from the known to the lived. And this approach is at least as old as the *Shema.*

May we merit to continue the project of those who came before us and not only be blessed in *what* we are building, but, perhaps more importantly, *how* we are building it. And may we be inspired by Rav Salanter to evolve this spiritual technology in line with the world evolving around us.

Justin Pines
February 2022
Ellul 5784 – August 2023

Hakarat HaTov (Acknowledgments)

I express my gratitude to the following individuals for their contributions, which made this book possible.

To Rav Yehuda Leib Nekritz, the other faculty, and the students of Beis Yosef Novardok Yeshiva in Boro Park during my college years from 1949 to 1953. They introduced me to R. Israel Salanter's life and teachings; initiated me into some of the Mussar practices with which to work on one's character and personal traits; inspired me with their personal model of kindness, respect for others, closeness to God, and continuous striving to improve character and sensitivity to others. I wanted to be like them, and they continue to influence me to this day.

To R. Justin Pines, who urged me to offer a course on Mussar at Yeshivat Chovevei Torah. After taking the course, he told me that he had been inspired by his studies of Mussar, and especially the teachings of R. Shlomo Wolbe. He was convinced that Mussar and its educational techniques could be important resources for contemporary religious education. In this spirit, he introduced experimental Mussar programs in professional settings and, later, in classes for students and their parents at the Ramaz School. After ordination, he worked with me as a fellow for two years to complete a new translation of and commentary on R. Israel Salanter's writings. In many ways, this book is the outcome of his encouragement and efforts.

To R. Elli Fischer who edited this entire book. His editorial skills and judgment considerably improved the translation and made the book more understandable and reader-friendly.

To Sender Cohen, who underwrote this publication in honor and memory of his father, Prof. Getzel Cohen, himself a model committed Jew who treasured Torah and Jewish education.

To Daniel Septimus, who believed in this book and worked out an arrangement to simultaneously publish it through Koren Publishers while making the text of this neglected classic available for free online as part of Sefaria's comprehensive collection of the extended Jewish library. And to Sara Wolkenfeld, who has worked closely with us on this project as well.

To Matthew Miller and the entire team at Koren Publishers who accepted this book for publication, and to David Silverstein, Yoel Finkelman, Nechama Untterman and Ita Olesker who did a superb job of copy editing, and guided us to clarify meanings and to upgrade the translation in many places. Also thanks to Ruth Pepperman who proofread the English and Avihai Gamdani who proofread the Hebrew.

To the original board members who set up the J.J. Greenberg Institute for the Advancement of Jewish Life – Sender Cohen, Felicia Herman, Darren Kleinberg, Lynn Kroll, Jeremy Pava, and Aryeh Rubin. This framework underwrote the two-year fellowship for Justin Pines, which enabled completion of the translation of R. Israel Salanter's writings.

To the partners of the J.J. Greenberg Institute for the Advancement of Jewish Life: they enabled JJGI, as a division of the Hadar Institute, to complete this project to present the writings and thought of R. Israel Salanter to an English-speaking audience and arrange its final publication; the Aviv Foundation – Steve and Chani Laufer; Jerry and Paula Gottesman; Moshe and Abbie Greenberg; Harold Grinspoon and Diane Troderman; the Micah Foundation – Jeremy and Anne Pava; Tali Rosenblatt-Cohen and Sender Cohen; Phil Darivoff; the Irvin and Sharna Frank Foundation – May Sheehan and Jacob Howland; the Genesis Philanthropy Group – Marina Yudborovsky; the Genesis Prize Foundation – Stan Polovets, chair; Michael and Linda Jesselson; Lynn Korda Kroll and Jules Kroll; Bobbie and Fran Lent; the Maimonides Fund – Mark Charendoff; Alan and Elisa Pines; Julie and Marc Platt; Aryeh and Raquel Rubin; Joe Kanfer; Lou Bravmann; the Gewurz Family Foundation – Ilan and Julie Gewurz; Tom and Elissa Katz; David and Sally Lowenfeld; Peter Joseph and Elizabeth Scheuer; the Robert

Russell Foundation and the Jack Chester Foundation – Norman Lipoff; Josh and Lizzie Scheinfeld.

To Blu Greenberg, who has sustained and anchored my life for sixty-five years, and whose personal example of giving to others and doing good without limit is a central way to imitate God in our lives, as R. Israel Salanter taught. To our children, Moshe and Abbie, David and Tamar, Deborah and Jonathan, Goody and Eric, who exemplify R. Salanter's teaching that "the Torah came to make a *mensch*," and to our son, J.J. *z"l*, whose personal example shapes me every day.

May their reward be the grace and blessing of God and that the *Shekhina*/Divine Presence be encountered in this work.

Yitz Greenberg

In addition to the gratitude and blessings expressed by Rav Yitz above to those who were partners in this project, I want to add my family, including my grandparents, Murray *z"l* and Lucy *z"l* Pantirer, and Eli *z"l* and Hilda Pinewski, who each survived the *Shoah*; my parents, Elisa and Alan Pines, and my siblings, who help shape the path which led me to Rav Yitz and Mussar; and the love of my life, Tali, and our children Olivia, Caroline, Aria, and Murray – who inspire me and help me to grow on a daily basis.

It is impossible to recognize all of the good which leads us to any moment. It is particularly difficult to recount the ways in which Rav Yitz has shaped my journey, through our direct relationship, through my family's relationship with him, and through the endless ways in which he has shaped the world in which we all live. I am grateful for the relationship he shared with my grandfather, Murray Pantirer, *z"l*, through their service together on the US Holocaust Memorial Council; that my father, Alan Pines, met and learned with Rav Yitz through the Wexner Heritage Program; that Rav Yitz and Rabbanit Blu once joined my childhood community, Etz Chaim, in Livingston, New Jersey, for the High Holy Days; and that the leadership of Yeshivat Chovevei Torah provided us with the opportunity to encounter and learn with Rav Yitz.

I thank Rav Yitz for his modeling the Jewish way, his mentorship and his friendship, and for the life-changing opportunity to learn one-on-one with him and to be a part of this project. I will never forget these experiences and take seriously the obligations which come with them.

Thank you to both Rav Yitz and Rabbanit Blu for welcoming me into their home. May the seeds they have planted continue to bring us all closer to aligning our actions with our covenantal mission.

Justin Pines

Appendix

SELECTED LIST OF CLASSIC AND MODERN MUSSAR WORKS AVAILABLE IN ENGLISH OR IN TRANSLATION[1]

Pirkei Avot (*Ethics of the Fathers*) (second century).[2]

Sefer Emunot VeDe'ot (*The Book of Beliefs and Opinions*), Saadia Gaon (933).

Ḥovot HaLevavot (*Duties of the Heart*), Rabbenu Baḥya ibn Pakuda (1040).

Shemona Perakim (*Eight Chapters*), Rambam (Maimonides; Rabbi Moses ben Maimon) (1168).

Hilkhot De'ot (*Laws of Moral Dispositions*), Rambam (1180).

HaMaspik LeOvdei Hashem (*The Guide to Serving God*), Abraham, son of Rambam (1230).

Iggeret HaRamban (*The Letter of Nahmanides*), Ramban (Rabbi Moses ben Nahman Girondi) (thirteenth century).

Shaarei Teshuva (*The Gates of Repentance*), Rabbenu Jonah of Girona (d. 1264).

Orḥot Tzaddikim (*The Ways of the Righteous*), Anonymous (c. 1440).

Tomer Devora (*The Palm Tree of Deborah*), Moses ben Jacob Cordovero (1588).

Meneket Rivka (*Rebecca's Nurse*), Rebecca bat Meir Tiktiner (1609).

---

1. For a more comprehensive list, visit sefaria.org/texts/Musar or mussarinstitute.org/mussar-classics/.
2. For R. Greenberg's translation and commentary of *Pirkei Avot*, see *Sage Advice: Pirkei Avot* (Jerusalem: Koren Publishers, 2016).

Mesillat Yesharim (*The Path of the Just*), Rabbi Moshe Ḥayim Luzzatto (1740).

Ḥeshbon HaNefesh (*Accounting of the Soul*), Menachem Mendel Lefin (1811).

Pele Yo'etz (*Wondrous Advisor*), Rabbi Eliezer Papo (1824).

Ohr Yisrael (*The Light of Israel*), edited by Rabbi Isaac Blazer, letters and essays by Rabbi Yisrael Salanter and additional material on Rabbi Salanter and on Mussar, written by Rabbi Blazer himself (1890).

Madregat HaAdam (*The Stature of the Human*), Rabbi Yosef Yozel Hurwitz (d. 1919).

Ḥovat HaTalmidim (*The Students' Obligation*), Rabbi Kalonymus Kalmish Shapira, the *Rebbe* of Piaseczna (1932).

Mikhtav MeEliyahu (published in English as *Strive for Truth!*), Rabbi Eliyahu Dessler (1959).[3]

Tenuat HaMussar (*The Mussar Movement: Its History, Leading Personalities and Doctrines*), Rabbi Dov Katz (1963).

Alei Shor, Rabbi Shlomo Wolbe (1968/1998).[4]

Sparks of Mussar: A Treasury of the Words and Deeds of the Mussar Greats, Rabbi Chaim Ephraim Zaitchik (1985).

Siḥot Mussar (*Reb Chaim's Discourses: The Shmuessen of the Mirrer Rosh Yeshiva, Rabbi Chaim Shmulevitz, Zt"l*), Rabbi Chaim Shmulevitz (1989).

Zeria UVinyan BeḤinukh (*Planting and Building: Raising a Jewish Child*), Rabbi Shlomo Wolbe (1995).

Mussar for Moderns, Rabbi Elyakim Krumbein (2005).

A Responsible Life: The Spiritual Path of Mussar, Rabbi Ira F. Stone (2006).[5]

Everyday Holiness, Alan Morinis (2008).[6]

Teshuva, Restoring Life, Rabbi Reuven Leuchter (2014).

3. Rabbi Dessler passed away in 1953, six years before the publication of *Mikhtav Me-Eliyahu*.
4. There is an audio translation only, available at: torahdownloads.com/c-12-alei-shor.html.
5. Visit contemporarymussar.org to learn more.
6. Visit mussarinstitute.org to learn more.

Changing the World from the Inside Out: A Jewish Approach to Personal and Social Change, Rabbi David Jaffe (2016).[7]
Nurture Their Nature: The Torah's Essential Guidance for Parents and Teachers, Rabbi Yosef Lynn and Rabbi Jack Cohen (2021).

SELECTED MODERN MUSSAR ORGANIZATIONS

The Center for Contemporary Mussar (contemporarymussar.org)
Inside Out Wisdom and Action (insideoutwisdomandaction.org)
Institute for Jewish Spirituality (jewishspirituality.org)
Meor (meor.org)
The Mussar Institute (mussarinstitute.org)

7. Kirva – The Inside Out Wisdom and Action Project makes Mussar wisdom and practice accessible to people working for social change, helping them integrate this wisdom into their organizing, advocacy, and service. Kirva's leadership cohorts, curricula, consulting, webinars, and practice groups are available to people from all backgrounds and experience with Mussar.

The fonts used in this book are from the Arno family

Maggid Books
The best of contemporary Jewish thought from
Koren Publishers Jerusalem Ltd.